# Communications in Computer and Information Science 2074

**Rationale**

The CCIS series is devoted to the publication of proceedings of computer science conferences. Its aim is to efficiently disseminate original research results in informatics in printed and electronic form. While the focus is on publication of peer-reviewed full papers presenting mature work, inclusion of reviewed short papers reporting on work in progress is welcome, too. Besides globally relevant meetings with internationally representative program committees guaranteeing a strict peer-reviewing and paper selection process, conferences run by societies or of high regional or national relevance are also considered for publication.

**Topics**

The topical scope of CCIS spans the entire spectrum of informatics ranging from foundational topics in the theory of computing to information and communications science and technology and a broad variety of interdisciplinary application fields.

**Information for Volume Editors and Authors**

Publication in CCIS is free of charge. No royalties are paid, however, we offer registered conference participants temporary free access to the online version of the conference proceedings on SpringerLink (http://link.springer.com) by means of an http referrer from the conference website and/or a number of complimentary printed copies, as specified in the official acceptance email of the event.

CCIS proceedings can be published in time for distribution at conferences or as post-proceedings, and delivered in the form of printed books and/or electronically as USBs and/or e-content licenses for accessing proceedings at SpringerLink. Furthermore, CCIS proceedings are included in the CCIS electronic book series hosted in the SpringerLink digital library at http://link.springer.com/bookseries/7899. Conferences publishing in CCIS are allowed to use Online Conference Service (OCS) for managing the whole proceedings lifecycle (from submission and reviewing to preparing for publication) free of charge.

**Publication process**

The language of publication is exclusively English. Authors publishing in CCIS have to sign the Springer CCIS copyright transfer form, however, they are free to use their material published in CCIS for substantially changed, more elaborate subsequent publications elsewhere. For the preparation of the camera-ready papers/files, authors have to strictly adhere to the Springer CCIS Authors' Instructions and are strongly encouraged to use the CCIS LaTeX style files or templates.

**Abstracting/Indexing**

CCIS is abstracted/indexed in DBLP, Google Scholar, EI-Compendex, Mathematical Reviews, SCImago, Scopus. CCIS volumes are also submitted for the inclusion in ISI Proceedings.

**How to start**

To start the evaluation of your proposal for inclusion in the CCIS series, please send an e-mail to ccis@springer.com.

Chao-Yang Lee · Chun-Li Lin ·
Hsuan-Ting Chang
Editors

# Technologies and Applications of Artificial Intelligence

## 28th International Conference, TAAI 2023
## Yunlin, Taiwan, December 1–2, 2023
## Proceedings, Part I

*Editors*
Chao-Yang Lee
National Yunlin University of Science and Technology
Douliou, Taiwan

Chun-Li Lin
National Yunlin University of Science and Technology
Douliou, Taiwan

Hsuan-Ting Chang
National Yunlin University of Science and Technology
Douliou, Taiwan

ISSN 1865-0929 ISSN 1865-0937 (electronic)
Communications in Computer and Information Science
ISBN 978-981-97-1710-1 ISBN 978-981-97-1711-8 (eBook)
https://doi.org/10.1007/978-981-97-1711-8



This Springer imprint is published by the registered company Springer Nature Singapore Pte Ltd.
The registered company address is: 152 Beach Road, #21-01/04 Gateway East, Singapore 189721, Singapore

# Preface

The Artificial Intelligence Society of the Republic of China aims to promote research, development, application, and exchange in the field of artificial intelligence and related areas. Since its establishment in 1995, over 20 years of dedicated effort has brought together numerous AI technology research and development talents from universities, research institutions, and industry in Taiwan. To facilitate the exchange of academic and practical experiences in artificial intelligence, the society has been organizing the International Conference on Artificial Intelligence annually since 1995, and since 1999 it has also been hosting an additional AI Forum each year. These events provide a platform for experts and scholars from domestic and international universities, research units, and industry to exchange AI technologies and application results. Participants in the past have included researchers and students from Taiwan, as well as experts and scholars from other countries such as mainland China, Japan, Thailand, India, Russia, Malaysia, USA, Singapore, Vietnam, Norway, and more. Over the past two decades, with the contributions and efforts of many, it has become the most important AI conference and academic exchange venue in Taiwan.

The International Conference on Technologies and Applications of Artificial Intelligence (TAAI) is committed to the technological development of artificial intelligence. With the efforts of many pioneers, it has become Taiwan's most important international AI academic conference, offering an annual event for experts and scholars in related fields from home and abroad to showcase research achievements and exchange research insights and experiences. This year's event, the 28th edition, was cohosted by the Artificial Intelligence Society of the Republic of China and the National Yunlin University of Science and Technology. In addition to calling for papers on related technologies for presentation, the conference also invited well-known experts and scholars from home and abroad for keynote speeches to discuss the current important trends in the field of artificial intelligence. A special feature of the event is the annual bilateral exchange with the Japanese Society for Artificial Intelligence (JSAI), with many members of JSAI attending the event. Additionally, the conference plans activities such as the AI CUP E.Sun Bank Artificial Intelligence Challenge, Young Woman Rising Star in AI, and High School Sessions, inviting Japanese scholars, industry experts, and young students to participate in the AI event. This conference received a total of 193 submissions, each of which was reviewed by three reviewers in a single-blind process, and finally 47 papers were accepted for publication.

December 2023 Prof. Chuan-Yu Chang

# Preface

# Organization

## Organizing Committee

### Honorary Chair

| | |
|---|---|
| Neng-Shu Yang | National Yunlin University of Science and Technology, Taiwan |

### General Chairs

| | |
|---|---|
| Chuan-Yu Chang | National Yunlin University of Science and Technology, Taiwan |
| Chuan-Kang Ting | National Tsing Hua University, Taiwan |

### Program Chairs

| | |
|---|---|
| Chien-Chou Lin | National Yunlin University of Science and Technology, Taiwan |
| Hung-Yu Kao | National Cheng Kung University, Taiwan |
| Tzong-Han Tsai | National Central University, Taiwan |

### Publication Chairs

| | |
|---|---|
| Hsuan-Ting Chang | National Yunlin University of Science and Technology, Taiwan |
| Chao-Yang Lee | National Yunlin University of Science and Technology, Taiwan |
| Chun-Li Lin | National Yunlin University of Science and Technology, Taiwan |

### Sponsorship Chair

| | |
|---|---|
| Shih-Yu Chen | National Yunlin University of Science and Technology, Taiwan |

**Special Session Chairs**

Yi-Lung Lin — National Yunlin University of Science and Technology, Taiwan
Dun-Wei Cheng — National Yunlin University of Science and Technology, Taiwan

**Public Relations Chairs**

Chian C. Ho — National Yunlin University of Science and Technology, Taiwan
Szu-Hong Wang — National Yunlin University of Science and Technology, Taiwan

**Publicity Chairs**

Jen-Chun Lin — Academia Sinica, Taiwan
Jun-Cheng Chen — Academia Sinica, Taiwan

**AI Competition Chair**

Tzong-Han Tsai — National Central University, Taiwan

**Game Tournament Chair**

Shi-Jim Yen — National Dong Hwa University, Taiwan

**Young Woman Star Session Chair**

Min-Chun Hu — National Tsing Hua University, Taiwan

**High School Chair**

Jen-Wei Huang — National Cheng-Kung University, Taiwan

**Advisory Committee**

He Zheng Xin — National Taiwan University of Science and Technology, Taiwan
Von-Wun Soo — National Tsing Hua University, Taiwan
Yau-Hwang Kuo — National Cheng-Kung University, Taiwan

| | |
|---|---|
| Wen-Lian Hsu | Asia University, Taiwan |
| Hsiang Jieh | National Taiwan University, Taiwan |
| S. M. Chen | National Taiwan University of Science and Technology, Taiwan |
| Chun-Nan Hsu | Academia Sinica, Taiwan |
| Vincent S. Tseng | National Yang Ming Chiao Tung University, Taiwan |
| Yung-jen Hsu | National Taiwan University, Taiwan |
| I-Chen Wu | National Yang Ming Chiao Tung University, Taiwan |
| Hui-Huang Hsu | Tamkang University, Taiwan |
| Chia-Hui Chang | National Central University, Taiwan |
| Hung-Yu Kao | National Cheng-Kung University, Taiwan |
| Chuan-Kang Ting | National Tsing Hua University, Taiwan |

## Program Committee

| | |
|---|---|
| Albert Bakhtizin | Central Economics and Mathematics Institute of Russian Academy of Sciences, Russia |
| Aldy Gunawan | Singapore Management University, Singapore |
| Andrea Salfinger | Johannes Kepler University Linz, Austria |
| Anthony Y. H. Liao | Asia University, Taiwan |
| Ayush Singhal | University of Minnesota, USA |
| Been-Chian Chien | National University of Tainan, Taiwan |
| Bi-Ru Dai | National Taiwan University of Science and Technology, Taiwan |
| Bor-Shen Lin | National Taiwan University of Science and Technology, Taiwan |
| Cameron Browne | Queensland University of Technology, Australia |
| Chang-Shing Lee | Engineer Ambitiously-NI, USA |
| Chang-Tien Lu | Virginia Polytechnic Institute and State University, USA |
| Chao-Chun Chen | National Cheng Kung University, Taiwan |
| Che Nan Kuo | CTBA Business School, Taiwan |
| Cheng-Fa Tsai | National Ping Tung University of Science and Technology, Taiwan |
| Cheng-Te Li | National Cheng Kung University, Taiwan |
| Cheng-Hsuan Li | National Taichung University of Education, Taiwan |
| Chen-Sen Ouyang | I-Shou University, Taiwan |
| Cheng-Zen Yang | Yuan Ze University, Taiwan |
| Chenn-Jung Huang | National Dong Hwa University, Taiwan |

| | |
|---|---|
| Chia-Hung Yeh | National Sun Yat-Sen University, Taiwan |
| Chia-Hui Chang | National Central University, Taiwan |
| Chien-Chou Lin | National Yunlin University of Science and Technology, Taiwan |
| Chien-Feng Huang | National University of Kaohsiung, Taiwan |
| Chih-Chieh Hung | National Chung Hsing University, Taiwan |
| Chih-Chin Lai | National University of Kaohsiung, Taiwan |
| Chih-Hua Tai | National Taipei University, Taiwan |
| Ching-Hu Lu | National Taiwan University of Science and Technology, Taiwan |
| Chih-Hung Wu | National University of Kaohsiung, Taiwan |
| Chih-Ya Shen | National Tsing Hua University, Taiwan |
| Chuan-Kang Ting | National Chung Cheng University, Taiwan |
| Chu-Hsuan Hsueh | National Yang Ming Chiao Tung University, Taiwan |
| Chung-Kuang Chou | National Taiwan University, Taiwan |
| Chung-Ming Ou | Kainan University, Taiwan |
| Chun-Hao Chen | National Taipei University of Technology, Taiwan |
| Chun Tsai | National Chung Hsing University, Taiwan |
| Chun-Chi Lai | National Yunlin University of Science and Technology, Taiwan |
| Chung-Hong Lee | National Kaohsiung University of Applied Sciences, Taiwan |
| Chung-Nan Lee | National Sun Yat-Sen University, Taiwan |
| Chun-Wei Lin (Jerry Lin) | Western Norway University of Applied Sciences, Norway |
| Chun-Wei Tsai | National Chung Hsing University, Taiwan |
| Churn-Jung Liau | Academia Sinica, USA |
| Dan Goldberg | Texas A&M University, USA |
| David L. Sallach | Argonne National Laboratory and the University of Chicago, USA |
| Daw-Tung Lin | National Taipei University, Taiwan |
| De-Nian Yang | Academia Sinica, Taiwan |
| Eri Sato-Shimokawara | Tokyo Metropolitan University, Japan |
| Frank S. C. Tseng | National Kaohsiung First University of Science and Technology, Taiwan |
| Fred Morstatter | University of Southern California, USA |
| Fu-Shiung Hsieh | Chaoyang University of Technology, Taiwan |
| Gene P. K. Wu | Hong Kong Polytechnic University, China |
| Grace Lin | Institute for Information Industry, Taiwan |
| Giuseppe D'Aniello | University of Salerno Fisciano, Italy |
| Guan-Ling Lee | National Dong Hua University, Taiwan |
| Hao-Chuan Wang | National Tsing Hua University, Taiwan |

| | |
|---|---|
| Hiroki Shibata | Tokyo Metropolitan University, Japan |
| Hiroshi Kawakami | Kyoto University, Japan |
| Hong-Han Shuai | National Yang Ming Chiao Tung University, Taiwan |
| Hong-Jie Dai | National Kaohsiung University of Science and Technology, Taiwan |
| Hsiao-Ping Tsai | National Chung Hsing University, Taiwan |
| Hsien-Chou Liao | Chaoyang University of Technology, Taiwan |
| Hsin-Chang Yang | National University of Kaohsiung, Taiwan |
| Hsin-Hung Chou | Chang Jung Christian University, Taiwan |
| Hsin-Min Wang | Academia Sinica, Taiwan |
| Hsiu-Min Chuang | National Defense University, Taiwan |
| Hsin-Te Wu | National Penghu University of Science and Technology, Taiwan |
| Hsuan-Tien Lin | National Taiwan University, Taiwan |
| Hsueh-Ting Chu | Asia University, Taiwan |
| Hsun-Ping Hsieh | National Cheng Kung University, Taiwan |
| Hsu-Yung Cheng | National Central University, Taiwan |
| H. T. Chu | Asia University, Taiwan |
| Huei-Fang Yang | National Sun Yat-Sen University, Taiwan |
| Hui-Ju Hung | The Pennsylvania State University, USA |
| Hung-Yi Lee | National Taiwan University, Taiwan |
| Hung-Yu Kao | National Cheng Kung University, Taiwan |
| I-Chen Wu | National Yang Ming Chiao Tung University, Taiwan |
| I-Fang Chung | National Yang-Ming University, Taiwan |
| I-Hsien Ting | National University of Kaohsiung, Taiwan |
| I-Shyan Hwang | Yuan Ze University, Taiwan |
| Jason Jung | Chung-Ang University, Korea |
| Jenn-Long Liu | I-Shou University, Taiwan |
| Jenq-Haur Wang | National Taipei University of Technology, Taiwan |
| Jen-Tzung Chien | National Yang Ming Chiao Tung University, Taiwan |
| Jen-Wei Huang | National Cheng Kung University, Taiwan |
| Jialin Liu | Lawrence Berkeley National Lab, USA |
| Jian-Sing Li | National University of Tainan, Taiwan |
| Jiann-Shu Lee | National University of Tainan, Taiwan |
| Jiun-Long Huang | National Yang Ming Chiao Tung University, Taiwan |
| Jose Luis Ambite | University of Southern California, USA |
| Jr-Chang Chen | National Taiwan University, Taiwan |
| Ju-Chin Chen | National Kaohsiung University of Science and Technology, Taiwan |

| | |
|---|---|
| Judy C. R. Tseng | Chung-Hua University, Taiwan |
| Jung-Kuei Yang | National Dong Hwa University, Taiwan |
| Kawuu W. Lin | National Kaohsiung University of Science and Technology, Taiwan |
| Kazunori Mizuno | Takushoku University, Japan |
| Keh-Yih Su | Academia Sinica, Taiwan |
| Keng-Pei Lin | National Sun Yat-sen University, Taiwan |
| Klaus Brinker | University of Applied Sciences Hamm-Lippstadt, Germany |
| Ko-Wei Huang | National Kaohsiung University of Science and Technology, Taiwan |
| Koong Lin | National University of Tainan, Taiwan |
| Kun-Ta Chuang | National Cheng Kung University, Taiwan |
| Kuo-Hsien Hsia | Far East University, Taiwan |
| Leilei Shi | Bank of China International (China), China |
| Li-Chen Cheng | National Taipei University of Technology, Taiwan |
| Lieu-Hen Chen | National Chi Nan University, Taiwan |
| Ling-Jyh Chen | Academia Sinica, Taiwan |
| Li-Wei Ko | National Yang Ming Chiao Tung University, Taiwan |
| Lung-Pin Chen | Tunghai University, Taiwan |
| Mark H. M. Winands | Maastricht University, Netherlands |
| Martin Michalowski | University of Minnesota, Twin Cities, USA |
| Marie-Liesse Cauwet | TAO, Inria Saclay-CNRS-LRI, University Paris Sud, France |
| Masakazu Muramatsu | The University of Electro-Communications, Tokyo, Japan |
| Matteo Gaeta | University of Salerno Fisciano, Italy |
| Mayank Kejriwal | University of Southern California, USA |
| Min-Chun Hu | National Tsing Hua University, Taiwan |
| Min Sun | National Tsing Hua University, Taiwan |
| Ming-Feng Tsai | National Chengchi University, Taiwan |
| Ming-Shun Tsai | Taiwan AI Academy, Taiwan |
| Min-Yuh Day | Tamkang University, Taiwan |
| Mitsunori Matsushita | Kansai University, Japan |
| Mi-Yen Yeh | Academia Sinica, Taiwan |
| Mong-Fong Horng | National Kaohsiung University of Applied Sciences, Taiwan |
| Mu-Chun Su | National Central University, Taiwan |
| Mu-En Wu | National Taipei University of Technology, Taiwan |
| Naohiro Matsumura | Osaka University, Japan |
| Po-Hsun Cheng | National Kaohsiung Normal University, Taiwan |
| Po-Ruey Lei | ROC Naval Academy, Taiwan |

| | |
|---|---|
| Po-Yuan Chen | Jinwen University of Science and Technology, Taiwan |
| Ray-Bing Chen | National Cheng Kung University, Taiwan |
| Rong-Ming Chen | National University of Tainan, Taiwan |
| Rung-Ching Chen | Chaoyang University of Technology, Taiwan |
| Sai-Keung Wong | National Yang Ming Chiao Tung University, Taiwan |
| Shan-Hung Wu | National Tsing Hua University, Taiwan |
| Sheng-Mao Chang | National Cheng Kung University, Taiwan |
| Shie-Jue Lee | National Sun Yat-sen University, Taiwan |
| Shih-Cheng Horng | Chaoyang University of Technology, Taiwan |
| Shih-Hung Wu | Chaoyang University of Technology, Taiwan |
| Shi-Jim Yen | National Dong Hwa University, Taiwan |
| Shing-Tai Pan | National University of Kaohsiung, Taiwan |
| Shirley Ho | National Chengchi University, Taiwan |
| Show-Jane Yen | Ming Chuan University, Taiwan |
| Shou-De Lin | National Taiwan University, Taiwan |
| Shun-Chin Hsu | Chang-Jung Christian University, Taiwan |
| Shunichi Hattori | Central Research Institute of Electric Power Industry (CRIEPI), Japan |
| Spencer Polk | Carleton University, Canada |
| Tao-Hsing Chang | National Kaohsiung University of Science and Technology, Taiwan |
| Thibaut Lust | UPMC-LIP6, France |
| Ting Han Wei | University of Alberta, Canada |
| Tsaipei Wang | National Yang Ming Chiao Tung University, Taiwan |
| Tsan-Sheng Hsu | Academia Sinica, Taiwan |
| Tsung-Che Chiang | National Taiwan Normal University, Taiwan |
| Tsung-Ting Kuo | University of California San Diego, USA |
| Tuan-Fang Fan | National Penghu University of Science and Technology, Taiwan |
| Tung-Kuan Liu | National Kaohsiung University of Science and Technology, Taiwan |
| Tzong-Han Tsai | National Central University, Taiwan |
| Tzong-Yi Lee | Chinese University of Hong Kong, Shenzhen, China |
| Tzu-Hsien Yang | National Cheng Kung University, Taiwan |
| Tzung-Pei Hong | National University of Kaohsiung, Taiwan |
| Waskitho Wibisono | ITS Indonesia, Indonesia |
| Wei-Guang Teng | National Cheng- Kung University, Taiwan |
| Wei-Min Liu | National Chung Cheng University, Taiwan |
| Wei-Shinn Ku | Auburn University, USA |

| | |
|---|---|
| Wei-Ta Chu | National Chung Cheng University, Taiwan |
| Wen-Chih Peng | National Yang Ming Chiao Tung University, Taiwan |
| Wen-Chung Shih | Asia University, Taiwan |
| Wen-Huang Cheng | National Yang Ming Chiao Tung University, Taiwan |
| Wen-Hung Liao | National Chengchi University, Taiwan |
| Wen-Yang Lin | National University of Kaohsiung, Taiwan |
| Wing-Kwong Wong | National Yunlin University of Science and Technology, Taiwan |
| Wu-Chih Hu | National Penghu University of Science and Technology, Taiwan |
| Vincent S. Tseng | National Yang Ming Chiao Tung University, Taiwan |
| Yao-Ting Huang | National Chung Cheng University, Taiwan |
| Yasufumi Takama | Tokyo Metropolitan University, Japan |
| Yen-Chieh Lien | University of Massachusetts Amherst, USA |
| Yi-Cheng Chen | National Central University, Taiwan |
| Yi-Cheng Chen | Tamkang University, Taiwan |
| Yi-Chung Chen | National Yunlin University of Science and Technology, Taiwan |
| Yih-Chuan Lin | National Formosa University, Taiwan |
| Yi-Hsin Ho | Takushoku University, Japan |
| Yi-Hsuan Yang | Academia Sinica, Taiwan |
| Yi-Hung Wu | Chung Yuan Christian University, Taiwan |
| Yi-Jen Su | Shu-Te University, Taiwan |
| Yi-Leh Wu | National Taiwan University of Science and Technology, Taiwan |
| Yi-Ling Chen | National Taiwan University of Science and Technology, Taiwan |
| Yin-Fu Huang | National Yunlin University of Science and Technology, Taiwan |
| Ying-Ping Chen | National Yang Ming Chiao Tung University, Taiwan |
| Yi-Ren Yeh | Chinese Culture University, China |
| Yi-Shin Chen | National Tsing Hua University, Taiwan |
| Yuan Gao | Northwest University, China |
| Yu-Chiang Wang (Frank Wang) | National Taiwan University, Taiwan |
| Yu-Da Lin | Penghu University of Science and Technology, Taiwan |
| Yue-Shi Lee | Ming Chuan University, Taiwan |
| Yuh-Ming Cheng | Shu-Te University, Taiwan |
| Yu-Huei Cheng | Chaoyang University of Technology, Taiwan |

| | |
|---|---|
| Yu-Ling Hsueh | National Chung Cheng University, Taiwan |
| Yung-Chun Chang | Taipei Medical University, Taiwan |
| Yung-jen Hsu | National Taiwan University, Taiwan |
| Yun-Nung Chen | National Taiwan University, Taiwan |
| Yu-Sheng Chen | National Taiwan University, Taiwan |
| Yusuke Nojima | Osaka Metropolitan University, Japan |
| Yu-Ting Wen | National Yang Ming Chiao Tung University, Taiwan |

# Contents – Part I

# Contents – Part II

# Proposal of Personal Value-Based User Modeling Using Latent Factors

Kaichi Nihira(✉), Hiroki Shibata, and Yasufumi Takama

Tokyo Metropolitan University, 6-6 Asahigaoka, Tokyo 191-0065, Hino, Japan
nihira-kaichi@ed.tmu.ac.jp, {hshibata,ytakama}@tmu.ac.jp

**Abstract.** This paper proposes a method for modeling users' personal values as latent factors through matrix factorization. The proposed method is applied to memory-based collaborative filtering (CF) and Factorization Machines (FM) to demonstrate its effectiveness. A recent trend in CF is to introduce additional factors than interaction history. A rate matching rate (RMRate) has been proposed for modeling user's personal values, and it has been shown to be effective for increasing diversity and recommending niche (long-tail or unpopular) items. On the other hand, the disadvantage of RMRate is that it needs an attribute-level evaluations in addition to rating (total evaluation) to items, which limits its applicability. To address this problem, personal value-based modeling method without using attribute-level evaluations has been proposed, which defines user's personal values as their tendency to select popular/unpopular items. Experimental results showed that this method was effective especially for users who rated a small number of items. However, this approach is difficult to extend for obtaining other types of personal values. To obtain different types of personal values of users only from a rating matrix, this paper proposes to calculate RMRate by regarding the product of user's and item's latent vectors as a pseudo attribute-level evaluation. Experimental results with two datasets show the RMRate calculated by the proposed method can improve precision, recall, and nDCG of memory-based CF and FM.

**Keywords:** Recommendation · Personal values · Collaborative filtering

## 1 Introduction

This paper proposes personal value-based modeling method using latent factors through matrix factorization. The task of recommender systems is to recommend appropriate information to users from a large amount of information, which has been increasing year by year. Most recommendation approaches are categorized into two types: a content-based approach [1] and collaborative filtering (CF) [2]. Content-based approach models the interests of target users based on the attribute values of items (e.g., genre, director, actor, etc. in movies). On the other hand, CF models users' interests only from the history of interaction


C.-Y. Lee et al. (Eds.): TAAI 2023, CCIS 2074, pp. 1–15, 2024.
https://doi.org/10.1007/978-981-97-1711-8_1

(e.g., purchase, browse, evaluation, etc.) with items. Compared to content-based approaches, the advantage of CF is that it can recommend a wide variety of items without knowing the attributes of items. CF is a valuable approach for building effective recommendation systems that cater to diverse user preferences and provide high-quality personalized recommendations.

CF are categorized into two types: memory-based CF and model-based CF. Memory-based CF predicts the target user's ratings by referring to the ratings of other users with similar interests and preferences. This approach can easily explain why an item is recommended to a user. The GroupLens algorithm is well known as a typical memory-based CF [2]. Model-based CF predicts the target user's rating by modeling relationship between users and items. This approach often achieves higher performance compared to memory-based CF, because it is able to capture complex relationships and dependencies by leveraging advanced mathematical models. Singular Value Decomposition (SVD) [3], Non-negative Matrix Factorization (NMF) [4], and Factorization Machines (FM) [5] are well-known as typical model-based CF.

This paper focuses on personal values, which are supposed to have the strong relation to potential consumer preferences. Personal values have been paid attention to in marketing [6], web intelligence [7], and other areas. In order to define personal values quantitatively, the rate matching rate (RMRate) has been proposed [8]. The effectiveness of employing RMRate has been shown by applying it to content-based CF [8], memory-based CF [9], and matrix-based CF [10]. On the other hand, RMRate has the problem that it cannot be used for datasets that does not have evaluation of item attributes (attribute-level evaluations). To extend the applicability of the personal values-based approach, personal values have been redefined in terms of the popularity of items [11]. As this method does not need attribute-level evaluations, it can be applied to datasets without such information. Its effectiveness has been shown by applying it to memory-based CF. However, this approach is difficult to extend for obtaining other types of personal values.

To obtain different types of personal value-based user models only from a rating matrix, this paper proposes for calculating RMRate on the basis of latent factors obtained by matrix factorization. The proposed RMRate regard the product of user's and the item's latent vectors as a pseudo attribute-level evaluation. The proposed method is evaluated by applying it to memory-based CF and FM. Experimental results with two datasets show that the precision, recall, and nDCG can be improved by introducing the proposed method.

This paper is organized as follows. Related work about memory-based CF, matrix-based CF, FM, and personal value-based user modeling for recommendation are introduced in Sect. 2. Section 3 proposes a personal value-based user modeling method using the latent factors obtained by NMF. The effectiveness of the proposed method is shown on the basis of the experimental results with two datasets in Sect. 4.

## 2 Related Works

### 2.1 Memory-Based Collaborative Filtering

In the GroupLens algorithm [2], the inter-user similarity $\rho_{i,t}$ between user $u_i$ and $u_t$ is calculated by Eq. (1) using the Pearson correlation coefficient.

$$\rho_{i,t} = \frac{\sum_{v_j \in V_{i,t}} (s_{i,j} - \bar{s}'_i)(s_{t,j} - \bar{s}'_t)}{\sqrt{\sum_{v_j \in V_{i,t}} (s_{i,j} - \bar{s}'_i)^2} \sqrt{\sum_{v_j \in V_{i,t}} (s_{t,j} - \bar{s}'_t)^2}}, \tag{1}$$

where $V_{i,t}$ is the intersection of $I(u_i)$ and $I(u_t)$, $I(u_i)$ is a set of items rated by user $u_i$, $s_{i,j}$ is the rating of $u_i$ on item $v_j$, and $\bar{s}'_i$ is $u_i$'s average rating of items in $V_{i,t}$.

After calculating the similarities, the predicted rating $\hat{s}_{i,j}$ of user $u_i$ on item $v_j$ is calculated by Eq. (2).

$$\hat{s}_{i,j} = \bar{s}_i + \frac{\sum_{u_t \in U(v_j)} \rho_{i,t}(s_{t,j} - \bar{s}_t)}{\sum_{u_t \in U(v_j)} \rho_{i,t}}, \tag{2}$$

where $\bar{s}_i$ is the average ratings of $u_i$ and $U(v_j)$ is the set of $u_i$'s neighborhood (similar) users who evaluated $v_j$. It is necessary to determine the lower and upper bounds on the size of $U(v_j)$. Decreasing the size decreases the bias (difference between actual ratings and predicted ratings) but increases the variance of prediction, and vice versa.

Cosine similarity can also be employed for calculating inter-user similarity, which is defined as Eq. (3). This paper uses this similarity in addition to the Pearson correlation coefficient in the experiments.

$$\rho_{i,t} = \frac{\sum_{v_j \in V_{i,t}} s_{i,j} s_{t,j}}{\sqrt{\sum_{v_j \in V_{i,t}} s_{i,j}^2} \sqrt{\sum_{v_j \in V_{i,t}} s_{t,j}^2}}. \tag{3}$$

### 2.2 Matrix-Based Collaborative Filtering

Koren et al. have proposed the method of Matrix Factorization [12]. Figure 1 shows an overview of matrix factorization. A rating matrix $\mathbf{S}$, consisting of $n$ users and $m$ items, is decomposed into a user matrix $\mathbf{U}$ of size $n \times k$ and an item matrix $\mathbf{V}$ of size $m \times k$. The predicted rating value $\hat{s}_{i,j}$ of $u_i$ on $v_j$ is calculated

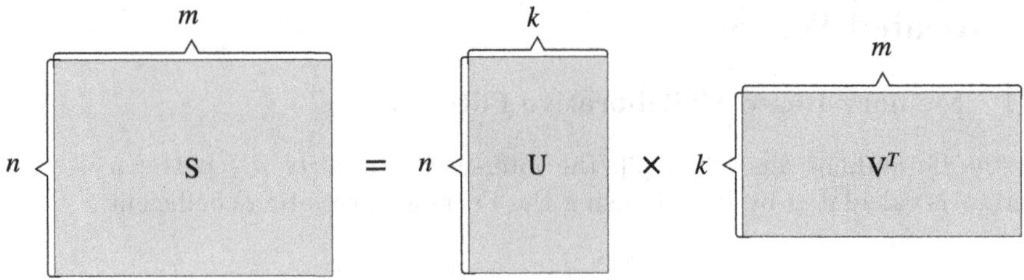


**Fig. 1.** Overview of matrix factorization.

by taking the dot product of the corresponding latent factor vectors $\mathbf{u}_i$ and $\mathbf{v}_j$ (Eq. (4)).

$$\hat{s}_{i,j} = \mathbf{v}_j^T \cdot \mathbf{u}_i. \tag{4}$$

For every rating value $s_{i,j} \in S$, the sum of the squared errors is employed as the objective function (Eq. (5)) and find $\mathbf{U}$ and $\mathbf{V}$ that minimize it.

$$L(\mathbf{U}, \mathbf{V}) = \sum_{s_{i,j} \in S} (s_{i,j} - \mathbf{v}_j^T \mathbf{u}_i). \tag{5}$$

To obtain $\mathbf{U}$ and $\mathbf{V}$, optimization methods such as Stochastic Gradient Descent (SGD) [12] and Alternating Least Squares (ALS) [13] are commonly used. Lee et al. proposed Non-negative Matrix Factorization (NMF), in which the latent factor matrix is obtained as a non-negative matrix [4]. Although the learning model and objective function remain the same as Eq. (4) and (5), respectively, constraints are imposed for the matrix elements to have nonnegative value.

### 2.3 Factorization Machines

FM is known to be an effective method for modeling interactions between features [5]. FMs learns low-dimensional embedding vectors for features and assigns weights to combinations of features for capturing their interactions. The prediction rating $\hat{s}$ is calculated by Eq. (6).

$$\hat{s}(\mathbf{x}) = w_0 + \sum_{i=1}^{n} w_i x_i + \sum_{i=1}^{n} \sum_{j=i+1}^{n} \langle \mathbf{v}_i, \mathbf{v}_j \rangle x_i x_j, \tag{6}$$

where $w_0$ is the global bias, $x_i$ is $i$-th feature in a feature vector $\mathbf{x}$, $w_i$ is the weight of $x_i$, and $\mathbf{v_i}$ is a $d$-dimensional embedding vector for $x_i$. $\langle \mathbf{v}_i, \mathbf{v}_j \rangle$ is the interaction between two features $x_i$ and $x_j$ which is calculated as the dot product of their corresponding embedding vectors $\mathbf{v}_i$ and $\mathbf{v}_j$.

FM can work with any real valued feature vectors, so various types of information can be considered. For example, a feature vector can include target users and target items, which are essential for prediction, ratings for other items previously rated by the user, and the most recent movie rated by the user before the target item [5].

### 2.4 Personal Value-Based User Modeling

Personal values are supposed to have the strong relation to potential consumer preferences. Hattori et al. have defined personal values as the effect of users' evaluation of item attributes on their evaluation (rating) of items in the context of recommendation [8]. For example, when a target item is an accommodation, its attributes are service, location, price etc. If a user always highly evaluates the service of a favorite accommodation, a service is supposed to have a strong effect on user's decision making. To define such personal values quantitatively, RMRate is defined as Eq. (7).

$$RMR_{i,a} = \frac{\sum_{v_j \in I(u_i)} \delta(p_{i,j}, p^a_{i,j})}{|I(u_i)|}, \tag{7}$$

where $p_{i,j} \in \{pos, neg\}$ is the polarity of the total rating of $u_i$ on $v_j$, and $p^a_{i,j} \in \{pos, neg\}$ is the polarity of the rating of $u_i$ on the *attribute* $a$ of $v_j$. If the rating is higher than neutral rating, it is regarded as *pos*, and *neg* otherwise. The function $\delta(p_{i,j}, p^a_{i,j})$ returns 1 if $p_{i,j}$ is equal to $p^a_{i,j}$, and 0 otherwise. It has been reported that the precision of recommendation in cold-start situations was improved by employing RMRate [8].

Takama et al. have proposed memory-based CF employing the RMRate [9]. This method represents a user's characteristics as the vector of the RMRate and calculates an inter-user similarity $\rho_{i,t}$ between user $u_i$ and $u_t$ based on the Pearson correlation coefficient. It has been reported that the user modeling employing the RMRate enables long-tail item recommendation while maintaining the precision [9]. Takama et al. have proposed matrix-based CF employing the RMRate [10]. It has been reported that this methods recommend many unpopular items than the state-of-the art matrix-based methods while keeping precision and recall [10].

While it is shown that recommender systems employing the RMRate are effective, there is a problem that RMRate cannot be calculated on datasets that do not have the attribute-level evaluations. To address this problem, personal value-based modeling method without using attribute-level evaluations has been proposed, which defines user's personal values as their tendency to select popular/unpopular items [11]. This method defines four attributes with the combination of {popular/unpopular items} × {average number of ratings/average rating} and another attribute defined as the ratio of popular items to all items rated by a user was also defined as an attribute. It has been reported that introducing these attributes can achieve higher precision and recall than conventional memory-based CF [11]. However, this method is difficult to extend for obtaining other types of personal values than those relating to the popularity of items.

## 3 Personal Value-Based User Modeling with Latent Factor

Although the effectiveness of recommender systems employing RMRate has been shown [8–10], RMRate cannot be calculated without attribute-level evaluations. To solve this problem, this paper proposes a method for calculating RMRate on the basis of latent factors obtained by NMF. This section describes how to calculate the RMRate from the latent factors and applies it to memory-based CF and FM. The procedure is described in the subsequent subsections.

### 3.1 Getting Personal Values by NMF

Let $\mathbf{U}(n \times k)/\mathbf{V}(m \times k)$ be the latent factor matrix of the user/item obtained by NMF. For user $u_i$ and item $v_j$, the element-wise multiplication $\mathbf{A}_{i,j}$ between the latent factors $\mathbf{u}_i \in \mathbf{U}$ and $\mathbf{v}_j \in \mathbf{V}$ is calculated by Eq. (8).

$$\begin{aligned} \mathbf{A}_{i,j} &= \mathbf{u}_i \odot \mathbf{v}_j \\ &= (u_{i,1}v_{j,1}, u_{i,2}v_{j,2}, \cdots, u_{i,k}v_{j,k}). \end{aligned} \tag{8}$$

The proposed method regards the product of $u_{i,a}$ and $v_{j,a}$ as pseudo attribute-level evaluation for latent attribute $a$ ($pae_{i,j,a}$) after applying min-max normalization (Eq. (9)).

$$pae_{i,j,a} = \frac{u_{i,a}v_{j,a} - \min \mathbf{A}_{i,j}}{\max \mathbf{A}_{i,j} - \min \mathbf{A}_{i,j}}. \tag{9}$$

Using the pseudo attribute-level evaluations, RMRate is defined as Eq. (10).

$$RMR_{i,a} = \frac{\sum\limits_{v_j \in I(u_i)} \delta(p_{i,j}, p_{pae_{i,j,a}})}{|I(u_i)|}, \tag{10}$$

where $p_{pae_{i,j,a}} \in \{pos, neg\}$ is the polarity of $pae_{i,j,a}$. If $pae_{i,j,a}$ is equal to or higher than threshold, it is regarded as $pos$, and $neg$ otherwise. In studies of recommendation systems, ratings which higher than a neutral rating are treated as a positive evaluation (e.g., 3 on a 5-point scale is neutral rating, 4 and 5 are positive). A similar threshold determination method has been employed in references [8–11]. Given that the maximum value of $pae_{i,j,a}$ is 1 and supposing 0 as a missing value (unrated), 4 and 5 in a 5-point scale correspond to 0.8 and 1.0, respectively. In this case, the threshold is set to 0.8.

### 3.2 Calculation of Inter-User Similarity

To calculate the inter-user similarity in the case of memory-based CF, the proposed method uses the Pearson correlation coefficient and cosine similarity, which are often used in memory-based CF. Using the Pearson correlation coefficient, the similarity between $u_i$ and $u_t$ is calculated by Eq. (11).

$$\rho_{i,t} = \frac{\sum_{a=1}^{k}(RMR_{i,a} - \overline{RMR_i})(RMR_{t,a} - \overline{RMR_t})}{\sqrt{\sum_{a=1}^{k}(RMR_{i,a} - \overline{RMR_i})^2}\sqrt{\sum_{a=1}^{k}(RMR_{t,a} - \overline{RMR_t})^2}}, \tag{11}$$

where $\overline{RMR_i}$ means the average RMRate of $u_i$.
The cosine similarity is calculated by Eq. (12).

$$\rho_{i,t} = \frac{\sum_{a=1}^{k} RMR_{i,a} RMR_{t,a}}{\sqrt{\sum_{a=1}^{k} RMR_{i,a}^2}\sqrt{\sum_{a=1}^{k} RMR_{t,a}^2}}, \tag{12}$$

### 3.3 Rating Prediction

The proposed memory-based CF calculates the predicted rating by applying the similarity described in Subsect. 3.2 to Eq. (2). The proposed FM-based models calculate the predicted rating by applying the feature matrix, which consists of row vectors $\mathbf{x}$ described in Sect. 2.3, $\mathbf{X}_{uirp}(k)$ and $\mathbf{X}_{uip}(k)$ to Eq. (6). $\mathbf{X}_{uirp}(k)$ and $\mathbf{X}_{uip}(k)$ are constructed as follows: $k$ is the number of the latent factors of NMF.

- $\mathbf{X}_{uirp}(k)$
  (1) Active user
  (2) Active item
  (3) Ratings to other items by the active user
  (4) RMRate of active user
- $\mathbf{X}_{uip}(k)$
  (1) Active user
  (2) Active item
  (3) RMRate of active user

Active user/item is represented using one-hot encoding. One variable is assigned to an item for representing the ratings to other items: if the active user rated an item, the corresponding variable has the value of his/her rating multiplied by 0.2, and 0 otherwise.

**Table 1.** Number of users per number of ratings.2–4 columns show the range of the number of ratings.

| Dataset | 1–10 | 11–20 | 21–40 | 41– |
|---|---|---|---|---|
| Yahoo! Movie | 1,053 (9.2%) | 4,933 (43.0%) | 2,818 (24.6%) | 2,661 (23.2%) |
| Rakuten Travel | 3,800 (15.8%) | 14,496 (60.1%) | 4,599 (19.1%) | 1,208 (5.0%) |

**Table 2.** Number of items per number of ratings.2–4 columns show the range of the number of ratings.

| Dataset | 1–10 | 11–20 | 21–40 | 41– |
|---|---|---|---|---|
| Yahoo! Movie | 663 (9.7%) | 1,837 (26.9%) | 1,648 (24.1%) | 2,679 (39.3%) |
| Rakuten Travel | 5,385 (45.6%) | 1,630 (13.8%) | 1,581 (13.4%) | 3,212 (27.2%) |

# 4 Experiment

## 4.1 Datasets

The experiments use two datasets, which are generated from rating data of the following websites: Yahoo! Movie[1] and Rakuten Travel[2]. The evaluated item of Yahoo! Movie dataset is a movie, and Rakuten Travel dataset is an accommodation. As both datasets employ 5-point scale, ratings of 4 and 5 are treated as a positive evaluation. As for preprocessing, users with ratings less than 10 were removed from both datasets. Yahoo! Movie dataset consists of 11,465 users, 6,827 items, and 473,339 total evaluations. The density of the rating matrix is 0.00605. Rakuten Travel dataset consists of 24,103 users, 11,808 items, and 437,969 total evaluations. The density of the rating matrix is 0.00154.

Table 1 and Table 2 respectively show the number of users and items per the number of evaluations. Both datasets have many users with 11–20 ratings. While Yahoo! Movie dataset has many items with many ratings, Rakuten Travel dataset has many items with few ratings.

## 4.2 Outline

To show the effectiveness of the proposed methods, the proposed memory-based CF is compared with the conventional memory-based CF, using Pearson correlation coefficient and cosine similarity for calculating inter-user similarity. Let

[1] https://movies.yahoo.co.jp/.
[2] https://rit.rakuten.com/data_release/.

$\mathrm{KNN_{rp}}$ and $\mathrm{KNN_{rc}}$ be KNN[3] with ratings that uses Pearson correlation coefficient and cosine similarity, $\mathrm{KNN_{pp}}(k)$ and $\mathrm{KNN_{pc}}(k)$ be KNN with the proposed RMRate calculated from the $k$ latent factors that uses Pearson correlation coefficient and cosine similarity. The proposed FM is compared with the FM using the feature matrix $\mathbf{X}_{uir}$, which consists of the active user/item and the ratings to other items rated by the active user. Let $\mathrm{FM_r}$ be FM using $\mathbf{X}_{uir}(k)$, $\mathrm{FM_{rp}}(k)$ be FM using $\mathbf{X}_{uirp}(k)$, and $\mathrm{FM_p}(k)$ be FM using $\mathbf{X}_{uip}(k)$.

The experiment supposes a task of recommending the top-$N$ items as a list, which contains items with the highest predicted ratings. In this paper, the $N$ is set to 3. The performance is evaluated by P@$N$ (precision at $N$, Eq. (13)), R@$N$ (recall at $N$, Eq. (14)), and nDCG@$N$ (normalized discounted cumulative gain at $N$, Eq. (15)).

$$\mathrm{P@}N(u_i) = \frac{\sum_{j=1}^{N} f(u_i, v_j)}{N}, \tag{13}$$

$$\mathrm{R@}N(u_i) = \frac{\sum_{j=1}^{N} f(u_i, v_j)}{|I^+(u_i)|}, \tag{14}$$

$$\mathrm{nDCG@}N(u_i) = \frac{\mathrm{DCG@}N(u_i)}{\mathrm{ideal\ DCG@}N(u_i)}, \tag{15}$$

where the function $f(u_i, v_j)$ returns 1 if $s_{i,j}$ (actual rating) is 4 or 5, and 0 otherwise. $I^+(u_i)$ is the set of items $u_i$ gave ratings 4 or more. DCG@$N$ serves as a robust metric for evaluating the accuracy of rankings, where higher values indicate superior ranking performance. nDCG is calculated by dividing DCG by the maximum value of DCG, also known as the ideal DCG for a given recommendation list. DCG is defined as Eq. (16).

$$\mathrm{DCG@}N(u_i) = G_1 + \sum_{j=2}^{N} \frac{G_j}{\log_2 j}, \tag{16}$$

where $G_j$ is the gain attributed to the item positioned at the $j$-th rank within the recommendation list. In this paper, the gain is defined as the rating given by the user. In the following, P@$N$, R@$N$, and nDCG@$N$ is treated as the average of all users. In addition, D@$N$ (diversity at $N$) is leveraged to evaluate the effectiveness of the proposed attributes and recommendation methods in facilitating the recommendation of diverse items. D@$N$ is the number of distinct items included in the top-$N$ recommendation list, which is equal to the number of items that has been recommended for one or more users.

Note that in the experiments, items with a predicted rating lower than 4 are excluded from the recommendation list. As a result, a user may receive less than

[3] KNN stands for K-Nearest Neighbor, which is often used to refer to memory-based CF.

three recommended items. In such cases, $N$ is adjusted to match the number of recommended items for those users.

The experiment is carried out by repeating double cross validation as follows.

(1) Divide a dataset $D$ into three subsets $D_i$.
(2) Do the following process for all combinations of hyperparameters.
 ($\alpha$) Divide a dataset $D' = D \backslash D_i$ into three subsets $D'_j$.
 ($\beta$) Calculate the RMSE of the predicted rating obtained by $\mathrm{KNN_{rp}}$, $\mathrm{KNN_{rc}}$, or $\mathrm{FM_r}$ of the validation data $D'_j$ using $D'' = D' \backslash D'_j$ as the training data.
 ($\gamma$) Calculate the average $\overline{\mathrm{RMSE}}$ over $D'_1$, $D'_2$, and $D'_3$.
(3) With the hyperparameters achieving the minimum $\overline{\mathrm{RMSE}}$ in (2), calculate the predicted rating of the test data $D_i$ using $D'$ as the training data. If $\mathrm{KNN_{rp}}$ is used in (2)($\beta$), either $\mathrm{KNN_{rp}}$ or $\mathrm{KNN_{pp}}(k)$ are used for prediction; if $\mathrm{KNN_{rc}}$ is used, either $\mathrm{KNN_{rc}}$ or $\mathrm{KNN_{pc}}(k)$ are used; if $\mathrm{FM_r}$ is used, either $\mathrm{FM_r}$, $\mathrm{FM_{rp}}(k)$, or $\mathrm{FM_p}(k)$ are used.
(4) Calculate P@3, R@3, nDCG@3, and D@3.
(5) Calculate the average P@3, R@3, nDCG@3, and D@3 over $D_1$, $D_2$, and $D_3$ (respectively denoted as $\overline{\text{P@3}}$, $\overline{\text{R@3}}$, $\overline{\text{nDCG@3}}$, and $\overline{\text{D@3}}$) as final result.

In (3), the proposed methods use the hyperparameters determined for its corresponding conventional methods in (2)($\beta$) in order to compare the proposed and conventional methods with the same settings while avoiding advantageous comparison for the proposed methods. KNN has two hyperparameters: lower and upper bounds on $U(x_j)$. If $|U(x_j)|$ is smaller than lower bound, the second term on the right-hand side of Eq. (2) is set to 0. FM has four hyperparameters which related to optimization: the number of iterations over the training set, the dimension of the embedding vector, and L2 penalty of the weight and the embedding vector for optimization, respectively. FM-based model used ALS for optimization [13].

### 4.3 Result

Table 3 shows $\overline{\text{P@3}}$, $\overline{\text{R@3}}$, $\overline{\text{nDCG@3}}$, and $\overline{\text{D@3}}$ for Yahoo! Movie dataset and Rakuten Travel dataset. In these tables, the results in bold indicate the best performance between $\mathrm{KNN_{rp}}$ and $\mathrm{KNN_{pp}}(k)$, between $\mathrm{KNN_{rc}}$ and $\mathrm{KNN_{pc}}(k)$, and between $\mathrm{FM_r}$, $\mathrm{FM_{rp}}(k)$, and $\mathrm{FM_p}(k)$. It is shown that for both datasets, $\mathrm{KNN_{pp}}(k)/\mathrm{KNN_{pc}}(k)/\mathrm{FM_p}(k)$ achieved higher $\overline{\text{P@3}}$, $\overline{\text{R@3}}$ and $\overline{\text{nDCG@3}}$ than $\mathrm{KNN_{rp}}/\mathrm{KNN_{rc}}/\mathrm{FM_r}$ in most cases regardless of $k$. On the other hand, no clear tendency is observed in terms of $\overline{\text{D@3}}$. It is observed that the difference of $\overline{\text{P@3}}$, $\overline{\text{R@3}}$ and $\overline{\text{nDCG@3}}$ between $\mathrm{FM_{rp}}(k)$ and $\mathrm{FM_r}$ is small compared to those between $\mathrm{FM_p}(k)$ and $\mathrm{FM_r}$ for both datasets. Since the number of proposed RMRate ($k$) is at most a hundred, which is fairly small relative to total number of feature variables of FM, the performance was not so affected.

To examine the effect of the number of ratings a user gave on $\overline{\text{P@3}}$, $\overline{\text{R@3}}$, and $\overline{\text{nDCG@3}}$, users are grouped based on their number of ratings, and $\overline{\text{P@3}}$, $\overline{\text{R@3}}$,

**Table 3.** Experimental result.

(a) Yahoo! Movie

| Method | $\overline{P@3}$ | $\overline{R@3}$ | $\overline{nDCG@3}$ | $\overline{D@3}$ |
|---|---|---|---|---|
| $KNN_{rp}$ | .489 | .225 | .538 | 3,096 |
| $KNN_{pp}(20)$ | .496 | **.231** | .539 | 3,118 |
| $KNN_{pp}(50)$ | **.498** | **.231** | .542 | 3,120 |
| $KNN_{pp}(100)$ | **.498** | **.231** | **.543** | **3,122** |
| $KNN_{rc}$ | .492 | .229 | .531 | **2,759** |
| $KNN_{pc}(20)$ | .518 | .242 | .559 | 2,591 |
| $KNN_{pc}(50)$ | .519 | .244 | .561 | 2,572 |
| $KNN_{pc}(100)$ | **.522** | **.245** | **.563** | 2,567 |
| $FM_{r}$ | .579 | .291 | .698 | 4,566 |
| $FM_{rp}(20)$ | .579 | .291 | .698 | 4,566 |
| $FM_{rp}(50)$ | .575 | .287 | .694 | 4,570 |
| $FM_{rp}(100)$ | .581 | .294 | .702 | **4,633** |
| $FM_{p}(20)$ | .583 | **.301** | **.722** | 4,543 |
| $FM_{p}(50)$ | **.584** | .300 | .718 | 4,546 |
| $FM_{p}(100)$ | **.584** | .299 | .717 | 4,537 |

(b) Rakuten Travel

| Method | $\overline{P@3}$ | $\overline{R@3}$ | $\overline{nDCG@3}$ | $\overline{D@3}$ |
|---|---|---|---|---|
| $KNN_{rp}$ | .581 | .410 | .611 | **7,661** |
| $KNN_{pp}(20)$ | **.733** | .436 | **.762** | 7,145 |
| $KNN_{pp}(50)$ | .729 | **.437** | .758 | 7,128 |
| $KNN_{pp}(100)$ | .728 | .435 | .756 | 7,116 |
| $KNN_{rc}$ | .702 | .440 | .731 | **7,386** |
| $KNN_{pc}(20)$ | .741 | .449 | .763 | 6,436 |
| $KNN_{pc}(50)$ | **.742** | **.450** | **.765** | 6,411 |
| $KNN_{pc}(100)$ | **.742** | **.450** | **.765** | 6,404 |
| $FM_{r}$ | .776 | .445 | .829 | 7,243 |
| $FM_{rp}(20)$ | .775 | .442 | .828 | 7,227 |
| $FM_{rp}(50)$ | .777 | .445 | .831 | 7,246 |
| $FM_{rp}(100)$ | .776 | .444 | .831 | 7,260 |
| $FM_{p}(20)$ | .779 | .450 | .831 | 7,248 |
| $FM_{p}(50)$ | .779 | .450 | .832 | 7,284 |
| $FM_{p}(100)$ | **.782** | **.453** | **.836** | **7,311** |

and $\overline{nDCG@3}$ are calculated for each group. Table 4, 5 and 6 respectively show the result for Yahoo! Movie dataset and Rakuten Travel dataset. It is shown that for both datasets, $\overline{P@3}$, $\overline{R@3}$, and $\overline{nDCG@3}$ of $KNN_{pp}(k)$/ $KNN_{pc}(k)/FM_{p}(k)$ tend to be higher than $KNN_{rp}/KNN_{rc}/FM_{r}$ regardless of $k$. In particular, this tendency is clear for users with 1 to 20 ratings.

The recommendation performance of CF-based model is decreased by the cold-start problem [14]. The cold-start problem is the difficulty of providing suitable recommendations for new users or the difficulty of recommending items that are newly introduced. Even so, the methods employing the proposed RMRate achieved higher $\overline{P@3}$, $\overline{R@3}$ and $\overline{nDCG@3}$ than the conventional methods when the number of ratings per user is small for both datasets. Therefore, it is expected that the methods employing the proposed RMRate can mitigate the cold-start problem.

## 5 Conclusion

This paper proposed a personal values modeling method using latent factors obtained by NMF. To define a personal values quantitatively, RMRate is calculated from the pseudo attribute-level evaluation that is calculated as the Hadamard product of user's and item's latent vectors. As the proposed RMRate can be calculated only from a rating matrix, the proposed method can be applied to datasets without item's attribute-level evaluations. Experiments using

**Table 4.** $\overline{\text{P@3}}$. 2–4 columns show the range of the number of ratings.

(a) Yahoo! Movie.

| Method | 1–10 | 11–20 | 21–40 | 41– |
|---|---|---|---|---|
| $KNN_{rp}$ | .382 | .478 | **.574** | **.687** |
| $KNN_{pp}(20)$ | .415 | .480 | .563 | .658 |
| $KNN_{pp}(50)$ | .416 | **.481** | .564 | .662 |
| $KNN_{pp}(100)$ | **.418** | .479 | .566 | .667 |
| $KNN_{rc}$ | .416 | .474 | .554 | .653 |
| $KNN_{pc}(20)$ | .432 | .498 | .589 | .694 |
| $KNN_{pc}(50)$ | .435 | .498 | .590 | .697 |
| $KNN_{pc}(100)$ | **.437** | **.501** | **.591** | **.702** |
| $FM_{r}$ | .514 | .579 | .636 | .680 |
| $FM_{rp}(20)$ | .510 | .576 | .642 | .684 |
| $FM_{rp}(50)$ | .504 | .574 | **.645** | .676 |
| $FM_{rp}(100)$ | .519 | .575 | .642 | .680 |
| $FM_{p}(20)$ | **.523** | .575 | .637 | .689 |
| $FM_{p}(50)$ | .521 | .576 | .639 | .699 |
| $FM_{p}(100)$ | .516 | **.582** | .636 | **.701** |

(b) Rakuten Travel.

| Method | 1–10 | 11–20 | 21–40 | 41– |
|---|---|---|---|---|
| $KNN_{rp}$ | .590 | .561 | .573 | .705 |
| $KNN_{pp}(20)$ | **.715** | **.741** | **.804** | **.846** |
| $KNN_{pp}(50)$ | .711 | .737 | .800 | .842 |
| $KNN_{pp}(100)$ | .712 | .733 | .797 | .838 |
| $KNN_{rc}$ | .679 | .715 | .784 | .835 |
| $KNN_{pc}(20)$ | .721 | .749 | .817 | **.867** |
| $KNN_{pc}(50)$ | **.723** | .750 | .818 | .864 |
| $KNN_{pc}(100)$ | **.723** | **.751** | **.819** | **.867** |
| $FM_{r}$ | .764 | .781 | .829 | .846 |
| $FM_{rp}(20)$ | .761 | .781 | .829 | .847 |
| $FM_{rp}(50)$ | .762 | .784 | .830 | .853 |
| $FM_{rp}(100)$ | .761 | .784 | .829 | .857 |
| $FM_{p}(20)$ | .766 | .785 | .832 | .852 |
| $FM_{p}(50)$ | .764 | **.788** | .831 | .866 |
| $FM_{p}(100)$ | **.769** | .787 | **.835** | **.869** |

**Table 5.** $\overline{\text{R@3}}$. 2–4 columns show the range of the number of ratings.

(a) Yahoo! Movie.

| Method | 1–10 | 11–20 | 21–40 | 41– |
|---|---|---|---|---|
| $KNN_{rp}$ | .271 | .259 | **.183** | **.087** |
| $KNN_{pp}(20)$ | .287 | **.261** | .181 | .083 |
| $KNN_{pp}(50)$ | .288 | **.261** | .180 | .084 |
| $KNN_{pp}(100)$ | **.289** | .259 | .180 | .085 |
| $KNN_{rc}$ | .288 | .258 | .176 | .081 |
| $KNN_{pc}(20)$ | .299 | .274 | .190 | .089 |
| $KNN_{pc}(50)$ | .302 | .274 | **.192** | .089 |
| $KNN_{pc}(100)$ | **.304** | **.277** | **.192** | **.090** |
| $FM_{r}$ | .348 | .338 | .238 | .103 |
| $FM_{rp}(20)$ | .349 | .336 | .240 | .104 |
| $FM_{rp}(50)$ | .343 | .331 | .240 | .103 |
| $FM_{rp}(100)$ | .362 | .334 | .239 | .103 |
| $FM_{p}(20)$ | **.366** | .347 | **.245** | .103 |
| $FM_{p}(50)$ | .363 | .347 | .244 | **.106** |
| $FM_{p}(100)$ | .359 | **.348** | .244 | **.106** |

(b) Rakuten Travel.

| Method | 1–10 | 11–20 | 21–40 | 41– |
|---|---|---|---|---|
| $KNN_{rp}$ | .479 | .364 | .179 | .100 |
| $KNN_{pp}(20)$ | .488 | **.410** | **.248** | **.132** |
| $KNN_{pp}(50)$ | **.489** | .409 | .245 | .131 |
| $KNN_{pp}(100)$ | .488 | .407 | .243 | .130 |
| $KNN_{rc}$ | .496 | .410 | .239 | .126 |
| $KNN_{pc}(20)$ | .503 | **.423** | .250 | **.133** |
| $KNN_{pc}(50)$ | **.504** | **.423** | **.251** | **.133** |
| $KNN_{pc}(100)$ | **.504** | **.423** | **.251** | **.133** |
| $FM_{r}$ | .492 | .424 | .271 | .143 |
| $FM_{rp}(20)$ | .487 | .422 | .273 | .143 |
| $FM_{rp}(50)$ | .490 | .427 | .272 | .144 |
| $FM_{rp}(100)$ | .488 | .426 | .274 | .145 |
| $FM_{p}(20)$ | .498 | .427 | .273 | .143 |
| $FM_{p}(50)$ | .496 | **.431** | .274 | .147 |
| $FM_{p}(100)$ | **.501** | **.431** | **.276** | **.148** |

**Table 6.** $\overline{\mathrm{nDCG@3}}$. 2–4 columns show the range of the number of ratings.

(a) Yahoo! Movie.

| Method | 1–10 | 11–20 | 21–40 | 41– |
|---|---|---|---|---|
| $\mathrm{KNN}_{\mathrm{rp}}$ | .450 | .528 | .609 | .697 |
| $\mathrm{KNN}_{\mathrm{pp}}(20)$ | **.488** | **.544** | **.617** | **.700** |
| $\mathrm{KNN}_{\mathrm{pp}}(50)$ | .476 | .527 | .596 | .679 |
| $\mathrm{KNN}_{\mathrm{pp}}(100)$ | .478 | .524 | .600 | .684 |
| $\mathrm{KNN}_{\mathrm{rc}}$ | .472 | .514 | .581 | .656 |
| $\mathrm{KNN}_{\mathrm{pc}}(20)$ | .488 | .544 | .617 | .700 |
| $\mathrm{KNN}_{\mathrm{pc}}(50)$ | .492 | .544 | **.620** | .704 |
| $\mathrm{KNN}_{\mathrm{pc}}(100)$ | **.493** | **.547** | **.620** | **.707** |
| $\mathrm{FM}_{\mathrm{r}}$ | .637 | .705 | .756 | .767 |
| $\mathrm{FM}_{\mathrm{rp}}(20)$ | .637 | .707 | .755 | .769 |
| $\mathrm{FM}_{\mathrm{rp}}(50)$ | .630 | .702 | .757 | .768 |
| $\mathrm{FM}_{\mathrm{rp}}(100)$ | .648 | .705 | .755 | .769 |
| $\mathrm{FM}_{\mathrm{p}}(20)$ | **.675** | **.731** | **.766** | .773 |
| $\mathrm{FM}_{\mathrm{p}}(50)$ | .667 | .727 | .761 | .779 |
| $\mathrm{FM}_{\mathrm{p}}(100)$ | .663 | .726 | .759 | **.781** |

(b) Rakuten Travel.

| Method | 1–10 | 11–20 | 21–40 | 41– |
|---|---|---|---|---|
| $\mathrm{KNN}_{\mathrm{rp}}$ | .632 | .582 | .565 | .674 |
| $\mathrm{KNN}_{\mathrm{pp}}(20)$ | **.753** | **.765** | **.802** | **.824** |
| $\mathrm{KNN}_{\mathrm{pp}}(50)$ | .748 | .761 | .798 | .822 |
| $\mathrm{KNN}_{\mathrm{pp}}(100)$ | .749 | .757 | .796 | .816 |
| $\mathrm{KNN}_{\mathrm{rc}}$ | .719 | .736 | .777 | .803 |
| $\mathrm{KNN}_{\mathrm{pc}}(20)$ | .753 | .766 | .807 | .837 |
| $\mathrm{KNN}_{\mathrm{pc}}(50)$ | **.755** | .768 | .807 | .836 |
| $\mathrm{KNN}_{\mathrm{pc}}(100)$ | **.755** | **.769** | **.809** | **.839** |
| $\mathrm{FM}_{\mathrm{r}}$ | .817 | .837 | .870 | .866 |
| $\mathrm{FM}_{\mathrm{rp}}(20)$ | .815 | .837 | .871 | .866 |
| $\mathrm{FM}_{\mathrm{rp}}(50)$ | .818 | .841 | .872 | .870 |
| $\mathrm{FM}_{\mathrm{rp}}(100)$ | .818 | .841 | .873 | .871 |
| $\mathrm{FM}_{\mathrm{p}}(20)$ | .820 | .839 | .872 | .873 |
| $\mathrm{FM}_{\mathrm{p}}(50)$ | .818 | .843 | .874 | .876 |
| $\mathrm{FM}_{\mathrm{p}}(100)$ | **.825** | **.844** | **.876** | **.880** |

two datasets were conducted to compare the memory-based CF and FM-based model employing the proposed RMRate with the conventional methods. As an overall tendency, $\mathrm{KNN}_{\mathrm{pp}}(k)/\mathrm{KNN}_{\mathrm{pc}}(k)/\mathrm{FM}_{\mathrm{p}}(k)$ achieved higher $\overline{\mathrm{P@3}}$, $\overline{\mathrm{R@3}}$ and $\overline{\mathrm{nDCG@3}}$ than $\mathrm{KNN}_{\mathrm{rp}}/\mathrm{KNN}_{\mathrm{rc}}/\mathrm{FM}_{\mathrm{r}}$ in most cases regardless of $k$. In addition, it was also confirmed that $\mathrm{KNN}_{\mathrm{pp}}(k)/\mathrm{KNN}_{\mathrm{pc}}(k)/\mathrm{FM}_{\mathrm{p}}(k)$ tend to achieve higher $\overline{\mathrm{P@3}}$, $\overline{\mathrm{R@3}}$ and $\overline{\mathrm{nDCG@3}}$ than $\mathrm{KNN}_{\mathrm{rp}}/\mathrm{KNN}_{\mathrm{rc}}/\mathrm{FM}_{\mathrm{r}}$ regardless of $k$. In particular, this tendency is clear for users with 1 to 20 ratings. Based on this result, the proposed RMRate is expected to be effective for the cold-start problem.

Future work is to investigate the characteristics of the proposed personal values. The experimental results showed that the number of latent factors $k$ in the proposed method did not affect the performance so much. Investigating the relationship between $k$ and the characteristics of the calculated RMRate in details may help improve recommendation performance. To avoid advantageous comparison for the proposed methods, this paper compared the proposed and conventional methods with the hyperparameters tuned with the conventional methods. However, there may be differences in appropriate lower and upper bounds on the size of neighborhood users between the proposed and the conventional methods. Therefore, hyperparameters suitable for the proposed approach will be set.

Another future direction is to introduce the proposed RMRate to matrix-based CF. It has been shown that matrix-based CFs employing RMRate calculated from item attribute-level evaluations achieved comparable recommendation accuracy to typical matrix-based CFs while recommending more unpopular items [10]. It is expected that those benefits can also be obtained by applying the proposed RMRate to matrix-based CF.

**Acknowledgements.** In this paper, we used "Rakuten Dataset" (https://rit.rakuten.com/data_release/) provided by Rakuten Group, Inc. via IDR Dataset Service of National Institute of Informatics. This work was partially supported by JSPS KAKENHI Grant Numbers 21H03553, 22H03698, and 22K19836.

## References

1. Pachet, F., Roy, P., Cazaly, D.: A combinatorial approach to content-based music selection. IEEE Multimedia **7**(1), 44–51 (2000). https://doi.org/10.1109/93.839310
2. Resnick, P., Iacovou, N., Suchak, M., Bergstorm, P., Riedl, J.: GroupLens: an open architecture for collaborative filtering of netnews. In: 1994 ACM conference on Computer Supported Cooperative Work, pp. 175–186. Association for Computing Machinery, New York (1994). https://doi.org/10.1145/192844.192905
3. Sarwar, B.M., Karypis, G., Konstan, J.A., Riedl, J.T.: Application of Dimensionality Reduction in Recommender System - A Case Study. Technical report, Retrieved from the University of Minnesota Digital Conservancy (2000). hdl.handle.net/11299/215429
4. Lee, D.D., Seung, H.S.: Algorithms for non-negative matrix factorization. In: 13th International Conference on Neural Information Processing Systems, pp. 535–541. MIT Press, Cambridge (2000)
5. Rendle, S.: Factorization machines. In: IEEE International Conference on Data Mining, pp. 995–1000. IEEE Press, Sydney (2010). https://doi.org/10.1109/ICDM.2010.127
6. Vinson, D.E., Scott, J.E., Lamont, L.M.: The role of personal values in marketing and consumer behavior. J. Mar. **41**(2), 44–50 (1977). https://doi.org/10.2307/1250633
7. Chen, J., Hsieh, G., Mahmud, J.U., Nichols J.: Understanding individuals' personal values from social media word use. In: 17th ACM Conference on Computer Supported Cooperative work & Social Computing, pp. 405–414. Association for Computing Machinery, New York (2014). https://doi.org/10.1145/2531602.2531608
8. Hattori, S., Takama, Y.: Recommender system employing personal-value-based user model. J. Adv. Comput. Intell. Intell. Inform. **18**(2), 157–165 (2014). https://doi.org/10.20965/jaciii.2014.p0157
9. Takama, Y., Chen, Y.-S., Misawa, R., Ishikawa, H.: Analyzing potential of personal values-based user modeling for long tail item recommendation. J. Adv. Comput. Intell. Intell. Inform. **22**(4), 506–513 (2018). https://doi.org/10.20965/jaciii.2018.p0506
10. Takama, Y., Shibata, H., Shiraishi, Y.: Matrix-based collaborative filtering employing personal values-based modeling and model relationship learning. J. Adv. Comput. Intell. Intell. Inform. **24**(6), 719–727 (2020). https://doi.org/10.20965/jaciii.2020.p0719
11. Nihira, K., Shibata, H., Takama, Y.: Proposal of personal value-based user modeling without attribute evaluation. In: 10th International Symposium on Computational Intelligence and Industrial Applications, C1–3. Beijing Institute of Technology, Beijing (2022)

12. Koren, Y., Bell, R., Volinsky, C.: Matrix factorization techniques for recommender systems. Computer **42**(8), 30–37 (2009). https://doi.org/10.1109/MC.2009.263
13. Zhou, Y., Wilkinson, D., Schreiber, R., Pan, R.: Large-scale parallel collaborative filtering for the Netflix prize. In: Fleischer, R., Xu, J. (eds.) AAIM 2008. LNCS, vol. 5034, pp. 337–348. Springer, Heidelberg (2008). https://doi.org/10.1007/978-3-540-68880-8_32
14. Schein, A.I., Popescul, A., Ungar, L.H., Pennock, D.M.: Methods and metrics for cold-start recommendations. In: 25th annual international ACM SIGIR Conference on Research and Development in Information Retrieval, pp. 253–260. Association for Computing Machinery, New York (2002). https://doi.org/10.1145/564376.564421

# Artificial Intelligence Model Interpreting Tools: SHAP, LIME, and Anchor Implementation in CNN Model for Hand Gestures Recognition

Chung-Chian Hsu[1,2], S. M. Salahuddin Morsalin[1(✉)], Md Faysal Reyad[2], and Nazmus Shakib[2]

[1] Department of Information Management, National Yunlin University of Science and Technology, Douliu, Taiwan
{hsucc,D10813004}@yuntech.edu.tw

[2] Graduate School of Artificial Intelligence, National Yunlin University of Science and Technology, Douliu, Taiwan
{m11023054,m11023053}@yuntech.edu.tw

**Abstract.** Explainable AI (XAI) are the tools and frameworks of artificial intelligence applications that make it easier to trust the results and outcomes produced by machine learning algorithms. Additionally, XAI helps with debugging, enhancing model performance, and describing the behavior of models to others. This paper presents an innovative approach for hand-gesture detection using an Explainable AI Convolutional Neural Network (XAI-CNN) and SHAP (Shapley Additive Explanations) values, LIME (Local Interpretable Model-agnostic Explanations), and Anchor as Explainable AI tools. The XAI-CNN model is specifically designed for ten different classes of hand-gesture accurate recognition, including palm moved, C, ok, I, fist, index, palm, thumb, down, and fist moved symbols. The proposed XAI-CNN architecture, built upon the previous CNN model, demonstrates an impressive accuracy of 99.98%. Furthermore, the SHAP (XAI tools) values, LIME, and Anchor integration enable the interpretation and visualization of the model's decision-making process separately, enhancing the transparency and trustworthiness in the hand-gesture recognition process. This research contributes to the robustness and interpretable AI systems for hand-gesture recognition, empowering users with accurate and understandable AI technology.

**Keywords:** Explainable AI · Shapley Additive Explanations · Local Interpretable Model-agnostic Explanation · Anchor · Hand-gesture Recognition · Image Classification · Convolutional Neural Network

## 1 Introduction

The XAI tool sophisticates the interpretability and transparency of complex machine learning models, such as Convolutional Neural Networks (CNNs) widely used for hand gesture recognition. The human body key-point detection and recognition [1] are challenging tasks in human-computer interaction and computer vision. XAI tool is an enabler


C.-Y. Lee et al. (Eds.): TAAI 2023, CCIS 2074, pp. 16–29, 2024.
https://doi.org/10.1007/978-981-97-1711-8_2

in many sectors and helps to make them auto-controlled from remote places. However, the complexity of recognizing hand gestures due to the diversity in shape, size, capturing angle, lighting conditions, and background distortion developed the Baseline CNN model [2]. XAI techniques provide insights into the decision-making process of these models, enabling users to understand the underlying factors contributing to predictions. We can create more potentiality, trustworthiness, and accountability by integrating XAI into the CNN model, empowering the users' capability to understand the performance and verify the model's results.

XAI tools integration techniques in the CNN model with SHAP values, LIME, and Anchor not only enhance the interpretability but also contribute to increasing the trustworthiness in hand gesture detection [3, 4]. By utilizing the CNN model, which excels at extracting complex spatial patterns from input data. We capture intricate hand-gesture features that might be challenging for traditional algorithms. When combined with XAI tools, which provide feature-level explanations, XAI-CNN models become more robust and precise in their predictions. The SHAP values, LIME, and Anchor implementation enable fine-tuning the XAI-CNN model's parameters for increased accuracy by finding the essential aspects that affect the model's decision-making process. This paper explores the synergistic relationship between XAI-CNN and XAI tools, demonstrating their effectiveness in enhancing hand-gesture detection accuracy while maintaining transparency and interpretability by following Trustworthiness in Artificial Intelligence (TAI) guidance.

## 2 Related Works

The capabilities of deep learning and its effectiveness in extracting and classifying the detail characteristics from input data have received more attention in recent work. An explainable artificial intelligence approach [5] for unsupervised fault detection models in industrial applications and SHAP has been implemented in rotating machinery. XAI has provided scientific insights about the variability of the signals, which enhances the acceptance and trustworthiness of users, and professionals in AI-power devices [6]. The AI model architecture becomes understandable by XAI tools' additive explanation and predictive results based on the local interpretable model-agnostic explanations to illustrate the deep-learning model [7]. The deep learning models can efficiently classify retinoblastoma and fundus images with high accuracy, recall, precision, and F1 scores on the test set. The SHAP, and LIME, visualizations provide local and global explanations for the model's predictions [8], highlighting important regions for classification. A CNN base model [9] detected the hand-based near-infrared pictures database, which offered accurate and efficient recognition of human hand motions. The paper [10] presents a method that uses XAI techniques to improve the Explainable details of a classifier for air-handling unit faults. The increasing expansion of deep learning algorithms in computer vision applications to combat noise and interference in the noise picture is growing using Sub-Pixel Layer and convolution ($1 \times 1$) [11] to amplify input features and fusion feature maps.

This method used an XGBoost algorithm for fault detection and classification. In addition, the XAI-based SHAP technique provides explanations for the fault's diagnosis.

We have followed a deep learning-based adaptive CNN model [12] for automatic hand gesture detection and movement recognition by injecting some modules. The proposed XAI-CNN model enhances trust-worthy in the hand-gesture recognition process model through Interpretable Model-agnostic Explanations. AI has revolutionized the way we live and work, but it can sometimes be difficult to understand how AI algorithms reach their decisions. This is where explainable AI comes in XAI provides a framework for understanding how an AI model makes decisions, increasing trust and accountability.

## 3 Proposed XAI-CNN Method

This section presents an overview of the previous Convolutional Neural Network (CNN) and our proposed Explainable Artificial Intelligence Convolutional Neural Network (XAI-CNN) architecture, working procedures, and a depiction comparison. Explainable AI is a set of tools and frameworks to help users understand and interpret predictions made by machine learning models, natively integrated with a number of products and services. This helps us to debug and improve the model performance, and assist others in understanding your models' behavior. Fortunately, this work offers a plethora of powerful tools and libraries that empower AI models and machine learning practitioners to address these challenges in head-on practices.

### 3.1 Traditional CNN for Hand Gesture Detection

The CNN model is a kind of artificial neural network designed to process data with a grid-like structure, such as images. It consists of multiple layers of interconnected nodes, including convolutional layers that extract relevant features by applying filters to local regions of the input. This hierarchical architecture enables CNNs to automatically learn and capture complex patterns and spatial relationships, making them highly effective in tasks like image recognition, including hand gesture detection. Pooling layers that minimize the spatial dimensions come after the convolutional layers and fully connected layers that carry out the final classification based on the retrieved features. By leveraging the inherently hierarchical and shared-weight structure, CNNs have revolutionized computer vision tasks and achieved good performance in various domains, for instance, object detection, recognition, classification, segmentation, and so on.

The structure of the previous CNN model consists of two convolutional layers, one convolutional 2D layer, two pooling layers, and two fully connected layers with Rectified Linear Unit (ReLU) as an activation function. The model has two stages: image preprocessing in the first stage and gesture recognition in the second stage using the CNN model with two distinct architectures. The previous model contains multiple layers with various parameters.

### 3.2 Proposed XAI-CNN Architecture

We have applied the tuning and adaptation approaches to the previous CNN model and modified it to robust the performance. After several optimizations of the model, we have reached our proposed XAI-CNN model structure that provided better generalization

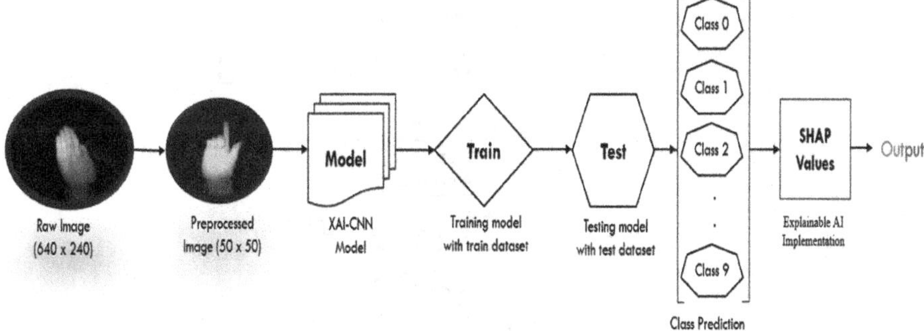


**Fig. 1.** Proposed XAI-CNN model work process.

capability than the previous CNN model. Figure 1 depicts the performing process of our proposed XAI-CNN model.

This transparency is crucial for regulatory compliance, ethical considerations, and gaining user acceptance. We have processed the image data, as seen in Fig. 1, before being sent to the model for training. The input data goes through the image conversion process of RGB to grayscale. Each image undergoes a Grayscale to RGB conversion before being produced. Moreover, its measurements were lowered from 640*240 to 50*50 for rapid processing. The network is then given the pre-processed picture dataset and instructed to learn features and classify the photos into the assigned ten classes. We have used 20% of the test data for the proposed XAI-CNN model testing, and it has measured up to 99.98% accuracy. Figure 2 demonstrates the proposed XAI-CNN model architecture. Interpretable models play a pivotal role in machine learning, promoting trust by shedding light on their decision-making mechanisms.

Data preprocessing: Our dataset contains almost 20,000 images of different hand gestures and the original image size was 640 × 240. As a result, we have decreased the size of the image to 50 × 50 and converted them into grayscale to perform efficiently by the machine. Model modification: We have modified the layers of the previous ADCNN model as follows:

- We have changed the feature maps of the first layer of 128 to increase the shallow features of the input.
- We have added 3 layers (Convolutional 2D, ReLU, MaxPooling (2 × 2), and Dropout layer) before the flattening layer. As a result, MaxPooling decreases the spatial feature size, reducing the number of parameters and computations in the network. The next layer is the dropout configuration to randomly exclude 20 percent of neurons to reduce overfitting.
- Next, we have added another dense layer and ReLU activation function to receive the previous feature map 128-dimensional output as the first fully connected layer.
- The final part of our proposed XAI-CNN structure is the output layer which comprises a Softmax activation function and contains 10 neurons, one for each hand gesture recognition and classification.

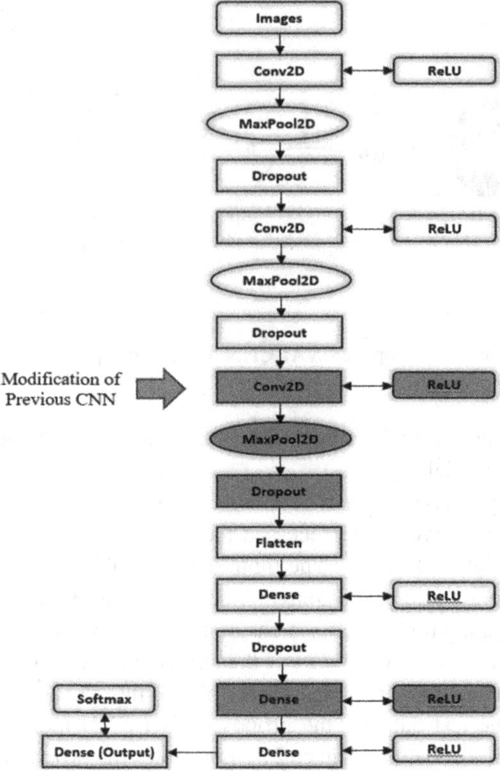


**Fig. 2.** Proposed XAI-CNN model structure.

### 3.3 Data Augmentation

Data augmentation addresses a variety of challenges when training the model, such as limited or imbalanced data, overfitting, and variation and complexity. This approach is essential to train the XAI-CNN model and improve its capacity to generalize variations in hand-gesture appearances. It also generates additional training data by applying various transformations to the original dataset, such as rotations, translations, scaling, and flipping. By augmenting the dataset, we increase diversity and variability, which helps the model generalize better and become more robust to variations in hand-gesture presences. Proper kernel initialization contributes to efficient training and prevents vanishing. Kernel regularization techniques, such as regularization, mitigate overfitting, allowing the model to generalize better and capture essential hand-gesture features. It also helps prevent overfitting, as it introduces noise and variations that discourage the model from relying too heavily on specific information or patterns in the original data. Moreover, data augmentation expands the dataset size, which is particularly beneficial when working with limited labeled data, improving CNN's ability to learn representative and discriminative hand-gesture features. We have modified hyper-parameters in our proposed module to customize the XAI-CNN model. All the final selected parameters as listed in Table 1.

**Table 1.** Proposed XAI-CNN Model parameters

| Layers | Configurations |
|---|---|
| Optimizer | Adam |
| Loss | categorical_crossentropy |
| Metrics | ['accuracy'] |
| Conv2D | 128 filters, 5 × 5 kernel, and ReLU |
| Max-Pooling | 2 × 2 kernel |
| Dropout | 20% |
| Conv2D | 32 filters, 3 × 3 kernel, and ReLU |
| Max-Pooling | 2 × 2 kernel |
| Dropout | 20% |
| Conv2D | 32 filters, 3 × 3 kernel, and ReLU |
| Max-Pooling | 2 × 2 kernel |
| Dropout | 20% |
| Flatten | – |
| Dense | 128 Neurons and ReLU |
| Dropout | 20% |
| Dense | 128 Neurons and ReLU |
| Dense | 64 Neurons and ReLU |
| Dense (Output) | Softmax 10 Classes |

# 4 Experimental Design

## 4.1 Dataset Arrangement

An AI accelerator [13] performs deep learning object recognition from camera raw data for real-time application. The interpretable model is trained to mimic the behavior of the black box model around the data point. AI has revolutionized work, but it can sometimes be difficult to understand how AI algorithms make decisions. This is where explainable AI comes in XAI provides a framework for understanding how an AI model makes decisions, increasing trust and accountability. The local model is trained to generate an explanation of the prediction, highlighting the most important features that contributed to the prediction. The idea behind XAI is to explain the prediction model by training a local, interpretable model around the data point. We trained and tested our proposed XAI-CNN model using data obtained by the leap motion controller on hand sign recognition, known as "leapGestRecog" [14]. Twenty thousand photographs of ten distinct hand gestures made by ten different subjects—five men and five women—are included in the collection. Each type of hand gesture has a corresponding symbol. The experiment comprised all 10 of the dataset's unique gesture photos. The hand gesture identification procedure is often challenging if the image of datasets does not belong to normal illumination. However, it might be difficult to distinguish specific hand actions in these photographs because of low lighting. We have divided 80% and 20 percent of the dataset into training datasets and testing sets. It led to a split of 16,000 photographs as training sets and 4,000 photos for testing all datasets. The picture format is PNG with 640 × 240 pixels resolution. Ten static hand gestures have been employed in the testing and recorded with various scale, rotation, and translation parameters, shown in Fig. 3.

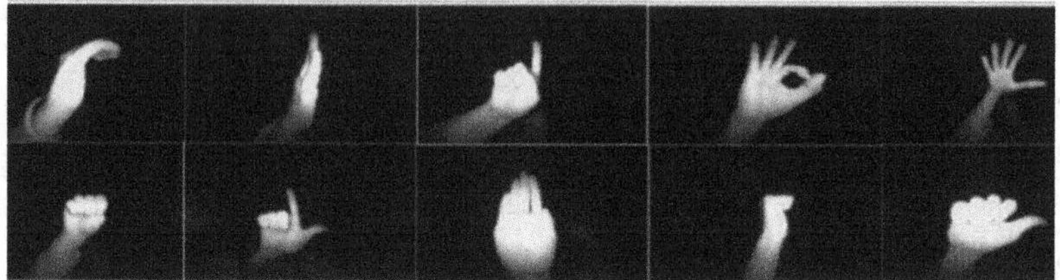

**Fig. 3.** Sample image of "leapGestRecog" dataset.

## 4.2 Image Processing

The photos are changed to grayscale for real-time classification, as seen in Fig. 4. As a result, the picture pre-processing lowers the number of parameters in the first convolutional layer and less the computational load. Additionally, we have used color space conversion and reshaping for one-color channel processing to compare three RGB channels.

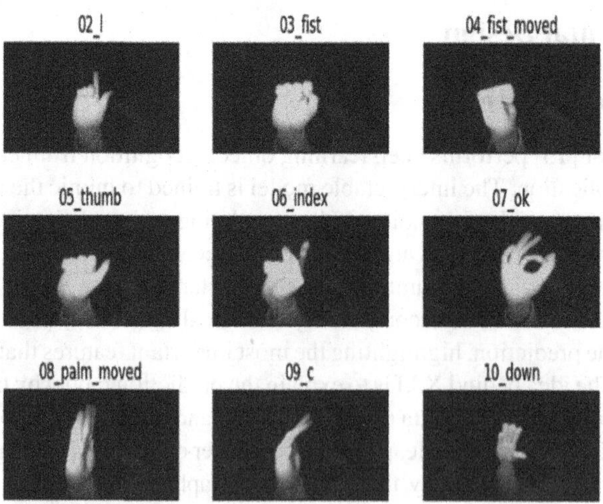


**Fig. 4.** Randomly selected images from training data.

### 4.3 Evaluation Metrics

We employed a variety of criteria to evaluate the performance of the previous CNN and XAI-CNN models. Accuracy, Precision, Recall, and F1-score were these. TP: True Positive, FP: False Positive, FN: False Negative, TN: True Negative.

Precision: Another term for it is the Positive Predictive Value. The proportion of accurate forecasts to all positively anticipated class values is known as precision. We calculate the accuracy by using the equation below.

$$\text{Precision} = \frac{TP}{TP + FP}. \tag{1}$$

Recall: It can be referred to as sensitivity. Calculating recall involves dividing the percentage of accurate predictions by the total number of correct class predictions. We calculate the Recall by the following equation below.

$$\text{Recall} = \frac{TP}{TP + FN}. \tag{2}$$

$$\text{F1} = \frac{2 \times \; Precision \times Recall}{Precision + Recall}. \tag{3}$$

$$\text{Accuracy} = \frac{TP + TN}{TP + TN + FP + FN} \times 100. \tag{4}$$

F1-score: The F1-score is also known as the F-measure or the F-score. The F1 score illustrates how Precision and Recall are balanced. Only when the values of Precision and Recall are both high values of the F1-score increase. Accuracy is the percentage of correct classifications.

## 5 Experimental Results

This section demonstrates the experimental outcomes of the proposed XAI-CNN architectures and the result comparison. We have used the Python platform to conduct the experiments utilizing the Numpy, Keras, and Scikit-learn modules. As explained in Section III, the training set from the "leapGestRecog" dataset was used to learn features from the training data and to test the models using the testing data. Figure 5 shows the comparison of traditional CNN and our proposed XAI-CNN confusion matrix result difference.

Figure 6(a) shows the proposed XAI-CNN model training loss. Figure 6(b) demonstrates the proposed XAI-CNN model accuracy.

**Table 2** lists all the performance comparisons of the previous CNN models and the proposed XAI-CNN based on the values of various performance parameters. The baseline CNN model got 95.73% accuracy, the adaptive CNN model had 99.73 percent accuracy, and the deep CNN model acquired 99.73% accuracy. Whereas the proposed XAI-CNN model has achieved the best accuracy of 99.98 percent for the same epoch numbers.

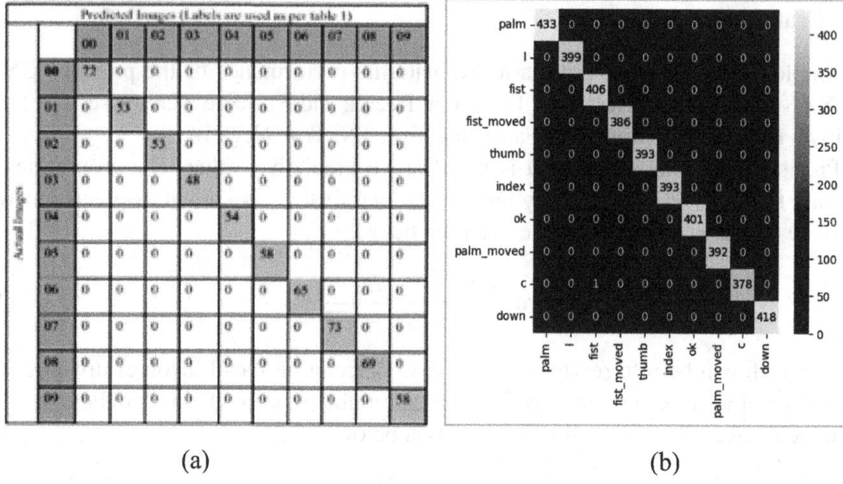


**Fig. 5.** Confusion matrix of (a) previous model, (b) proposed XAI-CNN.

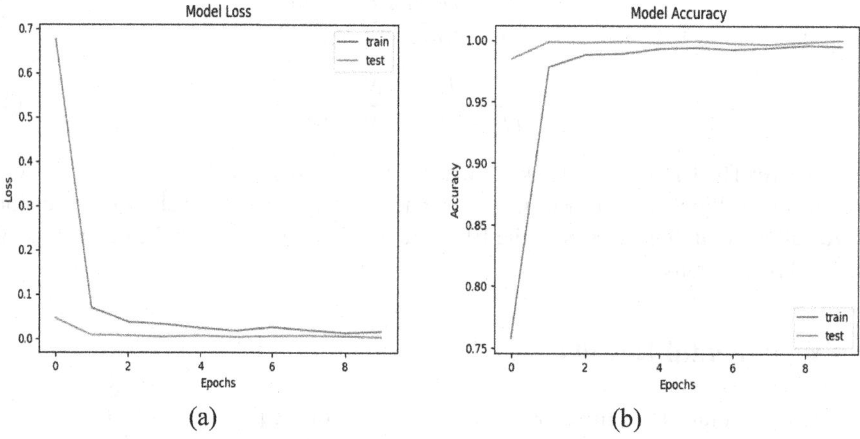


**Fig. 6.** Performance of the proposed XAI-CNN (a) Model loss, (b) Model accuracy.

### 5.1 Shapley Additive Explanations

The SHAP is a valuable XAI tool for training our proposed XAI-CNN model for hand-gesture detection and computer vision tasks. SHAP values illustrate the contribution or the importance of each feature on the prediction of the model. These values provide insights into the contribution of each feature to the model's output prediction. While dealing with image data, the SHAP (Shapley Additive Explanations) values provide insights into the contribution of each pixel or region of the image to the model's output prediction. These values quantify the importance and relevance of different image features for the decision-making process of the model. The method can be applied to visualize

**Table 2.** Performance comparison of the CNN model.

| Parameters | Baseline CNN | Adapted CNN | Deep CNN | Proposed XAI-CNN |
|---|---|---|---|---|
| Epoch | 10 | 10 | 10 | 10 |
| Precision | 0.96 | 0.98 | 0.98 | 0.99 |
| Recall | 0.96 | 0.99 | 0.99 | 0.99 |
| F1 Score | 0.96 | 0.99 | 0.99 | 0.99 |
| Accuracy | 95.73 | 99.73 | 99.75 | 99.98 |

the Shapley values, identify the most important features, and quantify the model's bias towards certain groups or classes.

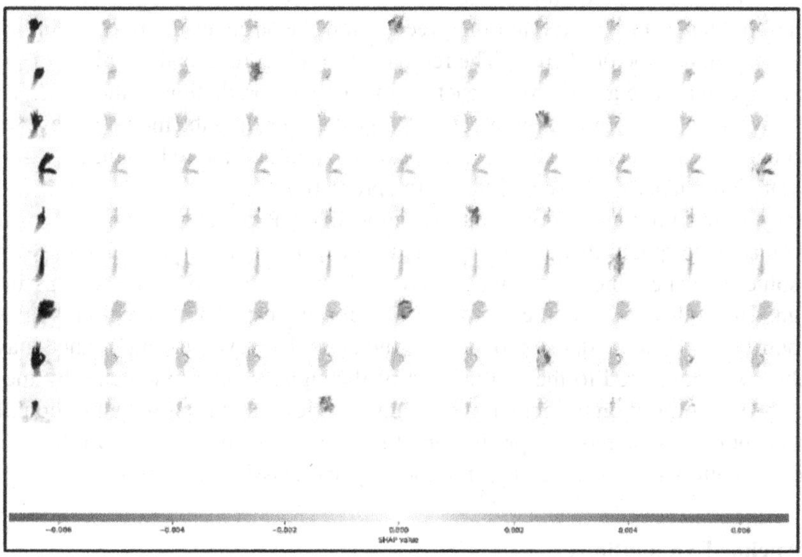

**Fig. 7.** SHAP Values implementation on XAI-CNN.

Figure 7 explains ten outputs (each class) for nine different images. Red pixels increase the model's output probability while blue pixels decrease the output probability. The input images are shown on the left and as nearly transparent grayscale backings behind each of the explanations. SHAP values show which pixels or areas of the input image have the most effects on the model's prediction of a specific hand motion in the context of hand gesture detection using an XAI-CNN model. We can comprehend the visual signals and patterns that the model uses to generate precise predictions by examining the SHAP values. The heat-map process flows to display the SHAP values for picture data, with brighter areas denoting regions with greater significance or contribution to the model's judgment. Users may check and trust the model's outputs thanks to this visualization, which aids in understanding and comprehending the logic behind the model's predictions.

In summary, SHAP values provide an interpretable and quantitative measure of the contribution of pixels or regions in an image towards the model's decision-making process, allowing for better understanding and transparency in image classification tasks such as hand-gesture detection.

## 5.2 LIME Explanations

In LIME's explanation for Fig. 8, the colors and their meanings typically represent the importance of different regions or pixels in the image for the model's prediction of the class. The colors provide insights into which parts of the image strongly influence the model's decision and which parts are less relevant. The green background likely indicates the regions or pixels in the image that have a positive impact on the model's prediction of the class. These regions are supportive of the model's decision and contribute to the model's confidence in predicting class.

The brighter or more saturated the green color, the stronger the positive influence of those regions on the prediction. The red background represents the regions or pixels in the image that have a negative impact on the model's prediction of the class. These regions might be misleading or contrary to the gesture, leading the model to have lower confidence in its prediction. The brighter or more saturated the red color, the stronger the negative influence of those regions on the prediction.

The yellow color border around the sign most likely represents the regions or pixels at the image's periphery that also contribute to the model's decision. While they might have some relevance, their importance may be lower compared to the regions inside the sign. The yellow color border around the circle suggests that this region is relevant and contributes to the model's prediction of the class. However, its importance may be slightly lower compared to the central part of the sign, which is indicated by the red color. The red color fill in the center of the sign signifies that this particular region plays a significant role in the model's prediction of the class. The model heavily relies on the features or patterns in this central part to identify and classify the gesture.

## 5.3 Anchor Explanations

In Anchor's explanation, the colors and their meanings typically represent the important regions or conditions in the image that influence the model's prediction of the "ok" class. Each color provides insights into the specific areas or features that are significant for the model's decision. The deep green background likely indicates the regions or pixels in the image that are strongly associated with the model's prediction of the class. These regions play a crucial role in the decision-making process, and the model heavily relies on them to classify the image. The light green color covering the palm of the hand suggests that this particular area is essential for the model's prediction of the class. The features or patterns present in the palm region significantly contribute to the model's ability to recognize the sign. The light blue and deep blue color borders around the upper part of all fingers indicate that these regions are relevant and contribute to the model's prediction of the class as shown in Fig. 9. The lighter blue color may represent a moderate influence,

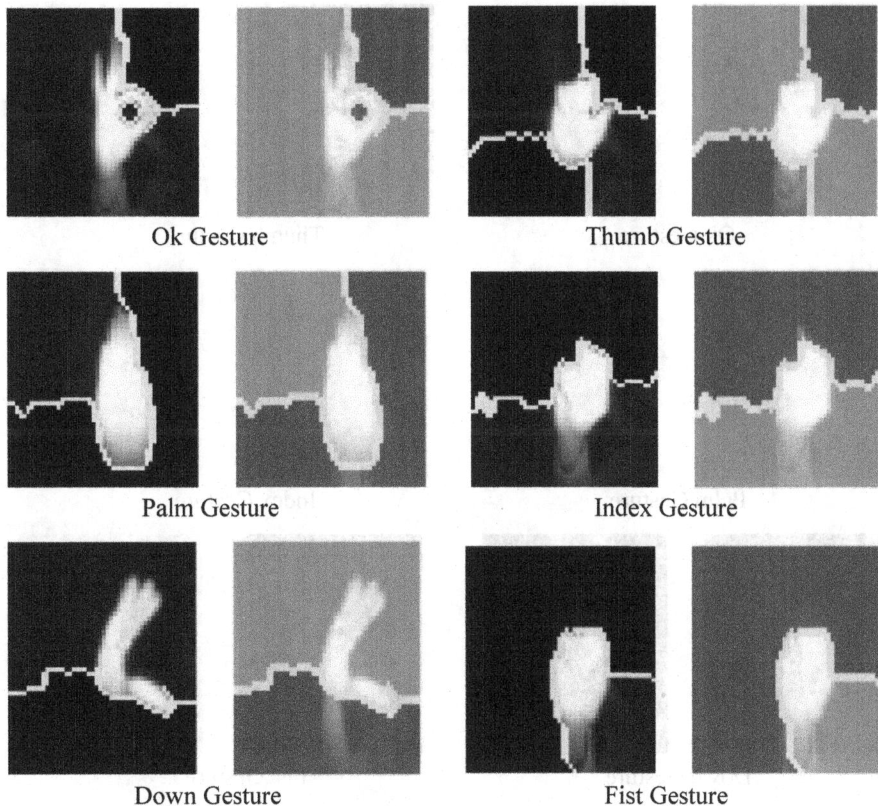


**Fig. 8.** LINE employment in proposed XAI-CNN.

while the deeper blue color suggests a stronger impact on the model's decision. The brown color borders around the upper left and lower left parts of the image signify that these areas are important for the model's prediction.

The specific features or conditions present in these regions contribute significantly to the model's ability to recognize the sign. The light blue color border around the circle suggests that this region is relevant to the model's prediction. While important, its influence may be slightly lower compared to the deep green background. The deep blue color fill in the center of the sign indicates that this central part of the circle plays a critical role in the model's prediction of the class. The model heavily relies on the features or patterns in this central area to identify and classify the gesture.

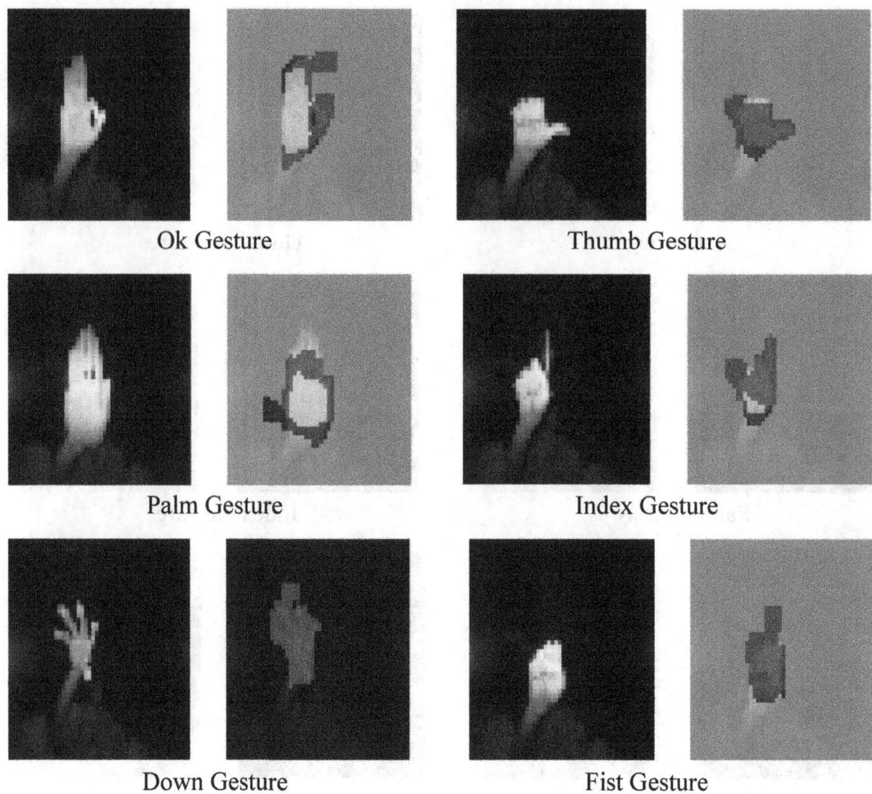


**Fig. 9.** Anchor execution in XAI-CNN model.

## 6 Conclusion

In conclusion, this paper highlights the significance of Explainable AI (XAI) tools techniques, specifically focusing on SHAP values, LIME, and Anchor integration in the proposed XAI-CNN model for hand gesture recognition. The SHAP values effectively extract and classify high-level features from data, enabling accurate recognition of hand gestures. In addition, LIME as an XAI tool enhances interpretability, transparency, and accountability in the decision-making process of the proposed XAI-CNN model. Integrating Anchor provides valuable insights into the contribution of individual hand gesture features, improving interpretability and facilitating trust in the model's outputs. Understanding the effects of feature characteristics, biases, and errors can be identified and addressed to refine the model's performance. Overall, the hand gesture recognition process becomes more precise and understandable when the XAI tools, notably SHAP values, LIME, and Anchor combined with the XAI-CNN model. This development improves our comprehension of the decision-making process and promotes AI and human cooperation. The experimental results have presented responsible and dependable AI systems by providing users with technology for accurate hand gesture recognition.

## References


1. Sheu, M.H., Morsalin, S.M.S., Hsu, C.C., Lai, S.C., Wang, S.H., Chang, C.Y.: Improvement of human pose estimation and processing with the intensive feature consistency network. IEEE Access **11**, 28045–28059 (2023)
2. Flores, C.J.L., Cutipa, A.E.G., Enciso, R.L.: Application of convolutional neural networks for static hand gestures recognition under different invariant features. In: 2017 IEEE XXIV International Conference on Electronics, Electrical Engineering and Computing (INTERCON), Cusco, pp. 1–4 (2017)
3. Ribeiro, M.T., Singh, S., Guestrin C.: "Why Should I Trust You?": explaining the predictions of any classifier. In: 2016 Conference of the North American Chapter of the Association for Computational Linguistics, San Diego, pp. 97–101 (2016)
4. Ribeiro, M.T., Singh, S., Guestrin, C.: Anchors: high-precision model-agnostic explanations. In: The Thirty-Second AAAI Conference (AAAI-2018), pp. 1527–1535 (2018)
5. Brito, L.C., Susto, G.A., Brito, J.N., Duarte, M.A.: An explainable artificial intelligence approach for unsupervised fault detection and diagnosis in rotating machinery. In: 2017 IEEE XXIV International Conference on Electronics, Electrical Engineering and Computing (INTERCON), Cusco, pp. 1–4 (2017)
6. Gozzi, N., Malandri, L., Mercorio, F., Pedrocchi, A.: An explainable artificial intelligence approach for unsupervised fault detection and diagnosis in rotating machinery. Mech. Syst. Signal Process. **163**, 108105 (2022)
7. Bhandari, M., Yogarajah, P., Kavitha, M.S., Condell, J.: Exploring the capabilities of a lightweight CNN model in accurately identifying renal abnormalities: cysts, stones, and tumors, using LIME and SHAP. Appl. Sci. **13**(5), 3125 (2023)
8. Aldughayfiq, B., Ashfaq, F., Jhanjhi, N., Humayun, M.: Explainable AI for retinoblastoma diagnosis: interpreting deep learning models with LIME and SHAP. Diagnostics **13**(11), 1932 (2023)
9. Mahmoud, A.G., Hasan, A.M., Hassan, N.M.: Convolutional neural networks framework for human hand gesture recognition. Bull. Electr. Eng. Inf. **10**(4), 2223–2230 (2021)
10. Meas, M., et al.: Explainability and transparency of classifiers for air-handling unit faults using explainable artificial intelligence (XAI). Sensors **22**(17), 6338 (2022)
11. Sheu, M.H., Morsalin, S.M.S., Wang, S.H., Shen, Y.T., Hsia, S.C., Chang, C.Y.: FIBS-unet: feature integration and block smoothing network for single image dehazing. IEEE Access **10**, 71764–71776 (2022)
12. Alani, A.A., Cosma, G., Taherkhani, A., McGinnity, T.M.: Hand gesture recognition using an adapted convolutional neural network with data augmentation. In: 2018 4th International Conference on Information Management (ICIM), Oxford, pp. 5–12 (2018)
13. Zhu, W.Y., Wong, W.K., Morsalin, S., Wang, S.H., Sheu, M.H.: Software and hardware integration system design with fruit identification for smart electronic scale applications. In: 2021 IEEE International Conference on Consumer Electronics-Taiwan (ICCE-TW), Penghu, pp. 1–2 (2021)
14. Sharma, H.K., Kumar, P., Ahlawat, P., Manchanda, Y.: Deep learning based accurate hand gesture recognition using enhanced CNN model. In: Second International Conference on Computing (2021)

# Proposal of Finding Potentially Valid Menus from Recipe Dataset Using Knowledge Graph Embedding

Aoi Ohta(✉), Hiroki Shibata, and Yasufumi Takama

Graduate School of Systems Design, Tokyo Metropolitan University, Hino, Tokyo, Japan
ota-aoi1@ed.tmu.ac.jp, {hshibata,ytakama}@tmu.ac.jp

**Abstract.** This paper proposes a method to find potentially valid menus which do not explicitly exist in the recipe dataset using knowledge graph embedding (KGE).KGE can predict the missing links in Knowledge Graphs (KGs) by embedding each entity and relation as a vector. Using this feature,the proposed method finds potentially valid menus from the recipe dataset. As it is impossible for a recipe KG to include all possible combinations of recipes that could be regarded as menus,finding potentially valid menus is necessary for realizing recipe recommender systems.This paper describes how to construct the recipe KG from the Cookpad dataset and find potentially valid menus by exploiting TransE.The effectiveness of the proposed method is shown based on the survey-based evaluation. Furthermore, this paper investigates the effect of additional learning.

**Keywords:** Knowledge graph embedding (KGE) · Recipe recommendation

## 1 Introduction

This paper proposes the method to find menus which are not registered in the recipe dataset using Knowledge Graph Embedding (KGE). Highly evaluated for its expressiveness, Knowledge Graph (KG) is widely used in a variety of topics related to artificial intelligence. Unlike other data structures, a graph can handle many kinds of relations between things: Therefore, it is suitable to express what the world is like. However, it is infeasible to enumerate and express all knowledge in a specific domain by KG: the amount of things and relations in a real world is enormous even in a specific domain. Furthermore, there is a huge amount of implicit knowledge we use in our daily life and expressing such knowledge as KG is a difficult task.

Knowledge Graph Embedding (KGE) can find knowledge that are not explicitly registered in KG by mapping KG elements into the embedding vector space. As KGE maps KG so that it can fulfill the semantic relationships on vector


C.-Y. Lee et al. (Eds.): TAAI 2023, CCIS 2074, pp. 30–45, 2024.
https://doi.org/10.1007/978-981-97-1711-8_3

calculation, it can be used to predict implicit relationships. This ability of KGE can be applied to many kinds of tasks such as recommendation, question answering, and information retrieval. It is also applied to domain-specific tasks such as medicine recommendation [6].

As for a food-related domain, the number of cooking recipes existing in the world is enormous and many new recipes have been created every other day. The number of menus, which are a combination of recipes, is also enormous. As a result, recipe posting sites have been popular means for us to access recipe information. Some of the sites also publish their recipe information as datasets [1]. Although some of the datasets contain menu information as well, only a part of possible combinations of recipe is explicitly registered.

The aim of this paper is to find hidden menus from recipe KG by applying KGE. The recipe KG is made from a dataset of the recipe posting site [1]. This paper uses three types of knowledge in the dataset: menus, categories of each recipe, and the hierarchical structure of the categories. The categories of recipes include detailed information such as the ingredients, seasons, and types of dishes. The constructed KG is mapped to the vector space by TransE [2], one of the widely-used KGE methods. Experimental result shows the obtained models can predict menus explicitly registered in the KG correctly. It is also confirmed that it can predict potentially valid menus that are not registered in the dataset. Moreover, as KGE is expected to do more valid prediction by increasing the density of the KG, this paper investigates the effect of additional learning.

The contribution of this paper is summarized as follows: it is shown that the obtained model using TransE can predict menus registered in KG. A survey was taken to examine the effectiveness of the proposed method for predicting potentially valid menus: the result shows that average precision of 0.8 was achieved. Furthermore, it is shown that user feedback can be incorporated into the model by additional learning.

The remainder of this paper is organized as follows: Sect. 2 introduces related work. Section 3 details the proposed method. Section 4 reports the experimental results. Section 5 investigates the effect of the additional learning. Section 6 discusses the experimental results. Section 5 presents the conclusions and future work.

## 2 Related Work

This section discusses related work including knowledge graph embedding and its application.

Knowledge graph embedding models learn embedding vectors of triples $(h, r, t)$. A variety of models has been developed, which are classified into three types depending on its optimization method: translation-based [2,4,8,16], bilinear [9], and neural network [3,13]. The quality of embeddings depends on the model parameters. Therefore, it is reported that old models could perform better than new ones by adjusting model parameters properly [11].

TransE is the first translation-based knowledge graph embedding model [2]. Translation-based model learns embedding vectors $\boldsymbol{h}, \boldsymbol{l}, \boldsymbol{t}$ of a triple $(h, l, t)$ :

$h, t \in E$ are respectively head and tail entities and $l \in L$ is a relation, where $E$ is a set of entities and $L$ is a set of relations. Each translation-based models have its own constraints that are considered in a learning phase. For example, TransE optimizes its embedding vectors so that $\boldsymbol{h}+\boldsymbol{l}$ can be close to $\boldsymbol{t}$ if a triple $(h, l, t)$ exists in the training set $S$. It is achieved by minimizing the value of the loss function $\mathcal{L}$ defined as Eq. (1). During the learning, $\boldsymbol{h}, \boldsymbol{l}, \boldsymbol{t}$ is updated based on the product of $\mathcal{L}$ and the learning rate.

$$\mathcal{L} = \sum_{(h,l,t)\in S} \sum_{(h',l,t')\in S'_{(h,l,t)}} [\gamma + d(\boldsymbol{h}+\boldsymbol{l},\boldsymbol{t}) - d(\boldsymbol{h'}+\boldsymbol{l},\boldsymbol{t'})]_+, \tag{1}$$

where $[x]_+$ means the positive part of of $x$ and $\gamma$ is a hyperparameter that determines the margin. $d(a, b)$ is a function to calculate the dissimilarity between vector $\boldsymbol{a}$ and $\boldsymbol{b}$, which is calculate with either $L_1$ or $L_2$ norm. $S'_{(h,l,t)}$ is a set of corrupted triples that is constructed according to Eq. (2). Corrupted triples are made by replacing either $h$ or $t$ by another entity which is randomly sampled from $E$.

$$S'_{(h,l,t)} = \{(h', l, t) | h' \in E \wedge h' \neq h\} \cup \{(h, l, t') | t' \in E \wedge t' \neq t\}. \tag{2}$$

Limitation of TransE is that it cannot recognize 1-N, N-1, and N-N relations. In particular, it tries to map different tail (head) entities of the triples to the same embedding vector when their heads (tails) and relations are the same. Several models have been proposed for mitigating this problem. For example, TransH maps triples to hyperplane so as to make each triple separately embedded [16].

By linear vector operations on the embedding space, KGE can predict missing links in KGs, which is called a link prediction task. Using link prediction, KGE can perform various tasks. For example, Palumbo et al. [10] have performed recommendations using link prediction and have shown that it can perform better than collaborative filtering such as SVD. Gong et al. have proposed a method for applying KGE to medicine recommendations for avoiding undesirable medicine-medicine interaction, especially intended for patients that have more than two diseases [6].

Massive amount of recipe data have been utilized to construct KGs [5,14]. Besides, to help the analysis of recipe data, a corpus has been created from the Cookpad dataset [7]. The constructed KGs has been utilized to such tasks as recommendation systems [15] and robotic cooking [12]. On the other hand, to the best of our knowledge, this paper is the first work that applies KGE to menu recommendation.

## 3 Proposed Method

This paper proposes a method to find potentially valid menus from the KG which is constructed from the Cookpad dataset. In particular, this paper focuses on the task of predicting the main dish that suits the specified side dish using KGE. The proposed method applies TransE to learn KG which includes following relationships: main dishes and side dishes registered as menus, recipe and its categories, and category and its parent category. The latter two relationships are used to express similarlity between recipes.

This paper defines three relations for expressing the above-mentioned relationships, which are shown in Table 1. fit_main represents relations of main dish and side dish, category_is represents relations of recipe and its category, and parent_is represents hierarchical structure of categories. In Table 1, columns Head and Tail show the type of entity in that position. The column Table shows the table of the Cookpad dataset mainly used for obtaining the relation. The column Number of triples shows the number of triples about the relation. When constructing KG from the Cookpad dataset, main dish and side dish can be distinguished by dish_type_id column in the dataset, which has value of either 1 (main dish) or 0 (side dish). "Category" means "recipe category" that each recipe belongs to. The number of "recipe category" in the Cookpad dataset is 1,099.

The name of recipes and categories are used as the entity names. Although it is possible to use IDs instead of strings (names) for identity assurance, it is expected that if two recipes with different IDs have the same name, their categories and suitable menus are supposed to be similar.

**Table 1.** Defined Relations

| Relation name | Head | Tail | Table | # of triples |
|---|---|---|---|---|
| fit_main | side dish | main dish | base_kondate_recipes | 108,345 |
| category_is | recipe | category | search_category_recipes | 164,912 |
| parent_is | sub category | parent category | search_categories | 1,095 |

Figs. 1-3 show how the triples are constructed. The structure of the Cookpad dataset is represented by tables in these figures. Double lines connect the columns that have the same elements between different tables.

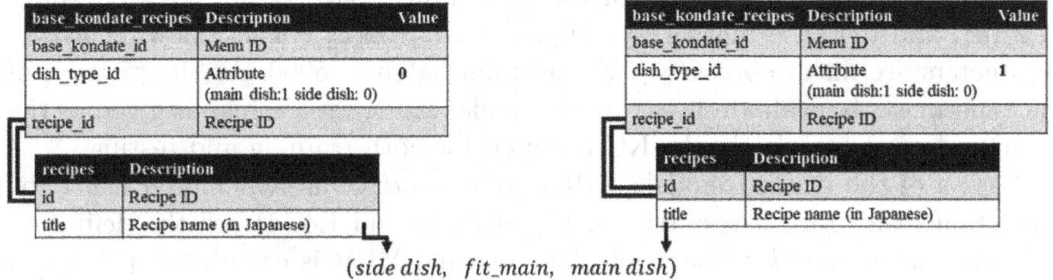


**Fig. 1.** Construction of fit_main

The model trained with the constructed KG predicts suitable main dishes to the specified side dish. By specifying any side dish as a head entity $h$ and

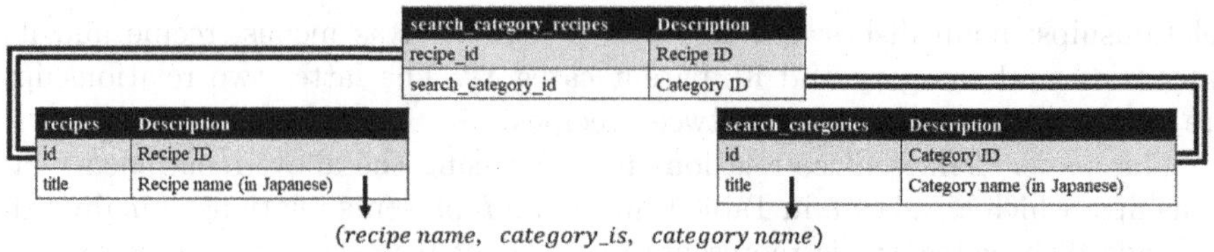


**Fig. 2.** Construction of category_is

| search_categories | Description |
|---|---|
| id | Category ID |
| title | Category name (in Japanese) |
| parent_id | Category ID of the parent category |

| search_categories | Description |
|---|---|
| id | Category ID |
| title | Category name (in Japanese) |
| parent_id | Category ID of the parent category |

*(category name, parent_is, category name)*

**Fig. 3.** Construction of parent_is

fit_main as relation $l$, the model finds the entity whose embedding vector is close to $\boldsymbol{h} + \boldsymbol{l}$.

# 4 Experiments

## 4.1 Outline of the Experiments

**First Experiment: Verification of Prediction Accuracy for Explicitly Registered Triples.** This paper aims to find potentially valid menus from the KG constructed from the Cookpad dataset by applying KGE. For that purpose, the first experiment is conducted to verify that TransE can learn the menus which are registered in the KG. At the same time, this experiment aims to choose the model to be used for the second experiment, which is described in Sec. 4.1.

The models are trained with a grid search using all triples in the constructed KG. The hyperparameters are selected from the following range: learning rate = {0.001, 0.01, 0.1}, dimension of the embedding space = {20,50}, margin = {1,2,10}, and distance measure = {$L_1$ norm, $L_2$ norm}. The following hyperparameters are fixed: epochs = 600 and mini batch = 5000. As the purpose of the experiment to evaluate how well the model can learn the menus given as the training data, all triples in the KG are used for both training and testing.

For all of the trained models, MRR' and $\overline{recall@k}$ are calculated using the prediction result for all test triples. Equation(3) and Eq.(4) are the definition of MRR' and $\overline{recall@k}$ respectively. The original MRR is calculated as follows: calculate the reciprocal rank of the first correct answer (main dish) in the list of entities sorted in descending order of predicting score, then average it over all test triples. This paper uses MRR' instead of MRR to evaluate the performance of models to find all correct answers.

$$MRR' = \frac{1}{Q}\sum_{i=1}^{Q}(\frac{1}{P_i}\sum_{j=1}^{P_i}\frac{1}{rank_{ij}}), \tag{3}$$

where $Q$ is the number of test triples, $rank_{ij}$ is the rank of $j$-th correct answer for the $i$-th test triple, and $P_i$ is the number of correct answers for the $i$-th test triple.

$$\overline{recall}@k = \frac{1}{Q}\sum_{i=1}^{Q}\frac{TP_i@k}{P_i}, \tag{4}$$

where $TP_i@k$ is the number of correct answers for the $i$-th test triple included in the top-k entities with higher prediction scores than others.

Among all 36 models, 10 models are selected based on the result of MRR' and $\overline{recall}@10$ so that models of various MRR' and $\overline{recall}@10$ can be compared. For each of the selected models, $\overline{precision}@10$ (Eq. (5)) is calculated for test menus. The menus to be used as test data are selected by randomly sampling 10 side dishes from the KG. In Eq. (5), $TP_i@10$ is the ratio of valid answers in the top 10 prediction results (main dishes) for each test data, which was judged by the authors. The correct answers that exist in the KG are obviously regarded as valid.

$$\overline{precision}@10 = \frac{1}{10}\sum_{i=1}^{10}\frac{TP_i@10}{10}. \tag{5}$$

The model that has the highest $\overline{precision}@10$ is used in the second experiment.

**Second Experiment: Evaluation** of the prediction accuracy for potentially valid menus. The model selected in Sec. 4.1 is evaluated through the survey to evaluate its ability to predict potentially valid main dishes.

Three side dishes are selected from the KG for the survey which fulfill the following conditions:

1. The recipe is available on Cookpad Website and the page URL is able to get.
2. When predicting tail entities using the side dish as the head entity of fit_main relation, more than 80% of correct answers are included in top10 prediction result.
3. It is easy to judge whether the prediction is correct or not. For example, its genre is obvious, or its taste can be imagined.

Condition 1 aims to provide detailed information on the recipe to the answerers. Condition 2 aims to guarantee that the model can predict the correct answers, which are registered in the KG, for the side dish. Condition 3 helps answerers to answer the survey with confidence.

For the survey, 15 main dishes are selected from each prediction results of the selected side dishes. Each from the top, middle, and bottom of the prediction rank, 5 main dishes are extracted which satisfy the following conditions:

1. The recipe is available on Cookpad website and the page URL is able to get.
2. The recipe is obviously a main dish.

During the survey, each of the main dish is evaluated by following 5 point evaluation in terms of the suitability for the selected side dish. Answerers must follow the link to the corresponding recipe page on cookpad web site to answer the survey.

- 5: very suitable combination as a menu
- 4: suitable combination as a menu
- 3: not sure
- 2: not suitable combination as a menu
- 1: completely not suitable combination as a menu

### 4.2 Results

Figure 4 shows the boxplot about the distribution of precision@10 over 10 side dishes by each of the 12 models. Table 2 shows MRR' and recall@10 of the models. Model numbers (horizontal axis) in Fig. 4 correspond to those shown in Table 2: models in Fig. 4 are lined up in descending order of MRR' and of recall@10 when MRR' is equal.

The result shows that models with higher MRR' and recall@10 tend to achieve higher precision@10, which supports the hypothesis that if the model can learn explicitly registered menus in the KG, it can also predict potentially valid menus.

As the model B achieves the highest $\overline{precision}$@10, it is used in the second experiment (Sec. 4.3).

**Table 2.** MRR' and recall@10 of the models

| Number | 1 | 2 | 3 | 4 | 5 | 6 | 7 | 8 | 9 | 10 | 11 | 12 |
|---|---|---|---|---|---|---|---|---|---|---|---|---|
| MRR' | 0.83 | 0.83 | 0.83 | 0.83 | 0.80 | 0.79 | 0.62 | 0.55 | 0.42 | 0.27 | 0.25 | 0.14 |
| recall@10 | 0.89 | 0.87 | 0.87 | 0.86 | 0.83 | 0.83 | 0.77 | 0.91 | 0.61 | 0.69 | 0.51 | 0.28 |

### 4.3 Result of the Second Experiment

Table 3 shows the survey results regarding one of the side dish: * 付け合せに♪ +きのこのバター醤油 *(* for garnish + mushrooms in butter and soy sauce *). Main dishes with boldface indicate that they are registered in the KG as

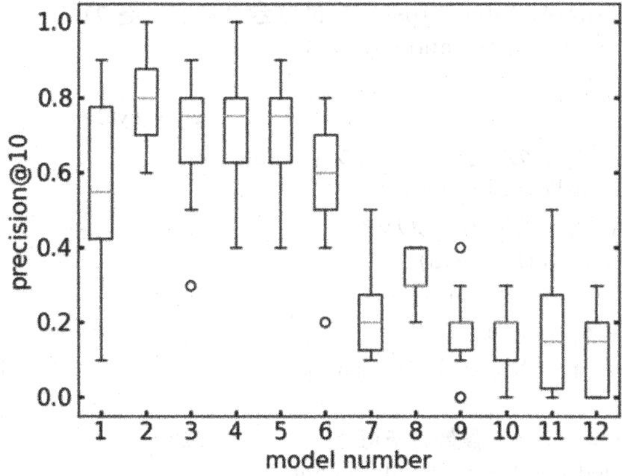


**Fig. 4.** The comparison of precision@10 between the models

the main dishes of the side dishes. The column Avg. evaluation represents the average of the evaluation by the answerers in terms of the suitability as described in Sec. 4.1. The column Model evaluation represents the position of the recipe in the prediction rank by the model.

As explained in Sec. 4.1, the recipes that are not main dish are excluded in the survey: the number of such excluded recipes in top, middle, and bottom rank is respectively 5, 22, and 65. This result indicates the validity of the model obtained by the proposed method.

It is shown in Table 3 that the main dish obtained the highest evaluation was predicted in bottom rank. On the contrary, the main dish obtained the lowest evaluation was predicted in top rank. The reason of this result is discussed in Sec. 5.

Figures 5 and 6 show the precision calculated from the result of the survey for "* 付け合せに♪＋きのこのバター醤油 *(* for garnish + mushrooms in butter and soy sauce *)" and "定番スープ@ヴィッシソアーズ (Classic Soup @Vissi Soars)", respectively. These figures compare the precision of the following three 'virtual' recommender systems:

- system A: recommend five recipes in top rank
- system B: recommend five recipes in middle rank
- system C: recommend five recipes in bottom rank

The horizontal axis of these figures represent the threshold: when the number of positive evaluation (4 or 5) is equal to or more than threshold, the recipe is regarded as valid as the main dish. In Fig. 6, when the threshold is 15 or less, all of the 15 recipes are regarded as valid, therefore the precision is 1.0 regardless of the system.

It is shown in Fig. 6 that every system has almost the same precision at every threshold. On the other hand, it is shown in Fig. 7 that the precision of system A is always higher than systems B and C. Although the precision of system B

**Table 3.** Result of survey forside dish: "* 付け合せに♪＋きのこのバター醤油 *(* for garnish + mushrooms in butter and soy sauce *)"

| Recipe name | Avg. evaluation | Model evaluation |
|---|---|---|
| たっぷりにんにくとトマトのシンプルパスタ (Simple pasta with plenty of garlic and tomato) | 4.04 | bottom |
| 見た目も爽やか！パセリとガーリックパスタ (refreshing! parsley and garlic pasta) | 4.00 | bottom |
| 野菜たっぷり♪ヘルシーキーマカレー (Plenty of vegetables♪Healthy keema curry) | 3.90 | top |
| 燻製器で作る本格ソーセージ (Authentic sausage made in a smoker) | 3.88 | bottom |
| 鮭とアスパラのペペロンチーノ風焼きそば ( Peperoncino style fried noodles with salmon and asparagus) | 3.84 | middle |
| 魅惑のキーマカレー (Enchanting keema curry) | 3.78 | top |
| **パプリカのキーマカレー (paprika keema curry)** | 3.74 | top |
| サクッとささみのスティックフライ (Crispy scissors stick fry) | 3.72 | bottom |
| お弁当に！ナゲットのチーズ挟み (For lunch! nugget cheese sandwich) | 3.64 | bottom |
| チキンのトマトスープカレー (chicken tomato soup curry) | 3.62 | top |
| コーンたっぷり。我が家のほくほくシチュー (Plenty of corn. Homemade steamed stew) | 3.60 | middle |
| 野菜と鶏肉の梅マヨサラダ風炒め (Stir-fried vegetables and chicken with plum mayo salad style) | 3.54 | middle |
| ＊キャラ弁おかず＊お花ハンバーグ (*Chara bento side dish *Flower-shaped hamburger) | 3.42 | bottom |
| ササミとワカメの蒸しロール (Steamed fillet and seaweed rolls) | 3.20 | middle |
| 茄子と豚肉とキノコの甘酢炒め (Sweet and sour stir-fried eggplant, pork and mushrooms) | 3.04 | top |

is lower than system C, as mentioned above, a lot of recipes in the bottom rank were excluded from the survey. Therefore, the precision of system B is originally higher than that of system C.

Figure 7 shows the relationship between the total amount of positive/negative answers and the average evaluation of the main dishes for "* 付け合せに♪＋きのこのバター醤油 *(* for garnish + mushrooms in butter and soy sauce *)" : a positive answer corresponds to 4 and 5, and a negative answer corresponds to 1 and 2. It is observed that the lower the average evaluation, the more controversial in the sense that the number of positive and negative answers are almost the same. It is also observed from the survey of all of three side dishes that the number of positive answers is obviously larger than that of negative answers when the number of positive answers is over 30. When the threshold for judging

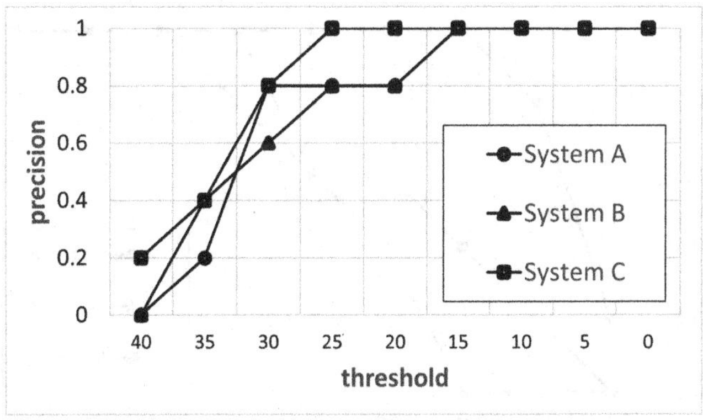


**Fig. 5.** The comparison of evaluation value

the validity is set to 30, the precision are 0.8, 0.8, and 1.0 for the side dishes "* 付け合せに♪十きのこのバター醤油 *(* for garnish + mushrooms in butter and soy sauce *)," "ほうれん草とお麩のかき玉みそ汁," and "定番スープ@ヴィッシソアーズ," respectively. These results support the hypothesis that if the model can learn menus explicitly registered in the KG, it can also predict potentially valid menus.

# 5 Discussion

This section discusses the experimental result based on the characteristics of TransE.

As described in Sec. 2, TransE tries to map head/tail entities which have the same relation to the same tail/head entity to the same embedding vectors. As a result, the proposed method tends to give high prediction score to the main dishes that satisfies this condition for the main dish having fit_main relation with the specified side dish. Although this characteristic will contribute to find potentially valid menus, it could lead to misprediction in other cases. The discussion below is delivered based on this perspective by citing experimental results.

In Table 3, a lot of curry recipes that were predicted in top rank obtained high evaluation as the main dish of "* 付け合せに♪十きのこのバター醤油 *" by the survey. In particular, the main dish "パプリカのキーマカレー (paprika keema curry)," which is predicted in top rank, obtained high evaluation value in the survey. This recipe is included in the following triple in the KG:
(パプリカのキーマカレー (paprika keema curry) , *category_is*, 挽肉を使ったカレー (Curry with minced meat))
Due to the characteristics of TransE as mentioned above, recipes which are the head entity (indicated as * in the triple) of the following triple will have similar embedding vector to "パプリカのキーマカレー (paprika keema curry)."

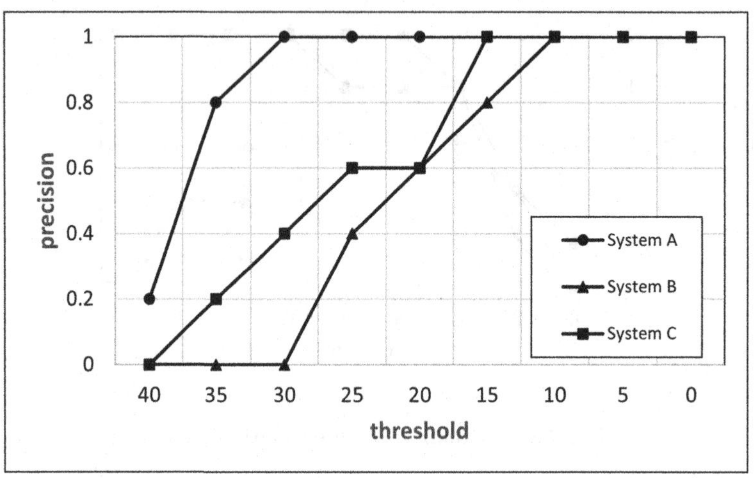


**Fig. 6.** The comparison of precision@10 between the supposed systems based on the result shown in Table 3

(*, *category_is*, 挽肉を使ったカレー (Curry with minced meat))
As a result, a lot of curry recipes are included in top rank as shown in Table 3.

On the other hand, in Table 3, "茄子と豚肉とキノコの甘酢炒め (Sweet and sour stir-fried eggplant, pork and mushrooms) ," which was included in top rank, obtained the worst evaluation by the survey. This recipe was included in the following triple:
(具沢山の味噌汁 (Miso soup with lots of ingredients), *fit_main*, 茄子と豚肉とキノコの甘酢炒め (Sweet and sour stir-fried eggplant, pork and mushrooms) )
Meanwhile, "パプリカのキーマカレー (paprika keema curry)" was included in the following triple:
(具沢山の味噌汁 (Miso soup with lots of ingredients), *fit_main*, パプリカのキーマカレー (paprika keema curry))
As both main dishes have fit_main relation to the same head entity, they will have a similar embedding vector. By adding triples that represent the difference between these two main dishes, it is expected that "茄子と豚肉とキノコの甘酢炒め (Sweet and sour stir-fried eggplant, pork and mushrooms)" will not have a similar embedding vector to "パプリカのキーマカレー (paprika keema curry)."

## 6 Additional Learning

### 6.1 Outline of the Experiment

This section investigates the effect of additional learning. As mentioned in Sec. 1, KGE is expected to do more valid prediction by increasing the density of the KG. In particular, it is expected to become more accurate by incorporating a feedback from human. In this section, the additional learning is conducted by using the result of the survey in Sec. 4.3 as a user feedback.

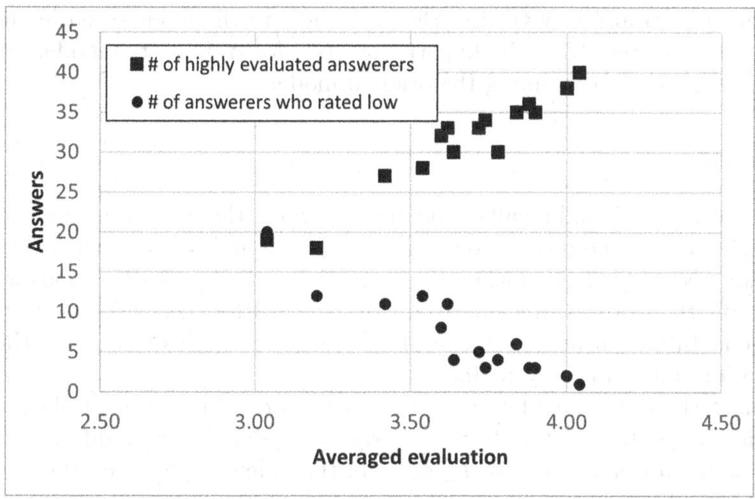


**Fig. 7.** The comparison of precision@10 between the supposed systems based on the result of the survey for "定番スープ@ヴィッシソアーズ (Classic Soup @Vissi Soars)"

User feedbacks are incorporated in three ways, which are shown in Table 4. The row Training represents the training data used for learning a model. "new triples" represents a set of triples generated from the survey result: when a main dish obtains 30 or more positive evaluation, it is linked with fit_main relation to the specified side dish. The number of generated triples was 25. "original" represents the KG constructed from the Cookpad dataset. In the row Method, "additional" means that the new embedding vectors are learned by updating the original model (trained by the original KG) based on additional learning with the training data. "new" means that the embedding vector are learned from scratch using the training data.

**Table 4.** Result of the additional learning

| | pattern 1 | pattern 2 | pattern 3 | original |
|---|---|---|---|---|
| Training | new triples | original + new triples | original + new triples | original |
| Method | additional | additional | new | new |
| MRR' | 0.34 | 0.832 | 0.833 | 0.830 |
| recall@10 | 1.0 | 0.870 | 0.870 | 0.870 |

In Table 4, Pattern 1 uses the original model as pre-trained model and updates it by additional learning with new triples. Pattern 2 uses the original model as pre-trained model as well, but uses the original KG as additional training data together with new triples. Pattern 3 trains a model from scratch with original KG and new triples. Original refers to the model used in the second experiment (Sec. 4.1). The hyperparameters for training the models are the same as those used for training the original model.

### 6.2 Result

Table 4 shows MRR' and recall of the models, where the test data is the same as the training data. The result shows that patterns 2 and 3 have almost the same prediction accuracy as the original model. Although the MRR' of pattern 1 is much lower than others, it cannot be compared with others because test data is different. In fact, it achieved a recall of 1.0, which means that all of the new triples were ranked in the top 10.

Figure 8 shows the boxplot about the distribution of the amount of change of the entity embedding vectors from the original model. The amount of change is defined as the absolute value of $L_2$ norm of the difference between the vectors.

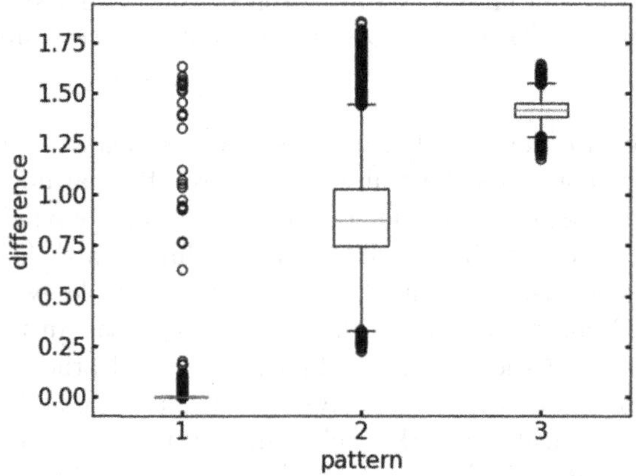


**Fig. 8.** The amount of change of entity embedding vectors

In pattern 1, most of the embedding vectors have not changed. This is because TransE updates the embedding vectors of the entities only in the training data. Pattern 2 had larger distribution than others. In pattern 3, all of the vectors have significantly changed. As shown in Table 4, patterns 2 and 3 have almost the same MRR' and recall as the original model. The comparison between patterns 2 and 3 shows that additional learning did not modify the original model so much while keeping the prediction accuracy.

Table 5 shows the 10 main dishes for the side dish "* 付け合せに♪＋きのこのバター醤油 *(* for garnish + mushrooms in butter and soy sauce *)," which was predicted by the model trained by pattern 2. Compared to Table 3, invalid predictions such as "茄子と豚肉とキノコの甘酢炒め (Sweet and sour stir-fried eggplant, pork and mushrooms)" have disappeared, while "燻製器で作る本格

**Table 5.** The prediction result trained with additional learning pattern 2 side dish:"*付け合せに♪＋きのこのバター醤油 *(* for garnish + mushrooms in butter and soy sauce *)"

| Recipe name |
|---|
| 野菜たっぷり♪ヘルシーキーマカレー (Plenty of vegetables ♪ Healthy keema curry) |
| チキンのトマトスープカレー (Chicken tomato soup curry) |
| パプリカのキーマカレー (Paprika keema curry) |
| 野菜たくさんドライカレー (Dry curry with lots of vegetables) |
| 豆なキーマ☆ (Bean keema curry☆) |
| 燻製器で作る本格ソーセージ (Authentic sausage made in a smoker) |
| バターチキンカレー (Butter chicken curry) |
| 我が家の定番☆トマト缶で作るカレー (A staple in our home ☆Curry made with canned tomatoes) |
| トマトたっぷりキーマカレー (Keema Curry with plenty of tomatoes) |
| すぐ美味しい20分でキーマカレー (Quick and delicious keema curry in 20 min) |

ソーセージ (Authentic sausage made in a smoker)," which was added as one of the new triples, has appeared. These results show that additional learning to the proposed method can improve the recommendation.

## 7 Conclusion

This paper proposed a method to find potentially valid menus from the recipe dataset using KGE. The proposed method uses TransE to learn the KG generated from the Cookpad dataset.

The effectiveness of the proposed method was evaluated through the survey. The result supports the hypothesis that if the model can learn explicitly registered menus in the KG, it can also predict potentially valid menus.

Through the evaluation experiment, it is shown that the model can predict potentially valid main dishes for the specified side dish. On the other hand, it is also shown that the model could predict irrelevant main dishes when a KG did not contain enough triples for showing the differences between triples, due to the characteristics of TransE. However, this paper also shows that user feedback about mis-predictions can be incorporated into the model by additional learning.

In future works, finding other KGE models suitable for predicting potentially valid menus, and improving the performance of additional learning, should be considered. Furthermore, to reflect personal preference to the KGE in any ways other than additional learning should also be considered. It is expected that more potentially valid menus can be found by expanding the proposed method.

**Acknowledgements.** In this paper, we used "Cookpad dataset" provided by Cookpad Inc. via IDR Dataset Service of National Institute of Informatics. This work was partly supported by JSPS KAKENHI Grant Numbers 21H03553, 22H03698, and 22K19836.

## References


1. Cookpad data. Informatics Research Data Repository, National Inst. Inform. (dataset). https://doi.org/10.32130/idr.5.1
2. Bordes, A., Usunier, N., Garcia-Durán, A., Weston, J., Yakhnenko, O.: Translating embeddings for modeling Multi-relational data. In: Proceedings of the 26th International Conference on Neural Information Processing Systems (NIPS26). vol. 2, pp. 2787–2795 (2013)
3. Dettmers, T., Minervini, P., Stenetorp, P., Riedel, S.: Convolutional 2D knowledge graph embeddings. In: Proceedings of the 25th Annual Conference on Artificial Intelligence(AAAI). vol. 32, pp. 1811–1818 (2018). https://doi.org/10.1609/aaai.v32i1.11573
4. Ebisu, T., Ichise, R.: TorusE: Knowledge graph embedding on a lie group. In: Proceedings of the 25th Annual Conference on Artificial Intelligence(AAAI). vol. 32, pp. 1819–1826 (2018). https://doi.org/10.1609/aaai.v32i1.11538
5. Gharibi, M., Zachariah, A., Rao, P.: FoodKG: a tool to enrich knowledge graphs using machine learning techniques. Frontiers in Big Data **3**, 12 (2020). https://doi.org/10.3389/fdata.2020.00012
6. Gong, F., Wang, M., Wang, H., Wang, S., Liu, M.: SMR: Medical knowledge graph embedding for safe medicine recommendation. Big Data Res. **23**, 100174 (2021). https://doi.org/10.1016/j.bdr.2020.100174
7. Harashima, J., Hiramatsu, M.: Cookpad parsed corpus: Linguistic annotations of japanese recipes. In: Proceedings of the 14th Linguistic Annotation Workshop(Law), pp. 87–92 (2020). https://api.semanticscholar.org/CorpusID:227230692
8. Lin, Y., Liu, Z., Sun, M., Liu, Y., Zhu, X.: learning entity and relation embeddings for knowledge graph completion. In: Proceedings of the 25th Annual Conference on Artificial Intelligence(AAAI). vol. 29, pp. 2181–2187 (2015). https://doi.org/10.1609/aaai.v29i1.9491
9. Nickel, M., Tresp, V., Kriegel, H.P.: A Three-Way model for collective learning on Multi-relational data. In: Proceedings of the 28th International Conference on Machine Learning(ICML), pp. 809–816 (2011)
10. Palumbo, E., Rizzo, G., Troncy, R., Baralis, E., Osella, M., Ferro, E.: Translational models for item recommendation. In: Proceedings of the 17th International Semantic Web Conference(ISWC), pp. 478–490 (2018)
11. Ruffinelli, D., Broscheit, S., Gemulla, R.: You CAN teach an old dog new tricks! on training knowledge graph embeddings. In: Proceedings of the 8th International Conference on Learning Representations(ICLR) (2020). https://openreview.net/forum?id=BkxSmlBFvr, 20 pages
12. Sakib, M.S., Paulius, D., Sun, Y.: Approximate Task Tree Retrieval in a Knowledge Network for Robotic Cooking. IEEE Robotics Autom. Lett.(RA-L) 7(4), 11492–11499 (2022). https://doi.org/10.1109/LRA.2022.3191068
13. Schlichtkrull, M., Kipf, T.N., Bloem, P., vanÂ den Berg, R., Titov, I., Welling, M.: Modeling relational data with graph convolutional networks. In: Proceedings of the 17th International Semantic Web Conference(ISWC), pp. 593–607 (2018)
14. Tian, Y., Zhang, C., Guo, Z., Ma, Y., Metoyer, R., Chawla, N.: Recipe2vec: Multi-modal recipe representation learning with graph neural networks. In: Proceedings of the 31st International Joint Conference on Artificial Intelligence(IJCAI), pp. 3448–3454 (2022). https://doi.org/10.24963/ijcai.2022/479

15. Tian, Y., Zhang, C., Metoyer, R., Chawla, N.V.: Recipe recommendation with hierarchical graph attention network. Frontiers in Big Data **4**, 778417 (2022). https://doi.org/10.3389/fdata.2021.778417
16. Wang, Z., Zhang, J., Feng, J., Chen, Z.: Knowledge graph embedding by translating on hyperplanes. In: Proceedings of the 21st Annual Conference on Artificial Intelligence(AAAI). vol. 28, pp. 1112–1119 (2014). https://doi.org/10.1609/aaai.v28i1.8870

# Strategic Pairwise Selection for Labeling High-Risk Action from Video-Based Data

Kuan-Ting Chen(✉), Bo-Heng Chen, and Kun-Ta Chuang

Department of Computer Science and Information Engineering, National Cheng Kung University, Tainan, Taiwan
{ktchen,bhchen}@netdb.csie.ncku.edu.tw, ktchuang@mail.ncku.edu.tw

**Abstract.** Accidental risk can occur anywhere in daily life, with typical examples including pedestrian accidents and concerns about child safety on school campuses. In response to these risks, the field of dangerous behavior detection technology has gained considerable attention. Such technology aims to minimize response times and mitigate the occurrence of harm through early detection of potentially dangerous behavior. However, when it comes to generating label data for these models, the diversity of human behavior and the subjective nature of defining dangerous behaviors make the labeling process challenging, often leading to ambiguous situations. To overcome this challenge, we introduce a labeling generation framework based on pair comparison called Strategic Pair Selection (SPS). SPS employs a comparative approach to assist annotators in determining ambiguous cases, thus enhancing the accuracy of the detection of dangerous behavior. Additionally, SPS combines video-based action analysis to learn distinctive features of dangerous behaviors, optimizing the selection of pairs for comparison. The experimental results on real data demonstrate that SPS outperforms other pairwise sampling baseline models, showing its attractive practicability.

**Keywords:** Data Labeling · Pairwise Sampling · Image Analysis

## 1 Introduction

In recent years, the occurrence of traffic accidents has become increasingly frequent, significantly affecting the safety of people's daily lives. According to data from the Ministry of Transportation, the incidence of traffic accidents has been continuously increasing in the past six years [1]. In addition to the realm of traffic [3], potential risks are widely discussed in various other areas, such as healthcare [17] and campus security [7].

Taking advantage of the advancement of artificial intelligence technologies, the detection of dangerous behaviors has emerged as a prominent research topic. This technology enables early detection of risks and reduces the response time to hazardous events, thus leading to growing demands and services in various areas of modern life.


C.-Y. Lee et al. (Eds.): TAAI 2023, CCIS 2074, pp. 46–60, 2024.
https://doi.org/10.1007/978-981-97-1711-8_4

Using images to identify dangerous behaviors is the main approach [18] due to its essential advantages. First, images can be applied across various fields, from traffic surveillance to industrial safety and healthcare facilities. Furthermore, images capture more comprehensive information. Finally, the increasing number of cameras has generated a substantial amount of video data.

However, although image acquisition is easily achieved, it is difficult to label whether an image contains risk behavior without human interpretation. First, different environments have different definitions of hazardous behavior. Second, the diversity of human behavior makes it difficult to establish clear danger criteria. These issues make annotation tasks more complicated. Therefore, the task of labeling data for the recognition of hazardous behavior is often confronted with ambiguous circumstances, making it hard for annotators to come to a definite conclusion or resulting in conflicting opinions.

To address this challenge, we design our framework based on pairwise comparison. Psychological theories have revealed a phenomenon where pairwise comparisons, such as binary labeling, often yield judgments that are more reliable and consensual than single evaluations. [22] Thurstone's law [8] is a psychological theory that introduces a model that allows the derivation of scale values from subjects' paired comparison results. For example, it can be used to compare the relative risk levels of different behaviors and infer the degree of danger associated with each behavior. This is seen as a suitable way to tackle matters of opinion that are controversial.

**Fig. 1.** An ambiguous case in pairwise comparing of risky actions. [12]

Pairwise comparison can help solve ambiguous situations. However, not all randomly selected pairs achieve the desired effects. The primary difficulty is to prevent the selection of pairs that are not sufficiently distinct, as it is difficult to differentiate between two similar choices. Consider the example depicted in Fig. 1, where the left image shows people playing the violin and the right image shows people playing the flute. In this scenario, annotators might struggle to determine which action poses a higher risk.

Pairwise active sampling can be used to capitalize on the advantages of paired comparisons in addressing ambiguous labeling tasks [6]. This method utilizes Bayesian information maximization and selects pairs with the highest information gain. Promising results have been achieved with this approach. However, existing methods mainly focus on non-video data, lacking discussions on video data. Our proposed approach aims to integrate video-based action feature embedding techniques into the pairwise comparison framework, enhancing pair selection strategies.

To overcome the aforementioned challenges, we introduce a Strategic Pair Selection (SPS) framework. This approach follows an interactive feedback structure, which utilizes user interactions to learn their perception of hazardous actions and determine which pairs to select. The learning process involves analyzing image data to learn action features and subsequently refining selection strategies based on user feedback.

The main contributions of our work are summarized as follows:

- We propose a strategic pair selector framework (SPS) based on video analysis.
- We provide a discrimination-based pair-selection approach.
- We offer a solution that integrates video analysis with pair comparison.

## 2 Related Works

In the application of preference aggregation in label ranking problems, implicit expressions of annotators' preferences can be leveraged through paired comparisons. Due to insights from psychology [2], it has been found that responses to paired comparison questions are more stable, as they are less susceptible to the influence of unrelated choices. Therefore, the use of paired comparisons in annotation tasks involving human participants has potential as a promising research area. In the following section, following the framework established by [16], we categorize related work into three groups: sorting, information gain, and matchmaking.

Sorting-based approaches in ranking methodologies leverage sorting algorithms, such as insertion sorting, to prioritize the selection of pairs with comparable quality. The objective is to ensure that pairs showing similar quality attributes are chosen more frequently compared to pairs with distinct quality characteristics. For example, in a study by Maystre and colleagues [15], the Quicksort algorithm was used for pairwise comparisons. Furthermore, in a recent investigation by Ponomarenko et al. [21], the Swiss system, originally used in chess competitions, was applied to rank subjective evaluations of visual quality. The Swiss system employs a two-fold approach, where random conditions are initially selected for comparison and subsequently sorted to identify pairs with similarity.

These techniques aim to maximize information by computing posterior probability distributions of quality scores and using utility functions such as the Kullback-Leibler divergence [13] to select comparisons. In particular, Crowd-BT [6] computes the entropy for each pair and incorporates the reliability of the annotator through alternating optimization. In [19], the score distributions are derived using the maximum likelihood estimation, but it is excluded due to numerical instability. [9] and [24] use a Bayesian framework to compute quality score distributions. Hybrid-MST [14] selects comparison batches for maximum information gain in a minimum spanning tree, optimizing computational efficiency. Finally, ASAP [16] introduces an improvement to Hybrid-MST. Calculate the posterior distribution of item scores using approximate message passing based on factor graphs to improve efficiency.

In the gaming domain, a pioneering matchmaking system was introduced, incorporating the TrueSkill algorithm [11]. The system's primary objective is to pair players on the basis of their closely aligned skill levels. By analyzing the skill distribution of pairs of players, the system predicts the expected outcome of their matches. For the purpose of our discussion, we shall refer to this approach as the TS-sampling method.

# 3 The SPS Framework

## 3.1 System Architecture

The framework shown in Fig. 2 employs an interactive feedback architecture to promote dynamic user-system interaction. This improves user perception and understanding. The system is able to gain knowledge from the feedback it receives, which in turn influences the selection of pairs. The learning process combines video data analysis, providing valuable visual information, and explicit user feedback. This interactive and data-driven method has the potential to improve framework performance and refine dangerous action analysis and decision-making.

At our framework's core is the strategic pair selector, comprising two elements: candidate selector and pair selector. They collaboratively choose pairs from unlabeled video data for user labeling. User responses form an answer pool, training both selectors iteratively. Binary labels accumulate with rounds, historical data enhancing selectors' performance. Sufficient binary labels trigger the pairwise-to-score method, converting results to scores. This iterative and adaptive approach progressively improves the accuracy of pair selection, yielding robust results.

Before diving into the intricacies of each component, it is essential to introduce the notation. Operating on unlabeled video data denoted as $N$, the candidate selector samples a pool of candidate pairs, represented by $C = \{p_0, p_1, ..., p_m\}$.

Subsequently, the pair selector chooses a subset from the candidate pool, denoted as $S = \{p_0, p_1, ..., p_s\}$, presenting these selected pairs as query tasks to the annotators for labeling. The pairwise label assigned by the annotators, denoted as $y_i$, signifies the comparison between pairs, with values of 1 or -1, indicating which action is perceived as more dangerous. As the annotation process progresses, provided answers are stored in the answer pool, forming the answer history $H$. This comprehensive notation framework facilitates effective communication and understanding of the various components and their interactions within the SPS framework.

Our proposed framework consists of two distinct phases: the Initial phase and the Iteration phase, which serve essential roles in the overall process. Specifically, the initial phase acts as the foundational stage, playing a pivotal role in initiating the framework training process. In this phase, a set of pairs is randomly selected and the user's initial answers are collected, laying the groundwork for subsequent training iterations. For the Iteration phase, it is characterized by an iterative feedback loop, where the framework continuously refines and improves its pair selection process. The framework adjusts the modules to improve performance by using binary labels and user feedback from prior rounds, resulting in more precise and reliable pair-selection results. This iterative process ensures that the framework progressively enhances its performance, providing a dynamic pair selection mechanism based on the annotations collected from the user.

## 3.2 Action Video Analysis

In the SPS framework, the selection of informative pairs relies heavily on video analysis techniques, which can be broadly categorized into two main approaches: image-based and skeleton-based analysis. Image-based analysis processes the video by using RGB

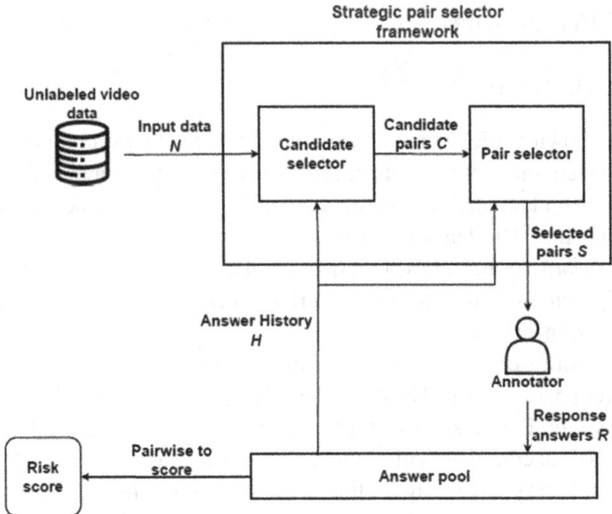


**Fig. 2.** System architectural design

or grayscale images. This approach has a notable drawback, because it can be affected by variations in image quality, potentially reducing the accuracy of the labeling process [20]. Considering the diverse nature of video sources in our framework, which may have suboptimal image quality, we therefore utilize skeleton-based analysis.

Skeleton representation uses the human action pose graph, a common skeletonbased video representation. Each node is a 2D/3D coordinate corresponding to a joint of a skeleton, connected by edges based on the body structure. OpenPose generates graphs $G = \{G_0, G_1,..., G_t\}$ from images, each $G_i = (V_i, E_i)$ with 18 joints. [5].

**Video-to-Image Processing for STGCN.** Consequently, we adopt ST-GCN (Spatio-Temporal Graph Convolutional Network) [23], which takes into account the temporal relationships of each image in video data, effectively extending the image data to the three-dimensional scale of video data. ST-GCN processes 3D skeleton graphs with graph convolutions, disseminating information across adjacent frames. It has been proven that it can capture spatial-temporal relationships that can effectively model behavior changes. ST-GCN handles multi-person videos, analyzing intricate interactions in shared contexts. This empowers our framework to extract spatiotemporal features efficiently, boosting the accuracy of analysis.

### 3.3 Candidate Selector

The candidate selector plays an essential role in SPS, and its core functionality is driven by the RankNet model [4], which is well known for its efficient pairwise ranking algorithm. This model thrives on training data that comprise pairwise comparisons, offering the versatility to adapt to various data types. In our specific application, we capitalize on the strengths of the ST-GCN to handle skeleton-based video data. This strategic choice enables us to extract meaningful features from the skeleton data, significantly enhancing the candidate selector's effectiveness in discerning relevant pairs for annotation.

To ensure that the RankNet model operates optimally, it first undergoes a specialized training phase. During this stage, the model is trained using annotated data that consist of pairwise comparisons of candidate pairs. Through these training data, the RankNet model gains the ability to distinguish the relative rankings and preferences of the pairs, empowering it to make well-informed decisions during the working phase of our framework. The training process is essential to refining the model's ability to accurately rank the candidate pairs, resulting in more effective and informative pair selection for annotation.

**Training Phase.** In SPS framework, the RankNet model is treated as a critical role. It works as a scoring function $s = f\ (x;\ w)$, where $x$ represents the input and $w$ represents the parameters. Consequently, the scores of action $x_i$ and document $x_j$ are computed as $s_i = f\ (x_i;\ w)$ and $s_j = f\ (x_j;\ w)$, respectively.

To determine the relative risk order between $x_i$ and $x_j$, RankNet adopts the pairwise method. This involves the use of a sigmoid function to define the probability that $x_i$ is riskier than $x_j$ as $\bar{P}ij = P\ (x_i > x_j) = \frac{1}{1+e^{-\sigma(s_i - s_j)}}$. Here, $\sigma$ is a parameter learned during the process, which is similar to logistic regression. A value of $P_{ij} > 0.5$ indicates that $x_i$ is considered riskier than $x_j$, while $P_{ij} < 0.5$ implies the opposite. The sigmoid function maps the probability that $x_i$ is riskier than $x_j$ to a real number within the range of [0, 1], allowing for a classificationbased approach to address the relative risk order problem.

The pairwise labels are defined as $\{+1, -1, 0\}$ and denoted as $\mathrm{y_{i,j}} \in 1, -1, 0$. These labels correspond to the true probability $\overline{\mathrm{P}}_{ij}$ as $\overline{\mathrm{P}}_{ij} = \frac{1}{2}\ (1 + \mathrm{y_{ij}})$. The cross-entropy loss function is then utilized to measure the discrepancy between the predicted probabilities $\overline{\mathrm{P}}_{ij}$ and the true labels $\mathrm{y_{ij}}$. By optimizing this loss function, the RankNet model effectively learns the underlying patterns and relationships in pairwise comparisons, enabling accurate ranking and prediction of risky actions.

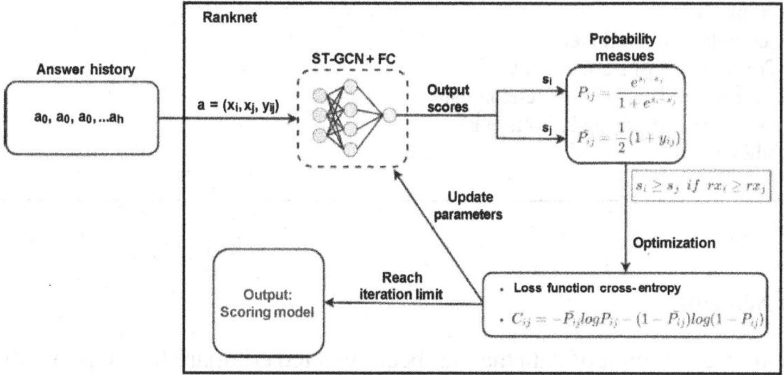


**Fig. 3.** Candidate selector in the training phase

Working phase In the working phase, shown in Fig. 3, the scoring model plays a vital role in the subsequent stages of the SPS framework. Once we obtain the scoring model through the training process, the next crucial step involves scoring and sorting all the unlabeled data based on the model's predictions. Taking advantage of the power of pairwise comparison and the knowledge acquired during training, the scoring model assigns scores to each action, reflecting their perceived levels of danger.

Through this sorting process, we identify the top k actions with the highest danger scores and the last k actions with the lowest danger scores. These top k actions represent the most critical and potentially hazardous activities that require close attention and analysis. On the contrary, the last k actions denote the least concerning activities in terms of danger.

The sorted data then facilitate the creation of candidate pairs for further annotation and comparison. Each candidate pair consists of both a dangerous and a nondangerous action, enabling more informative and insightful comparisons during the annotation process. This strategic approach improves the efficiency and effectiveness of the framework in identifying and labeling risky actions.

The strategic design of our candidate selector is based on the unique predictive capabilities of RankNet, which allows it to distinguish two distinct sets with significant differences: the most dangerous actions and the least dangerous actions. Using the scoring model generated by RankNet, we can effectively identify actions that span a wide range of danger levels. Consequently, when forming candidate pairs, we strategically combine actions from these two sets to ensure diversity and avoid unnecessary similarities or confusion. Algorithm 1 outlines the process of the candidate selector working phase, showcasing the systematic selection of informative and diverse candidate pairs. This approach enhances the efficiency and effectiveness of the pair selection process in the SPS framework.

**Algorithm 1** Candidate selector

```
Data: Label history H, skeleton_data
Result: candidate
RankNet.train(H)
Rank skeleton_data by RankNet
top_k ← Top k subset of skeleton_data
bottom_k ← Bottom k subset of skeleton_data
candidate ← Permutation(top_k, bottom_k)
return candidate
```

### 3.4 Pair Selector

Due to the limited amount of data that has been selected compared to all population data, it affects the training quality of RankNet at an early stage. RankNet might occasionally predict low-risk actions as high-risk, and vice versa. To enhance our framework, we introduced a pair selector. This selector identifies pairs of candidates that truly exhibit discriminatory patterns. To achieve this, we utilize a deep Q-network (DQN) [10] architecture that incorporates both dueling-Q and double-Q techniques. This combination enables our pair selector to capture the expected long-term user perception from the current state and to learn an optimal decision-making strategy. As such, we enhance the general effectiveness and precision of our system.

In the context of the pair selector, three fundamental components are crucial: action, state, and reward. The action involves selecting a pair from the candidate pool, while the reward is derived from the user's answer. However, defining the state poses a unique challenge. Ideally, the state should encapsulate the user's perception of danger, but it remains inherently subjective and is not directly observable.

To overcome this challenge, our framework adopts a solution that uses the sequence of past answers as the state representation. This sequence effectively captures the historical context of user responses, providing valuable insights into the user's evolving perception of danger during the reinforcement learning (RL) process. While the user's true state of mind is intangible, this surrogate representation allows our framework to adapt and learn from the user's feedback, continually refining its decision-making process over time.

The SPS labeling framework facilitates iterative updates to the model's parameters in a sequential process. At each time step t, the agent acquires the user state representation st based on observations ot. Subsequently, the agent receives a reward rt based on user feedback, and the experience tuple (ot, it, rt, ot + 1) is stored in the replay memory M. To enhance the performance of the Q network, a mini-batch of experiences is sampled from M, and the mean square loss function is minimized during the training process. Algorithm 2 provides a detailed description of the overall training process of the pair selector. This iterative learning approach enables the agent to continuously assimilate information from user interactions, adapt its decision-making strategy, and continually refine the pair selection process. As a result, the framework becomes more adept at accurately and effectively labeling risky actions over time, empowering users with valuable insights and enhanced risk assessment capabilities.

**Algorithm 2** Train Pair Selector

```
Data: all human behavior skeleton data
Initialize memory M ← {}
Initialize the action experience E ← {}
for step to last_step do
|  if E is empty then
|  |  action ← random selection form skelet_data
|  else
|  |  candi_pool ← candi selector(M, skelet_data)
|  L  action ← the candidate in candi_pool with maximum Q value
|  reward, action_label ← user response(action)
|  Set state ← E
|  Append action label to E
|  Set new state ← E
|  Push (state, action, reward, new_state, candi_pool) to M
|  if M is full then
L  L  DQN.learn(M)
```

## 3.5 Pairwise to Score

Once the aforementioned process is finished, a large collection of results from pairwise comparisons, shown as binary labels, is created. As the framework progresses, these binary labels accumulate critical information regarding the hierarchical order of perilous actions. However, to harness the full potential contained within this dataset and to achieve a more comprehensive grasp of the extent of the danger, a mechanism is indispensable to transform these binary labels into meaningful scores.

The Bradley-Terry model is a widely used statistical approach in the area of pairwise comparison analysis and is the focus of this study. This model has the potential to measure the relative scores or probabilities of outcomes in a set of pairwise comparisons. It is specifically designed for this purpose.

Within the confines of the Bradley-Terry model, the probability of elevating one action i above another action j is formulated as expounded in Formula 1. Here, si and sj represent the strengths or scores linked to actions i and j, respectively. These scores cover latent variables that encapsulate the relative performance or desirability of actions. Significantly, the Bradley-Terry model customarily gauges these scores through the optimization of a likelihood function that arises from observed pairwise comparisons. The likelihood function is represented by Formula 2, as shown.

$$P(i > j) = \frac{S_i}{S_i + S_j} \tag{1}$$

$$L(s) = \sum\nolimits_i^n \sum\nolimits_j^n \ln\left(\frac{S_i}{S_i + S_j}\right) \tag{2}$$

As our labeling process progresses through several rounds, a substantial amount of pairwise labels is collected. We convert the accumulated pairwise comparison results into meaningful ranking scores. The set of ranking scores serves as a comprehensive representation of the risk levels associated with each action observed throughout the labeling process. The Bradley-Terry model enables us to quantify the relative levels of danger among different actions, enhancing our ability to make informed decisions and conduct in-depth analysis in the context of risky human actions.

## 4 Experiments

To comprehensively evaluate the effectiveness of our proposed framework, we conducted a series of experiments using an open dataset. The evaluation goal is designed to answer the following questions.

1. Does our proposed framework outperform other competing methods which are well-known pairwise sampling methods?
2. How does the performance of our proposed framework change as the number of queries increases?
3. How do the components in our proposed framework affect performance?

### 4.1 Datasets and Experimental Setup

**Datasets.** The DeepMind Kinetics human action dataset [12] consists of 300,000 video clips from Youtube, covering 400 categories of human motion, including daily activities, sports scenes, and complex interactions. Every video clip is about 10 s long and comprises 300 frames, with a frame rate of 30 frames per second.

The dataset only provides raw video clips without joint locations. However, our framework needs skeleton-based data. To obtain the joint locations, we utilize OpenPose, which is an open-source tool, to estimate the positions of 18 joints in each frame of the video clips, with each joint represented as a tuple. In multiperson scenarios, we select the person with the highest joint confidence. The clips are converted to a tensor of shape (18, 3, T) and padded to ensure that all clips have the same length of T = 300. This allows our framework to maintain a uniform input dimension.

**Experimental Settings.** We tested our framework by creating categorized datasets and comparing them to datasets generated by baseline techniques. Data labeling involved 20 query rounds, each with 100 pairwise tasks, collecting 2000 labels in a session.

**Table 1.** Testing data categories

| Top 10 high risk action labe | Top 10 low risk action label |
|---|---|
| archery | curling hair |
| high jump | canoeing or kayaking |
| side kick | crying |
| breakdancing | hugging |
| tobogganing | singing |
| springboard diving | playing recorder |
| parkour | counting money |
| breakdancing | tasting beer |
| clean and jerk | cleaning floor |
| jumpstyle dancing | braiding hair |

Using these labeled data, we trained a binary classification model using the ST-GCN framework. To assess the accuracy of the model, we created a separate test set consisting of 10 categories of actions representing the high-risk class and the other 10 categories for the low-risk class, as detailed in Table 1. The performance of the model is determined by its ability to classify actions correctly into their risk categories.

To evaluate the quality of the labeled data generated by our framework and baselines, we trained several classification models using the labeled data generated by our framework and other baselines separately. The evaluation metrics used for these classification models are precision, recall, and accuracy. High accuracy indicates the acquisition of high-quality labeled data. Except for random selection, other baseline methods cannot handle such a large amount of data due to computational limitations. Therefore, we randomly selected 1000 data points as a sample for the baseline methods in addition to random.

### 4.2 Performance Comparison

Table 3 compares the performance of binary classification models trained with labeled data created by different pair selection methods, including our proposed SPS framework and other baseline approaches. The results show that our method consistently outperforms the baseline methods in all evaluation metrics. Additionally, an in-depth analysis of the accuracy of various high-risk action classes is presented in Fig. 4(a) and Table 2. The results demonstrate that our SPS framework is significantly superior to other baseline methods in most cases.

It is worth noting that, despite SPS having the best predicted results in the majority of action classes, there is still the possibility that other baselines may outperform it in some categories with small sampled cases. It is because that when the number of actions sampled in a particular category is small, the result may not be statistically reliable due to the lack of sufficient data.

Interestingly, we observed that the random method achieved comparable or even better performance than other baseline methods in some cases. This unexpected result can be explained by the disparity in the magnitude of the data. The random method has the advantage of selecting pairs from the entire dataset, whereas other methods are constrained to a subset of 1000 samples due to computational limitations.

In light of the phenomenon we observed and the potential influence of data size, we conducted an additional experiment to investigate the impact of data size on the performance of our SPS method. In this experiment, we restricted the SPS method to select pairs from a subset of data, similar to the other baseline methods.

The goal was to see whether this constraint would lead to a decrease in performance. The results, as shown in Table 3, revealed a significant decrease in the performance of the SPS method. This decline was evident not only in the overall evaluation metrics but also in the precision of the individual high-risk action classes, as illustrated in Fig. 4(b).

The significance of having a large and comprehensive dataset is highlighted by these results, especially when trying to label the risks associated with human behavior. Human risk behavior can exhibit considerable variations, and a comprehensive understanding of high-risk actions requires a dataset that encompasses a wide range of behaviors and contexts.

**Table 2.** Testing model performance

| Method | Precision | Recall | Accuracy |
|---|---|---|---|
| SPS | 0.780 | 0.737 | 0.778 |
| TrueSkill | 0.481 | 0.660 | 0.504 |
| ASAP | 0.560 | 0.580 | 0.587 |
| Hybrid-MST | 0.497 | 0.503 | 0.526 |
| Random | 0.555 | 0.571 | 0.599 |

**Table 3.** Testing model performance with same subset data

| Method | Precision | Recall | Accuracy |
|---|---|---|---|
| SPS(1000 samples) | 0.671 | 0.592 | 0.671 |
| TrueSkill | 0.481 | 0.660 | 0.504 |
| ASAP | 0.560 | 0.580 | 0.587 |
| Hybrid-MST | 0.497 | 0.503 | 0.526 |
| Random | 0.555 | 0.571 | 0.599 |

### 4.3 Effect on Query Rounds

The results of our experiment, as shown in Table 4, consistently show that the performance of the testing model improves with an increasing number of query rounds. This finding highlights the positive impact of having more labeled data on the model's performance in the risk labeling scenario. Moreover, we noticed that the performance growth rate gradually converges after the 15 rounds of queries. This suggests that when the amount of labeled data is increased, there is a noticeable improvement in performance, however, the additional benefits become less noticeable as more data is added.

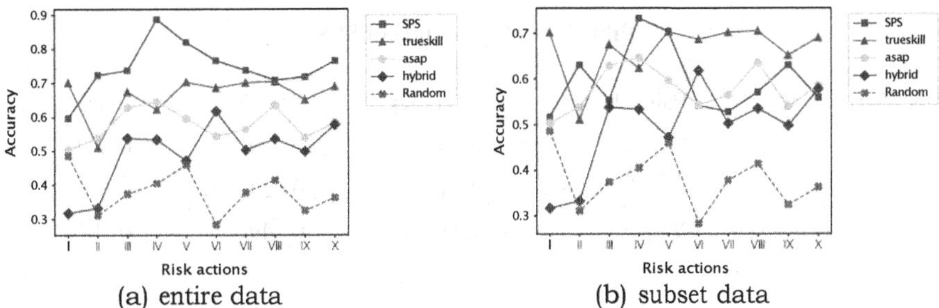


**Fig. 4.** Accuracy comparison in different high-risk action classes. I: wrestling, II: capoeira, III: pole vault, IV: American football, V: dodgeball, VI: hammer throw, VII: gymnastics tumbling, VIII: dunking basketball, IX: shot put, X: javelin throw

**Table 4.** Performance of testing model in different query rounds

| Rounds | Precision | Recall | Accuracy |
|---|---|---|---|
| 5 | 0.658 | 0.381 | 0.614 |
| 10 | 0.687 | 0.467 | 0.648 |
| 15 | 0.765 | 0.702 | 0.758 |
| 20 | 0.779 | 0.738 | 0.778 |

### 4.4 Comparison of Components in SPS

As discussed earlier, our framework incorporates two essential components: the candidate selector and the pair selector. The combination of these components is essential to improve the effectiveness and efficiency of our strategy. The role of the pair selector in aiding the candidate selector is of great importance, resulting in a more comprehensive and precise selection of pairs. We conducted an ablation study to evaluate the effect of this design, comparing the performance of different SPS variants. We thoroughly examined and compared the different SPS variants to identify their individual advantages and disadvantages, providing us with useful information for our strategy. The results are summarized in Table 5.

The results presented in Table 5 demonstrate the essential role of the candidate selector in improving the system performance, particularly in terms of recall. This particular feature is credited to the model's specialized ability to detect, which enables it to recognize potentially dangerous activities and consequently direct the selection of pairs with a decrease in misjudgment.

The incorporation of the pair selector as a supplementary element has been extremely successful, leading to remarkable improvements in performance, and thus confirming its essential role in the entire system. The results are indisputable, demonstrating the pair selector's remarkable capacity to pick pairs from the potential group, thereby affirming its critical role in the whole procedure.

**Table 5.** Ablation study of SPS

| Candidate selector | Pair selector | Accuracy | Precision | Recall |
|---|---|---|---|---|
| | | 0.594 | 0.619 | 0.367 |
| V | | 0.641 | 0.623 | 0.604 |
| V | V | 0.782 | 0.749 | 0.781 |

## 5 Conclusions

In this paper, we introduce and emphasize the importance of pairwise comparison in risk labeling scenarios. We propose a novel strategic pair selection framework to tackle the challenge of labeling risky human actions in a pairwise manner. The core of the proposed SPS framework contains two essential components: the candidate selector and the pair selector. The integration of these two components enables SPS to sample discriminative pairs, which leads to a more precise and effective identification of risky behaviors. This technique simplifies the categorization procedure and boosts the general accuracy of label acquisition. In our experiments, we found that our method was superior to other baselines, demonstrating its effectiveness.

**Acknowledgement.** This paper was supported in part by Ministry of Science and Technology, R.O.C., under Contract 112-2221-E-006-158 and 1122622-8-006-010-TD1.

## References

1. Data query of ministry of transportation. https://roadsafety.tw/Dashboard/Custom
2. Ailon, N.: Reconciling real scores with binary comparisons: a new logistic based model for ranking. In: NIPS (2008)
3. Bortnikov, M., Khan, A., Khattak, A.M., Ahmad, M.: Accident recognition via 3d cnns for automated traffic monitoring in smart cities. In: Advances in Intelligent Systems and Computing (2019)
4. Burges, C.J.C., et al.: Learning to rank using gradient descent. In: Proceedings of the 22nd International Conference on Machine Learning (2005)
5. Cao, Z., Hidalgo Martinez, G., Simon, T., Wei, S., Sheikh, Y.A.: Openpose: realtime multi-person 2d pose estimation using part affinity fields. IEEE Trans. Pattern Anal. Mach. Intell. (2019)
6. Chen, X., Bennett, P.N., Collins-Thompson, K., Horvitz, E.: Pairwise ranking aggregation in a crowdsourced setting. In: Proceedings of the sixth ACM International Conference on Web Search and Data Mining (2013)
7. Cohen, J.: School safety and school violence: trends. Int. J. Appl. Psychoanal. Stud. **18**, 246–251 (2021)
8. Culyer, A.J.: Thurstone's law of comparative judgment (2014)
9. Glickman, M.E., Jensen, S.T.: Adaptive paired comparison design. J. Stat. Plan. Inference **127**, 279–293 (2005)
10. Hasselt, H.V., Guez, A., Silver, D.: Deep reinforcement learning with double q-learning. In: AAAI Conference on Artificial Intelligence (2015)
11. Herbrich, R., Minka, T.P., Graepel, T.: Trueskilltm: A bayesian skill rating system. In: NIPS (2006)
12. Kay, W., et al.: The kinetics human action video dataset. ArXiv abs/1705.06950 (2017)
13. Kullback, S., Leibler, R.A.: On information and sufficiency. Ann. Math. Stat. **22**, 79–86 (1951)
14. Li, J., Mantiuk, R.K., Wang, J., Ling, S., Callet, P.L.: Hybrid-mst: a hybrid active sampling strategy for pairwise preference aggregation. In: Neural Information Processing Systems (2018)
15. Maystre, L., Grossglauser, M.: Just sort it! a simple and effective approach to active preference learning. In: International Conference on Machine Learning (2015)
16. Mikhailiuk, A., Wilmot, C., P´erez-Ortiz, M., Yue, D., Mantiuk, R.K.: Active sampling for pairwise comparisons via approximate message passing and information gain maximization. In: 2020 25th International Conference on Pattern Recognition (ICPR), pp. 2559–2566 (2020)
17. Mishra, P.K., Iaboni, A., Ye, B., Newman, K., Mihailidis, A., Khan, S.S.: Privacy-protecting behaviours of risk detection in people with dementia using videos. BioMed. Eng. OnLine **22** (2022)
18. Özyer, T., Ak, D.S., Alhajj, R.: Human action recognition approaches with video datasets—a survey. Knowl.-Based Syst. **222**, 10695 (2021)
19. Pfeiffer, T., Gao, X.A., Chen, Y., Mao, A., Rand, D.G.: Adaptive polling for information aggregation. In: Proceedings of the AAAI Conference on Artificial Intelligence (2012)
20. Pham, H.H., Salmane, H., Khoudour, L., Crouzil, A., Zegers, P., Velastin, S.A.: Spatio–temporal image representation of 3d skeletal movements for view-invariant action recognition with deep convolutional neural networks. Sensors (Basel, Switzerland) **19**, 1932 (2019)
21. Ponomarenko, N.N., et al.: Image database tid2013: peculiarities, results and perspectives. Signal Process. Image Commun. **30**, 57–77 (2015)
22. Tarlow, K.R., Brossart, D.F., McCammon, A.M., Giovanetti, A.J., Belle, M.C., Philip, J.: Reliable visual analysis of single-case data: a comparison of rating, ranking, and pairwise methods. Cogent Psychol. **8** (2021)

23. Yan, S., Xiong, Y., Lin, D.: Spatial temporal graph convolutional networks for skeleton-based action recognition. In: AAAI Conference on Artificial Intelligence (2018)
24. Ye, P., Doermann, D.S.: Active sampling for subjective image quality assessment. In: 2014 IEEE Conference on Computer Vision and Pattern Recognition, pp. 4249–4256 (2014)

# Modeling Transitions of Inter-segment Patterns for Time Series Representation

I.-Fu Sun, Lo Pang-Yun Ting, Ko-Wei Su, and Kun-Ta Chuang(✉)

Department of Computer Science and Information Engineering, National Cheng Kung University, Tainan, Taiwan
{ifusun,lpyting,kwsu}@netdb.csie.ncku.edu.tw, ktchuang@mail.ncku.edu.tw

**Abstract.** Against the backdrop of technological advancements, we are now equipped to collect and analyze time series data in unparalleled ways, offering significant value across various fields. However, traditional time series data analysis often leans heavily on expert insight. This study introduces a novel approach to time series data analysis based on the shapelet evolution graph, designed to intuitively capture core patterns and characteristics within the data without the need for expert intervention. Comparative analysis reveals that our approach excels in scenarios with explicit pattern transitions. Our research not only offers a fresh perspective and methodology for time series data analysis, through comparison with other baseline methods, but also provides foundational knowledge to predict whether a dataset exhibits pattern transition phenomena.

**Keywords:** Time Series · Shapelets · Graph Embedding · Classification Problems · Pattern Transition · Representation Learning

## 1 Introduction

Advancements in technology have enabled us to collect and analyze data in unprecedented ways. Whether in industrial applications, healthcare, or energy management, time series data has become an essential tool to understand the world and make better informed decisions. For example, in manufacturing [1], sensors can collect various data such as machine temperature, pressure, speed, and so on. We can use this information to predict machine failures and perform maintenance in advance, thereby enhancing production efficiency and reducing downtime. In terms of energy management [2], the use of smart meters allows us to understand the power usage of each household. This information can help power companies better manage the power supply.

Many studies have found that time series data analysis often requires expert knowledge for proper preprocessing and analysis of data, such as considering seasonal factors [3] and human routines [4] in power research. However, for an increasing number of new time series data, this expert knowledge is often not readily available. Therefore, a modeling method that is used for time series and designed to be interpretable is necessary. Shapelets, which represent a type of time series subsequence [5], provide direct,


C.-Y. Lee et al. (Eds.): TAAI 2023, CCIS 2074, pp. 61–74, 2024.
https://doi.org/10.1007/978-981-97-1711-8_5

interpretable, and explanatory information in classification scenarios. Shapelet-based models have been proven to have potential in various practical fields [6].

However, using shapelets directly for classification tasks can have some problems. In most complex classification tasks, time series data is composed of many different parts, which may cause some biases if classification tasks are solely based on shapelets. In Time2Graph [7], the authors emphasized the transition of shapelets. They constructed the transition pattern of the shapelets into a graph to explore the deeper meaning of each shapelet. Moreover, the authors constructed shapelet evolution graphs for power data for different months. As the example illustrated in Fig. 1, there are significant differences in the shapelet evolution graphs of January and July constructed from the same shapelet set. The power data of households have seasonal characteristics, and the graphs of their evolution from different months show that this modeling technique can accurately capture seasonal features, even without the need to input any timestamps. However, if one directly computes the shapelet evolution graph for the entire year's electricity data, it would not reflect the differences between different months.

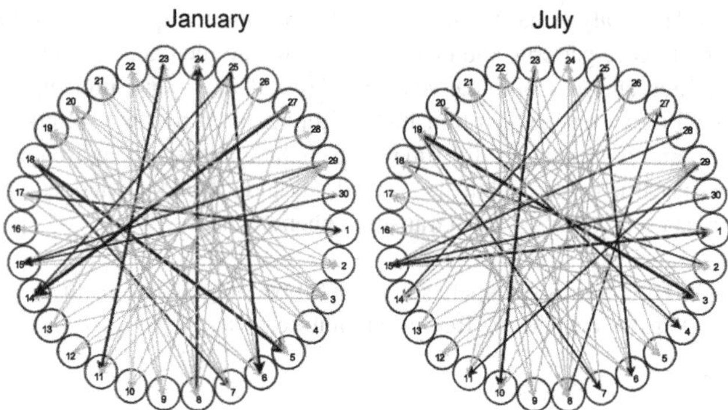


**Fig. 1.** Shapelet evolution graphs at different times. The thickness of the edge represents the transition probability of the shapelet.

This illustrates the necessity of applying different shapelet evolution graphs in different situations. Even if the time span is not several months long, many time series data still have such characteristics. For example, in the initial investigation that introduced the concept of shapelets [8], the author transforms the contour of a leaf into a type of time series. However, a leaf can be clearly divided into left and right parts, and therefore, the time series converted from the leaf can be divided into two subtime series, left and right.

In many time series data, we can observe the pattern transition. Pattern transitions are typically due to time series data displaying different behaviors or characteristics in certain segments due to external factors. Understanding whether there is a pattern transition in the data is crucial because it can help us decide which analysis method or model to use. By comparing our approach with the original Time2Graph method and other baseline methods, we can better determine whether a particular time series dataset has this characteristic of pattern transition. A simple idea is to directly divide the time series data into two patterns for consideration. Therefore, we first conducted tests, slicing the time series data into various combination patterns and testing them individually. Based on our experimental results in some datasets, we found pattern settings that are better than the original methods. For example, the earthquake wave dataset (EQS). This finding matches our hypothesis. As illustrated in 2, a seismic wave consists of several types of waves that arrive in succession, such as P-wave, S-wave, and Surface wave. These three waves each have their unique wave patterns and arrive in sequence. The patterns of the three waves differ significantly. Some shapelet transitions that are normal in the P-wave might be abnormal in the S-wave (Fig. 2).

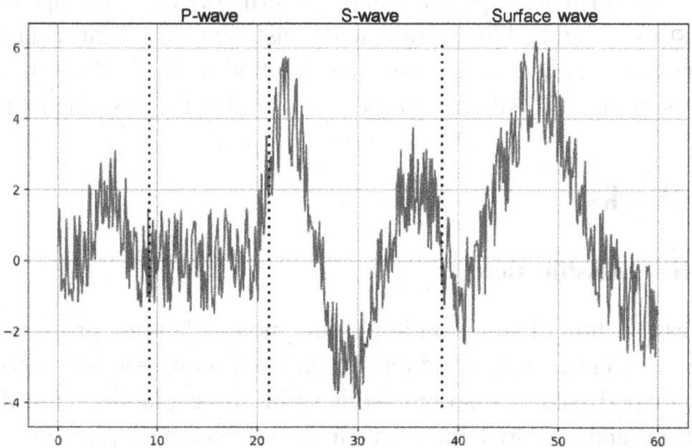


**Fig. 2.** Seismic waves exhibit a fixed and continuous pattern transform. This data naturally exhibits pattern transitions. A high amplitude in the S-wave is abnormal for the P-wave, yet it's difficult to represent this when drawing a unified shapelet evolution graph.

Meanwhile, it is quite difficult to find a pattern setting that exceeds the original method in specific datasets. For example, in the dataset composed of strawberry purees on the food spectrometer, all the pattern settings we tested lag behind the original Time2Graph method. Due to the strawberry puree production method, the spectral data of strawberry purees can be considered to have almost no pattern transition phenomena. This indicates that repeatedly testing different pattern settings can help determine whether there is a pattern transition in the time series data and find an appropriate segmentation method.

However, even for a dataset with a pattern transition, in most cases, this leads to results that are not as good as the original method. It should be noted that the chosen patterns can overlap, which means that the possibility of patterns is $O(\frac{L}{\tau} 2n)$, where L is the length of the time series, $\tau$ is the chosen segment length, and n is the chosen number of patterns. Trying to obtain the optimal result from this large number of choices is quite a challenge. The introduction of expert knowledge can effectively solve this problem, but it contradicts our premise. This suggests that this approach is not suitable for determining whether there is a pattern transformation in the time series.

Therefore, we need a simpler method that does not rely on complex pattern settings and performs better in datasets with a pattern transform. We reconstructed the shapelet evolution graph proposed in Time2Graph. We divided the time span into different patterns and defined two parts of the graphs separately.

**Sub-shapelet Evolution Graph**: Compute the shapelet evolution graph for each pattern. A shapelet evolution graph that operates within a local time span allows us to calculate transitions from a local perspective.

**Inter-pattern Edge**: Compute the edges between the correlations of two patterns. This results in each sub-shapelet evolution graph not being a completely independent graph from one another.

Using multiple graphs, we can obtain the internal meaning of each shapelet in the corresponding pattern. Simultaneously, by connecting different patterns with inter-pattern edges, we can distinguish the importance and similarity of different shapelets in different subparts, and apply the embedding results to downstream classification tasks. We tested the effectiveness of our time series modeling method in seven datasets and achieved higher F1 scores in most classification tasks compared to the baseline method.

## 2 Related Works

### 2.1 Time Series Classification

Time series classification (TSC) is an important and challenging problem in data mining. Most research can be categorized into several directions, including distance-based, feature-based, shape-based, and so on. We have briefly explained these different TSC research directions and tried to demonstrate to the readers the application scenarios and pros and cons of this field. Some of these methods will also be used in our experiments.

**Distance-Based:** Distance-based methods mainly rely on measuring the distance between time series. Calculating pairwise distances among all time series data and then performing classification using a 1-NN (one-nearest neighbor) approach is a common method, and it is difficult to outperform this technique [9]. In distance-based methods, the choice of the method used to calculate the distance between two time series is crucial. Common practices include Euclidean Distance (ED) [10], and Dynamic Time Warping (DTW) [11]. Generally, each has its own use cases, but the ED and DTW methods remain the most widely used. Most distance-based methods struggle to handle noise-related issues [12]. Equation 1 and 2 describe how the calculations for these two methods are implemented.

$$\mathrm{D(p,q)} = \sqrt{\sum\nolimits_{i=1}^{n} (q_i - p_i)^2}. \tag{1}$$

$$\mathrm{D(I,j)} = \mathrm{d(I,j)} + \min\begin{cases} D(i-1,j-1), \\ D(i-1,j), \\ D(i,j-1). \end{cases} \tag{2}$$

**Feature-Based**: Feature-based methods extract features from original time series and use these features to describe and classify time series [13]. These features may include but are not limited to, statistical characteristics, frequency domain characteristics, and other more complex features, such as the parameters of autoregressive models. The feature-based method can significantly reduce the complexity of time series for efficient computation and is also resistant to noise. However, the selection of features often requires a high level of domain knowledge to assist. Selecting the most representative and meaningful features is a great challenge. Some typical algorithms, such as Xgboost [14] and Bag-of-Patterns. Among these feature-based methods, we chose Xgboost as a representative to serve as a baseline.

**Shape-Based**: Shape-based methods focus primarily on the shape and patterns of the time series. These methods regard time series as a shape and perform classification through matching and comparing shapes. This method has high recognition for some time series with explicit periodicity or patterns. Directly using shapelets for classification is also a common approach, such as Learn Time Series Shapelets [15] and Fast Shapelets [16]. Time2Graph [7] is also an extension of this method.

## 2.2 Shapelet

A shapelet v represents a segment that belongs to a certain class. Essentially, the goal of finding a shapelet is to find a segment that enhances the classification effect, meaning that it should be close to the positive samples and distant from the negative samples. This concept can be formalized as:

$$L = -g(Spos(v, T), Sneg(v, T)), \tag{3}$$

where the function $S*(v, T)$ calculates the distance of v from the set $T*$. The function g measures the distance between these two sets, using metrics such as information gain, or some measure of the disparity in the set, such as the KL divergence. Finally, we obtain L, a measure of the quality of the shapelet results.

## 2.3 Shapelet Evolution Graph

A shapelet evolution graph is a directed and weighted graph $G = (V, E)$ whose objective is to express the probability that one shapelet immediately follows another shapelet. Any graph can be represented as a matrix with dimensions corresponding to the number of nodes. We can use a matrix G to represent a shapelet evolution graph, where aij is the probability of transition from shapelet i to shapelet j. We will present the detailed shapelet evolution graph construction method in Sect. 3. G is constructed by traversing all adjacent segments of the dataset. Unlike a regular state machine, we cannot know exactly which shapelet a certain time period corresponds to, and we can only calculate the probability of the corresponding shapelet. Therefore, what we actually compute is the confidence score of the transition.

## 2.4 Graph Embedding

Graph embedding is a technique that maps nodes, edges, or the entire graph to a low-dimensional vector space. It includes many types of method. Among them, the random walk-based methods are more consistent with the physical meaning described by the shapelet evolution graph than other methods.

**DeepWalk** [17]**:** DeepWalk employs random walk techniques to generate paths, learning the vector representations of nodes based on their cooccurrence relationships within the graph. This concept is very similar to word2vec, which treats the nodes in the graph as words, and the results of random walks as sentences. This approach is particularly useful for learning node representations in large-scale information networks.

## 3 Methodology

In this section, we propose a novel representation learning algorithm for time series modeling based on the designed pattern transition graph. We apply this representation to classification tasks to demonstrate the effectiveness of our algorithm.

### 3.1 Preliminaries

**Time Series Classification**: Time series classification uses supervised machine learning to analyze multiple labeled classes of time series data and then predict or classify the class to which a new dataset belongs. Each time series data Xu, with label Y, can be represented as Xu = $\{x_1^u, x_2^u, \ldots, x_L^u\}$, where N is the total length of the time series and $u \in U$ contain all date series.

Our goal is to learn a function $f$: $X_u \rightarrow Y_u$, which maps each time series data to its corresponding label $Y_u \in \{0, 1\}$. A segment $s$ can be defined as $s = \{x_i, x_{i+1}, \ldots, x_{i+\tau-1}\}$, where $\tau$ is the length of each segment. In our work, $\tau$ is a hyperparameter. After deciding $\tau$, the time series data $X$ can be simply divided into N segments of length $\tau$. Therefore, we can rewrite the input data as:

$$X_u = \{s_1, \ldots, s_N\}, \tag{4}$$

and

$$s_i = \{x_{i*\tau}, \ldots, x_{(i+1)*\tau}\}, \tag{5}$$

where $\tau * N = L$.

**Pattern:** For ease of explanation, we have formulated the concept of a "pattern". A pattern refers to a subset within time series data. For patternAB, it encompasses all time data from time point A to time point B. As shown in Fig. 3, the patterns do not need to cover all time points, and different patterns may overlap. For a time series dataset with a length equivalent to N segments, there are n(n − 1)/2 different patterns. Therefore, for a dataset, there exist a wide number of pattern combinations.

### 3.2 System Architecture

Our method calculates the assignment probability vector with a selected shapelet set on all time segments and then generates the transition matrix between segments. In Time2Graph work, the author considers all the transition matrices of the positive samples at the same time to construct the shapelet evolution graph. In our work, we treat different sections separately. As depicted in Fig. 4, we generate multiple sub-shapelet evolution graphs. This approach allows the graph embedding to capture both local and global characteristics of the shapelet.

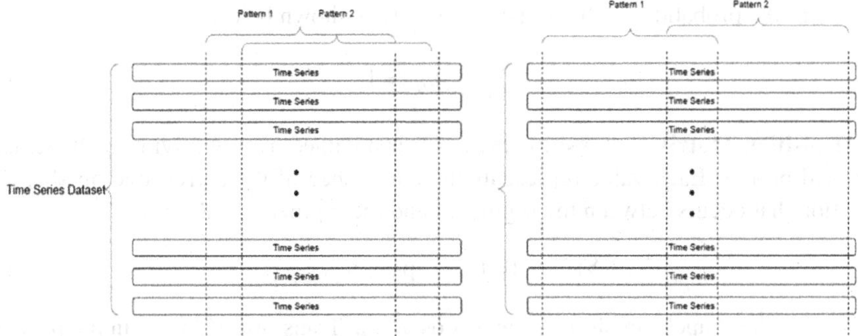


**Fig. 3.** Pattern is a sub-dataset of time series dataset. The left figure represents the possible outcomes when randomly selecting two patterns, while the right figure represents the selection method we used in our experiments.

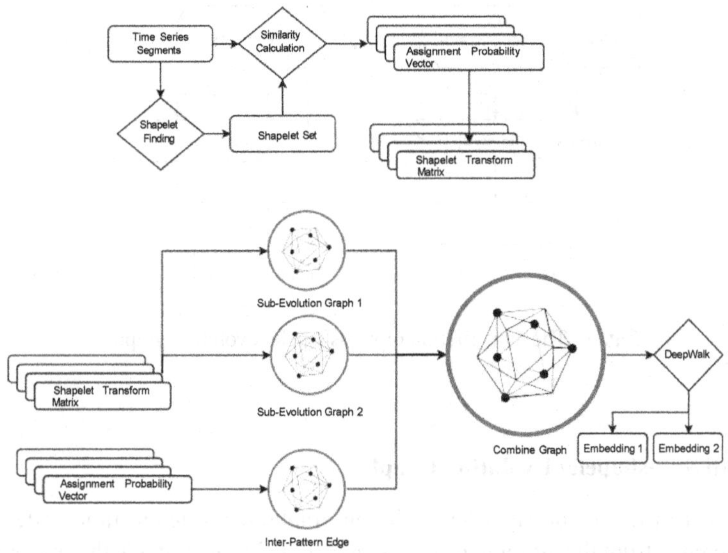


**Fig. 4.** Inter-segment pattern with sub-shapelet evolution graph architecture.

### 3.3 Shapelet Evolution Graph

To create a shapelet evolution graph, we must first have a shapelet set S, in which there are n shapelets. How to find shapelets accurately and quickly is a challenge, but in our case, we do not need the measure of the quality of the shapelet results to be high. Therefore, the idea is to create a candidate set and choose shapelets from it.

**Assignment Probability:** The probability of assignment $p_{ij}$ refers to the probability that the segment $i$ corresponds to the shapelet $j$. It is determined by the maximum and minimum distances between all shapelets and the segment $i$. The closer the shapelet, the higher the probability. The distance calculation method used is DTW (Dynamic Time Warping). The relevant formula is in Eq. 2. Because it is a probability representation, the sum of the probabilities should be equal to 1, as shown below:

$$\sum_{j \in S} p_{ij} = 1 \tag{6}$$

**Transition Matrix**: A transition matrix Ti is obtained by multiplying each element in pi and pi + 1. Each value represents the confidence of the corresponding shapelet transition that occurs between the segment i and the segment i + 1.

$$\forall \mathrm{t_{xy}} \in \mathrm{T_i}, \mathrm{t_{xy}} = \mathrm{p_{ix}} * \mathrm{p_{(i+1)y}}. \tag{7}$$

Finally, the shapelet evolution graph adds all the Transition Matrices in the positive samples together. Since this is just a subgraph of our work, we do not perform normalization, leaving it to be handled after the calculation of the remaining parts is completed. Figure 5 is a schematic diagram of the construction of a sub-shapelet evolution graph.

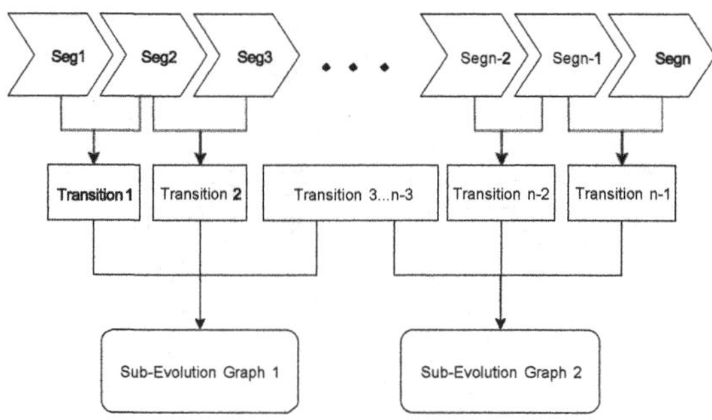


**Fig. 5.** The construction of sub-shapelet evolution graph.

### 3.4 Multi Sub-shapelet Evolution Graph

We construct different sub-shapelet evolution graphs for different time patterns. The main difference from the aforementioned shapelet evolution graph is that we only need time segments that are in the corresponding pattern. In this way, we can obtain several sub-shapelet evolution graphs. At this stage, each subgraph is independent of the others, and each subgraph is an N × N size matrix, where N is the size of the shapelet set.

Since the graphs do not share nodes, all subgraphs can be simply merged into one matrix using block diagonal matrices, as shown in the two blocks in the upper left and lower right in Fig. 6.

### 3.5 Inter-pattern Edge

We define the inter-pattern edge to connect different patterns. For each interpattern edge eij, i and j will never be in the same pattern. These edges will link different patterns together, so that when performing a random walk, the path can potentially jump across different patterns.

A simple idea is that if the patterns before and after are similar enough, then some shapelets between them have a higher probability of being similar. We employ an element-wise multiplication method to calculate the shapelet transition probability between two segments, based on their corresponding distribution probabilities. The algorithm steps are illustrated in Fig. 7.

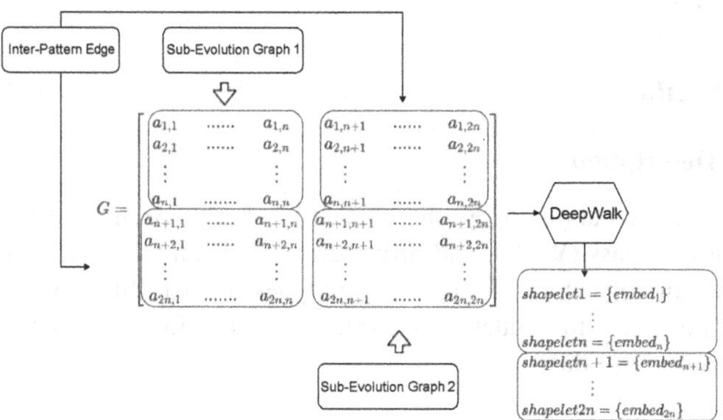


**Fig. 6.** Combination of inter-pattern edge and sub-shapelet evolution graph.

After calculating all inter-pattern edges, we can concatenate them with the sub-shapelet evolution graph. At this point, we have obtained a directed weighted graph that considers shapelets as different nodes for different patterns. Its size is AN × AN, where A is the number of patterns and N is the number of shapelets. Since we are going to perform graph embedding calculations similar to DeepWalk next, we normalize each row to ensure that they sum up to 1.

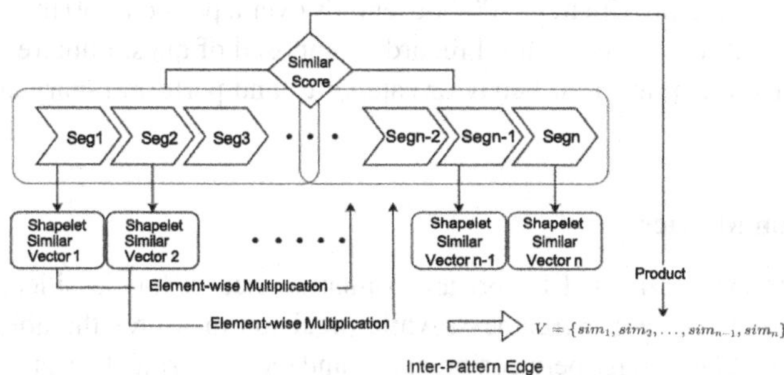


**Fig. 7.** Inter-pattern edge calculation.

### 3.6 Graph Embedding

DeepWalk, an efficient graph embedding method, traditionally does not cater to directed weighted graphs. With a minor adjustment to the walk, we adapt it without altering other aspects. Expanding the original shapelet evolution graph from N × N to AN × AN results in embedding groups of AN. These are applied to the A patterns, each having N embedding vectors.

After obtaining the shapelet embeddings, we validate their efficacy through classification tasks. In our approach, the decision tree is chosen as the classifier, optimized over various hyperparameters. The classifier does not influence the embedding, allowing faster parallel processing.

# 4 Experiments

## 4.1 Dataset Description

We used three public datasets from the UCR Time Series Archive [18]: Earthquakes (EQS), WormsTwoClass (WTC), and Strawberry (STB) and the dataset of real world electricity consumption records (ECR) with four types of labels (Sleep, Out, Other, Meal) from a power company, to validate our proposed model. Table 1 shows the summary statistics for these seven datasets.

**Table 1.** Overall statistics of 7 datasets in the experiments.

| | EQS | UCR WTC | STB | Sleep | ECR | | Meal |
|---|---|---|---|---|---|---|---|
| | | | | | Out | Other | |
| positive ratio | 18% | 58% | 64% | 37% | 26% | 35% | 5% |
| #(time series) | 461 | 258 | 983 | 7680 | 7680 | 7680 | 7680 |

We provide a brief introduction to the ECR dataset. This dataset includes data from electrical meters for approximately 100 households over a period of 50 to 150 days. For most users, there is a set of behavioral records composed of questionnaire surveys. We briefly categorize them into four behavior categories and perform binary classification tasks for each.

## 4.2 Evaluation Metrics

Precision, accuracy, recall, and F1 score are evaluation metrics for classification models. Accuracy measures general correctness, while precision measures the ability to avoid misclassification. The balance between precision and recall is critical because optimizing one may affect the other. Therefore, the F1 score, which takes both into account, is our main reference indicator.

## 4.3 Baseline Methods

We selected a few representative classifiers from many general-purpose classifiers to serve as our baselines. For each classifier, we used 5-fold cross-validation to fine-tune the hyperparameters to obtain the best results.

**DTS:** The decision tree is a supervised learning algorithm using a tree structure to represent decision rules.

**LR:** Logistic regression is a supervised learning algorithm and uses a logistic function to predict a binary variable.

**XGB:** XGBoost implements the gradient-boosting decision tree algorithm and has features such as automatic handling of missing values and adaptability to unbalanced datasets.

**SVM:** Support Vector Machine (SVM) is used to find a decision boundary that maximizes the margin between two classes of samples.

**RF:** Random forest constructs multiple decision trees and combines their results to make a final prediction. It can handle a large number of input variables and is not prone to overfitting.

**T2G** [7]**:** Time2Graph constructs a shapelet evolution graph and transforms the time series into an embedded representation.

### 4.4 Experimental Results

In the experimental results in Table 2, it can be seen that our method (T2GPattern) achieved the best performance in four of the seven datasets.

The ECR datasets are generally influenced by the homeowner as an external factor, so they typically perform better than other baselines. Among them, the only dataset in which we did not achieve better results was the ECR-Sleep dataset, likely because the homeowner had already gone to sleep, leading to subpar performance. Such results align with our initial hypothesis, which is "the performance should be better in the presence of a pattern transform but worse if there is not a clear and common pattern transform in the dataset".

Our hypothesis was also well validated in the UCR dataset. Our method achieved better results in the EQS dataset (fixed pattern transform) and worse results in the STW dataset (without a pattern transform). This demonstrates that our method can not only achieve better results than general-purpose classifiers in many situations without domain knowledge, but also suggests that the effectiveness of our method largely depends on whether the dataset exhibits a pattern transform.

### 4.5 Ablation Study

In our research, we mainly propose two concepts:

1. Applying shapelet evolution graph to different sub-time intervals.
2. Connecting different sub-shapelet evolution graphs by considering the similarity of different phases.

In this section, we compare three sets of experiments, as shown below:

1. **T2G:** The original Time2Graph method.
2. **T2G-Pair:** Considering two sub-time intervals but not connecting the two sub-shapelet evolution graphs.

**Table 2.** F1 score of different classifiers and our method.

| | EQS | UCR STW | WTC | Sleep | ECR | | Out |
|---|---|---|---|---|---|---|---|
| | | | | | Meal | Other | |
| DTS | 0.47 | 0.95 | 0.77 | 0.54 | 0.10 | 0.46 | 0.39 |
| LR | 0.43 | 0.91 | 0.62 | 0.55 | 0.10 | 0.40 | 0.36 |
| SVM | 0.4 | 0.76 | 0.72 | *0.57 | 0.08 | 0.47 | 0.38 |
| RF | 0.19 | *0.97 | *0.78 | 0.51 | 0.09 | 0.40 | 0.34 |
| T2G | 0.21 | 0.99 | *0.78 | 0.51 | 0.10 | 0.44 | 0.35 |
| XGB | 0.30 | 0.97 | 0.74 | 0.33 | 0.05 | 0.27 | 0.28 |
| T2G-Pattern | ***0.5** | **0.96** | **0.77** | **0.56** | ***0.14** | ***0.51** | ***0.43** |

3. **T2G-Pattern:** Our method which considers two sub-time intervals and connecting the two sub-shapelet evolution graphs.

Our experiments demonstrate the effectiveness of our approach when considering different sub-time intervals and connecting these sub-shapelet evolution graphs. The results are shown in Tables 3 and 4.

**Table 3.** F1 score of different methods on UCR.

| Dataset | EQS | | | UCR STW | | | WTC | | |
|---|---|---|---|---|---|---|---|---|---|
| Evaluation | Accu | Recall | F1 | Accu | Recall | F1 | Accu | Recall | F1 |
| T2G | 0.73 | 0.14 | 0.21 | *0.98 | *0.98 | *0.99 | *0.74 | 0.80 | *0.78 |
| T2G-Pair | *0.75 | 0.09 | 0.15 | 0.94 | 0.95 | 0.95 | 0.72 | 0.74 | 0.79 |
| T2G-Pattern | **0.74** | ***0.51** | ***0.5** | **0.95** | **0.96** | **0.96** | **0.71** | ***0.82** | **0.77** |

In this experiment, even after exploring numerous possible pattern settings, facing simple datasets (UCR-STW) without a pattern transform still results in a decrease in performance. This suggests that T2G-Pair is not the bound for such methods. However, in most of the datasets, T2G-Pair still achieved better results than the original Time2Graph method. It should be noted that, in the ECR-Meal dataset, our method surpassed the other two algorithms in all evaluation metrics. Mealing is also an activity that clearly involves multiple operations. During the process, several appliances are often involved, including the refrigerator, television, oven, microwave, computer, and air conditioning, all of which could potentially be used during this activity.

This results in the meal dataset being one that has a pattern transform but without a general transformation rule (for example, in UCR-EQS where the P-wave cannot occur after the S-wave). Due to the bidirectional setup of the inter-pattern edge, this issue is addressed to some extent.

**Table 4.** F1 score of different methods on ECR.

| | Sleep | | | Meal | | |
|---|---|---|---|---|---|---|
| | Accu | Recall | F1 | Accu | Recall | F1 |
| T2G | *0.5269 | 0.6545 | 0.5088 | 0.7138 | 0.3373 | 0.0969 |
| T2G-Pair | 0.5252 | 0.7072 | 0.5273 | 0.7155 | 0.3614 | 0.1036 |
| T2G-Pattern | **0.4572** | ***0.9736** | ***0.5626** | ***0.7902** | ***0.3626** | ***0.1350** |
| | Other | | | Out | | |
| | Accu | Recall | F1 | Accu | Recall | F1 |
| T2G | 0.5159 | 0.5769 | 0.4716 | 0.5296 | 0.4886 | 0.3539 |
| T2G-Pair | 0.5477 | *0.6296 | *0.5104 | 0.4753 | *0.6195 | 0.3838 |
| T2G-Pattern | ***0.5863** | **0.5900** | **0.5053** | ***0.5977** | **0.5880** | ***0.4285** |

## 5 Conclusions

In this paper, we explore the issue of distinct shapelet evolution graphs produced for different areas within time series data, and we expound on their necessity. Furthermore, we propose the phase transition matrix to differentiate the similarities and differences in shapelets' performance across different patterns. This matrix is composed of two key components: sub-shapelet evolution graph and inter-pattern edge. By leveraging these components, the matrix can compute graph embeddings after connecting different sub-shapelet evolution graphs, thereby achieving embedding results considering a different pattern.

In our experiments, the results indicate that our method outperforms other baseline methods in datasets that exhibit a pattern transform, while it ranks below the baseline in other datasets. This suggests that our approach can distinguish whether a dataset has a pattern transformation even without the presence of expert knowledge.

In future work, we plan to integrate deep learning. Instead of using simple segmentation methods, our aim is to leverage the capabilities of deep learning techniques. Specifically, we are looking to explore the potential of Recurrent Neural Networks (RNN) in this regard. RNNs have the ability to recognize sequential data patterns and may offer a more powerful and insightful approach to understanding the evolution of shapelets over time.

**Acknowledgement.** This paper was supported in part by Ministry of Science and Technology, R.O.C., under Contract 112-2221-E-006-158 and 1122622-8-006-010-TD1.

## References

1. Huang, S., Guo, Y., Liu, D., Zha, S., Fang, W.: A two-stage transfer learning based deep learning approach for production progress prediction in IoT-enabled manufacturing. IEEE Internet Things J. **6**(6), 10627–10638 (2019)

2. Wu, Z., Mu, Y., Deng, S., Li, Y.: Spatial–temporal short-term load forecasting framework via K-shape time series clustering method and graph convolutional networks. Energy Rep. **8**, 8752–8766 (2022)
3. Alberg, D., Last, M.: Short-term load forecasting in smart meters with sliding window-based ARIMA algorithms. Vietnam J. Comput. Sci. **5**(3–4), 241–249 (2018)
4. Devlin, M.A., Hayes, B.P.: Non-intrusive load monitoring and classification of activities of daily living using residential smart meter data. IEEE Trans. Consum. Electron. **65**(3), 339–348 (2019)
5. Ye, L., Keogh, E.: Time series shapelets: a novel technique that allows accurate, interpretable and fast classification. Data Min. Knowl. Disc. **22**(1–2), 149–182 (2010)
6. Yan, W., Li, G., Wu, Z., Wang, S., Yu, P.S.: Extracting diverse-shapelets for early classification on time series. World Wide Web **23**(6), 3055–3081 (2020)
7. Cheng, Z., Yang, Y., Wang, W., Hu, W., Zhuang, Y., Song, G.: Time2Graph: revisiting time series modeling with dynamic shapelets. In: Proceedings of the AAAI Conference on Artificial Intelligence, vol. 34, no. (04), pp. 3617–3624 (2020)
8. Ye, L., Keogh, E.: Time series shapelets. In: Proceedings of the 15th ACM SIGKDD International Conference on Knowledge Discovery and Data Mining (2009)
9. Bagnall, A., Lines, J., Bostrom, A., Large, J., Keogh, E.: The great time series classification bake off: a review and experimental evaluation of recent algorithmic advances. Data Min. Knowl. Disc. **31**(3), 606–660 (2016)
10. Danielsson, P.-E.: Euclidean distance mapping. Comput. Graph. Image Process. **14**(3), 227–248 (1980)
11. Müller, M.: Information Retrieval for Music and Motion. Springer, Heidelberg (2007). https://doi.org/10.1007/978-3-540-74048-3
12. Abanda, A., Mori, U., Lozano, J.A.: A review on distance based time series classification. Data Min. Knowl. Disc. **33**(2), 378–412 (2018)
13. Wu, J., Yao, L., Liu, B.: An overview on feature-based classification algorithms for multivariate time series. In: 2018 IEEE 3rd International Conference on Cloud Computing and Big Data Analysis (ICCCBDA) (2018)
14. Yu, B., et al.: SubMitoXGBoost: predicting protein submitochondrial localization by fusing multiple feature information and eXtreme gradient boosting. Bioinformatics **36**(4), 1074–1081 (2019)
15. Grabocka, J., Schilling, N., Wistuba, M., Schmidt-Thieme, L.: Learning time-series shapelets. In: 20th ACM SIGKDD International Conference on Knowledge Discovery and Data Mining (2014)
16. Rakthanmanon, T., Keogh, E.: Fast shapelets: a scalable algorithm for discovering time series shapelets. In: Proceedings of the 2013 SIAM International Conference on Data Mining (2013)
17. Perozzi, B., Al-Rfou, R., Skiena, S.: DeepWalk. In: Proceedings of the 20th ACM SIGKDD International Conference on Knowledge Discovery and Data Mining (2014)
18. Dau, H.A., et al.: The UCR time series archive. IEEE/CAA J. Automatica Sinica **6**(6), 1293–1305 (2019)

# From SMOTE to Mixup for Deep Imbalanced Classification

Wei-Chao Cheng, Tan-Ha Mai, and Hsuan-Tien Lin(✉)

Department of Computer Science and Information Engineering, National Taiwan University, Taipei, Taiwan
{d10922024,htlin}@csie.ntu.edu.tw

**Abstract.** Given imbalanced data, it is hard to train a good classifier using deep learning because of the poor generalization of minority classes. Traditionally, the well-known synthetic minority oversampling technique (SMOTE) for data augmentation, a data mining approach for imbalanced learning, has been used to improve this generalization. However, it is unclear whether SMOTE also benefits deep learning. In this work, we study why the original SMOTE is insufficient for deep learning, and enhance SMOTE using soft labels. Connecting the resulting soft SMOTE with Mixup, a modern data augmentation technique, leads to a unified framework that puts traditional and modern data augmentation techniques under the same umbrella. A careful study within this framework shows that Mixup improves generalization by implicitly achieving uneven margins between majority and minority classes. We then propose a novel margin-aware Mixup technique that more explicitly achieves uneven margins. Extensive experimental results demonstrate that our proposed technique yields state-of-the-art performance on deep imbalanced classification while achieving superior performance on extremely imbalanced data. The code is open-sourced in our developed package https://github.com/ntucllab/imbalanced-DL to foster future research in this direction.

**Keywords:** Deep Learning · Imbalanced Classification · Margin · Mixup · Data Augmentation

## 1 Introduction

Imbalanced classification is an old yet practical research problem for the machine learning and artificial intelligence community. For example, fraud detection applications [1, 2] are often characterized by data imbalance, because there are far fewer fraudulent cases than normal ones. Another example is real-world image data for computer vision, which often exhibits long-tail properties, where minority classes occur less frequently [3–5].

One immediate challenge in imbalanced classification is that minority classes are under-represented in the objective function, which can result in underfitting to these minority classes. This is typically addressed via re-weighting [6, 7] or re-sampling [8, 9] techniques. Re-weighting techniques belong to the family of algorithm-oriented


C.-Y. Lee et al. (Eds.): TAAI 2023, CCIS 2074, pp. 75–96, 2024.
https://doi.org/10.1007/978-981-97-1711-8_6

approaches, which directly modify the objective function and optimization steps. Resampling techniques, on the other hand, belong to the family of data-oriented approaches, which manipulate the data being fed to the learning model.

Among algorithm-oriented techniques, re-weighting by inverse class frequencies stands out as one of the simplest methods, as discussed in previous works [10]. Other approaches assign weights in various ways as [7, 11]. For instance, in the study by Cui et al. [7], a theoretical framework is developed to calculate the effective number of examples for each class, subsequently assigning suitable weights based on this calculated value. More sophisticated approaches in the algorithm-oriented family modify the objective function to favor minority classes. For instance, the label-distribution aware margin (LDAM) loss proposed in [12] is based on a theoretical framework that gives minority classes a larger margin. LDAM achieves state-of-the-art performance on benchmark datasets. Nevertheless, it is harder to optimize LDAM loss across general deep learning models due to its sophisticated design.

The most basic approaches in the data-oriented family involve oversampling minority classes or downsampling majority classes [8] in an attempt to make the data distribution less skewed. Compared with re-weighting approaches, such sampling approaches tend to be less stable. Moreover, oversampling or downsampling from the original data brings no new information to the learning model. Advanced approaches in the data-oriented family are thus based on synthetic (or virtual) examples, such as the well-known synthetic minority oversampling technique (SMOTE) [8]. As its name suggests, SMOTE synthesizes virtual examples for minority classes to improve imbalanced classification. Its concept has inspired various follow-up studies that also synthesize virtual examples for imbalanced classification [9, 13]. SMOTE and its follow ups are closely related to data augmentation techniques commonly used in modern deep learning [14–16]. Nevertheless, despite the practical success of SMOTE for nondeep models [13, 17], SMOTE has not been thoroughly studied for its validity when coupled with modern deep learning models.

A recent follow-up to SMOTE, designed for addressing imbalanced learning in the context of modern deep learning, is DeepSMOTE [18]. This method leverages the concept of Generative Adversarial Networks (GANs) [19] for oversampling. Effective SMOTE-based generation of synthetic examples is achieved by utilizing a deep encoder-decoder model to convert the original data into a lower-dimensional representation space. It allows DeepSMOTE to perform better on complex data than the original SMOTE. DeepSMOTE is claimed to produce high-quality synthetic examples to assist imbalanced classification. Somehow to the best of our knowledge, DeepSMOTE needs more benchmarks to demonstrate its practical potential.

Another oversampling technique is Major-to-minor Translation (M2m) [20]. M2m also addresses class imbalance by augmenting less-frequent classes through sample translation from more-frequent ones. It employs a pre-trained model to identify potential samples by introducing random noise to majority-class images; in case, the pre-trained model does not identify synthetic data, it uses existing minority samples to achieve balance. By leveraging and integrating the diversity of majority information, this approach enables the classifier to acquire more generalized features from the minority classes.

Despite its benefits, M2m is computationally intensive and complex to implement due to the translation process.

In this work, we examine the SMOTE approach to understand its disadvantages when coupled with modern deep learning models. We correct these disadvantages via a soft variant of SMOTE that achieves competitive performance on benchmark datasets. We then show that the soft variant of SMOTE is coincidentally connected with Mixup [16], a modern and popular augmentation technique for deep learning, which however was not originally proposed for imbalanced classification. Although a recent workshop paper [21] proposes a variant that modifies Mixup [16] to improve deep imbalanced classification, the effectiveness and rationale of Mixup and its variants for deep imbalanced classification have not been adequately studied, to the best of our knowledge.

Inspired by LDAM [12], which successfully improves deep imbalanced classification with uneven margins, we study the effectiveness of Mixup via margin statistics analysis. We introduce a new tool called the margin gap between the majority and minority classes. The gap is empirically demonstrated to be loosely correlated to the accuracy in deep imbalanced classification. We find that Mixup [16] implicitly improves the margin gap, which constitutes a new piece of empirical evidence that explains its effectiveness. We further demonstrate that the gap can be more explicitly fine-tuned by making Mixup margin-aware when synthesizing the inputs and output of the virtual example. The proposed margin-aware Mixup (MAMix) approach empirically achieves state-of the-art performance on common imbalanced classification benchmarks and achieves significantly better performance than Mixup and LDAM for extremely imbalanced datasets. The results validate the usefulness of our study and our proposed approach.

To make deep imbalanced learning easier for researchers and real-world users, we further develop an open-sourced python package called imbalanced-DL for this community. From our experience, we observed that to tackle deep imbalanced classification effectively, a single model may not be sufficient, thus we provide several strategies for people to use. The package not only implements several popular deep imbalanced learning strategies, but also provides benchmark results on several image classification tasks. We hope that our research findings along with our developed software can not only help with reproducibility but also shed lights on more comprehensive research in this community in the future.

We summarize our contributions as the following: (i) We systematically design and study the variants of the SMOTE algorithm for deep learning, (ii) We are first to utilize margin statistics to analyze whether a model has learned proper representations through uneven margins for deep imbalanced classification, (iii) We determine that a direct application of the original Mixup [16] already achieves competitive results for imbalanced learning by implicitly enforcing uneven margins, (iv) We further develop a simple yet effective algorithm that guides Mixup to take margins into account more explicitly, and show that the algorithm works particularly well when the data is extremely imbalanced.

## 2 Related Work

In this section, we first define the imbalanced learning problem and review existing solutions. Then we discuss studies that are closely related to our approach. For a more comprehensive survey, see [22].

## 2.1 Problem Setup and Notations

We consider the imbalanced K-class classification problem. Let x ∈ Rd denote the input and y ∈ {1, ..., K} denote the corresponding label. Given the training data D = $\{(x_i, y_i)_{i=1}^n\}$ generated from some unknown P(x, y) independently, our goal is to learn a classifier f(x): Rd → {1, ..., K}, which predicts the correct label from a given input x. Let nj be the size of class j. We assume the training data to be imbalanced. That is, the size of the largest class maxi ni is very different from the size of the smallest class mini ni. The larger classes are generally called the majority, and the smaller ones are called the minority. After learning f(x), we follow [12] to evaluate its accuracy on a balanced test set generated from the same P(x | y) for each class. The evaluation essentially equalizes the importance of each class.

In this work, we adopt two standard benchmark settings to generate controllable synthetic datasets from real-world datasets [12, 23]. Both settings first decide the target size of each class by some parameters, and randomly sample within the real-world dataset to obtain the corresponding synthetic dataset under the target sizes. Both settings are based on the parameter of class imbalance ratio, which is the ratio between the size of the largest (head) class and that of the smallest (tail) class, that is, ρ = maxi ni/minini. The parameter characterizes the difficulty level of the dataset.

The first setting is called step imbalance, defined by ρ and another parameter μ. Step imbalance requires that μK of the classes be the minority, and the other (1 − μ)K be the majority. All the minority classes are of the same size, and so are all the majority classes. Following the class imbalance ratio, the size of the majority classes is ρ times larger than that of the minority ones.

The second setting is called long-tailed imbalance [7, 12] defined by ρ, where the sizes of the classes follow an exponentially decreasing sequence with a decreasing constant of ρ1/(K − 1). The constant ensures that the class imbalance ratio is exactly ρ. An illustrative example for long-tailed and step imbalance is in Fig. 1.

## 2.2 Algorithm-Oriented Approach

Traditionally, many classification approaches are designed from the principle of empirical risk minimization (ERM), which minimizes the summation of some loss function on each example. For the imbalanced classification, the ERM principle easily leads to underfitting the minority classes, as they are under-represented in the summation.

Approaches that improve ERM for the imbalanced classification problem can be roughly divided to two categories: algorithm-oriented and data-oriented. One possible algorithm-oriented approach, known as cost-sensitive learning, gives a higher cost when mis-classifying the minority class [24]. Cost-sensitive learning can also be carried out by giving larger weights to the minority examples. For instance, the class balance (CB) loss [7] re-weights each class by calculating its effective number of examples. Re-weighting increases the importance of the minority examples in the loss function, therefore preventing underfitting the minority classes. [12] shows that learning with re-weighting from the beginning of training can result in degraded representations because of early overfitting to the minority classes, making the performance of the reweighting even worse than ERM. To solve the overfitting issue, [12] also proposed the deferred re-weighting

(DRW) technique. DRW splits the one-stage training of deep learning into two phases. In the first phase, ERM without any re-weighting is used to learn a good representation, with the hope of not overfitting to the minority classes. Then, the training continues with an annealed (smaller) learning rate on a re-weighted loss, such as CB loss, in the second phase.

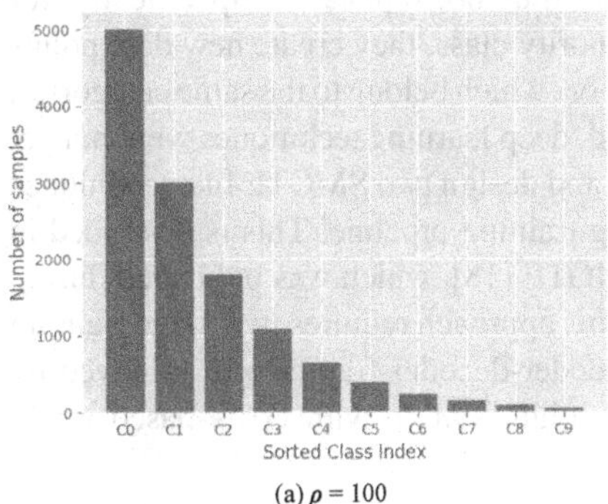


(a) $\rho = 100$

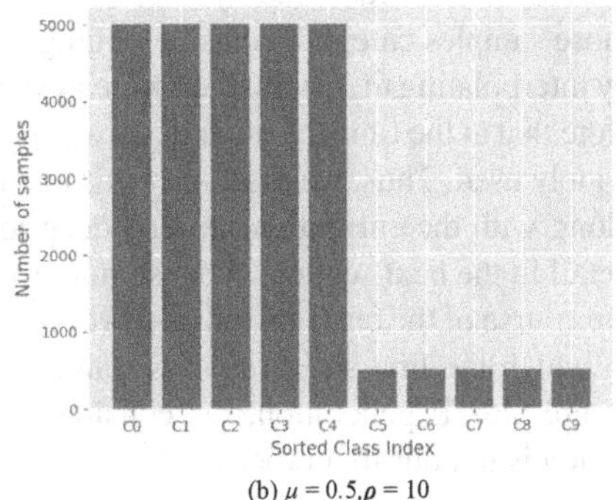


(b) $\mu = 0.5, \rho = 10$

**Fig. 1.** Number of training samples per class in synthetically generated imbalanced CIFAR-10 datasets for (a) long-tailed imbalance with $\rho = 100$ and (b) step imbalance with $\rho = 10$, $\mu = 0.5$.

With the DRW technique, some other algorithmic attempts are used to improve ERM. Label-distribution-aware margin (LDAM) [12] follows the rich literature of margin classifiers [25, 26] and proposes a loss function that encourages class-dependent margins to tackle the class imbalance issue. The ideal margin τi for each class is theoretically derived to be proportional to $n_i^{1/4}$. That is,

$$\tau_i = \frac{C}{n_i^{1/4}} \tag{1}$$

with some constant C. The ideal margin hints the need to enforce larger margins for the minority classes.

With the definition of τi, the authors of LDAM propose a margin-aware loss function that can be used in both the ERM phase and the re-weighting phase of DRW.

Combining LDAM and DRW with the CB loss in the second phase results in a state of-the-art approach for imbalanced learning [12], which will serve as the baseline of our comparison.

### 2.3 Data-Oriented Approach

A common approach for imbalanced multi-class classification at the data level is undersampling for majority classes or oversampling for minority classes. One such approach is SMOTE [8], which essentially oversamples minority classes by creating artificial examples through k-nearest neighbors within the same class. In the context of deep learning, this kind of oversampling can be viewed as a type of data augmentation. Also note ADASYN [9] and LoRAS [13], SMOTE extensions that address class imbalance using machine learning approaches. In this work, we revisit SMOTE and incorporate it into a modern deep learning pipeline.

**SMOTE**

Traditional replication-based oversampling techniques are prone to overfitting. To account for this, [8] proposes oversampling by creating synthetic examples for minority classes; in this case, the synthetic examples are thus not replicated. Specifically, for those samples categorized as belonging to a minority class, they create new data points by interpolating them with their k-nearest neighbors which belong to the same categories. Note that at the time this technique was proposed, deep learning techniques were not yet widely used. Thus, we first study this technique and design two SMOTE like techniques along with the current end-to-end deep learning training pipeline. This is described in detail in the next section. We also note DeepSMOTE [18], which was published during the course of the current study. However, since this approach requires two-stage training in which the first stage requires training an encoder-decoder framework, followed by DeepSMOTE generation, we consider it to be aligned more with GAN-based work, which is not our main focus.

### 2.4 Mixup-Based Techniques

**Mixup**

One of the most famous regularization—or data augmentation—techniques in deep neural networks for image classification problem is Mixup [16], which constructs virtual training examples via simple linear combinations as:

$$x^{\sim} = \lambda x_i + (1 - \lambda)x_j \tag{2}$$

$$y^{\sim} = \lambda y_i + (1 - \lambda)y_j, \tag{3}$$

in which (xi, yi) and (xj, yj) are two examples drawn uniformly from the training data and $\lambda \in [0, 1)$. Mixup-based techniques have been shown to mitigate the memorization of corrupt labels, increase robustness to adversarial training, and improve the generalizability of deep networks, which has led to state-of-the-art performance on tasks such as image classification.

## 3 Main Approach

We observe that Mixup [16] can generalize to a general framework, in the sense that they both train with similar fashion. We term this Mixup framework (Fig. 2), and describe the training algorithm for Mixup framework in Algorithm 1.

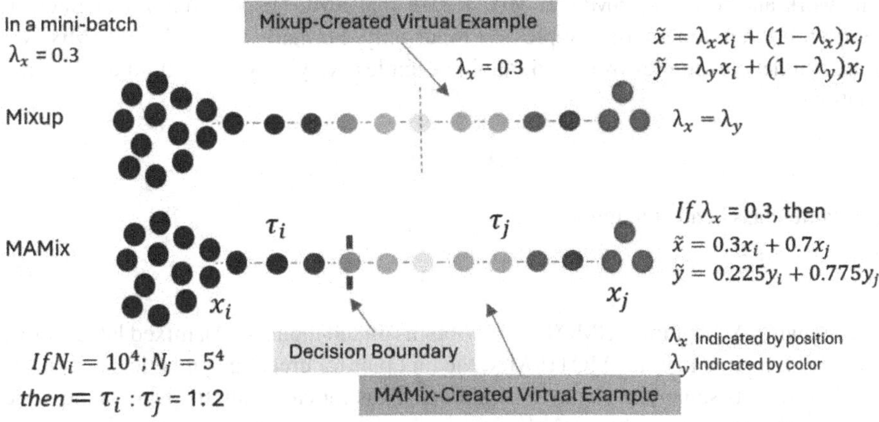


**Fig. 2.** Mixup Framework Illustration

**Algorithm 1:** Mixup Framework Training Algorithm

**Required** Dataset $D = \{(x_i, y_i)\}_{i=1}^{n}$ , model with parameter $\theta$
Initialize;
**while** *training* **do**
  Sample $\{(x_i, y_i), (x_j, y_j)\}_{m=1}^{M}$ From D;
  Sample $\lambda_x \sim Beta(\alpha, \alpha)$;
  **for** $m=1toM$ **do**
    (a)Obtain mixed input $\tilde{x}$;
    (b)Obtain $\lambda_y$;
    (c)Obtain mixed label $\tilde{y}$;
  **end**
  $L(\theta) \leftarrow \frac{1}{M} \sum_{(\tilde{x}, \tilde{y})} L((\tilde{x}, \tilde{y}); \theta)$;
  $\theta \leftarrow \theta - \delta \nabla_\theta L(\theta)$;
**end**

Specifically, within this Mixup Framework, the main difference between each method lies in three steps during mini-batch training, that is, (a) How to obtain mixed input (b) How to obtain label mixing factor λy and (c) How to obtain mixed label.

With this Mixup Framework, we design new methods through two perspectives. First, we design two SMOTE-like techniques—SMOTE-Mix and Neighbor-Mix—within this framework to examine the effectiveness of SMOTE in modern deep learning from input mixing perspective, and this is described in the following Approach 1. Secondly, we propose to incorporate the idea of uneven margin into this Mixup framework to better tackle deep imbalanced learning, which will be illustrated in Approach 2. Our proposed Approach 2 can be viewed from non-uniform label mixing perspective.

### 3.1 Approach 1: SMOTE-Like Techniques

We introduce two SMOTE-like techniques from input mixing perspective in SMOTE-Mix and Neighbor-Mix. First, we perform SMOTE-like input mixing under Mixup framework and term this SMOTE-Mix. Recall that SMOTE performs linear interpolation with their same-class samples on input only. Formally, with SMOTE-Mix, we create synthetic examples from two training samples (xi, yi), (xj, yj) with the following equations:

$$x^{\sim} = \lambda x_i + (1 - \lambda)x_j \tag{4}$$

$x_j$ = same-class nearest neighbor of $x_i$

$$y^{\sim} = y_i. \tag{5}$$

Following Algorithm 1, SMOTE-Mix obtains mixed input by (4), mixed label by (5), and λy = λx. Note that in SMOTE-Mix, the mix pair for creating synthetic examples is sampled from its same-class nearest neighbors. Thus for each pair, the label is the same (yi = yj); that is, they are hard labels.

We then further relax the above idea by not restricting xj to be the same class as xi; that is, we still create synthetic samples through the nearest neighbors, but due to the fact that data are in a high dimensional space, its nearest neighbors may not belong to the same categories. We term this relaxed version Neighbor-Mix, and formulate it as:

$$x^{\sim} = \lambda x_i + (1 - \lambda)x_j \tag{6}$$

$x_j$ = nearest neighbor of $x_i$

$$y^{\sim} = \lambda y_i + (1 - \lambda)y_{xj}. \tag{7}$$

Following Algorithm 1, Neighbor-Mix obtains mixed input by (6), mixed label by (7), and λy = λx. Note that for ˜y, Neighbor-Mix is soft-label, as xj may belong to other categories.

We discuss the empirical results of SMOTE-Mix and Neighbor-Mix on modern long-tailed image datasets in Table 1 to verify the effectiveness of SMOTE in deep learning. Now we further propose our main strategy within the Mixup framework to address deep imbalanced classification.

### 3.2 Approach 2: Margin-Aware Mixup (MAMix)

Inspired by the attempt to achieve uneven margins through a well-designed LDAM loss [12], we propose incorporating the concept of uneven margins into Mixup-based data augmentation techniques. We adopt the common definition and define the margin of an example (x, y) as:

$$\gamma(x, y) = f(x)_y - \max_{j \neq y} f(x)_j. \tag{8}$$

The margin for class j is defined as the average margin of all examples in the class:

$$\overline{\gamma_j} = \frac{1}{n_j} \sum_{i:y_i=j} \gamma(x_j, y_j), \tag{9}$$

Recall that the optimal class-distribution-aware margin trade-off follows (1) [12]. Suppose that (xi, yi) and (xj, yj) are two samples of different classes. Define ηi as the distance from xi to the decision boundary between class i and j, and define ηj similarly. Motivated by (1), we set:

$$\eta_{\mathrm{i}} = 1/\,\mathrm{n}_{\mathrm{i}}^{\omega};\ \eta_{\mathrm{j}} = 1/\,\mathrm{n}_{\mathrm{j}}^{\omega}. \tag{10}$$

We tune the hyper-parameter ω to strike the best trade-off in the proposed margin aware Mixup. The sensitivity of this hyper-parameter is discussed in detail in the Appendix A.

The proposed margin-aware Mixup (MAMix) is formulated as:

$$x^{\sim}MAM = \lambda_x x_i + (1-\lambda_x)x_j \tag{11}$$

$$y^{\sim}MAM = \lambda_y y_i + (1-\lambda_y)y_j. \tag{12}$$

Note that here, λx and the Mixup-selected pair (xi, yi) and (xj, yj) are obtained as in the original Mixup, whereas we compute λy for each Mixup-selected pair based on the following formula, where λy ∈ [0, 1]:

$$\lambda_y = \begin{cases} 1 - \dfrac{(1-\lambda_x)\times 0.5}{\eta_i/(\eta_i+\eta_j)}, \\ \dfrac{(0.5)\times(\lambda_x)}{\eta_j/(\eta_i+\eta_j)}, \quad \text{if}\, \lambda_x < \eta_j/(\eta_i+\eta_j) \end{cases} \tag{13}$$

Therefore, with Algorithm 1, our proposed MAMix obtains mixed input by (11), mixed label by (12), and λy through (13). Essentially, we obtain the optimal mixing factor by ηj /(ηi + ηj); note that ηi, ηj are obtained via (10). If the mixing factor λx is exactly the same as ηj / (ηi + ηj), the probability to output this synthetic example should be exactly 50% for class i and 50% for class j. Also, if the mixing factor λx is larger or smaller than ηj / (ηi + ηj), we compute its corresponding λy using (13), where the core idea is to use arithmetic progression to ensure that the classifier favors minority classes and therefore achieves uneven margins.

Recall that in original Mixup, the mixing factor λx is the same for synthetic x and y, that is, λx = λy. The core idea for Mixup to better account for class-imbalanced learning is by making y not uniform. Our proposed method achieves this by incorporating margin-aware concepts.

## 4 Experiments

### 4.1 Experiment Setup

We follow [12] in creating synthetic datasets for CIFAR-10 [27], CIFAR-100, and Tiny ImageNet. Additionally, our approach is aligned with the guidelines presented in [21] to ensure comprehensive coverage across CINIC-10 and SVHN datasets. To further enhance the depth of our study, we also examine CIFAR-10 and CINIC-10 datasets with extreme imbalance ratios to simulate extremely imbalanced scenarios. Furthermore, we adopt the protocol detailed in [12] with a fixed μ = 0.5 for step imbalance.

For a more comprehensive description about the dataset preparation, please refer to the Appendix B.

**Table 1.** Top-1 validation accuracy (mean ± std) on long-tailed imbalanced CIFAR-10 with ratio $\rho = 100$ with ResNet32 using SMOTE and its two variants

| Method | Accuracy |
|---|---|
| ERM | 71.23 ± 0.51 |
| SMOTE | 72.68 ± 1.41 |
| DRW | 75.08 ± 0.61 |
| M2m | 76.15 ± 0.72 |
| DeepSMOTE | 76.66 ± 0.57 |
| SMOTE-Mix–DRW | 77.46 ± 0.64 |
| Neighbor-Mix–DRW | 80.44 ± 0.32 |
| Mixup–DRW | 82.11 ± 0.57 |

### 4.2 Compared Methods

We compared our method with the baseline training methods: (1) Empirical risk minimization (ERM) loss, where we use standard cross-entropy loss with all examples sharing the same weights. (2) Deferred re-weighting (DRW), proposed by [12], where we train with standard ERM in the first stage and then apply re-weighting in the second stage with the final learning rate decay. (3) The margin-based state-of-the-art work of LDAM-DRW [12]. (4) The recent Mixup-based Remix [21]. Note that following the notation of [12], when two methods are combined, we abbreviate their acronyms with a dash. Our main proposed method is margin-aware Mixup (MAMix). For all experiments, we report the mean and standard deviation over 5 runs with different seeds. We computed the margin gap $\gamma$gap (introduced in the Appendix A) on the validation sets and our proposed method was developed using PyTorch.

## 5 Results and Analysis

In this section, we discuss SMOTE-like techniques—SMOTE-Mix and Neighbor-Mix—for imbalanced deep learning.

When directly using SMOTE for oversampling, the performance gain from around 71% to 72% is not competitive enough (Table 1). Previous studies [12, 28] show that training with re-weighting or re-sampling-based approaches is harmful for representation learning with deep models. Therefore, direct incorporation of SMOTE into deep learning achieves only limited performance improvements. However, SMOTE-Mix and Neighbor-Mix are effective when coupled with DRW (Table 1). Neighbor-Mix coupled with DRW achieves a greater performance improvement over SMOTE-Mix, whereas the performance of Neighbor-Mix is still inferior to that of Mixup, as demonstrated in Table 1, in which the performance difference lies in how to select the Mixup pair during training.

Motivated by the competitive results of SMOTE-Mix and Neighbor-Mix, we further relaxed Neighbor-Mix back to the original form of Mixup to examine the effectiveness of this approach on imbalanced data. Mixup is a modern data augmentation technique that is widely recognized to be effective in the deep image classification literature. However, the datasets are usually balanced; the effect of Mixup for imbalanced datasets has not been widely studied. Therefore, by simply applying Mixup on imbalanced learning settings, we expect to see improvement over a non-Mixup counterpart. For example, in long-tailed imbalanced CIFAR-10 with an imbalance ratio of $\rho = 100$, we can see that the top-1 validation accuracy improves from 72% to around 74% (Table 4) when applying Mixup, which is expected. However, when Mixup is deployed with DRW, the performance boosts from 72% to around 82% (Table 4) under the same setting, which exceeds the previous state-of-the-art result on imbalanced learning of LDAM-DRW [12]. The comprehensive results for imbalanced CIFAR-10 and CIFAR100 are given in Tables 4 and 5; those for imbalanced CINIC-10 are given in Table 6. The detailed results for imbalanced SVHN and imbalanced Tiny-ImageNet, please refer to the Appendix B.

**Table 2.** Top-1 validation accuracy (mean ± std) on extremely long-tailed imbalanced CIFAR-10 using ResNet32

| Imbalance ratio | 200 | 250 | 300 |
|---|---|---|---|
| Mixup–DRW | 77.02 ± 0.53 | 76.33 ± 0.78 | 73.39 ± 0.47 |
| Remix–DRW | 77.23 ± 0.61 | 75.39 ± 0.72 | 73.79 ± 0.29 |
| MAMix–DRW | **78.08 ± 0.23** | **76.34 ± 0.71** | **74.85 ± 0.29** |
| MAMix-Remix–DRW | 78.01 ± 0.23 | 76.25 ± 0.63 | 74.87 ± 0.56 |

**Table 3.** Top-1 validation accuracy (mean ± std) on extremely imbalanced CINIC-10 using ResNet18

| Dataset Imbalance ratio | Long-tailed | Step |
|---|---|---|
| | 200 | 200 |
| ERM | 56.22 ± 1.46 | 52.01 ± 0.52 |
| DRW | 58.97 ± 0.30 | 57.87 ± 1.01 |
| LDAM–DRW | 63.09 ± 0.54 | 65.47 ± 0.63 |
| Mixup–DRW | 66.86 ± 0.50 | 65.61 ± 0.59 |
| Remix–DRW | 66.46 ± 0.51 | 66.61 ± 0.27 |
| MAMix–DRW | **67.59 ± 0.37** | **67.34 ± 0.32** |

Note that Mixup-based methods demonstrate their highest efficacy when combined with DRW. Traditional re-weighting or re-sampling approaches have been shown to harm feature extraction when learning with imbalanced data [12, 28]. As a result, DRW provides a training scheme which first learns a good representation and further accounts for minority classes by re-weighting at later training stages.

In general imbalanced settings where the imbalance ratios are not extreme (e.g., $\rho < 200$), the original Mixup coupled with DRW already achieves competitive results, with the results among different Mixup-based approaches comparable to each other. However, our proposed MAMix outperforms the original Mixup and Remix in extremely imbalanced cases (e.g., $\rho \geq 200$), as demonstrated in Tables 2, and 3. When the imbalance ratio is extreme, our method consistently achieves results superior to those of Mixup and Remix, demonstrating the effectiveness of our method as well as the necessity of our algorithm in extremely imbalanced scenarios. Moreover, MAMix also serves as a general technique used to improve over Mixup or Remix; when deploying MAMix on top of Remix (MAMix–Remix–DRW in Table 2), there is also improvement (Table 2). However, simple deployment of MAMix already yields superior results. We also discuss Mixup-based approaches [16, 21] and their effects on margin statistics compared with margin-based state-of-the-art work in LDAM [12]. A comprehensive analysis of it has been provided in detail in the Appendix A.

**Table 4.** Top-1 validation accuracy (mean ± std) on imbalanced CIFAR-10 using ResNet32

| Dataset | Long-tailed | | | Step | | |
|---|---|---|---|---|---|---|
| Imbalance ratio | 100 | 50 | 10 | 100 | 50 | 10 |
| ERM | 71.23 ± 0.51 | 77.33 ± 0.74 | 86.72 ± 0.36 | 65.64 ± 0.82 | 71.41 ± 1.21 | 85.02 ± 0.33 |
| Mixup | 74.03 ± 0.96 | 78.79 ± 0.16 | 87.79 ± 0.42 | 66.91 ± 0.74 | 72.84 ± 0.60 | 85.50 ± 0.37 |
| Remix | 75.18 ± 0.26 | 80.21 ± 0.26 | 88.36 ± 0.36 | 69.26 ± 0.48 | 74.50 ± 1.16 | 86.68 ± 0.38 |
| MAMix | 74.74 ± 0.76 | 80.00 ± 0.24 | 88.17 ± 0.15 | 68.24 ± 0.43 | 73.88 ± 0.35 | 85.91 ± 0.33 |
| LDAM | 74.01 ± 0.68 | 78.71 ± 0.38 | 86.43 ± 0.32 | 65.64 ± 0.52 | 72.37 ± 0.61 | 84.74 ± 0.26 |
| DRW | 75.08 ± 0.61 | 80.11 ± 0.67 | 87.52 ± 0.25 | 72.02 ± 0.59 | 78.17 ± 0.27 | 87.73 ± 0.15 |
| M2m | 76.15 ± 0.72 | 80.71 ± 0.17 | 88.01 ± 0.24 | 72.91 ± 0.90 | 79.12 ± 0.21 | 87.85 ± 0.11 |
| DeepSMOTE | 76.66 ± 0.57 | 80.60 ± 0.38 | 87.60 ± 0.25 | 72.47 ± 0.64 | 77.52 ± 0.42 | 87.33 ± 0.07 |
| LDAM–DRW | 77.75 ± 0.39 | 81.70 ± 0.22 | 87.67 ± 0.39 | 77.99 ± 0.65 | 81.80 ± 0.39 | 87.68 ± 0.38 |
| Mixup–DRW | 82.11 ± 0.57 | 85.15 ± 0.27 | 89.28 ± 0.23 | 79.22 ± 0.98 | 83.28 ± 0.50 | 89.24 ± 0.15 |
| Remix–DRW | 81.82 ± 0.14 | 84.73 ± 0.23 | 89.33 ± 0.36 | 80.31 ± 0.70 | 83.61 ± 0.24 | 89.10 ± 0.15 |
| MAMix–DRW | **82.29 ± 0.60** | 85.11 ± 0.32 | 89.30 ± 0.14 | 80.02 ± 0.27 | 83.47 ± 0.19 | **89.29 ± 0.29** |

Additionally, we also compared our method with two additional methods: (1) Major-to-minor translation (M2m) [20]. (2) Fusing deep learning and SMOTE for imbalance data (DeepSMOTE) [18] to have a variety of comparisons. The results reveal that our proposed method performs better on all five datasets CIFAR10, CIFAR100, CINIC10 (Tables 4, 5, 6), SVHN, Tiny-ImageNet (in the Appendix B).

**Table 5.** Top-1 validation accuracy (mean ± std) on imbalanced CIFAR-100 using ResNet32

| Dataset | Long-tailed | | | Step | | |
|---|---|---|---|---|---|---|
| Imbalance ratio | 100 | 50 | 10 | 100 | 50 | 10 |
| ERM | 38.46 ± 0.36 | 43.51 ± 0.55 | 56.90 ± 0.13 | 39.56 ± 0.31 | 42.81 ± 0.21 | 55.09 ± 0.21 |
| Mixup | 40.69 ± 0.39 | 46.07 ± 0.60 | 59.63 ± 0.32 | 39.89 ± 0.10 | 41.09 ± 0.16 | 55.79 ± 0.35 |
| Remix | 42.46 ± 0.51 | 47.81 ± 0.48 | 60.71 ± 0.41 | 40.27 ± 0.18 | 42.97 ± 0.24 | 58.77 ± 0.23 |
| MAMix | 42.59 ± 0.22 | 47.89 ± 0.87 | 60.86 ± 0.55 | 40.02 ± 0.19 | 41.85 ± 0.44 | 57.39 ± 0.40 |
| LDAM | 40.49 ± 0.62 | 44.69 ± 0.37 | 56.06 ± 0.44 | 40.56 ± 0.29 | 43.11 ± 0.09 | 54.29 ± 0.41 |
| DRW | 40.40 ± 0.80 | 45.19 ± 0.49 | 57.23 ± 0.33 | 42.97 ± 0.24 | 46.78 ± 0.38 | 56.82 ± 0.38 |
| M2m | 41.92 ± 1.01 | 46.25 ± 0.15 | 58.34 ± 0.07 | 45.66 ± 0.02 | 49.54 ± 0.06 | 59.08 ± 0.22 |
| DeepSMOTE | 38.87 ± 0.19 | 44.70 ± 0.34 | 56.97 ± 0.25 | 42.27 ± 0.16 | 46.22 ± 0.39 | 55.45 ± 0.20 |
| LDAM–DRW | 41.28 ± 0.43 | 45.61 ± 0.41 | 56.42 ± 0.38 | 43.51 ± 0.61 | 46.81 ± 0.29 | 56.07 ± 0.30 |
| Mixup–DRW | 46.91 ± 0.46 | 51.75 ± 0.20 | 62.18 ± 0.24 | 47.56 ± 0.34 | 53.50 ± 0.47 | 62.91 ± 0.53 |
| Remix–DRW | 46.00 ± 0.48 | 51.16 ± 0.23 | 61.63 ± 0.25 | 48.91 ± 0.29 | 53.75 ± 0.26 | 62.47 ± 0.35 |
| MAMix–DRW | **46.93 ± 0.24** | **51.92 ± 0.20** | **62.30 ± 0.33** | 48.87 ± 0.36 | **53.87 ± 0.62** | **62.84 ± 0.18** |

## 6 Conclusion

In this work, we are first to utilize margin statistics to analyze whether the model has learned a proper representation under a class-imbalanced learning setting from a margin perspective. We propose achieving uneven margins via Mixup-based techniques. We first show that coupled with DRW training, the original Mixup implicitly achieves uneven margins in general imbalanced multi-class classification. However, in the case of extreme data imbalance (for example, CINIC-10 with an imbalance ratio $\rho \geq 200$), the proposed margin-aware Mixup outperforms Mixup by explicitly controlling the degree of uneven margins, and also outperforms the proposed Remix [21]. Therefore, in practice, we suggest using the original Mixup for good results on general imbalanced tasks; for extremely imbalanced tasks, we offer the proposed method to better account for such data imbalance. In sum, our study connects SMOTE to Mixup in deep imbalanced classification, while shedding light on a novel framework that combines both traditional [8] and modern [16, 21] data augmentation techniques under the same umbrella. Future work is needed to examine the theoretical aspects of these Mixup-based approaches. With this method and our developed software, we hope that our work can serve as a starting point for future research in the community.

**Table 6.** Top-1 validation accuracy (mean ± std) on imbalanced CINIC-10 using ResNet18

| Dataset | Long-tailed | | | Step | | |
|---|---|---|---|---|---|---|
| Imbalance ratio | 100 | 50 | 10 | 100 | 50 | 10 |
| ERM | 61.08 ± 0.55 | 66.17 ± 0.37 | 77.64 ± 0.08 | 57.29 ± 0.73 | 62.26 ± 0.42 | 75.39 ± 0.30 |
| DRW | 63.75 ± 0.22 | 69.35 ± 0.35 | 78.66 ± 0.10 | 64.34 ± 0.25 | 68.73 ± 0.27 | 78.24 ± 0.21 |
| M2m | 64.20 ± 0.22 | 69.84 ± 0.41 | 78.67 ± 0.11 | 63.99 ± 1.25 | 69.82 ± 0.20 | 78.66 ± 0.03 |
| LDAM–DRW | 68.15 ± 0.22 | 72.34 ± 0.42 | 79.03 ± 0.17 | 70.09 ± 0.32 | 73.16 ± 0.48 | 79.07 ± 0.10 |
| Mixup–DRW | 71.40 ± 0.25 | 75.02 ± 0.16 | 81.36 ± 0.09 | 71.33 ± 0.23 | 74.74 ± 0.20 | 81.37 ± 0.18 |
| Remix–DRW | 71.15 ± 0.24 | 74.68 ± 0.09 | 81.27 ± 0.13 | 71.48 ± 0.50 | 74.91 ± 0.21 | 81.26 ± 0.08 |
| MAMix–DRW | **71.76 ± 0.29** | **75.27 ± 0.17** | **81.46 ± 0.08** | **71.91 ± 0.23** | **75.26 ± 0.08** | **81.39 ± 0.08** |

**Authors' Contributions.** Cheng contributes to detailed literature survey, the initial idea of studying Mixup for deep imbalanced classification, experimental comparison, code implementation and release and initial manuscript writing; Ha rigorously reviewed the code implementation, addressed issues and bugs, and expanded the scope of experimental comparison by incorporating additional methods like DeepSMOTE and M2m; Lin contributes to the bigger picture of linking SMOTE and Mixup, the initial idea of the margin-aware extension, and suggestions on the research methodology.

**Funding.** The work is mainly supported by the MOST of Taiwan under 107-2628E-002-008-MY3.

**Availability of Data and Material.** Experiments are based on public benchmark data.
Code availability: released at open-source at https://github.com/ntucllab/imbalanced-DL.

Conflicts of interest/Competing interests: n/a
Ethics approval: n/a
Consent to participate: n/a
Consent for publication: n/a

## Appendix A Margin Statistics Analysis

We discuss Mixup-based approaches [16, 21] and their effects on margin statistics compared with margin-based state-of-the-art work in LDAM [12].

### A.1 Margin Perspectives

To better analyze and quantify the effect of different learning algorithms on the majority- and minority-class margins, we define the margin gap metric $\gamma_{gap}$ as:

$$\gamma_{gap} = \frac{\sum_i n_i \cdot \overline{\gamma_i}}{\sum_i n_i} - \frac{\sum_j n_j \cdot \overline{\gamma_j}}{\sum_j n_j} \tag{A1}$$

where $i, j$ belong to majority and minority classes, respectively. To decide which class belongs to a majority class, and which belongs a minority class, we set a threshold: if the class sample numbers exceed $1/K$ of the total training samples, we categorize them as majority classes; the others are viewed as minority classes.

Hence a large margin gap corresponds to majority classes with larger margins and minority classes with smaller margins, and hence poor generalizability for the minority classes. We hope to achieve a smaller margin gap when given unbalanced classes. Note that this metric can be negative, as the margins for minority classes are larger than those of majority classes. To better determine whether this is a good indicator of the correlation between the margin gap and top-1 validation accuracy, we further evaluate with Spearman's rank order correlation $\rho$ in Fig. A1.

A.1.1 Spearman's Rank Order Correlation. We demonstrate the results of analysis using Spearman's rank order correlation in Fig. A1. We note a negative rank order correlation between validation accuracy and margin gap $\gamma_{gap}$, as our definition of margin gap reflects the trend in which the better the model generalizes to the minority class, the lower the margin gap is. That is, better models produce smaller margin gaps between majority and minority classes. As seen in Fig. A1, Spearman's rank order correlation is $-0.820$, showing that although it is sometimes noisy, in general $\gamma_{gap}$ is a good indicator for top-1 validation accuracy. Note that we will discuss the noisy part later in the next subsection.

A.1.2. Uneven Margin. Given the superior empirical performance of mixup-based methods, we further analyzed this from a margin perspective to demonstrate the effectiveness of our method. first, we establish our baseline margin gap when the model is trained using ERM. Then, we examine the margin-based LDAM work in which larger margins are enforced for minority classes [12]. As seen in Table A1, the margin gap for ERM is the highest; that is, for deep models trained using ERM, majority classes tend to have higher margins than minority classes, resulting in poor generalizability for minority classes. LDAM-DRW [12] demonstrates its ability to shrink the margin gap, reducing the generalization error for the minority class through margin-based softmax training. Moreover, we observe that in long-tailed imbalance, the original Mixup alone yields competitive results, as the margin gaps are similar between the original Mixup, Remix, and our proposed method. This observation is consistent with remix, for which similar performance is reported in a long-tailed imbalance setting. However, in a step imbalance setting, the superiority of our method is evident, as it not only achieves better performance but also shrinks the margin gap more than the original Mixup.

Note that in Table A1, we see that for the long-tailed scenario, the margin gap of Remix-DRW is $-1.598$ and that of MAMix-DRW is $-1.136$. However, as shown in Table 4, their respective validation accuracies are 81.82 and 82.29. This is an example of the noisy part that is mentioned in the previous context. Here Remix-DRW yields a smaller margin gap than that of MAMix-DRW but poorer validation accuracy, because Remix tends to enforce excessive margins in minority classes, whereas our method strikes a better trade-off.

To further study why excessive margins in minority classes do not help with validation accuracy, we first decompose the margins into two parts: $\gamma \geq 0$ and $\gamma < 0$ part, where validation accuracy is decided by the $\gamma < 0$ part ($\gamma < 0$ determines the validation error).

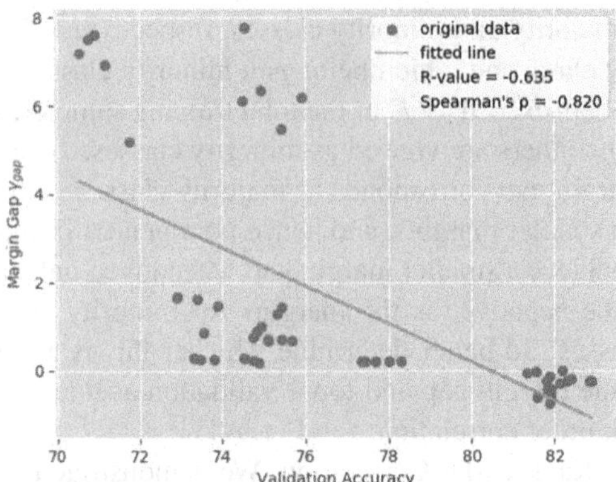


**Fig. A1.** Relationship between margin gap and validation accuracy for long-tailed imbalanced CIFAR-10 with imbalance ratio $\rho = 100$ using ResNet32

**Table A1.** Margin gap on imbalanced CIFAR-10 with $\rho = 100$ using ResNet32

| Dataset | Long-tailed | Step |
|---|---|---|
| Imbalance ratio | 100 | 100 |
| ERM | 7.645 | 8.515 |
| DRW | 6.089 | 7.086 |
| LDAM–DRW | 0.171 | 0.056 |
| Mixup–DRW | −0.978 | −0.481 |
| Remix–DRW | −1.598 | −1.870 |
| MAMix–DRW | −1.136 | −1.798 |

**Table A2.** Margin gap for extremely imbalanced CIFAR-10 with $\rho = 300$ using ResNet32

| Method | Margin gap |
|---|---|
| Remix–DRW | −0.101 |
| MAMix–DRW | −0.487 |

The detailed decomposition result is in Table A3, where we take all $\gamma < 0$ margins and report the average among majority classes and minority classes for each method, and we compute $\gamma \geq 0$ part the same way. From our observation, $\gamma < 0$ part is generally similar between Remix and our MAMix, thus there is only slight accuracy difference, however, the $\gamma \geq 0$ part is generally higher for Remix, as we can see from Table A3. Therefore, the reason why in this case Remix has lower margin gap lies in the fact that it enforces more margins in $\gamma \geq 0$ part of minority classes, as we can see the $\gamma \geq 0$ part is 4.891 for Remix minority classes, and 4.213 for that of MAMix counterpart.

**Table A3.** Margin decomposition on long-tailed imbalanced CIFAR-10 with $\rho = 100$ using ResNet32 (Majority: Class 0 to Class 2; Minority: Class 3 to Class 9)

| Average Margin | $\gamma < 0$ | $\gamma \geq 0$ |
|---|---|---|
| Remix–DRW Majority | −1.587 | 2.371 |
| MAMix–DRW Majority | −1.523 | 2.308 |
| Remix–DRW Minority | −1.933 | **4.891** |
| MAMix–DRW Minority | −1.875 | **4.213** |

From this observation, we identify that there seems to be *excessive margins* in minority classes for Remix, but—Do these excessive margins help or not ?—Previous research [29] has indicated that overly optimizing the margin may be an over-kill, in which the performance may be worse. We further answer this question by examining the difference between theoretical and practical margin distribution.

Recall that LDAM [12] derives a theoretically optimal ratio (1) for per class margin distribution, where such a ratio hints the need to *not over-push* the margin of minority classes. To further analyze how close the practical per class margin distribution of different methods are than that of theoretical margin distribution, we fit theoretical margin by practical margin, and since there is a constant multiplier $C$ in theoretical margin, as in the form of (1), we choose to use linear regression without bias. We set $C = 1$ and compare the fitting ($L_2$) error in Table A4. As we can see from Table A4, our proposed MAMix shows the smallest $L_2$ error, hinting that the per class margin distribution produced by our method is the *closest* to the theoretical margin distribution derived by [12], while the per class margin distribution produced by Remix [21] is slightly inferior than ours in terms of $L_2$ error between theoretical and practical margin, which is due to the excessive margins in minority classes as shown in *Remix_DRW Minority* $\gamma \geq 0$ part in Table A3. Moreover, from Table A4 and Table 4, we observe that the closer practical margin is to theoretical margin, the higher the validation accuracy. Therefore, from the above evidence, we argue that we not only need to enforce larger margin for minority classes, but also need to not over-push minority margins, indicating the need for our method to strike for the better trade-off.

Note that in Table A2—the extremely imbalanced setting—our method brings the margin gap closer than Remix, verifying that our method consistently outperforms Remix.

Therefore, from a margin perspective, we first establish the baseline: when trained with ERM for imbalanced learning, the margins for majority classes are significantly larger than those for minority classes. Second, the recently proposed LDAM loss indeed shrinks the margin gap significantly, suggesting that their approach is effective. To answer the original question—Can we achieve uneven margins for class-imbalanced learning through data augmentation?—the answer is positive, as we observe that applying the original Mixup implicitly closes the gap from a margin perspective, achieving comparable results. We further achieve uneven margins explicitly through the proposed MAMix.

**Table A4.** $L_2$ error on long-tailed imbalanced CIFAR-10 with $\rho = 100$ using ResNet32

| Method | $L_2$ Error |
|---|---|
| ERM | 0.435 |
| LDAM–DRW | 0.195 |
| Mixup–DRW | 0.0133 |
| Remix–DRW | 0.0179 |
| MAMix–DRW | **0.0126** |

**Table A5.** Per Class Accuracy in long-tailed imbalanced CIFAR-10 with $\rho = 100$ using ResNet32

| Method | C0 | C1 | C2 | C3 | C4 | C5 | C6 | C7 | C8 | C9 |
|---|---|---|---|---|---|---|---|---|---|---|
| ERM | 0.94 | 0.97 | 0.83 | 0.71 | 0.76 | 0.61 | 0.72 | 0.61 | 0.46 | 0.48 |
| LDAM–DRW | 0.95 | 0.97 | 0.79 | 0.73 | 0.82 | 0.69 | 0.78 | 0.70 | 0.63 | 0.66 |
| MAMix–DRW | 0.89 | 0.94 | 0.79 | 0.71 | 0.82 | 0.76 | 0.85 | **0.81** | **0.79** | **0.82** |

A.1.3. Per Class Accuracy Evaluation. To further demonstrate the effectiveness of our proposed method, we can see from Table A5 for detailed per class accuracy evaluation. As we can see from Table A5, with ERM, the minority classes (i.e, C7, C8, C9), the accuracy for those classes are low, with C8 and C9 to be 0.46 and 0.48 respectively. And we can see that previous state-of-theart in LDAM–DRW improved those two minority classes to 0.63 and 0.66. However, our proposed MAMix–DRW further elevated the per class accuracy of C8 and C9 and 0.79 and 0.82 respectively, without sacrificing the performance of the majority classes, which can be another evidence that shows the effectiveness of our algorithm.

A.1.4. Hyper-parameter $\omega$ in margin-aware MixupAs seen in Table A6, in the proposed MAMix, we can simply set $\omega$ to to 0.25, which is consistent with that suggested for LDAM [12]; however, the performance changes little when using different settings for $\omega$, demonstrating that the proposed method is easy to tune.

# Appendix B Implementation Details

## B.1 Implementation Details for CIFAR

We followed [12] for CIFAR-10 and CIFAR-100. We also followed [12] to perform simple data augmentation described in [30] for training, where we first padded 4 pixels on each side, then a 32 × 32 crop was randomly sampled from the padded image, or its horizontal flip. We also used ResNet-32 [30] as our base network. We trained the model with a batch size of 128 for 200 epochs. We use an initial learning rate of 0.1, then decay by 0.01 at the 160 and 180th epoch. We also use linear warm-up learning rate schedule for the first 5 epochs for fair comparison.

**Table A6.** Sensitivity of $\omega$ in long-tailed extremely imbalanced CIFAR-10 with $\rho = 300$ using ResNet32

| Method | Accuracy |
|---|---|
| MAMix–DRW ($\omega = 0.125$) | $74.64 \pm 0.17$ |
| MAMix–DRW ($\omega = 0.25$) | $74.85 \pm 0.28$ |
| MAMix–DRW ($\omega = 0.5$) | $74.7 \pm 0.75$ |
| MAMix–DRW ($\omega = 1.0$) | $74.66 \pm 0.36$ |
| MAMix–DRW ($\omega = 2.0$) | $74.21 \pm 0.56$ |
| MAMix–DRW ($\omega = 4.0$) | $74.05 \pm 0.50$ |
| MAMix–DRW ($\omega = 8.0$) | $73.52 \pm 0.52$ |

### B.2 Implementation Details for CINIC

We followed [21] for CINIC-10 where we used ResNet-18 [30] as our base network. As the training scheme provided by [21] we also trained the model for 200 epochs, with a batch size of 128, and initial learning rate of 0.1, followed by decaying the learning rate by 0.01 at the 160 and 180th epochs. We also use linear warm-up learning rate schedule. When DRW was deployed, it was deployed at the 160th epoch. When LDAM was used, we enforced the largest margin to be 0.5.

### B.3 Implementation Details for SVHN

We followed [31] for SVHN. We adopted ResNet-32 [30] as our base network. We trained the model for 200 epochs, with initial learning rate of 0.1 and batch size of 128. We used linear warm-up schedule, and decay the learning rate by 0.1 at the 160th, and 180th epochs. When DRW was deployed, it was deployed at the 160th epoch. When LDAM was used, we enforced the largest margin to be 0.5.

The detailed results for imbalanced SVHN is given in Table B7.

### B.4 Implementation Details for Tiny ImageNet

We followed [12] for Tiny ImageNet with 200 classes. For basic data augmentation in training, we first performed simple horizontal flips, followed by taking random crops of size $64 \times 64$ from images padded by 8 pixels on each side. We adopted ResNet-18 [30] as our base networks, and used stochastic gradient descent with momentum of 0.9, weight decay of $2 \cdot 10^{-4}$. We trained the model for 300 epochs, with initial learning rate of 0.1 and batch size of 128. We used linear warm-up rate schedule, and decay the learning rate by 0.1 at the 150th epoch and 0.01 at the 250th epoch. When DRW was deployed, it was deployed at the 240th epoch. When LDAM was used, we follow the original paper to enforce largest margin to be 0.5. Note that we cannot reproduce the numbers reported in [12].

The detailed results for imbalanced Tiny-ImageNet is given in Table B8.

**Table B7.** Top-1 validation accuracy (mean ± std) on imbalanced SVHN using ResNet32

| Dataset | Long-tailed | | | Step | | |
|---|---|---|---|---|---|---|
| Imbalance ratio | 100 | 50 | 10 | 100 | 50 | 10 |
| ERM | 79.91 ± 0.67 | 83.42 ± 0.15 | 88.43 ± 0.22 | 76.38 ± 0.93 | 81.33 ± 1.11 | 87.89 ± 0.31 |
| Mixup | 81.57 ± 0.68 | 85.16 ± 0.48 | 90.75 ± 0.28 | 76.62 ± 1.03 | 82.88 ± 1.06 | 89.79 ± 0.61 |
| Remix | 82.37 ± 0.67 | 86.27 ± 0.41 | 91.07 ± 0.21 | 78.89 ± 1.30 | 83.57 ± 0.63 | 90.20 ± 0.45 |
| Ours | 82.39 ± 0.45 | 86.75 ± 0.37 | 91.09 ± 0.25 | 77.83 ± 1.87 | 83.91 ± 0.97 | 90.68 ± 0.32 |
| LDAM | 81.96 ± 0.69 | 85.31 ± 0.29 | 89.40 ± 0.36 | 77.93 ± 1.00 | 83.84 ± 0.62 | 89.45 ± 0.37 |
| DRW | 80.68 ± 0.32 | 83.66 ± 0.49 | 88.64 ± 0.26 | 76.33 ± 2.00 | 82.29 ± 1.17 | 88.18 ± 0.45 |
| M2m | 77.68 ± 0.45 | 82.25 ± 0.36 | 88.39 ± 0.38 | 76.10 ± 0.83 | 80.46 ± 1.96 | 87.84 ± 0.77 |
| DeepSMOTE | 81.12 ± 0.58 | 83.62 ± 0.55 | 88.06 ± 0.49 | 78.67 ± 0.88 | 82.08 ± 0.52 | 87.73 ± 0.19 |
| LDAM–DRW | 83.48 ± 1.11 | 86.17 ± 0.54 | 89.85 ± 0.26 | 79.24 ± 1.19 | 84.79 ± 0.65 | 90.11 ± 0.41 |
| Mixup–DRW | 85.19 ± 0.32 | 87.43 ± 0.63 | 90.14 ± 0.23 | 80.73 ± 1.72 | 87.32 ± 0.87 | 90.84 ± 0.24 |
| Remix–DRW | 84.52 ± 0.62 | 87.27 ± 0.37 | 90.11 ± 0.53 | 80.90 ± 1.96 | 87.09 ± 0.85 | 90.80 ± 0.23 |
| MAMix–DRW | **85.41 ± 0.56** | **87.79 ± 0.45** | **90.59 ± 0.52** | **81.71 ± 1.28** | **87.62 ± 0.36** | 90.57 ± 0.23 |

**Table B8.** Top-1 validation accuracy (mean ± std) on imbalanced Tiny-ImageNet using ResNet18

| Dataset | Long-tailed | | Step | |
|---|---|---|---|---|
| Imbalance ratio | 100 | 10 | 100 | 10 |
| ERM | 32.86 ± 0.22 | 48.90 ± 0.43 | 35.44 ± 0.25 | 48.23 ± 0.13 |
| DRW | 33.81 ± 0.49 | 49.99 ± 0.27 | 37.79 ± 0.11 | 50.13 ± 0.30 |
| M2m | 34.33 ± 0.42 | 49.39 ± 0.63 | 37.02 ± 0.68 | 50.11 ± 0.24 |
| LDAM | 31.13 ± 0.36 | 46.90 ± 0.19 | 35.88 ± 0.09 | 47.91 ± 0.19 |
| LDAM–DRW | 31.90 ± 0.13 | 47.15 ± 0.31 | 36.75 ± 0.19 | 48.17 ± 0.16 |
| Mixup–DRW | 37.97 ± 0.38 | 52.51 ± 0.40 | 40.45 ± 0.21 | 54.46 ± 0.29 |
| Remix–DRW | 36.89 ± 0.61 | 52.13 ± 0.23 | 41.07 ± 0.37 | 53.58 ± 0.23 |
| MAMix–DRW | 37.73 ± 0.18 | 52.53 ± 0.34 | **41.46 ± 0.38** | 54.37 ± 0.29 |

## References


1. Awoyemi, J.O., Adetunmbi, A.O., Oluwadare, S.A.: Credit card fraud detection using machine learning techniques: a comparative analysis. In: 2017 ICCNI, pp. 1–9 (2017). https://doi.org/10.1109/ICCNI.2017.8123782
2. Roy, A., Sun, J., Mahoney, R., Alonzi, L., Adams, S., Beling, P.: Deep learning detecting fraud in credit card transactions. In: 2018 SIEDS, pp. 129–134 (2018). https://doi.org/10.1109/SIEDS.2018.8374722
3. Horn, G.V., Perona, P.: The devil is in the tails: fine-grained classification in the wild. CoRR abs/1709.01450 (2017). https://arxiv.org/abs/1709.01450

4. Lin, T.-Y., et al.: Microsoft COCO: common objects in context. In: Fleet, D., Pajdla, T., Schiele, B., Tuytelaars, T. (eds.) Computer Vision – ECCV 2014. LNCS, vol. 8693, pp. 740–755. Springer, Cham (2014). https://doi.org/10.1007/978-3-319-10602-1_48
5. Zhong, Y., et al.: Unequal training for deep face recognition with long-tailed noisy data. In: 2019 CVPR, pp. 7804–7813 (2019). https://doi.org/10.1109/CVPR.2019.00800
6. Huang, C., Li, Y., Loy, C.C., Tang, X.: Deep imbalanced learning for face recognition and attribute prediction. TPAMI **42**(11), 2781–2794 (2020). https://doi.org/10.1109/TPAMI.2019.2914680
7. Cui, Y., Jia, M., Lin, T.-Y., Song, Y., Belongie, S.: Class-balanced loss based on effective number of samples. In: CVPR (2019)
8. Chawla, N., Bowyer, K., Hall, L.O., Kegelmeyer, W.: SMOTE: synthetic minority over-sampling technique. J. Artif. Intell. Res. **16**(1), 321–357 (2002)
9. He, H., Bai, Y., Garcia, E.A., Li, S.: ADASYN: adaptive synthetic sampling approach for imbalanced learning. In: 2008 IEEE International Joint Conference on Neural Networks, pp. 1322–1328 (2008). https://doi.org/10.1109/IJCNN.2008.4633969
10. Huang, C., Li, Y., Loy, C.C., Tang, X.: Learning deep representation for imbalanced classification. In: 2016 CVPR, pp. 5375–5384 (2016). https://doi.org/10.1109/CVPR.2016.580
11. Liu, X., Zhou, Z.: The influence of class imbalance on cost-sensitive learning: an empirical study. In: ICDM 2006, pp. 970–974 (2006). https://doi.org/10.1109/ICDM.2006.158
12. Cao, K., Wei, C., Gaidon, A., Arechiga, N., Ma, T.: Learning imbalanced datasets with label-distribution-aware margin loss. In: NeurIPS (2019)
13. Bej, S., Davtyan, N., Wolfien, M., Nassar, M., Wolkenhauer, O.: LoRAS: an oversampling approach for imbalanced datasets. CoRR abs/1908.08346 (2019). https://arxiv.org/abs/1908.08346
14. DeVries, T., Taylor, G.W.: Dataset augmentation in feature space. In: ICLR 2017, Toulon, France, 24–26 April 2017, Workshop Track Proceedings (2017). https://openreview.net/forum?id=HyaF53XYx
15. Inoue, H.: Data augmentation by pairing samples for images classification (2018). https://openreview.net/forum?id=SJn0sLgRb
16. Zhang, H., Cisse, M., Dauphin, Y.N., Lopez-Paz, D.: Mixup: beyond empirical risk minimization. In: ICLR (2018). https://openreview.net/forum?id=r1Ddp1-Rb
17. Mathew, J., Luo, M., Pang, C.K., Chan, H.L.: Kernel-based SMOTE for SVM classification of imbalanced datasets. In: IECON 2015, pp. 001127–001132 (2015). https://doi.org/10.1109/IECON.2015.7392251
18. Dablain, D., Krawczyk, B., Chawla, N.: DeepSMOTE: fusing deep learning and smote for imbalanced data. IEEE Trans. Neural Netw. Learn. Syst., 1–15 (2022). https://doi.org/10.1109/TNNLS.2021.3136503
19. Goodfellow, I.J., et al.: Generative Adversarial Networks (2014). Accessed 8 Jan 2017
20. Kim, J., Jeong, J., Shin, J.: M2m: imbalanced classification via major-to-minor translation, pp. 13893–13902 (2020). https://doi.org/10.1109/CVPR42600.2020.01391
21. Chou, H.-P., Chang, S.-C., Pan, J.-Y., Wei, W., Juan, D.-C.: Remix: rebalanced mixup. arXiv (2020). 2007.03943
22. Johnson, J., Khoshgoftaar, T.: Survey on deep learning with class imbalance. J. Big Data **6**, 1–54 (2019)
23. Buda, M., Maki, A., Mazurowski, M.A.: A systematic study of the class imbalance problem in convolutional neural networks. Neural Netw. **106**, 249–259 (2018). https://doi.org/10.1016/j.neunet.2018.07.011
24. Khan, S.H., Hayat, M., Bennamoun, M., Sohel, F.A., Togneri, R.: Cost-sensitive learning of deep feature representations from imbalanced data. IEEE Trans. Neural Netw. Learn. Syst. **29**(8), 3573–3587 (2018). https://doi.org/10.1109/TNNLS.2017.2732482

25. Liu, W., Wen, Y., Yu, Z., Yang, M.: Large-margin softmax loss for convolutional neural networks. In: ICML, pp. 507–516 (2016)
26. Wang, F., Cheng, J., Liu, W., Liu, H.: Additive margin softmax for face verification. IEEE Sig. Process. Lett. **25**(7), 926–930 (2018). https://doi.org/10.1109/LSP.2018.2822810
27. Krizhevsky, A., Hinton, G.: Learning multiple layers of features from tiny images. Master's thesis, Department of Computer Science, University of Toronto (2009)
28. Ye, H.-J., Chen, H.-Y., Zhan, D.-C., Chao, W.-L.: Identifying and compensating for feature deviation in imbalanced deep learning. arXiv (2020). 2001.01385
29. Reyzin, L., Schapire, R.E.: How boosting the margin can also boost classifier complexity. In: Proceedings of the 23rd International Conference on Machine Learning. ICML 2006, pp. 753–760 (2006). https://doi.org/10.1145/1143844.1143939
30. He, K., Zhang, X., Ren, S., Sun, J.: Deep residual learning for image recognition. In: 2016 CPVR, pp. 770–778 (2016). https://doi.org/10.1109/CVPR.2016.90
31. Yang, Y., Xu, Z.: Rethinking the value of labels for improving class-imbalanced learning. In: NeurIPS (2020)

# Assessing Personality Factors for Recommendation Systems of Learning Method

Madoka Hagiri[1(✉)], Shoji Yamamoto[1], Aoi Ohta[2], and Yasufumi Takama[2]

[1] Tokyo Metropolitan College of Industrial Technology, 8-17-1, Minamisenju, Arakawa-ku, Tokyo 116-0003, Japan
s22030@g.metro-cit.ac.jp

[2] Tokyo Metropolitan University, 6-6 Asahigaoka, Hino, Tokyo 191-0065, Japan

**Abstract.** In recent years, with the spread of COVID-19, remote classes have started to operate in many universities as a useful method for successive education. Remote classes can provide a place and location for free learning, students can learn at their own pace based on self-directed study. However, it is necessary to make the follow-up system for students who are struggling with self-directed learning, since the remote classes is performed without complementary support and the self-directed learning requires autonomy. Therefore, in this research, we have developed a practical system that can recommend learning methods suitable for individual students. In order to match the individual student, we focus on each personality as their feature in recommending a study method. Calculation and memorization skills were measured as basic learning abilities, while the personality profiler test proposed by Yatabe-Gilford was performed at the same time. As a first step, this paper will discuss whether a correlation exists between personality and learning abilities for analyzing the adaptability in self-directed learning.

**Keywords:** Recommendation system · Personality · Learning Methods

## 1 Introduction

In recent years, with the spread of COVID-19, remote classes have started to operate in many universities. Even now that the infection of COVID-19 is under control, almost students yet have to study on their own initiative, since many classes still require self-directed study, such as online classes. Before, they obtained benefits about essential knowledge of lecture from teacher directly, and unclear points could be resolved through the communication among students. Although the self-directed study was only an assisting in lecture, unfortunately, this study is main task in online classes. The understanding of lecture content and practice of assignments must be accomplished by each student individually. Therefore, students who struggle with self-directed study may not fully understand the lecture content even when the class progresses. Also, significant individual difference in learning skills arise among students whether or not they are capable of studying initiatively.


C.-Y. Lee et al. (Eds.): TAAI 2023, CCIS 2074, pp. 97–109, 2024.
https://doi.org/10.1007/978-981-97-1711-8_7

Active learning may be a good method to learn how to study independently. This learning method is not a one-way lecture-style class, but a way for students to actively think and learn. They can learn how other students used to study method and how they acquire their skills in this class. However, it is difficult to judge whether the learning method of another student is appropriate for you. Some people prefer to learn all at once in a concentration, while others prefer to learn through daily repetitive practice. Suitable study methods vary to each one's own and we assumed that it depends mainly on each personality. Therefore, in this paper, we analysis the initiative ability for self-directed study with practical task, and develop a recommend system for the method of self-directed study based primarily on each personality.

## 2 Relate Studies

In previous research reports, many researchers have proposed support methods of self-directed study on e-learning. Nakayama et al. [1] analyzed the timing of studying in their daily activities, and proposed a system to recommend studying in their free time. On the other hand, Kurihara et al. [2] developed a recommendation system which can make a suggestion for educational materials based on cumulative similar user. These methods only provide an appreciate timing and material that have been effective in others. It is assumed that improving the initiative for self-directed study by recommending study opportunities is difficult. We consider that incorporating psychological factors is essential to improve the motivation of student.

In the research of psychophysical study, Tomas et al. [3] reported that Neuroticism and Conscientiousness, one of the personality, were effective to predict the result of academic performance. Their assertion makes sense to us that students with Conscientiousness are better suited to learn steadily every day, and students with Neuroticism will concentrate on their studies until they have reached a certain milestone. As the other studies focusing on personality, Su, J.-H. et al. [4] developed a recommender system that suggests cross-domain courses based on personality. Furthermore, Amany Said et al. [5] assess self-directed learning readiness level and personality traits among nursing students. These researches also concluded that the choice of subjects and methods based on personality affects learning performance.

Therefore, in this research, we focused on the relationship between personalities and academic performance for self-directed approach. If the approach of self-directed study can be classified according to personality, it may be possible to recommend a learning approach that matches students with same personality. Here, personality measurement is an important factor for our research. Big Five personality traits [6] is the most famous even if many methods for measuring personality are proposed in the field of psychology. Unfortunately, this method is summarized in five personality categories, it is concerned that the number of features is small for building a recommendation system. As a consequence, we focused on the Yatabe-Guilford personality test [7], which can make personality judgments similar to Big Five and has a large number of features. This test (hereinafter, this is called "YG personality test") is widely used as a test in the psychophysical field in Japan, since this test has an advantage which is easy to perform and process scoring.

## 3 Material and Methods

### 3.1 Measuring Personality

As mentioned above, we used the YG personality test to measure personality. This test includes 120 simple questions, such as "I look forward to meeting and discussing with a variety of people.", and participants reply with either "Yes," "No," or "Neither." The answers to the questions are evaluated as 12 personality traits which are indicated in Table 1. In this research, these traits are used as features of the participants' personalities.

**Table 1.** Personality traits List proposed by Guilford

| Personality traits | Abbreviation | Description |
|---|---|---|
| Depression | D | Character is depressed, gloomy, lethargic |
| Cyclic tendency | C | Emotional, agitated |
| Inferiority feelings | I | A sense of inferiority (awareness in which one is inferior to others) |
| Nervousness | N | Nervousness (easily affected by small things) |
| Objectivity | O | Subjectivity, dogmatic, and not listening to others' opinions |
| Cooperativeness | Co | Uncooperative and careful towards others |
| Agreeableness | Ag | Aggressive, proactive, ambitious, hasty, short-tempered |
| General activity | G | Active, agile, do everything on their own without other people's help |
| Rhathymia | R | Carefree, quick to decide, laid-back, impulsive |
| Thinking extroversion | T | Planless, not caring about small things |
| Ascendance | A | Domineering, leadership, and self-expression |
| Social extroversion | S | Likes to socialize with people, likes people |

Figure 1 shows an example of the results in YG personality test. As shown in this figure, it is found that this test can quantify each personality trait on a 20-point scale.

### 3.2 Measuring Learning Ability

Next, we have to evaluate learning ability for student in order to recommend a learning approach. Here, it is difficult to ensure that all learning capacities are covered because students learn so many kind of contents, Therefore, we selected calculation and memory task which are assumed that these two major abilities have common importance in the study of any contents.

As the measurement of calculational ability, we used the "Uchida-Kraepelin performance test" (hereinafter, this is called "UK-test"). This test was improved by Uchida based on Kraepelin's psychometric test [8]. Figure 2 shows an overview of the UK-test.

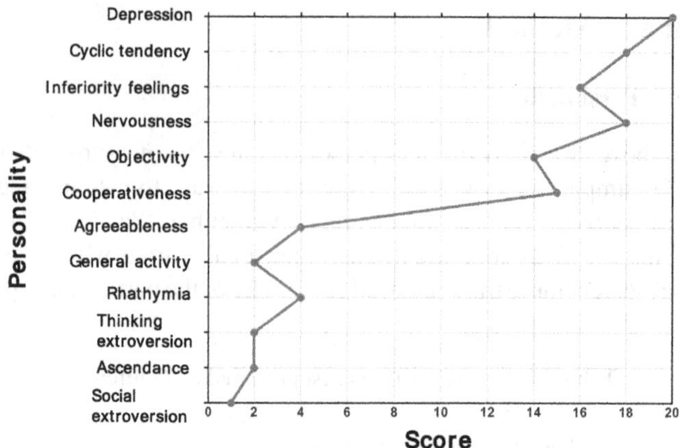


**Fig. 1.** Example of the results in YG personality test

In this test, participants perform a simple addition. Two single-digit numbers appear on the screen, and the participant answers only the last digit. As a time constraint, each line is changed in one-minute units, and total execution time is 30 min. Here, we had a 5 min break for the UK-test. Namely, participants perform 15 min of calculation, and after the break, they perform the remaining 15 min of calculation. The attempt of this rest is to clarify the effect of the 5-min break on the recovery of calculational performance. From the result of calculational examination, we expect to understand the participant's characteristics such as calculational ability, processing efficiency, and even concentration. The rate of error in the calculations may obtain an indication of the carelessness of participants. Furthermore, we have implemented the UK-test so that it can be performed remotely. The visual number display of UK-test is realized with JavaScript programming, and the answers from participant can be retrieved as text files. Since subjects can perform this test anywhere via the Internet, we have been able to obtain the result of UK-test from a large number of subjects.

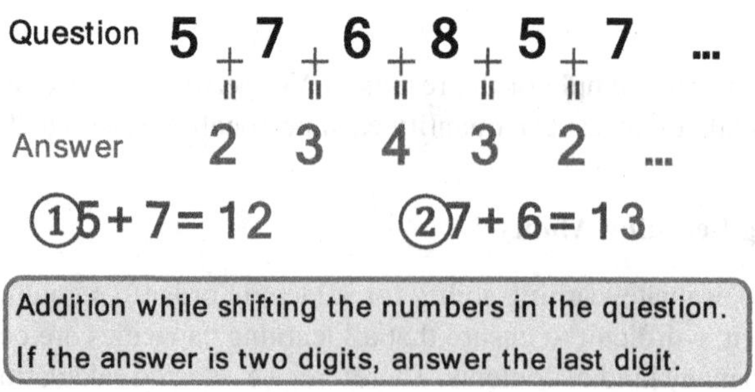

Question 5 + 7 + 6 + 8 + 5 + 7 ...

Answer 2 3 4 3 2 ...

① 5 + 7 = 12 ② 7 + 6 = 13

Addition while shifting the numbers in the question.
If the answer is two digits, answer the last digit.

**Fig. 2.** Overview of visual number display in UK-test

Subsequently, we examined our assessment methods for memory. It is well known that there are three types of human memory, which are sensory memory, short-term memory, and long-term memory. These memory linkages are known as the Multi Store Model of Memory, which was proposed by Atkinson and Shiffrin et al. [9].

First, sensory information such as light and sound is detected by sensory receptors and processed by neurons in brain. This sensory information is stored in sensory memory and after a while is transferred to short-term memory. Moreover, repeated information of short-term memory is eventually stored as long-term memory. While this long-term memory is capacity of memory we use in learning, it is difficult to assess long-term memory because the rehearsal conditions of memory are unclear. Therefore, we focused on short-term memory, which is the first stage of long-term memory. This attempt is based on an assumption that if short-term memory capacity is high, long-term memory is also excellent.

Many researches have been designed to assess short-term memory. Among them, the serial position effect is often used in psychophysical fields such as dementia screening [10]. This effect can quantify memory capacity by measuring our tendency to recall the first and last items in a series best, and our inability to remember the middle items. It is expected that participants with higher scores on the series position effect have better recognition and comprehension skills, as well as the ability to maintain concentration. These comprehension and concentration skills can be related to personality traits such as nervousness and perseverance. Therefore, in this research, we employed the series position effect as a guideline for quantifying memory capacity.

Figure 3 shows an overview of the experimental system for memory examinations. In this experiment, five figures are displayed in time sequence at fixed time intervals. These figures are different in shape and color, and consist of five different shapes and eleven different color combinations. The size of these figures is large enough to be recognized regardless of visual acuity, with at least a 2-degree field of view. The display intervals for five different figures were 1, 5, 10, and 15 s. After displaying the five figures, participants are asked to respond to the shape and color of figures in the displaying order. The score of memory ability was evaluated as percentage of correct answers for five displayed figures. In addition, we attempted to insert an interference between displaying and answering in order to assess tolerance to temporal memory. Since another operation that uses the brain is suitable as an interference, we employed the UK-test, which is used by a calculational test.

In the actual experiment, a personality test, a calculation test, and a memory test were administered in a series. A flowchart of entire experiment is shown in Fig. 4. A total of 20 participants, 18 males and 2 females, were asked to take part in the experiment. All were healthy students in their 20 s.

## 4 Evaluation of Relationship Between Personality and Learning Ability

### 4.1 Correlation Between Personality and Calculational Ability

Figure 5 shows an example of the results of calculational ability test. The horizontal axis is the number of trials, which is the same as testing the time, since each trial takes one minute. The vertical axis is the number of calculations completed per minute. It is

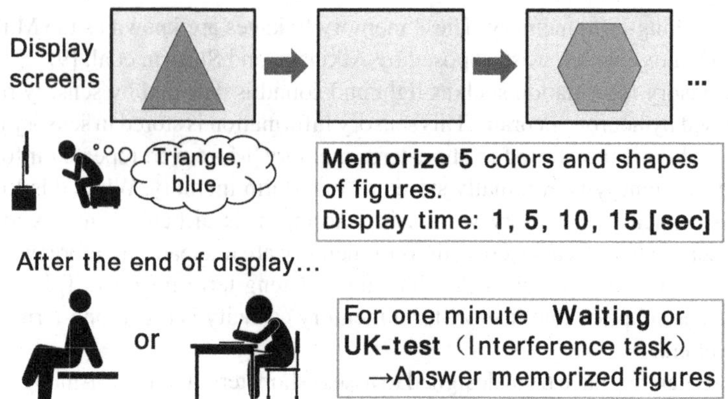


**Fig. 3.** Overview of memory test based on the serial position effect

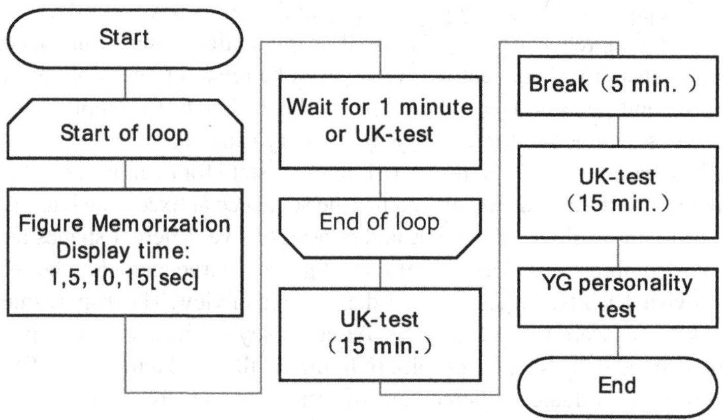


**Fig. 4.** Flowchart of all experiment to measure the personality and learning ability

noted that there will be a 5-min break after 15 rounds. The color of the bar in this graph indicates the percentage of correct answers: blue indicates correct answers and orange indicates incorrect answers.

Based on the above results, we adopted the following six types of features as calculational abilities.

- Overall average number of calculational trial
- Overall average number of correct answers
- Average percentage of correct answers in calculational trials
- Average percentage of incorrect answers in calculational trials
- Quantity of variation in calculational trials
- Quantity of variation in the number of correct answers

Figure 6 shows the results of correlation analysis between personality and calculational ability. The vertical column shows the feature of calculational ability, and the

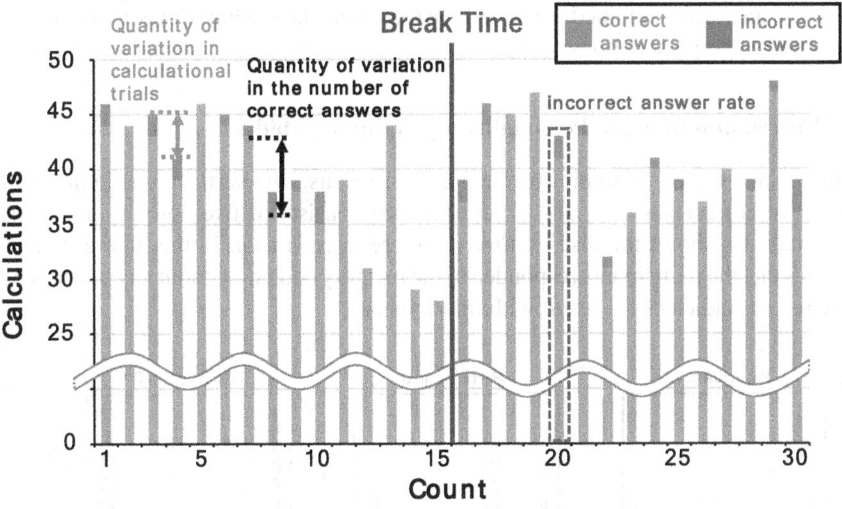


**Fig. 5.** Typical result of UK-test (Count = 1 min) (Color figure online)

horizontal column shows the abbreviation of personality features as shown in Table 1. The numbers in the colored boxes indicate the correlation coefficients, with red color becoming darker as the positive correlation increases. Conversely, the higher the negative correlation, the darker blue color of the box.

| Calculational ability | D | C | I | N | O | Co | Ag | G | R | T | A | S |
|---|---|---|---|---|---|---|---|---|---|---|---|---|
| Overall average number of calculational trial | 0.17 | 0.42 | 0.073 | 0.15 | -0.12 | -0.079 | 0.012 | -0.056 | 0.14 | -0.37 | -0.012 | -0.11 |
| Overall average number of correct answers | 0.12 | 0.35 | 0.085 | 0.11 | -0.15 | -0.055 | -0.012 | 0.0062 | 0.1 | -0.34 | -0.012 | -0.043 |
| Average percentage of correct answers in calculational trials | 0.11 | -0.031 | 0.33 | 0.65 | -0.086 | 0.24 | -0.77 | 0 | -0.73 | -0.42 | -0.26 | -0.17 |
| Average percentage of incorrect answers in calculational trials | -0.11 | 0.031 | -0.33 | -0.65 | 0.086 | -0.24 | 0.77 | 0 | 0.73 | 0.42 | 0.26 | 0.17 |
| Quantity of variation in calculational trials | -0.012 | 0.16 | 0.097 | 0.42 | -0.1 | 0.18 | -0.33 | 0.019 | -0.4 | 0.2 | -0.14 | 0.18 |
| Quantity of variation in the number of correct answers | 0.11 | 0.47 | 0.018 | 0.43 | -0.031 | 0.073 | -0.073 | -0.1 | -0.13 | 0.1 | -0.085 | 0.031 |

Personality

**Fig. 6.** Correlation between personalities and calculational ability. (Color figure online)

Overall, we were unable to find distinctive feature of calculational ability that correlated with all of the feature of personality. However, although locally, some computability scores have been observed to be highly correlated with the features of personality. For example, Agreeableness (Ag) and Rhathymia (R), the incorrect answer rate is high, and people with mood variability have uneven work. Since this partial high correlation case can be satisfactorily explained, it is clear that there is a relationship between calculational ability and some personalities.

## 4.2 Correlation Between Personality and Memory Ability

Figure 7 shows some examples of memory test results. The vertical axis indicates the number of correct answers, and a perfect score consists of five correct answer. The horizontal axis shows the display time of figure in each trial. In this figure, blue bar indicates that the participants responded to the memory content without any interference, while red bar indicates the result with interference.

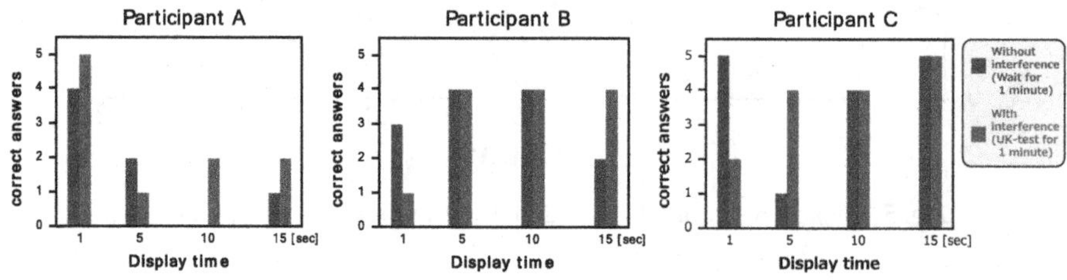


**Fig. 7.** Example of result in memory test. (Color figure online)

As for the overall trend in the number of correct answers, memory ability showed no characteristic trend with respect to display time. Some participants were better at memorizing the shorter display times, while others were better at memorizing the longer display times. Furthermore, there was little difference in results with and without interference.

Based on the above results, we adopted the following six types of features as memory abilities.

**※All features are averages.**

| Memory ability | D | C | I | N | O | Co | Ag | G | R | T | A | S |
|---|---|---|---|---|---|---|---|---|---|---|---|---|
| Without interference | -0.0023 | -0.14 | -0.11 | -0.17 | 0.24 | -0.11 | 0.06 | -0.057 | 0.24 | -0.038 | 0.11 | 0.2 |
| With interference | 0.1 | 0.07 | 0.099 | -0.053 | 0.28 | 0.32 | 0.14 | 0.13 | 0.23 | -0.31 | 0.1 | 0.19 |
| Display time 1[sec] | 0.53 | 0.26 | 0.39 | 0.27 | 0.46 | 0.32 | -0.09 | -0.4 | 0.062 | 0.0046 | -0.53 | -0.49 |
| Display time 5[sec] | -0.037 | -0.16 | -0.16 | -0.14 | 0.15 | 0.13 | 0.28 | 0.18 | 0.19 | -0.35 | 0.31 | 0.29 |
| Display time 10[sec] | -0.063 | -0.071 | 0.031 | -0.2 | 0.17 | -0.093 | 0.041 | 0.053 | 0.45 | 0.089 | 0.26 | 0.34 |
| Display time 15[sec] | -0.018 | 0.15 | -0.048 | -0.2 | 0.26 | 0.14 | 0.19 | 0.36 | 0.26 | -0.28 | 0.11 | 0.42 |

Personality

**Fig. 8.** Correlation between personalities and memory ability

- Average number of correct answers for with or without interference task (UK-test)
- Average number of correct answers for each displayed time (1, 5, 10, 15 [s])

Figure 8 shows the results of correlation analysis between personality and memory ability. However, no highly correlated personality was found in memory ability.

# 5 Discussion: Relationships with Classification

## 5.1 Re-evaluation by Classification of Personality Features

In the previous chapter, we found only a partial relationship between calculational and memory abilities and personality. However, the results in Fig. 6 and 8 are for all participants, and it is difficult to find highly correlated features when a large variation exists in personality. Therefore, we challenge to re-evaluate the results by classifying them into groups with similar personalities.

Hierarchical clustering is used in this study to classify them into groups with similar personalities. This clustering is one of an unsupervised learning method that groups samples sequentially based on their similarity in the feature space. In this case, we apply this method to features related to personality and obtained results as shown in Fig. 9.

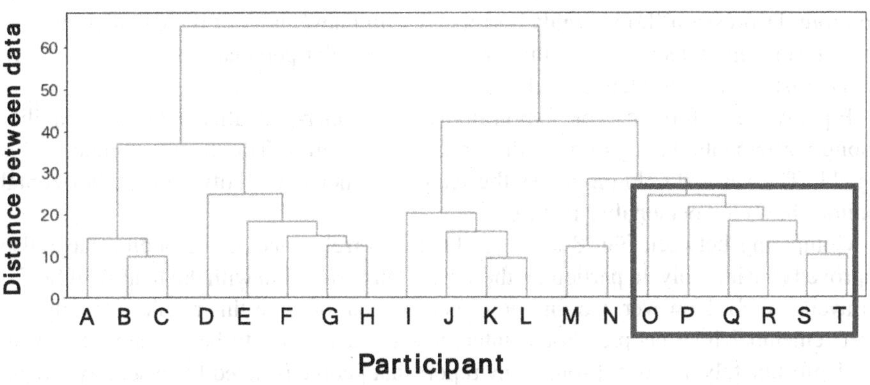


**Fig. 9.** Result of grouped personality by using hierarchical clustering

The horizontal axis in Fig. 9 shows the participants and the vertical axis shows the distance between the features. The result indicates that this method is able to group data that are close to each other in order. Here, this test, which is based on YG personality test, is capable of classifying personality into five categories. Therefore, we divided the personalities into five groups. The participants from O to T with the largest number of people were treated as the same personality group, and correlation analysis with learning ability was conducted again.

Figure 10 shows the results of correlation analysis between the features of personality and calculational ability among participants with groups with similar personalities.

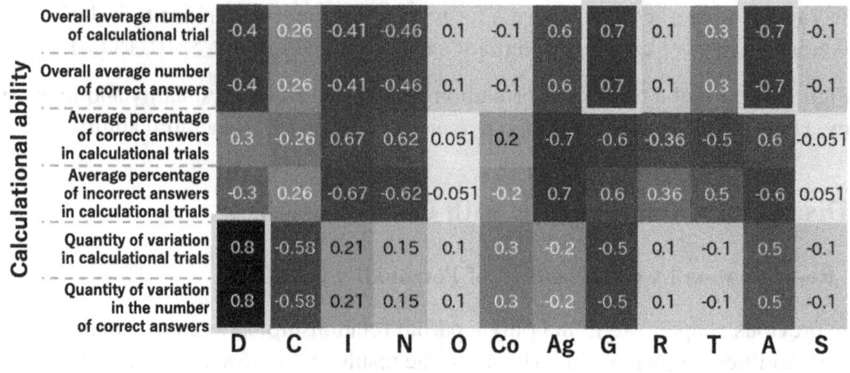


**Fig. 10.** Correlation between personalities and calculational ability in similar personality group

Owing to the grouping effect, it is clear that the overall correlation coefficient increases. In particular, the correct/incorrect response rate shows the presence of a significant positive/negative correlation for most of personalities. General activity (G) and Ascendance (A) are highly correlated with the activation of calculational tasks. Furthermore, Depression (D) is highly correlated with unevenness of the calculation task. These results allow us to inspect that groups with similar personalities have distinctive characteristics in their calculational abilities.

Equally, we performed a correlation analysis between personality and memory ability among participants with groups with similar personalities. This result is indicated as Fig. 11. The vertical column shows the feature of memory ability and the horizontal column shows the personality features.

Comparing between Fig. 8 and Fig. 11, the correlations with grouping have also improved considerably. In particular, there is a high correlation with the feature of Social extraversion (S). However, we find no direct implication with this result. Actually, we must remember how people should interact with each other to have a smooth social life. Unfortunately, it has not found any report that people isolated from society having poor memory ability. Since social extraversion includes a wide variety of situations, we presume that it is difficult to find a direct implication in this direct correlation analysis. Therefore, an additional factor analysis is performed in the next chapter to add to the results of this memory ability.

## 5.2 Factor Analysis for Memory Ability

Factor analysis methods were used to infer memory abilities related to personality. This is an analytical method that explores what latent variables are associated with the observed variables. In this study, we have investigated latent features that affect memory ability but cannot be observed in practice.

Figure 12 shows the results of factor analysis. The horizontal axis shows display time of the figure in each trial. Here, it is noted that horizontal axis is districted between left

※All features are averages.

| Memory ability | D | C | I | N | O | Co | Ag | G | R | T | A | S |
|---|---|---|---|---|---|---|---|---|---|---|---|---|
| Without interference | 0.14 | -0.12 | -0.35 | -0.14 | 0.46 | 0.26 | -0.029 | -0.086 | 0.64 | -0.43 | 0.2 | 0.93 |
| With interference | 0.2 | -0.059 | -0.26 | 0.23 | 0.67 | 0.6 | 0.2 | 0.086 | 0.67 | -0.6 | 0.49 | 0.72 |
| Display time 1[sec] | 0.52 | -0.44 | -0.22 | -0.59 | -0.15 | -0.03 | 0.03 | -0.15 | -0.031 | 0.46 | -0.52 | -0.22 |
| Display time 5[sec] | 0.47 | -0.39 | 0 | 0.12 | 0.66 | 0.55 | -0.17 | -0.2 | 0.4 | -0.64 | 0.38 | 0.75 |
| Display time 10[sec] | -0.016 | 0.079 | -0.46 | -0.016 | 0.25 | 0.093 | 0.031 | -0.19 | 0.75 | -0.31 | 0.42 | 0.88 |
| Display time 15[sec] | -0.34 | 0.22 | -0.21 | 0 | 0.53 | 0.2 | 0.058 | 0.32 | 0.47 | -0.58 | 0.1 | 0.88 |

Personality

**Fig. 11.** Correlation between personalities and memory ability in similar personality group

and right side with and without interference. The vertical axis indicates factor loadings, which indicate the value between −1 and 1. The factor loadings allow us to understand which variables are most closely associated with a particular factor. In other words, the more positive the factor loadings value is, the more positively correlated the factors and features are. As the result, the analysis revealed three distinct latent factors for the memory ability as shown in Fig. 12.

The first factor has high factor loadings for most features, except for display time of 1 s regardless of the presence or absence of interference. Usually, the longer display time, the more concentration is required, then this factor can be considered "persistence of concentration".

The second factor has a particularly low factor loading for 15-s display time, regardless of the presence or absence of interference. In this case, it is inferred that participants need to be patient, because they have to observe and memorize the same figure for 15 s. Here, it is considered to be the opposite "lack of patience" since it is a negative value as a factor loading.

The third factor has a large factor loading when there are no interfering issues. This factor may indicate a characteristic of forgetting the contents of memory due to interference. In other words, it is assumed to be "poor memory organization".

These three latent factors are considered to have a significant impact on the evaluation of memory ability. Therefore, we investigated correlations between three latent factors and personality. Figure 13 shows the results of correlation analysis.

From this analysis, it is found that some highly correlated area with personality exist. For example, people with Depression (D) tend to be less patient, and Rhathymia (R) people are less able to organize their memories. Although partly, it is clear that these personality traits are related to memory ability.

Finally, from the results of this factor analysis, it can be inferred that evaluation of memory ability needs to be improved. This indicates that the features initially setting

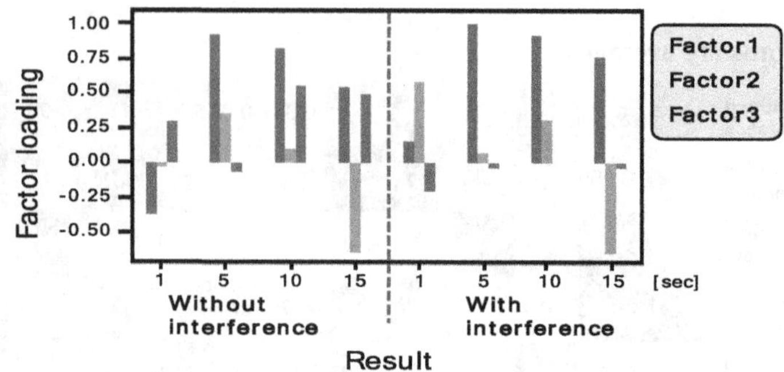


**Fig. 12.** Results of the factor analysis for memory ability

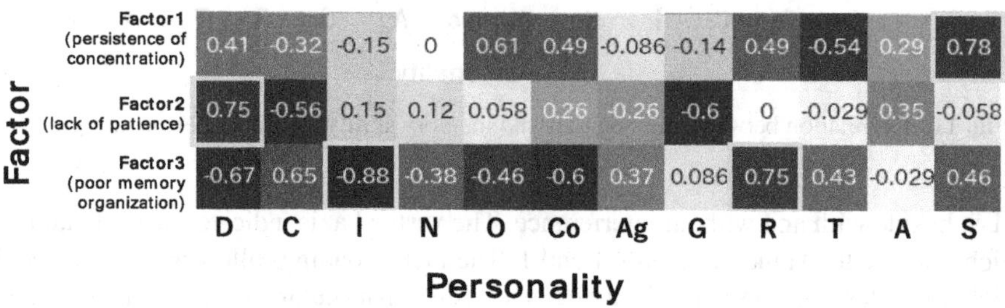

Factor
Factor1 (persistence of concentration)
Factor2 (lack of patience)
Factor3 (poor memory organization)
0.41 -0.32 -0.15 0 0.61 0.49 -0.086 -0.14 0.49 -0.54 0.29 0.78
0.75 -0.56 0.15 0.12 0.058 0.26 -0.26 -0.6 0 -0.029 0.35 -0.058
-0.67 0.65 -0.88 -0.38 -0.46 -0.6 0.37 0.086 0.75 0.43 -0.029 0.46
D C I N O Co Ag G R T A S
Personality


**Fig. 13.** Correlation between personalities and latent factors

for memory ability do not adequately reflect practical memory ability. Therefore, it is planned that we have search the useful features for memory ability and reevaluate the correlation with personality.

## 6 Conclusion

In this research, we tried to develop a recommendation system to support students who have difficulty with self-directed study. In order to find an appropriate study method for each individual, we started to identify learning abilities associated with personality. For the measurement of learning ability, we focused on two aspects of learning ability: calculation and memory ability. These two major abilities have common importance in the study of any contents.

On the other hand, the features of calculational ability were decided by the result of Uchida-Kraepelin performance test. The features of memory ability were selected based on the results of the serial position effect test. For the measurement of personality, we employed YG personality test used in the psychophysical field. Using these results, correlation analyses were performed between personality and each learning ability to evaluate each relationship.

As a result, the features of a slightly higher partial correlation were found between each ability and personality. To stand out these features, participants were grouped according to personality. The effect of this grouping was significant, and we were able to find several features that were well correlated. Therefore, we believe that it is possible to identify the features of learning ability based on their personality. Furthermore, there is a possibility to recommend the appropriate learning methods for each participant.

Reflecting on this study, it is little difficult to select features for personality and learning ability. Some features of the YG personality test are unrelated to learning, and they introduce noise. This limitation would result in a loss of precision for a recommendation system for the method of self-directed study. Therefore, we need to select each feature and focus on effective features deeply as the most recent items for next consideration. Moreover, we also plan a multifaceted analysis in the future. For the learning process, the emotional strength, such as attention, endurance and concentration, is very important. We continue to challenge our task that this improvement will contribute to the recommendation of a learning method with matching the personality and characteristics of the individual.

**Acknowledgments.** This research was partially supported by the Grant-in-Aid for Corporative Research of Tokyo Metropolitan University and College, and Grant-in-Aid for Scientific Research(C), 18K11540 (2021), respectively.

## References

1. Nakayama, K., Shimada, A., Minematsu, T., Yamada, M., Taniguchi, R.: Recommendation of personalized learning materials based on learning history and campus life sensing, companion. In: Proceedings 10th International Conference on Learning Analytics & Knowledge, pp. 649–654 (2020)
2. Kurihara, R.: Relationship between knowledge of Nominators and learning effect of nominee (in Japanese). In: Proceedings of the 74th National Convention of IPSJ, vol. 2012, no. 1, pp. 963–964 (2012)
3. Tomas, C.P., Adrian, F.: Personality predicts academic performance: evidence from two longitudinal university samples. J. Res. Pers. **37**(4), 319–338 (2003). https://doi.org/10.1016/S0092-6566(02)00578-0
4. Su, J.-H., Liao, Y.-W., Xu, J.-Z., Zhao, Y.-W.: A personality-driven recommender system for cross-domain learning based on Holland code assessments. Sustainability **13**(7), 3936 (2021). https://doi.org/10.3390/su13073936
5. Abd El Aziz, A.S., Taha, E.E.S., Ramadan, F.H., Badr, O.E.: Self-directed learning readiness level and personality traits among nursing students. Alexandria Sci. Nurs. J. **24**(3), 40–50 (2022). https://doi.org/10.21608/ASALEXU.2022.267754
6. Goldberg, L.R.: The development of markers for the big-five factor structure. Psychol. Assess. **4**(1), 26–42 (1992). https://doi.org/10.1037/1040-3590.4.1.26
7. Yatabe, T.: Construction of new self diagnostic inventories (in Japanese). Memoirs of the Department of Literature, Kyoto University, vol. 3, pp. 71–167 (1954)
8. Kashiwagi, S.: Studies on the work curve of Uchida-Kraepelin test. Percept. Mot. Skills **18**(3), 876 (1962). https://doi.org/10.2466/pms.1964.18.3.876
9. Atkinson, R.C., Shiffrin R.M.: Human memory: a proposed system and its control processes. Psychol. Learn. Motiv. **2**, 89–195 (1968). https://doi.org/10.1016/S0079-7421(08)60422-3
10. Glanzer, M., Cunitz, A.R.: Two storage mechanisms in free recall. J. Verbal Learn. Verbal Behav. **5**(4), 351–360 (1966). https://doi.org/10.1016/S0022-5371(66)80044-0

# IMF-PSO: A Particle Swarm Optimization Algorithm for Feature Selection in Classification

Cheng-Ju Lu and Tsung-Che Chiang(✉)

Department of Computer Science and Information Engineering, National Taiwan Normal University, Taipei, Taiwan (R.O.C.)
tcchiang@ntnu.edu.tw

**Abstract.** Feature selection is an important step in classification. Its goal is to find a set of features that can lead to high classification accuracy with a smaller number of features. This paper addresses feature selection as an optimization problem and solves it by a particle swarm optimization (PSO)-based approach. In the proposed PSO, we adopt three algorithmic components to enhance its performance: feature space adjustment, multi-swarm search, and local-best-guided improvement. We examine the effects of these components using seven data sets from the UCI repository. We also compare our algorithm with two existing algorithms. Experimental results show that the incorporated algorithmic components improve the algorithm performance and our algorithm outperforms the compared algorithms.

**Keywords:** Feature Selection · Particle Swarm Optimization · Classification

## 1 Introduction

Classification is a task of assigning data samples to proper classes based on the features of samples. With the ease of collecting data in the current digital era, the number of features of data could be very large. Since the number and quality of features have strong impact on the performance of classification algorithms, selection of relevant and useful features becomes a very important step in classification. Feature selection has been formulated as an optimization problem and solved by metaheuristics [1, 2]. In this research domain, there are three types of approaches: filter, wrapper, and embedded approaches. The wrapper approaches interact with classification algorithms to evaluate the set of selected features and can find the feature sets with high classification performance. Among the metaheuristics for feature selection, PSO [3] is the most widely adopted algorithm due to its promising performance [2]. In this paper, we propose a wrapper approach based on PSO for feature selection. The objective is formulated as (1), where $X$ denotes the set of selected features, $f_{\text{acc}}(X)$ denotes the accuracy of $X$, $f_{\text{size}}(X)$ denotes the number of selected features in $X$, and $D$ denotes the total number of all features. The parameter $\theta$ controls the relative weight between the accuracy and the feature size. Figure 1 illustrates the process flow of the proposed approach.

$$F(X) = \theta \times f_{\text{acc}}(X) + (1-\theta) \times (1 - f_{\text{size}}(X)/D) \tag{1}$$


C.-Y. Lee et al. (Eds.): TAAI 2023, CCIS 2074, pp. 110–125, 2024.
https://doi.org/10.1007/978-981-97-1711-8_8

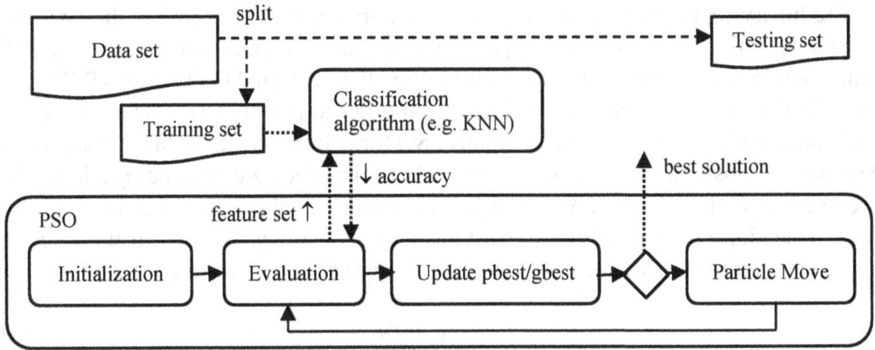


**Fig. 1.** The process flow of applying PSO for feature selection

The rest of this paper is organized as follows. Section 2 will present the literature review. Section 3 will elaborate our proposed PSO algorithm. Experiments and results will be given in Sect. 4. Section 5 will conclude this study and provide some directions for future research.

## 2 Literature Review

### 2.1 Solution Representation

Metaheuristics like PSO solve an optimization problem by alternating between searching in the encoded representation space and evaluating in the decoded solution space. Deciding the solution representation is the first and perhaps the most important step in the design of metaheuristics. In this sub-section, we will review several solution representation schemes in the literature.

Considering feature selection as an optimization problem, we want to select a subset of useful features from all features of the target data set. It is essentially an optimization problem with binary variables (selecting a feature or not), and hence several researchers adopted binary PSO [4] to do feature selection [5–7]. Equation (2) shows the standard equation for updating the speed of particles, where $x_i$ denotes the position of a particle $i$, $v_i$ denotes the speed, $pbest_i$ denotes the best position ever found by the particle $i$, and $gbest$ denotes the global best over all $pbest_i$. Algorithm parameters $w$, $c_1$, and $c_2$ control the magnitude of inertia, cognitive movement, and social movement, respectively; random variables $r_1$ and $r_2$, whose values fall in the interval [0, 1], add randomness to the moving direction. In the binary PSO, the values of binary position variables $x_{ij}$ are determined based on particle speed $v_{ij}$ and a sigmoid function, as shown in (3), where $rand$ is a random value falling in the interval [0, 1].

$$v_{ij} = w \times v_{ij} + c_1 \cdot r_1 \cdot (pbest_{ij} - x_{ij}) + c_2 \cdot r_2 \cdot (gbest_j - x_{ij}) \tag{2}$$

$$x_{ij} = \begin{cases} 0, 1/\left(1 + e^{-v_{ij}}\right) < rand \\ 1, otherwise \end{cases} \tag{3}$$

The binary representation fits the task of feature selection better than the continuous representation. As mentioned in [1], however, the concept of direction, speed, and momentum in the continuous PSO cannot be directly transferred to the binary PSO. The binary PSO must be designed very carefully in order to perform well. Thus, there are much more studies applying the continuous PSO for feature selection. In the continuous PSO, particle positions are represented by real vectors. They are updated by adding the speed vector, as shown in (4). A typical way to convert a real position vector to a binary feature selection vector is a threshold-cut mechanism. Simply speaking, if the value of $x_{ij}$ is greater than a predefined threshold value (e.g. 0.6), the $j_{th}$ feature is selected.

$$x_{ij} = x_{ij} + v_{ij} \tag{4}$$

Either binary or continuous, the typical representation aims to decide which features must be selected. Some other studies proposed special representations. For example, Lin et al. [8] adopted a representation that consists of the feature selection vector and two extra hyperparameters of SVM. Tran et al. [9] proposed a representation that searches for the cut points of the discretization procedure.

## 2.2 Solution Generation

The search space of PSO is determined after the representation scheme is chosen. The next step is to generate a swarm of particles. Xue et al. [10] proposed four initialization methods: purely-random, few-feature, many-feature, and mixture of few-feature and many-feature methods. Their experimental results showed that mixed initialization method is the best one. Li et al. [11] calculated a feature weight vector by the mutual information (MI) measure. These weight values were normalized and then transformed into probability by the sigmoid function. Features were selected according to the probability. Song et al. [12] proposed a similar method, where the weights of features were measured by the symmetrical uncertainty (SU).

In addition to the standard PSO move operator, many researchers incorporated crossover and mutation operators from evolutionary algorithms into their PSO. Zhang et al. [13] proposed a crossover operator. Roughly speaking, it replaces some position elements of a particle with the corresponding elements of a randomly chosen personal best particles. Song et al. [14] performed the arithmetic crossover between high-quality particles and a temporary particle. The temporary particle was generated by selecting the most important features, where the SU measure was used as the importance degree. Nguyen et al. [15] applied a mutation operator to the global best particle when the global best particle was not improved after a number of iterations. The mutation operator flips the position elements $x_{ij}$ in the probability that reflects how far $x_{ij}$ is away from the threshold value of selecting a feature. Chen et al. [16] proposed a more complicated way of controlling the flipping probability in the mutation operator. They used ReliefF to calculate the weights of features and then converted normalized weight values through a sin function to be probabilities. Xue et al. [17] selected five out of 25 move operators and adaptively used these operators based on their successful rates of generating better particles.

## 2.3 Reduction of Search Space and Evaluation Cost

The number of features decides the size of the search space. When the number of features gets large, we need advanced techniques to make our PSO search effectively and efficiently. Tran et al. [18] proposed the first variable-length PSO to do feature selection. They first ranked features based on the SU measure. Then, they applied multiple equal-size swarms to search in spaces with different number of features. When the global best particle was not updated for a certain number of iterations, the authors applied a length changing procedure. Song et al. [14] adopted similar concepts as Tran et al. did. The key difference is in that Song et al. used variable-size swarms to search in spaces of the same size. They set the size of each swarm based on the total importance of the features in the space the swarm searched. Li et al. [19] also ranked features and divided the search space, but they only used a single swarm. The swarm began the search process from the smallest space, and the space increased periodically. Li et al. [11] proposed a method that reduces the search space dynamically during the search process. Their method periodically identifies the features that are not selected by all personal best particles are removes them from the search space.

The number of features affects the search space, and the number of instances affects the evaluation cost of the selected features. Some studies addressed the high computational cost caused by a large number of instances. For example, Nguyen et al. [20] grouped training instances by the agglomerative clustering method. The cluster of instances that provided the minimal error of fitness when comparing with the full set of instances was used to evaluate particles. Chen et al. [16] used the $K$-nearest neighbor ($K$-NN) method to select the $K$ closest particles in the previous iteration and took the average fitness of these particles as the surrogate fitness of the new particle. Only new particles with good surrogate fitness values were evaluated by the training instances.

## 2.4 Optimization Objectives

The simplest objective of feature selection is to achieve the highest accuracy. Chuang et al. [5], Lin et al. [8], Zhang et al. [13], and Song et al. [14] designed their algorithms with this single objective. Besides achieving high accuracy, it is also important to reduce the number of selected features. Xue et al. [21] proposed a weighted objective function that combines the accuracy and the number of features, as shown in Eq. (1). This function was adopted in [11, 15, 16, 19, 20]. We also used this function as the particle fitness in this paper. Tran et al. [22] proposed another weighted objective function that combines the accuracy with their proposed distance measure, which was also adopted in [9, 18].

In PSO, the objective function is used to decide whether a new particle is better and can replace the personal best particle and global best particle. Xue et al. [10] proposed a hierarchical method to compare two particles in terms of the accuracy and the number of features. It was also adopted in [12, 17]. Another way is through the Pareto approach, which is based on the concept of dominance and seeks for a set of non-dominated solutions. Zhang et al. [7], Xue et al. [21], Xue et al. [23], and Zhang et al. [24] followed this way. A difference between [24] and the previous three studies is that the cost associated with features (instead of the number of features) in considered in [24].

## 3 The Proposed Particle Swarm Optimization Algorithm

### 3.1 Overview

In this paper we propose a wrapper-based PSO for feature selection. It seeks an optimal or near-optimal set of selected features and evaluates the candidate feature sets through a classification method (K-NN in this paper). We introduce three ideas in our PSO algorithm: Feature space adjustment, Multi-swarm search, and local-best-guided Improvement. Algorithm 1 is an overview of our algorithm. We call it IMF-PSO.

Feature space adjustment ranks the features and puts them into the search space gradually (lines 1 – 3 and 17 – 22). It aims to help our algorithm to search effectively in a large search space. The search space may contain several local optima, and thus we use multiple swarms to search in parallel (lines 8 – 13). At last, the local-best-guided improvement is an extra move mechanism that helps to improve low-quality particles (line 14). More details will be given in the following sub-sections.

**Algorithm 1:** The proposed IMF-PSO

*F*: the vector of feature indices sorted by the classification accuracy of a single feature
*FS*: the feature space (features currently considered in optimization)
$n_{stg}$: the number of stages for feature space adjustment; $n_{pop}$: the number of particles in a swarm
*PS*: the set of swarms; *PS*[*i*]: the $i^{th}$ swarm of particles; *A*: the archive
*ffe*: the number of fitness evaluations consumed
*MaxFFE*: the maximum number of fitness evaluations

```
1   F ← RankFeatures()
2   m ← 1
3   FS ← AdjustFeatureSpace(F, m, n_stg)
4   P, A, e ← Initialize(FS, n_pop)
5   ffe ← e, ffe_threshold ← MaxFFE/n_stg
6   PS ← {P}
7   while ffe < MaxFFE do:
8      if not all swarms are in stagnation:
9         i ← SelectSwarm(PS)
10     else:
11        S ← GenerateNewSwarm(PS, A, GV, n_pop)
12        PS ← PS ∪ {S}
13        i ← |PS|
14     PS[i], A, e ← UpdateParticles(PS[i], A, GV)
15     GV ← GenerateGuidingVector(PS, i)
16     ffe ← ffe + e
17     if ffe ≥ ffe_threshold:
18        m ← m + 1
19        NFS ← AdjustFeatureSpace(F, m, n_stg)
20        PS, e ← Reinitialize(PS, FS, NFS)
21        FS ← NFS
22        ffe ← ffe + e, ffe_threshold ← ffe_threshold + MaxFFE/n_stg
23  Output the best particle with the maximal fitness
```

### 3.2 Particle Encoding, Decoding, and Initialization

We adopt the continuous representation in our PSO. When $d$ features are considered in search, the position of a particle is a vector of $d$ real values. Take Fig. 2 as an example. FS denotes the current feature space to search, where six features are considered. (These features are ranked and ordered. The ranking method will be described in the next subsection.) A particle $x$ is a 6-D real vector. To decode a particle (i.e. to decide which features are selected), we check the value of each element of $x$; if the value is greater than a threshold $p_{\text{thre}}$, the corresponding feature is selected. In the example, $bv(x)$ is the decoded binary vector of $x$, where features 4, 5, and 3 are selected.

Whenever the feature space is adjusted (lines 3 and 19 in Algorithm 1), the elements of particle positions corresponding to the newly introduced features are randomly initialized.

| | | | | | | |
|---|---|---|---|---|---|---|
| *FS* | 4 | 2 | 1 | 5 | 6 | 3 |
| *x* | 0.65 | 0.23 | 0.45 | 0.88 | 0.33 | 0.71 |
| *bv(x)* | 1 | 0 | 0 | 1 | 0 | 1 |

**Fig. 2.** Particle representation (assuming selection threshold $p_{\text{thre}} = 0.6$)

### 3.3 Initialization and Adjustment of Search Space

As mentioned, we adjust/enlarge the feature space gradually during the search process. We adopt the method of [19] for the adjustment. First, the features of the data set are ranked by the classification accuracy of each single feature from the highest to the lowest. The accuracy of a single feature is obtained by using it as the only feature in $K$-NN to classify the data instances.

Let $F = \{f_1, f_2, \ldots, f_D\}$ denote the vector of feature indices sorted by the accuracy, where $D$ is the total number of features of the data set. We divide $F$ into $n_{\text{stg}}$ equal-size segments. (The last segment may have a smaller size than the others.) At the beginning of the search process, we consider only the first segment of features (lines 2 – 3 in Algorithm 1). When $100/n_{\text{stg}}\%$ more computational resource is consumed, we add one more segment, i.e. $D/n_{\text{stg}}$ more features are added into the search space (lines 17 – 22).

Figure 3 is an example where the data set has eight features ($D = 8$) and the number of adjustment stages is two ($n_{\text{stg}} = 2$). $F$ denotes the ordered list of features; feature 7 is the one with the highest accuracy and feature 3 is the one with the lowest accuracy. Initially, our PSO considers only the top four ($D/n_{\text{stg}} = 8/2 = 4$) features. The size of the position vector of a particle $x$ is four. When $100/n_{\text{stg}}\%$ ($100/2 = 50\%$) computational resource is consumed, we put the remaining four features into the search process (The size of the position vector of a particle becomes eight.) The ranking of features and the gradual increase of feature space help our PSO to put more focus on important features and search efficiently.

$n_{stg} = 2$ (there are two stages of adjustment of search space)

| $F$ | 7 | 2 | 1 | 6 | 5 | 4 | 8 | 3 |
|---|---|---|---|---|---|---|---|---|

$m = 1$ (stage1: only considering the first four features)

| $FS$ | 7 | 2 | 1 | 6 |
|---|---|---|---|---|
| $x$ | 0.32 | 0.72 | 0.64 | 0.11 |

$m = 2$ (stage2: considering all eight features)

| $FS$ | 7 | 2 | 1 | 6 | 5 | 4 | 8 | 3 |
|---|---|---|---|---|---|---|---|---|
| $x$ | 0.32 | 0.72 | 0.64 | 0.11 | 0.55 | 0.81 | 0.14 | 0.27 |

**Fig. 3.** Illustration of adjustment of search space ($D = 8$ and $n_{stg} = 2$)

### 3.4 Particle Evaluation

Given a particle $x$, first we decode it and obtain the set of selected features (see Fig. 2). Then, we use this set of features in K-NN (K = 5 in this paper) to get the average accuracy of classification through 5-fold cross-validation. Finally, we calculate the fitness of a particle by the weighted average of the average classification accuracy and the number of features, as shown in Eq. (1).

The calculation of classification accuracy may take long computation time. To save time, we add a cache in our PSO. We record the sets of selected features and the corresponding accuracy. If a decoded set of features is found in the cache, we use the recorded accuracy directly and this does not consume the fitness function evaluation. (Note that the number of fitness function evaluations, *ffe* in Algorithm 1, is used in the criterion for adjusting the feature space and in the stopping criterion.) For example, after we evaluate a particle [0.7, 0.4, 0.8, 0.2], we use its fitness directly for particles [0.8, 0.1, 0.9, 0.4] and [0.9, 0.3, 0.7, 0.5] (assuming $p_{thre} = 0.6$) since they all choose the same set of features.

### 3.5 Elite Archive Update

The purpose of the elite archive ($A$ in Algorithm 1) is to store high-quality and diverse particles for generating new swarms in case the existing swarms are in stagnation. At the beginning of the algorithm, the archive is set by the initial swarm. Then, it is updated after a swarm of particles finish movement at the end of each generation. Each particle $x$ in the swarm checks the difference $d(x, y)$ between its set of selected features and that of particles $y$ in $A$. If $d(x, y)$ is smaller than $p_{ham} \cdot |FS|$, the particle $y$ is collected in $Y$. FS denotes the current feature space, and $p_{ham}$ is an algorithm parameter. From all particles in $Y$, the particle $y^*$ that has the smallest hamming distance to $x$ is taken for comparison. If the fitness of $x$ is better than that of $y$, $x$ will replace $y$ in $A$. By considering both distance and fitness, we can keep high-quality and diverse particles in the archive.

### 3.6 Swarm Selection

Our PSO begins with a single swarm of particles, and new swarms might be produced as the search process goes. We say that a swarm is in stagnation when both of the following conditions are met:

- no particle updates its own personal best position in two consecutive generations;
- the number of fitness function evaluations does not increase in two consecutive generations.

In each generation, we select one non-stagnant swarm to move (line 9 in Algorithm 1). If the swarm that contains the global best particle is not stagnant, it is selected; otherwise, we select the non-stagnant swarm in a first-in-first-out order. When all swarms are in stagnation, we will generate a new swarm. Details are given in the next two sub-sections.

### 3.7 Guiding Vector

Inspired by [25], we introduce a guiding vector in our PSO. The guiding vector ($GV$) is a vector that represents the selection probability of features of the best particles in the swarms. It is used in the generation of new swarms (Sect. 3.8) and in the local-best-guided improvement (Sect. 3.9). When there is only a single swarm, the guiding vector is the same as the decoded binary vector of the global best particle. When there is more than one swarm, the guiding vector records the selection probability of the best particles in the swarms excluding the currently moving swarm. (In line 15 in Algorithm 1, swarm $i$ is the currently moving swarm.)

Figure 4 is an example, where three features are considered and the number of swarms is four. Assume that swarm 3 is the currently moving swarm, and thus we update the elements of $GV$ by considering only the best particles $gbest_1$, $gbest_2$, and $gbest_4$ from swarms 1, 2, and 4. All these three particles select the first feature, and hence the value of the first element of $GV$ is 1.0. Only one of the three particles selects the second feature, and hence the value of the second element of $GV$ is 1/3 = 0.33. The value of the third element is calculated in the same way. We exclude the best particle of the currently moving swarm to reduce its impact so as to get more diverse particle in the generation of new swarms and the local-best-guided movement.

| | | | |
|---|---|---|---|
| $bv(gbest_1)$ | 1 | 0 | 0 |
| $bv(gbest_2)$ | 1 | 1 | 1 |
| $bv(gbest_3)$ | 1 | 1 | 0 |
| $bv(gbest_4)$ | 1 | 0 | 1 |

| | | | |
|---|---|---|---|
| $GV$ | 1.0 | 0.33 | 0.67 |

**Fig. 4.** Example of calculating the guiding vector when there are more than one swarm (assume the current swarm is swarm 3, i.e. $i = 3$ in line 15 of Algorithm 1)

### 3.8 Swarm Generation

When all existing swarms are in stagnation, we generate a new swarm (line 11 in Algorithm 1). Note that the existing swarms are not discarded since they can serve as good initial solutions when the feature space is enlarged after adjustment. Algorithm 2 shows the steps of swarm generation. It actually consists of two main steps: finding the reference particle (lines 1–10 in Algorithm 2) and generating new particles around the reference particle (lines 11–17 in Algorithm 2).

The reference particle is expected to have high fitness and be located away from the current (stagnant) swarms. Recall that we maintain an elite archive that stores high-quality and diverse particles. Thus, we choose a particle from the archive to be the reference particle. We calculate the average distance from each archived particle $A[a]$ to the best particles of the swarms. The distance between two particles is calculated by the hamming distance of the decoded binary vectors of the particles. The score of a particle in $A$ is the sum of its fitness and the average hamming distance. The particle with the highest score is selected as the reference.

Figure 5 is an example, where we have three swarms and two particles in the archive $A$. We calculate the average hamming distance between $A[1]$ and the three best particles by $(0 + 1 + 3)/3 = 1.33$. In this example, particle $A[2]$ has a larger score and is selected as the reference particle.

| | | | | $d(gbest_i, A[1])$ | $d(gbest_i, A[2])$ |
|---|---|---|---|---|---|
| $bv(gbest_1)$ | 1 | 1 | 0 | 0 | 3 |
| $bv(gbest_2)$ | 1 | 1 | 1 | 1 | 2 |
| $bv(gbest_3)$ | 0 | 0 | 1 | 3 | 0 |

| | | | | $mean(d(A[j]))$ | $fit(A[j])$ | $score(A[j])$ |
|---|---|---|---|---|---|---|
| $bv(A[1])$ | 1 | 1 | 0 | 1.33 | 0.40 | 1.73 |
| $bv(A[2])$ | 0 | 0 | 1 | 1.67 | 0.85 | 2.52 |

**Fig. 5.** Example of finding the reference solution for new swarm generation

Now we have two helpers for generating a new swarm: the guiding vector and the reference particle. The guiding vector represents the selection probability of features based on other swarms; the reference particle represents a real solution that is expected to be different from the best solutions in all swarms and have high quality. To generate a particle in the new swarm, we follow the rules:

- If half of the best solutions in all swarms (excluding the currently moving swarm) select feature $j$ ($GV[j] \geq 0.5$) and the reference particle also selects feature $j$ ($ref[j] \geq p_{\mathrm{thre}}$), the new particle selects feature $j$ (line 14 in Algorithm 2).
- If half of the best solutions do not select feature $j$ and the reference particle does not select it, the new particle does not select the feature (line15).
- Otherwise, the new particle selects the feature randomly.

**Algorithm 2: GenerateNewSwarm**(*PS*, *A*, *GV*, $n_{pop}$)

```
    PS: the set of swarms; PS[i]: the i^th swarm of particles
    A: the archive; GV: the guiding vector; n_pop: the swarm size
    ref: the reference particle; FS: the feature space (features considered in optimization)

ref, score ← A[0], 0
for a from 1 to |A| do:
   d ← 0
   for i from 1 to |PS| do:
      gb ← FindBestParticle(PS[i])
      d ← d + HammingDistance(gb, A[a])
   sc ← fit(A[a]) + d/|PS|
   if sc > score:
      ref ← A[a]
      score ← sc
S ← ∅
for i from 1 to n_pop do:
   for j from 1 to |FS| do:
      if GV[j] >= 0.5 and ref[j] >= p_thre: x[j] ← random(p_thre, 1)
      else if GV[j] < 0.5 and ref[j] < p_thre: x[j] ← random(0, p_thre)
      else: x[j] ← random(0, 1)
   S ← S ∪ {x}
return S
```

## 3.9 Particle Update

When a swarm is moving, each particle takes two types of moving actions – the basic PSO movement and the oppositional movement. In addition, the worst particles also take the proposed local-best-guided movement. The basic PSO movement is shown in (2) and (4). The oppositional movement aims to increase the population diversity. For each position $x[j]$ of a particle $x$, we change its value from $x[j]$ to $1 - x[j]$ in probability $1/|FS|$, where *FS* is the current feature space for search.

The local-best-guided improvement extends the crossover operator in [25], which only used the guiding vector. We select $(p_{\mathrm{nb}} \cdot 100)\%$ of particles randomly from the swarm and then take the best one as a local best particle. Based on two local best particles $q$ and $r$ and the guiding vector *GV*, we adjust bad particles $x$ by Algorithm 3. We sort the particles from the worst fitness to the best fitness and apply the improvement to $n_{\mathrm{nm}}$ worst particles. Values of parameters $n_{\mathrm{nm}}$ and $p_{\mathrm{nb}}$ are given in Sect. 4.

**Algorithm 3: LocalBestGuidedImpovement**(*x*, *q*, *r*, *GV*)

```
for j from 1 to |FS| do:
   if q[j] >= p_thre and r[j] >= p_thre: selected = 1
   else if q[j] < p_thre and r[j] < p_thre: selected = 0
   else if random(0, 1) <= GV[j]: selected = 1
   else: selected = 0
   if selected == 1 and x[j] < p_thre: x[j] ← random(p_thre, 1)
   else if selected == 0 and x[j] >= p_thre: x[j] ← random(0, p_thre)
return x
```

# 4 Experiments and Results

## 4.1 Data Sets and Performance Indicator

We adopted seven data sets from the UCI machine learning repository [26]. Table 1 summarizes the basic information of these data sets. The number of classes ranges from 2 to 13, and the number of features ranges from 60 to 6400. We followed many studies to use Eq. (1) as the performance indicator and set θ by 0.9 [19, 20].

**Table 1.** Seven data sets used in the experiments

| Data set | #Instancess | #Features | #Classes | Data set | #Instances | #Features | #Classes |
|---|---|---|---|---|---|---|---|
| Sonar | 208 | 60 | 2 | Arrhythmia | 452 | 279 | 13 |
| Musk1 | 476 | 166 | 2 | LSVT | 126 | 310 | 2 |
| Urban | 675 | 147 | 9 | Synthetic Control | 600 | 60 | 6 |
| DriverFace | 606 | 6400 | 3 | | | | |

## 4.2 Experimental Setting

Our IMF-PSO contains two groups of parameters. One group is required by the standard PSO, such as the population size ($n_{pop}$) and the inertia weight ($w$); the other group is required by our proposed mechanism, such as the threshold in the decoding procedure ($p_{thre}$) and the number of stages of adjusting the search spaces ($n_{stg}$). Table 2 summarizes the parameter setting of the proposed IMF-PSO. The values of the parameters in the first group were set by following the literature [10], while the values of the parameters in the second group were set based on pilot runs of experiments.

In the following experiments, each algorithm (or algorithm variant) searched for the optimal set of features for each data set for 30 runs. In each run, we split the instances of the data set by 70% training instances and 30% testing instances. The training sets were different in 30 runs, but the same 30 training sets were used when we tested different algorithms in order to reduce the effect of randomness. At the end of each run, we took the best solution in terms of Eq. (1) and calculated its classification accuracy by the testing instances. The number of features and the testing accuracy were recorded. We checked the significance of difference between two algorithms by the Wilcoxon rank sum test with the level of significance of 0.05.

## 4.3 Effects of Feature Ordering

Recall that before we divide the feature vector into multiple segments to build search sub-spaces, we order the features by the classification accuracy of each single feature from the highest to the lowest (see Sect. 3.3). In this experiment, we examine the effects of the feature ordering mechanisms upon the algorithm performance. We compared two

**Table 2.** Parameter setting of the proposed IMF-PSO

| Parameters of Standard PSO | | Parameters of Proposed Mechanisms | |
|---|---|---|---|
| Parameter | Value | Parameter | Value |
| $MaxFFE$ | 3000 | $p_{thre}$ (used in the decoding procedure, Sect. 3.2) | 0.6 |
| $n_{pop}$ | 30 | $n_{stg}$ (the number of divisions of search space, Sect. 3.3) | 5 |
| $w$ | 0.7298 | $p_{ham}$ (used in collecting solutions in the archive, Sect. 3.5) | 0.2 |
| $c_1, c_2$ | 1.49618 | $p_{nb}$ (used in selecting neighbors, Sect. 3.9) | 0.2 |
| $vmax_d$,$vmin_d$ | 6, 0 | $n_{nm}$ (the number of neighbors in the local-best-guided movement, Sect. 3.9) | 1 |
| $xmax_d$,$xmin_d$ | 1, 0 | | |

algorithm variants, one of which orders the features from the highest accuracy to the lowest accuracy (Forward-PSO) and the other orders the features in the opposite way (denoted by Backward-PSO).

In Table 3, the symbol $A$ denotes the testing accuracy, and the symbol $F$ denotes the number of features. The mean and standard deviation of the two measures ($A$ and $F$) over 30 runs are reported. The better results between the two algorithm variants are marked in bold. The symbols +, −, and = represent that the result of Forward-PSO is significantly better than, significantly worse than, and equal to the result of Backward-PSO, respectively. The experimental results show that the feature ordering mechanism has a strong impact on the number of selected features. The Forward ordering mechanism is helpful for keeping the accuracy using a much smaller number of features.

### 4.4 Effects of Swarm Generation

Recall that when all swarms are in stagnation, our IMF-PSO will generate a new swarm. The particles in the new swarm are generated with the help of reference particles and a guiding vector. In this experiment, we compared two algorithm variants, one using the proposed swarm generation mechanism (denoted by RPGV) and the other using a random initialization mechanism (denoted by RI). RPGV is significantly better than RI for three data sets in terms of accuracy and for two data sets in terms of the number of features. It is worse only for one data set in terms of the number of features. The results show that our swarm generation mechanism improves the performance moderately. Due to the limitation of space, detailed numerical results are omitted here.

**Table 3.** Performance comparison between two feature ordering mechanisms

| Dataset | | Backward-PSO | | Forward-PSO | |
|---|---|---|---|---|---|
| | | mean | std | mean | std |
| Sonar | *A* | **0.830** | 0.062(=) | 0.823 | 0.048 |
| | *F* | 18.900 | 4.566(+) | **14.167** | 3.064 |
| LSVT | *A* | 0.767 | 0.085(=) | **0.769** | 0.056 |
| | *F* | 60.433 | 22.320(+) | **27.933** | 11.873 |
| Urban | *A* | 0.777 | 0.034(+) | **0.796** | 0.027 |
| | *F* | 54.700 | 10.613(+) | **19.533** | 6.334 |
| Musk1 | *A* | **0.848** | 0.033(−) | 0.828 | 0.027 |
| | *F* | 34.733 | 15.131(+) | **21.267** | 6.638 |
| Arrhythmia | *A* | 0.540 | 0.043(=) | **0.556** | 0.035 |
| | *F* | **59.233** | 24.568(−) | 65.833 | 28.538 |
| Synthetic Control | *A* | 0.942 | 0.018(=) | **0.944** | 0.018 |
| | *F* | 19.533 | 3.830(+) | **16.667** | 3.010 |
| DriverFace | *A* | **0.968** | 0.014(=) | **0.968** | 0.011 |
| | *F* | 393.167 | 58.317(+) | **366.567** | 53.759 |
| +/−/= | *A* | 1/1/5 | | | |
| | *F* | 6/0/1 | | | |

## 4.5 Effects of Local-Best-Guided Improvement

This experiment examine the effects of the proposed local-best-guided improvement procedure. We compared two algorithm variants, one (IMF-PSO) with and the other (MF-PSO) without the improvement procedure. In terms of accuracy, IMF-PSO is equal to MF-PSO for six data sets and is worse for just one. As for the number of features, IMF-PSO is significantly better than MF-PSO for all seven data sets. We tested two values, 1 and 20, for the parameter $n_{\mathrm{nm}}$ (the number of particles carrying out the improvement procedure). Although using a higher $n_{\mathrm{nm}}$ reduced the mean of the number of features further, there was no significant difference. In summary, the proposed improvement procedure is helpful, and we do not need to spend too much computation effort. Due to the limitation of space, detailed results are omitted here.

## 4.6 Comparison with Existing Algorithms

In the last experiment, we compared our IMF-PSO with existing algorithms. Based on our experience, the training and testing instances could have a large impact on the algorithm performance; thus, we cannot compare the results of our algorithm with the results in other papers directly. We need to run the codes of compared algorithms with the same training sets and testing sets to make a fair comparison. We found the source codes of two algorithms, 2-DUPSO[1] [27] and SaPSO[2] [17], and used them to avoid any potential mistake in the re-implementation. (We did a slight modification to let them use the same objective function as ours.) Table 4 presents the numerical results of the three algorithms. Comparing with these two algorithms, our IMF-PSO can find a significantly smaller number of features to reach equal or better classification accuracy.

**Table 4.** Performance comparison between three PSO algorithms

| Dataset | | 2-DUPSO | | SaPSO | | IMF-PSO | |
|---|---|---|---|---|---|---|---|
| | | mean | std | mean | std | mean | std |
| Sonar | *A* | 0.760 | 0.078(+) | 0.794 | 0.055(=) | **0.813** | 0.050 |
| | *F* | 12.133 | 5.151(=) | 23.600 | 3.597(+) | **11.700** | 3.535 |
| LSVT | *A* | 0.782 | 0.070(=) | **0.802** | 0.062(=) | 0.792 | 0.062 |
| | *F* | 34.333 | 15.406(+) | 124.000 | 8.702(+) | **10.433** | 3.559 |
| Urban | *A* | 0.775 | 0.065(=) | **0.799** | 0.027(=) | 0.788 | 0.028 |
| | *F* | 19.333 | 5.962(+) | 57.000 | 5.693(+) | **11.500** | 4.652 |
| Musk1 | *A* | 0.803 | 0.064(=) | 0.817 | 0.030(=) | **0.830** | 0.037 |
| | *F* | 22.900 | 9.697(+) | 67.200 | 7.667(+) | **16.533** | 5.770 |
| Arrhythmia | *A* | **0.602** | 0.071(=) | 0.600 | 0.036(=) | 0.588 | 0.041 |
| | *F* | 20.300 | 8.918(=) | 109.833 | 8.205(+) | **17.500** | 9.637 |
| Synthetic Control | *A* | **0.959** | 0.005(=) | 0.935 | 0.007(=) | 0.944 | 0.017 |
| | *F* | 16.333 | 5.307(+) | 26.200 | 2.722(+) | **14.533** | 2.255 |
| DriverFace | *A* | 0.951 | 0.018(+) | 0.958 | 0.013(=) | **0.964** | 0.013 |
| | *F* | 132.967 | 89.513(+) | 2537.133 | 29.106(+) | **37.700** | 28.824 |
| +/−/= | *A* | 2/0/5 | | 0/0/7 | | | |
| | *F* | 5/0/2 | | 7/0/0 | | | |

## 5 Conclusions

In this paper we addressed the feature selection problem by a PSO-based wrapper approach. The approach is based on a continuous PSO, and we incorporated three algorithmic components to enhance its performance. Firstly, we dynamically adjusted feature space during the search process. By ranking features based on their significance, we privilege the inclusion of higher-importance features earlier in the search space. This allocates computational resources to focus on the more critical features. Secondly, we applied

[1] https://github.com/XuesenYang/2-D-Particle-Swarm-based-feature-selection.

[2] https://github.com/xueyunuist/Self-Adaptive-Particle-Swarm-Optimization-for-Large-Scale-Feature-Selection-in-Classification.

multiple swarms to search different promising areas in the search space. New swarms are created when existing swarms fall in stagnation. Lastly, we proposed a new move operator to improve low-quality solutions. The operator modifies solutions based on local best solutions and a guiding vector that collects the information from all swarms. The experimental results confirmed the positive effects of components and superior performance of the whole algorithm.

For future work, the current version of algorithm has a lot of parameters and needs some efforts on parameter tuning. Thus, the next step is to investigate adaptive control mechanisms to make our algorithm easier to use. We also attempt to incorporate multiobjective and large-scale optimization techniques into our algorithm. The former enables our algorithm to find multiple sets of features that balance between classification accuracy and the number of features; the later strengthens the search ability of our algorithm to deal with the data sets of large number of features.

## References

1. Nguyen, B.H., Xue, B., Zhang, M.: A survey on swarm intelligence approaches to feature selection in data mining. Swarm Evol. Comput. **54** (2020). Article 100663
2. Rostami, M., Berahmand, K., Nasiri, E., Forouzandeh, S.: Review of swarm intelligence-based feature selection methods. Eng. Appl. Artif. Intell. **100** (2021). Article 104210
3. Kennedy, J., Eberhart, R.: Particle swarm optimization. In: Proceedings of ICNN 1995 - International Conference on Neural Networks, vol. 4, pp. 1942–1948 (1995)
4. Kennedy, J., Eberhart, R.C.: A discrete binary version of the particle swarm algorithm. In: Proceedings of 1997 Conference Systems Man and Cybernetics, pp. 4104–4108 (1997)
5. Chuang, L.Y., Chang, H.W., Tu, C.J., Yang, C.H.: Improved binary PSO for feature selection using gene expression data. Comput. Biol. Chem. **32**(1), 29–38 (2008)
6. Xue, B., Cervante, L., Shang, L., Browne, W.N., Zhang, M.: A multi-objective particle swarm optimization for filter-based feature selection in classification problems. Connect. Sci. **24**(2–3), 91–116 (2012)
7. Zhang, Y., Gong, D., Gao, X., Tian, T., Sun, X.: Binary differential evolution with self-learning for multi-objective feature selection. Inf. Sci. **507**, 67–85 (2020)
8. Lin, S.W., Ying, K.C., Chen, S.C., Lee, Z.J.: Particle swarm optimization for parameter determination and feature selection of support vector machines. Expert Syst. Appl. **35**(4), 1817–1824 (2008)
9. Tran, B., Xue, B., Zhang, M.: A new representation in PSO for discretization-based feature selection. IEEE Trans. Cybern. **48**(6), 1733–1746 (2018)
10. Xue, B., Zhang, M., Browne, W.N.: Particle swarm optimization for feature selection in classification: novel initialization and updating mechanisms. Appl. Soft Comput. **18**, 261–276 (2014)
11. Li, A.D., Xue, B., Zhang, M.: Improved binary particle swarm optimization for feature selection with new initialization and search space reduction strategies. Appl. Soft Computi. **106** (2021). Article 107302
12. Song, X., Zhang, Y., Gong, D., Sun, X.: Feature selection using bare-bones particle swarm optimization with mutual information. Patter Recogn. **112** (2021). Article 107804
13. Zhang, Y., Gong, D.W., Hu, Y., Zhang, W.: Feature selection algorithm based on bare bones particle swarm optimization. Neurocomputing **148**, 150–157 (2015)
14. Song, X., Zhang, Y., Guo, Y., Sun, X., Wang, Y.: Variable-size cooperative coevolutionary particle swarm optimization for feature selection on high-dimensional data. IEEE Trans. Evol. Comput. **24**(5), 882–895 (2020)

15. Nguyen, H.B., Xue, B., Andreae, P., Zhang, M.: Particle swarm optimization with genetic operators for feature selection. In: Proceedings of IEEE Congress on Evolutionary Computation (CEC), pp. 286–293 (2017)
16. Chen, K., Xue, B., Zhang, M., Zhou, F.: Correlation-guided updating strategy for feature selection in classification with surrogate-assisted particle swarm optimization. IEEE Trans. Evol. Comput. **5**(26), 1015–1029 (2022)
17. Xue, Y., Xue, B., Zhang, M.: Self-adaptive particle swarm optimization for large-scale feature selection in classification. ACM Trans. Knowl. Discovery Data **13**(5), 1–27 (2019)
18. Tran, B., Xue, B., Zhang, M.: Variable-length particle swarm optimization for feature selection on high-dimensional classification. IEEE Trans. Evol. Comput. **23**(3), 473–487 (2019)
19. Li, A.D., Xue, B., Zhang, M.: A forward search inspired particle swarm optimization algorithm for feature selection in classification. In: Proceedings of IEEE Congress on Evolutionary Computation (CEC), pp. 786–793 (2021)
20. Nguyen, H.B., Xue, B., Andreae, P.: PSO with surrogate models for feature selection: static and dynamic clustering-based methods. Memetic Comput. **10**, 291–300 (2018)
21. Xue, B., Zhang, M., Browne, W.N.: Multi-objective particle swarm optimization (PSO) for feature selection. In: Proceedings of Genetic and Evolutionary Conference (GECCO), pp. 81–88 (2012)
22. Tran, B., Zhang, M., Xue, B.: A PSO based hybrid feature selection algorithm for high-dimensional classification. In: Proceedings of IEEE Congress on Evolutionary Computation (CEC), pp. 3801–3808 (2016)
23. Xue, B., Zhang, M., Browne, W.N.: Particle swarm optimization for feature selection in classification: a multi-objective approach. IEEE Trans. Cybern. **43**(6), 1656–1671 (2013)
24. Zhang, Y., Gong, D.W., Cheng, J.: Multi-objective particle swarm optimization approach for cost-based feature selection in classification. IEEE/ACM Trans. Comput. Biol. Bioinf. **14**(1), 64–75 (2017)
25. Tian, Y., Liu, R., Zhang, X., Ma, H., Tan, K.C., Jin, Y.: A multipopulation evolutionary algorithm for solving large-scale multi-modal multi-objective optimization problems. IEEE Trans. Evol. Comput. **25**(3), 405–418 (2020)
26. UCI machine learning repository. http://archive.ics.uci.edu/ml. Accessed 31 July 2023
27. Hafiz, F., Swain, A., Patel, N., Naik. C.: A two-dimensional (2-D) learning framework for particle swarm based feature selection. Pattern Recogn. **76**, 416–433 (2018)

# Integration of Convolutional Neural Networks and Autoencoding for Generating Reconfigurable Intelligent Surfaces

Shih-Hsun Weng, You-Cheng Chen, Alan Liu, Shih-Cheng Lin, Sheng-Fuh Chang, and Yu-Jun Lai(✉)

Department of Electrical Engineering, National Chung Cheng University, Chiayi, Taiwan
andylai@alum.ccu.edu.tw

**Abstract.** This paper presents a method utilizing convolutional neural networks (CNN) and autoencoding for generating a reconfigurable intelligent surface (RIS) based on information like beam angles and radiation patterns. It reports how to solve a complex problem in communications with artificial intelligence through requirements analysis and designing of models. Generating a RIS for meeting the strict requirements of beam-steering is challenging since beamforming depends on the elements on the surface which can be arranged in a vast amount of combinations. A deep learning approach has been considered, but finding a suitable model is also a difficult task. This paper introduces a method of generating a small-size RIS and gradually introduces different design tactics to apply the model to solve the problem of larger RIS which is able to handle different incoming and outgoing beam angels. The design rationales of architecture and functions are introduced in the method and the corresponding experiments so that the practitioners can follow our method to construct an RIS. We employed various architectural improvement approaches in a sequential manner, utilizing a step-by-step method to enhance our neural network models. These modifications were carried out to demonstrate the model's capability in feature extraction and its increased generalization capacity. This was substantiated through the use of two distinct sizes of RIS, showcasing a notable enhancement in both feature-capturing ability and overall generalization performance.

**Keywords:** deep learning · reconfigurable intelligent surface · convolutional neural network · autoencoder · phase distribution · radiation pattern

## 1 Introduction

With the advent of the sixth-generation mobile network (6G), it is expected to support more extensive applications than 5G. Compared to 5G, 6G communication connects hundreds of thousands of users and devices simultaneously, providing higher channel capacity, throughput, reliability, and lower latency [1]. Therefore, many studies have worked on transmission architectures to meet communication demands. However, the energy problem is also crucial in 6G communication. Reconfigurable intelligent surfaces (RIS) have been introduced as a low-cost and high-performance technology in.


C.-Y. Lee et al. (Eds.): TAAI 2023, CCIS 2074, pp. 126–138, 2024.
https://doi.org/10.1007/978-981-97-1711-8_9

6G communication and used to control the wireless propagation environment. Artificial intelligence (AI) has gained popularity in many fields, but providing a good solution to a complex problem still is challenging. In recent times, AI technology has been steadily integrated into a range of communication applications, spanning electromagnetic and electric potential fields, intelligent beamforming, and considerations of materials and structures for RIS.

In this paper we transformed the knowledge of electromagnetic waves into the concept of waveform images, allowing these images to retain information about incident and reflected waves. Utilizing an autoencoder architecture, we extracted features from these images and then reconstructed them. Through this approach, we successfully trained a model that identifies relationships between RIS units and waveforms. Additionally, we effectively applied this technique to overcome the lengthy computations when using formulas to calculate phase distribution for multiple RIS units. Furthermore, this method enables us to ensure uniform computational time across different quantities of RIS units.

Through the strategic utilization of deep learning models and innovative architectural designs, we proficiently handle the intricate data derived from incoming and outgoing beam angles. It is worth noting that as the complexity of the problem space increases, the challenges faced by the model become more pronounced. To address this, we conducted experiments involving RIS, validating our approach and effectively resolving the issue of inadequate learning capacity within the model.

Our findings demonstrate the efficacy of our methodology in overcoming limitations in the model's learning capacity. Moreover, we enhance the CNN model's capabilities in feature extraction and generalization, as evidenced by the results from the RIS experiment. This success empowers the model to tackle complex, high-dimensional problems, highlighting the practicality and effectiveness of our strategy.

We also acknowledge the potential for complex and dense images to impact the encoding capacity of the autoencoder, particularly on the encoder side. To mitigate this, adjustments were made to the decoder architecture to enhance feature extraction capabilities. Additionally, we aimed to establish the model's robust inference capabilities with minimal data. Therefore, we incorporated experimental methods aimed at improving the model's ability to generalize. The effectiveness of these methods have been thoroughly validated.

## 2 Background and Related Work

### 2.1 Reconfigurable Intelligent Surface

A RIS consists of an array of elements (units) as shown in Fig. 1. Each element has a different phase for reflecting the beam to a designated direction to avoid signal loss by a receiver. Beamforming as shown in Fig. 2 is to reflect electromagnetic signals for pointing to a designated direction, and the signals from the interference among elements can be controlled to achieve beamsteering [2]. The phase $\phi_{RA}$ of each element is based on (1), in which $k_0$ is the wavenumber written as $k_0 = 2\pi/\lambda$, the subscript $i$ shows the $i^{th}$ element.

$$\phi_{\mathrm{RA}} = \mathrm{k_0}\left[\mathrm{R_i} - \left(\mathrm{x_i}\cos\varphi_{\mathrm{b}} + \mathrm{y_i}\sin\varphi_{\mathrm{b}}\right)\sin\theta_{\mathrm{b}}\right] \tag{1}$$

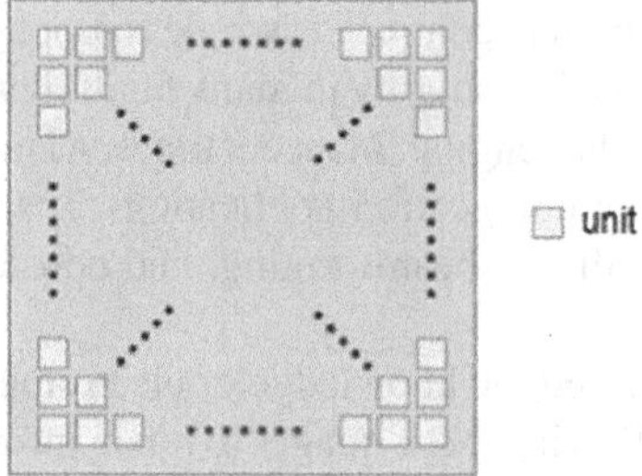


**Fig. 1.** Units arrangement of RIS in a 2D array

As shown in Fig. 2, Ri is the distance from signal source (Feed Horn), (xi, yi) represents the coordinate of an element, and $(\theta_b, \varphi_b)$ is the spherical angle of reflected beamforming. Using (1) and considering the incoming and outgoing angles of RIS, we can form an M × N array with the values of unit phases. Under a fixed frequency, we can obtain a phase distribution corresponding to the given pairs of angles.

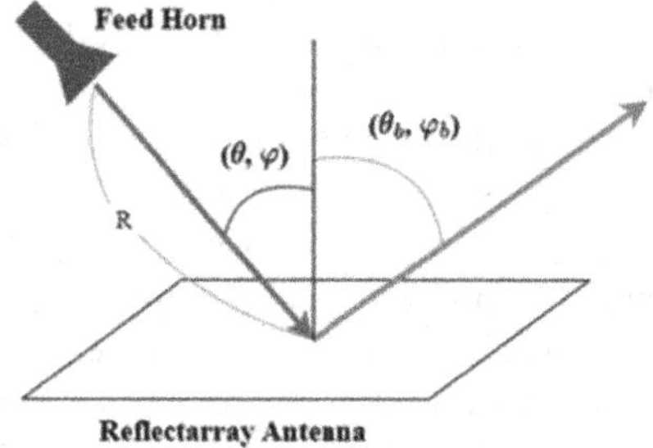


**Fig. 2.** Angles and distance information in beamforming

The Array Factor determines the gain and beam direction of a RIS, it represents the geometry structure and distance between elements of a RIS and is closely related to phase distribution. By applying (1), we have (2) for a RIS with a size M by N.

$$AF(\theta, \varphi) = \sum_{m=1}^{M}\sum_{n=1}^{N} e^{jk_0 d(msin\theta\cos\varphi + n\sin\theta\sin\varphi)} \\ e^{j\phi_{RA}} \cdot e^{-jk_0 R_i} \tag{2}$$

In order to provide a more flexible platform for beamsteering, the elements of RIS need to be controlled independently. With different combinations of switchable elements, beams can be steered to different directions with the best radiation pattern, and we use (2) to generate the radiation pattern Fig. 3. (right). Such features can be applied in serving moving targets or accommodating specifications of beamforming [3]. The concept of RIS may be realizable with the phase distribution that can meet the requirements of direction [4]. Such metasurface consists of a two-dimensional array with metamaterials, and they can be used in expanding frequency, beamforming, and controlling signals. Our study focuses on the RIS which is able to perform beamforming, in which each element is implemented as an embedded and adjustable for phase change taking place between the range of 0° and 180° as shown in (3), considered as the 1-bit RIS.

$$\begin{cases} 0^\circ, & 0^\circ = \varphi_{\min} < 180^\circ \\ 180^\circ, & \text{elsewhere} \end{cases} \tag{3}$$

The left-hand side of Fig. 3. (left) shows the phase distribution of a RIS. The current approach to RIS design depends on (1), However, this will not be sufficient to handle dynamic changes in using RIS. Thus, customizing an RIS promptly becomes an important issue.

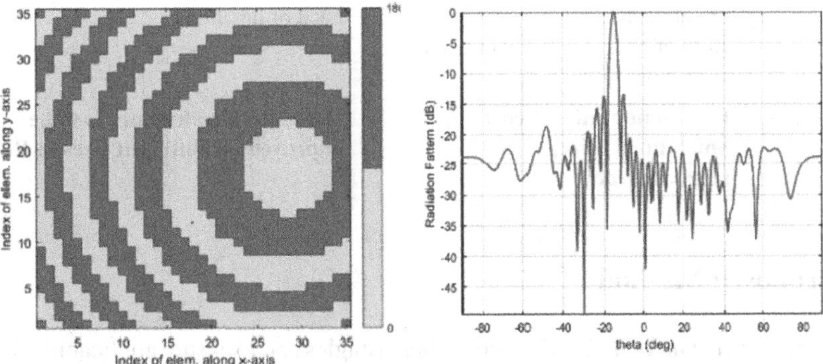


**Fig. 3.** (left) Phase distribution of RIS with the incidence angle $30^\circ$ an reflection angle $-15^\circ$, , and (right) radiation pattern in calculated result.

## 2.2 Related Work

Our study uses a deep learning approach to construct a model to produce a phase distribution. Some approaches use neural network models to perform inverse design engineering from radiation patterns to produce phase distributions. Using a traditional method of calculation using a formula in producing phase distribution is time-consuming [5], so the AI approaches are expected to produce phase distribution fast, efficiently, and cost-effective.

Qiu et al. [6] utilize neural network models to address beam requirements, but their models are large and require extensive training time. Ghorbani et al. [5] propose an autoencoding method for feature extraction with reduced computational demands, yet its multi-stage processing impacts accuracy. Shan et al. introduce a deep-learning strategy to program a beam-steering metasurface [7], yielding accurate results with optimized radiation patterns. Nonetheless, the extensive parameter count leads to time-consuming and costly training. The AMID model computes metasurfaces based on desired design targets [8], featuring low computational expense and efficient feature extraction via autoencoders. However, this approach compromises accuracy and design flexibility (Table 1).

**Table 1.** Comparison of Related Work

| | Advantages | Disadvantages |
|---|---|---|
| [6] | Simple network,<br>Beam requirements | Large model and parameter size, Long training time |
| [5] | Low calculation,<br>Auto encoding for efficient feature extraction | Separate stages,<br>Low accuracy |
| [7] | High accuracy,<br>Optimized radiation patterns using metaheuristics methods | Large model parameter size,<br>High computational cost,<br>Slow training time |
| [8] | Low computational cost,<br>Small model size,<br>Auto-encoder for efficient feature extraction | Lower accuracy,<br>Lack of flexibility |
| Our work | **Low computational cost,**<br>**Small model size,**<br>**High accuracy** | **Model architecture needs to be improved for different sizes of RIS** |

## 3 Proposed Method

To cater to diverse incoming and outgoing beam angles and to ensure applicability across various RIS sizes, our approach takes inspiration from the autoencoder concept used in the AMID model [8]. We have devised a model that leverages end-to-end training to swiftly generate phase distributions for the RIS. One of the most salient benefits of employing the autoencoder is its innate aptitude to disentangle complex relationships between inputs and outputs. In our pursuit, we seek to decipher the intricate interplay between the RIS discrete unit configurations and the distinct radiation patterns they induce. This is a nontrivial endeavor due to the high dimensionality and nonlinearity inherent in both elements. The autoencoder's intrinsic ability to distill meaningful features from the data not only simplifies the analysis but also empowers us to navigate through the convolution of factors influencing the radiation patterns.

### 3.1 Data Generation

Our proposed method is organized into three phases: Data Preprocessing, Model Improvement, and Data post-processing as shown in Fig. 4. Our dataset contains the data consisting of pairs of a phase distribution produced from Eq. (1) and its corresponding radiation pattern. A phase distribution is organized as an array. As for a radiation pattern, it is considered an image and is processed as a single-channel graph.

We use an autoencoding method to take the radiation pattern into a wave-oriented two-dimensional image as an input. The output then is the phase distribution of a RIS, and the gradual transformation is shown in Fig. 5. The phase distribution is a label-oriented way of processing the data. For generating the necessary data, we have repeatedly created pairs of phase distributions and corresponding radiation patterns. The incoming beam angles range from –60° to 60° and the outgoing beam angle is from 0° to 60° with one-degree intervals for a total of 7381 combinations. In addition to the numeric data, we have prepared radiation patterns as greyscale image files in the size of 256 × 256 to show the waves.

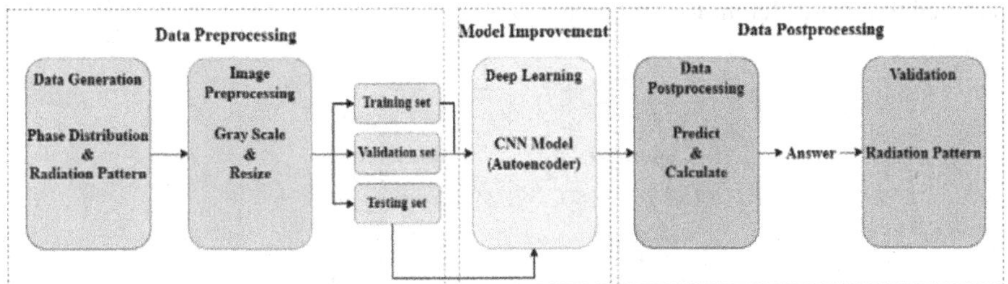


**Fig. 4.** Proposed Approach

### 3.2 End-to-end Autoencoder Architecture Tailored to RIS Requirements

End-to-end training in machine learning simplifies the training process by directly connecting inputs to desired outputs. This has advantages, such as learning complex features from data without manual engineering. Optimizing the entire model as a unified entity enhances performance by considering interactions between components, this approach compromises accuracy and design flexibility.

However, challenges arise from the inherent complexity and nonlinearity of end-to-end models, potentially affecting interpretability and leading to overfitting. In our study, we focus on two types of RIS in sizes of 10x10 and 32x32, exploring different design aspects including phase distribution and radiation patterns. To address these challenges, we tailor and modify the autoencoder and its associated components to meet the specific requirements of RIS design.

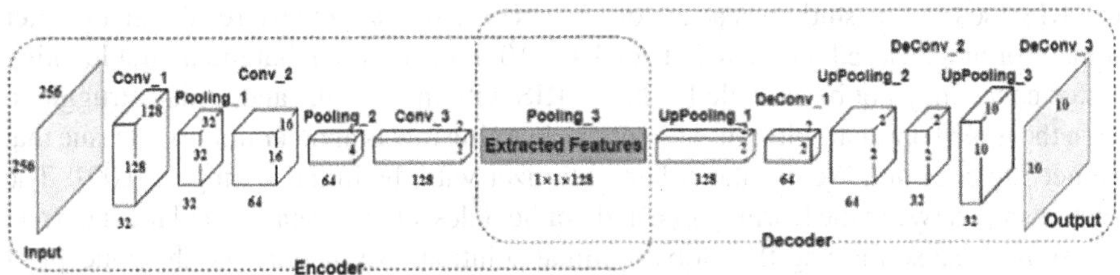


**Fig. 5.** Autoencoder for a 10 × 10 RIS

The front-end encoder utilizes convolutional and pooling layers, taking advantage of the substantial advancements convolutional neural networks have achieved in image-related tasks. Within these layers, effective feature extraction and efficient feature compression are carried out. The ultimate goal is to identify distinctive features within the waveform for the purpose of learning. Conversely, the back-end decoder employs upsampling and deconvolution techniques in image processing as shown in Fig. 5. The objective here is to leverage the extracted features for reconstruction, facilitating the efficient recovery of the phase distribution of the reconstructed intelligent surface. This phase distribution recovery stands as a pivotal focus of this study.

Figure 6 shows a sample of our 10 × 10 model, and the pink components are to be modified to meet different Requirements.

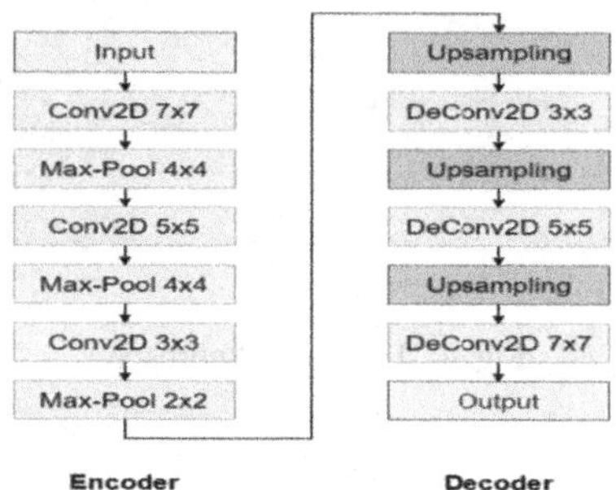


**Fig. 6.** 10 × 10 RIS generation

As for the 35 × 35 RIS, using the combination of 5 × 5 and 7 × 7 has caused a feature loss, and the learning process was terminated. It has led us to consider the possibility of 32 × 32 instead. By using upsampling layers with 2 × 2, 4 × 4, and 4 × 4, the learning features became more effective. For our proposed architecture, we use the Sigmoid function as the activation function which provides a nonlinear behavior in the range of 0 and 1 to determine the output of each node in the network, and the loss function we use is mean_squared_error. This is suitable for the binary output of an element in RIS.

### 3.3 Model Adjustment and Improvement

The RIS used in this study has a size of M × N, where a larger size results in a greater number of units. Based on the results of 10 × 10, it is observed that the model learning performance may not be suitable for larger RIS with more units, and it may struggle to learn the global optimal solution. Though the learning rate is another important issue that we need to consider. We use the Adam optimizer with the initial setting of 0.001. The relationship between the learning rate and gradient descent is essential, and the incorrect setting may cause missing the global optimal solution. We incorporate the concept of learning rate scheduling like the learning rate decay introduced in ResNet [9] with the decay rate of 0.1 for every 30 epochs. A typical learning rate scheduling is to slow down the learning in order to find the solution, and it can be shown as (4), in which $\eta$ is the learning rate, $\eta_0$ the initial learning rate, t the time or epoch, and k the decay rate set as 0.96 in our case.

$$H_t = \eta_0^{\circ} \cdot e^{-k \cdot t} \quad (4)$$

In order to avoid overfitting, usually the number of data is to be increased, or refined data is used with techniques like dropout and batch normalization. We follow the guidance of using batch normalization in CNN [10]. For batch normalization [11], we repeat the process of normalizing the features for training in each layer of the network model.

Some applications require the use of a fully connected model for increasing the accuracy of extracting all features to perform classification, but our goal is to extract features that are closely related to the radiation patterns associated with phase distribution and to find the phase distribution based on the features of the radiation patterns. Thus, we did not consider fully connected model. We utilize the idea of $1 \times 1$ convolution kernel in [12] and [13] for handling dimension reduction and nonlinear characteristics. By incorporating a nonlinear activation function with $1 \times 1$ convolution, the network becomes deeper for better feature detection. As illustrated in Fig. 8, compared to the use of $3 \times 3$ convolution, the feature map is kept with more distinguished features in using $1 \times 1$ convolution. As shown in Fig. 7, we have updated the architecture in Fig. 6 with different adjustments and improvements for the $32 \times 32$ RIS.

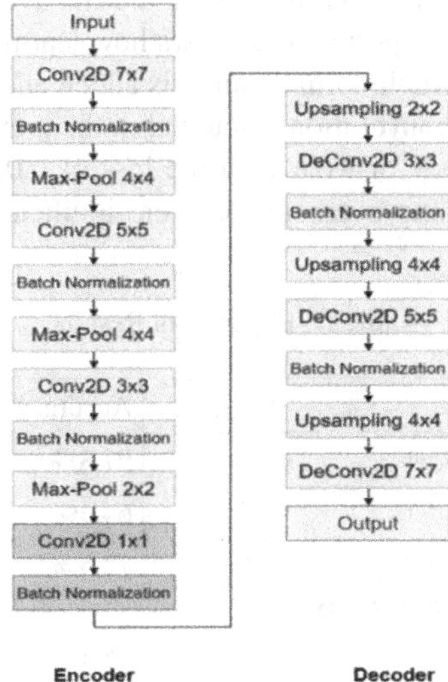


**Fig. 7.** $32 \times 32$ RIS generation

### 3.4 Postprocessing and Evaluation.

For converting to the one-bit representation, we set a threshold. If the value is over the threshold, then the value is set to 1; otherwise, it is set to 0. For visual analysis, we fed the phase distribution into Eq. (2) to calculate and draw the radiation pattern. Finally, we use the main beam, side lobe, and beam width to check if the produced RIS meets the requirements.

## 4 Experiments

### 4.1 Experiments Setup and Results

The experiments are conducted with the following parameter setting.

(a). Signal parameters

- Frequency of electromagnetic wave: 5.6 GHz
- Range of incoming angles: 0° – 60°
- Range of outgoing angles: -60° – 60°

(b). RIS parameters

- Number of elements: $10 \times 10$; $32 \times 32$
- Distance between elements: 0.5cm

Table 2 shows the results of four experiments with the accuracy and loss information associated with the models derived. Experiment 1 creates the initial models for $10 \times 10$ and $32 \times 32$ RIS. The results shown in Table 2 are the averages after performing the same experiments 20 times. Experiment 2 shows how learning rate decay can improve accuracy. In Experiment 3, batch normalization is added and the accuracy is improved. In Experiment 4, the $1 \times 1$ convolution discussed in the previous section is added, and the model yields the accuracy of 91% with the loss of 0.05. Compared to the initial model in Experiment 1, the improvement has been significant.

**Table 2.** Experiment Results

| | Model | Accuracy | Loss |
|---|---|---|---|
| Exp1 | 10 × 10 model | **97.5%** | 0.02 |
| | 32 × 32 model | 64.5% | 0.20 |
| Exp2 | 32 × 32 model + **Learning Rate Decay** | 77.5% | 0.14 |
| Exp3 | 32 × 32 + Learning Rate Decay + **Batch Normalization** | 85.9% | 0.09 |
| Exp4 | 32 × 32 model + Learning Rate Decay + Batch Normalization + **1 × 1 Conv2D** | **91%** | 0.05 |

### 4.2 RIS Design Examples Through Autoencoder

The experiments presented the results in terms of accuracy. In addition, we can use the RIS generated by Array Factor to compare to the RIS generated by our proposed method.

The images of phase distributions and corresponding radiation patterns are provided side by side for examination.

Table 3 shows the 10 × 10 RIS for handling incoming and outgoing beam angles both set as 0°. We see a close resemblance of two-phase distributions except for two misplaced elements. The radiation patterns are matched with the main beam, width, and side lobes.

**Table 3.** Incoming and outgoing beam angles with 0° for 10x10 RIS

| | **Using Array Factor** | **Proposed Method** |
|---|---|---|
| Phase Distribution | Index of elem. along y-axis; Index of elem. along x-axis; 0–180 | Index of elem. along y-axis; Index of elem. along x-axis; 0–180 |
| Radiation Pattern | Radiation Pattern (dB); theta (deg) | Radiation Pattern (dB); theta (deg) |

Tables 4 and 5 show the 32 × 32 RIS for handling different incoming and outgoing beam angles, one with 0° for both incoming and outgoing beam angles and the other with an incoming beam angle of 10° and outgoing angle of 60°. The phase distributions generated by Array Factor show smooth and uniform wave-like patterns, but the RIS generated by our proposed method are scattered. However, the radiation patterns show that the main beams and gains satisfy the requirements.

In addition, Table 6 shows that no extra time was required for the process, although there is a tenfold difference in the number of units between the 10x10 and 32x32 RIS, the computation time does not exhibit significant disparity. This can be attributed to the simultaneous calculation of the phase values for each point on the reconstructed intelligent surface in this study.

**Table 4.** Incoming and outgoing beam angles with 0° for 32 × 32 RIS

| | Using Array Factor | Proposed Method |
|---|---|---|
| Phase Distribution | 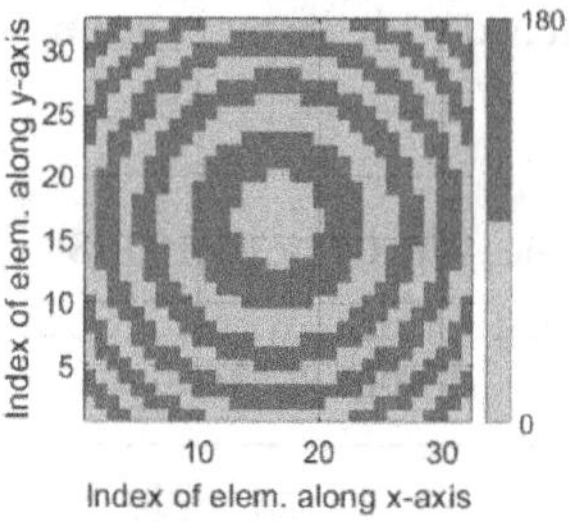 Index of elem. along y-axis; Index of elem. along x-axis; 0–180 | 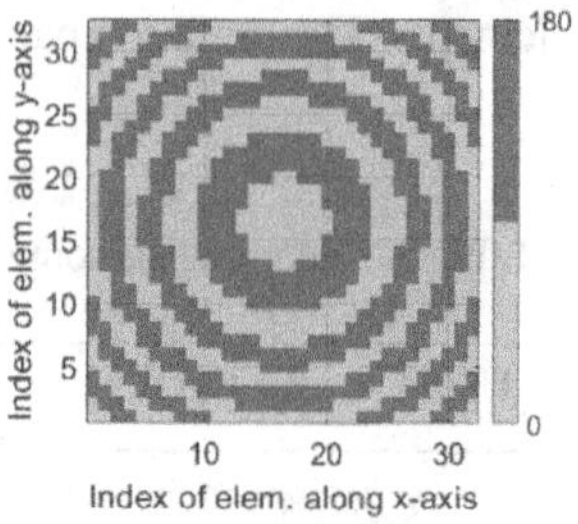 Index of elem. along y-axis; Index of elem. along x-axis; 0–180 |
| Radiation Pattern | 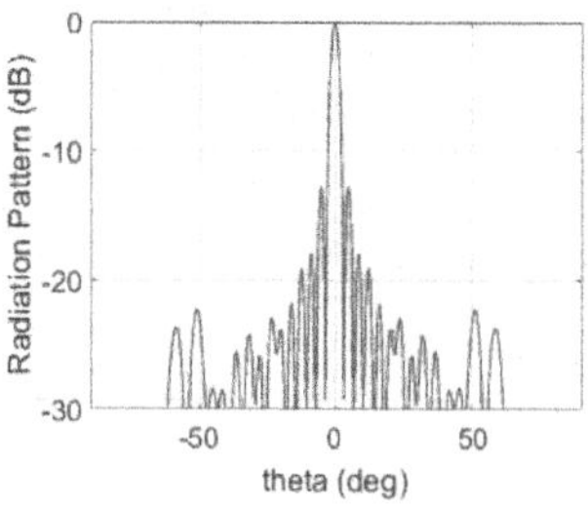 Radiation Pattern (dB); theta (deg) | 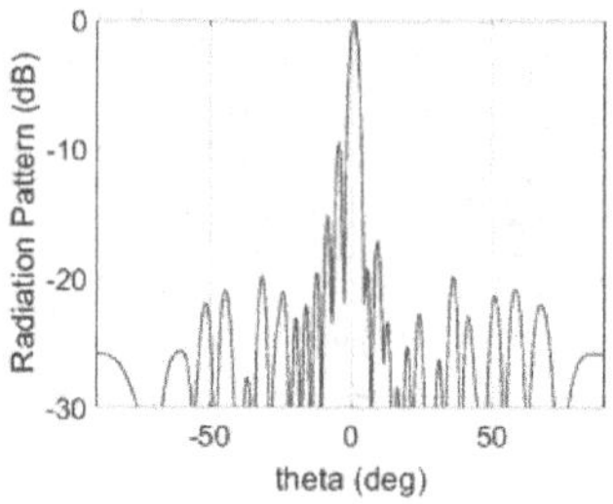 Radiation Pattern (dB); theta (deg) |

## 4.3 Observation

We demonstrate impressive learning results for a 10x10 RIS while indicating limitations for the larger 32x32 RIS due to potential convergence challenges. Experiment addresses this by adjusting learning rates through exponential decay, successfully mitigating convergence issues, yet introducing overfitting risks.

And we also enhance the architecture improving generalization and reducing overfitting. Introduces 1x1 convolutions after the encoder, boosting feature extraction capabilities and model accuracy. These enhancements collectively elevate the accuracy of the 32x32 RIS model, the result also enables us to ensure uniform computational time across different quantities of RIS units in Table 6.

The results validate the effectiveness of the proposed model architecture for generating the 10x10 RIS model, effectively learning its phase distribution and radiation pattern. However, while improvements are observed for the 32x32 RIS model, challenges remain in accurately capturing side lobes of the radiation pattern. The side-by-side comparison of the RIS generated by the Array Factor and our proposed method showed that the RIS may become more irregular as the size grows. However, it is promising that the corresponding radiation patterns contained acceptable performance in the main beam and width. While the compact model excels for smaller RIS, larger RIS requires deeper architectures for optimal performance.

**Table 5.** Incoming beam angle with 0° and outgoing beam angles with 60° for 32 × 32 RIS

| | **Using Array Factor** | **Proposed Method** |
|---|---|---|
| Phase Distribution | Index of elem. along y-axis (5, 10, 15, 20, 25, 30); Index of elem. along x-axis (10, 20, 30); colorbar 0–180 | Index of elem. along y-axis (5, 10, 15, 20, 25, 30); Index of elem. along x-axis (10, 20, 30); colorbar 0–180 |
| Radiation Pattern | Radiation Pattern (dB) (0, -10, -20, -30); theta (deg) (-50, 0, 50) | Radiation Pattern (dB) (0, -10, -20, -30); theta (deg) (-50, 0, 50) |

**Table 6.** Time required for model generation

| Models | Generation Time | Postprocessing Time |
|---|---|---|
| 10 × 10 model | 790 ms | 52.5 ms |
| 32 × 32 model + adjustment | 788 ms | 50.4 ms |

## 5 Conclusion

This paper has proposed a method for generating a RIS to meet the requirements of given incoming and outgoing angles. In addition, the method can also be applied to a larger size of RIS by adjusting the autoencoder. We have introduced the importance of the relationship between RIS and radiation patterns for building a deep-learning model. One important contribution is the effective design of RIS with information like the incoming and outgoing angles. We have processed the waves in radiation patterns as images. By using images to train a model, the features in a wave pattern are extracted to show the corresponding phase distribution. This paper shows how the requirements change of the problem can be reflected in the adjustment in the AI models. With the requirements of different RIS sizes, the architecture of the model needs to be redesigned. We have shown the design rationales through experiments, so that the readers may understand the reasons for choosing particular components. This paper has shown the techniques of using angles to generate an RIS, and our future work is to extend the work to larger sizes.

**Acknowledgments.** This work was supported by the Ministry of Science and Technology of Taiwan under Grants MOST 111-3114-E-194-001 and 111-2218-E-194-004. It is also supported by the Advanced Institute of Manufacturing with High-tech Innovations (AIM-HI) at National Chung-Cheng University.

## References

1. Alsabah, M., et al.: 6G wireless communications networks: a comprehensive survey. In: IEEE Access, pp. 148191–148243 (2021)
2. Dahri, M.H., Jamaluddin, M.H., Khalily, M., Abbasi, M.I., Selvaraju, R., Kamarudin, M.R.: Polarization diversity and adaptive beamsteering for 5G reflectarrays: a review. IEEE Access **6**, 19451–19464 (2018)
3. Pan, C., et al.: Reconfigurable intelligent surfaces for 6G systems: principles, applications, and research directions. IEEE Commun. Mag. **59**(6), 14–20 (2021)
4. Ayanoglu, E., Capolino, F., KSwindlehurst, A.L.: Wave-controlled metasurface-based reconfigurable intelligent surfaces. IEEE Wirel. Commun. **29**(4), 86–92 (2022). https://doi.org/10.1109/MWC.005.2100401
5. Ghorbani, F., et al.: Deep neural network-based automatic metasurface design with a wide frequency range. Sci. Rep. **11**(1), 7102 (2021)
6. Qiu, T., et al.: Deep learning: a rapid and efficient route to automatic metasurface design. Adv. Sci. **6**(12), 1900128 (2019)
7. Shan, T., Pan, X., Li, M., Xu, S., Yang, F.: Coding programmable metasurfaces based on deep learning techniques. IEEE J. Emerg. Sel. Top. Circ. Syst. **10**(1), 114–125 (2020)
8. Shi, X., Qiu, T., Wang, J., Zhao, X., Qu, X.: Metasurface inverse design using machine learning approaches. J. Phys. D Appl. Phys. **53**(27), 275105 (2020)
9. He, K., Zhang, X., Ren, X., Sun, J.: Deep residual learning for image recognition. In: 2016 IEEE Conference on Computer Vision and Pattern Recognition (CVPR), pp. 770–778, June 2016
10. Garbin, C., Zhu, X., Marques, O.: Dropout vs. batch normalization: an empirical study of their impact to deep learning. Multimed Tools App.l **79**(19), 12777–12815 (2020)
11. Ioffe, S., Szegedy, C.: Batch normalization: accelerating deep network training by reducing internal covariate shift. In: Proceedings of the 32nd International Conference on Machine Learning, pp. 448–456, June 2015
12. Lin, M., Chen, Q. and Yan, S.: Network in network. In: International Conference on Learning Representations (ICLR) (2014)
13. Szegedy, C., et al.: Going deeper with convolutions. In: IEEE Conference on Computer Vision and Pattern Recognition (CVPR), pp. 1–9 (2015)

# Comparison of Vocabulary Features Among Multiple Data Sources for Constructing a Knowledge Base on Disaster Information

Megumi Yasuo(✉) and Mitsunori Matsushita

Graduate School of Informatics, Kansai University, 2-1-1, Ryozenji-Cho, Takatsuki, Osaka 569-1095, Japan
{k290993,mmat}@kansai-u.ac.jp

**Abstract.** This research aims to develop a framework for smoothly obtaining disaster information from multiple web services through a knowledge base of disaster information. In Japan, where natural disasters occur frequently, there is a need for a system that can utilize disaster information transmitted on the Web from various locations in disaster-stricken areas for rescue operations and disaster recovery when a disaster occurs. Since such information is posted to many web services, searchers must refer to multiple web services to obtain the desired infor mation. In this study, we propose understanding the characteristics of disaster information posted on each web service and using them as a guide for searchers to obtain disaster information smoothly. To achieve this goal, we tried to construct a vocabulary set of disaster information by acquiring textual information from two different data sources and using word embedding and clustering. Comparison of the acquired disaster information revealed two points: The composition of dis aster information categories differs among data sources. Even texts in the same category have different characteristics of words depending on the data source.

**Keywords:** disaster information · multiple data sources · word embedding · text clustering

## 1 Introduction

Japan is often called a disaster-prone nation, facing significant disasters yearly. When disasters strike, people in disaster-stricken areas disseminate information about disaster-related information, including damage information, rescue requests, and the delivery status of relief supplies, with various social media, such as Twitter and Face book. Regarding the Osaka north earthquake in 2018, approximately 220,000 tweets in Japanese containing the word "Jishin (earthquake)" were posted in the first 10 min after the earthquake occurred [1]. A significant characteristic of these posts is that they originate directly from people in the disaster-stricken area. Information shared by those directly impacted

M. Yasuo and M. Matsushita—These authors contributed equally to this work.


C.-Y. Lee et al. (Eds.): TAAI 2023, CCIS 2074, pp. 139–150, 2024.
https://doi.org/10.1007/978-981-97-1711-8_10

is rapid, aiding in obtaining information about the disaster-stricken area faster than compilation by mass media. Moreover, information that mass media may not cover can be collected if someone shares it. To support rescue and disaster recovery activities quickly, it is essential to have a framework for efficiently collecting and organizing such information. Utilizing such shared informa tion by individuals, one can swiftly acquire information that traditional newspaper articles, news reports, or local government websites might not capture.

To achieve this objective, it is necessary to identify differences in disaster infor mation posted on various web services. Among the types of disaster information are requests for assistance, traffic updates, and data regarding the locations affected by the disaster. Collecting all these pieces of information from a single resource is difficult. Therefore, those searching for disaster information will focus on resources relevant to their tasks. Such information retrieval assumes that the searcher possesses prior knowledge about collecting disaster information. However, searchers needing this pre requisite knowledge must refer to various web services to obtain the information they seek.

Enabling people to access information easily will help them collect information more effectively. This paper aims to acquire metadata about the content in each web service and use it as a guide for searchers. As the first step, this study analyzes vocabulary acquired from different resources. It examines two aspects: whether there are differences in information acquired between web services and how the content of posted information differs among web services.

## 2 Related Works

This research aims to acquire and store disaster information from the web and use it as knowledge. To achieve this goal, we extract disaster information from text infor mation on web services and compare its contents to investigate the differences in the knowledge acquired from each resource. In this chapter, we review research on the use of information on the web in the event of a disaster and research on information extraction from text and define the position of this research.

### 2.1 Research on the Use of Information on the Web in the Event of a Disaster

Research using disaster information posted on web services has been attempted for var ious purposes, such as assessing the damage from disasters and collecting information on disaster-stricken areas [2–4]. In particular, there is a high demand for collecting disaster information from large-scale general-purpose social networking services such as Twitter, and several studies have been conducted so far [5–7]. One of the disaster information analysis systems based on Twitter information is "DISAANA," developed by the National Institute of Information and Communications Technology (NICT) [8]. The system analyzes information posted by Twitter users in real-time, extracts what is happening where, and includes a 5W1H search function and a "contradictory post" function for information whose facts are unclear.

When extracting disaster information from SNS, information unrelated to the dis aster is often mixed in as noise. In particular, entertainment-related information, such as games, tends to be posted on SNS. A survey of tweets in Japanese reported that 60% of tweets posted during normal times contained entertainment information1[1].

Some studies have analyzed noise postings on SNS from the task of extracting disaster information. Morino et al. extracted disaster information from SNS postings at the time of a disaster and analyzed the noise contained in results [9]. This study examined the types of noise in the mix and tested whether these noises could be separated from lexical features. It suggests that information about "games" is highly separable. On the other hand, we reported that it is difficult to separate noise with lexical features that are not biased toward specific contents, such as "merchandise items."

User-posted information has been considered unverifiable, unreliable, and unsuit able for use by large organizations in actual rescue operations. This point is discussed in some papers [10], including interviews conducted by Tapia et al. with NGO human itarian organizations [11]. Tapia et al. suggest that the methods to obtain information with acceptable reliability from microblogs include extracting valuable data using text classification techniques and acquiring and automatically classifying information from major geographical areas. Concerning this problem, a disaster information col lection system that considers the government's information collection process has been proposed [12]. This system is designed to enable users at the disaster site to report the location of damage smoothly via the web and to ensure the report's reliability by adding location information when the damage is reported.

### 2.2 Research on Information Extraction Using Text Clustering

Acquiring textual features using word embeddings is one of the effective methods for information extraction. Word embedding is a method of acquiring distances between words with word vectorization in a set of documents. While this method is widely used for document classification, there are attempts to use these methods to acquire latent knowledge. Magno et al. attempted to identify cultural characteristics and values by country using 1.7 billion tweets posted on Twitter [13]. This attempt classifies the cultural characteristics of 59 countries based on 22 perspectives, including "religion" and "science." The study revealed cultural characteristics and values by country, and correlations with actual cultural characteristics were pointed out in several indicators. Word embeddings were widely used in the research described in the previous section, which was oriented toward information recommendation. Park et al. attempted to recommend sightseeing routes according to the profile of tourists by using word-of mouth information on travel sites for designing sightseeing tour routes [14]. This study analyzed reviews posted on TripAdvisor, a travel review site, and found that each reviewer's profile had unique challenges. Debanjan et al. attempted to extract more valuable reviews from many reviews posted on e-commerce sites by using word variance representation [15]. This study aims to link the subset of good review sentences that mention a product from multiple perspectives with the emotional polarity derived from the review sentences. While many general e-commerce sites provide a function to evaluate the usefulness of the review sentences themselves, the advantage of estimating usefulness scores directly from the review sentences is that it can also be applied to newly posted

[1] https://www.biglobe.co.jp/pressroom/release/2011/04/27-1.

review sentences. An example of cross-domain use of word embeddings is the lyrics recommendation method by Han et al. [16]. This study recommends lyrics similar to the user's environment in a tourist destination by sharing word embeddings of reviews of tourist attractions and song lyrics. Conventional song recommendation methods use meta-information such as genre and artist, but using word embeddings across domains, they recommend lyrics appropriate for the listening environment.

Previous studies on web-based information in the event of a disaster have focused on collecting damage and rescue requests, indicating a high need to obtain disaster information on the Web. On the other hand, several studies on web-based informa tion resources about disasters have pointed out the need to ensure the reliability of web-based information for disaster recovery assistance and the need for knowledge acquisition support systems using text classification technology. Our research focuses on supporting the acquisition of disaster information. It aims to smoothly present information that matches the needs of a searcher who collects information about the disaster that needs to be dealt with quickly from multiple data sources. Previous studies using text clustering have shown that knowledge acquisition based on word embedding is helpful for knowledge extraction and information retrieval based on text. This paper examines building a word set by clustering words using these methods.

## 3 Collecting Disaster Information Using a Combination of Data Sources

When a large-scale disaster occurs, people post a variety of information about the disaster to web services. At this time, posters need to change the form and content of the information according to the specifications of each web service. For example, when posting to a web service such as Instagram, designed to post information with images attached, the contributor must prepare the images to be posted. Even in the same text media, there is a difference between sites where people share their impressions of an article (e.g., Hatena bookmark[2]), sites where contributors verbalize their claims and interpretations in long sentences (e.g., note[3]), and sites where contributors tend to express their impressions and experiences in short sentences (e.g., Twitter), the tendency of the contents of the posts will be different. This difference in form creates a difference in the information stored in each web service. Even when attempting to extract information on disaster information, the information obtained will differ among web services. Therefore, selecting a web service that provides information in line with the collection intention as an information source when acquiring information that meets a specific purpose is necessary. Under the above consideration, this study aims to construct a knowledge base of disaster information to match search queries and target web services to be extracted.

There are several types of large-scale disasters, such as earthquakes, volcanic eruptions, and lightning strikes, but the actual damage caused by these disasters differs from case to case. For example, in the case of a major earthquake, a landslide may occur as a secondary disaster, or a large-scale fire may cause damage. Both of these can be

[2] https://b.hatena.ne.jp/.

[3] https://note.com/.

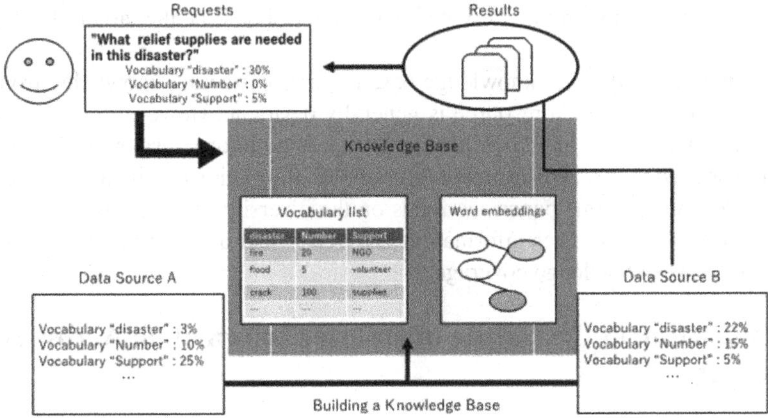


**Fig. 1.** Knowledge acquisition model for disaster information in multiple sources.

considered earthquake-related disasters, but the countermeasures and rescue policies required are different. Therefore, to obtain the necessary information for each disaster, a search framework that considers the disaster's characteristics is necessary. Information retrieval through the knowledge base of disaster information can estimate possible secondary disasters based on the characteristics of the disaster to be retrieved and present them to the searcher.

The knowledge base for handling disaster information is built from a vocabulary set clustered by word meaning and a set of sentences labeled based on disaster-related categories. The vocabulary sets are clustered based on the semantic similarity of the words obtained from the disaster information. The vocabulary sets are obtained for each type of disaster. The set of sentences is constructed by dividing the text acquired from web services such as SNS and news articles into sentences and classifying them as disaster information based on the content of the sentences. Once a distributed representation is obtained from the set of sentences, a sentence vector based on the vocabulary set is calculated for each sentence. The sentence vectors are associated with labels assigned to the original sentences. The knowledge base we aim to build in this research is statistical information on sentence vectors for each disaster category. With this knowledge base, it is possible to analogize the relevant disaster category from the input text's features and perform similarity search and information extraction based on semantic distance.

The process of acquiring information using the disaster information knowledge base is shown in Fig. 1. This figure shows the relationship between the searcher's information request, the knowledge base, and each data source. When a searcher makes an information request through the search system, the knowledge base analyzes which cluster features are included in the information request and returns appropriate knowledge and data sources as search results according to the features. The advantage of this method over general query matching and similarity search is that it can present search results considering the semantic distance per data source. As mentioned above, the tendency of information stored in web services varies depending on the design of the web service. The semantic distance of a data source to an information request can be used to determine whether the information in the presented data source should be the target of a detailed search.

Since building a disaster knowledge base requires extracting knowledge from vast data, having more data as a resource is generally desirable. However, processing vast data to build a knowledge base requires enormous computational resources. To con struct a helpful knowledge base, ensuring the diversity of information obtained from each data source is desirable. In this paper, we focus on the diversity of information in building a knowledge base of disaster information and verify that using multiple data sources together improves knowledge coverage.

## 4 Comparison of the Nature of Disaster Information Across Data Sources

In this paper, we obtained disaster information from two websites and analyzed their contents to clarify the differences in the information obtained from each site. Disaster information includes images and video data showing the damage, text data such as damage reports and requests for help, and numerical data such as location information. In this paper, text data is used as the target of analysis as the information to be acquired. As an analysis method, this paper uses a combination of word embedding and clustering to compare the characteristics of the words in each resource. This method is used to analyze trends in a dataset based on the semantic similarity of words. Text data on disasters are extracted from two web services, morphological analysis is performed to extract the part-of-speech of the words to be analyzed, a word distribution representation is obtained, and then clustering is performed to obtain semantically similar word clusters. The characteristics of the words in each data source are then compared to determine whether there are any differences between the data sources and their characteristics.

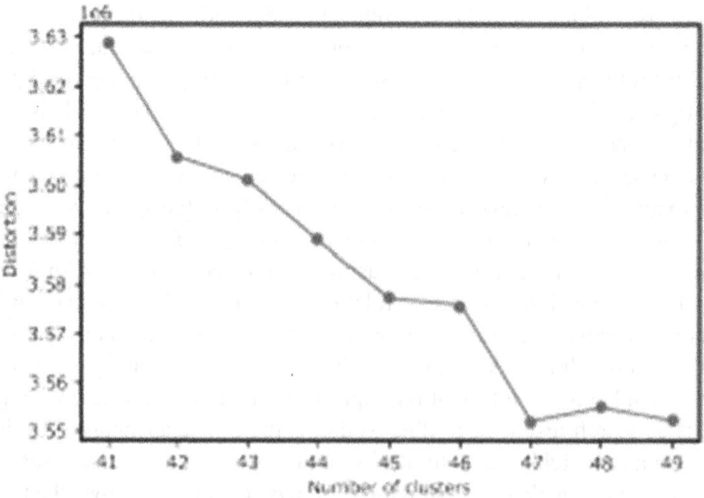


**Fig. 2.** Determining the number of cluster divisions using the elbow method.

**Table 1.** Examples of label names and words in each class.

| Label Name | Words |
|---|---|
| abbreviation | ROCK, ETC, DO, NR, RU, JET, SS |
| mood | subtle, hard, intense, grandiose, vivid, sufficient, crippled |
| operation | management, destruction, delivery, placement, removal, construction |
| number | 7, three, 1, hundred, six, one, five, two |

### 4.1 Extracting Disaster-Related Words

This study focused on the July 2020 torrential rainstorm in Japan from July 3 to July 31, 2020 (hereafter, the Kumamoto torrential rainstorm disaster)[4]. This disaster caused extensive damage, mainly in the Kyushu region, where 84 people died. The data source used was 9,206 Japanese-language tweets about the July 2020 torrential rain collected from Twitter, which was manually verified for content after eliminating retweets and tweets with duplicate content. In addition, among news articles reported during the same period, articles containing "Kumamoto torrential rainstorm disaster" in the title were extracted from the Mainichi Shimbun Article Search Service[5]. As a result, 271 articles were extracted. Then, nouns, adjectives, and adverbs for analysis and generated word variance representations were extracted using the Japanese Wikipedia entity vector[6]. The data were analyzed by Mecab (Ver. 0.996) [17], a mor phological analysis engine for Japanese, and mecab-ipadic-NEologd (Ver. 0.0.7)[7], a Japanese dictionary and the target words extracted. As a result, a vocabulary of 13,305 words and 7,362 words were obtained from Twitter data and news articles, respectivly.

The total number of unique words, excluding duplicates from each data source, was 17,896. The acquired words were subjected to cluster divisions using the k-means++ method for cluster numbers ranging from 2 to 70, and the progression of the sum of squared errors (SSE) was calculated. Figure 2 shows the results. Based on this figure, the elbow method was applied to estimate the optimal cluster number, revealing that a cluster number of 47 was determined to be an appropriate choice for the division.

Appropriate cluster names were then assigned to the clusters created manually. The labeling task was performed by four university students from the informatics faculty (hereafter, labeler). Thirty words were randomly selected from the acquired words classified into each cluster. Four labelers were requested to assign the most appropriate cluster name to represent words in each cluster. Words in the collected responses that were identical for two or more labelers were allowed to overlap with other clusters and were used as label names. Items that were not uniquely defined were not assigned a label name and were excluded from the analysis. Table 1 shows examples of the label names and some words included in each class. Finally, label names were assigned to 42 of the 47 clusters.

---

[4] https://www.data.jma.go.jp/kumamoto/shosai/kakusyusiryou/20200708kumamoto.pdf.

[5] https://mainichi.jp/contents/edu/maisaku/

[6] http://www.cl.ecei.tohoku.ac.jp/~m-suzuki/jawikivector.

[7] https://github.com/neologd/mecab-ipadic-neologd.

## 4.2 Analysing Disaster-Related Words Appeared

The proposal in this paper is to use multiple data sources together to build a knowledge base of disaster information, aiming at acquiring knowledge that is difficult to obtain from a single data source. To verify the proposal's validity, it is necessary to experimentally demonstrate that the nature of the information obtained from different data sources is different and that by using them together, information that cannot be obtained from a single data source can be collected. To verify the proposal, we observed the text acquired from each data source and assigned labels to them qualitatively. We compared their composition ratios to observe whether there was a difference in the type of information acquired across data sources.

First, to observe what kind of information each data source contained, we divided the data sources and assigned each sentence a classification label based on its textual content (hereafter, sentence label). For this process, we divided the tweet data into sentences, and the news article data was divided based on the punctuation points.

The nine sentence labels assigned are "disaster information," "traffic information," "support information," "human damage reports," "weather & warning information," "physical damage reports," "evacuation information," and "others." Table 2 shows the criteria for the assignment of sentence labels. To clarify whether there is a difference in the expression of disaster information among data sources, the composition ratio of the assigned sentence labels was compared among the data sources. Finally, we validated 30 news articles (including 426 sentences) and 1436 tweets for about 10% of the data used to build the lexical set.

Figure 3 shows the composition ratios of sentence labels assigned to each data source. The top 5% of all the sentences in each data source were labeled "support information," "human damage report," and "physical damage report" for the news articles group, and "disaster information," "human damage report," and "evacuation information" for the tweets group.

**Table 2.** Labels attached to the sentences and their criteria.

| Label | Contents |
|---|---|
| disaster information | an overview of the disaster, such as an outline of the disaster. |
| traffic information | public transportation and the availability of public roads |
| support information | relief supplies and volunteers |
| human damage reports | injuries, isolation, and other damage caused by the disaster |
| weather & warning information | weather information and warnings issued or lifted |
| physical damage reports | damage to homes and public facilities |
| evacuation information | evacuation centers, evacuees and evacuation status |
| others | contents that fall outside the above categories. |

Next, we analyzed the relationship between sentence labels and each cluster to reveal the differences in word characteristics between data sources. We calculated the proportion of words corresponding to each cluster for each data source, normalized the number of corresponding words by the number of sentences, and then calculated the differences between data sources. The calculated results are presented in Table 3. Larger values indicate a higher frequency of vocabulary usage in tweets for the corresponding cluster,

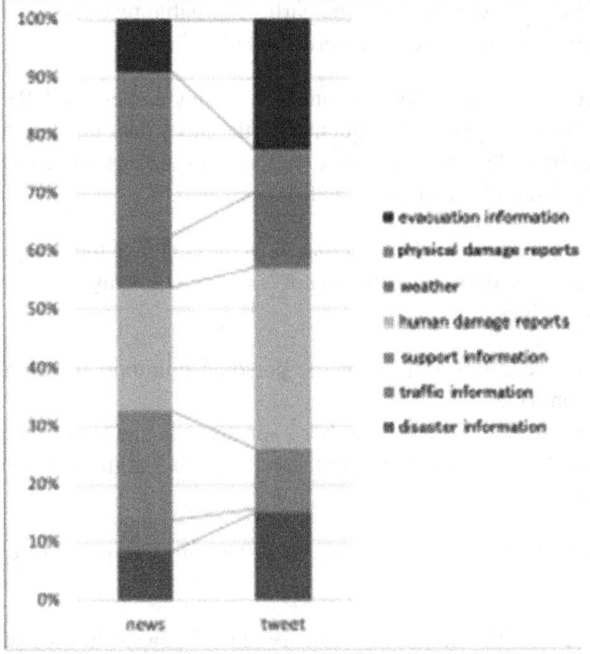


**Fig. 3.** Sentence label composition ratio among data resources.

while smaller values suggest a higher frequency of vocabulary usage in news articles. Based on this data, we qualitatively examined items falling within the 3-σ range of the standard deviation of the calculated results and considered the observed features unique to each data source.

**Table 3.** An excerpt of correlation biases between word cluster labels and disaster categories.

| label | abbreviations | mood | Kanji | operation | number |
|---|---|---|---|---|---|
| disaster information | 0.4561 | 0.2578 | 0.1533 | 0.0847 | -0.1602 |
| traffic information | 0.4167 | **-0.5000** | **0.6667** | **0.5833** | -0.1667 |
| support information | **0.6282** | 0.3034 | -0.0557 | 0.0420 | **-0.4164** |
| human damage reports | 0.4397 | -0.0071 | -0.1773 | 0.0780 | **-0.6809** |
| weather & wearing information | 0.2076 | 0.0466 | 0.1076 | 0.1746 | -0.3788 |
| physical damage reports | 0.4542 | 0.2997 | 0.2502 | 0.2890 | -0.3819 |
| evacuation information | 0.2392 | -0.1353 | -0.1275 | 0.2490 | **-0.5245** |
| ohers | 0.2254 | 0.1056 | 0.0230 | -0.0149 | -0.1874 |

Words in the cluster labeled "abbreviation" were frequently found in the tweet data labeled "support information:" The words in the "abbreviation" cluster were observed in 34 of the 47 sentences labeled "support information." An example sentence is as follows:

"KDDI and Okinawa Cellular are implementing support measures for customers in areas where the Disaster Relief Law has been applied due to the recent heavy rains in Kyushu. We sincerely hope for the earliest possible restoration of operations. For more information, please click here → [URL]"

These sentences included abbreviations of company names and URLs. Words in the cluster labeled "mood" appeared frequently in the news data labeled "traffic information:" The words in the "mood" were observed in 10 of the 12 sentences labeled "Traffic Information." An example sentence is as follows:

"When the reporter entered the Issachi area in the center of the village, which had become inaccessible due to the severing of National Highway 219 and other roads, he was left speechless."

In these sentences, descriptions of the personal opinions and impressions of the describer were confirmed.

Words in the cluster labeled "number" appeared in the news data labeled "support information," "human damage report," and "evacuation information:" An example sentence is as follows:

"The number of evacuees has risen to 2,099 in four prefectures, including Kumamoto."

In these sentences, the number of evacuees and damaged houses were included in the sentence.

## 5 Discussion

In the experiment in the previous chapter, we obtained disaster information from two different data sources and compared their contents to clarify "whether it is possible to obtain disaster information of different nature from multiple data sources" and "how the obtained disaster information differs among data sources." The differences in the composition of the sentence labels indicate that the nature of the disaster information available among the data sources is different. The results show that news articles provide mainly information on relief and material damage, while tweets provide information on general disasters and evacuation. This result indicates that the type of knowledge stored in each web service is different, meaning that by using multiple resources together to build a knowledge base of disaster information, it is possible to acquire knowledge that cannot be acquired with a single resource. The analysis of lexical features among data sources revealed that each data source has its characteristic descriptions. In particular, a comparison of data labeled "traffic information" suggested that the available information differs among the resources, even when the same label is used. This result indicates that the same event contains references from different perspectives. This result indicates that, when searching for disaster information, it is essential to use different data sources according to the problem to be solved.

This method has the limitation that it cannot be used for content that includes other modalities, such as images and videos. Especially for tweet data, we often observe references to other URLs or postings that assume the user is viewing the attached image.

By considering methods for acquiring knowledge from such complex information, the construction of a more practical knowledge base should be considered. In addition, the data in this paper was extracted based only on the period and key words, but it includes automatic posting by bots and reportage articles. In building a knowledge base, constructing a knowledge base with less noise should be considered by combining more advanced data cleansing methods.

## 6 Conclusion

This study aimed to facilitate access to disaster information by constructing a knowledge base on disaster information. It examined the significance of constructing a knowledge base using multiple data sources. Textual data were obtained from two different data sources, and the differences in the knowledge obtained from each data source were analyzed using word embedding and clustering. The analysis revealed that the composition of the available data differs between the data sources and that the knowledge acquired differs between the data sources, even for references to the same event. These results suggest the appropriateness of using multiple data sources on the Web to build a knowledge base of disaster information. It also suggests that it is possible to supplement the knowledge acquired from a single data source with information from different perspectives.

## References

1. Yamada, S., Utsu, K., Uchida, O.:"An analysis of tweets during the 2018 osaka north earthquake in japan -a brief report. In: 2018 5th International Confer ence on Information and Communication Technologies for Disaster Management (ICT-DM), pp. 1–5 (2018)
2. Houston, J.B., et al.: Social media and disasters: a functional framework for social media use in disaster planning, response, and research. Disasters **39**(1), 1–22 (2015)
3. Gerald, M., Yamamoto, L.: Flood disaster management system for situation awareness and response using twitter data. In: Sasaki, J., Murayama, Y., Velev, D., Zlateva, P. (eds.) Information Technology in Dis aster Risk Reduction, pp. 35–48. Springer International Publishing, Cham (2022)
4. Cui, Q., Shoyama, K., Hanashima, M., Usuda, Y.: Early estimation of heavy rain damage at the municipal level based on time-series analysis of sns information. J. Disaster Res. **17**(6), 944–955 (2022)
5. Alexander, D.E.: Social media in disaster risk reduction and crisis management. Sci. Eng. Ethics **20**(3), 717–733 (2014)
6. Chair, S., Charrad, M., Saoud, N.B.B.: Towards a social media-based framework for disaster communication. Proc. Comput. Sci. **164**, 271–278 (2019)
7. Ishii, T., Nakayama, H., Onuma, R., Kaminaga, H., Miyadera, Y., Nakamura, S.: A framework for promoting the experience of novices in examining articles that alert dangers of disaster on social media. Int. Conf. Comput. Sci. Comput. Intell. (CSCI) **2022**, 2081–2085 (2022)
8. Mizuno, J., et al.: "WISDOM X, DISAANA and D-SUMM: Large-scale nlp systems for analyzing textual big data. In: Proceedings of COLING 2016, the 26th Interna tional Conference on Computational Linguistics: System Demonstrations, pp. 263–267 (2016)

9. Morino, Y., Matsushita, M.: "Investigation of contamination by entertainment content in disaster information gathering. In: Information Processing Society of Japan, Special Interest Group on Entertainment Computing (IPSJ-SIGEC), vol. 2022-EC-65, no. 33, pp. 1–2 (2022, in Japanese)
10. Alajmi, B.M., Khalil, O.: The extent of and motivation for disaster informa tion seeking behavior via social networking sites. J. Electron. Resour. Librariansh.Resour. Librariansh. **34**(3), 219–244 (2022)
11. Tapia, A., Bajpai, K., Jansen, J. and Yen, J.: "Seeking the trustworthy tweet: Can microblogged data fit the information needs of disaster response and humanitarian relief organizations. In: Proceedings of the 8th International ISCRAM Conference, January 2011
12. Yasuo, M., Kitamura, S., Matsushita, M.: "Basic study on information sharing system for gathering damage situation in large scale disaster. In: Proceedings of Human Communication Symposium 2018, no. B-6–2 (2018, in Japanese)
13. Magno., G., Almeida, V.: "Measuring international online human values with word embeddings. ACM Trans. Web. **16**(2), 1–38 (2021)
14. Park, S.-T., Liu, C.: A study on topic models using lda and word2vec in travel route recommendation: focus on convergence travel and tours reviews. Pers. Ubiquit. Comput.Ubiquit. Comput. **26**(2), 429–445 (2022)
15. Paul, D., Sarkar, S., Chelliah, M., Kalyan, C., Sinai Nadkarni, P.P.: "Recom mendation of high quality representative reviews in e-commerce. In: Proceedings of the Eleventh ACM Conference on Recommender Systems. Association for Computing Machinery, pp. 311–315 (2017)
16. Han, Y., Yamanishi, R., Nishihara, Y.: "Music retrieval focusing on lyrics with summary of tourist-spot reviews based on shared word-vectors. In: 2020 International Conference on Technologies and Applications of Artificial Intelligence, pp. 73–78 (2020)
17. Kudo, T., Yamamoto, K., Matsumoto, Y.: "Applying conditional random fields to Japanese morphological analysis. In: Proceedings of the 2004 Confer ence on Empirical Methods in Natural Language Processing. Association for Computational Linguistics, pp. 230–237 (2004)

# An Improved Algorithm with Azimuth Clustering for Detecting Turning Regions on GPS Trajectories

Kuo-Si Huang[1], Yu-Chen Lin[2], Chang-Biau Yang[2], Ho-Chun Lin[3], Yung-Hsing Peng[4](✉), and Szu-Hsuan Wang[5]

[1] Department of Business Computing, National Kaohsiung University of Science and Technology, Kaohsiung, Taiwan

[2] Department of Computer Science and Engineering, National Sun Yat-Sen University, Kaohsiung, Taiwan
cbyang@cse.nsysu.edu.tw

[3] Chang Shen Tea Factory, Taoyuan, Taiwan

[4] Digital Transformation Research Institute, Institute for Information Industry, Kaohsiung, Taiwan
pengyh@iii.org.tw

[5] Myshine Technology Co., Ltd., Kaohsiung, Taiwan

**Abstract.** According to the latest report released by the Ministry of Agriculture (MOA) of Taiwan, the number of agriculture machinery in Taiwan exceeds 200,000. To keep track of these machinery, there are some research units making their efforts in devising GPS for agricultural application. Recently, Peng *et al.* proposed the turning region detection (TRD) problem for the GPS data obtained in the tea industry, which can be used to measure the working efficiency of agricultural machinery. To solve the TRD problem, Peng *et al.* tried to devise a linear time algorithm, which is easy to implement. However, the accuracy of their algorithm is far from expectation, which calls for further improvement. By adopting the concept of azimuth clustering, in this paper we propose a new algorithm for solving the TRD problem, which achieves better accuracy. The experimental results show that our new algorithm has an average accuracy 85%, which is better than the average accuracy 70% achieved with the previous algorithm. In addition, the proposed algorithm is not difficult to implement and is suitable for providing derivative services and analysis to agricultural managers in the future.

**Keywords:** GPS · Agri-machinery · Trajectory Analysis · Turning Region Detection

## 1 Introduction

In Taiwan agriculture, agricultural machinery (agri-machinery) is extremely important to farmers because of the labor shortage [3, 8, 14]. Therefore, in recent years the Taiwan government adopts a strategic raise for agri-machinery subsidies. Back to 2019, the


C.-Y. Lee et al. (Eds.): TAAI 2023, CCIS 2074, pp. 151–161, 2024.
https://doi.org/10.1007/978-981-97-1711-8_11

total subsidies for Taiwanese farmers to purchase agri-machinery was first raised from NT$50 million to NT$1,600 million, which revealed the purpose of government to help farmers. Next, an annual investment of NT$2,300 million was issued from 2022 to 2025 to support the development of intelligent and energy-saving agri-machinery, aiming to increase the international competitiveness of Taiwan agriculture. To accomplish this goal, the collaboration between enterprises and research units is of high necessity.

Briefly, the research and development for agri-machinery can be categorized into two main types, which are the hardware construction [3, 7] and the software establishment [5]. However, for the case in Taiwan, we notice that the development for agri-machinery software has not yet been widely discussed. In other words, the research for agri-machinery software remains worthy to be investigated. According to the statistics from the Ministry of Agriculture (MOA), there are more than 200,000 agri-machinery in Taiwan [8]. By using the global positioning system (GPS) [4, 12, 13], some researchers attempted to propose solutions for tracking the usage of agri-machinery, and most of them involve the techniques of data processing and computing algorithms [6, 11]. Recently, by referring to the WAGRI platform [9], Peng et al. proposed the idea of agri-machinery data bank [10], which is designed to share machine data for developing agri-machinery services in the future. In their paper, Peng et al. collaborate with domestic companies to devise a GPS tracker suitable for agri-machinery, so that the trajectories of agri-machinery can be obtained and stored in the data bank.

In the practical application of trajectories, the turning region detection (TRD) problem needs to be solved. In the TRD problem, the input is a GPS trajectory containing n points, and the output is a bit string of length n–1, where 0 and 1 denote the straight tag and turning tag for a point, respectively. One can see that by solving the TRD problem, the working efficiency of agri-machinery can then be estimated by computing the straight speed and turning speed, which is helpful for agri-machinery management. In the previous result, Peng et al. devised a linear time algorithm that is easy to implement, and then utilized the algorithm to build cloud services for the agri-enterprise Chang Shen Tea Factory (CSTF). However, they mentioned that the accuracy of their algorithm requires improvement, according to their experimental results. In this paper, we propose an improved algorithm for the TRD algorithm, which is more feasible for developing cloud services for agri-machinery. Our new algorithm adopts the concept of azimuth clustering, so that the features of turning regions can be extracted more precisely. Experimental results show that our new algorithm outperforms the previous method, with the average accuracy improved from 70% to 85%.

The organization of this paper is as follows. In Sect. 2, we provide explanations for our method, including the formal definition of TRD problem and the detailed algorithm of our azimuth clustering approach. Section 3 presents the experimental results. Finally, we give conclusions and some future studies in Sect. 4.

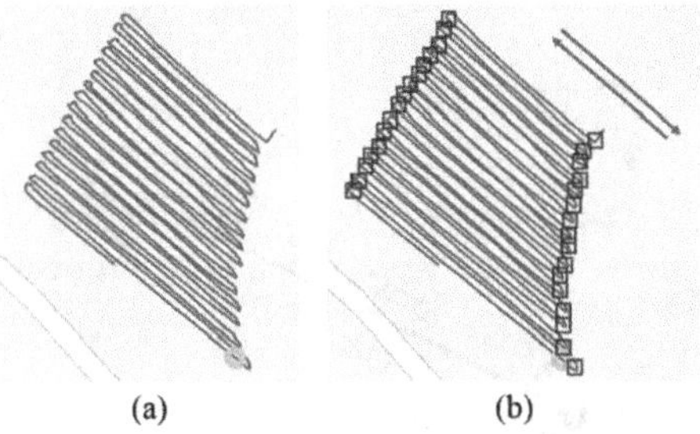


**Fig. 1.** A visual example of the sample trajectory with 3122 points in the database uploaded by the GPS tracker [10]. (a) The visualization for the machine trajectory in the red points. (b) Turning regions indicated by the blue squares. (Color figure online)

# 2 Methodology

## 2.1 GPS Trajectory and Turning Region Detection

For agricultural management, automatic collection of agricultural activities is very important when it comes to the labor shortage issue. Therefore, in previous research Peng et al. [10] devised a GPS tracker that can record and report the movement of agricultural machine. This GPS tracker adopts the u-blox NEO-M8 series module, and the tracker is available to be used in our paper. For ease of understanding, here we begin the explanations for variables. First, the GPS tracker collects the data in the form of (ID, t, lat, lon) and automatically upload the data to the server. For a record (ID, t, lat, lon), ID represents the unique identification of the GPS tracker, t refers to the recorded time of this record, lat and lon are the latitude and longitude of that corresponding location, respectively. Given a GPS trajectory containing n points, the turning region detection (TRD) problem [10] tries to output a bit-sequence of length n, where 0 and 1 denote the straight tag and turning tag for a point, respectively. Figure 1 shows a visual example of the sample trajectory with 3122 points in the database uploaded by the GPS tracker. In Fig. 1, the red points and blue squares (Fig. 1(b)) refer to the trajectory and turning regions of this machine.

Once the trajectories of working machinery are collected, we can evaluate the experience and analyze the efficiency by examining the driving behavior for straight regions and turning regions. In turning regions, newcomers would be less effective than experienced drivers. In the TRD problem, P = {p1, p2, ..., pn} denotes a trajectory of n ordered GPS points, where pi = (lati, loni), the ith point in P, composed of its latitude lati and longitude loni. Given a trajectory P, the TRD problem tries to obtain a binary sequence to indicates that if pi is in a turning region or not. In fact, if we plot the points in trajectory P on a map, one can easily identify turning regions based on this visualization. In Fig. 1(b), the blue squares are artificially marked with human examination. However, it is obviously a waste of time for human to process a large number of trajectories. Therefore, the TRD algorithm is very useful for developing automatic processing approach with computer analysis.

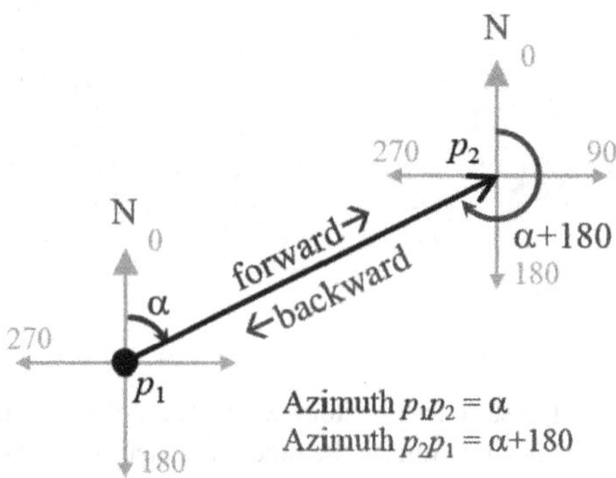


**Fig. 2.** An example of the forward and backward azimuths of $p_1p_2$, where $p_1$ and $p_2$ are the source and the destination, respectively.

### 2.2 Azimuth and Navigation

Azimuth or whole circle bearing (WCB) [2] is widely used in conjunction with the prismatic compass or the modern GPS for navigation. The azimuth, usually denoted α, is a horizontal angle measured clockwise from a north base line or meridian. It varies from 0 to 360 degrees in the clockwise direction relative to the north, where north, east, south, and west directions refer to 0, 90, 180, and 270 degrees, respectively. In addition, $p_1p_2$ means from point $p_1$ to point $p_2$, that is, $p_1$ and $p_2$ are source and destination. Figure 2 shows the forward and backward azimuths corresponding to the azimuths of $p_1p_2$ and $p_2p_1$, respectively.

In cartography, the forward azimuth of $p_1p_2$ in decimal degrees can be calculated by the cartographic coordinates of two points $p_1 = (x_1, y_1)$ and $p_2 = (x_2, y_2)$ in a flat plane as Eq. 1.

$$\alpha(p_1, p_2) = \frac{180}{\pi}\text{atan2}(x_2 - x_1, y_2 - y_1) \quad (1)$$

### 2.3 Working Direction and Displacement

On the farmland, the tea trees are planted in rows with working pathways between them. These pathways give spaces for farmers and equipment to move and operate. It can be observed that there are parallel straight lines in Fig. 1, and they follow some specific directions. We refer to these specific directions as the working azimuth $z^*$. Additionally, the forward and backward azimuths share specific departure and return pathways and we can operate along both directions. Taking Fig. 1 as an example, in the trajectory, one can observe that many segments share the two azimuths of the two green arrows in Fig. 1(b). Heavy agricultural machinery must move on the farm pathways according to the working direction $z^*$ or the complementary direction of $z^*$, otherwise it will destroy some tea trees.

The movement speed of the machine is another important indicator of its working state. A steady movement speed can indicate that it is in a normal operating state. If the movement speed is unstable, it indicates that the machine may encounter abnormal events in the tea garden, such as obstacles in the pathway, malfunctions of machine, or out of fuels. Additionally, drivers often slow down when making turns, which is a common behavior. The working speed corresponds to the displacement under a certain time between two points $p_i$ and $p_{i+1}$. Equations 2 and 3 give the haversine formula hav($p_1$, $p_2$) and its corresponding formula $\Delta(p_1, p_2)$ for calculating the displacement between $p_1 = (x_1, y_1)$ and $p_2 = (x_2, y_2)$ via their latitudes and longitudes, where 6371000 is the mean radius of the earth in meters (6371km) [2].

$$\text{hav}(p_1, p_2) = \sin^2\left(\frac{x_2 - x_1}{2}\right) + \cos(x_1) \times \cos(x_2) \times \sin^2(\frac{y_2 - y_1}{2}) \tag{2}$$

$$\Delta(p_1, p_2) = 6371000 \times 2 \times \text{atan2}(\sqrt{\text{hav}(p_1, p_2)}, \sqrt{1 - \text{hav}(p_1, p_2)}) \tag{3}$$

## 2.4 Our Algorithms

Based on the above preliminaries, the main steps of our TRD algorithm are described as follows, which is a variant and improved version of the TRD algorithm [10] proposed by Peng *et al.* Based on the output binary sequence *B*, it can be used to identify each point $p_i$ in the turning or working area. We can also compress *B* by run-length encoding to count revolutions.

**Algorithm 1** TRD: Turning Regions Detection.

**Input:** A trajectory $P=\{p_1, p_2, \ldots, p_n\}$ of *n* ordered GPS points, where $p_i=(lat_i, lon_i)$.
**Output:** A binary sequence $B=\{b_1, b_2, \ldots, b_{n-1}\}$, $b_i=1$ if $p_i$ is in a turning region.

1. Calculate the direction sequence $Z = \{z_1, z_2, \ldots, z_{n-1}\}$ with $z_i = \alpha(p_i, p_{i+1})$, where $z_i$ denotes the local moving direction from $p_i$ to $p_{i+1}$.
2. Calculate the displacement sequence $R = \{r_1, r_2, \ldots, r_{n-1}\}$ with $r_i = \Delta(p_i, p_{i+1})$, where $r_i$ denotes the local displacement from $p_i$ to $p_{i+1}$.
3. Determine the pivotal working direction $z^*$ by segment clustering in meaningful *Z* and *R*.
4. Set a threshold $\theta$. Report $b_i = 0$ if $z_i$ is close to $z^*$ within $\theta$. Otherwise, report $b_i = 1$.
5. **Return** *B*.

In Algorithm 1, Steps 1 and 2 calculate the local moving direction $z_i$ and displacement $r_i$ from $p_i$ to $p_{i+1}$, which take linear time. In order to obtain the working direction $z^*$, many algorithmic strategies in machine learning (ML), deep learning (DL) and artificial intelligence (AI) can be applied, such as linear discriminant analysis (LDA), *k*-means clustering, and decision tree [1]. Many ML and AI algorithms and strategies can be used to solve difficult problems, but they can be computationally expensive. Since Steps 1 and 2 can be done in linear time, and the input *P* of the TRD problem is a sequence, we tend to use linear time or sub-quadratic time algorithms to find the $z^*$.

In the input trajectory $P$, each $p_i = (lat_i, lon_i)$ is a pair of floating points. Note that in $Z$, each $z_i$ is a value of an azimuth limited to a range between 0 and 360, which can be transformed from trajectory $P$. One can see that it is much easier to deal with the sequence $Z$ of one-dimensional elements than the sequence $P$ of two-dimensional elements. In addition, we develop Algorithm 2 to detect the pivotal working direction $z^*$, where $z^*$ is the most frequently occurring direction in $Z$.

**Algorithm 2** zStar: Pivotal Direction Detection.

**Input:** A sequence $Z = \{z_1, z_2, \ldots, z_{n-1}\}$ of azimuth values.
**Output:** The pivotal working direction $z^*$.

1. Convert each $z_i \in Z$ to its nearest integer, obtaining the integer sequence $U = \{u_1, u_2, \ldots, u_{n-1}\}$, where $u_i$ denotes the corresponding integer of $z_i$.
2. Set $q$ buckets, then count the occurrence of azimuths in $U$ by using the buckets, and $z^*$ or its complementary will be in the bucket with most occurrences.
3. Check the most frequently occurring azimuth buckets to make $z^*$ meaningful.
4. **Return** $z^*$.

In fact, one can easily apply the modulo operation to put integers $u_i \in U$ into corresponding buckets by a single linear scan, or apply the concept of counting sort. Therefore, Algorithm 2 can be completed in O($n$) time, satisfying the linear time requirement of Algorithm 1. Due to the characteristics of farmland, such as the shape or topography of tea gardens, especially that in mountainous areas, there may be several pivotal working directions. This means that for a trajectory $P$, there may be multiple working directions of pathways existing in a tea garden. In Algorithm 2, the variables can be modified to suit the requirements of different situations.

## 3 Experiments

The experimental dataset is provided by the Chang Shen Tea Factory (CSTF), a well-known agri-enterprise in tea industry. The CSTF has won many agricultural awards from the Ministry of Agriculture, and also has a strong interest in developing smart agricultural services. With the approval of CSTF, we can analyze individual trajectories collected from machines and tea gardens. The experimental criteria and results are presented as follows.

### 3.1 Experimental Results

Based on the definition of the TRD problem, the pivotal working direction $z^*$ and the binary sequence $B$ are two main outputs in this paper. They can be used to indicate the turning and straight regions in trajectory $P$. In our experiments, we compare the number of turns for each case with the number of turns labeled by humans. This comparison can be used to evaluate the performance of related algorithms and understand gaps in practical applications.

The TRD algorithm proposed by Peng *et al.* [10] requires a threshold $\theta$ to obtain the binary sequence $B$. The threshold $\theta$ affects the result of the number of turns. There is another threshold $l$ to determine whether a possible turn can be ignored when the turning time (run length) is less than a certain limitation. According to the actual observation in the tea garden, it usually takes more than 10 s to make a normal turn. In this paper, we take the threshold $(l,\theta) = (10,5)$ to implement Peng's algorithm, which represents the best results in the previous paper [10].

In our experiments, there are 12 cases provided by the CSTF, and the first six cases are the same with those used in Peng's paper. Table 1 shows the comparison of Peng's TRD algorithm [10] and the proposed algorithm. The value in Table 2 indicates the number of turns for each test case. The value in column $\#S_H$ indicates the number of turns confirmed by manual inspection. In other words, the values in column $\#S_H$ are the targets of the proposed algorithms. Experimental results show that the proposed algorithm outperforms the previous TRD algorithm. More precisely, the proposed algorithm has an average accuracy 85%, better than the average accuracy 70% achieved with previous algorithm.

**Table 1.** Comparison of experimental results with 12 cases, where TRD (5,10) represents the TRD algorithm [10] with $(l,\theta) = (5,10)$.

| Cases | Length $n = \|P\|$ | $\#S_H$ (obj.) | TRD (5,10) [10] | Our Algorithm |
|---|---|---|---|---|
| (1) | 3122 | 32 | 26 | 32 |
| (2) | 4061 | 26 | 22 | 24 |
| (3) | 6039 | 37 | 63 | 30 |
| (4) | 7241 | 80 | 100 | 86 |
| (5) | 5309 | 46 | 33 | 53 |
| (6) | 4192 | 19 | 50 | 30 |
| (7) | 3868 | 64 | 58 | 61 |
| (8) | 2651 | 40 | 45 | 45 |
| (9) | 3427 | 10 | 33 | 11 |
| (10) | 3762 | 45 | 56 | 41 |
| (11) | 2201 | 8 | 28 | 9 |
| (12) | 5156 | 21 | 46 | 23 |

### 3.2 Visualization from Trajectory to Azimuth

In order to present the azimuth effect in the visualization, we take Fig. 3 to show the azimuth sequence $Z$ of Case (1), where Case (1) has 3122 points with azimuth values between 0 to 360. It is not difficult to see that in the turning area, the azimuth values change greatly; while in the working pathway, the azimuth values are similar. By observing Fig. 3, we can easily conclude that there are 32 turns in Case (1).

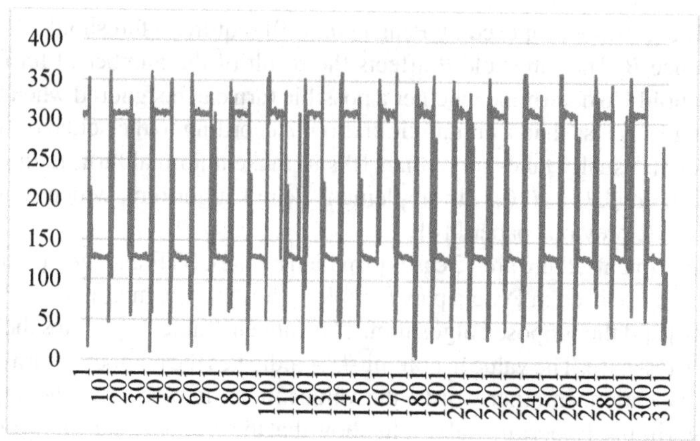

**Fig. 3.** A visualization for azimuth sequence $Z$ of Case (1), where $n = 3122$.

### 3.3 Visualization from Trajectory to Azimuth with Displacement

Figure 4 shows the azimuth sequence $Z$ of Case (2), where Case (2) has 4061 points and each $z_i \in Z$ is between 0 to 360. In the first 200 points, it is difficult to determine if each point in the area is in the turning region or not. By calculating and observing the displacement sequence $R$ associated with the local speed, we find that small displacement and low moving speeds occur in the first 200 points. The machine may be stationary while its engine is running, so the GPS may report a different position due to vibration.

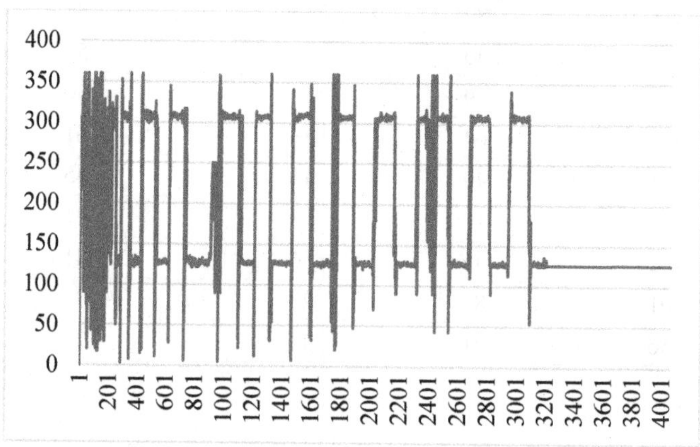

**Fig. 4.** A visualization of azimuth sequence $Z$ of Case (2), where $n = 4061$.

Figure 5 shows the azimuth sequence $Z$ and displacement sequence $R$ for each point, where it is possible that the first 200 points might be in stationary status when the engine is running. Based on the observation, we try to use the displacement sequence $R$ as an additional condition to detect turning regions. In the preliminary experiments, if $r_i < 0.2$ (m/s), we consider it is not in the working state. We design a filtering rule by combining displacement $R$ with threshold $\delta$, $(((r_i < \delta)?0:1) + ((r_i = 0)?1:0))$, and apply this rule as shown in Fig. 6. Therefore, in Fig. 6, the orange points hide some azimuth points. It can be seen that there are 23 working segments in the exposed area, so we conclude that there are 24 turns in Case (2).

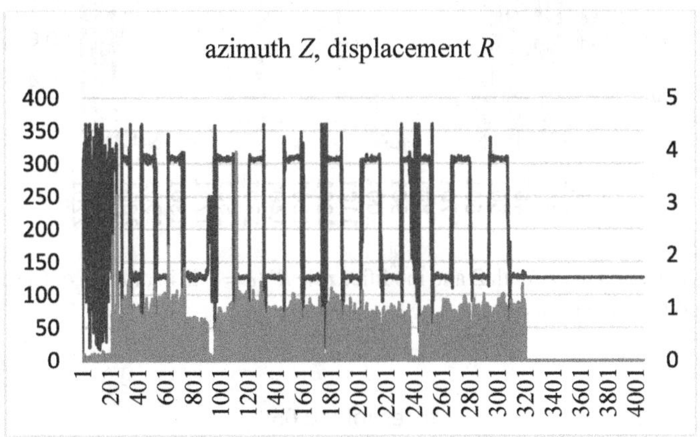


**Fig. 5.** A visualization of azimuth $Z$ and displacement sequence $R$ (meters, in red) of Case (2).

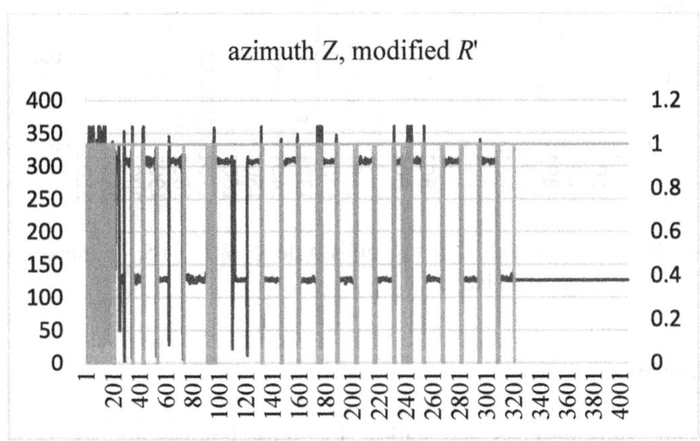


**Fig. 6.** A visualization of azimuth $Z$ and modified rule $R'$ ($\delta = 0.2$, in orange) of Case (2).

Figure 7 and 8 show the comparison of 12 cases for thresholds $\delta = 0.2$ and $\delta = 0.05$. In the visual comparison, it can be seen that the smaller threshold $\delta = 0.05$ can be used to hide more noise points, so that the points in the pathways can be easily identified.

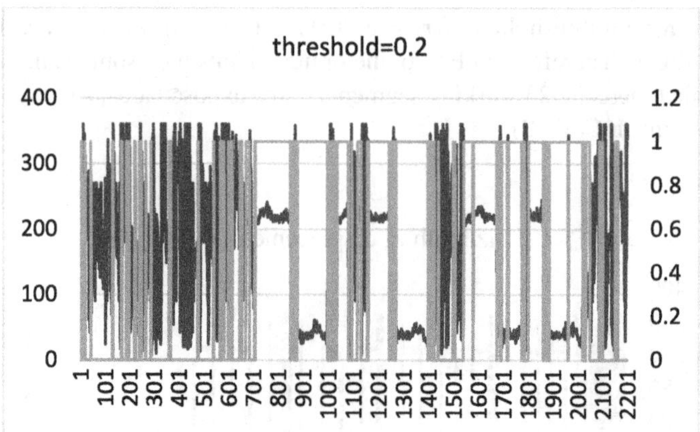


**Fig. 7.** A visualization of azimuth $Z$ and modified rule $R'$ ($\delta = 0.2$, in orange) of Case (11), where $n = 2201$. (Color figure online)

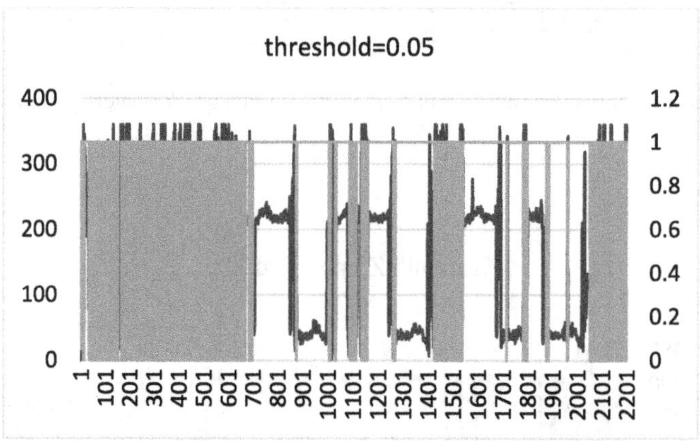


**Fig. 8.** A visualization of azimuth $Z$ and modified rule $R'$ ($\delta = 0.05$, in orange) of Case (11), where $n = 2201$. (Color figure online)

## 4 Conclusions

There are many study on GPS application. Recently, Peng *et al.* (2023) proposed the turning region detection (TRD) problem for the GPS trajectories obtained in the tea industry, which can be used to measure the working efficiency of agricultural machinery. To solve the TRD problem, Peng *et al.* tried to devise a linear time algorithm, which is easy to implement. In this paper, we take consideration of the azimuth and displacement from the original trajectory, and show that they can be used to improve the original result. By combining the azimuth and displacement of each point in the trajectory, we propose a new algorithm for the TRD problem. The experimental results show that the proposed algorithm has an average accuracy 85%, which is better than the average accuracy 70% achieved with previous algorithm. In addition, the proposed algorithm is also not difficult to implement, which is suitable for providing derivative services and analysis to agricultural managers.

There are some possible ways for future study. One may try to optimize the threshold $\delta$ with more test cases to improve the accuracy by other machine learning (ML) algorithms or strategies. In addition, we can try to design algorithms with higher complexity to obtain better results, such as the convex hull finding and pattern matching. Finally, according to the fact that our experiment involves the number of turns inspected by human, it is worthwhile to investigate and involve deep learning (DL) algorithms and artificial intelligence (AI) for future improvement.

## References


1. Alpaydın, E.: Introduction to Machine Learning. 4th edn. The MIT Press, Cambridge (2020)
2. DiBiase, D.: Nature of Geographic Information: An Open Geospatial Textbook. Pennsylvania State University, College of Earth and Mineral Sciences (2014)
3. Huang, W.Y., Liu, T.L.: The development of a new cutting machine for tea harvester. In: The Professional Report of Tea Industry in Taiwan. vol. 122, pp. 13–14, December 2022. https://www.tbrs.gov.tw/ws.php?id=4131
4. Jiang, L., Chen, C.X., Chen, C.: L2MM: learning to map matching with deep models for low-quality GPS trajectory data. ACM Trans. Knowl. Discov. Data **17**(3), 1–25 (2023)
5. Kurdi, M.M., Elzein, I.A.: Trajectory and motion for agricultural robot. In: 2022 International Conference on Decision Aid Sciences and Applications (DASA), pp. 1430–1434. Thailand, March 2022
6. Lo, S.F., Tseng, K.T., Yang, C.B., Huang, K.S.: A diagonal-based algorithm for the longest common increasing subsequence problem. Theoret. Comput. Sci. **815**, 69–78 (2020)
7. Manikandan, S., Kaliyaperumal, G., Hakak, S., Gadekallu, T.R.: Curve-aware model predictive control (C-MPC) trajectory tracking for automated guided vehicle (AGV) over on-road, in-door, and agricultural-land. Sustainability **14**(19), 12021 (2022)
8. Ministry of Agriculture, Taiwan: Taiwan Agricultural Statistics Website. https://agrstat.moa.gov.tw/sdweb/public/inquiry/InquireAdvance.aspx
9. National Agriculture and Food Research Organization (NARO), Japan: The WAGRI Platform in Japan. https://wagri.naro.go.jp/
10. Peng, Y.H., Chen, Y.H., Lin, H.C., Huang, P.C., Lee, C.P.: The development of agricultural machinery data bank with GPS as an application study. In: Proceedings of the 40th Workshop on Combinatorial Mathematics and Computation Theory (CMCT2023). Taoyuan, Taiwan, 19–20 May 2023
11. Peng, Y.H., Yang, C.B.: Finding the gapped longest common subsequence by incremental suffix maximum queries. Inf. Comput. **237**, 95–100 (2014)
12. Wang, C.Z., Kong, L.W., Jiang, J., Lai, Y.C.: Machine learning-based approach to GPS antijamming. GPS Solut. **25**(3), 115 (2021)
13. Wei, X., Wang, Y., Sun, C.: PerDet: machine-learning-based UAV GPS spoofing detection using perception data. Rem. Sens. **14**(19), 4925 (2022)
14. Wu, H.C.: Discussion on the structure of current agricultural human resources. In: The seasonal report of technical service in Taiwan Agriculture Research Institute (TARI), vol. 118, pp. 36–39, June 2019. https://scholars.tari.gov.tw/bitstream/123456789/11963/1/30-2-8.pdf

# A Pilot Study on AI-Assisted Code Generation with Large Language Models for Software Engineering

Hsiao-Chuan Liu, Chia-Tung Tsai, and Min-Yuh Day(✉)

Graduate Institute of Information Management, National Taipei University, New Taipei City, Taiwan
{s711136108,s711136106,myday}@gm.ntpu.edu.tw

**Abstract.** The field of code generation, influenced by deep learning, has become crucial in contemporary software engineering, facilitating the conversion of natural language to executable code. A noticeable knowledge gap exists, prompting an exhaustive examination of the current methodologies and innovations. The primary objective of this research is to offer a thorough literature review, illuminating the current state of deep learning-powered code generation. A rigorous systematic review was employed, wherein 28 influential papers from essential academic databases were recognized. An analytical approach was adopted to discern trends, understand the significance of numbers, and draw meaningful conclusions from the data. These papers were then analyzed using a structured methodology. The study unveils insights into large language model code generation, potentially bridging the prevailing knowledge gap and offering direction for future innovations in the domain.

**Keywords:** AI · Code Generation · Large Language Model · Software Engineering · Systematic Literature Review

## 1 Introduction

In recent years, there has been increasing attention in the software engineering field to code generation engines related to generic data processing, especially with the emergence of various deep learning and natural language processing (NLP) technologies over the past decade [5]. Through code generation technology, it's possible to produce source code in specific programming languages based on developers' natural language requirements.

The software development process has become increasingly complex, requiring advanced skills and a significant amount of time investment. Beginners face the high cost of learning multiple programming languages. At the same time, due to the complexity of software architectures, even experienced expert developers may find it challenging to read and understand the code written by their peers [11]. However, the continuous advancements in deep learning for software engineering tasks have proven that pre-trained models are particularly effective in code generation tasks [14]. For instance, the


C.-Y. Lee et al. (Eds.): TAAI 2023, CCIS 2074, pp. 162–175, 2024.
https://doi.org/10.1007/978-981-97-1711-8_12

emergence of writing tools like ChatGPT and GitHub Copilot has provided developers with higher efficiency and productivity amid these complexities.

The objective of this study is to undertake a comprehensive systematic literature review in the domain of code generation, encompassing the organization of relevant databases and models. By extensively searching four major academic databases: Scopus, IEEE Xplore, ACM Digital Library and ProQuest, we identified 28 papers closely aligned with the topic. In reviewing these papers, we aim to spotlight core issues, research methodologies, and the most recent technological breakthroughs in the domain, thereby laying a robust foundation for future research.

## 2 Methodology

To ensure the rigor of the research, this study adopted the systematic review methodology recommended in [18]. In the field of code generation, especially regarding deep learning-related studies, there are only a few papers currently conducting bibliometric or comprehensive literature discussions. To bridge this research gap, we did not limit ourselves to a single database but expanded our search to prominent academic databases like Scopus, IEEE Xplore, ACM Digital Library and ProQuest, conducting an in-depth and comprehensive literature exploration and review.

### 2.1 Planning the Review

In this systematic literature review, four sequential stages were employed: formulation of research questions, identification of pertinent bibliographic databases, determination of search criteria through specific keywords, and finally, application of the PRISMA guideline 2020 [22] to rigorously refine the extracted literature (refer to Fig. 1).

### 2.2 Research Questions

This literature review aimed to highlight current writings on technological trends in code generation and present a bibliographic exploration of the subject. In simpler terms, this study seeks to answer the following queries:

- What's the latest in the world of code generation?
- Which terms often pop up in papers about code generation?
- Which programming language is frequently associated with these models?
- What foundational structures exist in the realm of code generation?

### 2.3 Related Academic Databases

In a scholarly article examining code generation, it is essential to maintain a broad perspective to capture a holistic view of the prevailing research. Initiating the review necessitates a careful selection of databases to maximize the likelihood of identifying relevant studies in the field. The literature search was conducted using the following esteemed academic databases:

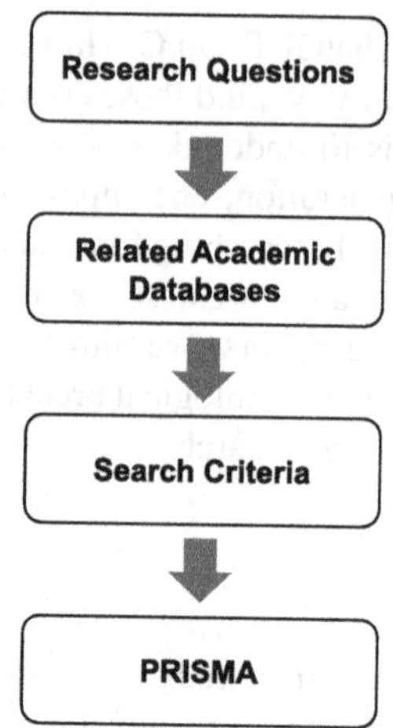


**Fig. 1.** The Planning Review of Systematic Review

- Scopus (https://www.scopus.com)
- IEEE Xplore (https://ieeexplore.ieee.org/Xplore/home.jsp)
- ACM Digital Library (https://dl.acm.org/)
- ProQuest (https://www.proquest.com/)

The selection of Scopus, IEEE Xplore, ACM Digital Library, and ProQuest was motivated by their extensive repository of works specifically related to code generation techniques and implementations.

## 2.4 Search Criteria

The current study used the main keywords, "coding," "code," "code generation," " coding assistance," "code automatic generation," "automatic programming," "pre-trained language model," "generative pre-trained transformer", "large language models," and "generative AI."

Table 1 displays our search results from the Scopus database. From this, we identified 1,262,125 articles associated with keywords related to code generation, indicating that this is an extensively broad query category. Based on these findings, we further incorporated the pre-trained language models and generative AI, which have been widely recognized in recent years, into our search criteria. In our final filtering, we specifically focused on the fields of computer science and engineering, as they are closely intertwined with code generation and AI technologies, and academically, they offer unique insights and research methodologies on this topic.

Table 2 displays our search results from the IEEE database. An initial search with coding-related keywords yielded 253,145 articles, highlighting the widespread attention coding techniques receive in academia. When we further incorporated trending AI research topics, the number of articles reduced to 72, underscoring the deep integration of AI with coding techniques. These articles not only reveal the latest developments in code generation and AI but also provide valuable direction and references for our research.

**Table 1.** Search Results – Scopus

| Set | Query String | Results |
|---|---|---|
| S1 | ( ABS ("coding") OR ABS ("code") OR ABS ("code generation") OR ABS ("coding assistance") OR ABS ("code automatic generation") OR ABS ("automatic programming")) | 1,262,125 |
| S2 | [S1] AND ( AND (TITLE-ABS-KEY ("pre-trained language model") OR TITLE-ABS-KEY ("generative ai") OR TITLE-ABS-KEY ("generative pre-trained transformer") OR TITLE-ABS-KEY ("large language models")) | 560 |
| S3 | [S2] AND (LIMIT-TO (SUBJAREA,"COMP") OR LIMIT-TO ( SUBJAREA,"ENGI"))) | 506 |

**Table 2.** Search Results - IEEE Xplore

| Set | Query String | Results |
|---|---|---|
| S1 | ("Abstract":"coding" OR "code" OR "code generation" OR "coding assistance" OR "code automatic generation" OR "automatic programming") | 253,145 |
| S2 | [S1] AND ("All Metadata": "pre-trained language model" OR "generative AI" OR "generative pre-trained transformer" OR "large language models") | 72 |

**Table 3.** Search Results - ACM Digital Library

| Set | Query String | Results |
|---|---|---|
| S1 | [[Abstract: "coding"] OR [Abstract: "code"] OR [Abstract: "code generation"] OR [Abstract: "coding assistance"] OR [Abstract: "code automatic generation"] OR [Abstract: "automatic programming"]] | 38,618 |
| S2 | [S1] AND [[Full Text: "pre-trained language model"] OR [Full Text: "generative ai"] OR [Full Text: "generative pre-trained transformer"] OR [Full Text: "large language models"]] | 243 |

Table 3 shows the results of our search in the ACM Digital Library. At first, when we looked for abstracts with our top six keywords, we found 38,618 matches. After adding terms about large language models, the number dropped to 243.

Table 4 presents the findings from our ProQuest search. We focused on 7 databases directly related to our topic, avoiding unrelated fields such as arts or social sciences. Initially, by ensuring every abstract and summary included our primary six keywords, the results tallied up to 329,249. Subsequently, by incorporating terms related to large language models, the count reduced to 1,024.

**Table 4.** Search Results - ProQuest

| Set | Query String | Results |
|---|---|---|
| S1 | SUMMARY("coding" OR "code" OR "code generation" OR "coding assistance" OR "code automatic generation" OR "automatic programming")<br>7 Databases Searched:<br>Canadian Business & Current Affairs Database<br>Coronavirus Research Database<br>Ebook Central<br>Library & Information Science Abstracts (LISA)<br>ProQuest Dissertations & Theses A&I<br>ProQuest Dissertations & Theses GlobalTrial<br>Publicly Available Content Database | 329,249 |
| S2 | [S1] AND ("pre-trained language model" OR "generative AI" OR "generative pre-trained transformer" OR "large language models") | 1,024 |

### 2.5 Prisma

During our search, we combined results from four databases. Any articles that appeared in more than one database were taken out to avoid repetition. Next, we got rid of articles that didn't fit our topic, just based on their titles. After this screening, we were left with 1,582 unique and fitting articles. In the end, we handpicked 28 articles that were closely related to our subject for a detailed look (refer to Fig. 2). Here's a breakdown of our process using the PRISMA flowchart:

1. We started with 1,845 articles from Scopus, IEEE Xplore, ACM Digital Library, and ProQuest.
2. We had 22 articles left after removing ones with unrelated titles, like "Proceedings - 2022 ACM/IEEE 44th International Conference on Software Engineering: New Ideas and Emerging Results, ICSE-NIER 2022" and "ICLR 2021 - 9th International Conference on Learning Representations."
3. After getting rid of duplicates, 1,823 articles were still in the running.
4. From these, we carefully chose and read 28 that were directly related to our study.

## 3 Literature Search Results

We analyzed data from 1,823 articles that made it through PRISMA's screening phase. In Fig. 3, there's an intersection matrix showing how the articles are spread across four databases. ProQuest has the most articles, while IEEE has the least.

### 3.1 Scopus

Scopus's collection, comprising 482 titles, overlaps with ProQuest by an impressive 17.22%. Its confluence with IEEE is recorded at 9.54% (46 titles), while with ACM, it

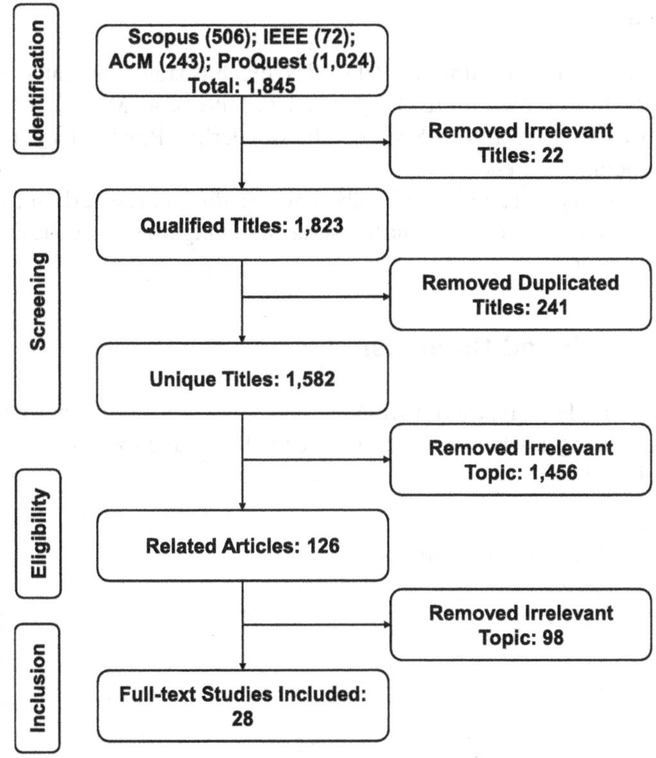


**Fig. 2.** The Search Flowchart of PRISMA for Systematic Review

stands at 8.92% (43 titles). These figures accentuate Scopus's commitment to fostering interdisciplinary research.

### 3.2 IEEE Xplore

IEEE, hosting 71 titles, demonstrates a 25.35% content overlap (18 titles) with ProQuest, emphasizing its alignment with major research trends. The database intersects with ACM at 5.63% (4 titles) and with Scopus at a rate of 64.79% (46 titles), signifying a broad coverage across technical domains.

### 3.3 ACM Digital Library

With a catalog of 243 titles, ACM's content is notably aligned with ProQuest, exhibiting a 9.47% overlap. Its intersections with IEEE and Scopus are marked at 1.65% (4 titles) and 17.70% (43 titles) respectively, showcasing ACM's pivotal role in bridging diverse research areas.

### 3.4 ProQuest

ProQuest, with a robust repository of 1017 titles, exhibits significant intersections with its counterparts. It overlaps with IEEE by 1.77% (18 titles), ACM by 2.26% (23 titles), and Scopus by 8.16% (83 titles). Such overlaps underline ProQuest's comprehensive and diverse scholarly content.

In summation, these databases not only maintain distinct scholarly niches but also demonstrate significant interdisciplinary overlaps, highlighting the cohesive nature of contemporary research.

## 4 Data Analysis and Discussion

From the 1,582 articles that passed PRISMA's screening, we carried out a data analysis. This included looking at when the articles were published and spotting commonly used keywords (Table 5).

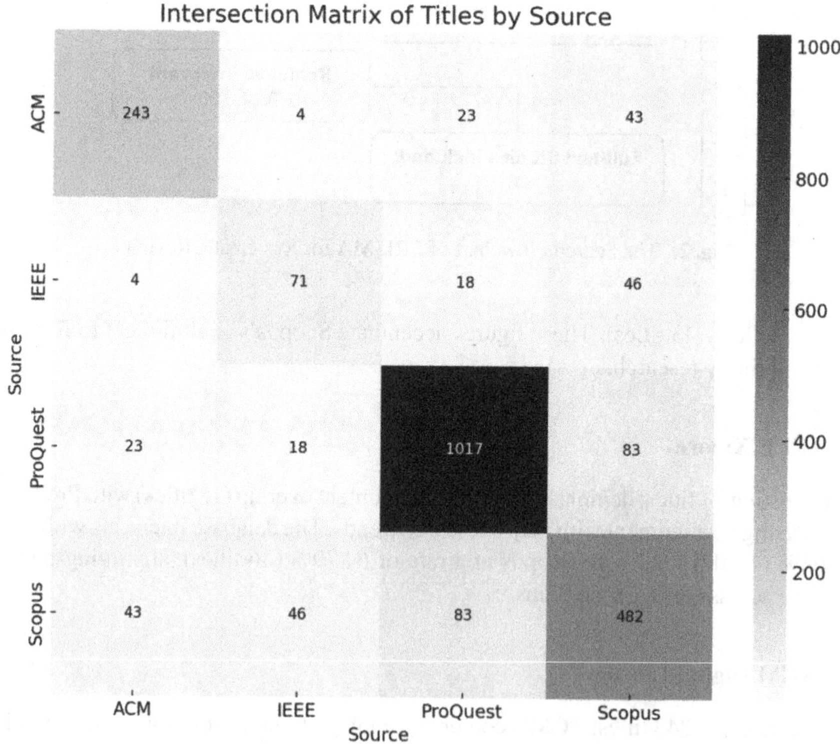


**Fig. 3.** Intersection Matrix of Titles Across Sources

**Table 5.** Code Generation Paper Types

| Document Type | Results |
|---|---|
| Working Paper | 793 |
| Conference Paper | 572 |
| Journal Article | 138 |
| Dissertation/Thesis | 59 |
| Feature | 9 |
| News | 3 |
| General Information | 2 |
| Packt Publishing eBooks | 2 |
| Review | 1 |
| Editorial | 1 |
| Magazines | 1 |

## 4.1 Distribution of the Year of Publication

Figure 4 provides a clear representation of the annual article count from 2009 to 2023. Starting from a modest number of just 1 article in 2009, there has been a significant growth in publications over the years. The most striking jump can be observed between 2022 and 2023, where the count surged from 371 to 1039 articles. This substantial increase might indicate a heightened interest or significant advancements in the field during that period. Despite the gradual rise in certain years, the overall trajectory showcases a pronounced upward trend, implying the increasing relevance and exploration of the subject matter.

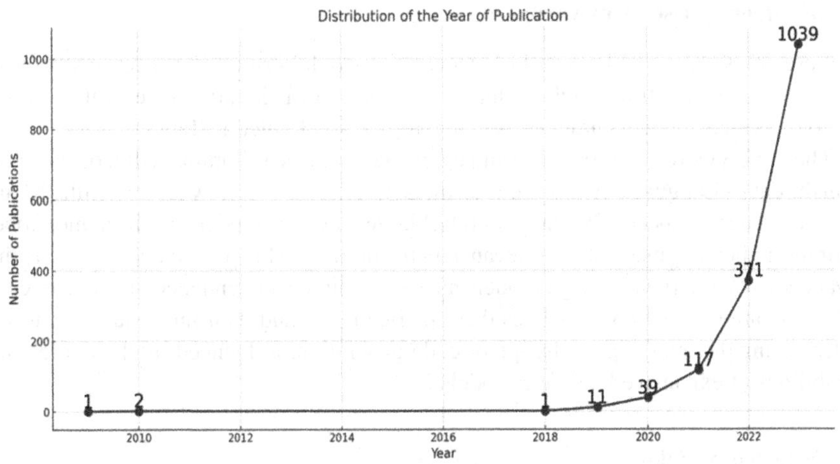


**Fig. 4.** Publication Year Distribution of Code Generation

## 4.2 Publication Types

The analysis of documents on code generation reveals a dominant presence of "Working Papers", accounting for a significant 50.13% of the total. This suggests that the topic is in its emergent phase, with many researchers sharing preliminary findings. "Conference Papers", contributing to 36.16%, further confirm the field's novelty, as conferences often serve as platforms for introducing new ideas. Traditional "Journal Articles" make up only 8.66%, hinting at the topic's recent emergence. The presence of "Dissertation/Thesis" at 3.73% indicates academic interest at the student level. The lower percentages for "Feature" and "Review" suggest the topic's infancy in broader discussions.

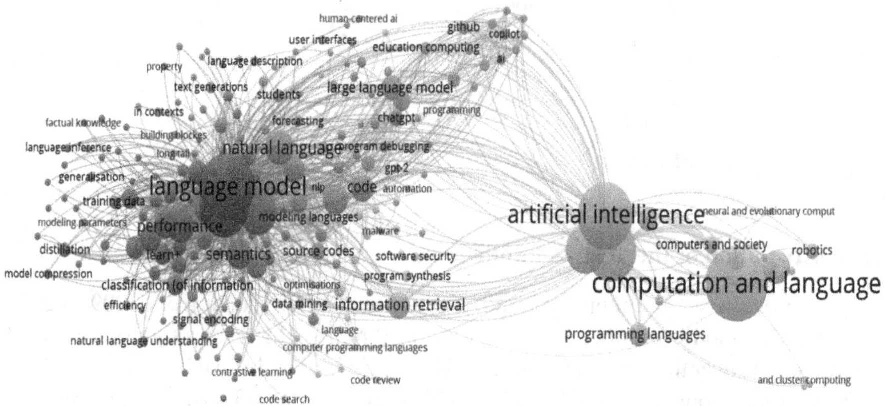


**Fig. 5.** Keyword Co-occurrences of Code Generation Articles

## 4.3 Frequently Used Keywords

The research scrutinized keyword co-occurrences to discern interconnections between terms in code generation articles. Out of 1,041 keywords identified, several stood out due to their recurrent appearances, with the top 10 spotlighted in Table 6.

The top keyword, "computation and language", echoes its dominant 466 occurrences from the data. "Language model" and "artificial intelligence" follow closely with 381 and 376 occurrences respectively. Interestingly, "large language model" has been mentioned 54 times, indicating its growing relevance in the domain. This prominence suggests that advancements in large language models have streamlined and enhanced the accuracy of code generation. Figure 5 visualizes these pivotal terms and their interrelations, further underscoring the evolving landscape of code generation, influenced by the burgeoning capabilities of expansive language models.

## 4.4 Selected Articles

In our literature review, we specifically examined datasets related to code generation. Table 8 lists the main datasets used in this field in recent years. From the table, these

**Table 6.** Frequently Used Keywords

| Keywords | Occurrences |
|---|---|
| computation and language | 466 |
| language model | 381 |
| artificial intelligence | 376 |
| computational linguistics | 307 |
| machine learning | 301 |
| software engineering | 187 |
| natural language processing | 168 |
| natural language | 102 |
| computer vision and pattern recognition | 94 |
| performance | 93 |

datasets mainly focus on the Python and Java programming languages. In particular, MultiPL-E [21], SOEval [23], ClassEval [19], and xCodeEval [13] were all released during this period, highlighting the active research in this domain.

It is worth noting that the SOEval dataset not only has 1,151 samples but is also open-source, providing researchers with a public link for access. Additionally, the APPS dataset, with 10,000 samples, is an ideal choice for large-scale research due to its vast sample size.

xCodeEval [13] is a massive dataset containing over 165B samples, covering more than 17 programming languages. The Stack [8] dataset is even more impressive, with a size reaching 3.1TB, covering over 300 programming languages. Meanwhile, The Vault [10] focuses on JavaScript, Java, and Python, boasting up to 40M samples.

Regarding licenses, most datasets allow commercial use, but the licensing agreements vary. For example, MultiPL-E adopts the BSD 3-Clause License but introduces restrictions on machine learning. In contrast, HumanEval, ClassEval, and APPS have opted for the more lenient MIT License.

Table 7 lists the primary models for code generation. PyCodeGPT [15] is based on the GPT-2 architecture and utilizes the CodeSearchNet [32] dataset for Python and Java. CodeT5 + (zero-shot) [31] is built on the T5 framework and covers multiple programming languages. Both Codex [1] and OctoGeeX [25] are trained on Python data from GitHub. PanGu-Coder2 [17] employs the PanGu-alpha structure and is trained on GitHub's Python data. Reflexion [20] uses the GPT-4 framework, while both phi-1-base [21] and Wizard-Coder [24] focus on Python. These models showcase the diversity and development trends in code generation technology.

**Table 7.** Code Generation Datasets

| Ref | Datasets | Year | Sample Size | Programming Language | Commercial Use | License |
|---|---|---|---|---|---|---|
| [1] | HumanEval | 2021 | 164 | Python | Yes | MIT License |
| [3] | APPS | 2021 | 10000 | Python | Yes | MIT License |
| [6] | PyTorrent | 2021 | - | Python | Yes | Only publicly available records of Python packages |
| [8] | The Stack | 2022 | 3.1TB | Over 300 | Yes | MIT or Apache 2.0 licenses |
| [10] | The Vault | 2023 | 40M | JavaScript/Java/Python | Yes | MIT license |
| [13] | xCodeEval | 2023 | 16.5B | Over 17 | Yes | CC BY-NC 4.0 license |
| [16] | Code4ML | 2023 | 2.5M | Python | Yes | Apache 2.0 license |
| [19] | ClassEval | 2023 | 100 | Python | Yes | MIT License |
| [21] | MultiPL-E | 2023 | 164 | Over 18 | Yes | BSD 3-Clause License with Machine Learning Restriction |
| [23] | SOEval | 2023 | 1151 | Python/ Java | Yes | It is open-source and publicly available at this link |

**Table 8.** Code Generation Models

| Ref | Model | Parameter | Backbone | Year | Pretrained Dataset | Size of Dataset | Programming Language |
|---|---|---|---|---|---|---|---|
| [1] | Codex | 12B | GPT-3 | 2021 | Python from GitHub | 100G | P, C + +, J, JS, Go |
| [2] | PolyCoder | 2.7B | GPT-2 | 2022 | Multi-Lingual Corpus | 249G | C, C#, C + +, Go, J, JS, PHP, P, R, Rust, Scala, TypeScript |

*(continued)*

**Table 8.** (*continued*)

| Ref | Model | Parameter | Backbone | Year | Pretrained Dataset | Size of Dataset | Programming Language |
|---|---|---|---|---|---|---|---|
| [4] | GPT-3.5 | - | GPT-3 | 2022 | - | - | P, C, C + +, J, JS, Go, Julia. Perl, R, Ruby, Smalltalk |
| [7] | PaLM | 540B | PaLM | 2022 | - | - | P |
| [9] | MarianCG | - | MarianMT | 2022 | CoNaLa and DJANGO | - | P, J |
| [12] | CodeMaster | - | CodeT5 | 2022 | - | - | P, J |
| [15] | PyCodeGPT | 110M | GPT-2 | 2022 | Python and Java from CodeSearchNet | 1.1M | P |
| [17] | PanGu-Coder2 15B | 317M/2.6B | PanGu-alpha | 2023 | Python from GitHub | 147G | P |
| [20] | Reflexion | - | GPT-4 | 2023 | - | - | P |
| [21] | phi-1-base | 1.3B | - | 2023 | Subset of The Stack and StackOverflow | 7B | P |
| [24] | WizardCoder | 15B | StarCoder | 2023 | - | 1T | P |
| [25] | OctoGeeX | 6B | - | 2023 | Python from GitHub | - | P, JS, J, Go, C + +, Rust |
| [26] | Code Llama | 34B | Llama-2 | 2023 | Proprietary dataset | - | Python |
| [27] | CodeGeeX | 13B | GPT | 2023 | Python from GitHub | 158B | 23 languages |
| [28] | CodeGen | 16.1B | - | 2023 | - | - | |
| [29] | SantaCoder | 1.1B | GPT-2 | 2023 | subset of The Stack | 268G | P, J, JS |
| [30] | StarCoder | 15B | StarCoder-base | 2023 | The Stack | 35B | 80 languages |
| [31] | CodeT5 + | 16B | T5 | 2023 | CodeSearchNet and C/C# datasets | 52B | R, JS, GO, P, J, PHP, C, C# |

Initials: P: Python, J: Java, JS: JavaScript, R: Ruby.

## 5 Conclusion

This study embarked on the critical endeavor of charting the landscape of code generation, particularly emphasizing the transformative role of deep learning technologies. Through an exhaustive review, 28 seminal papers were identified, revealing core challenges, methodologies, and state-of-the-art innovations in the realm of software engineering and automated programming. These findings underscore the potential of large language models, offering a new frontier for developers and researchers alike. The significance of this research is multifaceted; not only does it provide a consolidated foundation for academics, but it also holds profound implications for the future trajectory of software development practices. However, it's essential to recognize the inherent limitations of this study, particularly its reliance on select academic databases, which may inadvertently omit other pivotal works in the field. While the contributions made are substantial, it is paramount to interpret the findings within this context of potential selection bias. Given the rapid advancements in the domain, there's a pressing need for continuous reviews, encompassing a broader spectrum of sources and further diving into the evolving methodologies and tools in code generation.

**Acknowledgments.** This research was supported in part by the National Science and Technology Council (NSTC), Taiwan, under grants MOST 110–2410-H-305–013-MY2 and NSTC 112- 2425-H-305–002-, and National Taipei University (NTPU), Taiwan under grants 112-NTPU-ORDA-F-003, 112- NTPU-ORDA-F-004, and NTPU-112A513E01.

## References

1. Chen, M., et al.: Evaluating large language models trained on code. arXiv preprint arXiv: 2107.03374 (2021)
2. Xu, F.F., Alon, U., Neubig, G., Hellendoorn, V.J.: A systematic evaluation of large language models of code. In: Proceedings of the 6th ACM SIGPLAN International Symposium on Machine Programming, pp. 1–10 (2022)
3. Hendrycks, D., et al.: Measuring coding challenge competence with APPS. CoRR abs/2105.09938, arXiv preprint arXiv:2105.09938 (2021)
4. Buscemi, A.: A comparative study of code generation using ChatGPT 3.5 across 10 programming languages. arXiv preprint arXiv:2308.04477 (2023)
5. Yin, P., Neubig, G.: A syntactic neural model for general-purpose code generation. arXiv preprint arXiv:1704.01696 (2017)
6. Bahrami, M., et al.: Pytorrent: a python library corpus for large-scale language models. arXiv preprint arXiv:2110.01710 (2021)
7. Chowdhery, A., et al.: Palm: scaling language modeling with pathways. arXiv preprint arXiv: 2204.02311 (2022)
8. Kocetkov, D., et al.: The stack: 3 TB of permissively licensed source code. arXiv preprint arXiv:2211.15533 (2022)
9. Soliman, A.S., Hadhoud, M.M., Shaheen, S.I.: MarianCG: a code generation transformer model inspired by machine translation. J. Eng. Appl. Sci. **69**(1), 1–23 (2022)
10. Manh, D.N., et al.: The vault: a comprehensive multilingual dataset for advancing code understanding and generation. arXiv preprint arXiv:2305.06156 (2023)
11. Shin, J., Nam, J.: A survey of automatic code generation from natural language. J. Inf. Process. Syst. **17**(3), 537–555 (2021)
12. Yu, T., Gu, X., Shen, B.: Code question answering via task-adaptive sequence-to-sequence pre-training. In: 2022 29th Asia-Pacific Software Engineering Conference (APSEC), pp. 229–238. IEEE (2022)
13. Khan, M.A.M., Bari, M.S., Do, X.L., Wang, W., Parvez, M.R., Joty, S.: xCodeEval: a large scale multilingual multitask benchmark for code understanding, generation, translation and retrieval. arXiv preprint arXiv:2303.03004 (2023)

14. Yang, Z., Chen, S., Gao, C., Li, Z., Li, G., Lv, R.: Deep learning based code generation methods: a literature review. arXiv preprint arXiv:2303.01056 (2023)
15. Zan, D., et al.: CERT: continual pre-training on sketches for library-oriented code generation. arXiv preprint arXiv:2206.06888 (2022)
16. Drozdova, A., Trofimova, E., Guseva, P., Scherbakova, A., Ustyuzhanin, A.: Code4ML: a large-scale dataset of annotated Machine Learning code. PeerJ Comput. Sci. **9**, e1230 (2023)
17. Shen, B., et al.: PanGu-Coder2: boosting large language models for code with ranking feedback. arXiv preprint arXiv:2307.14936 (2023)
18. Tranfield, D., Denyer, D., Smart, P.: Towards a methodology for developing evidence-informed management knowledge by means of systematic review. Br. J. Manag.Manag. **14**(3), 207–222 (2003)
19. Du, X., et al.: ClassEval: a manually-crafted benchmark for evaluating LLMs on class-level code generation. arXiv preprint arXiv:2308.01861 (2023)
20. Shinn, N., Cassano, F., Labash, B., Gopinath, A., Narasimhan, K., Yao, S.: Reflexion: language agents with verbal reinforcement learning. arXiv preprint arXiv:2303.11366 (2023)
21. Cassano, F., et al.: MultiPL-E: a scalable and polyglot approach to benchmarking neural code generation. IEEE Trans. Softw. Eng.Softw. Eng. **49**(7), 3675–3691 (2023). https://doi.org/10.1109/TSE.2023.3267446
22. Gunasekar, S., et al.: Textbooks are all you need. arXiv preprint arXiv:2306.11644 (2023)
23. Page, M.J., et al.: The PRISMA 2020 statement: an updated guideline for reporting systematic reviews. Int. J. Surg. **88**, 105906 (2021)
24. Siddiq, M.L., Casey, B., Santos, J.: A lightweight framework for high-quality code generation. arXiv preprint arXiv:2307.08220 (2023)
25. Luo, Z., et al.: WizardCoder: empowering code large language models with evol-instruct. arXiv preprint arXiv:2306.08568 (2023)
26. Muennighoff, N., et al.: OctoPack: instruction tuning code large language models. arXiv preprint arXiv:2308.07124 (2023)
27. Rozière, B., et al.: Code llama: open foundation models for code. arXiv preprint arXiv:2308.12950 (2023)
28. Zheng, Q., et al.: CodeGeeX: a pre-trained model for code generation with multilingual benchmarking on HumanEval-X. In: Proceedings of the 29th ACM SIGKDD Conference on Knowledge Discovery and Data Mining, pp. 5673–5684 (2023)
29. Nijkamp, E., et al: Codegen: an open large language model for code with multi-turn program synthesis. arXiv preprint arXiv:2203.13474 (2022)
30. Allal, L.B., et al: SantaCoder: don't reach for the stars! arXiv preprint arXiv:2301.03988 (2023)
31. Li, R., et al.: StarCoder: may the source be with you! arXiv preprint arXiv:2305.06161 (2023)
32. Wang, Y., Le, H., Gotmare, A.D., Bui, N.D., Li, J., Hoi, S.C.: Codet5+: open code large language models for code understanding and generation. arXiv preprint arXiv:2305.07922 (2023)
33. Zheng, Q., et al.: Codegeex: a pre-trained model for code generation with multilingual evaluations on humaneval-x. arXiv preprint arXiv:2303.17568 (2023)

# A System to Display the Intention Behind Shogi AI's Move as a Series of Reading Sequences

Shun Okuhama(✉) and Takeshi Ito

The University of Electro-Communications, Chofu Tokyo 182-8585, Japan
o2231027@gl.cc.uec.ac.jp, taito@mbc.nifty.com

**Abstract.** In recent years, Shogi AI has reached a level far beyond that of humans. As a result, it has become difficult to understand the meaning of Shogi AI moves. In this study, we propose a system that highlights the aim of a natural move by displaying the reading of the move. In order to achieve a natural move, the tuned AI was trained to select a move that is easy for amateurs with the highest playing population rating to choose. This allowed the system to represent the intention of a particular move as a series of reading sequences.

**Keywords:** Shogi AI · Deep Learning · Intention of Moves

## 1 Introduction

Thanks to advances in hardware and machine learning methods, Shogi AI reached a level close to that of professional players in the 2010s [1, 2], and around 2015, Yoshiyuki Kotani showed by objective measures that it outperformed top human players by statistically analyzing the results of games against professional players [3]. In 2017, Ponanza won two consecutive games against then Meijin Amahiko Sato, proving that Shogi AI was at a level beyond humans. Since then, the Shogi AI Strength competitions have continued and become stronger every year. Furthermore, more and more programs are incorporating deep reinforcement learning techniques and are now reaching a level far beyond human tops [4]. As a result, the moves made by Shogi AI are sometimes beyond human comprehension, making it difficult to understand their meaning. A method is needed to explain the meaning of Shogi AI moves in an easy-to-understand way.

This research purpose to facilitate the understanding of difficult Shogi AI moves for humans. Shogi commentaries often promote understanding by showing the successful sequential of moves that follow the move to demonstrate the merits of a move. Therefore, we propose a method that mimics this technique to aid understanding by showing the successful sequential of moves.

## 2 Related Works

One of the reasons why Shogi AI is challenging for humans to understand is the difference in thinking between humans and Shogi AI. Ito's research comparing the differences between human and Shogi AI thinking can be cited [5]. Ito showed the same game to


C.-Y. Lee et al. (Eds.): TAAI 2023, CCIS 2074, pp. 176–186, 2024.
https://doi.org/10.1007/978-981-97-1711-8_13

a human and a Shogi AI and compared their thinking processes. He pointed out that Shogi AI performs a massive tree search to find the next move, while humans discover it intuitively based on the overall view. Shogi AI moves are often said to be "intuitively difficult to play," which is thought to be due to this difference in thought process. While Shogi AI discovers the next move based on a vast, unreadable search, humans tend to think intuitively, narrowing down activities and, therefore, tend to need help thinking of candidate moves that are difficult to play intuitively.

On the other hand, some studies suggest that Shogi is a game that places more emphasis on search than Go. Takahashi conducted a study investigating the recognition process of Shogi and Igo game positions [6]. It was found that the more experienced players become, the fewer eye movements they make when recognizing game situations in Shogi compared to Go. This indicates that professional Shogi players can recognize game situations instantly and that their primary thought process is carried out by searching. This suggests that to understand the meaning of a move in Shogi, it is necessary to represent the move itself and the expected state of the board.

One of the studies that attempted to annotate Shogi game records automatically is the work of Kaneko [7]. In this research, we analyzed the game records of professional Shogi players using GPS Shogi, an open-source program, and built a system to post the readings of the game on Twitter. The evaluation results of the 27 publicly broadcast games showed that more than half of the predicted moves were correct, and the evaluation values generally represented the game's flow. This study also used the method of showing a series of reading sequences to aid in understanding the game record, suggesting the effectiveness of showing a series of reading sequences.

## 3 A Series of Reading Sequences

The goal of this research is to represent the goal of the Shogi AI's moves as readings. The technique of understanding the meaning of a move is easy to understand by showing how choosing that move can improve the situation. In Shogi courses and commentaries, professional players often show successful moves on a large board to demonstrate the intention of the move.

An example is shown below. For example, Fig. 1(a) shows a typical framing move phase in Shogi, known as the Oni-Goroshi strategy. From this point on, the player's success in the framing moves is evidenced by the fact that the rear player performs a series of seemingly natural activities in succession. Specifically, Fig. 1(b) shows the phase that proceeded with "▽S-6b, ▲P-7e, ▽P-6d, ▲Bx2b+, ▽Sx2b, ▲B*5e, ▽S-3c, ▲Bx6d, ▽G6a-5b, ▲P-7d, ▽G-6c, ▲R-7h, ▽Gx6d, ▲Nx7c+, ▽Sx7c, ▲Px7c+. If we proceed to this position, we can see that the exchange is between the first player's bishop & knight and the second player's silver. However, this promoted pawn is in a good position, indicating that this position is promising for the first move.

In this way, the intention can be emphasized by showing the progression of moves relatively naturally. In this study, we will construct a system that aids comprehension by providing a series of reading sequences.

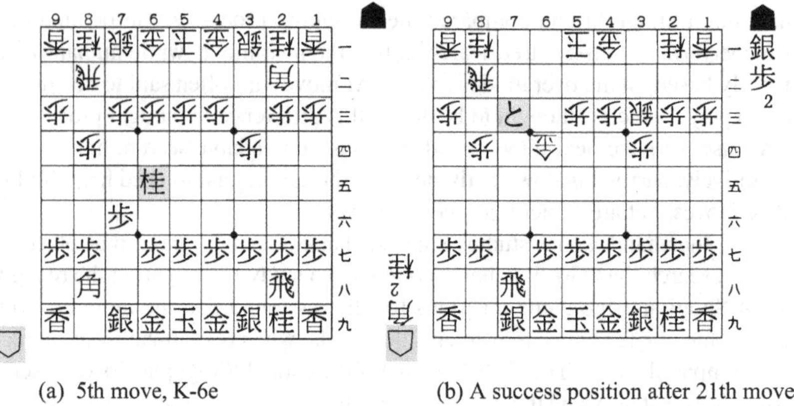

(a) 5th move, K-6e (b) A success position after 21th move

**Fig. 1.** Example of the Oni-Goroshi strategy

## 4 Purposed System

### 4.1 Design Policy

In this study, to understand the meaning of advanced Shogi AI moves, we first propose a moderately strength-tuned AI (hereafter referred to as "the tuning AI") to generate a "natural response move" to that move. This adjusted AI is required to generate moves that feel natural to the amateur being explained.

To achieve this, it is necessary to realize an AI that generates moves most easily chosen by the amateur player being explained. First, we assume that the inexperienced players to be described are the most populous amateur players. Then, the move that the player has the highest probability of selecting is determined by machine learning and is used as the tuning AI. The tuning AI then plays against the move chosen by the strong AI in a particular phase and moves forward until the difference between the strong and the tuning AI exceeds a specific evaluation value. The procedure of such moves is presented as intention readings. This will achieve the goal of this study.

### 4.2 Survey of Ratings with the Largest Player Population

This study focuses on amateur players on an online game server called "Shogi-Quest," a smartphone-based online game server [8]. Shogi-Quest is one of the most popular free-to-play online game sites in Japan.

With the cooperation of Shogi Crest management, we obtained game record data. All players' accounts that played within the last month were included. This was done to exclude dormant players who are not currently playing. In addition, accounts with less than 50 games were excluded. This was because players who played fewer games had large rating fluctuations, so only players who played more than 50 games and had stable ratings were included. The number of accounts that met these criteria was approximately 38,000. The ratings were divided into 100 intervals, as shown in Fig. 2. The horizontal axis shows the ratings, and the vertical axis indicates the number of accounts. This shows that it almost follows a normal distribution. In this population, the rating with the highest number of reports is between 1,300 and 1,400, so we will build the tuning AI for the level of players in this rating.

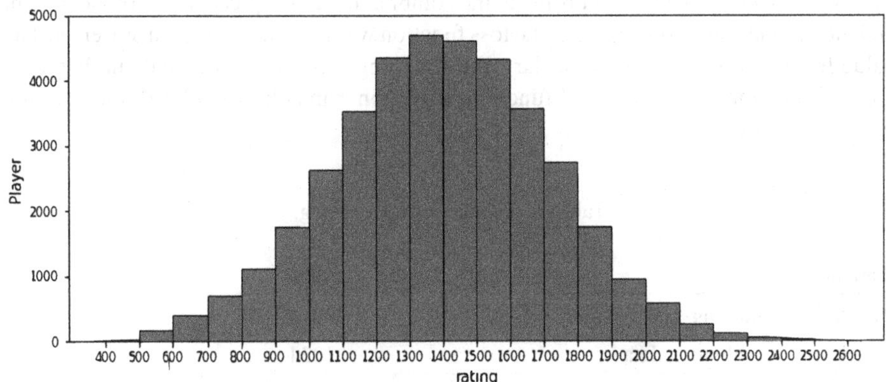


**Fig. 2.** Distribution of player population in Shogi-Quest.

### 4.3 Tuning AI

From 4.2, the ratings of amateurs to be studied were set to 1300–1400. Excluding the beginning of the game. This is because the game's early stages are standardized and may reflect something other than the player's game ability. We also excluded Bot games running in ShogiQuest.

For the game records that satisfy these conditions, we perform supervised learning, in which the policy function for predicting moves and the value function for predicting winning probability are simultaneously trained as a single neural network. Here, the input and intermediate layers are shared, and the strategy and value functions are output at the output layer, respectively.

The input layer is a convolutional layer with a filter size of 3 x 3 and 192 filters. Then, ReLU was used as the activation function. The inputs to the two parts are 9 x 9 binary images showing the coordinates of the pieces, and a binary image channel is constructed for each element on the board and each piece held. The articles on the board have 14 tracks, considering the details in the same position as the pieces on the board. The number of channels for the pawns is 38 since the maximum number of channels is allocated for each type of piece. Therefore, the total number of input channels is 104, the sum of each element on the board and the pawns held by the first and second players, respectively.

The middle layer is a Residual Network, and the convolution layer has a filter size of 3 x 3, 192 filters, and an activation function of ReLU. This Residual Network was repeated for ten blocks.

The output layer of the policy function was a convolution layer with a filter size of $1 \times 1$ and several filters of 27. The activation function was a softmax function. The output layer of the value function was a convolutional layer with a size of $1 \times 1$ and several 27 filters, plus an all-coupled layer with 256 units and, finally, an all-coupled layer with 1 unit. The activation function was then sigmoid.

The output of the policy function was a multiclass classification problem in which 2187 labels were classified according to the combination of the piece's type of movement and the destination's coordinates. The loss function was then the cross-entropy error. The value function outputs a single scalar value that ranges from 0 to 1 actual number. And the loss function used a sigmoid function. Based on Yamaoka's book [9], the learning options were defined as Table 1.

**Table 1.** Parameters for learning.

| Parameter | Value |
|---|---|
| Batch size of training data | 1024 |
| Batch size of evaluation data | 1024 |
| Learning rate | 0.01 |
| Optimization method | SGD |

In this study, the move agreement rate with amateur players in each phase is used as an indicator for developing the coordination AI, and an attempt is made to learn to improve the move agreement rate. The definition of the move agreement rate is as follows.

$$(Move\ agreement\ rate) = \frac{(Number\ of\ agreed\ positions)}{(All\ positions)} \tag{1}$$

In addition, the number of playouts in the search is adjusted to improve the move agreement rate. As a reason for incorporating search, we cite Ogawa's study that showed that the move agreement rate improved by more than 0.3% by using search when selecting moves [10]. Therefore, it is expected that the use of investigation will improve the move agreement rate of amateur players.

## 5 Experiments for the Development of the Tuning AI

### 5.1 Optimal Number of Epochs in Supervised Learning

From about 22,000 games of each player with a rating of 1300–1400, 90% were trained as training data and 10% as evaluation data. The move agreement rate with the evaluation data was calculated for each epoch as shown in Fig. 3.

The horizontal axis represents the number of epochs, and the vertical axis represents the start match rate. The move agreement rate increased until epoch number 8, after which the move agreement rate decreased. This is thought to be a decrease in the move agreement rate after epoch 9 due to overlearning. In this learning model, the highest start match rate was 45.5% at epoch 8.

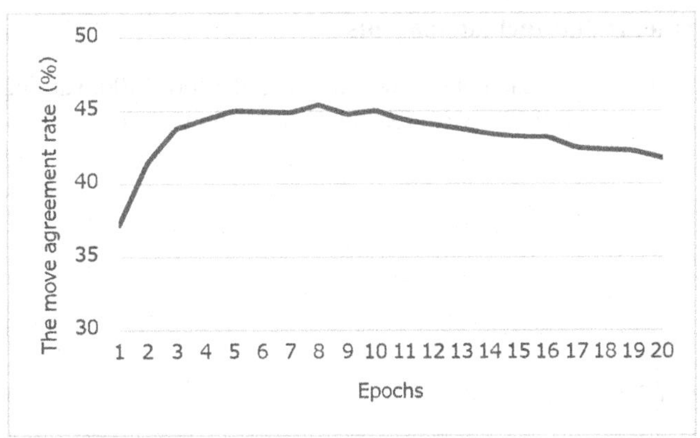


**Fig. 3.** Trends in the percentage of agreement with the evaluation data.

### 5.2 Model Evaluation

Based on the results of 5.1, the model with the highest start match rate, epoch number 8, was used to evaluate the start match rate with the other ratings. In this case, the ratings were separated by 100 and covered 1100–1600. Each rating was based on 500 games different from the evaluation data. The move agreement rate for each rating was calculated as shown in Fig. 4.

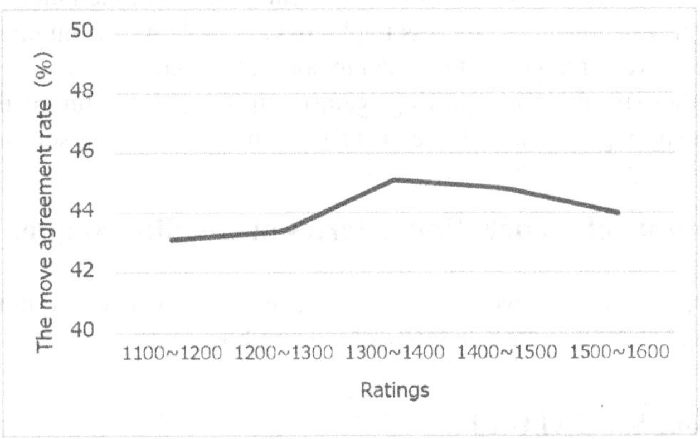


**Fig. 4.** Trends in the move agreement rate against rating.

The horizontal axis shows the rating and the vertical axis shows the move agreement rate. The highest move agreement rate was observed at a rating of 1300–1400 (45.1%). The move agreement rate decreased at both higher and lower ratings, confirming that the learning was appropriate for the 1300–1400 rating.

### 5.3 Improvements that Include Playouts

We searched 100 games of each player with a rating of 1300–1400, varying the number of playouts, and obtained the move agreement rate as shown in Fig. 5.

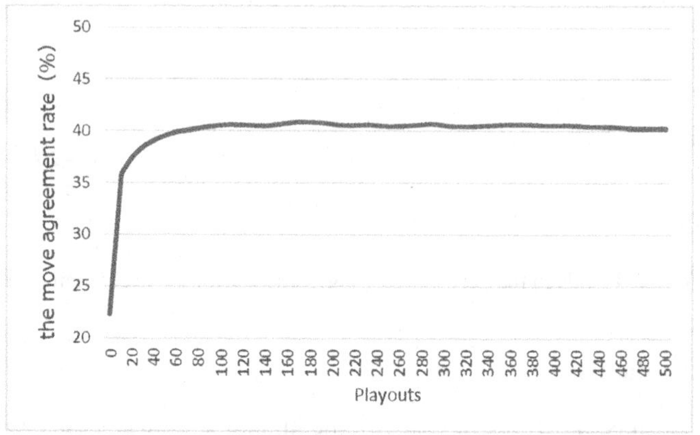


**Fig. 5.** Movement of the move agreement rate by the number of playouts.

The number of playouts was adjusted from 0 to 500 because learning tends to converge around 500 playouts. The vertical axis represents the number of playouts and the horizontal axis represents the move agreement rate. When the number of playouts was 170, the move agreement rate was the highest at 41%. As the number of playouts increased, the move agreement rate tended to converge around 40%.

Based on these results, when playing against a strong AI in the future, the number of playouts of the tuning AI should be set to 170 and moves should be selected by search.

## 6 An Example of Generating a Series of Reading Sequences

Using the proposed system, we will present the intentions behind two moves made by top professional chess players as a series of reading lines.

### 6.1 The Strong Shogi AI Used

As a strong Shogi AI, we use "Suisho5", the latest version of "Suisho", which won the 3rd World Shogi AI Denryu Tournament [11]. The number of nodes for the move search is assumed to be 1 million.

### 6.2 S*4a by Sota Fujii

**An Example of Target Move**

Let us take for example the game between Sota Fujii 2-Crown and Ayumu Matsuo 8-dan in the second group ranking game of the 34th Ryu-ou Tournament. In this game, the

57th move, S*4a in Fig. 6 is said to be the move that is difficult to understand at first glance but is said to be a strange move that will go down in history [12, 13]. It is also the move that Suisho5 chose as the best move. The meaning of this move was analyzed by the proposed system.

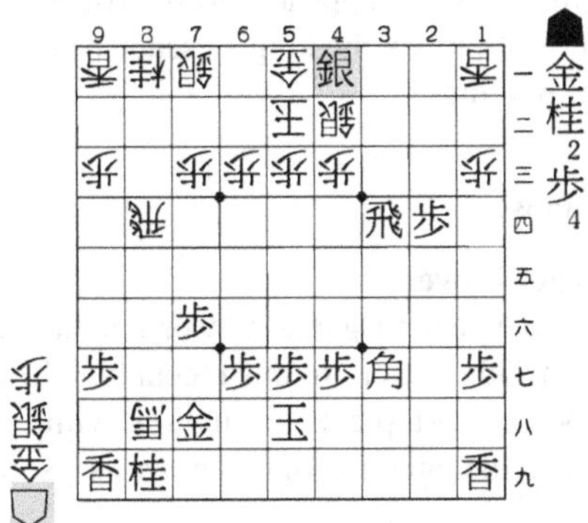

**Fig. 6.** The position of the 57th move.

**Analysis After S*4a**

The tuning AI chose the move Gx4a as the best move for the 58th move, as shown in Fig. 7(a). From this position, the first player used Suisho5 and the second player used the tuning AI, and proceeded to play until the evaluated values were more than 1,000 points apart. As a result, the following procedure progressed to (b), which clearly shows an example of a sequence of readings in which the first move gains the upper hand.

▽Gx4a, ▲R-8d, ▽B + 7h, ▲N*5e, ▽G*3h, ▲R-8b +, ▽S*6b, ▲Nx6c +, ▽Kx6c, ▲R*6d, ▽K-5b, ▲G*6c (b).

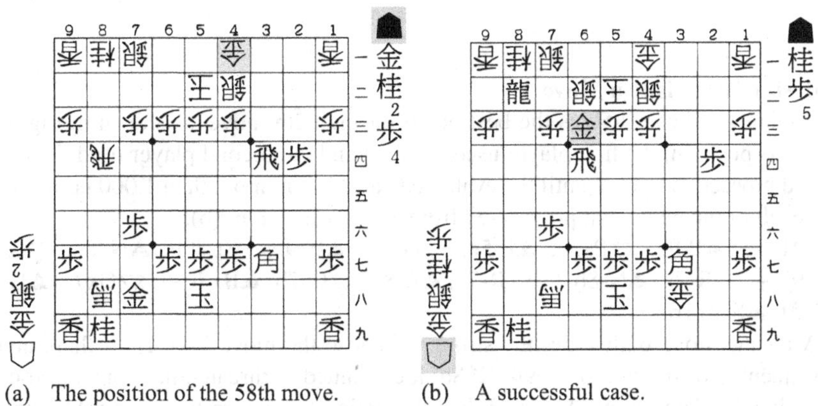

(a) The position of the 58th move. (b) A successful case.

**Fig. 7.** Display of success cases using the series of reading sequences.

After the 58th move Gx4a, Suisho5 chose the 59th move Rx8d, capturing the tuning AI's rook and targeting the tuning AI's bishop. The tuning AI chose the move Bx7h + to avoid losing the bishop and capturing Suisho5's gold. However, Suisho5 continued its attack, and from the move 63th R-8b +, it maintained a check, resulting in an advantage for Suisho5.

At first glance, 57th move, S*4a, appeared to be just throwing away silver, but it turned out to be a good move to block the king's escape route by letting him take it for gold from the sequence of readings.

### 6.3 B*4h by Takuya Nagase

**Another Example of Target Move**

Let's take the example of the second game between Sota Fujii Ryu-ou and Takuya Nagase Oza in the 71st Oza Title Match. In this recent match, the move "B*4h" on the 61st move in Fig. 8 has become a topic of discussion, with commentators expressing surprise [14]. We will present the intention of this move as a series of reading sequences with the proposed system.

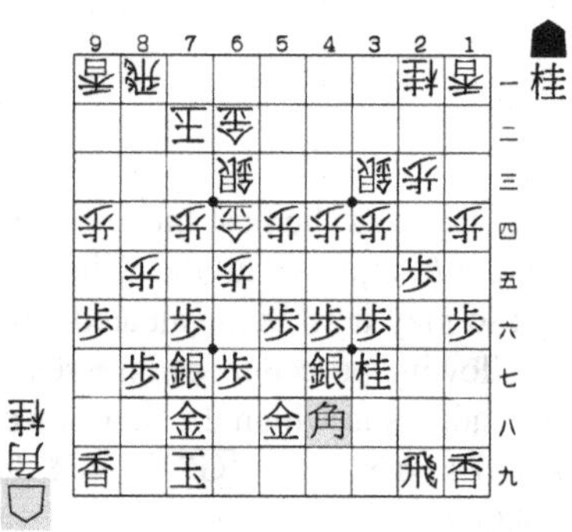

**Fig. 8.** The position of 61th move.

**Analysis of Exquisite a Move**

The tuning AI chose P-5e as the best move for the 62th move, as shown in Fig. 9(a). From this position, the first player used Suisho5 and the second player used the tuning AI, and proceeded to play until the evaluated values were more than 1,000 points apart. The result of the game that progressed from S*4a is shown in (b).

▽P-5e, ▲P-9e, ▽Px5e, ▲P-5e, ▽Gx5e, ▲P*9b, ▽Lx9b, ▲N*8d, ▽K-6a, ▲Nx9b +, ▽R-7a, ▲N-8b +, ▽R-7c, ▲B-8d, ▽G-7b, ▲Bx7c +, ▽Gx7c, ▲L*5g, ▽P*5f, ▲Sx5f (b).

After the move 62th P-5e, the strong AI chose the move P-9e for a flank attack. Subsequently, from the move 69th K*8d, it continued to threaten the king and rook of the tuning AI. The tuning AI's rook had the option to capture the strong AI's knight, but immediately after that, it would lose its rook to the strong AI's bishop. Therefore, it chose the move 70th K-6a to move the king away. Following this, the strong AI's bishop

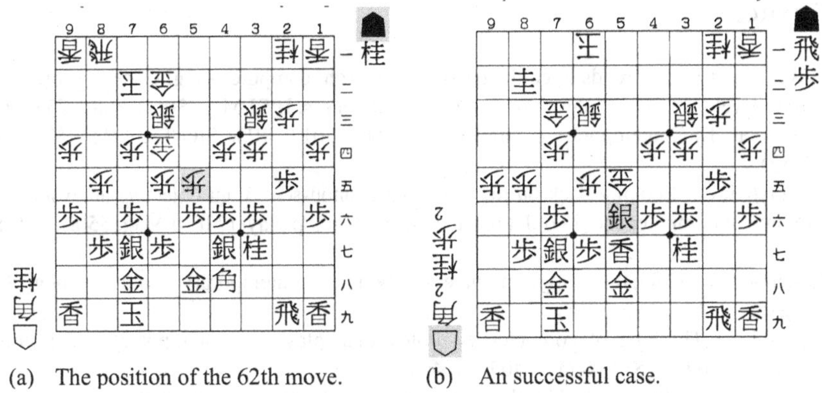

(a) The position of the 62th move. (b) An successful case.

**Fig. 9.** Display of success cases using the series of reading sequences.

promoted, capturing the tuning AI's rook and breaking its formation. This resulted in an advantage for the strong AI.

From the reading lines, it became apparent that move 61th B*4h served as the starting point to capture the tuning AI's rook and disrupt its formation.

## 7 Conclusion and Future Works

We proposed a system targeting Shogi Quest players with ratings between 1300 and 1400. This system uses a tuning AI to display the intentions behind moves made by a strong AI as a series of reading sequences. We demonstrated that the tuning AI can learn for the target ratings and further improved move agreement rates through search. As a result, we were able to present an example of a system that displays the intentions behind moves in specific positions as a series of reading sequences.

While we generated reading sequences for two moves in this study, it's important to note that for more complex moves, the number of sequences generated may increase, potentially making them harder to understand. Additionally, when there are multiple candidate moves for each move, the system needs to account for each of them. Therefore, our future work will involve analyzing existing shogi literature and magazines to devise algorithms for generating reading sequences. We will also explore methods for presenting reading sequences that are easier for amateur players to understand.

Ultimately, our goal is to evaluate whether this system can genuinely help amateur players understand the moves of challenging AI opponents, particularly when it's challenging to discern their intentions. To assess the effectiveness of the devised algorithms, we are planning experiments for the future.

**Acknowledgements.** We would like to thank Mr. Yasushi Tanase of Shogi Quest for providing us with the game record data used in this study.

## References

1. Takenobu, T.: New trends in computer shogi research: computer shogi close to professional player level - disclosing algorithms and its effectiveness. IPSJ Mag. **50**(9), 868–873 (2009)
2. Takenobu, T.: Contemporary computer shogi (May 2013). IPSJ SIG Tech. Rep. **30**(1), 1–8 (2013)
3. Yoshiyuki, K.: Looking back on the 3rd shogi dennou-sen: 3. an objective analysis on the strength of computer shogi - did it reach to the human top player? IPSJ Mag. **55**(8), 851–852 (2014)
4. Takenobu, T.: Computer shogi continues evolving: 1 contemporary computer shogi. IPSJ Mag. **59**(2), 144–152 (2018)
5. Takeshi, I.: Thinking of computer vs professional players -contemporary and future of computer shogi. IPSJ J. **48**(12), 4033–4040 (2007)
6. Katsuyoshi, T., Takeshi, I., Masakazu, M., Hitoshi, M.: Analysis on go players' recognition when they are thinking next moves. IPSJ J. **52**(12), 3796–3805 (2011)
7. Tomoyuki, K.: Evaluation of real-time commentary generated by computer shogi program. IPSJ J. **53**(11), 2525–2532 (2012)
8. ShogiQuest (2022). http://questgames.net/shogi10. Accessed 26 Dec 2022
9. Tadao, Y.: How to Create a Strong Shogi Software: Deep Learning Shogi AI Implemented in Python, Mynavi (2021)
10. Ogawa, T., Hsueh, C.H., Ikeda, K.: Improving the human-likeness of game AI's moves by combining multiple prediction models. In: ICAART, pp. 931–939 (2023)
11. Suisho5 (2023). https://github.com/mizar/YaneuraOu/releases/tag/v7.0.0. Accessed 30 Jun 2023
12. JBpress (2023). https://jbpress.ismedia.jp/articles/-/65464. Accessed 06 Oct 2023
13. Mynavi (2023). https://book.mynavi.jp/shogi/detail/id=121989. Accessed 06 Oct 2023
14. Japan Shogi Association (2023). http://live.shogi.or.jp/ouza/kifu/71/ouza202309120101.html. Accessed 07 Oct 2023

# Viewing on Google Maps Using Yolov8 for Damaged Traffic Signs Detection

Yahaya Ibrahim Garta, Wei-Kai Chao, Rung-Ching Chen(✉), and Shao-Kuo Tai

Chaoyang University of Technology, Taichung, Taiwan
crching@cyut.edu.tw

**Abstract.** The essence of object detection in Computer Vision is to identify and precisely locate an object in a scene. In transportation management, it detects traffic signs for application in autonomous vehicles and other road users. Traffic objects and the scene must also be documented and monitored for efficient traffic management. The signs are prone to damage and occlusion, which may compromise road safety, thus the need to detect, document, and monitor traffic signs. This paper proposed a traffic signs detection and recognition model using the state-of-the-art YOLOv8 model and an inventory management system for keeping traffic records. We also proposed a monitoring technique by viewing traffic scenes uploaded on customized Google My Map and Google Map, made possible by geolocation information of traffic signs. Our trained model achieved 87.1% mAP50 and 61.2% mAP50-95 on our dataset. We compared the performance of our model to other versions of YOLOv8.

**Keywords:** Computer Vision · YOLOv8 · Google Maps · Traffic Sign

## 1 Introduction

The traffic signs play a vital role to road users by regulating and maintaining road traffic, thereby ensuring road safety. Pedestrians and autonomous-driving, semi-autonomous, human-driven vehicles are road users guided by traffic signs while using the road. Essential information, warnings, direction, and guide hugely helps in maintaining an orderly flow of traffic. Because of the importance of traffic signs, most authorities institute a body with the sole responsibility of monitoring, maintaining, and keeping records of designated signs. Road maintenance encompasses regular inspections of traffic signs to identify damaged or missing signs and promptly address the issue. The signs are sparsely located along Trunk A, B, and C roads.

Previously, we identified and located traffic signs using object detection methods [1, 2]. For holistic management of traffic signs that encompasses all road users, detailed information and the location of each sign needs to be kept, and proper and efficient monitoring mechanisms must be applied. These are feasible through proper inventory management and devising means of monitoring the scene.

With the advent of machine learning, researchers use machine learning algorithms to detect and recognize traffic signs and markings which can be implemented for monitoring purposes, assisting drivers and in advanced driver assistance systems [3]. A more


C.-Y. Lee et al. (Eds.): TAAI 2023, CCIS 2074, pp. 187–197, 2024.
https://doi.org/10.1007/978-981-97-1711-8_14

advanced approach is using deep learning methods in computer vision to detect and recognize traffic signs easily and accurately. Unlike the traditional system, which uses vehicular monitoring, satellite and camera is employed for monitoring traffic signs.

## 2 Related Work

Researchers in computer vision have proposed many techniques to detect traffic signs. David, M. et al. proposed a camera-based system mounted on vehicles for detecting specific traffic signs [4]. The authors used You Only Look Once (YOLO) v3, and it achieved high performance when tested on a dataset of images captured in different weather conditions. A YOLOv3 algorithm was proposed by Vinothkumar, S et al. to detect and recognize traffic signs to improve road safety and reduce accidents [5]. The YOLOv3 algorithm combines features learned from training data with the ResNet algorithm to make predictions more accurate and efficient. Experimental results show that the YOLOv3 approach performs better than other algorithms in accuracy.

Xilin, Z. proposed a YOLO V3 algorithm for traffic sign recognition [6]. The proposed model was compared to R-CNN series algorithms. The results shows that YOLO V3 is faster and more accurate in traffic sign recognition. Haowei, Z. et al. improved neural network called YOLOv7-WCN for detecting traffic signs in challenging conditions was proposed based on YOLOv7 [7]. They are adding a CHB module to the backbone network of YOLOv7 to enrich the image information and incorporate a Normalization-based Attention Module (NAM) to enhance the network, which focuses on a target region.

The loss function of YOLOv7 was replaced by Wasserstein Distance Loss aims to improve the training process of the algorithm. The accuracy improved from 85.5% to 89.0% in detection performance. Zhehui, Y. et al. proposed a comparison of three algorithms (Mask R-CNN, YOLOx, and YOLOv7) for large-scale road facility detection using the Mapillary dataset, with YOLOv7 performing the best [8]. The results demonstrate the generalization ability of the models trained on the dataset and provide insights into the strengths and limitations of the latest networks in multiclass object detection on street-level datasets. Jesus, B. et al. introduces a new approach for mapping traffic signs using data from a Mobile Mapping System (MMS), which includes images and point clouds [9]. Images are processed faster and utilize optimized artificial intelligence techniques, while point clouds allow for more precise positioning. The method combines image-based detection and classification with point cloud-based geo-referencing, resulting in high accuracy and efficiency for mapping traffic signs. Zeliang, L. et al. proposed a method for improving the detection of traffic signs in road scenes using an enhanced version of the YOLOv4 algorithm [10]. Proposed the use of deep learning and object detection technology to automate the detection and classification of street signs captured in Google Street View images. By training a custom object detection model and leveraging the Street View API, the authors were able to detect and classify Stop and Give Way signs with high accuracy. This approach has the potential to assist local government authorities in monitoring and maintaining traffic sign infrastructure, and it can be scaled to detect other types of signs in different locations.

The method combines the MLP architecture with a convolutional neural network to enhance object detection and incorporates same-level connections within PANet to improve feature extraction. Experimental results demonstrate that the improved YOLOv4 algorithm increases the detection accuracy of sample images and meets real-time detection requirements, showing advantages compared to similar algorithms. Andrew, C. et al. proposes the use of deep learning and Google Street View images to autonomously detect and classify traffic signs, aiding in monitoring and maintenance [11]. By combining object detection, photogrammetry, and GIS, the proposed approach achieves high accuracy in detecting and locating street signs, offering a scalable solution for asset management systems.

Emin, G. et al. proposed a portable and image-based advanced driver assistance system (ADAS) that uses the YOLO v5 algorithm for real-time detection of traffic signs, vehicles, and pedestrians [12]. The system was trained on a Tesla P100 Graphics Processing Unit GPU, achieving high detection speed and accuracy. The study compares the model's performance on different embedded platforms and computers, demonstrating its efficiency and suitability for real-time road object detection. Domen, T. et al. proposed a convolutional neural network (CNN) approach called mask R-CNN to detect and recognize many traffic sign categories, addressing the challenge of automating traffic sign inventory management [13]. Their system achieves below 3% error rates and shows promise for practical applications in traffic sign management.

Christoph, G. et al. proposed a system that uses artificial neural networks and 360° camera equipment to automatically detect and classify different types of traffic signs in images [14]. These signs are then linked to a database, allowing for semi-automatic inventory and off-site inspections of traffic signs. Changbin, Y. et al. proposed a new technique for detecting and inspecting damaged traffic signs in natural scenes using mobile laser scanning (MLS) data, including images and point clouds [15]. The proposed model involves training a deep learning network called Fast R-CNN to detect traffic signs followed by rough detection of the sign area in MLS point clouds. An accurate traffic sign is then detected, and placement parameters are measured for damage inspection and inventory purposes.

Jing, Z. et al. proposed algorithm combines a Progressive multi-scale residual network (PMRNet) for image de-raining and a CoT-YOLOv5 algorithm for sign recognition in rainy weather conditions, improving accuracy by extracting rain mark features and enhancing global modeling capability. Experimental results demonstrate the effectiveness of the PMRNet algorithm and the improved performance of the CoT-YOLOv5 algorithm compared to the original YOLOv5 [16].

Cheng, P. C. et al. propose a mobile mapping system (MMS) equipped with lidar, a camera, and Global Navigation Satellite System (GNSS) / Inertial Navigation System (INS) integration (GNSS/INS), which incorporates ground control points and a refinement technique called Normal Distribution Transform Simultaneously Localization and Mapping (NDT SLAM) to improve the accuracy of the reconstructed point cloud [17].

A deep neural network identifies traffic signs and uses the intersection of lidar scan points and detected objects to obtain accurate 3D geodetic coordinates of the traffic signs. Experimental results demonstrate the effectiveness of their approach in reducing labor work and improving accuracy in HD map creation. The methods above need to address the following.

i. Use a state-of-the-art model that can accurately detect traffic signs.
ii. An inventory system for keeping traffic records includes location information of traffic signs for monitoring.
iii. A system can efficiently monitor the status and conditions of traffic signs for proper monitoring by a team.

We aim to reduce the stated research gaps as follows.

i. (1) Used State-of-The-Art (SOTA) YOLOv8 to detect and recognize traffic signs.
iv. (2)Proposed an inventory management system for keeping records and easy retrieval of traffic signs
v. Proposed traffic signs views on Google My Map for recognition, monitoring, and location of traffic signs for efficient tracking.

Apart from the abstracts, introduction, and related work, the remainder of this paper includes viz: methodology, experiment, result and analysis, conclusion, acknowledgment, and references.

## 3 Methodology

We created a simple inventory management records system using Excel 2016 format to keep records of our traffic signs dataset. A Google Map account was created to view traffic signs' locations over an area. We used YOLOv8l to detect and recognize traffic signs.

### 3.1 Dataset

We obtained seven hundred and seventy-two (772) traffic sign images online and used the Sony Xperia Model G3426 GPS location-enabled to capture five (5) geolocation traffic sign images. We used seven hundred and seventy-seven (777) traffic signs images.

### 3.2 Preprocessing

We used the Roboflow platform to preprocess our dataset, including annotation and data augmentation tasks. The augmented resulted in one thousand six hundred and thirty-two (1632) traffic sign images, which we used to train, test, and validate our model. The dataset was split in the ratio of 70% for training, 20% for testing, and 10% for validation.

### 3.3 Preprocessing

An inventory record system was created using Excel 2016 format for storing and retrieving traffic signs images. We used Excel 2016 because it can be exported to a database server. Information on the traffic signs is stored in Excel format, as shown in Table 1 while the images are stored in a folder as input.

In Table 1, the attributes of each data are stored with these fields: image_id is the identification number of traffic signs, gps_lat, and gps_long. are the latitude and longitude, respectively, of each traffic sign. Where gps_alt. is the altitude of each traffic sign and status indicates the condition of each traffic sign to get detailed information on each traffic sign for ease of reference and location.

The traffic signs are uploaded to Google My Map via Google Photos. Each traffic image, after that, automatically placed itself on the map based on the attributes in Table 1 and displayed as shown in Fig. 1; detailed information about the images can be accessed on the map, and shareable links are provided for sharing. The images can also be viewed on Google Earth. These can be used to monitor traffic signs across sparsely located areas properly.

**Table 1.** Records of information of our dataset in the proposed inventory system

| image_id | gps_lat | gps_long | gps_alt | status |
|---|---|---|---|---|
| DSC_0228 | 24;10.08999999999504 | 120;42;55.332600000023 | 161 | good |
| DES_0231 | 24;4;8.057499999995325 | 120;42;56.980500000005 | 162 | good |
| DCS_0229 | 24;4;10.076199999995854 | 120;42;56.733400000026 | 162 | good |
| DCS_0235 | 24;4;2.976299999994811 | 120;42;58.6284999999911 | 162 | good |
| DCS_0223 | 24;4;8.970700000005304 | 120;42;53.986800000013 | 0 | good |
| ts_01 | nil | nil | nil | good |
| ts_02 | nil | nil | nil | occluded |
| ts_03 | nil | nil | nil | damaged |

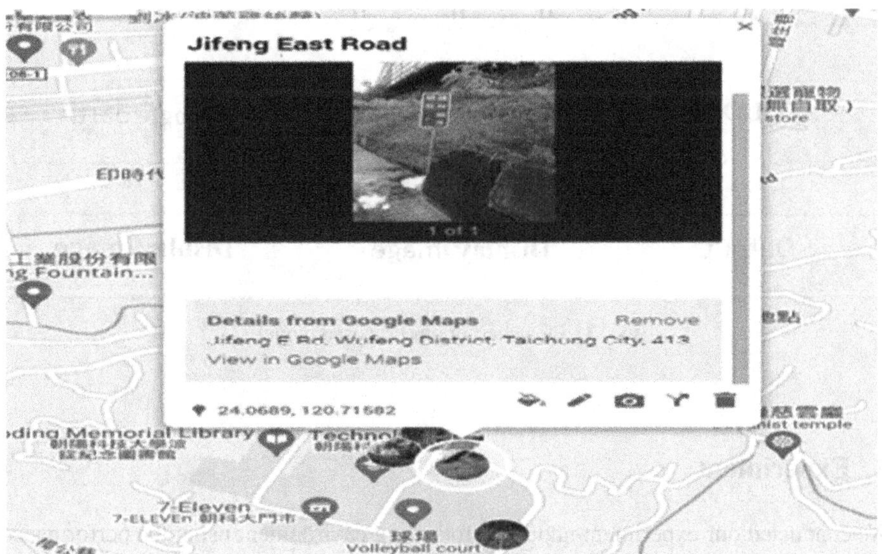


**Fig. 1.** Display of a traffic sign on Google My Maps.

### 3.4 YOLOv8

YOLOv8 architecture is the latest version of the YOLO object detection family model, which introduces improvements to its predecessors. A neural network architecture that combines Feature Pyramid Network (FPN) and Path Aggregation Network (PAN) was introduced. FPN helps detect objects at different scales and resolutions by reducing the image resolution and increasing the number of feature channels. In contrast, PAN aggregates features from different network levels to accurately detect objects of various sizes and shapes. It also introduces a labeling tool on the Roboflow platform, which simplifies the annotation process for training the model.

### 3.5 The Model

Our proposed model is based on YOLOv8l architecture because of the introduced features, which are suitable for modeling traffic signs that may accurately detect sparsely distributed traffic signs under various conditions. Figure 2 shows the flow graph of our proposed model. We adopt the loss function and optimizer of the model.

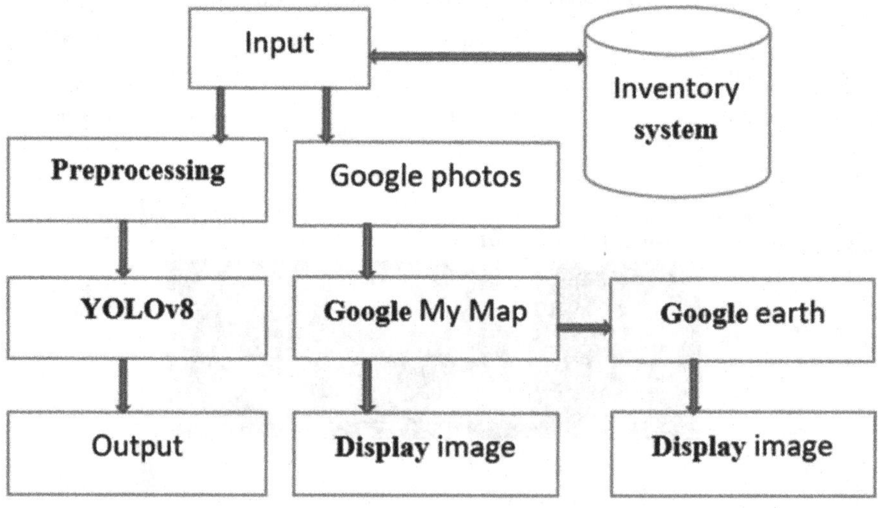


**Fig. 2.** Flowchart of our proposed model.

## 4 Experiment

We conducted our experiment under the following environment using the performance evaluation metrics of YOLO models.

### 4.1 Experimental Set-Up

We trained our model on Windows 10 Education version 22H2 with 16.0 GB RAM, Intel(R) Core(TM) i7-4790 CPU @ 3.60GHz 3.60 GHz, and used Google Colab Python 3.10.12 with GPU, NVIDIA-SMI 525.105.17, CUDA 12.0. The software includes Ultralytics YOLOv8.0.134, Python 3.10.6, torch 2.0.1+cu118. CUDA:0 (Tesla T4, 15102MiB).

### 4.2 Evaluation Metrics

YOLOv8 uses mean average precision (mAP), precision, and recall as performance evaluation metrics. There are two (2) mAPs viz mA50 and Map50-90. The mathematical representation of these metrics is given below.

$$\text{Precision} = \frac{\text{TP}}{\text{TP} + \text{FP}} \tag{1}$$

$$\text{Recall} = \frac{\text{TP}}{\text{TP} + \text{FN}} \tag{2}$$

$$\text{mAP} = \sum\nolimits_{i=1}^{n} \text{AP}i/\text{n} \tag{3}$$

where TP represents the successful detection of objects where the model's predictions match the actual objects (correct detection), false Positive (FP) is the number of bounding boxes that the model incorrectly predicts as targets but do not match the ground truth bounding boxes of any targets (incorrect detection). At the same time, False Negative (FN) refers to the number of undetected targets (missed detection). AP is the average precision. These are represented in the confusion metrics shown in Fig. 3.

### 4.3 Analysis of Results

Figure 3 shows graphs of evaluation metrics recorded after 100 epochs on our dataset. It shows losses during training, indicating a significant reduction at the end of the training. The graph also shows precision, recall, mAP50, and m AP50-95. Figure 4 shows validation images of our trained model indicating the bounding boxes on each validation dataset. Figure 5 is the inference showing the bounding boxes of some traffic signs.

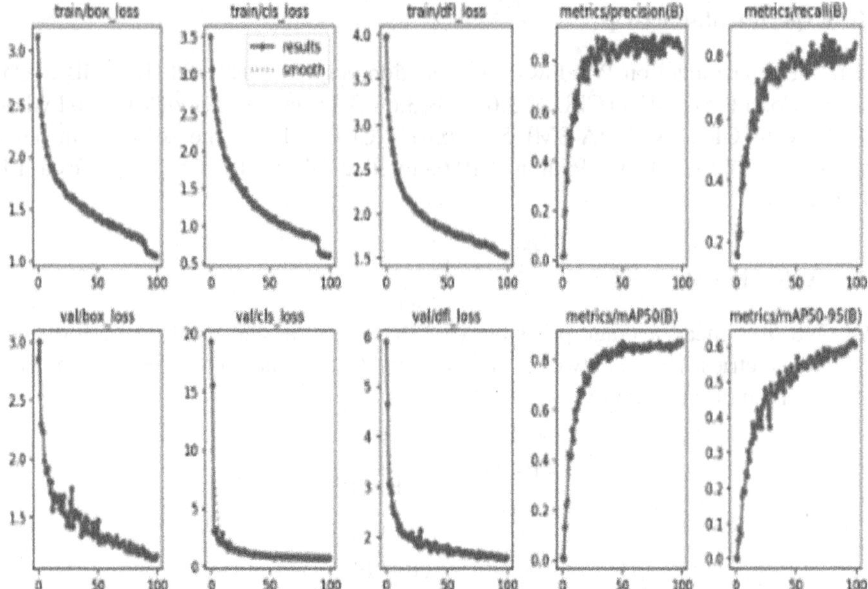


**Fig. 3.** Graphs of performance metrics.

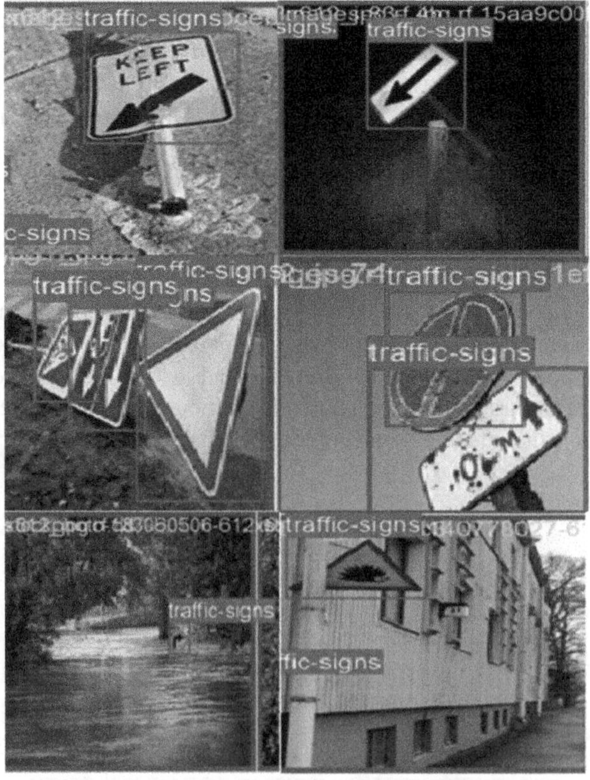


**Fig. 4.** The images of validation damaged traffic sign.

**Table 2.** Performance evaluation metrics.

| model | mAP50 | mAP 50-95 | R | P |
|---|---|---|---|---|
| YOLOv8n | 0.867 | 0.577 | 0.802 | 0.869 |
| YOLOv8s | 0.875 | 0.604 | 0.843 | 0.820 |
| YOLOv8m | 0.849 | 0.579 | 0.831 | 0.807 |
| YOLOv8l | 0.871 | 0.612 | 0.792 | 0.883 |
| YOLOv8x | 0.863 | 0.587 | 0.839 | 0.828 |

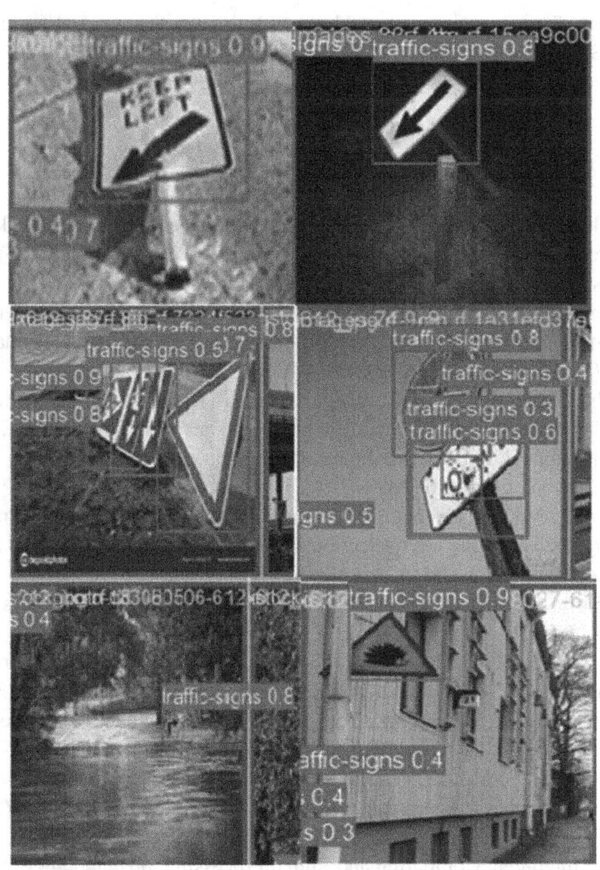


**Fig. 5.** The images of inference result showing bounding boxes on detected damaged traffic signs.

Table 2 compares performance evaluation metrics of YOLOv8 versions trained with our traffic signs. YOLOv8l recorded 87.1% mAP50 and 61.2% m AP50-95%, indicating good dataset performance.

## 5 Conclusion

We have proposed an inventory management system for keeping records and quickly retrieving traffic signs. Each traffic sign in the database has attributes that can be used to locate its position on Google My Map or Google Earth for proper monitoring. A state-of-the-art YOLOv8 model was proposed tYOLOv8l o detect and recognize traffic signs which recorded good performance across evaluation metrics with mAP50 of 87.1% and m AP50-95 of 61.2%. For future work, a real-time database will be developed where all traffic signs can be kept, and access and trained images can be stored and uploaded via Google My Map and Google Earth for implementation.

**Acknowledgment.** This paper is supported by the Ministry of Science and Technology, Taiwan. The Nos are MOST-112-2221-E-324-003 -MY3 and MOST-112-2221-E-324-011 -MY2, Taiwan.

## References

1. Dewi, C., Chen, R.C., Jiang, X., Yu, H.: Deep convolutional neural network for enhancing traffic sign recognition developed on Yolo V4. Multimed. Tools Appl. **81**(26), 37821–37845 (2022). https://doi.org/10.1007/s11042-022-12962-5
2. Dewi, C., Chen, R.C., Jiang, X., Yu, H.: Robust detection method for improving small traffic sign recognition based on spatial pyramid pooling. J. Ambient Intell. Human Comput. **14**, 8135–8152 (2023). https://doi.org/10.1007/s12652-021-03584-0
3. Dewi, C., Chen, R.C., Zhuang, Y.C., Jiang, X., Yu, H.: Recognizing road surface traffic signs based on YOLO models considering image flips. Big Data and Cogn. Comput. **7**(1), 54 (2023)
4. David, M., Matteo, B., Mario, V., Ratko, G.: Traffic sign detection using YOLO v3. In: Consumer Electronics, pp. 1–6 (2020)
5. Vinothkumar, S., Varadhaganapathy, S., Shanthakumari, R., Pradeev, S., Pragatheeswaran, S., Annamalai, K.S.: Traffic sign detection using hybrid network of YOLO and Resnet. In: Computer Communication and Informatics, pp. 1–7 (2023)
6. Xilin, Z.: Traffic sign detection based on YOLOv3. In: Power, Electronics and Computer Applications, pp. 1044–1048 (2023)
7. Haowei, Z., Aiqing, H., Yan, R., Xue, J.: Traffic sign detection based on improved YOLOv7. In: Intelligent Control, Measurement and Signal Processing, pp. 71–75 (2023)
8. Zhehui, Y., Chenbo, Z., Hiroya, M., Yoshihide, S.: Development of a large-scale roadside facility detection model based on the mapillary dataset. Sensors **22**(9992), 1–12 (2022)
9. Jesus, B., Elena, G., Pedro, A., David, C.: Novel approach to automatic traffic sign inventory based on mobile mapping system data and deep learning. Remote Sensor **12**(3), 1–15 (2020)
10. Zeliang, L., Huawen, W., Yasenjiang, M.: Detection of traffic sign based on improved YOLOv4. In: Intelligent Computing and Signal Processing, pp. 444–448 (2022)
11. Andrew, C., Alan, B., Qian, C.S.: Detecting and mapping traffic signs from Google street view images using deep learning and GIS. Comput. Environ. Urban Syst. **77**(101350), 1–11 (2019)
12. Emin, G., Cuneyt, B., Batuhan, C.: An implementation of real-time traffic signs and road objects detection based on mobile GPU platforms. IEEE Access **10**, 86191–86203 (2022)
13. Domen, T., Danijel, S.: Deep learning for large-scale traffic-sign detection and recognition. Intell. Transp. Syst. **21**(4), 1427–1440 (2020)

14. Christoph, G., Wolfgang, B.: Neural network-based traffic sign recognition in 360∘ images for semi-automatic road maintenance inventory. In: Intelligent Transportation System, pp. 1–7 (2020)
15. Changbin, Y., Chenglu, W., Huan, L., Cheng, W., Jonathan, L.: Rapid traffic sign damage inspection in natural scenes using mobile laser scanning data. Intell. Transp. Syst. **23**(10), 17809–17818 (2022)
16. Jing, Z., Haoliang, Z., Ding, L., Yuguang, X., Hong-an, L., Xuewen, L.: Research on rainy day traffic sign recognition algorithm based on PMRNet. Math. Biosci. Eng. **20**(7), 12240–12262 (2023)
17. Cheng, P.C., Chen, C.H., Wei, Y.W.: Mobile mapping system for automatic extraction of geodetic coordinates for traffic signs based on enhanced point cloud reconstruction. IEEE Access **10**, 117374–117384 (2022)

# Neural Networks to Infer Traditional Chinese Medicine Prescriptions from Indications

Ping-Kan Liao[1(✉)] and Von-Wun Soo[1,2]

[1] Institute of Information Systems and Applications, National Tsing Hua University, 101 Section 2 Kuan-Fu Road, Hsinchu 30043, Taiwan, ROC
sinloten17@gmail.com, soo@cgu.edu.tw

[2] Department of Artificial Intelligence, Chang-Gung University, 259 Wen-Hwa 1st Road, Kwei-Shan333, Tao-Yuan, Taiwan, ROC

**Abstract.** Ith increasing digitization of Chinese medicine-related books and extraction and analysis of the ingredients in herbs, it now becomes feasible to use big data analysis and deep learning techniques to learn the regularities from previous vague experience and knowledge of traditional Chinese medicine. We combine the Compendium of Materia Medica, Traditional Chinese Medicine Integrated Database (TCMID) and Traditional Chinese Medicine Systems Pharmacology Database (TCMSPD) and uses a pre-trained ensemble convolutional neural networks to infer Chinese medicine prescriptions from Chinese medicine indications. We constructed multiple biological networks including indications, target proteins and chemical compounds, and inferred the ingredients using a random walk algorithm from indications, and the potential Chinese medicine prescriptions are generated by a combination of herbs that cover the inferred ingredients. A pre-trained ensemble CNN is used to filter out unlikely prescriptions. Even under extreme incomplete information of the domain knowledge, the blind evaluation by human experts on the prescriptions proposed by our system being categorized as "suitable" or "very suitable" against "not suitable" and "very unsuitable" is overall 38.00%.

**Keywords:** traditional Chinese medicine · convolutional neural networks · random walk algorithms · prescriptions · homogeneous and heterogeneous biological networks

## 1 Introduction

Traditional Chinese medicine (TCM) has several thousand years of history and has a huge influence in Chinese culture. The use of TCM, such as medicated diet, diet therapy, medicated bath, etc., has long been regarded as part of daily health care in Asian and Chinese communities. And due to some of its efficacy is confirmed by clinical practices, western countries have gradually recognized and accepted it, and it has now become one of the new medical trends. However, even with the advancement of modern science and technology in biology and medicine, the underlying mechanisms and


C.-Y. Lee et al. (Eds.): TAAI 2023, CCIS 2074, pp. 198–216, 2024.
https://doi.org/10.1007/978-981-97-1711-8_15

effectiveness of the TCM have still been skeptical and questioned due to its complexity. In contrast to the precision treatment of Western medicine that typically uses single pill with chemical components whose ingredients and functions are clearly understood and tested, TCM uses a prescription which is composed by a variety of herbs for holistic treatment. Western medicine, on the other hand, has focused on high specificity and precision of a chemical drug compound to act on certain target protein, while TCM is in general a multi-target treatment system concept. Western medicine has developed precise knowledge on chemical compound structures of drugs, drug target relations in complex pathways and processes, gene and disease relations, and also elaborated disease taxonomy and ontology. It seems to be feasible that if we can map the multi-compounds and multi-targets of TCM as complex compound-target networks, plus the corresponding relationship between the indications and the targets, we can simulate and infer potential prescriptions given the indications. However, in actually dealing with the multi-drugs and multi-target interactions in TCM, it has become very challenging to analyze and understand. Because not all chemical compound ingredients in Chinese herbs are known or can be extracted, not to mention the knowledge of their targets and interactions in the physiological processes in patients. Besides most existing TCM prescriptions are based on empirical and clinical experience from old ancient Chinese medicine practitioners and the concepts and terminologies are quite different from Western medicine.

## 2 Related Work

In Liu et al. [1] and Kuo et al. [2]'s work, they constructed networks including drugs, target paths, disease, and adopted a random walk model to predict new indications for drugs. They have established heterogeneous networks of drug-drug similarity networks, drug-disease networks, drug target networks, protein-protein interaction networks, target-disease networks and disease-disease networks so that they can conduct random walk inference over these heterogeneous networks. Since the random work model can be applied in any direction in a network, it intuitively follows that the random walk model can infer in a reverse order, namely infer drug given the disease.

In our work, we established heterogeneous networks of indications-indications similarity networks, target-protein to target-protein interaction networks, chemical compounds-chemical compounds similarity networks, indications to target-protein networks, indications-chemical compounds networks and target-protein to chemical compounds networks. The random walk model inference processes in the order of running through the indications similarity networks, the target-protein interaction networks and the chemical compounds similarity networks.

### 2.1 Indications for TCM

In medicine, the indications are the scope and standard notions on diseases for the treatment methods of drugs and surgery that are supposed to deal with the diseases. In TCM, it refers also to some symptoms that are phenomena observed in some disease development [3]. For example, heat clearing and damp-drying (清熱燥濕). And the indications in TCM may not share the same terms and notions as the disease ontology in western medicine. This makes it difficult to combine knowledge of both sides to understand the relations between TCM and West medicine. We have to apply conversion terms of indications used in TCM and map into western concepts in an approximate manner that could potentially fuzzy the system to infer precisely as western medicine.

### 2.2 The Construction of Biological Networks

With the development of genetics, proteomics, and chemical messenger, the relationship between diseases and these information is gradually revealed. For example, Online Mendelian Inheritance in Man(OMIM) provides the association between diseases and genes [4], Traditional Chinese Medicine Systems Pharmacology Database(TCMSP) provides information on some chemical compounds of Chinese herbs and related diseases and target proteins [5]. It is helpful for simulating or predicting the effects and correlations between chemicals, proteins and diseases to use the information to build the networks. However, most chemical compounds of Chinese herbs are so rich and unknown. Even the knowledge of their constituents are just beginning to increase through many modern extraction processes and compound structure analytic instruments such as mass spectrum in western medicine technology, it is still far more than complete. Our work on accurate prediction will somewhat be constrained by the incomplete information on constituents of Chinese herbs.

**Chemical-Based Networks**

The chemical-based networks can be divided into the chemical similarity and the chemical interaction. The similarity of chemical compounds is the structure's similarity.

The molecular structure of chemical compounds usually use Simplified Molecular Input Line Entry Specification(SMILES) to describe [6]. Molecular fingerprint are also a common representation for the structure of method chemical compounds [7]. It contains two-dimensional and three-dimensional structure information.

The methods commonly used in calculating the similarity of chemical compounds are Jaccard similarity, Euclidean distance, Cosine similarity.

**Target-Based Networks**

The target protein sequences are usually recorded in FASTA format, in which each amino acid and nucleic acid is represented by a single letter. The commonly methods for calculating sequence similarity are Basic Local Alignment Search Tool(BLAST) and Smith-Waterman algorithm [8].

**Indication-Based Networks**

The correlation between the indications can be calculated by using disease models established by gene or protein-protein interaction, but this method is not suitable for symptoms that are not caused by this or diseases with incomplete information [9]. Another method is to use phenotypes to calculate semantic similarity [10].

## 3 Overview of the System Architecture

In order to infer prescriptions on the combination of herbs to cope with indications in terms of Chinese medicine, several information modules have to be established.

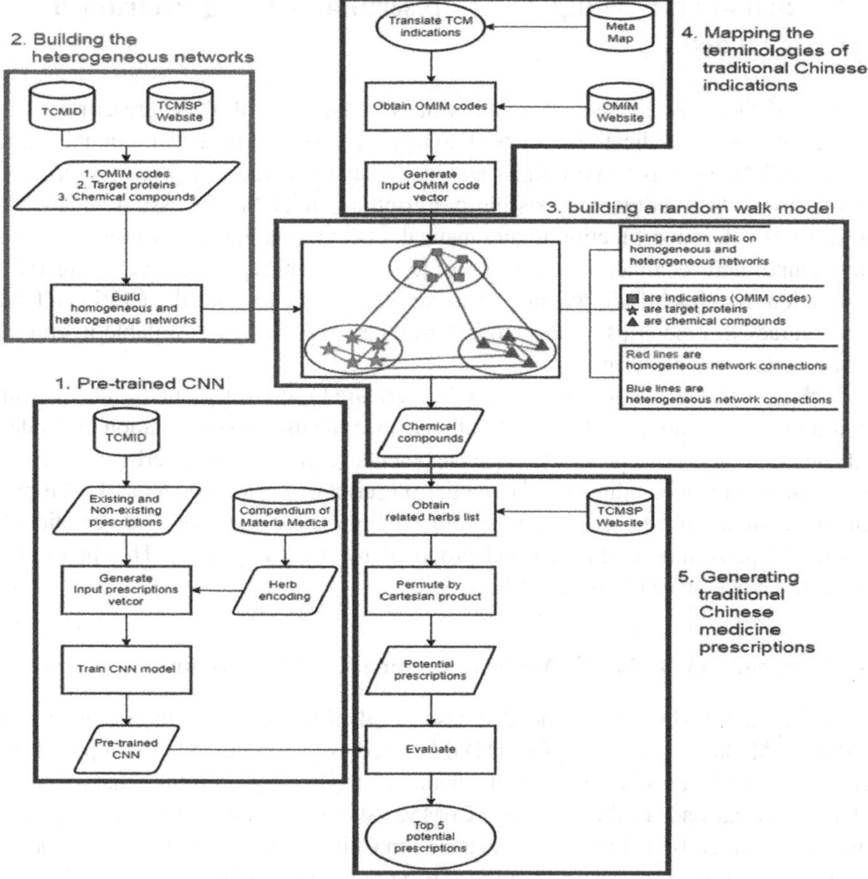


**Fig. 1.** System architecture

The scheme and methodologies of our work is mainly divided into five main steps: 1. Pre-train a CNN that can predict whether a proposed prescription of herb combination is similar to the existing traditional medicine, 2. Build both homogeneous and heterogeneous networks by integrate biological knowledge of western medicine on chemical compound, proteins and phenotype that allows to infer the drug ingredients associated with their target proteins/genes that can be further associated with phenotypes and disease indications, 3. Build a random walk model on to conduct the probabilistic inference on the multiplex heterogeneous networks and homogeneous networks, 4. Map the terminologies of TCM into western medicine terminologies using MetaMap tool so that the indications of Chinese medicine can be mapped to the corresponding OMIM codes of western terms, and 5. Generate TCM prescriptions by covering the chemical compounds (ingredients) inferred by the random walk inference by a combination of herbs. The overall architecture is shown in Fig. 1. The detailed descriptions of each step are to be described in the subsequent sections.

## 4 Prediction on Existing TCM Prescriptions Using Pretrained CNN Models

Since TCM literature consists of a somewhat big data size of TCM prescriptions in dealing with various indications, we wish to take advantage of the convolutional neural network (CNN) models to be trained as a classifier to decide if a given prescription is likely to be "similar" to the existing prescriptions in TCM. We assume this CNN can serve as a decision function to automatically decide if a given new prescription is truly "sound" and "complete" in some sense to be acceptable as a typical existing TCM prescription. But first of all, we have to make sure the accuracy of the CNN can have high accuracy to predict using the ground truth data reported and available in current TCM literature and prescriptions.

Luckily, we have a large data from TCM literature to serve as ground truth. To train a pretraining CNN model with ground truth data, we can use cross-validation method to evaluate its prediction accuracy. Because the potential combination of herbs can become plenty and too many candidates of potential prescriptions can be generated. The pre-trained classifier can be then used as a filter to eliminate those "no good" candidates of potential prescriptions inferred and proposed by our AI systems. This pretrained ensemble CNN is to be discussed in Sect. 8.1.

### 4.1 Compendium of Materia Medica Encoding (CoMM-Encoding)

In this study, the herbs that are encoded based on their features from the Compendium of Materia Medica (本草綱目) (CoMM)to be used as the input, and the output of the CNN model is a binary classification of whether it is indeed a prescription that is similar to the traditional ones in the literature. CoMM lists many properties of herbs, plants, animals and minerals [11] hierarchical catalog in Chinese medicine, and each recorded herb has a flavor tropism and indications. Using these data and the word classification of indications, herbs can be summarized as 148 features as in Table 1, which can be converted into one-hot encoding with a 148 dimension vector. It turns out that 1,425 herbs can be successfully encoded in our work. The encoding of a prescription is the sum of all CoMM-encoding of each herb in the prescription.

**Table 1.** Attributes in the CoMM-encoding vector

| Attribute Name | Quantity |
|---|---|
| Tropism of Flavor | 12 |
| Catalog of CoMM | 109 |
| Word Classification of Indications of Single Herb | 27 |

### 4.2 The TCMID Data Set

Traditional Chinese Medicine Integrated Database (TCMID) [12] is a database that provides information about herbs and prescriptions. The data sheet prescription-TCMID.v2.01 records the detailed information of 46,930 prescriptions, such as name, composition, indication, use method and reference. To reduce the complexity, we ignore the dosage, ways of preparing process and the original source sites of the herbs. For conducting the training data for binary classification of prescriptions, we have to generate counter-part of negative examples of prescriptions (fake prescriptions) for training the CNN classification model. We assume randomly generate a combination of herbs is unlikely to be a prescription in comparison to the currently existing ones. But if we combine existing herbs with an arbitrary random selection, it will be too easy for the CNN to recognize that it is a fake prescription that is not our purpose. To make the classifier more precise and sensitive to the subtle change, therefore, we need to generate random fake prescriptions whose probability distribution is as close to the real existing prescriptions as possible. Therefore, we prepare a set of positive and negative prescription data as existing and non-existing classes as follows.

- Existing prescriptions

  We filter out these prescriptions based on the herbs recorded in the CoMM [11] that cannot be completely encoded, and these filtered prescriptions are used as our the part of training data set. After filtering, the number of prescriptions is 3,435.
- Non-existing (fake) prescriptions

  Based on the existing prescriptions, we calculate the distribution of the number of herbs in the prescriptions and the occurrence frequency distribution of individual herbs. Using these two distributions, we can sample according to the probability distribution and generate the set of fake prescriptions as negative data for our training data set.

According to the statistics on the TCMID data set, 657 herbs appear at least once, and 768 herbs never appear at all in the 1,425 herbs of CoMM. To make the evaluation feasible, we must compromise with data that appear both only.

The training data set is composed of existing prescriptions (positive examples) and non-existing prescriptions (negative examples), the order is sorted randomly to ensure the balance of the data. The total number of training data set is 6,870, with each number of existing and non-existing prescriptions is balanced 3,435 respectively.

## 5 Building the Biological Heterogeneous and Homogeneous Networks Based on Western Medicine Knowledge

The biological networks include homogeneous networks and heterogeneous networks as shown in 0. Homogeneous networks are connections between the same types of component data, such as chemical compounds connected to chemical compounds; heterogeneous networks are connections between different types of component data, such as target protein connected to chemical compounds. In biological knowledge networks from western medicine, the pathways may contain interaction direction between components. However, they are far from complete and sometimes hard to obtain. We build the networks by ignoring such directions and also use an assumption to augment the networks based on a concept of "similarity" which means "similar components tend to have similar causality effects". In a large scale of implementation, it makes it easier to build the networks in an efficiently manner and conduct the random walk inference without losing much information on interactions among components.

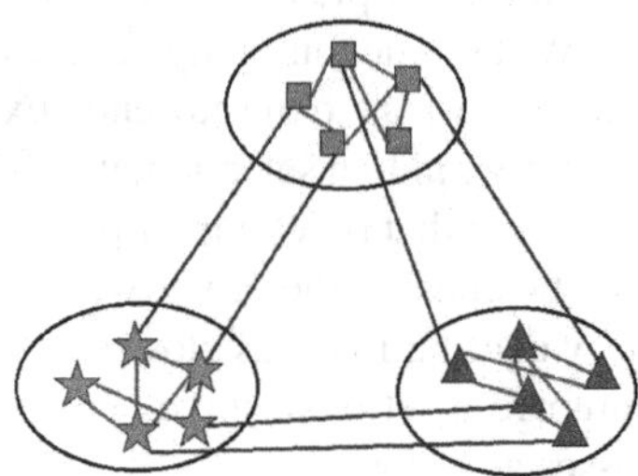

**Fig. 2.** Heterogeneous and homogeneous networks construction

Figure 2 shows the networks structure including the connections between the indications (green square icon), the target protein (orange star icon) and the chemical compounds (purple triangle icon). Red line indicates the homogeneous network connections and the blue line indicates the heterogeneous network connections.

In this work, the input of the networks is encoded vector representation of indications, and it initiates the random walk inference processes in the order of running through the indications similarity networks, the target-protein interaction networks and the chemical compounds similarity networks. The heterogeneous networks of the indications to the chemical compounds will serve as a reference standard for determining an inference threshold for the random work model. The networks will predict the chemical compounds whose likelihood probability are higher than the given inference threshold as the proposed candidate components that may be effective responses to the input indications.

### 5.1 Data Sources

In TCMID, the data sheet ingredient targets disease drug-TCMID.v2.03 records the relationship between chemical compounds, target protein and diseases [12]. Also, Traditional Chinese Medicine Systems Pharmacology Database (TCMSP) [5] provides the relationship between herbs, chemical compounds and target proteins. We can use the information to build homogeneous networks and heterogeneous networks.

### 5.2 Building the Homogeneous Networks

The diseases recorded in the data sheet ingredient targets disease drug-TCMID.v2.03 are OMIM code [4], and there are 4,308 OMIM codes in total. Since there is a corresponding relationship between OMIM codes (genetic disease codes) and chemical compounds, for two OMIM codes, if the corresponding chemical compounds are the same or overlapping to some extent, it means they tend to have more or less similar functions. Therefore, we can use this concept to calculate Jaccard similarity between two OMIM codes as Eq. 1 where $O$ indicates the OMIM code, and $C$ is the chemical compound.

$$sim\left(O_i, O_j\right) = \frac{\left|(C \in O_i) \cap \left(C' \in O_j\right)\right|}{\left|(C \in O_i) \cup \left(C' \in O_j\right)\right|} \tag{1}$$

The target proteins recorded in the data sheet ingredient targets disease drug-TCMID.v2.03 are UniProt [13] code, and there are 13,340 UniProt codes in total.

In order to calculate the sequence similarity between target proteins, first, we obtain the sequence of a target protein by searching UniProt through its UniProt code. Second, we use Biostrings package [14] from R-programming language to calculate the sequence similarity between target proteins. The sequence similarity is calculated based on the Smith-Waterman alignment algorithm [8].

The chemical compound recorded in the data sheet ingredient targets disease drugTCMID.v2.03 are chemical compound names, and there are 1,110 chemical compound names in total. Also, there are 6,465 chemical compound names in TCMSP. After merging the chemical compound names of TCMID and TCMSP and removing duplicate items, there are 6,734 in total.

In order to calculate the structural similarity of between chemical compounds, first, we obtain the SMILES of chemical compounds by searching PubChem through chemical compound names. SMILES can map a chemical compound molecular topology into a unique string language expression so that the structure of a chemical compound can be compared in terms of the character sequence in the string.

Second, we use RxnSim package [15] from R-programming language to calculate SMILES Jaccard similarity between two chemical compounds $X$ and $X\prime$ which are expressed in terms of SMILES string sequences as in Eq. 2.

$$sim\left(x, x'\right) = \frac{\left|X \cap X'\right|}{\left|X \cup X'\right|} \tag{2}$$

## 5.3 Building the Heterogeneous Networks

According to the data sheet ingredient targets disease drug-TCMID.v2.03, we can obtain the corresponding relationship between OMIM code and target protein. Therefore, if there is the corresponding relationship between OMIM code $O_i$ and target protein $F_j$, the association is 1, otherwise it is 0.

$$OF(i,j) = \begin{cases} 1; & if\ O_i\ has\ F_j \\ 0; & else \end{cases} \tag{3}$$

According to the data sheet ingredient targets disease drug-TCMID.v2.03, we can obtain the corresponding relationship between OMIM codes and chemical compounds. Therefore, if there is the corresponding relationship between a OMIM code $O_i$ and a chemical compound $C_j$, the connection association is 1, otherwise it is 0.

This heterogeneous network will be used as the ground truth reference for determining the threshold.

$$OC(i,j) = \begin{cases} 1; \ if \ O_i \ has \ C_j \\ 0; \quad else \end{cases} \tag{4}$$

According to the data sheet ingredient targets disease drug-TCMID.v2.03 and TCMSP, we can obtain the corresponding relationship between target proteins and drug chemical compounds. Therefore, if there is the corresponding relationship between a target protein $F_i$ and a chemical compound $C_j$ the association is 1, otherwise it is 0.

$$FC(i,j) = \begin{cases} 1; \ if \ F_i \ has \ C_j \\ 0; \quad else \end{cases} \tag{5}$$

# 6 The Random Walk Inference Models on Complex Heterogeneous Networks

In this study, the indications will be firstly converted into OMIM Code and then be entered as the input into the homogeneous and heterogeneous networks that have been established based on the similarity concept, and then use the random walk models to infer the affected chemical compounds given indications. The networks make the final decision on the chemical compounds whose likelihood probability exceeding a given threshold.

Since the entire networks contain the information transmission of homogeneous and heterogeneous networks, we use the random walk models proposed by Huang et al. [16] and Hwang and Kuang [17]. At every inference step in the networks, the influence between homogeneous and heterogeneous networks must be considered before updating the information.

About the transmission of the network, define the probabilistic transition matrix as S in terms of the original matrix M as in Eq. 6. The sum of each row of the transition matrix should be 1.

$$S(i,j) = \frac{M(i,j)}{\sum_k M(i,j)} \tag{6}$$

The transfer process of a single network is defined in Eq. 7.

$$p^t = \alpha S p^{t-1} + (1-\alpha)p^0 \tag{7}$$

In formula 7, $p^t$ is the state probability at step $t$, $p^0$ is the initial state probability, $p^{t-1}$ is the state probability before $p^t$, and $\alpha$ is the diffusion coefficient. $\alpha S p^{t-1}$ can be regarded as the iterative transfer of previous state probability, and $(1-\alpha)p^0$ can be regarded as the random walk in the initial state and then restart.

If $\alpha$ is 0, then the state probability will always be the initial probability and cannot be extended to other nodes; if $\alpha$ is not 0, after $t$ iterations, the probability will tend to stabilize and reach convergence. The $\alpha$ of indications networks, target-protein networks and chemical-compounds networks are 0.5, 0.25 and 0.25 respectively.

We combined random walk formula of both the homogeneous and heterogeneous network and derived the Eq. 8 [16].

$$p_i^t = \alpha_i S_i p_i^{t-1} + (1 - \alpha_i)\left[a_i \sum_{i \neq j} S_{ij} p_j^0 + (1 - \alpha_i) p_i^0\right] \tag{8}$$

In the formula 8, $\alpha_i S_i p_i^{t-1}$ is the transition of the previous state probability in the homogeneous network; $(1 - \alpha_i)\left[a_i \sum_{i \neq j} S_{ij} p_j^0 + (1 - \alpha) p_i^0\right]$ is the initial state probability updated from heterogeneous networks.

## 7 Converting TCM Indications Terms into Western Medicine Concepts

Since the input of the random walk model must be related to the OMIM code, to enable the input descriptions of TCM indications which are taken from the data sheet of TCMIDv203, we use MetaMap [18] by National Library of Medicine (NLM) to help us map the descriptions of traditional Chinese medicine indications to the Unified Medical Language System (UMLS) medical concepts, and then use the UMLS concepts to search for relevant OMIM codes.

MetaMap [18] can map biomedical texts to the conceptual vocabulary of UMLS, and each mapped vocabulary contains different semantic types and semantic groups. The same mapped vocabulary may have multiple semantic types. For example, if we input "cold", it could be mapped to "cold temperature" (Natural Phenomenon or Process),"common cold" (Disease or Syndrome), and "cold sensation" (Organism Function). By filtering the semantic types, the vocabulary could be mapped into a specific standardized semantic range. The semantic types we choose is either "diseases", "syndromes and signs" or "symptoms" to ensure mapping into indication related standard western medicine terms in UMLS. Table 2 illustrates an example of using MataMap to map the traditional Chinese medicine indications.

**Table 2.** Results of TCM Indications that are Translated into English Using MetaMap Mapping

| TCM indications | English | MetaMap Mapping |
|---|---|---|
| 濕疹, 皮炎, 燒傷, 潰瘍。 | Eczema, dermatitis, burns, ulcers | Eczema<br>Dermatitis<br>Burn injury<br>Ulcer |

# 8 Experimentation

## 8.1 The Performance of the Pre-Trained Ensemble CNN Classifier

In order to train a pre-trained CNN as the classifier to distinguish whether the TCM prescriptions is similar to the existing prescriptions, we divide data into training set, validation set and test set with total data 6,870. The 5-fold average performance of the pre-trained CNN is 81.72% as shown in Table 3.

**Table 3.** Training and evaluation of pre-trained ensemble CNN models

| Fold-N | Validation accuracy | Evaluation accuracy |
|---|---|---|
| 1 | 0.809216 | 0.818049 |
| 2 | 0.806791 | 0.820961 |
| 3 | 0.784964 | 0.815138 |
| 4 | 0.809871 | 0.822416 |
| 5 | 0.820388 | 0.809316 |
| Average | 0.809216 | **0.817176** |

In order to boost the performance of pre-trained CNN, we use voting, a way of ensemble learning. First, we increase our data set by vector-shifting 1 to 3 bits, vector-flipping left and right, and swapping the front and back halves of the vector. These processes can generate additional 12 different data sets. This is to avoid the position bias for the herbs the appear in the input. Second, we use these data set to train CNN individually. After training, we use test data set to obtain prediction accuracy of each CNN individually. Here, including the Pre-trained CNN, we can obtain a total of 13 prediction accuracies for 13 CNN runs. We calculate voting weight for each model based on these prediction accuracy. The total sum of voting weight is 1.

$$w_i = \frac{p_i}{\sum_{n=1}^{n=max} p_n} \tag{9}$$

In the formula, $w_i$ is the voting weight of model $i$, $p_i$ is the prediction accuracy of model $i$, $\sum_{n=1}^{n=max} p_n$ is the sum of prediction accuracy of models, $max$ is the total number of models. Table 4 shows the voting weight of each model.

Finally, we enter the test data and obtain 92.43% prediction accuracy by weighted voting from 13 CNN models. Compare with the 81.72% prediction accuracy of single pre-trained CNN, this result shows the benefit of ensemble learning.

**Table 4.** Voting weight of each CNN

| Model Name | Prediction accuracy | Voting weight |
|---|---|---|
| Pre-trained CNN | 0.835517 | 0.079085 |
| Shift 1 bit | 0.800582 | 0.075778 |
| Shift 2 bits | 0.806405 | 0.076329 |
| Shift 3 bits | 0.807860 | 0.076467 |
| Flip-shift 1 bit | 0.820961 | 0.077707 |
| Flip-shift 2 bits | 0.809316 | 0.076605 |
| Flip-shift 3 bits | 0.816594 | 0.077294 |
| Swap-shift 1 bit | 0.813683 | 0.077019 |
| Swap-shift 2 bits | 0.812227 | 0.076881 |
| Swap-shift 3 bits | 0.812227 | 0.076881 |
| Swap-flip-shift 1 bit | 0.812227 | 0.076881 |
| Swap-flip-shift 2 bits | 0.810771 | 0.076743 |
| Swap-flip-shift 3 bits | 0.806404 | 0.076330 |
| Total | 10.564774 | 1.000000 |

### 8.2 Experiment of Random Walk Inference

**Test Data for Random Walk Models**

Although TCM dataset consists of a lot of data, to be able to have the data match with western medicine knowledge to be able to be conduct random walk inference over biological networks for evaluation, the TCM indications used as evaluation data must meet the following conditions:

1. It must be complete or most of them can be converted into UMLS medical concepts.
2. Its OMIM codes in conceptual vocabulary of UMLS must be completely found in order to cover all indications.

Therefore, we tentatively choose 8 indications from the data sheet prescription-TCMID.v2.01 as the test data as shown in Table 5.

After the chemical compounds are proposed by the random walk algorithms, we can obtain related herbs by searching on the TCMSP online platform [19] that covers the inferred chemical compounds. In Table 6, X means that no related herbs were found, and the chemical compounds are sorted in descending order which is based on their probabilities that exceed the threshold.

**Table 5.** Test data set for random walk

| Case Index | Indications | MetaMap Mapping | OMIM Code |
|---|---|---|---|
| 1 | 血痢。 | Hemorrhagic dysentery | 175050 |
| 2 | 癲狂、五癇、眩暈, 氣血虛, 挾風痰鬱火, 時作時止, 痰涎壅盛, 心神昏憒。 | Seizures<br>Dizziness<br>Malnutrition<br>Flatulence | 121200<br>310700<br>155310<br>223100 |
| 3 | 口舌糜爛, 及走馬牙疳等證。 | Oral cavity Malnutrition | 311200<br>155310 |
| 4 | 瘟疫, 鼻中出血後, 飲水瀉痢。 | Plague Diarrhea | 123320<br>304790 |
| 5 | 濕疹, 皮炎, 燒傷, 潰瘍。 | Eczema<br>Dermatitis<br>Burn injury<br>Ulcer | 301000<br>605803<br>608572<br>600263 |
| 6 | 跌打損傷。 | Bruises | 232400 |
| 7 | 瘡癬。 | Tinea | 615598 |
| 8 | 頭痛。 | Headache | 141500 |

**Table 6.** The searching result using TCMSP online platform

| 17alpha-estradiol | aminoacetic acid | 1-butanol | glycerin |
|---|---|---|---|
| X | Largehead Atractylodes Rhizome (白朮) | Chinese Lobelia Herb (半邊蓮) | Giant Typhonium Tuber (白附子) |
| | Ternate Pinellia (半夏) | Pilose Asiabell Root (黨參) | Greenish Lily Bulb (百合) |
| | Common Jujube (大棗) | Medicinal Morinda Root (甘草) | Indigowoad Root (板藍根) |
| | Dan-shen Root (丹參) | Rosewood Heart Wood (降香) | Chinese Thorawax Root (柴胡) |
| | Mongolian Snakegourd Fruit (瓜蔞) | Chinese Trumpetcreeper (凌霄花) | Japanese Climbing Fern Spore (海金沙) |

(*continued*)

**Table 6.** *(continued)*

| 17alpha-estradiol | aminoacetic acid | 1-butanol | glycerin |
|---|---|---|---|
| | Mung beans (綠豆) | White Mulbeery Root - bark (桑白皮) | Common Floweringquine Fruit (木瓜) |
| | Great Burdock Fruit (牛蒡子) | Mulberry Leaf (桑葉) | Costusroot (木香) |
| | Gordon Curyale Seed (芡實) | Muskroot - like Semiaquilegia Root (天葵子) | Ginseng Leaf (人參葉) |
| | Common Yam Rhizome (山藥) | Ginkgo Leaf (銀杏葉) | Mullberry Fruit (桑椹) |
| | Common Macrocarpium Fruit (山茱萸) | Herb of Shortscape Fleabane (燈細辛) | Fructus Hippophae(沙棘) |
| | Blessed Thistle (水飛薊) | | Villous Amomum Fruit (砂仁) |
| | Sandalwood (檀香) | | Fresh Ginger (生薑) |
| | Tabasheer (天竺黃) | | |

## 8.3 Evaluation on Generating TCM Prescriptions

Herbs may have many other names and since one chemical compound may have several related herbs. After obtaining the herbs to cover ingredients inferred by the random walk inference, we filter them based on the herbs recorded in the CoMM. We then use the Cartesian product to generate all possible combination of herbs as prescriptions. To narrow down the possible number of prescriptions, we can also select only the top three herbs according to the distribution of occurrence frequency of individual herbs as the permutation of the combinations of herbs. Therefore, we will have the following three possible versions of generating prescriptions:

- The baseline that is based on the herbs that cover the ingredients that are associated with indications in the heterogeneous networks that are recorded in OMIM.
- The random walk (RW) model: prescriptions of herbs that cover all ingredients inferred by the random walk model.
- The random walk + occurrence frequency of individual herbs(RW+O):

After random walk inference, there are many ingredients that are to be covered by combination of herbs. In the Table 7, we show the number of herb combinations from the three versions of prescription generation.

The pre-trained CNN can predict which combinations of herb are similar to TCM prescriptions, and the results are shown in Table 8. We find many test data whose values turn out to be all 0's. The possible reasons are: 1. Since we use CoMM-encoding as the input of the pre-trained CNN, we filter out most of the existing prescriptions as the

**Table 7.** Number of herb combinations

| Case Index | Baseline | RW | RW + O |
|---|---|---|---|
| 1 | 31,104 | 12,096 | 486 |
| 2 | 18,433 | 1,512 | 162 |
| 3 | 21,888 | 3,276 | 81 |
| 4 | 103,680 | 108 | 18 |
| 5 | 5,806,080 | 144 | 27 |
| 6 | 216 | 30 | 9 |
| 7 | 51,840 | 3,024 | 54 |
| 8 | 96 | 36 | 18 |

data set, and the number dropped from 46,930 to 3,435. 2. Although TCMSP provides 13,729 chemical compounds and 502 herbs, there are still many chemical compounds that no related corresponding herbs can be found in TCMSP.

However, even under this extremely incomplete information condition, the systems can still infer the effectiveness by the random walk model on case index 3, 5 and 7.

**Table 8.** The number of predicted prescriptions

| Case Index | Baseline | RW | RW + O |
|---|---|---|---|
| 1 | 137 | 0 | 0 |
| 2 | 0 | 0 | 0 |
| **3** | **17** | **172** | **15** |
| 4 | 6 | 0 | 0 |
| **5** | **1,587** | **61** | **9** |
| 6 | 5 | 0 | 0 |
| **7** | **12,437** | **1,168** | **30** |
| 8 | 0 | 0 | 0 |

In order to fairly compare with the baseline, we enlarge the number of combination of herbs for each version to the same number as the baseline, the number of predicted as prescriptions will follow the same proportion to be enlarged. For example, take a look at case index 3 in Table 7. We want to enlarge the RW number (3,279) to the same number as the baseline (21,888), the enlarged ratio should be 6.68 times (namely 21,888/3,279). Similarly, we obtain the ratio for cases 5 and 7. Table 9 shows the enlarged ratio of each version to the baseline. As shown in the Table 10, versions based on the random walk algorithms tend to perform better than the baseline in all cases in the sense that they can generate more prescriptions. However, with so large number of feasible prescription candidates, we have to further narrow down the most effective ones.

**Table 9.** The enlarged ratio of each version to baseline

| Case Index | RW to Baseline | RW + O to Baseline |
|---|---|---|
| 3 | x6.68 | x270.22 |
| 5 | x40,320 | x215,040 |
| 7 | x17.14 | x960 |

**Table 10.** The number of predicted prescriptions (enlarging)

| Case Index | Baseline | RW | RW+O |
|---|---|---|---|
| 3 | 17 | 1,149 | **4,053** |
| 5 | 1,587 | **2,459,250** | 1,935,360 |
| 7 | 12,437 | 20,022 | **28,800** |

### 8.4 Expert Subjective Evaluation by Questionnaire

Since truly biological evaluation on whether a prescription is indeed effective for a given set of indications is very costly. At this academic study, we can only conduct subjective evaluation by questionnaire to get the first sense as to how the models perform. We invited 5 experts as Chinese medical physicians and pharmacists to subjectively evaluate the Top 5 prescriptions of version RW+O by questionnaire. The experts are all above five years of professional experience in their domains. There are 8 questions in the questionnaire, each of question is a description of the indication with 7 prescriptions. Among the 7 prescriptions, five are Top 5 prescriptions, one is non-Top 5 prescription, and one is TCMID standard prescription. The purpose of adding the latter two to the options is to ensure the evaluation is blind that no evaluator has an idea whether prescriptions are computer generated. There are 4 options for each prescription for the evaluators to select, which are "very unsuitable", "unsuitable", "suitable", and "very suitable". According the chart in Fig. 3, the proportion of "suitable" plus "very suitable" is 38.00%. Considering that we are in the case of extreme incomplete data, this blind evaluation result is quite satisfactory in the sense that the model builder is quite naive in the Chinese medicine domain.

Take a closer look at the responses to the questions in Table 11. In question 2, 4, 6, 7, and 8, among the 5 prescriptions the CNN predicted, the number of prescriptions being approved by all Chinese medical physicians is 1, 2, 4, 5, and 2 respectively. Even though the number of predicted of prescriptions by pre-trained CNN is 0 because none of the prescriptions passed the threshold like case 2, 4, 6 and 8, the model's top five predictions by our system are still approved by all Chinese medical physicians. This shows that the system can indeed discover some potential prescriptions that Chinese medical physicians and pharmacists tend to consider as feasible according to their expertise and experience. However, the ground truth effects of the proposed prescriptions by the systems have

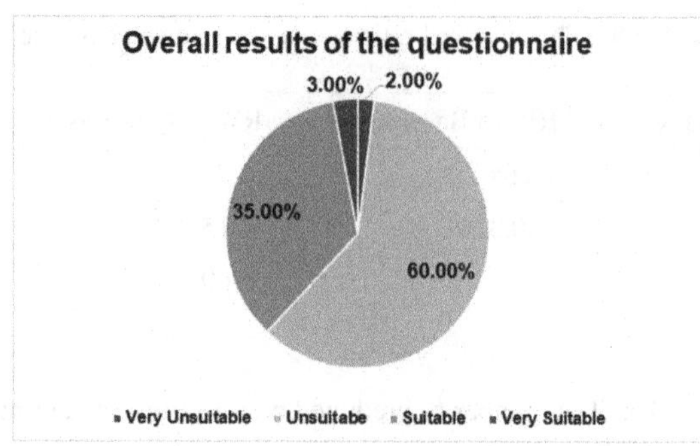


**Fig. 3.** Overall results of the questionnaire

to go through more rigorous clinical evaluations to be validated which could be a very costly process.

**Table 11.** The number of approved by all Chinese medical physicians

| Question Index | Number of predicted Prescriptions | Number of Approved Prescriptions |
|---|---|---|
| 1 | 0 | 0 |
| **2** | **0** | **1** |
| 3 | 15 | 0 |
| **4** | **0** | **2** |
| 5 | 9 | 0 |
| **6** | **0** | **4** |
| **7** | **30** | **5** |
| **8** | **0** | **2** |

## 9 Conclusion

We established homogeneous and heterogeneous networks by OMIM codes, target protein sequences and chemical compounds, then use a random walk algorithm to infer possible potential TCM prescriptions from the descriptions of TCM indications. In order to establish a deep learning model that can classify prescriptions as "feasible", we pretrain an ensemble CNN model, so that it can learn to classify a "true" prescriptions from the "fake" ones. We obtain an overall pre-trained ensemble CNN with the average prediction accuracy being 92.43%.

Finally, we conducted subjective evaluations on the potential prescriptions proposed by our systems using questionnaires. The blind evaluation by human experts on the prescriptions proposed by our system being categorized as "suitable" or "very suitable" against "not suitable" and "very unsuitable" is overall 38.00%. Considering the available data are quite incomplete at many stages, this result is quite surprising and satisfactory. Although under extreme incomplete information such as the ingredients of Chinese herbs, it often makes results deteriorate, we still obtain preliminary results for further investigation and evaluation.

In addition to making the information more complete as we encountered many gaps between the Chinese medicine and western medicine as future work. The mapping of indications of Chinese medicine with western disease ontology definitely is a non-trivial task that needs to take more domain expert knowledge. Besides, the inference over the biological networks can be elaborated if the construction of biological networks can be refined even more precisely.

## References

1. Liu, H., Song, Y., Guan, J., Luo, L., Zhuang, Z.: Inferring new indications for approved drugs via random walk on drug-disease heterogenous networks. BMC Bioinform. **17**(539), 3712–3714 (2016)
2. Kuo, Y., Soo, V.: Predictions on indications of traditional Chinese medicine based on a random walk model. In: CSCE-BIOCOMP (2019)
3. Marshall, A.C.: Traditional Chinese medicine and clinical pharmacology. In: Hock, F.J., Gralinski, M.R. (eds.) Drug Discovery and Evaluation: Methods in Clinical Pharmacology, pp. 455–482. Springer, Cham (2020). https://doi.org/10.1007/978-3-319-68864-0_60
4. Hamosh, A., Scott, A.F., Amberger, J., Valle, D., McKusick, V.A.: Online Mendelian inheritance in man (OMIM). Hum. Mutat. **15**(1), 57–61 (1999)
5. Jinlong, R., et al.: TCMSP: a database of systems pharmacology for drug discovery from herbal medicines. J. Cheminform. **6**(1), 13 (2014). https://doi.org/10.1186/1758-2946-6-13
6. David, W.: Smiles, a chemical language and information system. 1. introduction to methodology and encoding rules. J. Chem. Inf. Comput. Sci. **28**(1), 31–36 (1988)
7. Cereto-Massagué, A., Ojeda, M.J., Valls, C., Mulero, M., Garcia-Vallvé, S., Pujadas, G.: Molecular fingerprint similarity search in virtual screening. Methods **71**, 58–63 (2015)
8. Pearson, W.R.: An introduction to sequence similarity ("homology") searching. Current Protocols Bioinform. **42**, 1–3 (2013)
9. Suthram, S., Dudley, J.T., Chiang, A.P., Chen, R., Hastie, T.J., Butte, A.J.: Network-based elucidation of human disease similarities reveals common functional modules enriched for pluripotent drug targets. PLoS Comput. Biol. **6**(2), 1000662 (2010)
10. Wang, X., Gulbahce, N., Yu, H.: Network-based methods for human disease gene prediction. Brief. Funct. Genomics **10**(5), 280–293 (2011)
11. Li, S.: Compendium of Materia Medica (1596)
12. Lin, H., et al.: TCMID 20: a comprehensive resource for TCM. Nucleic Acids Res. **46**(D1), 1117–1120 (2017)
13. Bateman, A., Bridge, A., Wu, C.: UniProt (website). https://www.uniprot.org/
14. Pagès, H., Aboyoun, P., Gentleman, R. and DebRoy, S.: Biostrings: efficient manipulation of biological strings (R package version 2.70.1). https://bioconductor.org/packages/release/bioc/html/Biostrings.html
15. Varun, G., Venkata, S.T., Myung, C.K., Yong, K.T., Anirban, B.: RxnSim: a tool to compare biochemical reactions. Bioinformatics **31**(22), 3712–3714 (2015)
16. Huang, Y., Yeh, H., Soo, V.: Inferring drug-disease associations from integration of chemical, genomic and phenotype data using network propagation. BMC Med. Genom. **6**(3), 1–14 (2013). https://doi.org/10.1186/1755-8794-6-S3-S4

17. Hwang, T., Kuang, R.: A heterogeneous label propagation algorithm for disease gene discovery. In: Proceedings of the 2010 SIAM International Conference on Data Mining, pp. 583–594 (2010)
18. Aronson, A.R.: Effective mapping of biomedical text to the UMLS Metathesaurus: the MetaMap program. In: Proceedings, AMIA Symposium, pp. 17–21 (2001)
19. Wang, Y.: Traditional Chinese medicine database and analysis platform (website). https://www.tcmsp-e.com/tcmsp.php

# Image Pseudo Label Consistency Exploitation for Semi-supervised Pathological Tissue Segmentation

Chien-Yu Chiou[1], Wei-Li Chen[1], Chun-Rong Huang[2], and Pau-Choo Chung[1](✉)

[1] Department of Electrical Engineering, National Cheng Kung University, Tainan, Taiwan
pcchung@ee.ncku.edu.tw

[2] Cross College Elite Program, and Academy of Innovative Semiconductor and Sustainable Manufacturing, National Cheng Kung University, Tainan, Taiwan

**Abstract.** Supervised deep learning-based segmentation methods help doctors to identify regions of human tissues and lesions on pathological images and diagnosis diseases. However, due to the huge sizes of pathological images and the fragile shapes of human tissues and lesions, labeling large scale training data for the supervised deep learning methods is prohibitive. Semi-supervised learning methods generate pseudo-labels of unlabeled data and utilize the information from both labeled and unlabeled data to reduce the required amount of labeled data for training. One of the critical issues of semi-supervised learning is to generate consistent pseudo-labels for similar samples. To improve the consistency of the pseudo-labels, we propose an image pseudo label consistency exploitation method to regularize the models to generate similar predictions for similar samples by considering the image consistent loss and set consistent loss with the help of data augmentations of the unlabeled images. The experiments on two pathological segmentation datasets show the superior of the proposed method over state-of-the-art methods.

**Keywords:** Pathological Image Analysis · Pathological Tissue Segmentation · Semi-supervised Learning · Semantic Segmentation

## 1 Introduction

In recent years, deep learning achieves success in many fields [9, 12, 23, 25, 27], and been gradually introduced to pathological image analysis to assist doctors diagnose disease [8, 10, 13]. Deep segmentation models [6, 28, 34] help doctors to identify regions of interested tissues and lesions on pathological images and diagnose diseases. However, it requires a large scale of labeled training data to train accurate and robust deep segmentation models. Labeling pathological images requires knowledge in pathology and to be operated by experienced pathologists. In addition, the sizes of pathological images are huge, while the interested tissues and lesions often have relatively small sizes and/or fragile shapes. Such situations increase the difficulties to accurately label the pathological images [10]. Therefore, it is very expensive and time-consuming to create a large scale labeled training set for pathological segmentation models.


C.-Y. Lee et al. (Eds.): TAAI 2023, CCIS 2074, pp. 217–226, 2024.
https://doi.org/10.1007/978-981-97-1711-8_16

To reduce the burden of labeling, making good use of abundant unlabeled data with limited amount of labeled training data becomes an important issue for the training of deep pathological segmentation models [10]. State-of-the-art semi-supervised learning (SSL) methods [21, 35] usually generate pseudo-labels for the unlabeled data with a teacher model and then train a student model utilizing both the information from the labeled and unlabeled training data to infer the segmentation results. One of the most critical issues of SSL is the quality of the generated pseudo-labels [1]. The teacher model may make wrong predictions for the unlabeled data and thus generate incorrect pseudo-labels. Learning with incorrect pseudo-labels will degrade the performance of the learned student model.

Based on the semi-supervised smoothness assumption [4] that similar objects should have similar labels, consistency regularization is often used to improve the learned student models and also help to increase the quality of pseudo-labels generated by the teacher model [15, 22, 26, 32]. To achieve consistency regularization, two or more perturbations of a training sample are made. Because the perturbations are generated from the same training sample, both teacher and student models should also make the consistent predictions. A consistency regularization loss is calculated based on the difference between the predictions. It encourages the models to generate consistent predictions for different perturbations of the same samples. However, when unlabelled samples are from the same class, consistency regularization cannot be applied to generate similar predictions for these samples. In pathological tissue segmentation, many tissues, such as cells or glands, will repeatedly appear in the pathological images. Conventional consistency regularization is then hard to retrieve effective information from these tissues.

To address this issue, we propose an image pseudo label consistency exploitation method to regularize the models to generate similar predictions for similar samples by considering the image consistent loss and set consistent loss with the help of data augmentations of the unlabeled images. The details of the proposed method will be described in Sect. 3.

## 2 Related Work

While most researchers focus on developing semi-supervised classification and segmentation methods for natural images [7, 21, 35, 38] and medical images [18, 36], semi-supervised segmentation methods for pathological images are not well discussed. Li et al. [19] consider self-loop uncertainty to provide the ground-truth for the unlabeled images for semi-supervised pathology image segmentation. Xie et al. [37] propose the pairwise relation-based semi-supervised method by combing a segmentation network with a pairwise relation network. Lai et al. [17] propose a semi-supervised active learning framework to expand the diversity of the labeled set to the unlabeled set. Jin et al. [14] propose a mean-teacher based hierarchical consistency enforcement framework to enhance the consistency among auxiliary and main decoders of the model. Shi et al. [29] propose a semi-supervised pixel contrastive learning framework to capture the cross-patch information by optimizing a contrastive loss.

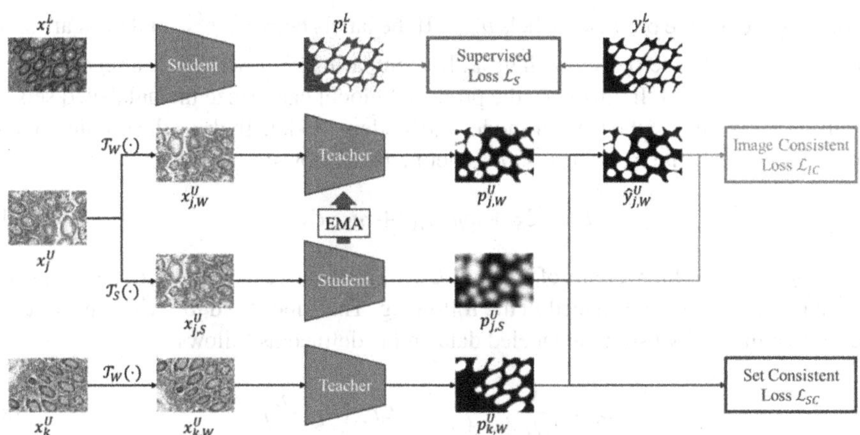


**Fig. 1.** Overview of the proposed method

# 3 Method

Given a partially labeled training set of pathological images, the labeled dataset $\mathcal{X}_L$ is defined as $\mathcal{X}_L = \{(x_i^L, y_i^L)\}_{i=1}^{N_L}$ with $N_L$ samples and the unlabeled dataset $\mathcal{X}_U$ is defined as $\mathcal{X}_U = \{x_j^U\}_{j=1}^{N_U}$ with $N_U$ samples, where $x_i^L$ denotes the $i$-th labeled image, $y_i^L$ denotes the label of the $i$-th image, and $x_j^U$ denotes the $j$-th unlabeled image. We aim to train a semantic segmentation model for pathological images by utilizing both the information from the labeled and unlabeled training data.

Figure 1 shows the overview of the proposed method. The proposed framework consists of a teacher model and a student model with the same architecture, which are initialized with the same pre-trained weights. The teacher model aims to provide pseudo labels of $\mathcal{X}_U$ for the student model, while the student model aims to learn information from the $\mathcal{X}_L$ and $\mathcal{X}_U$ by using the proposed losses. To propagate the information learned by the student model and improve the teacher model, the teacher model is updated by using exponential moving average (EMA) from the student model's weights.

The labeled images are learned by using the student model with supervised loss $\mathcal{L}_S$. Given an unlabeled image $x_j^U$, we pass $x_j^U$ to two random augmentation functions $\mathcal{T}_W(\cdot)$ and $\mathcal{T}_S(\cdot)$ to generate two random augmentations $x_{j,W}^U$ and $x_{j,S}^U$. Because $x_{j,W}^U$ and $x_{j,S}^U$ are generated from $x_j^U$, the predicted labels of $x_{j,W}^U$ and $x_{j,S}^U$ should be consistent. Let the predicted labels of $x_{j,W}^U$ by using the teacher model be $p_{j,W}^U$. Let the predicted labels of $x_{j,S}^U$ by using the student model be $p_{j,S}^U$. $p_{j,W}^U$ and $p_{j,S}^U$ should be consistent. Based on the consistent constraint, we propose an image consistent loss $\mathcal{L}_{IC}$ to ensure the consistency between the predicted labels of the teacher model and the student model.

To further utilize the remaining unlabeled images, we consider the correlations among the $x_j^U$ and the remaining unlabeled images in $\mathcal{X}_U$. Given an unlabeled image $x_k^U$, $k \neq j$, it is also passed to the random augmentation function $\mathcal{T}_W(\cdot)$ and the teacher model to generate the predicted labels $p_{k,W}^U$. If the labels between $p_{j,W}^U$ and $p_{k,W}^U$ are similar, $p_{j,S}^U$ should also be similar with $p_{k,W}^U$. By comparing $p_{j,W}^U$ with $p_{k,W}^U$, a set consistent loss $\mathcal{L}_{SC}$ is computed. In this way, the proposed model can utilize the unlabeled sets to enhance the training of the teacher model and student model. To drive the training of the proposed network, the loss function $\mathcal{L}$ is defined as follows:

$$\mathcal{L} = \mathcal{L}_S + \omega_{IC}\mathcal{L}_{IC} + \omega_{SC}\mathcal{L}_{SC}, \tag{1}$$

where $\omega_{IC}$ and $\omega_{SC}$ the weights of $\mathcal{L}_{IC}$ and $\mathcal{L}_{SC}$. The detailed definitions of the proposed loss functions will be introduced in the following. The supervised loss $\mathcal{L}_S$ aims to learn the student model by using the labeled data and is defined as follows:

$$\mathcal{L}_S = \frac{1}{N_L}\sum\nolimits_{x_i^L, y_i^L \in \mathcal{X}_L} \mathcal{L}_{CE}\left(p_i^L, y_i^L\right), \tag{2}$$

where $p_i^L$ is the predicted labels of the student models of the labeled dataset, and $\mathcal{L}_{CE}(\cdot)$ is the cross entropy function.

To apply the information of the unlabeled dataset, we propose the image consistent loss $\mathcal{L}_{IC}$ which aims to ensure the label consistency of $p_{j,W}^U$ and $p_{j,S}^U$ generated by using the teacher model and the student model as follows:

$$\mathcal{L}_{IC} = \frac{1}{N_U}\sum\nolimits_{x_j^U \in \mathcal{X}_U} \mathcal{L}_{CE}\left(p_{j,S}^U, \hat{y}_{j,W}^U\right), \tag{3}$$

where $\hat{y}_{j,W}^U$ is the pseudo-label of $x_j^U$ generated by the one-hotting teacher model prediction $p_{j,W}^U$. By considering the image consistency between predicted results of the teacher model and the student model of the same unlabeled image, the models are enforced to learn effective features to represent both of the weak and strong augments of the unlabeled image.

In addition to the image consistent loss, we propose the set consistent loss to further improve the consistency of the predicted labels between two similar samples $x_j^U$ and $x_k^U$. To reduce the computation complexity, we represent each sample by using the average predictions of different augmentations as $\overline{p}_{j,W}^U, \overline{p}_{k,W}^U, \overline{p}_{j,S}^U$. Here, we explore the set of similar samples $x_k^U$ with high confidence for each $x_j^U$ by using the following criteria: $x_k^U$ that has $\overline{p}_{j,W}^U > t_{conf}$ and $\overline{p}_{k,W}^U > t_{conf}$. The similarity between two samples $\overline{p}_{j,W}^U$ and $\overline{p}_{k,W}^U$ is defined by using the Bhattacharyya coefficient [2] as follows:

$$f_{sim}\left(\overline{p}_{j,W}^U, \overline{p}_{k,W}^U\right) = \sqrt{\overline{p}_{j,W}^U}^{\mathrm{T}} \cdot \sqrt{\overline{p}_{k,W}^U}. \tag{4}$$

For the pairs $(j, k)$ with high similarity $f_{sim}\left(\overline{p}_{j,W}^U, \overline{p}_{k,W}^U\right) > t_{sim}$, we consider that these pairs form a set of the same class. Based on the set of each unlabeled data $x_j^U$, we compute the set consistent loss $\mathcal{L}_{SC}$ as follows:

$$\mathcal{L}_{SC} = \sum\nolimits_j \boldsymbol{I}_{\boldsymbol{conf}}(j) \sum\nolimits_{k \neq j} \boldsymbol{I}_{\boldsymbol{conf}}(k) \boldsymbol{I}_{\boldsymbol{sim}}(j, k)\left(1 - f_{sim}\left(\overline{p}_{j,S}^U, \overline{p}_{k,W}^U\right)\right), \tag{5}$$

where $\boldsymbol{I}_{\boldsymbol{conf}}(j)$ indicates if $\overline{p}_{j,W}^{U} > t_{conf}$ and $\boldsymbol{I}_{\boldsymbol{sim}}(j,k)$ indicates if $f_{sim}\left(\overline{p}_{j,W}^{U}, \overline{p}_{k,W}^{U}\right) > t_{sim}$. If $\overline{p}_{j,W}^{U} > t_{conf}$, $\boldsymbol{I}_{\boldsymbol{conf}}(j) = 1$, otherwise $\boldsymbol{I}_{\boldsymbol{conf}}(j) = 0$. Similarly, if $\overline{p}_{k,W}^{U} > t_{conf}$, $\boldsymbol{I}_{\boldsymbol{conf}}(k) = 1$, and otherwise $\boldsymbol{I}_{\boldsymbol{conf}}(k) = 0$. If $f_{sim}\left(\overline{p}_{j,W}^{U}, \overline{p}_{k,W}^{U}\right) > t_{sim}$, $\boldsymbol{I}_{\boldsymbol{sim}}(j,k) = 1$, otherwise $\boldsymbol{I}_{\boldsymbol{sim}}(j,k) = 0$. Finally, the similarity between $\overline{p}_{j,S}^{U}$ and $\overline{p}_{k,W}^{U}$ is defined as follows:

$$f_{sim}(\overline{p}_{j,S}^{U}, \overline{p}_{k,w}^{U}) = \sqrt{\overline{p}_{j,S}^{U}}^{\mathrm{T}} \cdot \sqrt{\overline{p}_{k,W}^{U}}^{\mathrm{T}}. \tag{6}$$

By considering the set consistent loss, our method can ensure the labels of unlabeled data of the same class to be consistent and thus it can help learn better features to segment the tissue regions.

# 4 Experiments

## 4.1 Datasets and Settings

**Datasets.** Two datasets including the GlaS [30] dataset and MoNuSeg dataset [16] were used for evaluation. The GlaS dataset [30] contains images of Hematoxylin and Eosin (H&E) stained slides of benign tissues and malignant tumours in the glandular epithelium with 165 images. The training set contains 37 benign images and 48 malignant images, and the testing set contains 37 benign images and 43 malignant images for the segmentation task. The MoNuSeg dataset [16] is a large dataset of H&E stained images for nuclear boundary segmentation from tissues of the tumors of different organs. There are 30 training images with around 22,000 nuclear boundary annotations and 14 testing images with around 7000 nuclear boundary annotations for training and evaluation.

**Table 1.** Segmentation Performance on the GlaS Dataset (IoU %)

| Method | 1/16 | 1/8 | 1/4 | 1/2 | 1 |
|---|---|---|---|---|---|
| U-Net [28] | - | - | - | - | 76.81 |
| Attention U-Net [24] | - | - | - | - | 77.53 |
| TransU-Net [5] | - | - | - | - | 79.10 |
| MedT [33] | - | - | - | - | 77.50 |
| SwinU-Net [3] | - | - | - | - | 79.86 |
| NMNet [31] | - | - | - | - | 82.13 |
| ReCo [21] | 61.68 | 62.84 | 64.59 | 66.57 | - |
| U$^2$PL [35] | 29.74 | 41.14 | 63.26 | 70.22 | - |
| Proposed | 68.98 | 69.83 | 78.18 | 83.37 | - |

**Settings.** To reduce the complexity of the proposed network, we used the segmentation network pre-trained on COCO dataset [20] with ResNet-50 [11] as the backbone and DeepLabv3 [6] as the decoder. For each dataset, we compared the proposed methods with the state-of-the-art semi-supervised methods [21, 35] and supervised methods [3, 5, 24, 28, 31, 33] under 1/2, 1/4, 1/8, and 1/16 partition protocols which are widely used in recent semi-supervised methods. In the experiments, the method is implemented under PyTorch 1.12.1 on a personal computer with an NVIDIA RTX3090 GPU. The batch size was set to 4. The weak augmentations included random scale in the range of [0.8, 1.5], random crop and horizontal flip. The strong augmentations included color jittering of the brightness factor of 0.2, the contrast factor of 0.2, the saturation factor of 0.2, and hue factor of 0.05, The EMA teacher decay was set to 0.99. The networks are updated by using the SGD optimizer with the initial learning rate of 1e-4, momentum 0.9 and the weight decay 1e-4. The learning rate is updated by using the cosine scheduler with the warmup scheme for the first epoch. In the first five epochs, only supervised loss is used to update the models. The weights $\omega_{IC}$ and $\omega_{SC}$ are set to 0.1 in the experiments. $t_{conf}$ And $t_{sim}$ are set to 0.9 to ensure the correlations between unlabeled data of the same class.

## 4.2 Quantitative Results

Table 1 shows the results of the competing methods and proposed methods in the GlaS dataset. The results of the state-of-the-art semi-supervised methods, U$^2$PL [35] and ReCo [21], are reported. Compared with ReCo, more training data in higher partition protocols can help generate better unreliable pseudo-labels for U$^2$PL. Similar situation also occurs for the proposed method because more training samples provide more evidence for computing the image consistent loss and the set consistent loss. By considering both losses, the consistency of the unlabeled dataset can be well exploited for semi-supervised semantic segmentation. The results of the supervised methods U-Net [28], Attention U-Net [24], transformer U-Net (Trans U-Net) [5], medical transformer (MedT) [33], SWinU-Net [3] and NMNet [31] reported in [31] are also listed in Table 1 for comparisons

**Table 2.** Segmentation Performance on the MoNuSeg Dataset (IoU %)

| Method | 1/16 | 1/8 | 1/4 | 1/2 | 1 |
|---|---|---|---|---|---|
| U-Net [28] | - | - | - | - | 59.81 |
| Attention U-Net [24] | - | - | - | - | 62.64 |
| TransU-Net [5] | - | - | - | - | 65.68 |
| MedT [33] | - | - | - | - | 65.73 |
| SwinU-Net [3] | - | - | - | - | 64.72 |
| NMNet [31] | - | - | - | - | 67.73 |
| ReCo [21] | 51.75 | 69.26 | 72.62 | 75.68 | - |
| U$^2$PL [35] | 58.86 | 69.04 | 64.59 | 69.77 | - |
| Proposed | 71.51 | 72.26 | 70.33 | 73.50 | - |

to show that our method with proposed losses can achieve comparable and even better results compared with supervised methods.

Table 2 shows the results of the competing methods and proposed methods in the MoNuSeg dataset. In the MoNuSeg dataset, more nuclei can be observed in the training images. ReCo can then learn more representative features from nuclei based on the pixel-level contrastive learning compared with $U^2$PL. In contrast, the proposed method considers the image level consistency information for label propagation for the unlabeled training set and thus achieves slightly worse results compared with ReCo. Nevertheless, the proposed method still outperforms $U^2$PL and competing supervised methods. Such results indicate discovering image and feature correlations of the content of unlabeled data helps retrieve more reliable feature representations for pathology image segmentation.

### 4.3 Qualitative Results

Figure 2 and Fig. 3 show the qualitative results of the GlaS and MoNuSeg datasets, respectively. The first column and the second column show the input image and the ground truth. The third column and fourth column show the results of $U^2$PL under the 1/4 and 1/2 protocols, while the fifth column and sixth column show the results of our method under the 1/4 and 1/2 protocols. As shown in Fig. 2, our method can achieve better results compared with $U^2$PL for both of the 1/4 and 1/2 protocols. Because $U^2$PL considers negative samples which are not available in the GlaS dataset, the feature learned by $U^2$PL cannot well represent the tissues of benign and malignant classes. In contrast, our image consistent loss and set consistent loss considers feature similarity between unlabeled images to attract images of the content to be consistent and thus will not be affected by insufficient negative samples in $U^2$PL. Similar problems also occur in the results of the MoNuSeg datasets as shown in Fig. 3 because of the lack of negative samples to distinguish the nuclei regions from background regions. As a result, our method can achieve better segmentation results in both datasets.

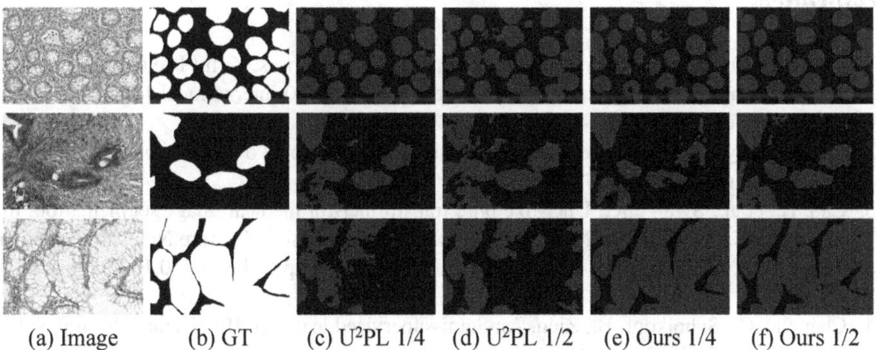


**Fig. 2.** Segmentation Results of the GlaS Dataset.

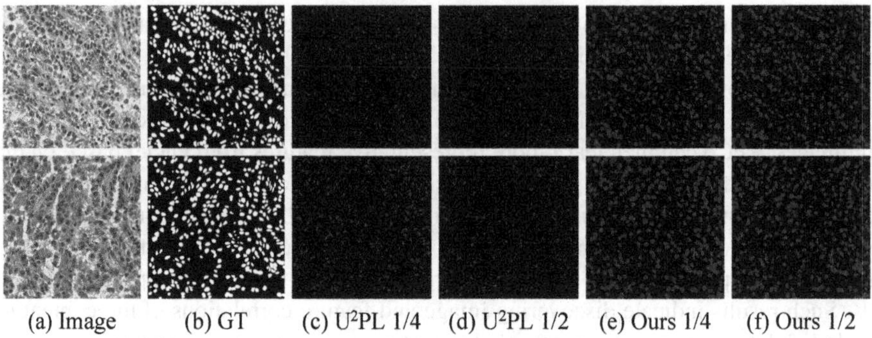


**Fig. 3.** Segmentation Results of the MoNuSeg Dataset.

## 5 Conclusions

In this paper, we propose an image consistent loss and set consistent loss for semi-supervised pathological tissue segmentation. By using these two losses, the generated pseudo labels are constrained in both image level and set level so the pseudo labels will be more consistent for regions of the same semantic labels. The experiments show the proposed method outperform the state-of-the-art semi-supervised and supervised semantic segmentation methods. In the future, we will further consider the similarity between unlabeled data to generate more robust feature representations.

**Acknowledgement.** This work was supported in part by the National Science and Technology Council, Taiwan under Grant NSTC 111-2634-F-006-012, NSTC 111-2628-E-006-011-MY3, and 112-2622-8-006-009-TE1, NSTC 112-2634-F-006-002. The authors would like to thank National Center for High-performance Computing (NCHC) for providing computational and storage resources.

## References

1. Arazo, E., Ortego, D., Albert, P., O'Connor, N.E., McGuinness, K. In: Pseudo-labeling and confirmation bias in deep semi-supervised learning. In: 2020 International Joint Conference on Neural Networks (IJCNN), pp. 1–8. IEEE (2020)
2. Bhattacharyya, A.: On a measure of divergence between two multinomial populations. Sankhy¯A: Indian J. Stat. 401–406 (1946)
3. Cao, H., et al.: Swin-Unet: Unet-like pure transformer for medical image segmentation. In: Karlinsky, L., Michaeli, T., Nishino, K. (eds.) Computer Vision. Lecture Notes in Computer Science, vol. 13803, pp. 205–218. Springer, Cham (2022). https://doi.org/10.1007/978-3-031-25066-8_9
4. Chapelle, O., Scholkopf, B., Zien, A.: Semi-supervised learning. IEEE Trans. Neural Netw. **20**(3), 542–542 (2009)
5. Chen, J., et al.: TransUNet: transformers make strong encoders for medical image segmentation. arXiv (2021)
6. Chen, L.C., Papandreou, G., Schroff, F., Adam, H.: Rethinking atrous convolution for semantic image segmentation. arXiv (2017)

7. Chen, X., Yuan, Y., Zeng, G., Wang, J.: Semi-supervised semantic segmentation with cross pseudo supervision. In: Proceedings of Conference Computer Vision and Pattern Recognition, pp. 2613–2622 (2021)
8. Chen, Y.C., Lu, C.S.: RankMix: data augmentation for weakly supervised learning of classifying whole slide images with diverse sizes and imbalanced categories. In: Proceedings Conference on Computer Vision and Pattern Recognition, pp. 23936–23945 (2023)
9. Chiou, C.Y., Lee, K.T., Huang, C.R., Chung, P.C.: ADMM-SRNet: alternating direction method of multipliers based sparse representation network for one-class classification. IEEE Trans. Image Process. **32**, 2843–2856 (2023)
10. Chung, P.C., Yang, W.J., Wu, T.H., Huang, C.R., Hsu, Y.Y.: Emerging research directions of deep learning for pathology image analysis. In: 2022 IEEE Biomedical Circuits and Systems Conference (BioCAS), pp. 100–104. IEEE (2022)
11. He, K., Zhang, X., Ren, S., Sun, J.: Deep residual learning for image recognition. In: Proceedings of Conference Computer Vision and Pattern Recognition, pp. 770–778 (2016)
12. Hsu, T.C., Liao, Y.S., Huang, C.R.: Video summarization with spatiotemporal vision transformer. IEEE Trans. Image Process. **32**, 3013–3026 (2023)
13. Huang, S.K., Yu, C.R., Liao, Y.S., Huang, C.R.: Evaluations of deep learning methods for pathology image classification. In: 2022 IEEE Biomedical Circuits and Systems Conference (BioCAS), pp. 95–99. IEEE (2022)
14. Jin, Q., et al.: Semi-supervised histological image segmentation via hierarchical consistency enforcement. In: Wang, L., Dou, Q., Fletcher, P.T., Speidel, S., Li, S. (eds.) Medical Image Computing and Computer Assisted Intervention, vol. 13432, pp. 3–13. Springer, Heidelberg (2022). https://doi.org/10.1007/978-3-031-16434-7_1
15. Ke, Z., Qiu, D., Li, K., Yan, Q., Lau, R.W.H.: Guided collaborative training for pixel-wise semi-supervised learning. In: Vedaldi, A., Bischof, H., Brox, T., Frahm, J.M. (eds.) ECCV 2020. LNCS, vol. 12358, pp. 429–445. Springer, Cham (2020). https://doi.org/10.1007/978-3-030-58601-0_26
16. Kumar, N., Verma, R., Sharma, S., Bhargava, S., Vahadane, A., Sethi, A.: A dataset and a technique for generalized nuclear segmentation for computational pathology. IEEE Trans. Med. Imaging **36**(7), 1550–1560 (2017)
17. Lai, Z., Wang, C., Oliveira, L.C., Dugger, B.N., Cheung, S.C., Chuah, C.N.: Joint semi-supervised and active learning for segmentation of gigapixel pathology images with cost-effective labeling. In: Proceedings of IEEE/CVF International Conference on Computer Vision Workshops, pp. 591–600 (2021)
18. Li, X., Lequan, Y., Chen, H., Chi-Wing, F., Xing, L., Heng, P.A.: Transformation-consistent self-ensembling model for semisupervised medical image segmentation. IEEE Trans. Neural Netw. Learni. Syst. **32**(2), 523–534 (2021). https://doi.org/10.1109/TNNLS.2020.2995319
19. Li, Y., Chen, J., Xie, X., Ma, K., Zheng, Y.: Self-loop uncertainty: A novel pseudo-label for semi-supervised medical image segmentation. In: Martel, Anne L., et al. (eds.) MICCAI 2020. LNCS, vol. 12261, pp. 614–623. Springer, Cham (2020). https://doi.org/10.1007/978-3-030-59710-8_60
20. Lin, T.-Y., et al.: Microsoft coco: Common objects in context. In: Fleet, D., Pajdla, T., Schiele, B., Tuytelaars, T. (eds.) Computer Vision – ECCV 2014: 13th European Conference, Zurich, Switzerland, September 6-12, 2014, Proceedings, Part V, pp. 740–755. Springer, Cham (2014). https://doi.org/10.1007/978-3-319-10602-1_48
21. Liu, S., Zhi, S., Johns, E., Davison, A.: Bootstrapping semantic segmentation with regional contrast. In: Proceedings of International Conference on Learning Representations (2022)
22. Liu, Y., Tian, Y., Chen, Y., Liu, F., Belagiannis, V., Carneiro, G.: Perturbed and strict mean teachers for semi-supervised semantic segmentation. In: Proceedings of Conference Computer Vision and Pattern Recognition, pp. 4258–4267 (2022)

23. Luo, K., Li, X., Lan, Y., Gao, M.: GradMa: a gradient-memory-based accelerated federated learning with alleviated catastrophic forgetting. In: Proceedings of Conference on Computer Vision and Pattern Recognition, pp. 3708–3717 (2023)
24. Oktay, O., et al.: Attention u-net: learning where to look for the pancreas. arXiv (2018)
25. OpenAI: Gpt-4 technical report (2023)
26. Ouali, Y., Hudelot, C., Tami, M.: Semi-supervised semantic segmentation with cross-consistency training. In: Proceedings of Conference on Computer Vision and Pattern Recognition, pp. 12674–12684 (2020)
27. Rombach, R., Blattmann, A., Lorenz, D., Esser, P., Ommer, B.: High-resolution image synthesis with latent diffusion models. In: Proceedings of Conference on Computer Vision and Pattern Recognition, pp. 10684–10695 (2022)
28. Ronneberger, O., Fischer, P., Brox, T.: U-net: convolutional networks for biomedical image segmentation. In: Navab, N., Hornegger, J., Wells, W.M., Frangi, A.F. (eds.) MICCAI 2015. LNCS, vol. 9351, pp. 234–241. Springer, Cham (2015). https://doi.org/10.1007/978-3-319-24574-4_28
29. Shi, J., Gong, T., Wang, C., Li, C.: Semi-supervised pixel contrastive learning framework for tissue segmentation in histopathological image. IEEE J Biomed. Health Inform. **27**(1), 97–108 (2023)
30. Sirinukunwattana, K., et al.: Gland segmentation in colon histology images: the glas challenge contest. Med. Image Anal. **35**, 489–502 (2017)
31. Song, E., Zhan, B., Liu, H., Cetinkaya, C., Hung, C.C.: NMNet: learning multi-level semantic information from scale extension domain for improved medical image segmentation. Biomed. Signal Process. Control **83**, 104651 (2023)
32. Tarvainen, A., Valpola, H.: Mean teachers are better role models: weight-averaged consistency targets improve semi-supervised deep learning results. In: Proceedings of Advances in Neural Information Processing Systems, vol. 30 (2017)
33. Valanarasu, J.M.J., Oza, P., Hacihaliloglu, I., Patel, V.M.: Medical transformer: gated axial-attention for medical image segmentation. In: de Bruijne, Marleen, et al. (eds.) MICCAI 2021. LNCS, vol. 12901, pp. 36–46. Springer, Cham (2021). https://doi.org/10.1007/978-3-030-87193-2_4
34. Wang, W., et al.: InternImage: exploring large-scale vision foundation models with deformable convolutions. In: Proceedings of Conference on Computer Vision and Pattern Recognition, pp. 14408–14419 (2023)
35. Wang, Y., et al.: Semi-supervised semantic segmentation using unreliable pseudo-labels. In: Proceedings of Conference on Computer Vision and Pattern Recognition, pp. 4248–4257 (2022)
36. Xia, Y., et al.: Uncertainty-aware multi-view co-training for semi-supervised medical image segmentation and domain adaptation. Med. Image Anal. **65**, 101766 (2020)
37. Xie, Y., Zhang, J., Liao, Z., Verjans, J., Shen, C., Xia, Y.: Pairwise relation learning for semi-supervised gland segmentation. In: Martel, A.L., et al. (eds.) MICCAI 2020. LNCS, vol. 12265, pp. 417–427. Springer, Cham (2020). https://doi.org/10.1007/978-3-030-59722-1_40
38. Yang, L., Qi, L., Feng, L., Zhang, W., Shi, Y.: Revisiting weak-to-strong consistency in semi-supervised semantic segmentation. In: Proceedings of Conference on Computer Vision and Pattern Recognition, pp. 7236–7246 (2023)

# Real-Time Prediction of Acute Kidney Injury in the Intensive Care Unit Using EDGE-AI Platform

Yu-You Xie[1(✉)], Wei-Hua Hou[1], Chun-Chieh Tsao[1], Szu-Hong Wang[1], Chia-Rong Lee[1], Ming-Sheng Hsu[2], Hsu-Yen Kuo[2], and Ting-Wei Wang[2]

[1] Department of Electronic Engineering, National Yunlin University of Science and Technology, Yunlin, Taiwan
{B11023212,B11023218,B11023229,wangsr,leecr}@yuntech.edu.tw
[2] School of Medicine, National Yang-Ming University, Taipei, Taiwan

**Abstract.** Acute kidney injury (AKI) is a common early stage of renal degeneration in Intensive Care Unit (ICU) patients and is usually diagnosed by medical professionals after 48 h. We propose that a weight sensor be installed on the patient's urine bag in order to calculate hourly urine output and integrate patient data. The Acute Kidney Injury Network examined the previous 30-h urine output. A deep learning model (CNN-LSTM) predicts the AKI risk rate in 6 h. If the risk is higher than the threshold, use the hospital's official machine to alarm medical professionals. The model evaluation criteria Area Under Curve (AUC) was 0.97 (±0.02), precision = 0.96, recall = 0.96. To predict AKI in ICU 6 h earlier by using edge AI of urine output alarms medical professionals. It will improve unsustainable monitoring and result in immediate treatment and a 15% reduction in dialysis rates and a 20% reduction in mortality rates.

**Keywords:** Acute kidney injury · deep learning · edge AI · predict · alarm

## 1 Introduction

Acute kidney injury (AKI) is a global public health concern. According to research, approximately 13.3 million people suffer from AKI each year, resulting in approximately 1.7 million deaths. Patients frequently require long hospital stays and have a high mortality rate [1]. The incidence rate in intensive care units (ICUs) ranges from 35% to 75%, with over 50% of cases requiring urgent dialysis. Even with emergency dialysis, mortality rates remain in the 50–80% range [2]. This means that once AKI is detected with delay, it is extremely difficult to reverse.

When the kidneys are compromised. Serum creatinine cannot be removed from the blood, resulting in decreased urine output. As a result, serum creatinine concentration or urine output is used to make a clinical diagnosis of AKI [3].

AKI is not immediately detected by medical professionals, because most patients of serum creatinine draw blood and track for two days. Urine output is observed for at least


C.-Y. Lee et al. (Eds.): TAAI 2023, CCIS 2074, pp. 227–237, 2024.
https://doi.org/10.1007/978-981-97-1711-8_17

six to twelve hours to achieve the diagnostic standard. For patients, the failure to detect AKI in time can lead to serious irreversible kidney damage and a high mortality rate [2].

For the reasons indicated previously. It necessitates a system capable of detecting threats 24 h a day, seven days a week. As indicated in Table 1, predict AKI and warn clinicians for examination and therapy before it happens. As a consequence, we put the "Alert Kidney System" in the hospital's ICU and attached a urine catheter to the patient's bedside for continuous monitoring. We can estimate the probability of AKI in patients in the next six hours using edge AI. A hospital business jet simulation that uses LINE notify to tell medical staff about high-risk patients. Early therapy is necessary in order to lower patient death and dialysis rates.

**Table 1.** Comparison between this system and traditional methods.

| Detect AKI methods | Ward round of doctor | AI model | Annotation |
|---|---|---|---|
| Labor costs | High | Low | Automated inspection of hardware equipment |
| Money cost | High | Middle | It has the advantage of being mobile and reusable with simple hardware equipment |
| Time costs | Middle | Low | urine output is easily overlooked by the medical professionals, |
| Accuracy | Middle | High | By automatic detection and analysis, the system a void human error |
| Full-time detection | Low | High | Artificial urine inspection is done about once every eight hours and draw blood is done about once every two days. The system can be monitored for a long time |
| Predict future risk | Low | High | Failure to detect and treat immediately can easily lead to dialysis or death |

## 2 Related Technologies

### 2.1 Acute Kidney Injury Network

AKIN is one of the medical criteria for diagnosing AKI, determined by continuous changes in creatinine and urine output, as shown in Table 2.

**Table 2.** Medical criteria AKIN [4]

| | Serum creatinine | Urine output |
|---|---|---|
| Stage2 | increase from 200 to 300% | <0.5 ml/kg/h for a period >12 h |
| Stage3 | increase higher than 300%, or equal to or greater than 4.0 mg/dl (≥354μmol/l) with an acute increase of at least 0.5 mg/dl (44μmol/l) | urine output <0.3 ml/kg/h for a period >24 h, or anuria for a period >12 h |

### 2.2 Receiver Operator Characteristic

ROC contrasts changes in True Positive Rate (TPR) and False Positive Rate (FPR) by adjusting judgment criteria. As a result, the model's accuracy, sensitivity, specificity, and other characteristics are evaluated. The aim is to get close to the ROC curve's upper-left corner (the best position for model training). The Area Under Curve (AUC) is close to one, showing that the model can clearly distinguish between genuine and false positives (the goal of this study is to identify between patients with and without AKI).

### 2.3 Long Short-Term Memory

LSTM mainly improves the problem of RNN Gradient Vanishing and Gradient Exploding with the characteristic of long-term memory. We use LSTM to process the time series data (patient's admitted urine volume). Which is mainly composed of four components.

**Input Gate.** When inputting data, the input gate can decide whether to input the value or not.
**Memory Cell.** Saves the calculated value for the next cell.
**Output Gate.** Determines whether the calculated value is output.
**Forget Gate.** Determines whether to clear the value of the Memory cell.

### 2.4 Citation of Journals

In machine learning, we used the technique of the Italian Society of Nephrology's magazine [5]. Figure 1 depicts the findings of this investigation. We collected characteristics from patients' hourly urine output patterns during their ICU stay. When patients were kept in the hospital for more than 30 h. We calculated moving averages and time series of hourly urine production using sliding windows ranging in size from 2 to 12 h. A feature (total of 11) was defined as the lowest value in each sliding window's moving average. To provide completely independent samples, just one set of features was chosen at random for each patient.

## 3 System Function and Design

### 3.1 System Situation

In the hospital ward, as illustrated in Fig. 2. Patients equipped with urinary catheters are positioned on their hospital beds. The Renal Guard system is affixed to the bedside, while the patient's urine bag is suspended from a hook on a weight sensor for measurement

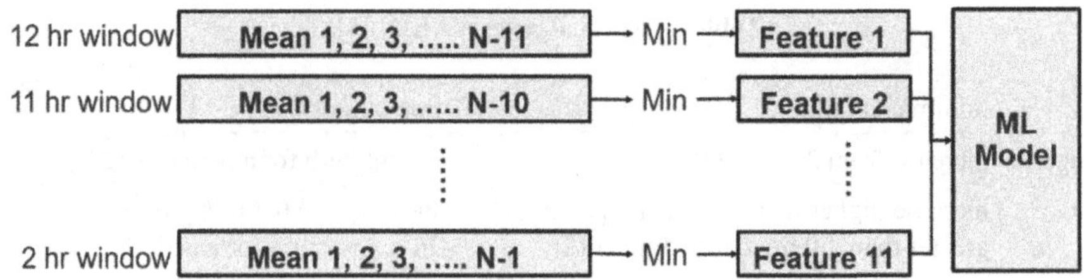


**Fig. 1.** Using sliding windows of 2 to 12 h to calculate the minimum value in the moving average as a feature.

purposes. The analysis is conducted utilizing an embedded system (KV260). Conversion is executed by an analog-to-digital converter (HX711), alerts are sent and data is uploaded to the hospital database via WiFi USB (RT5370).

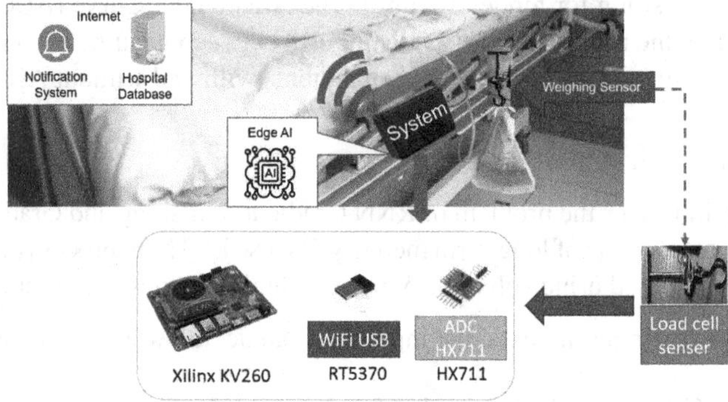


**Fig. 2.** Context Diagram

### 3.2 System Process

Figure 3. Shows the System Architecture Diagram, which operates in the following steps.

**Step 1**. Configure the system environment, start the program, and Load the Cell sensor to monitor the weight of the urine bag every 5 minutes.
**Step 2.** Convert the weight of the urine bag to a digital signal and calculate the urine volume per hour.
**Step 3.** The KV260 reads the value and uploads it to the hospital's information system for medical staff to track the patient's condition.
**Step 4.** Take the patient's first 30 hours of urine volume and perform edge calculations to predict the probability of AKI after 6 hours.
**Step 5.** If the system predicts that the patient will have AKI. Using LINE NOTIFY to simulate the hospital's public machine to alert the healthcare staff of the high-risk patient, and then follow up.

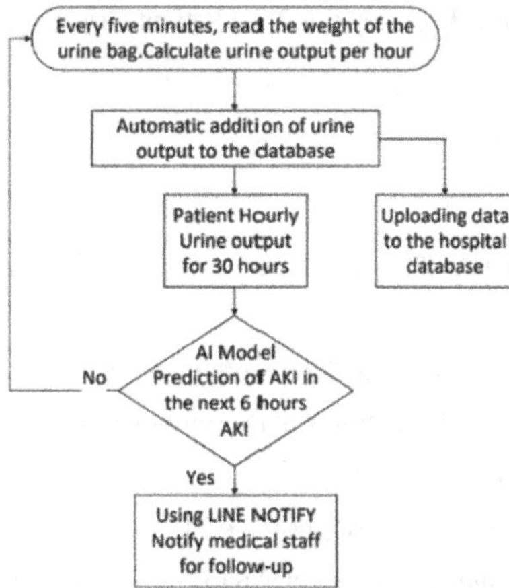


**Fig. 3.** System Architecture Diagram

### 3.3 Data Analysis

MIMIC-III [6], a publicly available American database, was used. To examine relevant data from 97 patients admitted to Beth Israel Deaconess Medical Center's Intensive Care Unit (ICU) between 2001 and 2012. We chose features that meet the criteria for training our AI model.

The data is split into 80% for training and 20% for testing. To aid model learning, the training set is used for observational analysis and feature extraction. The testing set is used to assess the model's performance.

### 3.4 Data Pre-processing

Table 3 converts the MIMIC-III data into time series. For urine output values with missing data of less than 9 h. The urine volume is divided by the total time and normalized into hourly urine output. Creatinine values with missing data of less than 4 days are used for data labeling following AKIN standard stage 2 or higher. These data are used for training the model.

The original dataset comprises a total of 11,320 records from 97 patients. After processing, as shown in Table 4. The dataset is reduced to 10,005 records, involving 58 patients, with 2,138 cases meeting the AKI criteria based on AKIN's urine volume standard.

'Subject_id' represents patient identifiers, 'chart-time' indicates the date of record, 'value' represents urine output in milliliters per hour (ml/h), and 'have_aki' indicates whether the patient has AKI (0 represents no, 1 represents yes).

### 3.5 Data Expansion

The total number of records in the dataset is 10,005. Approximately 80% of this data, or 6,353 records, is used for model training. There are over 1,300 records indicating the presence of AKI (the number varies due to random sampling). The number of AKI-positive

**Table 3.** Analyzing ICU Patient Criteria [5]

| ICU length of stay < 24 h |
|---|
| sCr baseline < 0.5 mg/dl |
| Community AKI |
| Patients requiring dialysis during ICU stay |
| ICU admission < 50 times |
| Incomplete urine output record (missing value more than 9 h) |
| Incomplete creatinine acid record (missing values more than 4 days) |
| Standardized time series (units per hour) |
| Standardize urine output to ideal body weight (IBW) [5] |
| Use of AKIN standardized annotation data for AKI stage 2 or higher (elevated creatinine acid, decreased urine output) |

**Table 4.** MIMIC pre-processing results table

| Subject_id | charttime | value | have_aki |
|---|---|---|---|
| 10001884 | 2131/1/11 11:00 | 100 | 0 |
| 10001884 | 2131/1/11 12:00 | 80 | 0 |
| 10001884 | 2131/1/11 13:00 | 75 | 0 |
| 10001884 | 2131/1/11 14:00 | 60 | 0 |
| 10001884 | 2131/1/11 15:00 | 50 | 0 |
| 10001884 | 2131/1/11 16:00 | 50 | 0 |
| 10001884 | 2131/1/11 17:00 | 30 | 0 |
| 10001884 | 2131/1/11 18:00 | 30 | 0 |
| 10001884 | 2131/1/11 19:00 | 37.5 | 0 |
| 10001884 | 2131/1/11 20:00 | 37.5 | 0 |

patients may vary from time to time). The percentage of positive samples (1300/6353) is approximately 20%. The model has a high accuracy of 98%, but it has a 0% correct classification rate for positive samples. This is because the vast majority of the data pertains to healthy patients. The model does not have enough data for patients with AKI to learn the features properly.

Suppose there are 1,000 individuals, with only 2 of them having AKI. If the model detects 3 people with AKI. Its accuracy is 999/1000 = 99.9%, which seems nearly perfect. However, if the equipment malfunctions one day and it examines another 1,000 individuals, none of whom have AKI, then the accuracy becomes 998/1000 = 99.8%. In other words, this model only recognizes patients with normal medical conditions [9].

In cases of data imbalance. It can lead to extremely high model accuracy while failing to distinguish the minority class in practical tests. To solve this problem. We applied Borderline SMOTE for data augmentation in the training set, as shown in Fig. 4. The concept is to artificially generate some samples with similar features in areas near the minority class samples [7].

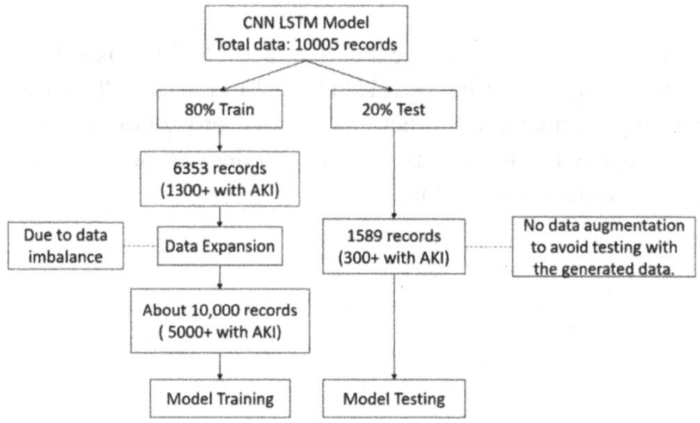


**Fig. 4.** Data flowchart

The image on the right in Fig. 5. Represents new samples obtained using the Borderline SMOTE method. This method addresses the issue of insufficient minority samples by preventing minority sample characteristics from being too similar to those of majority samples. As a result, these minority samples have more representative features, making model training easier.

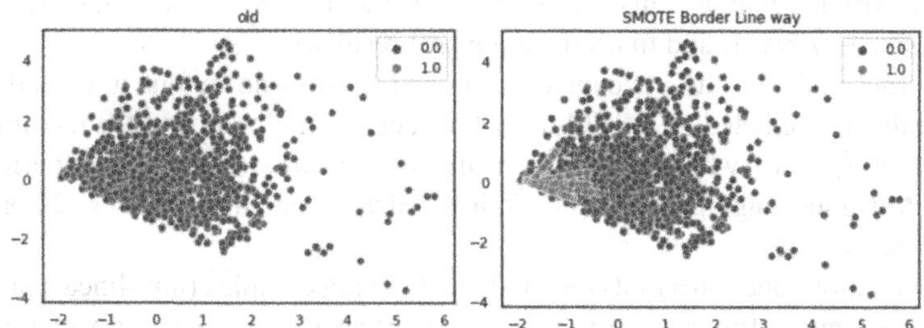


**Fig. 5.** Comparison of data augmentation (Blue dots are patients without AKI, and orange dots are patients with AKI) (Color figure online)

The test results indicate whether hospital patient data can be arbitrarily expanded. The data in the training set was only supplemented. During model testing, the original data was preserved. This practical approach helps model training, which leads to higher recognition rates.

After expanding about 10,000 (5,000 with AKI) for model training and 1,589 (300 with AKI) for model testing.

### 3.6 Proposed CNN LSTM Model

CNN LSTM is used in the deep learning model. The input is made up of the patient's hourly urine output over a 30-h period. The output forecasts the AKI risk rate for the next 6 h.

Convolution 1D is used for feature extraction, and LSTM is used for classification. Filters = 32, kernel_size = 7, strides = 1, LSTM = 20, epochs = 30, activation function = sigmoid, optimizer = adam, loss function = binary_crossentropy.

Because the data is a one-dimensional time series, as shown in Fig. 6. we use convolution 1D to extract subtle features.

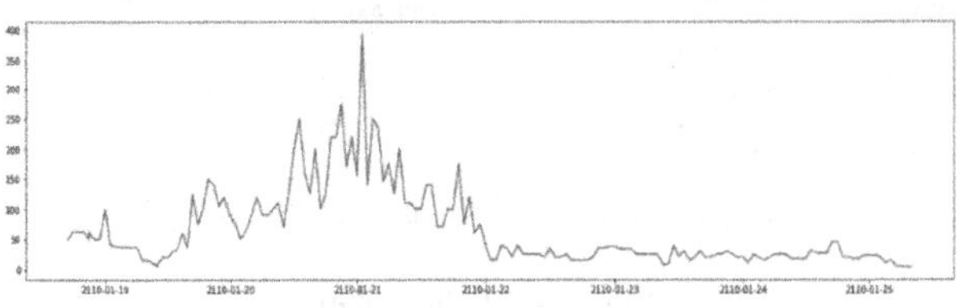

**Fig. 6.** Change in continuous urine output (x-axis is a date, y-axis is urine output).

We applied the approach from the machine learning journal to this study, extending the concept of eleven features. Testing with filters greater than 11 and multiples of four. The model's performance was evaluated using filters = 16 or filters = 32. It was discovered that filters = 32 produced the best results.

We followed the journal's lead and used a sliding time window. The window size was tested with the middle value (2 + 12) / 2 = 7 and kernel sizes of 5, 6, 7, 8, and 9. A kernel size of 7 was found to produce the best results.

In journal patients, the concept of sustained 30-h urine output is extended. The optimal value is predicted by LSTM to be between the midpoint and the maximum. 30 (urine output) / 2 = 15, where 15 represents the optimal value of 30. After experimenting with LSTM values ranging from 15 to 29, it was determined that LSTM = 20 produced the best results.

The activation function assists the model in learning complex (non-linear) problems. Relu, sigmoid, and softmax are common options. Because we need binary classification (with or without AKI), sigmoid is appropriate for this scenario and produces probabilities ranging from 0 to 1.

### 3.7 AKI Risk Rate Criteria

How do you know when to notify healthcare professionals about a patient's AKI risk? As shown in Fig. 7, we exhaustively considered probabilities ranging from zero to one for analysis. The optimal threshold was determined through empirical testing to be 0.8.

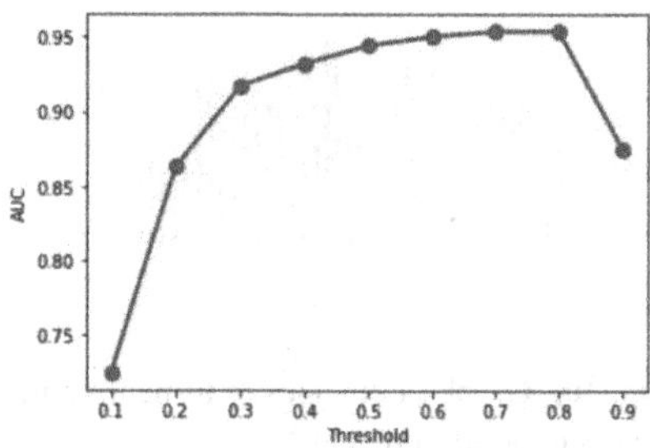


**Fig. 7.** AKI Risk Rate Threshold Discrimination Chart

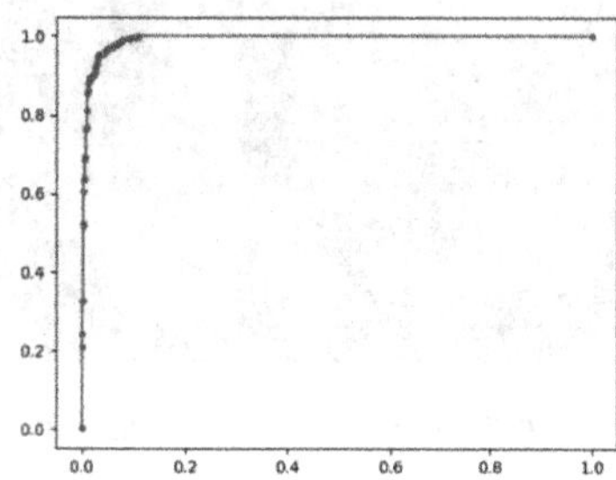


**Fig. 8.** ROC Curve

# 4 Experimental Results

The model evaluation criteria Area Under Curve (AUC) is 0.99 as shown in Fig. 8. Precision = 0.96, Recall = 0.96, F1-Score = 0.96, Loss Function (loss) = 0.14, Accuracy = 0.97.

The model predicted that over 1,200 cases would be normal, and they were (true negatives - tn). It predicted normal in nine cases, but they actually had AKI (false negatives - fn). Over 330 cases were correctly predicted to have AKI, and they did (true positives - tp). It also predicted AKI in 89 cases that were actually normal (false positives - fp).

The model identified 420 patients as having AKI risk, and 330 of them developed AKI. In contrast, AKI occurred in 9 of the 1,210 patients who were not thought to be at risk.

Until now, numerous teams [7–9] have worked to develop AI models for predicting AKI based on various patient characteristics. However, there has been no evidence of these models being used in clinical settings.

In terms of technological innovation, we conducted tests using water instead of urine, as shown in Fig. 9. However, urine and water have different densities. The normal specific gravity of urine ranges from 1.005 to 1.030 g/cm3. For a healthy adult weighing 70 kg, the standard for oliguria is a urine volume of 35 ml per hour, which is equivalent to a weight of approximately 35.2g to 36.1g. The highest margin of error is only 3.1%. In cases of oliguria, urine weight and volume can be approximated as values similar to that of water.

Making predictions using data the model hasn't seen before, as shown in Fig. 10. The model issued an alert at the 36 h, while the doctor didn't notice until the 41st hour, as depicted in Fig. 11. This doesn't include the time required for blood sampling and urine volume analysis.

As shown in Fig. 12. When the model predicts that a patient is at risk of AKI in the next 6 h. We simulate the hospital's public machine for notification with Line notify.

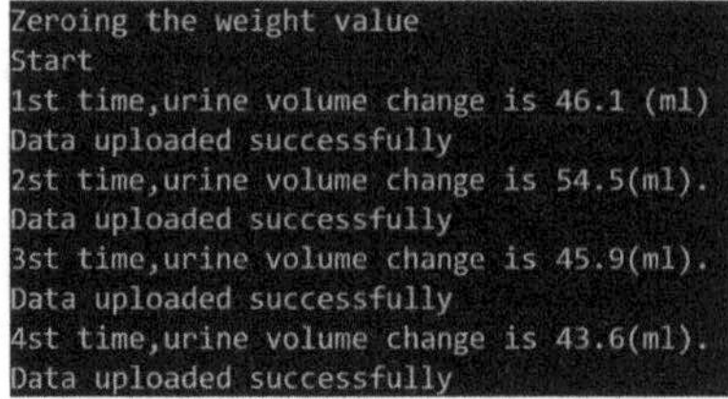
Zeroing the weight value
Start
1st time,urine volume change is 46.1 (ml)
Data uploaded successfully
2st time,urine volume change is 54.5(ml).
Data uploaded successfully
3st time,urine volume change is 45.9(ml).
Data uploaded successfully
4st time,urine volume change is 43.6(ml).
Data uploaded successfully

**Fig. 9.** Measurement diagram

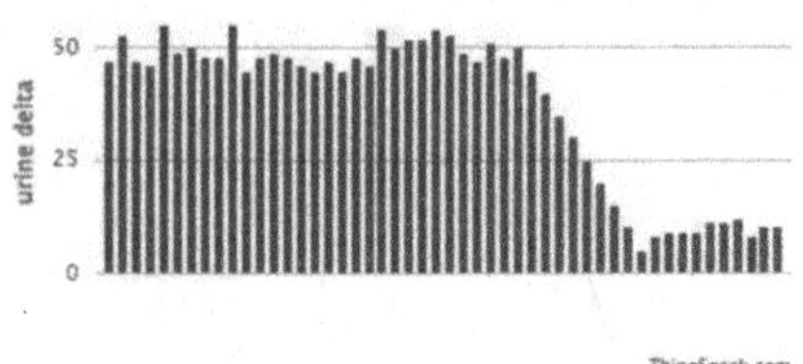


**Fig. 10.** Graph of changes in urine output, x-axis in hourly units [10]

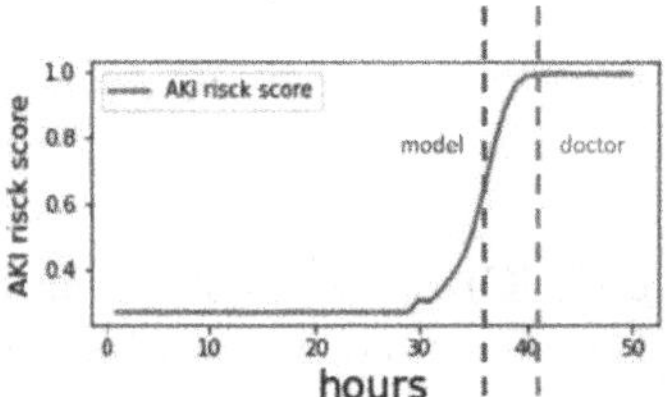


**Fig. 11.** Test Results

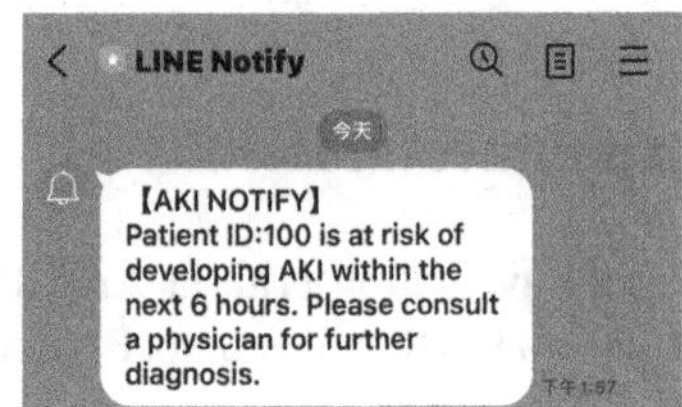


**Fig. 12.** Line notify schematic

## 5 Conclusion

Traditional healthcare providers frequently fail to detect AKI in a timely manner, resulting in severe and irreversible kidney damage. In this study, we installed a weight sensor on the patient's urine bag to create a renal monitoring system. Using edge computing to analyze changes in urine volume. We were able to predict acute kidney injury (AKI) in the intensive care unit (ICU) six hours ahead of time and alert healthcare personnel immediately. This enhancement addresses the problem of late monitoring. According to the British Medical Journal. It can help reduce kidney dialysis rates by 15% and patient mortality rates by 20% [11].

**Acknowledgements.** This study would like to thank the National Yunlin University of Science and Technology's Intelligent Identification Industry Service Research Center, as well as the Ministry of Education's Deep Plowing Project and others for their financial support.

## References

1. Palevsky, P.M., Zhang, J.V., O'Connor, T.Z., et al.: Intensity of renal support in critically ill patients with acute kidney injury. N. Eng. J. Med. **359**(1), 7–20 (2008)
2. Consortium for Acute Kidney Injury and Renal Diseases (CAKS) Registration
3. Nat Rev Dis Primers. Jul 15;7(1), 52 (2021)
4. Palevsky, P.M., et al.: KDOQI US commentary on the 2012 KDIGO clinical practice guideline for acute kidney injury. Am. J. Kidney Dis. **61**(5), 649–672 (2013)

5. Alfieri, F., Ancona, A., Tripepi, G., et al.: A deep-learning model to continuously predict severe acute kidney injury based on urine output changes in critically ill patients. J. Nephrol. **34**, 1875–1886 (2021)
6. Johnson, A., Pollard, T., Mark, R.: MIMIC-III Clinical Database (version 1.4). PhysioNet (2016)
7. Tran, N.K., et al.: Artificial intelligence and machine learning for predicting acute kidney injury in severely burned patients: a proof of concept. Burns **45**, 1350–1358 (2019)
8. Zhang, Z., Ho, K.M., Hong, Y.: Machine learning for the prediction of volume responsiveness in patients with oliguric acute kidney injury in critical care. Crit. Care **23**, 112 (2019)
9. Zimmerman, L.P., et al.: Early prediction of acute kidney injury following ICU admission using a multivariate panel of physiological measurements. BMC Med. Inform. Decis. Mak.Mak. **19**, 16 (2019)
10. Thing Speak. https://thingspeak.com/
11. Postgraduate Med. J. **92**(1083), 9–13 (2016)

# Facial Nerve Disorder Rehabilitation via Generative Adversarial Network

Donald Jasper Su, Chia Cheng Lin, and Fang Yu(✉)

Management Information Systems Department, National Chengchi University, Taipei, Taiwan
{109306091,109306066}@g.nccu.edu.tw, yuf@nccu.edu.tw

**Abstract.** With the rapid growth in the number of patients with facial nerve disorders, the cost of therapy is continually increasing, thus placing both physical and financial burdens on patients. Patients with facial nerve paralysis can benefit from facial massages and facial muscle exercises, which enhance tissue blood circulation and oxygen uptake, thereby ameliorating facial muscle stiffness and pain. Consequently, this paper proposes a demonstration of a rehabilitation system designed to lessen the burdens borne by patients while encouraging a greater dedication and readiness to engage in rehabilitation. Leveraging Facemesh technology, we can accurately identify facial landmarks of individuals, thereby facilitating the assessment of the precision in the exercises performed by patients. Additionally, the GANimation model is employed to create user-specific instructional imagery derived from their facial attributes. The effectiveness of our proposed system is underscored through a live demonstration bolstered by rigorous experimental validation.

**Keywords:** Generative Adversarial Network · Healthcare · Facial Nerve Paralysis

## 1 Introduction

Facial nerve paralysis has emerged as a prevalent and challenging condition in modern society, with an incidence of 40 cases per 100,000 individuals per year [13]. This condition adversely affects the physical and emotional well-being of an affected person. The adage "disease is a goad, and recovery is a blessing" aptly describes the challenges the affected individuals face during their recovery period, which involves extensive rehabilitation and therapy. The cost of treatment for facial nerve paralysis varies based on the severity of the symptoms, with an average price of USD 1,000 per treatment, leading to an emerging rehabilitation market.

Recent studies have shown that facial muscle exercises can improve inter-tissue blood circulation and oxygen intake, alleviating symptoms such as stiffness, numbness, and pain in facial muscles [13]. Despite the potential benefits of facial muscle exercises, the recovery process can be arduous and overwhelming, given facial neuropathy's physical and psychological effects. Thus, several mobile applications, such as Winzig1 and Sports Injury Rehabilitation, have been published for home rehabilitation.


C.-Y. Lee et al. (Eds.): TAAI 2023, CCIS 2074, pp. 238–249, 2024.
https://doi.org/10.1007/978-981-97-1711-8_18

However, most applications focus on physical rehabilitation, such as traumatic Brain Injury, Stroke, and Orthopedic Disorders, instead of supporting those clients suffering from facial nerve disorders. Therefore, this paper proposes a demonstration for online rehabilitation in facial nerve paralysis, with two major challenges. *1) How to correctly evaluate the patient's facial movements for the exercise requirement?* and *2) How can the user get better guidance during the recovery process?*

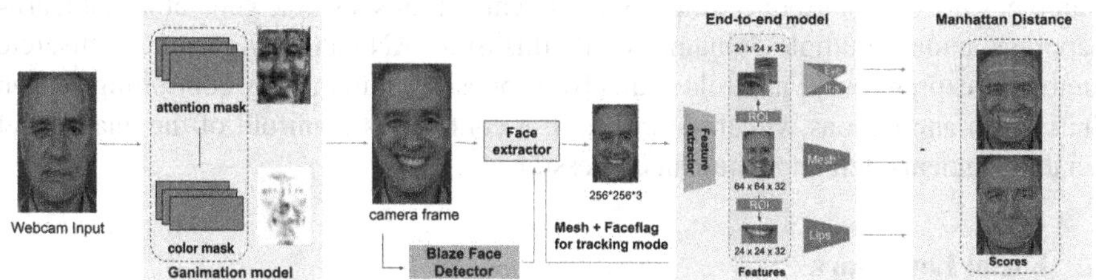


**Fig. 1.** Illustration of our advanced framework's architecture, which amalgamates methodologies influenced by GANimation [16] and FaceMesh [12]. This synergy seeks to augment the quality of real-time video streaming. Additionally, the Manhattan distance metric is employed for computing the final score.

Figure 1 illustrates the overall architecture of our framework, with two major components. First, we adopt *Facemesh* [12] from Google, a lightweight 3D face landmark detection model that can extract 468 anchors on mobile devices. After deriving the anchors, we compare the similarity between the facial motions of the subject and that of the instruction image to determine whether the patients correctly finished the exercise. Second, to improve user experience, we synthesize realistic and personalized rehabilitation instructions via Gamination [16], which can model the lighting changes on facial expressions. Gamination is a conditional Generative Adversarial Network (GAN) [4] based on Action Units annotations that describe the anatomical facial movements defining in a continuous manifold a human expression. Therefore, our users can follow the instructions synthesized from their faces.

To prove the efficacy of our proposed framework, develop a real-time system for autonomous facial expression rehabilitation with a user-friendly interface. Each user is asked to follow a series of rehabilitation introductions generated from Ganimation. Then, the system will track their facial landmarks via Facemesh to calculate their scores. We conduct extensive user studies to evaluate our system and 86% of them show positive feedback on our app.

## 2 Related Works

### 2.1 Image-to-Image Translation

The goal of the image-to-image translation is to convert an input image from a source domain to a target domain by preserving the intrinsic source content and transferring the extrinsic target style. Specifically, image-to-image translation has been adopted for various applications, including image segmentation [11], style transfer [21], image inpainting

[3], Super-resolution [9], image/video colorization [7], and Domain adaptation [2]. To synthesize high-quality images, Generative Adversarial Networks (GANs) [4], which establish a zero-sum game between a generator network, i.e., generating the fake but plausible images, and a discriminator network, i.e., distinguishing between real and fake images. During training, GANs iteratively update two models' parameters until the model converges, i.e., the generated images are similar to the real instances. Image-to-Image translation could also be adopted in synthesizing human facial expressions. For example, Choi et al. introduce SrarGAN [1], which trains a single generator that learns mappings among multiple domains. While this SrarGAN can only generate a discrete number of expressions, Pumarola et al. [16] propose Ganimation by controlling Action Units (AU) annotations, which describes in a continuous manifold of the anatomical facial movements defining a human expression.

## 2.2 Facial Landmark

Facial landmark detection aims to detect the location of predefined facial landmarks, such as the corners of the eyes, eyebrows, and nose tip, which can be applied to a large variety of tasks, including face recognition [22, **?**] head pose estimation [19], facial reenactment [18]. Generally, conventional facial landmark detection algorithms aim to fit a deformable face mesh, such as Active Shape Model (ASM), Active Appearance Model (AAM), and Constrained Local Model (CLM), which is based on statistical information, and thus offers underwhelming performance for most types of in-the-wild images. Typically, the direct regression methods [8]adopted various pre-trained backbone models, such as ResNet, MobileNet, and ShuffleNet. On the other hand, heatmap- based methods commonly use Hourglass network architecture, including HRNet and CU-Net. This paper uses FaceMesh [12] from MediaPipe, a lightweight direct coordinate regression method based on the MobileNet with the Single Shot Multibox Detector. Compared to heatmap-based methods. FaceMesh directly predicts coordinates, which is more computationally efficient and requires less training data, which is much more suitable for a mobile device with limited computational resources.

## 2.3 AI for Rehabilitation

With the rapid growth of mobile services and robust sensor techniques, AI-empowered rehabilitation has attracted significant attention from both industrial and research fields. Nayak et al. [15] investigated the application of AI in prosthetic and orthotic rehabilitation to aid in the recovery of limbs. Meng et al. [14] presented a study on robust iterative feedback tuning control of rehabilitation robots for repetitive ankle training to facilitate the recovery of limbs. With the recent advance in facial recognition systems, Guanoluisa et al. [5] propose a passive stereoscopic vision to capture facial information for facial paralysis rehabilitation. However, this work measures the correctness of the patient's facial expressions without considering two essential dimensions of the rehabilitation process: *interaction*, (i.e., the patient is involved in real-time), and *immersion* (i.e., the patient is easy to follow instructions).

# 3 Method

## 3.1 Facial Landmark for Rehabilitation Evaluation

To effectively evaluate the correctness of the rehabilitation exercise, we adopt the pre-trained facial landmark models, FaceMesh [12], to extract the 468 anchor points from the videos of those patients with facial nerve paralysis. Compared to the conventional facial landmark model, FaceMesh utilizes a graph-based representation of the face, which captures the spatial relationships between landmarks, e.g., cheeks, forehead, mouth, eyes, and better handles occlusions and variations in facial expressions, thus leading to a more accurate and robust representation of facial landmarks.

First, FashMesh adopts the MobileNetV2 for feature extraction, a lightweight CNN backbone to extract the image features. To achieve better efficiency, MobileNetV2 replaces the redundant convolution layer with the bottleneck convolution layer, i.e., $1 \times 1$-convolution neural network, which can learn the importance of each channel. While stacking multiple convolutional layers may sacrifice some detail of the image, MobileNetV2 adopts the residual connection between the bottlenecks to preserve the fine-grained information from the input data, which can also alleviate the gradient vanishing problem. After extracting the image feature from MobileNetV2, FashMesh used Single Shot MultiBox Detector (SSD) to predict the 468 landmarks, which utilizes the multi-scale feature maps for detection. The objective of SSD consists of localization loss to evaluate the position of the landmarks, and confidence loss to determine the label.

Summing up, we obtained 468 landmark set $\mathrm{V} = \{v_i\}_{i \in [1,468]}$, where each landmark can be denoted as $v_i = (x_i, y_i, z_i, p_i)$. $x_i, y_i \in [0, 1]$ are the coordinates of the landmark which are normalized by the image width and height, respectively. $z_i$ denotes the landmark's depth according to the head's center. Since FaceMesh also encodes the geometric relationships between landmarks, it can further predict the presence $p$ of the landmark for those occlusions images. Note that the value of $v_i$ is normalized according to the central point of each face to align the landmark for different faces.

It's worth noting that we further propose the group normalization is to describe the local geometric patents for each face. Specifically, we divide the anchor points into $K$ groups, i.e., $\{c^k\}_{k \in [1,K]}$, where each anchor point $v_i$ belongs to only one of them. Then, we normalize $x_i$ and $y_i$ as follows.

$$x_i = \frac{x_i - \mu_x^k}{\sigma_x^k}, \text{ and } y_i = \frac{y_i - \mu_y^k}{\sigma_y^k},$$

where $\mu^k$ and $\sigma^k$ are the average and standard derivation of the group $c^k$, respectively. Given the landmarks set V of the user image and the landmark set $\hat{\mathrm{V}}$ of the introduction image, we the Manhattan distance [10] to evaluate the correctness of the rehabilitation exercise as follows.

$$d(\mathrm{V}, \widehat{\mathrm{V}}) = \frac{1}{468} == \left(p_i \wedge \hat{p}^{\hat{i}}\right)\Big)\left(a|x_i - \hat{x}_i| + \beta\left|y_i - \hat{y}^{\hat{i}}\right|\right), \tag{1}$$

where $\alpha$ and $\beta$ determine the penalty of distance by the $x-$ and $y-$axis. With a higher distance, the user exercise is farther away from the rehabilitation instruction. Conversely, a smaller loss indicates that the predicted facial landmark is closer to the ground truth landmark. Therefore, a smaller Manhattan distance loss indicates more accurate facial landmark predictions in our model.

### 3.2 GANimation for Prototype Image Synthesis

While we have correctly evaluated the exercise via FascMesh, we further adopt GANimation [16] to synthesize the personalized instructions for rehabilitation to achieve better user immersion. Specifically, GANimation is a conditional generative adversarial network (CGAN) that can transform the face shots of patients by controlling the Action Units (AUs), i.e., the contractions of specific facial muscles in a fine-grained manner. In contrast, conventional CGANs employ a discrete label to describe the facial expression as the conditional variable. Therefore, we adapt the GANimation to generate images to guide the patients in rehabilitation step-by-step instead of giving a single image as the final goal.

Following the standard GAN paradigm, GANimation consists of a generator network $G$ to synthesize the photo-realistic image by considering the condition and a discriminator network $D$ to evaluate the quality of the generated results. Given the input user image $\mathbf{I} \in \mathrm{R}^{W \times H \times 3}$, the actions units of $\mathbf{I}$ can be denoted as $y$, which encodes the expression of user image gesture expression in a $N$ -dimensional vectors. The goal of GANimation is to learn a generator $G$ to translate the user image $\mathbf{I}$ into an output image $\hat{\mathbf{I}}$ with the target expression $\hat{y}$ but keep the identity of input $\mathbf{I}$. The objective of GANimation can be defined as follows.

$$G^* = \arg \min_G \max_D L(\mathbf{I}, y, \hat{y}), \tag{2}$$

where the generator $G$ learns to translate $\mathbf{I}$ into the target image $\hat{\mathbf{I}}$ by minimizing the loss function $L$ and the discriminator $D$ has to distinguish the quality of transformed image $\hat{\mathbf{I}}$.

Instead of directly regressing a full image, the generator $G$ in GANimation outputs two masks, an attention mask $\mathbf{A}$ form a sub-network $G_A$, and color mask $\mathbf{C}$ a subnetwork $G_C$, to construct the translated images as follows.

$$\hat{I} = (1 - A) \cdot C + A \cdot I, \tag{3}$$

where mask $A = G_A(I|y) \in \mathrm{R}^{W \times H}$ and $\mathbf{C} = G_C(I|y) \in \mathrm{R}^{W \times H \times 3}$. The mask $\mathbf{A}$ indicates to which extent each pixel of the $\mathbf{C}$ contributes to the output image $\hat{\mathbf{I}}$. Therefore, the generator does not need to render static elements and can focus exclusively on the pixels defining the facial movements, leading to sharper and more realistic synthetic images.

The first discriminator $D_I$ adopts the WGAN-GP [6] as the adversarial image loss to enable the model to distinguish the real and synthesized image.

$$\mathrm{E}_{\mathbf{I}\sim\mathrm{P}}\left[D_I\left(G\left(\mathbf{I}|y^{\wedge}\right)\right)\right]\mathrm{E}_{\mathbf{I}\sim\mathrm{P}}[D_I(\mathbf{I}|)] + \lambda_{gp}\mathbf{E}\ {}_{\sim\mathbf{I}\sim\mathrm{P}^{\sim}}\left[\left\|\nabla D(\tilde{\mathbf{I}})\right\|_2 - 1\right], \tag{4}$$

where P denotes the input image distribution and $\tilde{\mathrm{P}}$ represents the random interpolation distribution. The first and second terms in Eq. (4) enable the discriminator $D$ to distinguish the generated image $\hat{\mathbf{I}} = G(\mathbf{I}|\hat{y})$ from the generator $G$ and the real input image $\mathbf{I}$.

The last part is the gradient penalty for the discriminator to stabilize the training process by preventing the gradient vanishing problem.

Then, GANimation employs another discriminator network $D_y$ with the Conditional Expression Loss ensures that the target AUs $y\hat{}$ are adequately encoded in the output image $\hat{\mathbf{I}}$, which can be illustrated as follows.

$$\mathrm{E}_{I\sim \mathrm{P}}[Dy(I) - y]^2/2 + \mathrm{E}_{I\sim \mathrm{P}}[Dy(G(I|y^\wedge)) - y^\wedge]^2/2, \tag{5}$$

where the former part ensure the original input image **I** can be correctly classified to its AUs $y$, and the second part aim to distinguish transformed image $\hat{\mathbf{I}} = G(I|y\hat{})$ is belongs to the target AUs $y\hat{}$ by $D_y$.

To retain the identity of the transformed image $\hat{\mathbf{I}}$ from the input image **I**, inspired by cycle-consistency [21], GANimation further adopts the Identity loss to guarantee that the face in both the input and output images corresponds to the same person. Without ground-truth supervision, the identity loss can be formally written as follows.

$$\mathrm{E}_{\mathbf{I}\sim \mathrm{P}}[\|G(G(I|y^\wedge)|y) - I\|_1]. \tag{6}$$

The fundamental idea behind the identity loss is that the input image $I$ is first transformed to the target image under the condition $y\hat{}$ via generator $G$. The generator $G$ is required to inverse the transformation process, i.e., $\hat{\mathbf{I}}$ can be transformed back to the input image **I** by the condition $y$.

### 3.3 Implementation Detail

Our live video streaming setup comprises standard consumer-level hardware. We capture live video with a built-in webcam. In our experimental setup, we utilized a Logitech StreamCam camera operating at 30 frames per second (FPS), which provided a favorable trade-off between seamless video output and minimized computational load. Furthermore, the camera was configured to capture video at a resolution of 640 × 480, rendering our approach compatible with any consumer-grade RGB camera. To improve the video streaming quality, we used Logitech-provided Logitech Capture auto-correction techniques to adjust brightness, contrast, and sharpness, thereby enhancing the user experience.

We select 80 representative facial landmarks with higher weight to enhance the effectiveness of rehabilitation measurement. Following the Yanagihara Grading System [17], we improved and permitted a hierarchical categorization of rehabilitation performance, ranging from 0 to 0.1, where 0 epitomizes optimal alignment. We categorize into four-grade levels, including excellent (0–0.025), medium (0.025–0.05), below average (0.05–0.075), and unsatisfactory (above 0.075). Each participant was instructed to hold a specified facial expression for 50 seconds, repeating the task twice consecutively. After the first successful attempt, a system indicator prompted the individual to resume a neutral facial expression before embarking on a second trial. Upon successful completion of the designated tasks, participants progressed to subsequent phases of the facial rehabilitation exercise regimen.

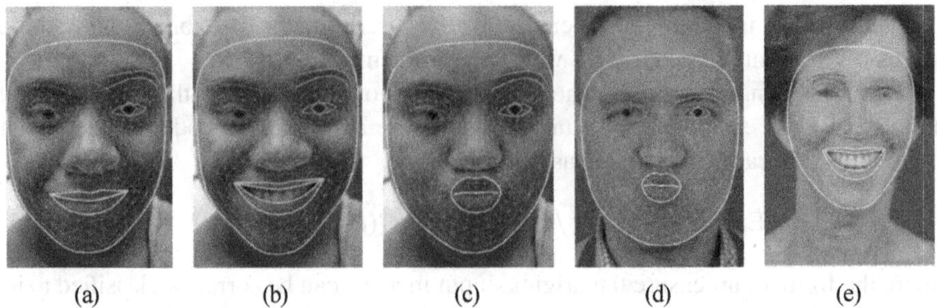

(a) (b) (c) (d) (e)

**Fig. 2.** (a) The original face of the black man. (b) A smiling face and (c) The pout face of the black man generated from Ganimation. (d) The pout face of a white man. (e) The smile face of a white woman.

**Table 1.** Evaluation of rehabilitation successful rate compared with the instruction photo via Ganimation which is analyzed by FashMesh from the introuction image in Fig. 2

| | (a) | (b) | (c) | (d) | (e) |
|---|---|---|---|---|---|
| (a) | 0.000 | 0.037 | 0.079 | 0.067 | 0.079 |
| (b) | 0.037 | 0.000 | 0.132 | 0.076 | 0.059 |
| (c) | 0.079 | 0.132 | 0.000 | 0.047 | 0.099 |
| (d) | 0.067 | 0.076 | 0.047 | 0.000 | 0.071 |
| (e) | 0.079 | 0.059 | 0.099 | 0.071 | 0.000 |

## 4 Experimental Results

### 4.1 Rehabilitation Evaluation via Facemesh

Figure 2 showcases the output of the GANimation for our prototype facial study. Upon examination, it becomes evident that the FaceMesh analysis is used to evaluate the success rate of the rehabilitation, juxtaposing it with the reference photograph through GANimation. When identical images are compared, the score naturally defaults to 0. Utilizing group normalization allows the analysis to accommodate a single individual exhibiting varied facial movements. It is observed that the score escalates as the disparity in facial expressions increases. Ideally, a good rehabilitation outcome score should be between 0 and 0.05; scores higher than this range will be considered a rehabilitation failure, necessitating a retry to achieve the intended goal.

As illustrated in Table 1, when comparing the facial expressions of a Black individual exhibiting a pouted face to a smiling face, and a White individual with a pouted face, it is observed that the score for the smiling Black individual is significantly higher. According to the pass/fail criteria, only a, b and c, d passed, which are slightly different in the angle of the mouth closure and both are pouted expressions but cross-tested for different individuals. This result emphasizes that our framework gives precedence to facial expressions over individual unique features, a strategy that holds the promise of enhancing accuracy in rehabilitation outcomes.

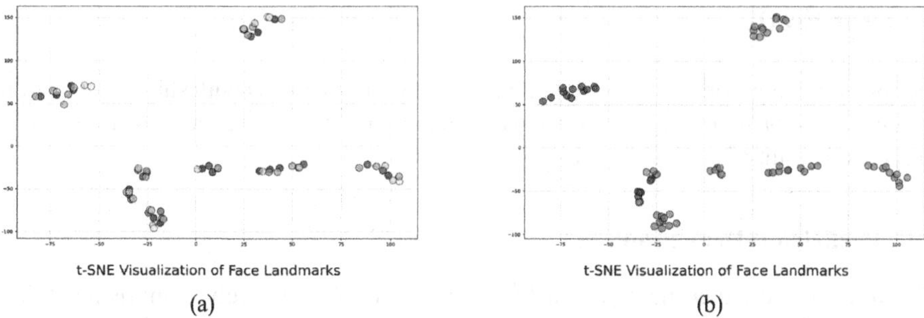


(a) (b)

**Fig. 3.** This t-SNE visualization illustrates classifications based on distinct categories: ethnicity and gender, and facial expression, each represented with unique color-coded clusters.

While the chart in Fig. 3a emphasizes classifications based on "Ethnicity & Gender", facilitating a detailed analysis through distinct clusters, the representation in Fig.3b focuses on "Facial Expression", allowing for a comparative study between the two classification paradigms.

### 4.2 Rehabilitation Instruction Generation via Ganimation

As illustrated in Fig 2, we showcase representative samples encompassing two distinct races and genders, amounting to a total of three subjects who exhibit symptoms of facial paralysis. Leveraging the proficiently trained GANimation model, our framework is capable of generating high-quality, realistic facial images that faithfully represent the user's specified facial movements and expressions.

Figure 3 utilizes t-SNE visualizations to evaluate the performance of our experimental framework. This framework is grounded on synthesized facial expressions derived from a cohort of 18 subjects who are genuine patients suffering from facial nerve disorders, encompassing a diverse range of ethnicities and genders. The expressions, with four moods, "pout," "gasp," "smile," and "unhappy," were synthesized utilizing GANnimation [16], culminating in a dataset of 72 unique data points demonstrated in each subplot. We opt for t-SNE representation for its proficiency in projecting highdimensional data into a 2D or 3D space, facilitating qualitative visual interpretation. This is particularly pertinent as our facial landmarks, sourced from *Facemesh* [12], are three-dimensional $(x, y, z)$ and are consequently dimensionality-reduced for this visualization. The chosen parameters for the t-SNE model are a perplexity of 3 and a random state of 42.

On the other hand, the four distinct facial expressions largely segregate into separate clusters in Fig. 3b. A minor degree of overlap between red and green data points with blue ones can be observed, attributed to the emphasis of all four expressions on mouth movements, causing minor deviations based on individual subject variations. Conversely, in Fig. 3a, we adjusted the visual offsets to distinguish the 18 color-coded clusters representing different ethnicities and genders. Despite the complexity, the clustering is coherent, with each cluster containing over 16 points and a deviation rate below 8%.

## 5 User Study

Our primary intention was to complement objective assessments with subjective human evaluations to provide a comprehensive understanding of the actual effectiveness of our proposed learning-based approach.

### 5.1 Participant Demographics

We initiated the experiment with a focus on a cohort exclusively comprising Asian students from the university, encompassing a sample size of 25 individuals aged between 18 and 22 years. The gender distribution within this cohort included 10 males and 15 females. Subsequent to the anticipated acceptance of this paper, we plan to recruit a more diverse participant pool, projected to be between 50 and 80 individuals. This pool will maintain a balanced gender distribution and draw from various backgrounds, including academic circles (universities), government offices, technology firms, and art centers, to foster a comprehensive perspective in our evaluations.

### 5.2 Study Procedure

Participants were required to evaluate a series of 24 test examples. These examples were organized into five stages, each containing five designated facial expression rehabilitation exercises. Upon the completion of all 24 exercises, which encompasses the entirety of the four stages, the participant successfully concludes the test. These participants were instructed to mimic the facial expressions characteristic of individuals suffering from grade I to III facial nerve paralysis, based on the categorizations outlined in [20], which encompasses symptoms such as incomplete eyelid closure, lack of forehead movement, and asymmetrical mouth movement. Each test example was structured as follows:

Participants were systematically instructed to follow the established protocol within our framework. For an accurate evaluation of the rehabilitation exercises' precision, participants calibrated facial landmarks using a real-time webcam. Once the subject's image was captured, our system generated 24 tailored rehabilitation tasks based on this image.

Discrepancies observed between the actual facial expressions of the participants and the intended post-rehabilitation expressions were analyzed in terms of the relative position and dimensions of facial features. This analysis signified the completion of the participant's training phase. In tandem with this, our system delivered instantaneous feedback. This guided users to make adjustments according to specific task categories within the six Difficulties Stage: 'Open Eyes', 'Smile', 'confound', 'Pout', 'hold breath' and 'Point Down'.

In the final phase, the system presented an aggregate report of the participant's training performance. This was evaluated using the Manhattan distance metric, offering insights into the participant's advancements during the rehabilitation process (Fig. 4).

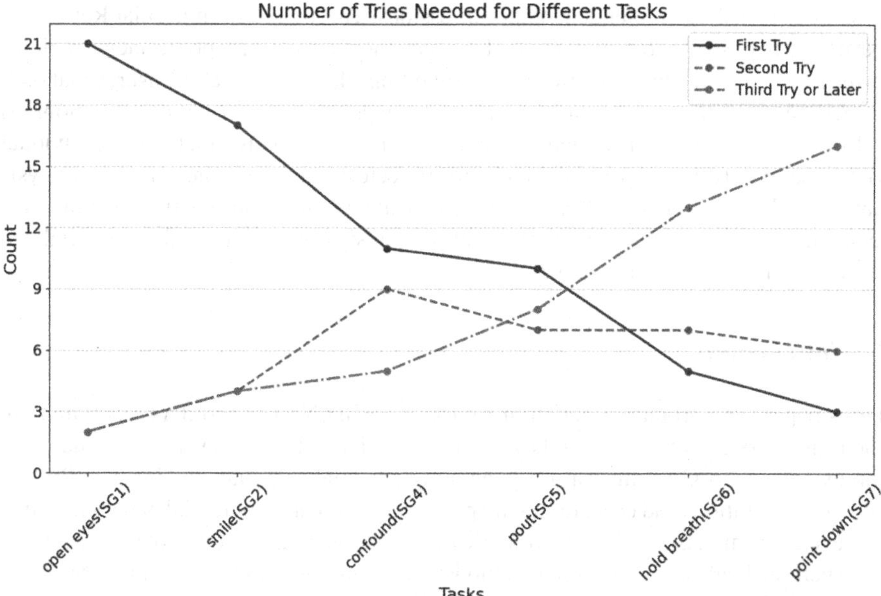


**Fig. 4.** A line chart illustrating the number of attempts required for distinct task categories within the six Difficulties Stage, namely: 'Open Eyes', 'Smile', 'confound', 'Pout', 'hold breath' and 'Point Down'.

### 5.3 Subject Feedback

In this section, we analyze the number of attempts required by the participants to successfully complete tasks across distinct categories within the "Six Difficulties Stage." The tasks were segregated into four categories: 'Open Eyes', 'Smile', 'Pout', and 'Point Down'. From our observations, tasks necessitating performances associated with the eyes and eyebrows—conducted in the initial stage—required the fewest attempts, with over 20 participants accomplishing them on their first try. However, a discernible increment in the number of attempts was observed as the subjects progressed through stages of escalating complexity. Remarkably, in the final stage of our experiment, over half of the cohort—representing more than 13 participants—needed three or more attempts to successfully fulfill the task requirements. This highlights a substantial increase in difficulty level, underscoring the necessity for greater precision and control in the execution of more complex facial movements.

## 6 Limitation and Discussion

Our framework has been devised to efficaciously assist individuals with facial palsy, enabling them to undergo rehabilitation remotely, be it away from hospital premises or via mobile devices, thereby enhancing convenience. However, it is paramount to note that our system plays a supplementary role. Misalignment in muscle activation can lead to facial movement distortions. In simpler terms, incorrectly activating incorrect facial muscles can result in unintended facial expressions. Through Neuromuscular Retraining (NMR), it is possible to facilitate cerebral reconnection to appropriate facial regions, thereby isolating and engaging the correct set of muscles. This process ensures that only the pertinent muscles are activated for a specific expression, fostering more harmonious and symmetrical facial movements. It is crucial to acknowledge that every individual with facial paralysis has a unique recovery trajectory. In cases where facial paralysis manifests abruptly, immediate emergency medical attention is imperative. If symptoms persist for 10 to 12 weeks, a comprehensive diagnosis is recommended at a specialized neurology and rehabilitation department.

## 7 Conclusion

In this paper, we introduce a new framework for Facial Nerve Disorders rehabilitation. The framework incorporates two key components: FaceMesh for evaluating rehabilitation exercises and GANimation for generating personalized guidance images. Results from demonstrations and user studies are promising, indicating potential patient benefits. However, it's emphasized that this framework is a supplementary tool, not a replacement for expert medical care. Additional methods like Neuromuscular Retraining (NMR) and self-physical rehabilitation can enhance its effectiveness. We hope this work can extend to support other rehabilitation and potentially revolutionize recovery.

## References


1. Choi, Y., Choi, M., Kim, M., Ha, J.W., Kim, S., Choo, J.: Stargan: unified generative adversarial networks for multi-domain image-to-image translation. In: Proceedings of the IEEE Conference on Computer Vision and Pattern Recognition, pp. 8789–8797 (2018)
2. Csurka, G.: Domain adaptation for visual applications: a comprehensive survey. arXiv preprint arXiv:1702.05374 (2017)
3. Elharrouss, O., Almaadeed, N., Al-Maadeed, S., Akbari, Y.: Image inpainting: a review. Neural Process. Lett. **51**, 2007–2028 (2020)
4. Goodfellow, I., et al.: Generative adversarial networks. Commun. ACM **63**(11), 139–144 (2020)
5. Guanoluisa, G.M., Pilatasig, J.A., Andaluz, V.H.: Gy medic: analysis and rehabilitation system for patients with facial paralysis. In: Seki, H., Nguyen, C.H., Huynh, V.-N., Inuiguchi, M. (eds.) IUKM 2019. LNCS (LNAI), vol. 11471, pp. 63–75. Springer, Cham (2019). https://doi.org/10.1007/978-3-030-14815-7_6
6. Gulrajani, I., Ahmed, F., Arjovsky, M., Dumoulin, V., Courville, A.C.: Improved training of wasserstein gans. Adv. Neural Inf. Process. Syst. **30**, 1–11 (2017)
7. Gupta, R.K., Chia, A.Y.S., Rajan, D., Ng, E.S., Zhiyong, H.: Image colorization using similar images. In: Proceedings of the 20th ACM International Conference on Multimedia, pp. 369–378 (2012)
8. Jin, Y., Li, Z., Yi, P.: Review of methods applying on facial alignment. In: 2022 IEEE 2nd International Conference on Electronic Technology, Communication and Information (ICETCI). pp. 553–557. IEEE (2022)
9. Kaji, S., Kida, S.: Overview of image-to-image translation by use of deep neural networks: denoising, super-resolution, modality conversion, and reconstruction in medical imaging. Radiol. Phys. Technol. **12**, 235–248 (2019)

10. Kim, H.W., Kim, H.J., Rho, S., Hwang, E.: Augmented emtcnn: a fast and accurate facial landmark detection network. Appl. Sci. **10**(7), 2253 (2020)
11. Li, R., Cao, W., Jiao, Q., Wu, S., Wong, H.S.: Simplified unsupervised image translation for semantic segmentation adaptation. Pattern Recogn. **105**, 107343 (2020)
12. Lugaresi, C., et al.: Mediapipe: a framework for building perception pipelines. arXiv preprint arXiv:1906.08172 (2019)
13. Luijmes, R.E., Pouwels, S., Beurskens, C.H., Kleiss, I.J., Siemann, I., Ingels, K.J.: Quality of life before and after different treatment modalities in peripheral facial palsy: a systematic review. Laryngoscope **127**(5), 1044–1051 (2017)
14. Meng, W., Xie, S.Q., Liu, Q., Lu, C.Z., Ai, Q.: Robust iterative feedback tuning control of a compliant rehabilitation robot for repetitive ankle training. IEEE/ASME Trans. Mechatron. **22**(1), 173–184 (2016)
15. Nayak, S., Das, R.K.: Application of artificial intelligence (ai) in prosthetic and orthotic rehabilitation. In: Service Robotics. IntechOpen (2020)
16. Pumarola, A., Agudo, A., Martinez, A.M., Sanfeliu, A., Moreno-Noguer, F.: Ganimation: Anatomically-aware facial animation from a single image. In: Proceedings of the European Conference on Computer Vision (ECCV), pp. 818–833 (2018)
17. Satoh, Y., Kanzaki, J., Yoshihara, S.: A comparison and conversion table of 'the house–brackmann facial nerve grading system'and 'the yanagihara grading system.' Auris Nasus Larynx **27**(3), 207–212 (2000)
18. Thies, J., Zollhofer, M., Stamminger, M., Theobalt, C., Nießner, M.: Face2face: Real-time face capture and reenactment of RGB videos. In: Proceedings of the IEEE Conference on Computer Vision and Pattern Recognition, pp. 2387–2395 (2016)
19. Wu, Y., Gou, C., Ji, Q.: Simultaneous facial landmark detection, pose and deformation estimation under facial occlusion. In: Proceedings of the IEEE Conference on Computer Vision and Pattern Recognition, pp. 3471–3480 (2017)
20. Yen, T.L., Driscoll, C.L., Lalwani, A.K.: Significance of house-brackmann facial nerve grading global score in the setting of differential facial nerve function. Otol. Neurotol. **24**(1), 118–122 (2003)
21. Zhu, J.Y., Park, T., Isola, P., Efros, A.A.: Unpaired image-to-image translation using cycle-consistent adversarial networks. In: Proceedings of the IEEE International Conference on Computer Vision, pp. 2223–2232 (2017)
22. Zhu, X., Lei, Z., Yan, J., Yi, D., Li, S.Z.: High-fidelity pose and expression normalization for face recognition in the wild. In: Proceedings of the IEEE Conference on Computer Vision and Pattern Recognition, pp. 787–796 (2015)

# Deep Learning for Journalism: The Bibliometric Analysis of Deep Learning for News Production in the Artificial Intelligence Era

Richard G. Mayopu and Long-Sheng Chen(✉)

Department of Information Management, Chaoyang University of Technology, Taichung 413310, Taiwan (R.O.C.)
lschen@cyut.edu.tw

**Abstract.** This research aims to evaluate the articles published from 2018 to 2023. We focused on the deep learning issues that have risen in the last decade. Deep learning is the popular approach in news research, especially in the classification or detection of the news. Moreover, in Artificial Intelligence (AI), numbers of applications are invented to help journalists to optimization their work. On the other hand, it can be the dark side of AI if used without wisdom. We have used the bibliometric method to extract the total data N = 69 to be analyzed, and we used several parameters such as scholarly landscape, keyword plus theme, co-networking, and evolution of research theme. The result of this research is that we found the matrix of research direction for future works, and it should be observed closely to the news classification and detection research. Since the large language model was invented, news production has changed and influenced journalism practices.

**Keywords:** Deep Learning · Journalism · News · Bibliometric · Artificial Intelligence

## 1 Introduction

The field of artificial intelligence (AI) has made significant strides in the information era that have changed many fields [1], including journalism and news reporting. A paradigm shift in the ways that news is produced, managed, and transmitted has occurred with the introduction of deep learning, a branch of AI [2]. In addition to increasing the precision and effectiveness of information extraction [3], deep learning techniques built on neural networks have also presented new difficulties and opportunities for the mass media sector. In order to shed light on the development of this intersection between AI and journalism, this article performs a thorough bibliometric investigation of the function and effects of deep learning in the field of news.

It is impossible to exaggerate the impact of deep learning on the distribution of news. Traditional media sources and internet platforms are rapidly using AI-driven algorithms to automate content creation, tailor content for users, and identify fake news [4]. As a


C.-Y. Lee et al. (Eds.): TAAI 2023, CCIS 2074, pp. 250–256, 2024.
https://doi.org/10.1007/978-981-97-1711-8_19

result, the incorporation of deep learning in news production has changed the dynamics of information flow, altering societal decision-making, public debate, and opinion formation. The purpose of this study is an in-depth exploration of both the aspects of this transition.

We use bibliometric analysis as the foundation of our methodology to fully understand the scope of this problem. With the help of this method, we are able to thoroughly study and evaluate the huge corpus of academic research related to deep learning and news [5]. We seek to present a thorough overview of the field's evolution, current state, and future directions by highlighting major trends, foundational research works, and influential personalities. Researchers and practitioners will be able to use our study as a valuable reference as well as gain an understanding of the role artificial intelligence will play in the delivery of news in the 21st century.

It is essential to understand how deep learning plays a role in the ecosystem of news in an age when information is a currency and a commodity. A core objective of this project is to unravel the intricate details of this relationship and to provide valuable insights into the future of news dissemination and journalism driven by artificial intelligence.

## 2 Literature Review

### 2.1 Deep Learning and Its Impact on Journalism.

Deep learning, a subfield of artificial intelligence (AI), has gained significant traction in the journalism domain. Researchers have shown that deep neural networks in tasks such as detecting type of news [6] sentiment analysis [3], summarization [7], and language translation [8], which are vital for news reporting. The infusion of deep learning techniques into journalism has not only enhanced the efficiency of content generation but has also raised questions about the credibility and ethics of AI-generated news articles.

### 2.2 Automating Content Creation and Curation

The application of deep learning in automating content creation and curation has been explored extensively [9]. Current research demonstrated how neural networks can generate news articles from structured data, reducing the burden on human journalists [10] also able to taking the responsibility of the media information. Additionally, research by Nguyen and Hekman [11] delved into the use of deep learning algorithms for content recommendation and personalization, reshaping the way news is consumed by users.

### 2.3 Fake News Detection and Mitigation

With the proliferation of misinformation, fake news detection has become a critical challenge. The recent research highlighted the effectiveness of deep learning models in identifying false information by analysing textual and visual content [12]. By detecting fake news, it can be mitigated or even prevented from spreading on a global scale.

### 2.4 Ethical and Social Implications

The intersection of deep learning and news has raised ethical concerns. Researchers examined the ethical implications of AI-generated news, addressing issues related to transparency, accountability, and responsibility of the engineer, designer in preparing the project and decide the which is the best algorithm to be used [13]. Moreover, the societal impact of AI-generated news on public opinion and decision-making processes has been discussed in order to determine the best approach to decide the ethical justification in using the AI-generated News.

## 3 Method

### 3.1 Data Source Selection

In our study, we employed bibliometric analysis to systematically assess the scholarly landscape at the intersection of deep learning and news. To ensure the comprehensiveness and reliability of our data, we turned to the Scopus database, a well-regarded repository of academic publications. Scopus, with its vast coverage of journals, conferences, and patents, provides an ideal platform for our bibliometric analysis.

### 3.2 Defining the Research Scope

To narrow down the focus of our study, we established a defined time frame of the last five years. This temporal constraint ensures that we capture the most recent developments in the field, considering the rapid evolution of both deep learning and news reporting during this period.

### 3.3 Search Queries and Keywords

Our data collection process began with the formulation of precise search queries. We utilized a combination of keywords and controlled vocabulary terms related to deep learning and news. These queries were designed to identify relevant publications, and conference papers published within the specified timeframe.

### 3.4 Data Extraction and Validation

After executing the search queries in Scopus, we retrieved a substantial dataset comprising academic articles, patents, and conference papers. It is important to note that Scopus provides extensive metadata for each publication, including author information, publication date, citation count, and affiliations. This dataset was subsequently validated to eliminate duplicates and ensure data accuracy.

### 3.5 Inclusion and Exclusion Criteria

To maintain the relevance of our analysis, we established inclusion and exclusion criteria. Publications that did not directly relate to the nexus of deep learning and news were excluded from our dataset. Conversely, any works that explored this intersection, whether from computer science, journalism, or related fields, were retained.

### 3.6 Data Preprocessing

Once our dataset was finalized, we conducted data preprocessing. This involved categorizing publications into relevant subfields (e.g., content generation, fake news detection, ethical considerations) based on their content and objectives. This step was crucial in structuring our analysis and identifying key research trends.

### 3.7 Deep Learning and Its Impact on Journalism

Our bibliometric analysis encompasses various parameters, including publication trends, authorship patterns, citation networks, and keyword co-occurrence. By examining these aspects, we aim to provide a comprehensive overview of the scholarly landscape, identifying influential authors, seminal works, emerging themes, and knowledge diffusion patterns within the field.

This bibliometric approach, anchored in data collected from the Scopus database over the past five years, enables us to conduct a robust and up-to-date analysis of the evolving relationship between deep learning and news, ultimately contributing valuable insights to the broader discourse on AI in journalism (Fig. 1).

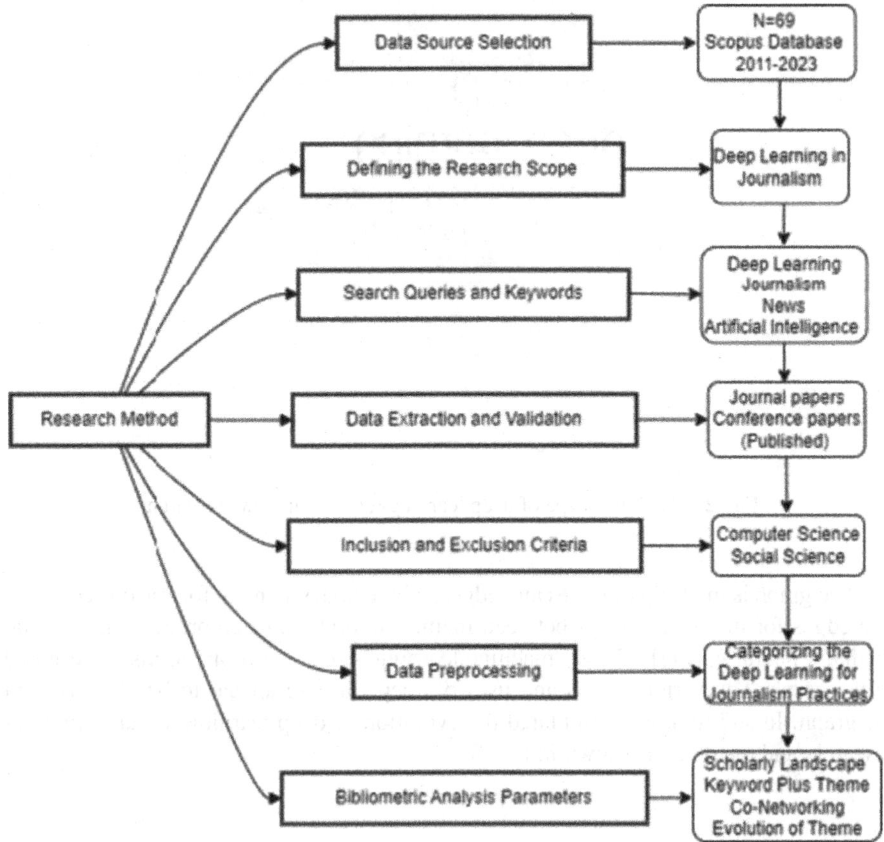


**Fig. 1.** Research method: the bibliometric of deep learning in journalism (step by step).

# 4 Discussion

## 4.1 Landscape and Evolution of Deep Learning Research in News Research

The parameter we used in this research is scholarly landscape, keyword plus theme, co-networking, and evolution of research theme. Figure 2 shows the landscape of scholarly research topics that are usually used in deep learning research related to news. Common techniques such as natural language processing (NLP) are the most common in news research.

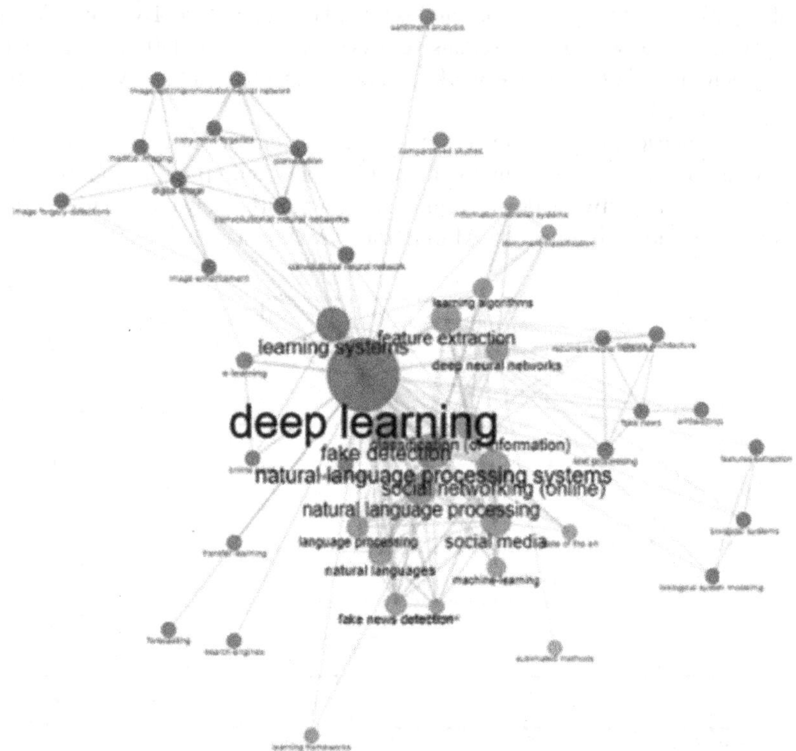


**Fig. 2.** The Landscape of deep learning research in news research.

The graph is made up of nodes and edges, where nodes stand in for various concepts and edges for the relationships between them. "Natural language processing," "social media," "neural networks," and "machine learning" are some of the terms represented in the graph. The various fields and uses of deep learning appear to be visualized in the graph. In addition, we formulated the evolution of deep learning research in news research, and the detail is shown in Fig. 3.

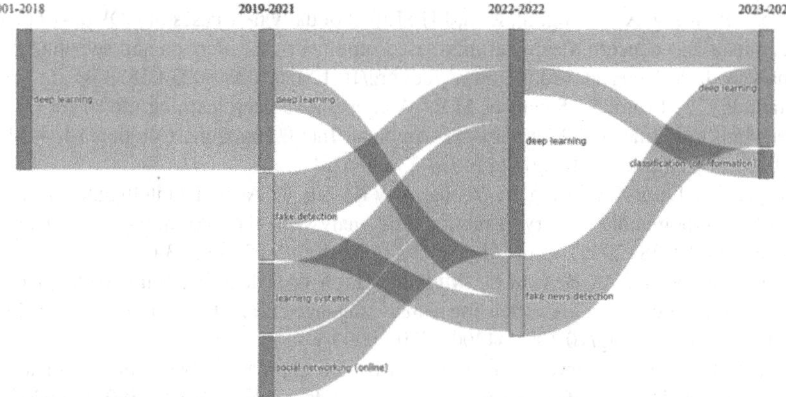


**Fig. 3.** The evolution of deep learning research in news research.

Figure 3 is the evolution of the deep learning research timeline graphic with four columns representing different periods. From 2001–2018, most research focused on deep learning topics in general, such as the model of CNN and RNN. In 2019–2021, most researchers developed their research into various fields that can implement deep learning in journalism, such as fake news detection. Social networking also became an interesting topic to be analyzed. Moving to 2022–2023, deep learning in fake news detection still became the favorite topic and research in classification information.

## 5 Conclusion

To conclude, our research has given critical, fresh perspectives on the scholarly environment of deep learning in the context of research in journalism, particularly news. We have highlighted the pervasive usage of NLP as a common technique in this domain by examining keywords, themes, co-networking, and the growth of research themes. Also, we demonstrate the interrelated ideas that allow deep learning to be applied.

**Acknowledgement.** This work was supported in part by Chaoyang University of Technology (CYUT) and the Ministry of Science and Technology of Taiwan, R.O.C. (Grant No NSTC 112-2410-H-324-004). We also express our thanks for supports from Chaoyang University of Technology.

## References

1. Caled, D., Silva, M.J.: Digital media and misinformation: An outlook on multidisciplinary strategies against manipulation. Springer Singapore (2022). https://doi.org/10.1007/s42001-021-00118-8
2. Greif, H.: Analogue models and universal machines. Paradigms of epistemic transparency in artificial intelligence. Minds Mach. **32**, 111–133 (2022). https://doi.org/10.1007/s11023-022-09596-9

3. Che, S.P., Wang, X., Zhang, S., Kim, J.H.: Effect of daily new cases of COVID-19 on public sentiment and concern: deep learning-based sentiment classification and semantic network analysis. J. Public Heal. (2023). https://doi.org/10.1007/s10389-023-01833-4
4. Mallick, C., Mishra, S., Senapati, M.R.: A cooperative deep learning model for fake news detection in online social networks. J. Ambient. Intell. Humaniz. Comput. **14**, 4451–4460 (2023). https://doi.org/10.1007/s12652-023-04562-4
5. Wong, K.F., Lam, X.Y., Jiang, Y., Yeung, A.W.K., Lin, Y.: Artificial intelligence in orthodontics and orthognathic surgery: a bibliometric analysis of the 100 most-cited articles. Head Face Med. **19**, 38 (2023). https://doi.org/10.1186/s13005-023-00383-0
6. Naeem, B., Khan, A., Beg, M.O., Mujtaba, H.: A deep learning framework for clickbait detection on social area network using natural language cues. J. Comput. Soc. Sci. **3**, 231–243 (2020). https://doi.org/10.1007/s42001-020-00063-y
7. Hou, S.-L., et al.: A survey of text summarization approaches based on deep learning. J. Comput. Sci. Technol. **36**, 633–663 (2021). https://doi.org/10.1007/s11390-020-0207-x
8. Fan, L.: Effectiveness model of automatic machine translation of publicity texts based on deep learning. Soft. Comput. (2023). https://doi.org/10.1007/s00500-023-08583-1
9. Carstensen, T., Ganz, K.: Gendered AI: German news media discourse on the future of work. AI Soc. (2023). https://doi.org/10.1007/s00146-023-01747-5
10. Bunz, M., Braghieri, M.: The AI doctor will see you now: assessing the framing of AI in news coverage. AI Soc. **37**, 9–22 (2022). https://doi.org/10.1007/s00146-021-01145-9
11. Nguyen, D., Hekman, E.: The news framing of artificial intelligence: a critical exploration of how media discourses make sense of automation. AI Soc. (2022). https://doi.org/10.1007/s00146-022-01511-1
12. Comito, C., Caroprese, L., Zumpano, E.: Multimodal fake news detection on social media: a survey of deep learning techniques. Soc. Netw. Anal. Min. **13**, 101 (2023). https://doi.org/10.1007/s13278-023-01104-w
13. Wellner, G., Mykhailov, D.: Caring in an algorithmic world: ethical perspectives for designers and developers in building AI algorithms to fight fake news. Sci. Eng. Ethics **29**, 30 (2023). https://doi.org/10.1007/s11948-023-00450-4

# Blockchain-Based Diagnostic Certificate System with Privacy Protection

Chun-Li Lin(✉)

Department of Computer Science and Information Engineering, National Yunlin University of Science and Technology, Douliou, Yunlin 64002, Taiwan, R.O.C.
cllin@yuntech.edu.tw

**Abstract.** Blockchain represents a novel form of information technology application. It offers promising potential for future transactions and practical applications, particularly through the implementation of smart contracts. To address the issue of the time and expenses incurred by patients when obtaining a diagnosis certificate from various hospitals or clinics, blockchain technology is leveraged to generate diagnostic certificates via smart contracts on the Ethereum platform. This application harnesses blockchain features to ameliorate the identified problems, and it also presents solutions for the various operational processes involved in doctors recording diagnostic certificates and patients accessing their diagnostic records.

**Keywords:** Blockchain · Ethereum · Smart Contract · Diagnostic Certificate · Privacy Protection

## 1 Introduction

This article is founded upon the premise of health insurance systems, wherein the public will require diagnostic certificates on specific occasions, such as routine health check-ups, medical insurance claims, or matters related to military service.

In the typical process of obtaining a diagnostic certificate, individuals are required to visit the registration desk at each hospital for registration. Additionally, registration fees and diagnostic certificate charges may vary slightly depending on the hospital. Subsequently, the applicant submits the diagnostic certificate request to the attending physician. Present-day hospitals typically levy fees for diagnostic certificate applications based on various requirements, and the application process concludes after data processing and the attending physician's endorsement. If a patient is admitted to the hospital or visits the emergency department but does not request a diagnostic certificate upon discharge, it becomes necessary to obtain a reissued diagnostic certificate in the future. This entails once again registering at an outpatient clinic, incurring additional registration and application fees, and obtaining the certificate from the original medical department's attending physician.

The expenses in terms of both money and time incurred during this process represent a burden for patients. In addition to the aforementioned financial outlays, patients typically invest time in commuting to and from the hospital or clinic and waiting for the


C.-Y. Lee et al. (Eds.): TAAI 2023, CCIS 2074, pp. 257–268, 2024.
https://doi.org/10.1007/978-981-97-1711-8_20

registration process to conclude. In comparison to the waiting times experienced during the application process, it is initially estimated that this wait may span several hours. To mitigate these costs, the initial concept revolves around digitization (see Fig. 1). In general, post-digitization, the information is typically stored within the databases of various local hospitals. When accessing this information, it necessitates retrieval from the relevant sources and diligent management. This process also involves a manpower requirement within the hospital.

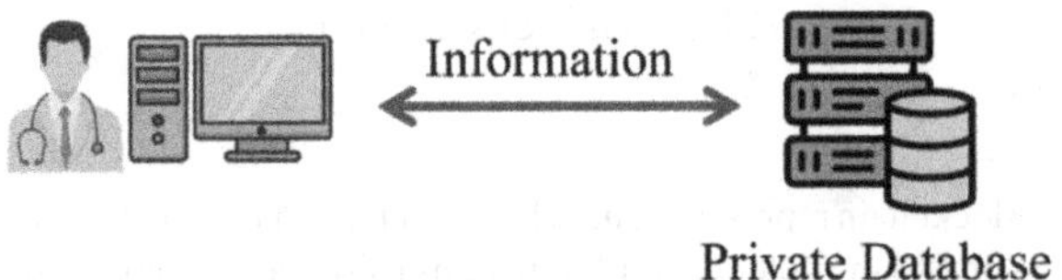


**Fig. 1.** General diagnostic information storage methods.

To facilitate easier access and utilization of diagnostic certificates for patients in the future, this article employs Ethereum [1] blockchain smart contracts [2] and encryption methods currently in common use for their application (see Fig. 2).

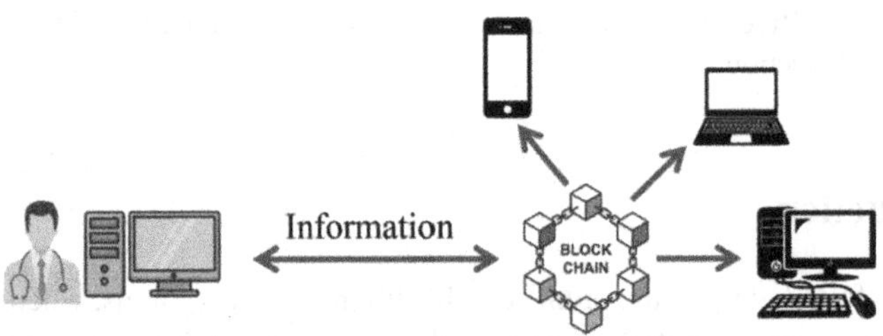


**Fig. 2.** Using blockchain to store diagnostic information.

Section 2 of this article will delve into the pertinent blockchain technology employed and outline its advantages. In Sect. 3, we will present the operational processes we propose for doctors to record diagnostic certificates and for patients to access and query their diagnostic certificates.

## 2 Related Research and Technical Background

### 2.1 Related Research

In the realm of current blockchain research in the medical field, there exists related research concerning medical insurance claims [3]. The specific goal of this research centers on enhancing the efficiency of insurance companies in processing claims, thereby expediting their review process. In contrast, the primary objective of this article is to address the timeliness and data preservation aspects inherent in the diagnostic certificate application process. The decision to employ the diagnostic certificate leans more towards the patient's discretion, and we also introduce concepts concerning the methods required for its utilization.

### 2.2 Blockchain

Initially, the concept of blockchain [4, 5] was predominantly associated with Bitcoin [6]. In a blockchain network, computers serve as nodes, and messages are distributed among them to transmit transaction data. The entire network of blockchain nodes collaboratively maintains records of these transactions in a decentralized manner. Before being permanently recorded, transaction data is temporarily stored. Nodes responsible for creating new blocks gather these transaction records and consolidate them into a single block, where the transaction information is then stored.

Blockchain functions akin to a public ledger where each transaction's details are recorded by all participants through a distributed computing method. This approach enhances efficiency, and the ledger is collectively supervised and maintained by everyone involved, thereby reducing costs. In terms of third-party verification costs, the information can be easily traced through queries, and it possesses the inherent feature of being tamper-resistant.

In the Bitcoin blockchain, each block employs a Merkle Tree [7] to store a digest of all its transaction messages. The Merkle tree, characterized by a binary tree structure, is formed by iteratively passing the hash value from one node to another. Each node in the tree holds the hash value computed from specific transaction information. This process continues from the bottom of the tree to the top until only one hash value remains. This uppermost node is referred to as the Merkle Root, which is used, via the Merkle tree path, to demonstrate the inclusion of a transaction message within the block (see Fig. 3).

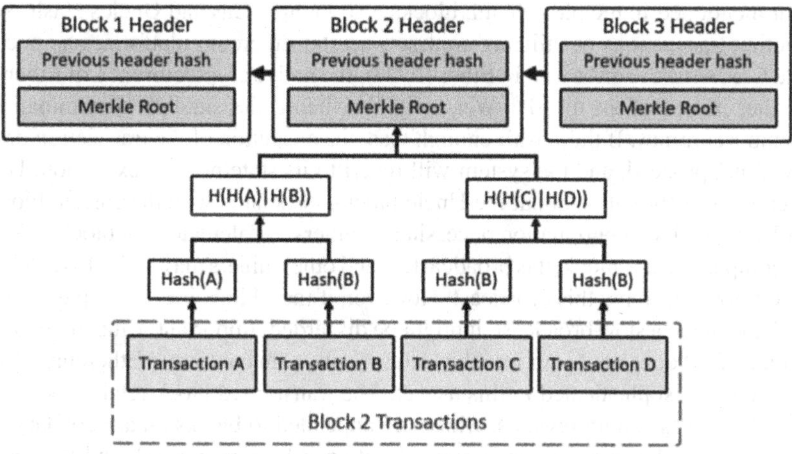


**Fig. 3.** The architecture of Merkle tree in the blockchain.

Blocks in the Bitcoin blockchain typically encompass more than just the Merkle tree. They also incorporate the hash value, timestamp, difficulty level, and Nonce value from the previous block's header. This collection of data is used to compute the new block's header, including its own hash value. Consequently, each new block continues the chain from the previous one, resulting in the formation of a blockchain.

The creation of the blockchain relies on miners who perform computational tasks, and anyone can engage in mining activities. These miners are responsible for calculating blocks on the main chain. To incentivize and reward those who perform this work, a proof-of-work mechanism [8] is employed. However, this mechanism consumes significant resources and electricity to operate. In the context of Bitcoin, if a miner successfully calculates a block and it is accepted onto the main chain, they receive a reward. Conversely, if the calculated block is not accepted, the resources and electricity expended during this operation are essentially lost without compensation.

In comparison to the proof-of-work (PoW) mechanism, Ethereum is actively developing a proof-of-stake (PoS) mechanism [9], known as the equity proof mechanism. This process can be likened to virtual mining. To prevent excessive energy consumption during mining, virtual tokens are utilized. Participants use these tokens to employ virtual computers, which then join the network to create new blocks and earn rewards, achieving the same effect as the PoW mechanism. However, in this PoS mechanism, the influence of a participant is determined by the amount of tokens they have invested. Miners are randomly selected to have the right to generate the next new block, and if a selected miner fails to do so within a specific timeframe, a second miner is chosen to carry out the task.

## 2.3 Ethereum

Ethereum is an open-source platform that utilizes blockchain technology, and the basic nature of its blockchain shares similarities with Bitcoin. However, there are distinctions in how Ethereum and Bitcoin operations function. In Ethereum, aside from the block content mentioned in the blockchain, blocks also include Gas and Uncles Hash. When conducting transactions or utilizing contracts on the Ethereum platform, one needs to expend Gas, which is measured in Ether (ETH), the native cryptocurrency of Ethereum. One Ether is equivalent to $10^{18}$ Wei, with Wei being the smallest denomination of Ethereum's currency. If there isn't enough Gas, the execution of the transaction or contract will not proceed, and the system will revert to its state prior to execution. Uncles Hash contains information about the Uncle blocks associated with the current block.

In Bitcoin, block continuation necessitates miners to calculate new blocks. When a miner computes a new block, it is broadcasted, and other miners may have also calculated a block before receiving this broadcast. However, if their block is not accepted onto the main chain due to a slow broadcast, it might be discarded. Importantly, the miner's computational effort does not factor into this determination. In contrast to Ethereum, Bitcoin is relatively less sophisticated in this aspect. The transmitted block retains its proof of work and receives certain rewards, which are appended to blocks on a secondary main chain. However, the transactions contained within it become invalid, and the rewards obtained do not encompass the transactions made by traders. This process consumes time, and the number of accepted proofs of work is limited.

When setting up an account on Ethereum, you are required to establish a password and obtain both the public key and the private key for the account. The account is identified by the public key, while the private key is generated during the account creation process. If you intend to utilize the private key, which is protected by the password you set, you'll need to enter the password to unlock it. This step is necessary for conducting regular monetary transactions and other operations within Ethereum.

Smart Contracts are a prominent feature of Ethereum. To create a smart contract, one must deploy the written contract code onto the Ethereum blockchain. Once deployed, the contract is assigned an address, which can be invoked whenever necessary for various purposes. This article utilizes Solidity, a commonly used programming language for writing smart contracts. After compilation, the contract code runs on the Ethereum Virtual Machine (EVM).

In this article, the utilization of smart contracts for diagnostic certificates will be implemented on the Ethereum platform. This involves handling user-sensitive information. To ensure the privacy and security of users, encryption measures are employed to safeguard this information. Present-day encryption technologies have reached a level of maturity, and healthcare professionals and patients typically select either symmetric key encryption or public key encryption based on the specific requirements of the application.

## 3 Research Methods

The symbols used in this article are depicted in the following Table 1.

**Table 1.** Symbol list.

| Symbol | Meaning |
|---|---|
| $K_{UD}, K_{RD}$ | Doctor's public key and private key |
| $K_{UP}, K_{RP}$ | Patient's public key and private key |
| $K_{UT}$ | Third Party's public key |
| $D_1$ | Diagnostic information in JSON format |
| $H_{D1}$ | Digest of diagnostic information |
| $S_D$ | Doctor's digital signature |
| $R_1, R_2$ | Random numbers |
| $E_{DS1}, E_{DS2}$ | Encrypted diagnostic information and signature |
| $E_{UR1}, E_{UR2}$ | Encrypted session key |
| TxN | Transaction record N |
| $Q_{ED}$ | QR Code of $E_{DS2}$ |
| $Q_{EK}$ | QR Code of $E_{UR2}$ |

The usage scenario is designed to apply to all individuals or entities possessing Ethereum accounts. When a doctor initiates system use for the first time, they will acquire both the public key $K_{UD}$ and the private key $K_{RD}$ dedicated to their professional activities. The doctor will secure the private key with a password of their own choosing. Using Ethereum's account-based method, one can access the doctor's basic information and the public key associated with their professional work on the internet.

Furthermore, when the doctor utilizes a patient's health insurance card, the patient's Ethereum account public key $K_{UP}$ and fundamental health insurance requirements will be automatically inputted. This usage scenario can be categorized into two primary functions: doctor-side operations and user-side inquiries and applications.

### 3.1 Doctor-Side Operation

The smart contract aspect primarily applies to the doctor's activities, as illustrated in Fig. 4, depicting the operational process. Once the doctor accesses the system interface by logging in, they employ the patient's health insurance card to access their personal information. After conducting a diagnosis, the doctor inputs the patient's symptoms, medical guidance, and other relevant details. Following verification, a smart contract is employed for the transmission of this information. During the initial processing of the information, it is stored in JSON format, creating D1 as shown in Fig. 5, outlining the content that has been saved.

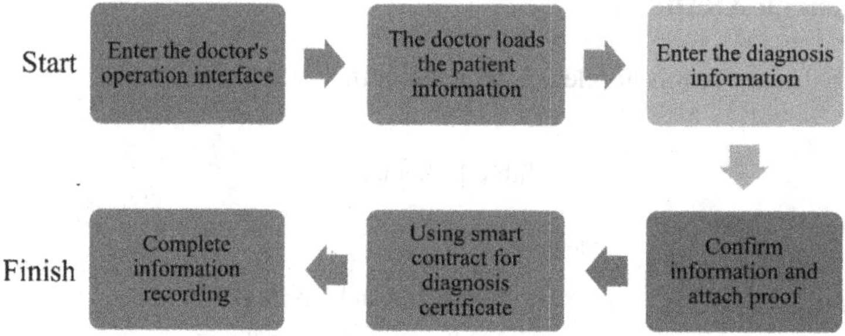


**Fig. 4.** Doctor-side operation flow chart.


```
[
  {
    "Patient name": “David Wang",
    "Medical record number": “012206",
    "ID number": “A123456789",
    "Gender": “Male",
    "Department": "Otolaryngology",
    "Medical treatment time": "2023-09-15 14:23:30",
    "Symptoms description": "Pharyngitis",
    "Doctor's orders": "Take medicine after meals",
    "Diagnostic doctor": “John Lee"
  }
]
```


**Fig. 5.** Patient information in JSON format.

Upon completing the format parameters, patient information is assembled. Information $D_1$ undergoes hashing to produce the digest $H_{D1}$. This digest is then signed using the doctor's private key $K_{RD}$, generating $S_D$. The doctor proceeds by generating a random number, denoted as $R_1$, which functions as the session key for this information. With the $R_1$ key, both $D_1$ and $S_D$ are encrypted, resulting in the creation of encrypted information $E_{DS1}$. Furthermore, the patient's public key $K_{UP}$ is employed to encrypt $R_1$, yielding the encrypted session key $E_{UR1}$, thereby ensuring the privacy and security of the information. Subsequently, $E_{DS1}$ and $E_{UR1}$ are converted into hexadecimal (Hex) format, yielding $E_{DS1}$ (Hex) and $E_{UR1}$ (Hex).

Following the conclusion of the conversion process, the smart contract is invoked. A specific method on the smart contract is utilized to store the converted message on the blockchain as a transaction TxN (as depicted in Fig. 6). After the successful completion of this transaction, the doctor transmits both the transaction and the hash value of the block header to the patient, serving as the foundation for subsequent inquiries.

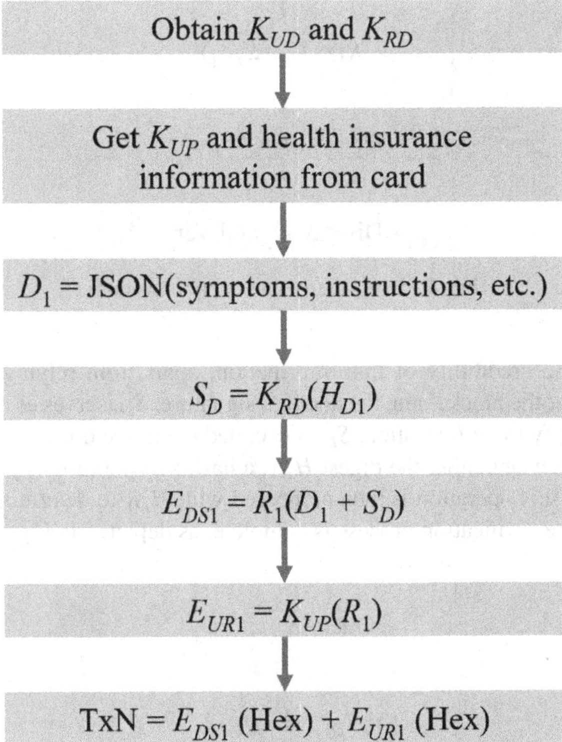


**Fig. 6.** Doctor-side system operating procedure.

### 3.2 User-Side Query

Once the information is securely stored in the blockchain, the user also receives the data transmitted by the doctor. Through the user interface, the user can input the necessary information for querying and employ a specific method to retrieve the data value of the transaction. The original encrypted information, $E_{DS1}$, and $E_{UR1}$, can be obtained by converting the hexadecimal data retrieved, $E_{DS1}$ (Hex) and $E_{UR1}$ (Hex).

$E_{UR1}$ is deciphered using the user's private key $K_{RP}$ to obtain the session key $R_1$. Subsequently, $R_1$ is used to decrypt $E_{DS1}$, revealing $D_1$ and $S_D$. At this point, $D_1$ is already in JSON format, and it can be displayed in the user interface to complete the query, as illustrated in Fig. 7.

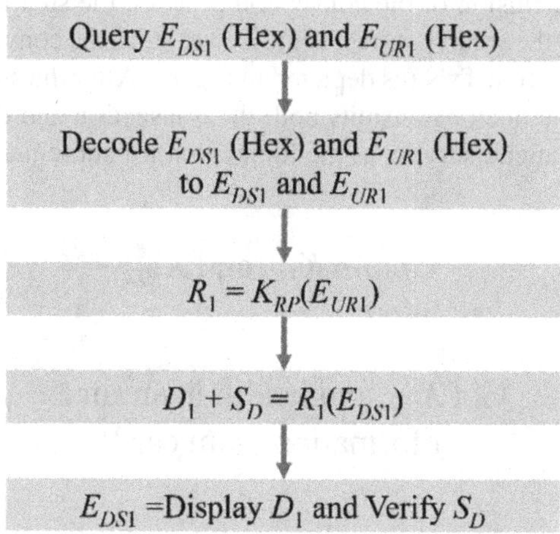


**Fig. 7.** User-side system query procedure.

Regarding the credibility of this information, apart from relying on the tamper-resistant nature of the blockchain, the doctor's signature, $S_D$, serves as a critical piece of evidence. To verify the information, $S_D$ is decoded using the doctor's public key $K_{UD}$. Subsequently, after obtaining the digest $H_{D1}$, a hashing operation is performed on $D_1$. The outcome of this operation is then compared with $H_{D1}$ to determine if they match, indicating that the verification process is complete, as depicted in Fig. 8.

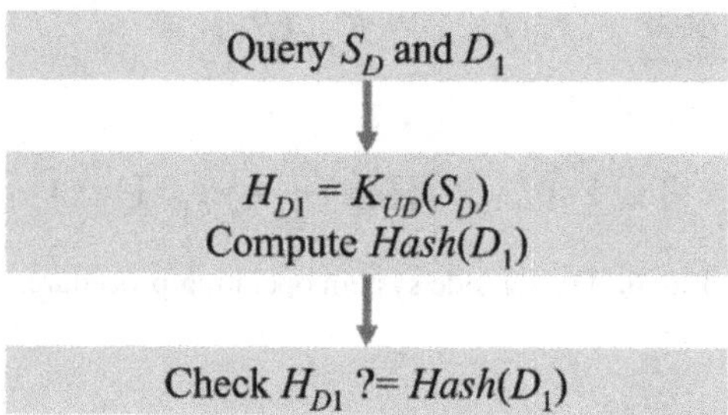


**Fig. 8.** Information verification procedure.

### 3.3 Application of User-Side Diagnostic Certificate

The user's application can be broadly categorized into two forms. One approach involves digital transmission, as illustrated in Fig. 9. When the user acquires $D_1$ in JSON format, a random number $R_2$ is generated, serving as the session key. $R_2$ is then employed to encrypt both $D_1$ and $S_D$, creating encrypted information $E_{DS2}$. Following that, the recipient's public key $K_{UT}$ is used to encrypt $R_2$, forming the encrypted session key $E_{UR2}$. At this stage, $E_{DS2}$ and $E_{UR2}$ can be transmitted to the other party for confirmation.

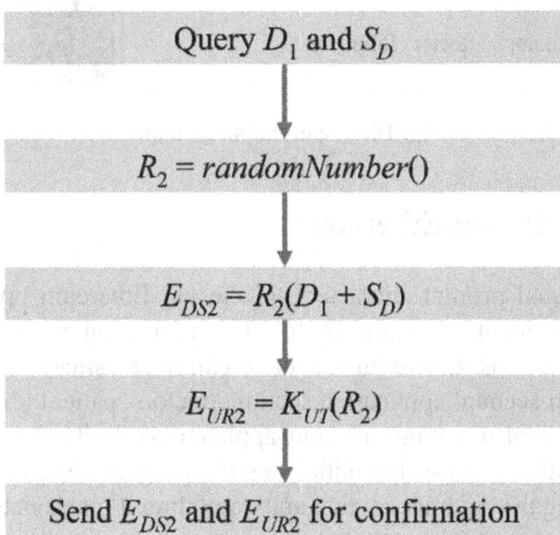


**Fig. 9.** User diagnostic certificate for third party.

Another method is to print the information on paper, with the receiving party having the necessary equipment to verify the blockchain data. The $D_1$ in JSON format is printed, and then the $E_{DS2}$ and $E_{UR2}$, which were calculated in the previous digital transmission process, are presented as QR Codes. The encrypted session key is represented by $Q_{EK}$, while the encrypted information and signature are represented by $Q_{ED}$. This serves as a form of information proof, similar to an attached seal. It can be printed on paper and provided to the other party for the purpose of information validation and verification (as shown in Fig. 10).

If the verifying party wishes to preserve the information in a pure paper format, the receiving end can use the organization's seal or undertake other organizational procedures after verifying the information.

| Medical record number: 012206 | | Medical treatment time: 2023-09-15 14:23:30 | | |
|---|---|---|---|---|
| David Wang | Male | ID number: A123456789 | | |
| Symptoms description: Pharyngitis | | Department: Otolaryngology | | |
| Doctor's orders: Take medicine after meals | | Signature | [QR code] | $Q_{EK}$ |
| Diagnostic doctor: John Lee | | | [QR code] | $Q_{ED}$ |

**Fig. 10.** Paper output example.

## 4 Implementation on Ethereum

We employ command prompt characters to execute Ethereum operations using the Ethereum platform client program, Geth. The application process can be broadly categorized into two steps: Ethereum account creation and smart contract deployment.

In the Ethereum account application section, doctors, patient users, and third-party entities are all required to submit account applications. Following the completion of the account application process, the initial step in the smart contract deployment phase involves configuring the contract content and compiling it (as depicted in Fig. 11).

```
> Tsource="contract HealthStatus {string PHealth = "Patient's Health Data";
function HSupload(string inputData) returns (string HealthStatus) { PHealth
= inputData;return PHealth;}}"
> Tcompiled=web3.eth.compile.solidity(Tsource)
```

**Fig. 11.** Set contract content.

Once the compilation is finished, it's necessary to configure the port and apply the corresponding settings to our smart contract, as illustrated in Fig. 12.

```
> abi=[{"constant":false,"inputs":[{"name":"inputData","type":"string"}],
"name":"HSupload","outputs":[{"name":"HealthStatus","type":"string"}
],"payable":false,"type":"function"}]
> MyHSContract=eth.contract(abi)
```

**Fig. 12.** Set port.

Finally, our smart contract is deployed on the blockchain and becomes accessible for use, as depicted in Fig. 13.

```
> HSContract=MyHSContract.new({from:doctor1,data:Tcompiled.code})
> HSContract.HSupload.call(input data)
```

**Fig. 13.** Deploy smart contract.

## 5 Conclusion

The approach we have proposed is grounded in blockchain technology. Leveraging the inherent characteristics of blockchain, where ledger records are collectively managed by all participants, patients no longer need to visit hospitals exclusively; they can make inquiries remotely, thereby enhancing user convenience. This increased flexibility reduces waiting times for administrative processes and commuting to hospitals, as well as lowers registration fees and the expenses associated with obtaining diagnostic certificates. Furthermore, for hospitals, the staff that previously handled diagnostic certificate-related tasks can now be redirected to attend to other medical needs. The immutability of blockchain technology also provides a certain level of data protection.

Regarding the utilization of smart contracts, our solution involves transmitting information to the smart contract, thus streamlining what were previously complex calculations through the operator interface. This optimization also reduces the amount of gas required for smart contract execution.

In addition to the advantages it offers, our method also transforms the existing record-keeping process for diagnostic certificates on the doctor's side. On the user's side, we have proposed both digital transmission and paper printing methods, enabling users to share diagnostic certificates with third parties.

While the primary focus of this method in this article is diagnostic certificates, it can similarly be applied to other types of credentials, such as skills certificates or graduation certificates. In the future, we can explore further applications, provided they comply with the requirements outlined in this article's usage scenario.

## References


1. Ethereum Homepage: https://ethereum.org/en/. Last accessed 14 Sep 2023
2. Ethereum Smart Contracts: Introduction to smart contracts. https://ethereum.org/en/smart-contracts/. Last updated 8 Sep 2023
3. Lin, C.M.: Streamlining Medical Insurance Claims Processing With Smart Contracts. Master's Thesis, National Chengchi University (2016)
4. Swan, M.: Blockchain: Blueprint for a New Economy, 1st edn. O'Reilly Media (2015)
5. Crosby, M., Nachiappan, P.P., Verma, S., Kalyanaraman, V.: BlockChain technology: beyond bitcoin. Appl. Innov. Rev. **2**, 6–10 (2016)

6. Nakamoto, S.: Bitcoin: A Peer-to-Peer Electronic Cash System. https://bitcoin.org/bitcoin.pdf (2009)
7. Chen, Y.C., Chou, Y.P., Chou, Y.C.: An image authentication scheme using Merkle tree mechanisms. Future Internet **11**(7), 149 (2019)
8. Wikipedia: Proof of work. https://en.wikipedia.org/wiki/Proof_of_work
9. Wikipedia: Proof of stake. https://en.wikipedia.org/wiki/Proof_of_stake

# Exploiting Style Transfer and Semantic Segmentation to Facilitate Infrared and Visible Image Fusion

Hsing-Wei Chang, Po-Chyi Su(✉), and Si-Ting Lin

Department of Computer Science and Information Engineering, National Central University, Taoyuan, Taiwan
pochyisu@csie.ncu.edu.tw

**Abstract.** Image fusion integrates different imaging sources to generate one with improved scene representation or visual perception, supporting advanced vision tasks such as object detection and semantic analysis. Fusing infrared and visible images is a widely studied subject, and the current trend is to adopt deep learning models. It is well known that training a deep fusion model often requires many labeled data. Nevertheless, existing datasets only provide images without precise annotations, affecting the fusion presentation and limiting further development. This research creates a dataset for infrared and visible image fusion with semantic segmentation information. We utilize existing image datasets specific to semantic segmentation and generate corresponding infrared images by style transferring. A labeled dataset for image fusion is formed, in which each pair of infrared and visible images is accompanied by their semantic segmentation labels. The performance of image fusion in target datasets can thus be improved.

**Keywords:** Image Fusion · Semantic Segmentation · Style Transfer

## 1 Introduction

### 1.1 Research Motivation

Due to varying filming conditions or hardware limitations, using a sensor with a single type may capture limited information and thus result in an incomplete depiction of the shooting scene. Image fusion is to extract complementary information from multiple images captured from the same scene and generate a fused image with the combined characteristics of each source through appropriate content integration. In various image fusion tasks, the fusion of infrared and visible images has received widespread attention. Visible sensors acquire reflected light information, providing rich texture details that closely resemble human visual perception. However, visible images cannot effectively capture objects of interest, e.g., pedestrians or vehicles in such complicated environments as nighttime, obstructions, smoke, etc. In contrast, infrared sensors collect thermal radiation information, effectively highlighting target objects even under extreme environmental interferences, compensating for the shortcomings of visible images, but they often


C.-Y. Lee et al. (Eds.): TAAI 2023, CCIS 2074, pp. 269–283, 2024.
https://doi.org/10.1007/978-981-97-1711-8_21

lack texture details. Based on the complementary nature of visible and infrared images, integrating the information of both images into a fused one contributes to advanced visual tasks such as object detection and semantic analysis, etc.

In recent years, numerous deep-learning-based methods for fusing infrared and visible images have been proposed, including such techniques as Auto-Encoders (AE), Convolutional Neural Networks (CNN), Generative Adversarial Networks (GAN), and others, and impressive results have been witnessed. Despite the breakthroughs in performance, most of the existing work has not fully addressed potential issues encountered in practical applications. For example, misalignment often occurs due to the differences in device settings for capturing infrared and visible images. Such disparity may result in severe distortions in the fusion outcomes. To address this problem, recent research, such as UMF-CMGR [1] and SuperFusion [2], has proposed aligning the input images before fusion to mitigate the effects of slight deformations on the fusion results. However, these methods require the input images to have the exact resolution, contradicting that the captured infrared and visible images may have disparities. Furthermore, most existing image fusion methods focus on improving visual quality and optimizing evaluation metrics, often overlooking the practicality of fusion results for subsequent higher-level visual tasks. Some research has recognized this problem and proposed solutions, such as TarDAL [3] and SeAFusion [4]. These methods introduce loss functions from higher-level visual tasks into the training process of fusion networks, guiding the network to generate images suitable for those tasks. These methods require the fusion network and the higher-level visual task to be trained simultaneously, implying that the training data should include precise annotations for that visual task. However, in current image fusion datasets, only a small portion of data includes object annotations or semantic segmentation labels, leading to unsatisfactory performance.

Additionally, we've noticed that images from different datasets are heavily influenced by the environment and capturing conditions, often exhibiting varying structural and textural features. For example, in Fig. 1 (a), infrared images from the RoadScene dataset retain more texture details than the other two datasets, LLVIP and MSRS, while as shown in Fig. 1 (c), the infrared images from the MSRS dataset exhibit lower brightness. Upon further examination of the average brightness and contrast of the datasets, we can observe that the MSRS dataset has lower values in both average brightness and contrast compared to the other two datasets. On the other hand, the RoadScene dataset has a noticeably higher average brightness than the other two datasets. Because of these variations among

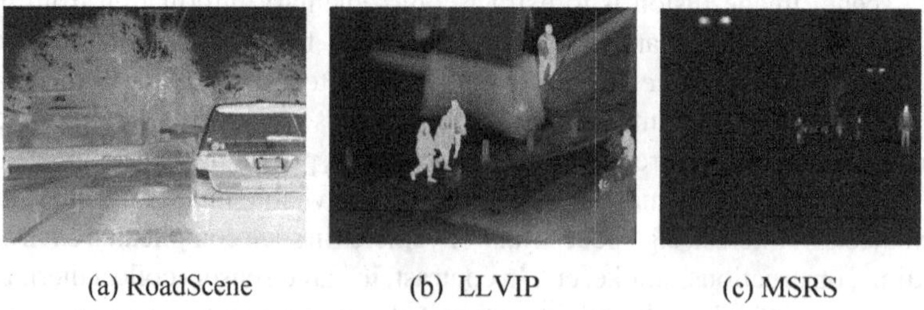

(a) RoadScene (b) LLVIP (c) MSRS

**Fig. 1.** Infrared and visible images from different datasets

different datasets, fusion networks trained on one dataset might not perform as expected when tested on other datasets.

### 1.2 Contribution of Research

This study proposes to establish a semantic segmentation dataset for infrared and visible image fusion. We utilize visible images from existing semantic segmentation datasets and generate corresponding infrared images using style transfer techniques. The resulting dataset is composed of image pairs, each containing an infrared image, a visible image, and their corresponding semantic segmentation labels. This approach tackles the scarcity of semantic segmentation labels in existing datasets for infrared and visible image fusion. To deal with the disparities between training and testing datasets, we train style transfer networks specifically for testing datasets. This strategy results in infrared images that closely match the characteristics of the testing data, thereby mitigating challenges arising from inconsistencies between training and testing sets.

### 1.3 The Organization of Paper

The paper is organized as follows: Section 1 introduces the research motivation and contributions. Section 2 discusses related research and datasets for infrared and visible image fusion. Section 3 presents the methodology proposed in this paper, including the establishment of the dataset and image fusion methods. Section 4 shows the research results and evaluations. Finally, Sect. 5 concludes the paper and outlines future work.

## 2 Related Work

### 2.1 Typical Infrared and Visible Image Fusion

Common methods for infrared and visible image fusion include Autoencoders (AE), Convolutional Neural Networks (CNN), and Generative Adversarial Networks (GAN). These methods decompose the fusion process into three subtasks: feature extraction, feature fusion, and image reconstruction.

#### 2.1.1 Fusion Methods Based on Auto-Encoder

Figure 2 (a) illustrates image fusion methods based on Auto-Encoders (AE). These methods often train an AE on publicly available datasets. The encoder is responsible for extracting features from input images, while the decoder reconstructs the input images based on these encoded features. The trained AE can subsequently be applied to tackle two subtasks in image fusion: feature extraction and image reconstruction. However, the feature fusion in this approach usually follows traditional fusion rules and lacks the ability to learn. For example, DenseFuse [6] and NestFuse [7] are two AE-based image fusion methods. Both of them train encoders and decoders on the MS-COCO dataset. DenseFuse introduces Dense Blocks into the encoder, connecting the output of each layer with the outputs of all other layers. This architecture enables the encoding process

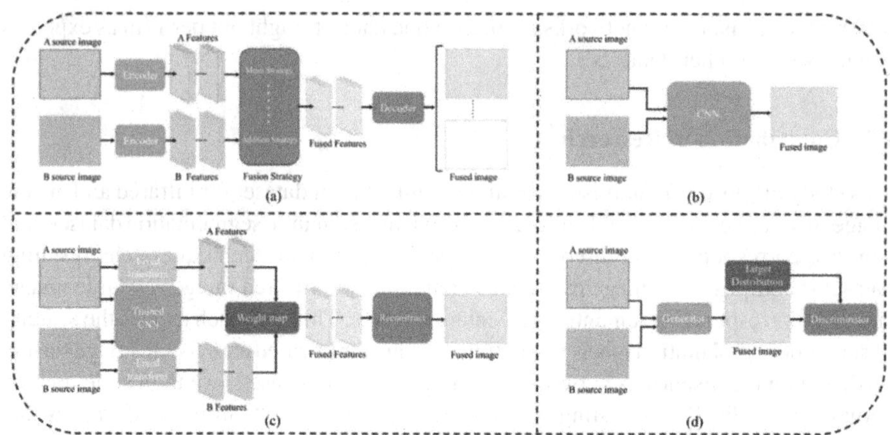


**Fig. 2.** Deep-learning-based fusion methods for infrared and visible images[5]

to capture more useful features from input images. Furthermore, DenseFuse designs two fusion strategies: Add and L1-norm, to fuse these features. The fused features are then reconstructed into an image by the decoder. On the other hand, NestFuse further enhances fusion performance by introducing nested connections and attention mechanisms. The nest connection-based network can preserve significant amount of information from input data in a multi-scale perspective.

### 2.1.2 Fusion Methods Based on Convolutional Neural Network

Convolutional Neural Network (CNN)-based image fusion methods are divided into two different forms. Firstly, there's an end-to-end approach that encompasses feature extraction, feature fusion, and image reconstruction, using carefully designed loss functions and network architectures, as illustrated in Fig. 2 (b). The other approach involves using pre-trained CNN models to formulate fusion rules and then performing feature extraction and image reconstruction using conventional methods, as illustrated in Fig. 2 (c). For instance, PIAFusion [8] designs an illumination-aware sub-network to estimate the illumination distribution and calculate the illumination probability. Subsequently, it utilizes the illumination probability to construct an illumination-aware loss to guide the training of the fusion network.

### 2.1.3 Fusion Methods Based on Generative Adversarial Network

Image fusion methods based on Generative Adversarial Networks (GANs) can implicitly accomplish feature extraction, feature fusion, and image reconstruction, as shown in n Fig. 2 (d). These methods mainly rely on two types of loss functions: content loss and adversarial loss. For example, FusionGAN [9] introduces the GAN mechanism. The generator generates the fused image, and the discriminator is used to enhance the preservation of rich details from visible images. In other words, the generator's objective is to produce a fused image that the discriminator struggles to distinguish from real visible images. This design compels the generator to learn useful features from both infrared and visible images and fuse them to generate high-quality fusion images. However, a single discriminator can lead to an imbalance in the information from infrared and visible images. To address this, DDcGAN [10] proposes using two discriminators to separately assess the structural differences between the fused image and each of the input images. This way aims to retain details from both infrared and visible images while ensuring a balanced representation between the two modalities.

### 2.2 High-Level Vision Task-Driven Image Fusion

To meet the requirements of image fusion for high-level vision tasks, TarDAL [3] and SeAFusion [4] proposed fusion methods for semantic segmentation and object detection, respectively. TarDAL introduces a dual-layer optimization formulation to address the joint problem of image fusion and object detection. It designs a target-aware dual adversarial learning network comprising a generator and two discriminators. The generator aims to find commonalities between the two input images and learn from their differences. This enables the generator to preserve structural information from the infrared image and texture details from the visible image. The two discriminators are tasked with separately evaluating the differences between the generator's output image and the two input images (infrared and visible). By utilizing this optimization formulation and a dual adversarial learning mechanism, TarDAL achieves the joint optimization of image fusion and object detection. This allows the fusion network to retain structural and detailed information in images better, resulting in excellent performance in object detection tasks. SeAFusion introduces a semantic-aware image fusion network aimed at enhancing the performance of fused images in high-level vision tasks. This method combines the image fusion network with a semantic segmentation network and guides semantic information back to the fusion network through loss functions, effectively improving the performance of fused images. Furthermore, SeAFusion introduces the Gradient Residual Dense Block (GRDB), a novel structure used to enhance the fusion network's ability to describe spatial details in images. GRDB can better capture local details and edge information in images, further enhancing fusion results. The combination of semantic awareness and the integration of the Gradient Residual Dense Block design in SeAFusion results in fused images that demonstrate improved performance in high-level vision tasks, as well as an enhanced capability to capture intricate image features.

### 2.3 Infrared and Visible Image Fusion Datasets

Common datasets for infrared and visible light image fusion include TNO [11], RoadScene [12], MSRS [8], M3FD [3], and LLVIP [13]. We list their settings in Table 1 and briefly describe their characteristics below.

The TNO dataset includes 261 pairs of daytime and nighttime images. Because of the small number of images, it is often used for testing and validating fusion methods. This dataset provides image pairs captured under various lighting conditions, making it valuable for evaluating the performance and effectiveness of fusion methods. The RoadScene dataset is one of the few datasets containing both aligned and unaligned data. It consists of 221 pairs of infrared and visible images captured in road scenes, containing

**Table 1.** Infrared and visible image fusion datasets

| Dataset | Image pairs | Resolution | Camera angle | Annotation |
|---|---|---|---|---|
| TNO | 261 | 768 × 576 | horizontal | None |
| RoadScene | 221 | 768 × 576 | driving | None |
| MSRS | 2999 | 640 × 480 | driving | Mask, Polygon |
| M3FD | 4200 | 1024 × 768 | driving | Bounding Box |
| LLVIP | 15488 | 1280 × 1024 | surveillance | Bounding Box |

various objects such as vehicles and pedestrians. The uniqueness of this dataset lies in its provision of both aligned and unaligned images, enabling the assessment of fusion methods under both alignment and un-alignment scenarios. The MSRS dataset is the only dataset with semantic segmentation annotations. It provides semantic segmentation labels for both infrared and visible images, which can be used for evaluating and validating research related to semantic segmentation. The M3FD dataset is introduced by TarDAL and provides bounding box annotations for objects, facilitating research related to object detection. The LLVIP dataset is designed for low-light object detection. It includes infrared and visible images captured under low-light conditions and provides bounding box annotations for objects.

## 3 Proposed Scheme

The proposed scheme is to establish the semantic segmentation dataset for infrared and visible image fusion, the alignment approach based on semantic segmentation masks, and the framework for infrared and visible image fusion. Section 3.1 presents the methodology employed for establishing the dataset. Section 3.2 introduces the image fusion framework.

### 3.1 Dataset Establishment

Considering the significant time and human resources required for pixel-level semantic segmentation labeling, we utilize an existing semantic segmentation dataset, Cityscapes [14], as our training data. The Cityscapes dataset offers a substantial collection of visible images along with corresponding semantic segmentation annotations. To generate the infrared images, we utilized the cross-modality perceptual style transfer network proposed by Wang et al. in UMF-CMGR [1]. This allowed us to transform the visible images from the Cityscapes dataset into infrared images to form the target training data.

#### 3.1.1 Cityscapes Dataset

The Cityscapes dataset is widely utilized in the field of computer vision and is primarily employed for tasks such as semantic segmentation, object detection, and instance segmentation in urban scenes. This dataset comprises high-resolution images with pixel-level accurate annotations, making it extensively used in research and competitions for model training and evaluation. The Cityscapes dataset contains images from various urban scenes across 50 cities in Germany. For the task of semantic segmentation, the dataset provides precise annotations for around 2000 images, encompassing 30 different semantic categories such as roads, pedestrians, buildings, trees, etc.

### 3.1.2 Cross-Modality Perceptual Style Transfer Network

The Cross-modality Perceptual Style Transfer Network (CPSTN) is introduced by Wang et al. in UMF-CMGR [1]. A style transfer network converts visible images into corresponding pseudo-infrared images. The objective of this approach is to mitigate the cross-modality differences between visible and infrared images. This is done to facilitate the subsequent image alignment steps, effectively addressing potential image misalignment issues that might arise during the fusion of infrared and visible images. CPSTN consists of two generators, G(A) and G(B), as well as two discriminators, $D_{ir}$ and $D_{vi}$. The generators adopt a U-net architecture with 9 ResNet blocks at the bottom. To enhance control over the style transfer outcomes, CPSTN proposes a learning strategy based on perceptual style transfer constraints. This strategy establishes the correlation between the two cyclic paths, preserving the precise structure and details of the generated images. This approach brings the generated images closer to the characteristic features of real infrared images.

### 3.1.3 Training CPSTN Using Different Datasets

Considering that the variations across different datasets can impact the subsequent alignment and fusion results, we perform separate training for each dataset to enhance adaptability. By training on each dataset individually, our network can capture the unique characteristics of that specific dataset, ensuring that the generated pseudo-infrared images closely match the visual features of the dataset.

## 3.2 Image Fusion

The proposed image fusion adopts the fusion framework from SeAFusion [4] as the foundation, as shown in Fig. 3. Adjustments are made to the loss functions and training strategies based on our training data.

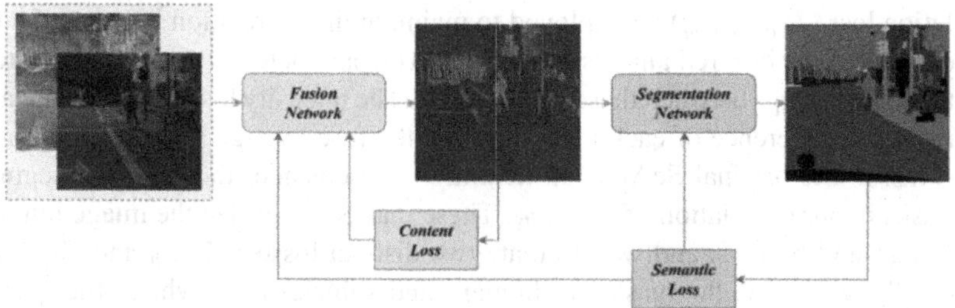


**Fig. 3.** The fusion framework of SeAFusion

### 3.2.1 Network Architecture

The SeAFusion consists of two parallel feature extractors and an image re-constructor. The feature extractors extracted features from the infrared and visible images. After feature extraction, the features are fused and passed to the image re-constructor for forming the fused features.

In the feature extractor, a 3 × 3 convolutional layer is included, and a Leaky ReLU is used as the activation function. Additionally, two Gradient Residual Dense Blocks (GRDB) are introduced. It consists of a dense block, which contains two 3 × 3 convolutional layers with Leaky ReLU as the activation function, and a 1 × 1 convolutional layer. Furthermore, a residual flow is introduced to compute the gradient, and a 1 × 1 convolutional layer is used to match its output dimensions to that of the dense block. For the image re-constructor, we concatenate the features from the infrared and visible and input them into the image re-constructor. The image reconstruction consists of three 3 × 3 convolutional layers and one 1 × 1 convolutional layer. The 3 × 3 convolutional layers use Leaky ReLU as the activation function, while the 1 × 1 convolutional layer uses Tanh as the activation function. Since Tanh restricts the output values to the range of − 1 to 1, we scale them by dividing them by 2 and adding 0.5 to confine the output values within the range of 0 to 1. Additionally, to avoid information loss, no down-sampling operations are performed in the fusion network, thus maintaining the output image size the same as the input image size.

### 3.2.2 Loss Function

We employ content loss and semantic loss for the fusion network. Specifically, the content loss encompasses intensity loss, texture loss, and correlation loss.

#### 3.2.2.1 Content Loss

To better integrate meaningful information into the fusion network, we redesign a content loss function, denoted as $\mathcal{L}_{content}$.. This loss function is composed of three components: intensity loss ($\mathcal{L}_{intensity}$), texture loss ($\mathcal{L}_{texture}$), and correlation loss ($\mathcal{L}_{correlation}$), defined as follows:

$$\mathcal{L}_{content} = \mathcal{L}_{intensity} + \alpha \mathcal{L}_{texture} + \beta \mathcal{L}_{correlation} \tag{1}$$

where the intensity loss ($\mathcal{L}_{intensity}$) constrains the overall brightness of the fused image, the texture loss ($\mathcal{L}_{texture}$) encourages the fused image to retain more texture details. The correlation loss ($\mathcal{L}_{correlation}$) is employed to maintain the correlation between the fused image and both the infrared and visible images. The parameters α and β are used to balance the relationships between these components. The intensity loss ($\mathcal{L}_{intensity}$) measures the brightness difference of each pixel between the fused image and the input images. In contrast to the original SeAFusion definition, we consider the semantic segmentation masks in our calculation of $\mathcal{L}_{intensity}$. These masks categorize the image into target and background regions, and we calculate two distinct losses: $\mathcal{L}_{target}$ and $\mathcal{L}_{background}$. Specifically, we define the masks for humans and vehicles as 1, while other parts are defined as 0, as shown below:

$$mask = \begin{cases} 1, \ if \ class = humans \ or \ vehicles \\ 0, \ otherwise. \end{cases} \tag{2}$$

As we would like the target objects to have high brightness and contrast with the background, $\mathcal{L}_{target}$, and $\mathcal{L}_{background}$ are defined as follows:

$$\begin{aligned}\mathcal{L}_{target} &= \frac{1}{HW} mask \otimes (I_{fuse} - max(I_{vi}, I_{ir}))_1 \\ \mathcal{L}_{background} &= \frac{1}{HW}(1 - mask) \otimes \left(I_{fuse} - I_{ir}\right)_1 \\ &+ \frac{1}{HW}(1 - mask) \otimes \left(I_{fuse} - I_{vi}\right)_1\end{aligned} \tag{3}$$

where H and W represent the height and width of the image, $\|\cdot\|_1$ denotes the $L_1 norm$, and $max(\cdot)$ represents element-wise maximum selection. $\mathcal{L}_{intensity}$ is defined as:

$$\mathcal{L}_{intensity} = \mathcal{L}_{target} + 0.5 \times \mathcal{L}_{background} \tag{4}$$

To preserve rich texture details in the fused image, we introduce the texture loss $\mathcal{L}_{texture}$, which encourages the fused image to retain more texture details, defined as follows:

$$\mathcal{L}_{texture} = \frac{1}{HW}\left|\nabla I_{fuse}\right| - max(|\nabla I_{vi}|, |\nabla I_{ir}|)_1 \tag{5}$$

where $\nabla$ represents the Sobel operator, used for calculating the image's texture details. $|\cdot|$ denotes the absolute value.

Finally, we aim to ensure that the fused image maintains the correlation between the input infrared and visible images. Thus, we introduce the correlation loss ($\mathcal{L}_{correlation}$), which is defined as follows:

$$\mathcal{L}_{correlation} = \frac{1}{corr\left(I_{fuse}, I_{ir}\right) + corr(I_{fuse}, I_{vi})} \tag{6}$$

where corr$(\cdot)$ represents the correlation operation.

**3.2.2.2 Sematic Loss**

Following the approach of SeAFusion [4], we also introduce the semantic loss into the loss function calculation of the fusion network. Similarly, we introduce a real-time semantic segmentation network [16] to perform semantic segmentation on the fused image. This network outputs main segmentation results $I_s$ and auxiliary segmentation results $I_{sa}$. The semantic loss is then composed of the main semantic loss and the auxiliary semantic loss, defined as follows:

$$\mathcal{L}_{main} = \frac{-1}{HW}\sum_{h=1}^{H}\sum_{w=1}^{W}\sum_{c=1}^{C} L_{so}^{(h,w,c)} log(I_s^{h,w,c}) \tag{7}$$

$$\mathcal{L}_{aux} = \frac{-1}{HW}\sum_{h=1}^{H}\sum_{w=1}^{W}\sum_{c=1}^{C} L_{so}^{(h,w,c)} log(I_{sa}^{h,w,c}) \tag{8}$$

where $L_{so}$ represents the ground truth. Finally, the semantic segmentation loss $\mathcal{L}_{semantic}$ is defined as follows:

$$\mathcal{L}_{semantic} = \mathcal{L}_{main} + \lambda \mathcal{L}_{aux} \tag{9}$$

where λ is used to balance the main semantic loss and the auxiliary semantic loss, as originally set to 0.1 in [16]. This loss function is not only applied to constrain the fusion network but also used to train the segmentation network. Finally, we define the loss function used to train the fusion network:

$$\mathcal{L}_{total} = \mathcal{L}_{content} + \gamma \mathcal{L}_{semantic} \tag{10}$$

where $\gamma$ is used to represent the importance of the semantic loss.

### 3.2.3 Training Strategy

In terms of training strategy, we adopt the joint low-level and high-level adaptive training strategy proposed by SeAFusion [4], iterating the training of the fusion network ($\mathcal{N}_{fusion}$) and the segmentation network ($\mathcal{N}_{segmentation}$). Initially, guided by the joint loss function $\mathcal{L}_{total}$, the fusion network parameters are updated using the Adam optimizer. Based on the current fusion results, the segmentation network parameters are updated through optimizing the semantic loss. With the increase in iteration steps, the alignment between the segmentation network and the fusion network improves, enabling the semantic loss to more accurately guide the training of the fusion network. The overall training process is illustrated in Fig. 4.

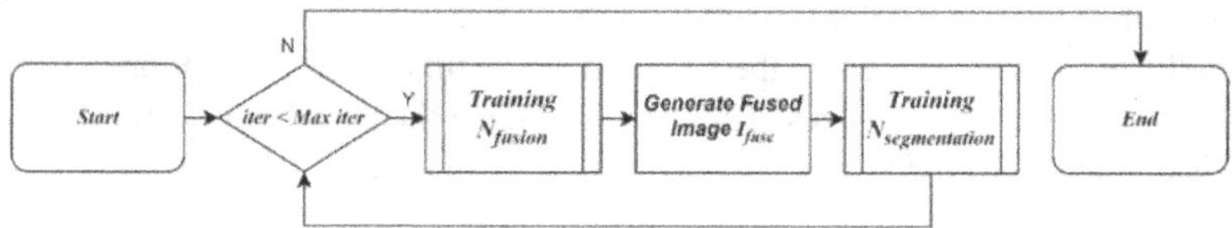


**Fig. 4.** Flowchart of training process

To ensure the convergence of the network, we initialize α, β, and $\gamma$ to 0 during the first iteration, which means only training the intensity loss $\mathcal{L}_{intensity}$. After the second iteration, we set α to 0.1, β to 0.05, and $\gamma$ is updated using the number of iterations.

## 4 Experimental Results

We utilized Python 3.7 as the programming language and employed PyTorch 1.10.1 and torchvision 0.11.2 as the deep learning framework. The operating system used was Ubuntu 18.04 LTS. In terms of hardware configuration, the CPU was Intel® Core™ i9-12900K @ 3.2 GHz with 64 GB of memory. The GPU was an NVIDIA GeForce RTX 3090. The versions of CUDA and cuDNN were 11.2 and 8.1, respectively. We used the RoadScene and LLVIP datasets for evaluation. The RoadScene dataset comprises 221 pairs of unaligned and aligned infrared and visible images. The LLVIP dataset consists of 12,025 pairs of training images and 3,463 pairs of testing images. CPSTN was trained for each dataset to ensure that the pseudo-infrared images resembled the original ones in that dataset. For the training details, we used the Adam optimizer with a learning rate of $2 \times 10^{-4}$, a batch size of 1, and training for 100 epochs. Figure 5 shows the generated infrared images for RoadScene and LLVIP datasets.

(a) Cityscapes (b) RoadScene (c) LLVIP

**Fig. 5.** Results of pseudo-infrared image generation

We retrained the SegFormer [15] model using the pseudo-infrared images generated from the above steps to improve the segmentation performance on infrared images. In terms of training details, we utilized the AdamW optimizer with an initial learning rate of $6 \times 10^{-5}$, a batch size of 1, and training for 160,000 iterations. The SegFormer model retrained using the pseudo-infrared images improved segmentation performance on real infrared images compared to the pre-trained model. As shown in Table 2, our retrained model enhanced segmentation accuracy for human and vehicle objects.

**Table 2.** Comparison of IoU and Accuracy for semantic segmentation results

| | Humans | | Vehicles | | Total | |
|---|---|---|---|---|---|---|
| | IoU | Acc | IoU | Acc | IoU | mAcc |
| Pretrained model | 44.51 | 62.73 | 53.99 | 62.22 | 21.15 | 30.34 |
| Ours | 41.05 | **63.86** | **57.61** | **67.75** | **23.31** | **32.51** |

The architecture for the fusion of infrared and visible images consists of two main parts: image fusion and semantic segmentation. In terms of training details for the image fusion network, we used the Adam optimizer with an initial learning rate of $10^{-3}$, a batch size of 8, and training for 2 epochs. For the segmentation network, we used SGD as the optimizer with an initial learning rate of $10^{-2}$, a batch size of 16, and trained for 20,000 iterations, and for 4 epochs. We compared the proposed method with five state-of-the-art fusion methods, DenseFuse [6], MFEIF [17], TarDAL [3], SeAFusion [4], and SuperFusion [2], on RoadScene dataset and LLVIP dataset. We evaluated the performance using 9 common metrics for fusion tasks: EN, MI [18], SF,

SD, VIF [19], AG, SCD [20], $Q^{AB/F}$ [21], and SSIM. The higher the values of the above-mentioned metrics, the better the performance of the image fusion method. Tables 3 and 4 present the evaluation results of these metrics for the RoadScene and LLVIP datasets, with **green**indicating the highest score, blueindicating the second-highest score, and *red*indicating the third-highest score. According to the tests, the proposed method has demonstrated excellent performance across various evaluation metrics, particularly in MI and VIF. This indicates that our fused images have retained more meaningful information from the input images. It is noteworthy that the introduction of gradient loss in our loss function has led to enhanced fusion results at image edges. As a result, our method also secured top-three rankings in metrics related to edge structure, such as SF, AG, and $Q^{AB/F}$. This suggests that our approach effectively preserves the edge structure of images, providing fused results with enhanced detail and clarity. With more examination of our fusion results on the RoadScene dataset, we can observe that our method effectively extracts valuable information from the infrared images to preserve object details when visible images are overexposed. For instance, in Fig. 6, we can see that the car within the red box is obscured by its headlights in the visible image, making it difficult to see. Our approach performs better at retaining the details of the car.

**Table 3.** Evaluation of fusion metrics for the RoadScene dataset

| | EN | MI | SF | SD | VIF | AG | SCD | $Q^{AB/F}$ | SSIM |
|---|---|---|---|---|---|---|---|---|---|
| **DenseFuse** | 6.8181 | 2.9100 | 0.0333 | 9.5284 | 0.6688 | 3.3183 | 1.3659 | 0.3804 | **0.7480** |
| **MFEIF** | 7.0488 | 3.2002 | 0.0375 | 10.1564 | 0.7564 | 3.7644 | 1.5965 | 0.4556 | *0.7407* |
| **TarDAL** | *7.2771* | *3.2343* | 0.0447 | 10.3056 | 0.7433 | 4.3243 | 1.4364 | 0.4181 | 0.7015 |
| **SeAFusion** | 7.3378 | 3.0308 | **0.0655** | **10.7103** | 0.8154 | **6.5238** | *1.5633* | *0.4926* | 0.6668 |
| **SuperFusion** | 7.1431 | 3.4889 | *0.0501* | *10.2810* | *0.7741* | *4.6301* | 1.4439 | 0.4939 | 0.7440 |
| **Ours** | **7.3645** | **3.9509** | 0.0609 | 10.2059 | **0.8530** | 5.9647 | **1.6429** | **0.5721** | 0.6823 |

Furthermore, benefiting from the combination of the target loss and the background loss, our approach achieves a well-balanced fusion of target and background information during the image fusion process. This balance allows us to retain background details while preserving the brightness of target objects. For instance, in Fig. 7, our method effectively retains the details of traffic lights in the background while ensuring that the brightness of the target object, in this case, a pedestrian, remains intact. This observation indicates that our method can adaptly capture and balance features from different image regions, achieving visual consistency between target objects and backgrounds throughout the fusion process.

**Table 4.** Evaluation of fusion metrics for the LLVIP dataset

| | EN | MI | SF | SD | VIF | AG | SCD | $Q^{AB/F}$ | SSIM |
|---|---|---|---|---|---|---|---|---|---|
| **DenseFuse** | 6.0575 | 2.4792 | 0.0451 | 9.8344 | 0.6601 | 3.2881 | 1.3765 | 0.3831 | 0.5216 |
| **MFEIF** | 7.0312 | 3.3109 | 0.0544 | 9.7961 | 0.8111 | 3.9454 | 1.5598 | 0.5329 | *0.6433* |
| **TarDAL** | 6.2663 | 2.7517 | 0.0390 | 7.7842 | 0.7910 | 2.9768 | 1.0448 | 0.2764 | 0.5662 |
| **SeAFusion** | **7.4025** | *4.0804* | **0.0772** | *9.8559* | 0.9042 | **5.4678** | **1.5867** | **0.6125** | 0.6497 |
| **SuperFusion** | *7.3092* | 4.2593 | 0.0684 | 9.8598 | *0.8481* | 4.6858 | 1.4637 | *0.5458* | **0.6612** |
| **Ours** | 7.3544 | **5.3530** | *0.0654* | **10.0727** | **0.9118** | *4.4213* | *1.5577* | 0.5576 | 0.6423 |

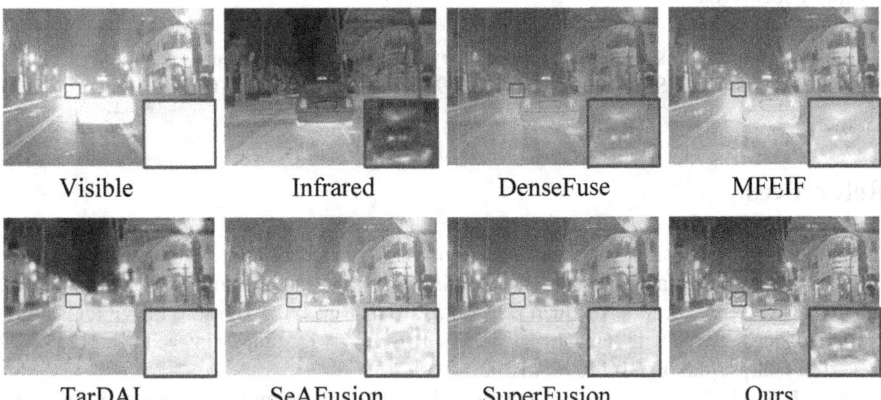


**Fig. 6.** The scene with overexposed visible images in the RoadScene dataset – 1

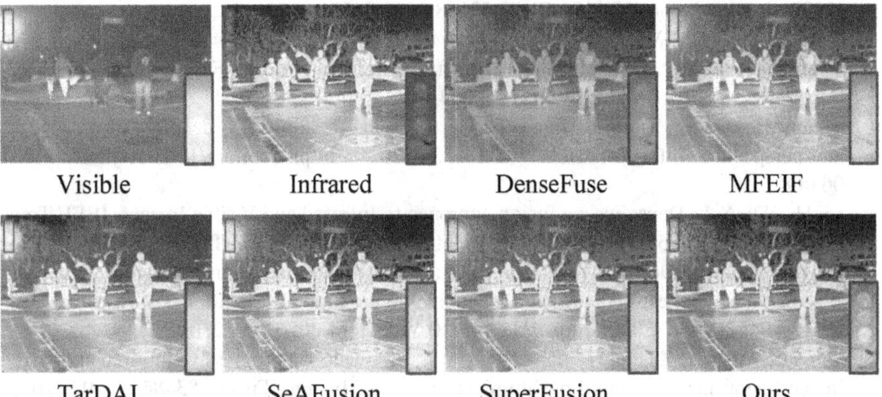


**Fig. 7.** The scenes with overexposed visible images in the RoadScene dataset – 2

## 5 Conclusion and Future Work

This paper proposes an approach for establishing a semantic segmentation dataset for infrared and visible fusion. This method utilizes style transfer and existing semantic segmentation datasets, effectively addressing the issue of traditional infrared and visible fusion datasets lacking high-level visual task annotations without additional manual labeling. In the current dataset establishment, we apply the style transfer only on infrared images while utilize the original Cityscapes images for the visible images. In future work, extending style transfer to visible images could be explored. This would allow the generation of diverse visible images from multiple datasets, making the dataset even richer and more diverse. Moreover, we observed that, under complex environmental conditions such as strong lighting or fog, the segmentation network might not perform very well. Future research could investigate the incorporation of manual annotations or the utilization of data augmentation techniques to enhance the model's accuracy in such complex scenarios.

**Acknowledgment.** This research is supported by the National Science and Technology Council, Taiwan, under Grants NSTC 111-2221-E-008-098 and 112-2221-E-008-077.

## References

1. Wang, D., Liu, J., Fan, X., Liu, R.: Unsupervised misaligned infrared and visible image fusion via cross-modality image generation and registration. arXiv preprint arXiv:2205.11876 (2022)
2. Tang, L., Deng, Y., Ma, Y., Huang, J., Ma, J.: SuperFusion: a versatile image registration and fusion network with semantic awareness. IEEE/CAA J. Autom. Sinica **9**(12), 2121–2137 (2022). https://doi.org/10.1109/JAS.2022.106082
3. Liu, J., et al.: Target-aware dual adversarial learning and a multi-scenario multi-modality benchmark to fuse infrared and visible for object detection. In: 2022 IEEE/CVF Conference on Computer Vision and Pattern Recognition (CVPR), 18–24 June 2022, pp. 5792–5801 (2022). https://doi.org/10.1109/CVPR52688.2022.00571
4. Tang, L., Yuan, J., Ma, J.: Image fusion in the loop of high-level vision tasks: a semantic-aware real-time infrared and visible image fusion network. Inform. Fusion **82**, 28–42 (2022). https://doi.org/10.1016/j.inffus.2021.12.004
5. Zhang, H., Xu, H., Tian, X., Jiang, J., Ma, J.: Image fusion meets deep learning: a survey and perspective. Inform. Fusion **76**, 323–336 (2021). https://doi.org/10.1016/j.inffus.2021.06.008
6. Li, H., Wu, X.J.: DenseFuse: a fusion approach to Infrared and Visible Images. IEEE Trans. Image Process. **28**(5), 2614–2623 (2019). https://doi.org/10.1109/TIP.2018.2887342
7. Li, H., Wu, X.J., Durrani, T.: NestFuse: an infrared and visible image fusion architecture based on nest connection and spatial/channel attention models. IEEE Trans. Instrum. Meas. **69**(12), 9645–9656 (2020). https://doi.org/10.1109/TIM.2020.3005230
8. Tang, L., Yuan, J., Zhang, H., Jiang, X., Ma, J.: PIAFusion: a progressive infrared and visible image fusion network based on illumination aware. Inform. Fusion **83–84**, 79–92 (2022). https://doi.org/10.1016/j.inffus.2022.03.007
9. Ma, J., Yu, W., Liang, P., Li, C., Jiang, J.: FusionGAN: a generative adversarial network for infrared and visible image fusion. Inform. Fusion **48**, 11–26 (2019). https://doi.org/10.1016/j.inffus.2018.09.004

10. Ma, J., Xu, H., Jiang, J., Mei, X., Zhang, X.P.: DDcGAN: a dual-discriminator conditional generative adversarial network for multi-resolution image fusion. IEEE Trans. Image Process. **29**, 4980–4995 (2020). https://doi.org/10.1109/TIP.2020.2977573
11. Toet, A.: The TNO multiband image data collection. Data in Brief **15**, 249–251 (2017). https://doi.org/10.1016/j.dib.2017.09.038
12. Xu, H., Ma, J., Jiang, J., Guo, X., Ling, H.: U2Fusion: a unified unsupervised image fusion network. IEEE Trans. Pattern Anal. Mach. Intell. **44**(1), 502–518 (2022). https://doi.org/10.1109/TPAMI.2020.3012548
13. Jia, X., Zhu, C., Li, M., Tang, W., Liu, S., Zhou, W.: LLVIP: A Visible-infrared Paired Dataset for Low-light Vision. arXiv e-prints, p. arXiv:2108.10831 (2021). https://ui.adsabs.harvard.edu/abs/2021arXiv210810831J
14. Cordts, M., et al.: The cityscapes dataset for semantic urban scene understanding. In: 2016 IEEE Conference on Computer Vision and Pattern Recognition (CVPR), 27–30 June 2016, pp. 3213–3223 (2016).s https://doi.org/10.1109/CVPR.2016.350
15. Xie, E., Wang, W., Yu, Z., Anandkumar, A., Alvarez, J.M., Luo, P.: SegFormer: simple and efficient design for semantic segmentation with transformers. Adv. Neural. Inf. Process. Syst. **34**, 12077–12090 (2021)
16. Peng, C., Tian, T., Chen, C., Guo, X., Ma, J.: Bilateral attention decoder: a lightweight decoder for real-time semantic segmentation. Neural Netw. **137**, 188–199 (2021). https://doi.org/10.1016/j.neunet.2021.01.021
17. Liu, J., Fan, X., Jiang, J., Liu, R., Luo, Z.: Learning a deep multi-scale feature ensemble and an edge-attention guidance for image fusion. IEEE Trans. Circuits Syst. Video Technol. **32**(1), 105–119 (2022). https://doi.org/10.1109/TCSVT.2021.3056725
18. Qu, G., Zhang, D., Yan, P.: Information measure for performance of image fusion. Electron. Lett. **38**(7), 313 (2002). https://doi.org/10.1049/el:20020212
19. Sheikh, H.R., Bovik, A.C.: Image information and visual quality. IEEE Trans. Image Process. **15**(2), 430–444 (2006). https://doi.org/10.1109/TIP.2005.859378
20. Aslantas, V., Bendes, E.: A new image quality metric for image fusion: the sum of the correlations of differences. AEU – Int. J. Electron. Commun. **69**(12), 1890–1896 (2015). https://doi.org/10.1016/j.aeue.2015.09.004
21. Xydeas, C., Petrovic, V.: Objective image fusion performance measure. Electron. Lett. **36**, 308–309 (2000). https://doi.org/10.1049/el:20000267

# Multi-action Prediction Using an Iterative Masking Approach with Class Activation Mapping

Chia-Ying Wu, Yu-Wei Tsay, and Arthur Chun-Chieh Shih(✉)

Institute of Information Science, Academia Sinica, Taipei 115, Taiwan
arthur@mail.iis.sinica.edu.tw

**Abstract.** While prediction techniques for multiple objects in images have become increasingly sophisticated, predicting multiple actions in videos remains challenging. Since most video training datasets only labeled a single action per clip, the trained three-dimensional convolutional neural network (3D CNN) model was limited to predicting a single action. To overcome this limitation, we propose an iterative method that combines a 3D CNN model with class activation mapping (CAM), which can achieve multi-object and multi-action prediction in videos. In each iteration, the action class with the highest score is output first. Then, the selected CAM method is applied to detect the primary action region. After masking this region in the input video, the masked video is re-input to the CNN model to predict actions occurring in other regions. In the experimental section, we used a video dataset of a single mouse with a single action label to train a 3D CNN model and tested the prediction performance using another set of composite videos of multiple mice with the same or different actions. The results demonstrate that the proposed method combined with Grad-CAM can correctly predict the individual actions of multiple mice in the videos. Moreover, we also analyzed a few of human action videos to illustrate the feasibility of this approach.

**Keywords:** Three-dimensional Convolutional Neural Network · Class Activation Mapping · Multiple Action Prediction

## 1 Introduction

Object recognition involves detecting and recognizing single or multiple targets in an image, whereas action recognition analyzes the dynamic context between image frames in a video [1, 2]. Due to the continuous development of various deep learning technologies, the former research has made a great progress in the recent years while the latter, action recognition, is still challenging.

The convolutional neural network (CNN) is a powerful deep learning model that can extract useful features from raw images and perform object recognition through a classifier. With the availability of several large-scale image databases that have been meticulously annotated [3], the multi-target prediction using two-dimensional (2D)


C.-Y. Lee et al. (Eds.): TAAI 2023, CCIS 2074, pp. 284–299, 2024.
https://doi.org/10.1007/978-981-97-1711-8_22

CNN models and related technologies has been widely applied in many fields, including autonomous driving [4], facial recognition [5], and other fields [6, 7].

In contrast, most of available video datasets for action recognition were only labeled single action at the clip level [8]. Therefore, the 3D CNN models were trained with the entire clip as input and a labelled action as output. In literature and our previous study [9], the prediction results of 3D CNN models indeed can achieve comparable accuracy with only one action per input video clip. However, how to use trained 3D CNN models to predict multiple actions in input videos with remains largely unknown.

Using the class activation mapping (CAM) to explain how deep learning systems perform object detection and recognition has become an emerging research topic in the field of machine learning. Selvaraju *et al.* first proposed the Grad-CAM method [10], which used a global average pooling and the feature map of the last convolutional layer. Through by backpropagation calculation, the regional heat map can be obtained, which can not only visually judge the classification, but also analyze the weight distribution of the focus area of the prediction result. In order to obtain more accurate positioning information for small targets, Grad-CAM++ proposed an improved method [11], claiming that the method can emphasize important features such as target categories and make the generated class activation maps more accurate. However, the major disadvantage of Grad-CAM++ is that the method often amplifies noise and affects positioning accuracy. In order to solve the noise problem and enhance the sensitivity of target detection, Score-CAM proposed a method that does not use the back propagation calculation method, but calculates the weight values with all filter channels for the summarization to obtain the CAM map [12]. These CAM methods were mainly used for image segmentation of 2D data [10, 13] and rarely applied to 3D video data analysis.

In this paper, we propose an iterative masking approach that combines a 3D CNN model with a CAM method to predict individual actions of multiple targets in an input video. The CNN model used in this study is firstly trained by the video clips labeled with only a single action. On the first prediction, the action with the highest score is chosen. The selected CAM method is applied to generate a mask map to erase the region for the predicted action in the original input video. The masked video is then re-input into the CNN model for the next prediction. In the results, we use a mouse action video dataset and a set of composite videos to predict individual actions of multiple mice in an experimental environment. Additionally, a few of human action videos are also analyzed to illustrate the feasibility of this approach.

## 2 Methods

### 2.1 Overview of the Proposed Method

The major steps of our proposed method include a 3D CNN model training, saliency map calculation, up-sampling, main action region detection, mask generation, and region masking (Fig. 1). In the initial step, a 3D CNN model is trained using a set of video clips each with an action label. When given a test clip as input, the CNN model generates a set of feature maps and output a vector of predicted scores. The class with the highest score is selected as the predicted class. Then, the saliency maps are calculated based on the feature maps through a CAM method. Since the size of the saliency map is the same as that of the feature map, the saliency map is then upsampled to the same size as the input video frame. The converted map is called heatmap where the area with the largest intensity value represents the location of predicted main action. Then, a simple method is applied to detect the main action region and a mask map is generated as a reference to erase this region in the input video. The masked video clip is then re-input to the CNN model for the second prediction, and the class with the highest score is output as the second predicted class. In what follows, we will describe each step in more details.

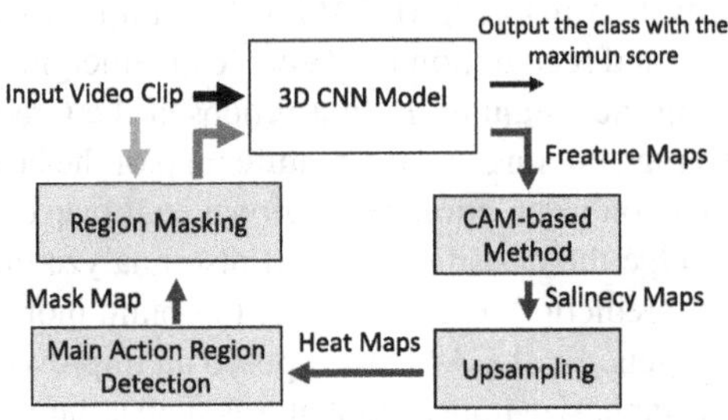


**Fig. 1.** Workflow of the proposed method.

## 2.2 Three-Dimension Convolutional Neural Network (3D CNN) Model

Given a 3D CNN model, let $A_k^d$ be the $d^{th}$ activation map of the $k^{th}$ filter channel for a specific class $c$ where $1 \leq d \leq D$ and $1 \leq k \leq K$ that $D$ and $K$ are the dimension of temporal reduction and the total filer number, respectively. The output score of class $c$, $Q^c$, can be defined as the linear combination of pooling all values from the activation maps as.

$$Q^c = \sum\nolimits_d \sum\nolimits_k w_k^{c,d} \cdot \sum\nolimits_{i,j} A_k^d(i,j), \tag{1}$$

where $A_k^d(i,j)$ is the value of $A_k^d$ at location $(i,j)$ and $w_k^{c,d}$ is the weight of the $k^{th}$ filter channel of the $d^{th}$ temporal reduction map for the class $c$.

In general, the final output scores are usually calculated by a softmax function to emphasize the maximum one as well as normalize all the output scores between 0 and 1. In Eq. 1, the score $Q^c$ is obtained before applying the softmax layer.

The architecture of the 3D CNN model implemented in our study was proposed by Tran *et al.* [17] where the dimension of temporal reduction, $D$, and the total filter number, $K$, are set to 2 and 512, respectively. Moreover, the dimensions of the feature maps are $2 \times 512 \times 7 \times 7$ where 2, 512, and $7 \times 7$ are the dimension of temporal reduction, the total number of filter channels, and activation map sizes, respectively. For all frames of the input videos, the rows and columns are normalized to 112 pixels. The frame rate is also resampled to 16 frames per second, similar to our previous works [9, 14].

### 2.3 CAM-Based Methods

For a general CAM method, the class-specific saliency map $S^{c,d}$ of the class $c$ and the temporal reduction dimension $d$ is defined as the relationship with the activation maps of all channels as below.

$$S^{c,d}(i,j) = \sum\nolimits_k g_k^{c,d} \cdot A_k^d(i,j), \tag{2}$$

where $g_k^{c,d}$ is the CAM weight of filer channel $k$ for the class $c$ and temporal reduction dimension $d$. Based on various criterions and derivations, several CAM methods have been proposed [10–13]. The originally proposed CAM method required retraining multiple classifiers again after training the initial model [15]. In the past few years, a few of methods without retaining have been proposed, such as Grad-CAM [10], Grad-CAM++ [11], Score-CAM [12], and so on. In what follows, the three methods applied in this study are introduced in detail.

**GradCAM**

Using the backpropagation approach, Grad-CAM method calculated the gradients of each output score over all activation maps firstly [11]. Then, the weighting scores were calculated by global average pooling of the gradient values. Given a filter channel $k$ and a specific class $c$, the weight $g_k^{c,d}$ was defined as below:

$$g_k^{c,d} = \frac{1}{B}\sum\nolimits_i \sum\nolimits_j \frac{\partial Q^c}{\partial A_k^d(i,j)}, \tag{3}$$

where B is the total pixel number of the activation map and the other variables have been defined in Eq. 1. Grad-CAM did not need to retrain and modify any part of the original CNN architecture. The visual explanation image can be obtained by upsampling a salient map and fused with the input image (or the 1st frame of the input video in this study). However, some studies pointed out that Grad-CAM may not be able to locate multiple targets with the same class in the input image [15]. Furthermore, the salient region generated by the unweighted average pooling of all derivatives may only partially cover the target object.

**GradCAM++**

For solving the unweighted problem, GradCAM ++ reformulated Eq. 3 and defined a revised formula as below:

$$g_k^{c,d} = \sum\nolimits_i \sum\nolimits_j \alpha_k^{c,d}(i,j) \cdot relu\left(\frac{\partial Q^c}{\partial A_k^d(i,j)}\right), \tag{4}$$

where *relu* was the rectified linear unit function and $\alpha_k^{c,d}(i,j)$ s were the weighting coefficients for the pixel-wise gradients for the class $c$. In order to simplify the computational complexity and implementation, the original score $Q^c$ was assumed to be the exponential function of the penultimate layer score $E^c$ as.

$$Q^c = \exp(E^c). \tag{5}$$

Then, the final equation of $\alpha_k^{c,d}(i,j)$ can be simplified as

$$\alpha_k^{c,d}(i,j) = \frac{B^2}{2 \cdot B^2 + B^3 \cdot \sum_a \sum_b A_k^d(a,b)}, \tag{6}$$

where $B = \frac{\partial E^c}{\partial A_k^d(i,j)}$. Finally, all $g_k^{c,d}$ values can be calculated by Eq. 4 through Eq. 6 one by one. In a saliency map, the value for each point was calculated by Eq. 1 and the negative part was ignored by a *relu* operator as below:

$$S^{c,d}(i,j) = relu\left(\sum_k g_k^{c,d} \cdot A_k^{c,d}(i,j)\right), \tag{7}$$

However, we found that a few of negative $A_k^{c,d}(i,j)$ with large magnitudes from some channels usually cause the total sum close to zero or be negative before applying *relu*. Thus, Eq. 7 was revised in this study as below:

$$S^{c,d}(i,j) = \sum_k g_k^{c,d} \cdot relu(A_k^{c,d}(i,j)). \tag{8}$$

**Upsampling**

The size of a saliency map obtained by the CAM method is the same as that of activation maps. In order to remap to the original video frames, an upsampling approach is required to expand the size. In this study, we use a linear interpolation method provided by the OpenCV Library to expand the size from $7 \times 7$ into $112 \times 112$. For convenience, the upsampled maps are called heatmaps in this study.

**Score-CAM**

Instead of employing the backpropagation method to calculate gradients, Score-CAM proposed a different approach to obtain saliency maps [12]. For each channel, the heatmap integrating with the input image is re-input to the CNN model again to obtain the score of the specific class $c$ as the weight for the channel. The saliency map is then obtained by the linear combination of the weights and activation maps.

Let $M_k^d = U\left(A_k^d\right)$ where $U$ is the upsampling operator that converts the activation map size of $A_k^d$ to the same size as the input and $N_k^d$ is the normalized map of $M_k^d$ where the values $N_k^d$ are all $\geq 0$ and $\leq 1$. Let $F_t$ be the $t^{\text{th}}$ frame of the input video $\boldsymbol{X}$ and $1 \leq t \leq p$ where $p$ is the total frame number of the input video. Because $d \leq D$ where $D$ is the temporal reduction of $p$, $\{N_k^d | 1 \leq d \leq D\}$ is expanded to $\{N_k^t | 1 \leq t \leq p\}$ by a repeat function provided by PyTorch. For each channel $k$, $G_k^t = N_k^t \circ F_t$ is computed where $\circ$ is the Hadamard product operator for each video frame. Then, an updated video $\{G_k^t | 1 \leq t \leq p\}$ is re-input to the 3D CNN model and the output score for class $c$ is treated as the CAM weight for channel $k$. After processing all channels, the final visualization maps are obtained by the linear combination of the weights and activation maps.

## 2.4 Detection of Main Action Region

In this study, two saliency maps obtained as well as two heatmaps will be generated. We combine the heatmaps into a single map, called the maximal heatmap, by selecting the maximum values between the heatmaps point by point. In order to find the predicted action region in the maximal heatmap, we use a fixed percentile as the threshold which was the $90^{th}$ percentile set in this paper, to binarize the maximal heatmap and obtain one or more possible regions. Then, for the region with the largest value in the maximal heatmap, called the main action region, all the points are set to 1 and the other points in the map were set to 0. Finally, the processed binary map is called the mask map.

## 3 Results

### 3.1 Experimental Datasets

In the experiment, we downloaded two different types of video data sets (including mice and humans) and trained two independent 3D CNN models separately. Additionally, some composite videos of multiple mice with the same and different actions were also synthesized for analyzing the prediction performance. All datasets are explained below.

**Mouse Dataset**

The experimental mouse video data set was downloaded from the Serre laboratory at Brown University [16]. The dataset includes 12 full-length videos, recorded during the day and night, for a total recording time of 10.6 h. After editing and annotation by professional technical personnel, 4,200 video clips were produced. The clipping dataset can be divided into eight actions, including Drink, Rear, Rest, Groom, Hang, Walk, Eat, and Head (Fig. 2a). The original frame size was 320 × 240 pixels and the frame rate per second was 30. To match the input specifications of the implemented 3D CNN model, the frame size and frame per second rate of all video clips were adjusted to 112 × 112 pixels and 20, respectively.

However, this dataset did not provide any video clip of multiple mice in a cage. To examine the correctness of the prediction results by the proposed method, we generated a set of composite video clips in which each one has two mice simultaneously in a cage performing the same or different actions. We first selected two video clips and checked the locations of one mouse in the video clip not overlapping with the corresponding regions of the other mouse in any frame in the other clip. Then, we identified an appropriate horizontal or vertical line to cut each video clip into two separated sub-clips, one with mouse and none for the other. After combining the sub-clips both with mice, a composite video clip with multiple mice was generated (Fig. 2b). Totally, 30 composite videos were generated including 15 for the mice with different actions on different sides, 10 for the mice with the same action on different sides, and 5 for the ones with different actions on the same side. In this study, we did not consider the overlap problem in the proposed method, and therefore did not compose videos of action intersections.

**Human Dataset**

We also downloaded the UCF101 video dataset of 101 human actions, which contains 13,320 video clips [8], and a pre-trained CNN model [17]. However, the human action clips were far more complex than the background and targets in the mouse dataset. Therefore, we only used some test videos from the dataset and YouTube-8M to test and analyze the proposed method, but did not provide a systematic comparison of prediction performance.

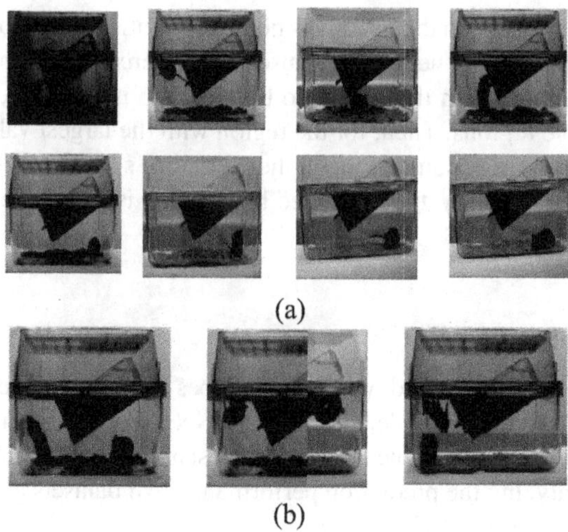

**Fig. 2.** Downloaded mouse dataset and our composite videos. (a) Screenshots of the mouse dataset, including 8 action classes of single mouse with a single action in each video clip. (b) Screenshots of three composite videos that simulated two mice with different actions on different sides (left), the same action on different sides (middle), and different actions on the same side (right).

### 3.2 Score Distributions for Single and Multiple Mouse Actions

With a 3D CNN model, the simplest way to predict single or multiple actions of multiple targets in a video clip was to directly select the highest-scoring class as the prediction result. In this paper, we called the method as "Top N selection", where N is the number of output action classes.

First, a video clip, Rear339, of a single Rear action (Fig. 3a) was input into the CNN model trained on the mouse dataset, and the distribution of the output scores showed that the action class with the maximum value was Rear (the bar chart in Fig. 3a). When a Groom action clip, Groom99, was input, the action class with the highest score according to the distribution of output scores was Groom (Fig. 3b). Therefore, the prediction results of single-target and single-action test data were both correct. When a composite video, Rear339 + Groom99, containing two mice with two different actions was input, the Rear action had the highest prediction score, and the Groom action had the second highest score, although the score was less than half of the highest score (Fig. 3c). Therefore, the action prediction results of the two mice through the Top 2 selection method were both correct.

When we tested using another set of video clips, Groom99 and Drink138, and their composite video, Groom99 + Drink138, by choosing the maximum value of the prediction score, the action prediction results of these two video clips were both correct (Figs. 3d and e). For their composite video, the action class with the highest prediction score was still Groom, while that with the second highest score was Rest instead of Drink (Fig. 3f). For this case, the multi-action prediction by the Top 2 selection method was incorrect.

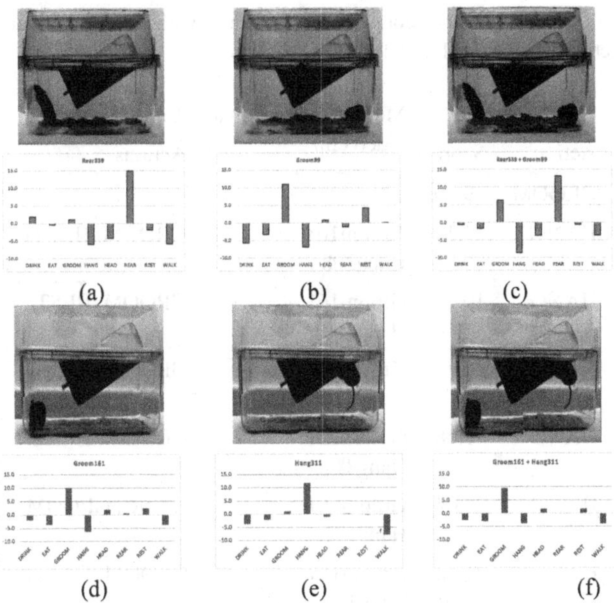


**Fig. 3.** Screenshots of the two data sets (a-c and d-f) of video clips and distribution plots of action prediction scores. Each data set includes two video clips of a single mouse with single action and their composite video. In each subfigure, a screenshot of the video clip is shown on the upper while the bar chart is the score distribution as shown on the below. For each bar chart, the vertical and horizontal axes represent the prediction score and the corresponding action class, respectively, and the numerical value appended to each action name in the title is the video clip number.

In order to study more cases, we used another video clip, Groom161, as a template fixed on one side and cut and spliced it with 10 video clips of Hang actions where the mice were all on the other side. For the single action video clips, the prediction results using the Top 1 selection method were all correct, and the scores were mostly higher than 10.0 (Table 1). However, when using the composite video clips of two mice with different actions as input, three prediction results were wrong by the Top 2 selection method and all top scores were lower than the predicted scores by single action videos. Furthermore, the second-highest scores in more than half of the results were much lower than their top 1 scores, but there were still three cases where the highest and second-highest scores were close (Table 1). Even though each of these 10 videos were composed with the same two different actions, and even one action on the same side was exactly the same half video clip, the prediction scores of these two actions still differed greatly between some videos. Therefore, the results show that relying solely on the score selection to predict multiple actions could be problematic.

**Table 1.** Prediction of actions and scores for single mouse with single action and multiple mice with different actions by the top 1 and 2 score selections.

| Single action | Top 1 selection | | Multiple actions in a video clip | Top 2 selection | |
|---|---|---|---|---|---|
| | Action | Score | | Actions | Top 2 Scores |
| Groom161 | GROOM | 9.89 | | | |
| Hang308 | HANG | 11.14 | Groom161 + Hang308 | GROOM, HANG | (9.00, 2.32) |
| Hang309 | HANG | 10.27 | Groom161 + Hang309 | GROOM, REST | (8.85, 1.26) |
| Hang310 | HANG | 10.44 | Groom161 + Hang310 | GROOM, HANG | (8.60, 2.75) |
| Hang311 | HANG | 11.68 | Groom161 + Hang311 | GROOM, HEAD | (9.37, 1.62) |
| Hang172 | HANG | 20.04 | Groom161 + Hang172 | HANG, GROOM | (12.46, 5.38) |
| Hang174 | HANG | 21.16 | Groom161 + Hang174 | GROOM, HANG | (7.88, 3.94) |
| Hang81 | HANG | 12.60 | Groom161 + Hang81 | GROOM, REST | (8.82, 2.34) |
| Hang017 | HANG | 10.46 | Groom161 + Hang017 | HANG, GROOM | (6.86, 6.34) |
| Hang018 | HANG | 12.98 | Groom161 + Hang018 | GROOM, HANG | (6.09, 6.05) |
| Hang019 | HANG | 12.95 | Groom161 + Hang019 | GROOM, HANG | (7.30, 6.46) |

### 3.3 Heatmaps and Mask Maps Generated by Three CAM Methods

In this subsection, we compare the visual explanation and mask maps generated by the three CAM methods. First, the composite video, Rear339 + Groom99, a fusion of two single action videos, Rear339 and Groom99, was input to the 3D CNN model. Then, we collected all output feature maps and applied Grad-CAM, Grad-CAM++, and Score-CAM to compute the saliency maps. Each heatmap was obtained from the saliency map after upsampling and then combined with the initial frame of the input video to generate a visual explanation map. As shown in the left two columns of Fig. 4, the areas of Rear action were all highlighted in the visual maps generated by the three CAM methods. Then, we detected the primary action regions in each maximal heatmap and obtained the mask maps through the CAM methods. We found that the mask areas in all three images covered the predicted action region of Rear (middle column in Fig. 4). By each mask map, all original video frames were masked with the primary action region and re-input to the 3D CNN model to predict actions again. After the second prediction, the highlighted areas in the visual explanation maps for Grad-CAM and score-CAM covered the regions of the other mice with Groom actions (columns 4 and 5 in Fig. 4a and c), appropriately. However, using Grad-CAM++, one visual explanation map had no highlighted areas, while the other one was highlighted almost the entire map (in the columns 4 and 5 in Fig. 4b).

For the output scores from the first prediction, the action of the highest score was Rear (Fig. 3c). After masking the primary regions by the three CAM-methods, the actions with the highest scores in the second prediction were all Groom (Fig. 5) and the scores were close to that obtained by predicting a single action alone (Fig. 3b).

When another video composed of two single action videos, Groom161 and Hang311, was input to the CNN model for action prediction, we found that the two highest scoring actions were Groom and Rest with the scores of 9.37 and 1.61, respectively, while the score for the action Hang was only − 3.85. Obviously, only one of the Top 2 selection was correct while the other was wrong.

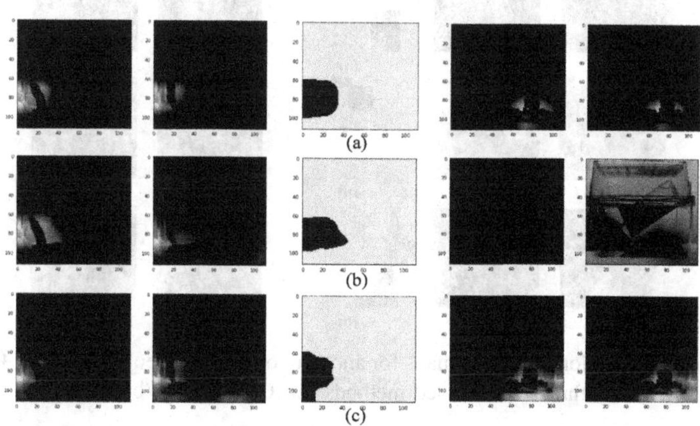


**Fig. 4.** The visual explanation and mask maps for the composite video, Rear339 + Groom99, generated by three CAM methods: (a) Grad-CAM, (b) Grad-CAM++, and (c) Score-CAM. The images in the 1st and 2nd columns are the visual explanation maps of the first 3D CNN prediction. In the 3rd column, the mask maps obtained by the CAM methods where the primary action regions are colored in black. The images in the right two columns are the visual explanation maps of the second CNN prediction.

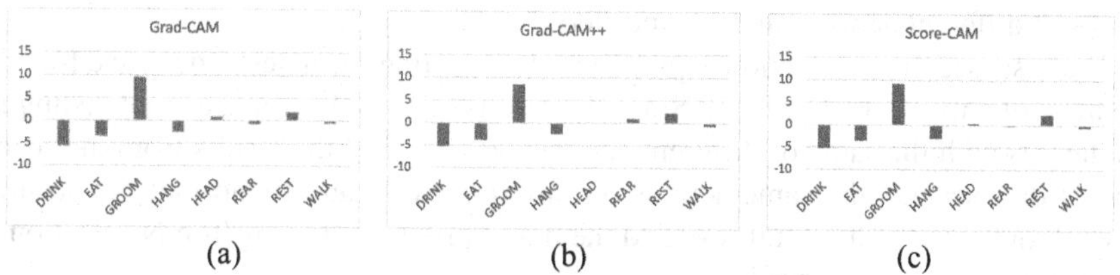


**Fig. 5.** The score distributions of the 2nd prediction with the re-input videos masking the primary action regions obtained by three CAM methods: (a) Grad-CAM, (b) Grad-CAM++, and (c) Score-CAM.

When applying our method, the first target action was selected the class with the highest score in the first prediction. Then, applying three CAM methods, the mask maps were obtained and used them to mask the main action regions in all frames of the original input video. In the second prediction, the masked videos were reinput to the 3D CNN model one by one. However, only for the video masked using Grad-CAM, the action with the highest prediction score was Hang, while the predicted classes for those masked by using Grad-CAM++ and Score-CAM were Groom and Head, respectively. As the mask maps shown in the middle column of Fig. 6, only the primary action region obtained by Grad-CAM looked reasonable, while that by Grad-CAM++ did not cover any mouse region, and that by Score-CAM only covered partial the mouse region. Therefore, Grad-CAM should be the most suitable CAM method for our proposed method.

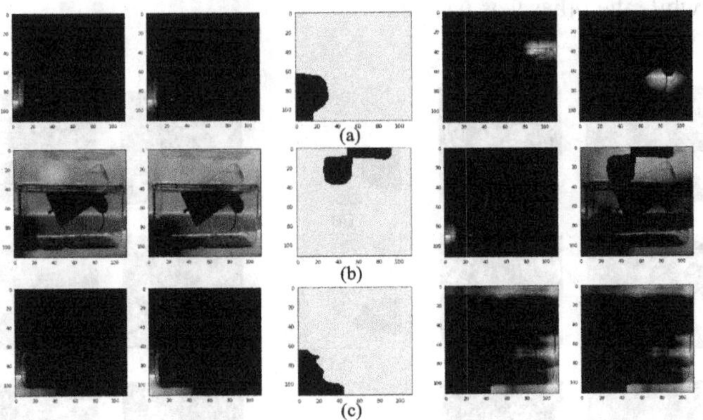


**Fig. 6.** Visual explanation and mask maps for another composite video, Groom161 + Hang311, that weregenerated by three CAM-based methods: (a) Grad-CAM, (b) Grad-CAM++, and (c) Score-CAM.

### 3.4 Multiple Mouse Action Prediction by Proposed Method

For comparing the prediction performance of the proposed approach with three CAM methods, we synthesized 30 multiple action mouse videos including 15 videos of different actions on different sides, 10 videos of the same actions on different sides, and 5 videos of different actions on the same side (Fig. 2b).

We first used Top 2 selection to predict multiple actions in all test videos and found an accuracy of only 50.0% (Table 2). Since the results selected by Top 2 cannot distinguish two targets with the same or different actions, we excluded the results from the second type of data set, i.e. the same actions on different sides, and found that the accuracy was still only 70%. The result revealed the major problem of using Top N selection for multi-target multi-action prediction.

When using the proposed method with Grad-CAM, we found the that prediction results were all correct for all test videos no matter for any type of the datasets (Table 2). If the method with Score-CAM, the accuracy rate was 0.80 while that by Grad-CAM++ was only 0.67 (Table 2). It indicated that the proposed method in cooperation with

**Table 2.** Prediction results of mouse action composite data by Top 2 selection and our method with Grad-CAM, Grad-CAM++, and Score-CAM.

| Sample Types | Sample No | Top 2 Selection | CAM-based Masking Approach | | |
|---|---|---|---|---|---|
| | | | Grad-CAM | Grad-CAM ++ | Score-CAM |
| Different Actions on Different Side | 15 | 11 | 15 | 9 | 11 |
| Same Action on Different Sides | 10 | 0 | 10 | 10 | 10 |
| Different Actions on Same Side | 5 | 3 | 5 | 1 | 3 |
| Total | 30 | 14 | 30 | 20 | 24 |

Grad-CAM can generate an appropriate mask map to mask predicted action regions effectively.

### 3.5 Analysis of Multiple Human Action Prediction by Our Method

In this part, we trained the other 3D CNN model by the human UCF101 database and analyzed the prediction ability of the proposed method through three human action videos where two videos of Fencing and Sumo Wrestling were selected from the same database, and a video "Piano" and "Quartet" was downloaded from the YouTube-8M dataset [18] (Fig. 7). In the beginning, we had applied all three CAM methods to compute visual explanation and mask maps. However, we found that the visual and mask maps obtained by Grad-CAM++ and Score-CAM were not as reasonable as Grad-CAM. Therefore, only the results obtained by Grad-CAM were presented in this subsection.

(a) (b) (c)

**Fig. 7.** Screenshots of three human action videos: (a) Fencing, (b) Sumo Wrestling, and (c) Piano and Quartet.

Using the fencing video as input (Fig. 7a), the output class with the largest score at the first prediction was Fencing. After calculating relevant maps via Grad-CAM, we found that both the fencers were highlighted in the visual explanation map, but compared to the other athlete, the fencer on the left was mostly covered by the highlighted area (Fig. 8a first and second columns). The detected primary action region was located on the left side of the mask map (middle column in Fig. 8a). After masking the action region, the masked video was reinput to the 3D CNN model. Selecting by the highest score, the output of the predicted class remained "Fencing" and the highlighted area in one of the visual explanation maps mostly covered the other athlete on the right (column 4 in Fig. 8).

Like fencing, sumo wrestling is a two-person sport, but there is often a referee in between. When using the sumo wrestling video (Fig. 7b) as input, the first prediction result was "Sumo Wrestling". But unlike the fencing case, only one athlete on the right side was highlighted in one of the visual explanation maps but not in the other one (first and second columns in Fig. 8b). The detected action region shown in the mask map was also located on the right side (middle column of Fig. 8b). Applying the masking procedure and feeding the masked video to the CNN model again, the output class was still "Sumo Wrestling" and another sumo wrestler on the left had been highlighted in one of the visual explanation maps at the 2nd prediction.

In addition to using videos from the same dataset UCF101, we downloaded a video Piano and Quartet [18] from the YouTube-8M dataset (Fig. 7c). On the first prediction, the highest-scoring class was "playing the cello." In the two visual explanation maps (the first and second columns in Fig. 8c), the highlighted area mainly covered the musician's hands playing the cello, and a meaningful mask map was obtained (middle column of Fig. 8c) to create a masked video for the next prediction. After the second prediction, the best class was "playing piano", and the highlighted area in the visual explanation map did cover the musician who played the piano.

In short, the above analysis results indicate that directly utilizing the 3D CNN model trained on single action clips by our approach could predict single or multiple actions of multiple targets in a video clip.

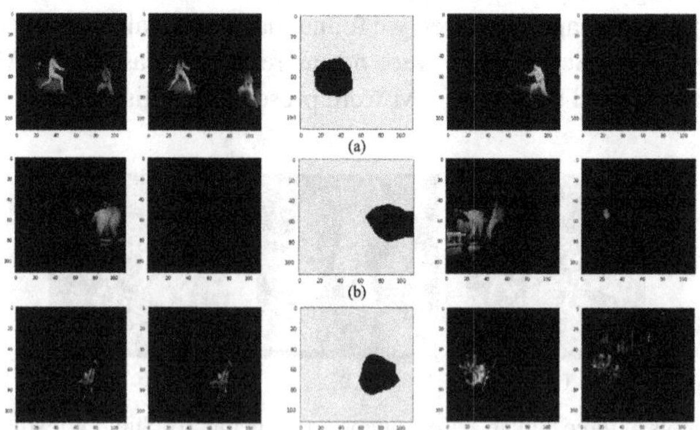


**Fig. 8.** The visual explanation maps generated by Grad-CAM at the 1st (the 1st and 2nd columns) and 2nd prediction (the 4th and 5th columns). The figures shown in middle columns are the mask maps obtained at the 1st prediction. The test videos used for each row are: (a) Fencing, (b) Sumo Wrestling, and (c) Musicians playing piano and cello.

## 4 Discussions and Conclusions

In this paper, we propose an iterative masking method with class activation mapping that can predict the individual actions of multiple targets in a video through a traditional 3D CNN model trained on a single action dataset without additional location and detailed labeling information. In addition, this method can also predict the action locations of individual targets in the video.

The main key to determining the correctness of the second prediction result in the proposed method is dependent on whether the mask map generated by the CAM method can effectively cover the predicted action area. We have applied three CAM methods to generate different mask maps and compared the prediction performance on mouse datasets. From the results, we found that the Grad-CAM++ method exhibited high sensitivity to noise, as the highlighted regions in the heatmaps were occasionally derived from noisy background regions rather than the target action areas. For Score-CAM, the time complexity was much higher than the others and the shapes of the main action regions were usually irregular that may need more post-processing steps to improve the part for mask generation. By contrast, the highlighted area in at least one visual explanation map generated by Grad-CAM showed that it covered the main area of the predicted action, and at the same time, the results of its second prediction were all correct. Although Grad-CAM was questioned to be unable to locate multiple objects of the same class in images [10]. However, the proposed method can predict the individual actions of multiple targets sequentially, rather than the actions of all targets simultaneously. This shortcoming has no impact on our method. Thus, Grad-CAM would be the most appropriate CAM method to incorporate in the proposed method.

In this study, we did not handle the inputs in which the distance between action targets was too close or overlapped each other. Since the saliency map obtained from the 3D CNN model have been reduced the location resolution, the targets acting too close may not be distinguished after down-sampling at low-resolution scales. Therefore, there may need to develop another method that can consider location information during the down- and up-sampling procedures.

Furthermore, the proposed method did not able to detect if there was no target class in the input or re-input video. For deep learning systems, the ability to detect inputs that do not belong to any class in the training set has been referred to as an open-set recognition problem. In our prior work, we have proposed a 3D CNN model combined with an open fuzzy min-max neural network to address this problem, enabling the detection of inputs not found in the training set [14]. Thus, our proposed method may need to combine with this previous work to tackle this issue in the future.

**Acknowledgment.** The work was partially supported by National Science and Technology Council (MOST 111-2221-E-001-018-MY2), Taiwan, and Institute of Information Science, Academia Sinica, Taiwan.

## References


1. Simonyan, K., Zisserman, A.: Two-stream convolutional networks for action recognition in videos. In: Ghahramani, Z., Welling, M., Cortes, C., Lawrence, N., Weinberger, K.Q. (eds.) NIPS 2014, vol. 27 (2014)
2. Feichtenhofer, C., Pinz, A., Zisserman, A.: Convolutional two-stream network fusion for video action recognition. In: Proceedings of the 2016 IEEE Conference on Computer Vision and Pattern Recognition (CVPR), pp. 1933–1941 (2016). https://doi.org/10.1109/CVPR.2016.213
3. Lin, T.Y. et al.: Microsoft COCO: common objects in context. In: Fleet, D., Pajdla, T., Schiele, B., Tuytelaars, T. (eds.) Computer Vision – ECCV 2014. ECCV 2014. LNCS, vol. 8693, pp. 1–13. Springer, Cham (2014)
4. Bojarski, M., et al.: End to End Learning for Self-Driving Cars. arXiv e-prints (2016)
5. Taigman, Y., et al.: DeepFace: closing the gap to human-level performance in face verification. In: Proceedings of the 2014 IEEE Conference on Computer Vision and Pattern Recognition (CVPR), pp. 1701–1708 (2014). https://doi.org/10.1109/CVPR.2014.220
6. Badrinarayanan, V., et al.: A deep convolutional encoder-decoder architecture for image segmentation. IEEE Trans. Pattern Anal. Mach. Intell. **39**(12), 2481–2495 (2017). https://doi.org/10.1109/TPAMI.2016.2644615
7. Kalchbrenner, N., Grefenstette, E., Blunsom, P.: A convolutional neural network for modelling sentences. In: Proceedings of the Annual Meeting of the Association for Computational Linguistics (2014)
8. Soomro, K., Roshan Zamir, A., Shah, M.: UCF101: A Dataset of 101 Human Actions Classes From Videos in The Wild. arXiv e-prints, arXiv:1212.0402 (2012). https://doi.org/10.48550/arXiv.1212.0402
9. Wu, C.-Y., et al.: Refined prediction of mouse and human actions based on a data-selective multiple-stage approach of 3D convolutional neural networks. In: Proceedings of the 2020 International Conference on Technologies and Applications of Artificial Intelligence (TAAI), pp. 242–247 (2020). https://doi.org/10.1109/TAAI51410.2020.00052
10. Selvaraju, R.R., et al.: Grad-CAM: visual explanations from deep networks via gradient-based localization. ICCV **2017**, 618–626 (2017). https://doi.org/10.1109/ICCV.2017.74
11. Chattopadhay, A., et al.: Grad-CAM++: generalized gradient-based visual explanations for deep convolutional networks. WACV **2018**, 839–847 (2018). https://doi.org/10.1109/WACV.2018.00097
12. Wang, H., et al.: Score-CAM: score-weighted visual explanations for convolutional neural networks. In: CVPRW 2020. IEEE/CVF (2020). https://doi.org/10.1109/CVPRW50498.2020.00020
13. Vinogradova, K., Dibrov, A., Myers, G.: Towards Interpretable Semantic Segmentation via Gradient-weighted Class Activation Mapping. arXiv e-prints (2020). https://doi.org/10.48550/arXiv.2002.11434
14. Wu, C.-Y., Tsay, Y.-W., Shih, A. C.-C.: Open action recognition by a 3d convolutional neural network combining with an open fuzzy min-max neural network. In: Proceedings of the 2022 International Conference on Advanced Robotics and Intelligent Systems (ARIS), pp. 1–6 (2022). https://doi.org/10.1109/ARIS56205.2022.9910444
15. Zhou, B., et al.: Learning deep features for discriminative localization. In: Proceedings of the 2016 IEEE Conference on Computer Vision and Pattern Recognition (CVPR), pp. 2921–2929 (2016). https://doi.org/10.1109/CVPR.2016.319

16. Jhuang, H., et al.: Automated home-cage behavioural phenotyping of mice. Nat. Commun. **1**(1), 68 (2010). https://doi.org/10.1038/ncomms1064
17. Ji, S., Xu, W., Yang, M., Yu, K.: 3D Convolutional neural networks for human action recognition. IEEE Trans. Pattern Anal. Mach. Intell. **35**(1), 221–231 (2013). https://doi.org/10.1109/TPAMI.2012.59
18. Abu-El-Haija, S., et al.: YouTube-8M: A Large-Scale Video Classification Benchmark. arXiv e-prints (2016). https://doi.org/10.48550/arXiv.1609.08675

# GraphSAGE-Based Spammer Detection Using Social Attribute Relationship

Bing-Yun Jin[1], Shiou-Chi Li[2], and Jen-Wei Huang[1](✉)

[1] Department of Electrical Engineering, National Cheng Kung University, Tainan, Taiwan
{jwhuang,jwhuang}@mail.ncku.edu.tw

[2] Institute of Computer and Communication Engineering, Department of Electrical Engineering, National Cheng Kung University, Tainan, Taiwan

**Abstract.** Spammers have existed since the birth of the Internet. They constantly pollute the social network environment, seriously degrade user experience and pose a threat to user account security. Finding spammers has become one of the most important tasks for social networking platforms. However, spammers use various methods to hide themselves from normal users, which makes it more difficult to detect spammers effectively. We propose a spammer detection method based on GraphSAGE Graph Neural Network, which distinguishes spammers from normal users based on the social attribute relationship of accounts. Even if spammers constantly change the content of their spam messages to avoid detection, they can still be identified by the different social attributes of spammers and normal users. In our method, user feature, relationship feature and behavior feature are designed and extracted to represent the social attribute relationship of users. At the same time, we have successfully and effectively utilized GraphSAGE to address the spammer detection problem. We prove the effectiveness of our method through experiments on the real-world dataset, and the results show that our performance is better than other comparison methods.

**Keywords:** Spammer Detection · Social Networks · Social Attribute Relationship

## 1 Introduction

With the continuous development of computers, mankind has entered the era of information. Since the emergence of the Internet, the way of information interaction and network communication has been changing all over the world. With the continuous improvement of social efficiency, human's desire to communicate is stimulated more and more strongly. This is when social networks, which help people communicate and communicate online, came into being.

However, the quality of the social networking platform and the user experience are damaged due to spam. The negative messages sent by spammers usually carry advertising links, false news and political propaganda for profit. These messages will not only reduce users' mailbox usage space but also waste users' reading time and screening time. As


C.-Y. Lee et al. (Eds.): TAAI 2023, CCIS 2074, pp. 300–313, 2024.
https://doi.org/10.1007/978-981-97-1711-8_23

proposed by Lee [19] *et al.*, these negative emails will continue to undermine users' use experience, and users will gradually lose confidence in social network platforms, eventually leading to the loss of users. Although these spams themselves cannot cause direct harm to users and social network platforms, they are often carried by social network platforms, and these spams with negative content bring great potential danger to social network platforms [14].

In the development process of social network platforms, how to find spammers has always been one of the key issues concerned by social network platforms. In the early stage of spam detection, social network platforms often rely on manual detection of email content. Since spam content is batch replicated and content similarity is high, this method is effective to a certain extent. However, this method also has great disadvantages. On the one hand, manual detection is very inefficient and cannot complete a large number of mail detection tasks. On the other hand, it will cause risks to the privacy of normal users and seriously damage the legitimate rights and interests of users. Therefore, with the development of the Internet, social network platforms gradually use machine learning methods to replace manual text detection. By analyzing the characteristics of mail contents, they can identify the spammers and then judge the spammers by the senders of these emails.

Meanwhile, as Cao [7] *et al.* have proved, in order to avoid detection, spammers tend to change their sent content over time. With the change of sent content, feature engineering needs to be selected and analyzed again. Meanwhile, relying on text content analysis will also damage users' privacy. So a content-based approach is not ideal.

With the development of social networks, the connection between users is more complicated. In this paper, we propose a method based on GraphSAGE [15] to detect spammers through Social Attribute Relationship (GSAR). We designed and extracted users' social attribute relationships and trained them with Graph-SAGE. Even if spammers constantly change the content of their spam messages to avoid detection, they can still be identified by the different social attributes of spammers and normal users.

The main contributions of our paper are as follows:

1. We propose a model to extract the social attribute relationship of users. We can find spammers based on the different social attributes of spammers and normal users, while avoiding the disclosure of users' privacy.
2. We leveraged the social attribute relationships of users as node features and carried out spammer detection based on GraphSAGE.
3. We prove the effectiveness of our method through experiments on the real-world dataset, and the results show that our performance is better than other comparison methods.

## 2 Related Works

### 2.1 Content-Based Spammer Detection

Content-based analysis method is to find spammers through feature extraction and feature analysis of mail contents. As reported by Kiliroor [17] *et al.*, the content-based method will judge spammers by looking for keywords in the content of articles, analyzing the degree of content repetition, calculating the number of special characters, the number of URL links carried and other content characteristics. Different researchers will focus on different content features. For example, some researchers will focus on keywords with emotional color in articles. Xia Hu [16] *et al.* focused on emotional information of contents and processed emotional information in email contents. Through analysis in the field of psychology, different situations of spammer and normal user are distinguished, and an optimization formula is proposed, which is applied to the method of spammer detection.

Carreras [8] *et al.* proposed to use AdaBoost algorithm to solve the problem of spam filtering. They used several variants of AdaBoost algorithm, and finally made the results better than Pupu Bayes. Debarr [10] *et al.* detected spam by optimizing the random forest model. They first used word frequency and reverse representation of documents to cluster the content, and then used the random forest to classify the labeled samples to achieve less labeling information but better results.

Markines [22] *et al.* analyzed six different features of spam contents and then applied these features to different machine learning algorithms for spammer detection. Benevenuto [2] *et al.* analyzed spam through features such as whether there were URL features in the content and the number of user posts. Lee [19] *et al.* searched for spammers by analyzing the number of posts of users, gender, age and other characteristics of users.

With the development of Internet technology, some researchers use semi-supervised or unsupervised methods to detect spam. Geng [13] *et al.* use semi-supervised learning to reduce the amount of data that needs to be tagged and combine traditional self-training and link learning to find spam. Li [20] *et al.* proposed a semi-supervised model based on multi-view to improve the accuracy of spam search through the combination of multiple views. El-Mawass [11] *et al.* proposed a hybrid method for detecting social spam using Markov Random Fields. Their approach combines user attributes with content-based similarities.

But in general, content-based approaches are not effective against spammers in the long run because spammers change the content of their spam messages over time to make them look more like normal users. Meanwhile, the content-based method will also pose a threat to users' privacy. Therefore, compared with the relationship-based method, the content-based method is not very ideal.

### 2.2 Relationship-Based Spammer Detection

Benevenuto [3] *et al.* marked spammers in the data set through manual discrimination, defined some of their social behavior characteristics after analyzing their behaviors, and then trained them with traditional machine learning methods to conduct spammer detection.

Krestel [18] *et al.* sought for spammers by expressing the relationship between users in a graph structure, and then proposed a method to calculate the spread score of spam on the graph structure. Yu [27] *et al.* proposed a semi-supervised technique based on matrix factorization, which integrates both user content and behavior for social spam detection.

Fakhraei [12] *et a*l. used the mixture of Markov models to find the relationship between normal users and users. Additionally, they introduced a model that utilizes hinge-loss Markov Random Fields (HL-MRFs) to facilitate collective reasoning, and the prediction ability of the noise abuse reporting system is successfully improved to find spammer. Recently, Yin [26] *et al.* proposed a method to extract the relationship characteristics of users according to their long-term dependency and short-term dependency. Logistic Regression and XG-Boost were used for training respectively to search for spammer. In the related works addressing multi-relation spammer detection issues, there hasn't been a comprehensive simultaneous consideration of the impact brought by both the users' account characteristics and the graph structure formed by interactions among users. For instance, in the case of MDM [26], they only focused on the long-term and short-term dependency relationships of user behavior at the individual and collective levels, overlooking information such as the registration time and registration age of users' accounts themselves.

# 3 Proposed Method

## 3.1 System Architecture

In the whole framework, we design and simultaneously extract user features, relationship features, and behavior features to represent the social attribute relationships of users. The user feature represents the inherent characteristics of users registered on the social networking platform. The relationship feature involves constructing different social networks based on users' various social relations and extracting features using different graph algorithms on each network. The behavior feature is derived from users' evolving actions on the social networking platform over time. We merge the features extracted from these three aspects to form the node features of users. Finally, we utilize node-level classification of GraphSAGE to model the users. The framework of our method is shown in Fig. 1.

# 4 Feature Selection

**User Feature.** In this paper, we use $F_U$ to represent user features. User feature refers to the characteristics that users have when they register on the social networking platform. In the dataset we use, user features include the gender, age and registration duration recorded by the platform, as well as the labels assigned to each user's identity.

Typically, the information provided by normal users during registration on the social networking platform reflects their real circumstances. On the other hand, spammers often register accounts with the intention of hiding their true identities or creating a large number of accounts rapidly, resulting in concentrated and patterned account information. Although user features are simple attributes associated with nodes, they play an important role in spammer detection. We use one-hot encoding to represent the gender, where a value of 1 corresponds to male and 0 corresponds to female. We normalized the age and registration duration of the users. The description of user information is shown in Table 1.

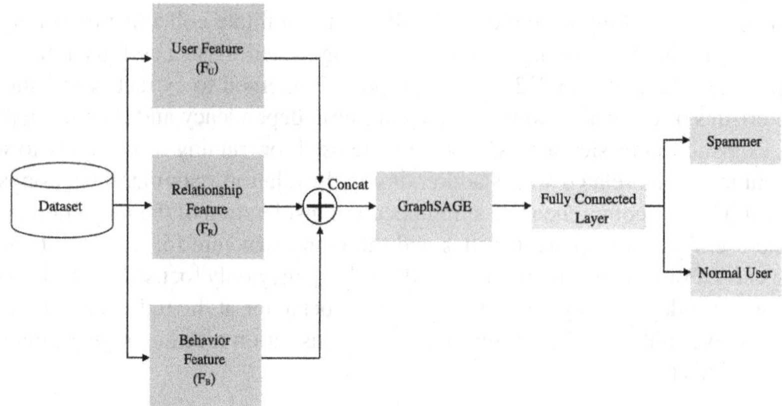


**Fig. 1.** The framework of GSAR

**Table 1.** The description of user information

| Content | Range | Description |
|---|---|---|
| ID | [0,539773] | Representing the account of each user |
| Gender | 0 or 1 | Representing male or female |
| Registration duration | [0,1] | The registration duration has been normalized |
| Age | [0,1] | The age has been normalized |

**Relationship Feature.** In this paper, we use $F_R$ to represent the relationship feature. We are aware that in real-life situations, users on social platforms often have more than one type of relationship. We define the relationships between users as *R*, which represents a collection of *K* relationships among users. In this paper, the number of relationships is 7, and Table 2 lists the descriptions of these 7 relationships.

**Table 2.** The description of relation information

| Relationship ID | Relationship Type |
|---|---|
| $r1$ | Give a Gift |
| $r2$ | Add Friend |
| $r3$ | View Profile |
| $r4$ | Send Message |
| $r5$ | Pet Game |
| $r6$ | Meet-Me Game |
| $r7$ | Report Abuse |

Based on the 7 different relationships between users, we created 7 directed graphs, where each graph has the same set of nodes representing users, and the edges represent the relationships between users. We used *Turi Create* to generate features for each node in the 7 directed graphs. We employed the following five graph analysis methods to uncover the features of users within different relationships: *Degree* [4], *PageRank* [23], *k-core* [1], *Weakly Connected Components* [25], *Triangle Count* [24]. We then merge these extracted features together as the final relationship features for each node. Fig. 2 shows the method for extracting relationship features.

The Degree represents the relationship between nodes. In each relationship graph, we calculate the in-degree and out-degree for each node, corresponding to the user's receiving behavior and sending behavior, respectively. A higher out-degree of a node indicates that the user has a greater number of outgoing actions, while a lower in-degree suggests that the user receives fewer incoming actions. Due to the significant differences in receiving and sending behavior between spammers and normal users, spammers typically have more sending behavior and less receiving behavior, while normal users have relatively balanced receiving and sending behavior.

PageRank is a commonly used link analysis algorithm originally designed to address the problem of web page ranking in the process of web recommendation. It calculates the importance of nodes based on the link relationships between them. The core idea is that the importance of a node depends on the degree to which it is connected to other important nodes. In other words, in PageRank, the importance of a node is determined by the number of links to it and the importance of the nodes linking to it. We compute the PageRank value for each node to reflect its importance in the graph, where a higher PageRank value indicates a more important node. The function for calculating the PageRank value is as follows:

$$PR(xi) = (1 - d) + d \sum_{xj \in P(xj)}^{L} \frac{PR(xi)}{L(xi)} \tag{1}$$

where $PR(x_i)$ represents the PageRank value of node $x_i$, $d$ is the damping factor, set to 0.85, it signifies that users are 85% likely to continue browsing web pages through links rather than randomly navigating to other pages, $P\ (x_j)$ refers to the set of nodes that link to $x_i$, $L(x_j)$ represents the count of outgoing links from node $x_i$.

The K-core is an important graph algorithm used for graph structure analysis and removal of redundant nodes. It is used to partition a large graph into subgraphs based on the K-core concept. The core idea of K-core is to gradually remove nodes with smaller degrees until the remaining nodes in the graph have at least K neighbors. We compute the Core-Number for each node to reflect its importance in the graph. The Core-Number indicates the number of neighbors that a node has after iterative pruning, and a higher Core-Number value indicates greater importance and centrality of the node in the graph.

The Weakly Connected Components is used to group nodes in a graph based on weak connectivity. Weak connectivity refers to considering the directed edges in a graph as undirected edges, such that if there is a path between two nodes, they are considered mutually reachable. If there exists a path between any two nodes in the graph, then the graph is a weakly connected graph. We extract the component-size as a feature for each node, which represents the number of nodes in each component. The size of the

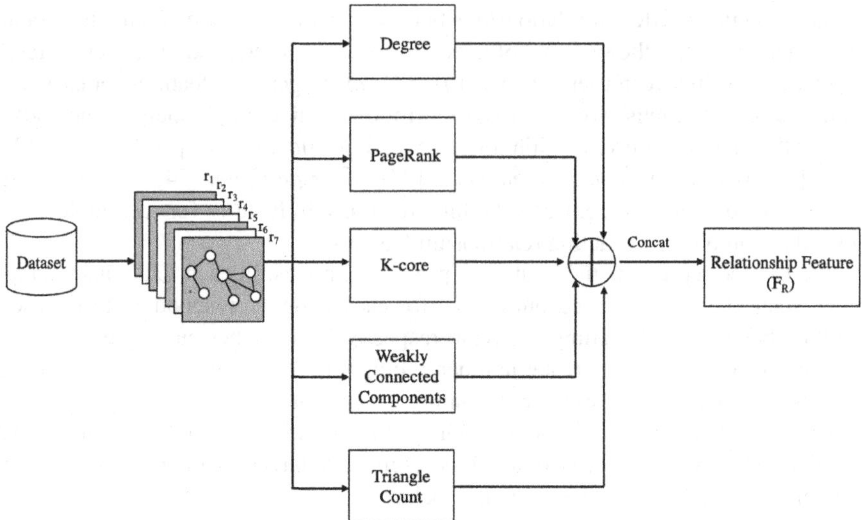


**Fig. 2.** The method for extracting relationship features

component-size can indicate the scale of different components. If a node belongs to a larger component-size, it implies that the node has stronger connectivity in the graph. In a social network, it indicates that the node is directly or indirectly connected to many individuals and has a greater influence.

The Triangle Count algorithm is a commonly used measure of connectivity in social network analysis. Its core idea is to count the number of triangles formed by a target node and its two adjacent nodes. In this algorithm, we ignore the direction of edges between nodes and treat the directed graph as an undirected graph. We extract the triangle count for each node as a feature. In a social network, when a user establishes triangular connections with two other users, it indicates that these three users mutually know each other, which aligns with the typical social behavior of normal users. Spammers, on the other hand, tend to engage in one-way, indiscriminate sending behavior towards other users, and the likelihood of strong associations between spammers and other users is generally low.

**Behavior Feature.** In this paper, we use $F_B$ to represent behavior features. Spammers and normal users have different purposes: Spammers aim to spread spam on a large scale, while normal users maintain social relationships with others. Consequently, there are significant differences in their behaviors on social networking sites. To uncover patterns in the diverse sending behaviors of users and extract behavior features, we employ the N-gram algorithm [5]. The N-gram algorithm is a commonly used technique in text analysis that involves breaking down a text into contiguous sequences of N elements. In our case, we split the user's behavior sequences and use them to identify distinct behavior patterns between spammers and normal users. To avoid high-dimensional feature space, we set $N = 2$, specifically using bi-gram.

We split the user's behavior sequence into consecutive pairs of elements, where each element corresponds to a relationship type. We then count the occurrences of all bi-grams to derive the user's behavior sequence feature. In our dataset, which consists of 7 types of relationships, for example, if a user performs the add Friend behavior followed by the send message behavior, the value for the sequence $r_2 - r_4$ will increase by one. The behavior sequence of spammer K is shown in Fig. 3.

## 5 GraphSAGE On Spammer Detection

In the context of spammer detection in social network analysis, traditional convolutional neural network (CNN) approaches are challenging to apply due to the non-Euclidean structure of graph data. Graph Neural Networks (GNN) [21] address this issue by updating node representations iteratively based on the features of the nodes themselves and their neighboring nodes. Compared to traditional machine learning methods, GCN has the ability to fully leverage the neighboring information of nodes. By aggregating feature information from neighboring nodes in the convolutional layers, GCN obtains richer information. This advantage empowers GCN in capturing complex relationships among nodes within graph structures. Additionally, GCN exhibits strong generalization capabilities as they can effectively extend to new nodes through weight sharing in the convolutional layers.

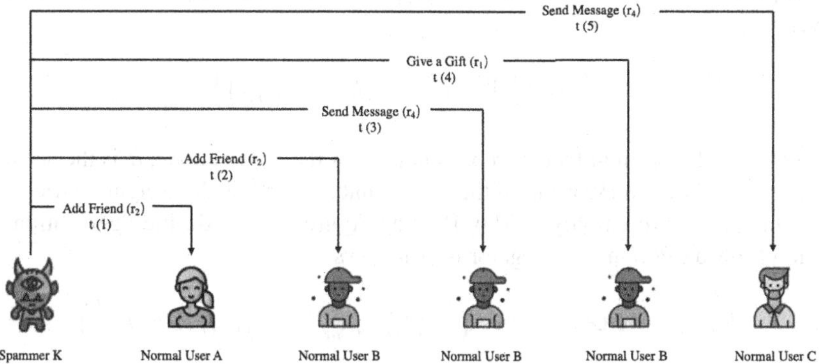


**Fig. 3.** The behavior sequence of spammer K

We propose using the GraphSAGE model for spammer detection, where each node's representation is obtained by aggregating the features of its neighboring nodes. In spammer detection, we focus more on analyzing the relationships between users and the users with whom they interact. This allows us to capture the local features of the nodes more effectively.

Given a graph $G = (M, E)$, where $M$ is the set of nodes representing users in the graph, and $E$ is the set of edges representing the sending relationships between connected users. Since spammers typically propagate spam through message sending, we choose to use a social network graph with the relationship

*Message*. $\{h_m, \forall m \in M\}$ represents the node features we have extracted. The main steps for performing spammer detection using GraphSAGE are as follows: Sampling, Aggregation and Classification.

**Sampling.** In our work, the center nodes are generated through random sampling. For each node, we divide the entire graph into $k$ layers. At each layer $g(1 \leq g \leq k)$ , we sample $N_g$, neighboring nodes. If the total number of neighboring nodes is less than $N_g$, we use the "With Replacement Sampling" method to ensure that the final number of sampled neighboring nodes is $N_g$. Typically, $k$ is set to 2.

**Aggregation.** After we have completed the sampling of nodes, we aggregate the features of neighboring nodes using different aggregation methods. During the aggregation process, the direction of aggregation is different from the direction of sampling. This means that we aggregate the features of first-layer neighboring nodes to their corresponding first-layer neighboring nodes, and then aggregate the features of first-layer neighboring nodes to the center node. As a result, the center node obtains the aggregated feature representation. The aggregation functions as follows:

$$h^k_{N(m)} = AGG_k\left(\left\{h^{k-1}_{m'}, \forall_{m'} \in N(m)\right\}\right) \tag{2}$$

where $k$ represents the layer at which the node is located, $h^k$ represents the feature representation obtained by aggregating the neighbors of node $m$, $N\ (m)$ is the set of neighbors in the $k$ layer, $m'$ is the sampled neighbor node, $h^{k-1}_{m'}$ is the representation of the sampled neighbor nodes in the $k-1$ layer, $AGG_k$ is the aggregation function in the $k$ layer.

$$h^k_m = \sigma\left(W^k \cdot Concat\left(h^{k-1}_m, h^k_{N(m)}\right)\right) \tag{3}$$

where $h^{k-1}$ is the original feature representation of the central node, $\sigma$ is the activation function, and in our work, we used the *ReLU* function, $W^k$ is the weight matrices.

In this paper, we employed Max Pooling Aggregator to do the aggregation. The function for Max Pooling Aggregator is as follows:

$$h^k_{N(m)} = AGG^{pool}_k = \max\left(\left\{\sigma\left(W_{pool}h^{k-1}_{m'} + b\right), \forall_{m'} \in N(m)\right\}\right) \tag{4}$$

$$h^k_m = \sigma\left(W^k \cdot Concat\left(h^{k-1}_m, h^k_{N(m)}\right)\right) \tag{5}$$

The final representation output is as follows:

$$z_m = h^k_m \tag{6}$$

where $\forall m \in M$ at $k$ layer, $z_m$ is the final representation output.

**Classification.** After obtaining $z_m$, we input it into a fully connected layer comprising multiple neurons, each of which is connected to the features in the node representation. The weight matrix of the fully connected layer performs a linear combination of these features, and the resulting linear combination is then non-linearly transformed using the *Sigmoid* activation function:

$$\hat{y}_m = Sigmoid(W \cdot z_m + b) \tag{7}$$

where $\hat{y}_m$ represents the final output, indicating the probability that the node. m belongs to the positive class, $W$ is the weight matrix of the fully connected layer, $b$ is the bias.

Our model is trained using a cross-entropy loss function, which is:

$$Loss = -(y \cdot \log(\hat{y}) + (1 - y) \cdot \log(1 - \hat{y})) \tag{8}$$

where $\hat{y}$ is the predicted probability of the sample being positive, $y$ is the sample label, which takes a value of 1 if the sample belongs to the positive class, and 0 otherwise.

# 6 Experiments

## 6.1 Dataset

The dataset used in this experiment was collected from a real-world dataset obtained from a social networking platform called Tagged. This social networking platform helps users meet new friends with shared interests and offers features such as messaging, gaming, and gift-giving. Tagged has over 100 million users, with millions of global monthly visits. In this dataset, there are 7 different types of relationships between users, as shown in Table 2. Users in this dataset are labeled as either normal users or spammers, with the labels manually assigned by domain experts. The dataset consists of 515 K normal users and 22 K spammers, accounting for 4.1% of the overall user population. The number of normal users is significantly larger than the number of spammers. Additionally, the dataset contains over 81 M actions, each associated with a timestamp. Statistics of the dataset are provided in Table 3.

**Table 3.** Dataset Statistics

| Dataset | Tagged.com |
|---|---|
| #user | 539774 |
| #normal user | 517428 |
| #spammer | 22346 |
| #actions | 81645631 |
| Proportion of spammer | 4.1% |

## 6.2 Evaluation Metrics

Since we have access to the true labels of each user, we use Precision ($P$), Recall ($R$), and F1-Score ($F1$) as the metrics to evaluate the performance of the model.

$$P = \frac{TP}{TP + TF}, R = \frac{TP}{TP + FN}, F1 = \frac{2PR}{P + R} \tag{9}$$

where $TP$ is the number of spammers that is detected accurately, $FP$ represents the number of incorrectly identified spammers, $FN$ represents the number of undetected spam senders by the model. The $F1$ is a metric that quantifies the balance between precision and recall. It is calculated as the weighted average of precision and recall.

### 6.3 Baseline

We compare our model with the other four baseline models RF [6], XGB [9], CSDE [12] and MDM [26]. For the RF, Random Forest is an ensemble technique rooted in decision trees. In the training process, it constructs several decision trees and amalgamates their outcomes to enhance prediction accuracy while mitigating overfitting concerns. Every tree is trained on a portion of the dataset, and the ultimate forecast is reached through the averaging or voting of results from each distinct tree. Additionally, Random Forest introduces an element of randomness by incorporating random features and data point subsets. This randomness aids in diminishing variance and fostering better generalization.

For the XGB, XGBoost stands as a sophisticated gradient boosting algorithm that harnesses the advantages of both boosting and gradient boosting machines. It's tailored for improved performance and scalability. In an iterative fashion, XGBoost constructs an ensemble of decision trees with a keen emphasis on rectifying the errors made in previous iterations. It integrates techniques such as regularization, parallel processing, and handling missing data to amplify its capabilities.

For the CSDE, they leveraged probabilistic modeling with a hybrid Markov model to capture relational sequence information. They developed a statistical relational model using hinge loss Markov random fields (HL-MRFs) and utilized boosted tree as the classifier. For the MDM, they capture user behaviors in terms of both long-term and short-term dependencies at individual and collective levels. At the individual level, the model focuses on a single recent behavior that may influence subsequent behaviors. On the other hand, at the collective level, the model considers the combined influence of multiple relations involved in the user's short-term behavior sequence. Meanwhile, they respectively utilize Logistic Regression and XGBoost as the classifiers.

### 6.4 Parameter Settings

In our experiment, we divided the dataset into proportions of 6:2:2 for the training set, validation set, and test set. We set the number of layers for sampling neighbors $K = 2$, number of samples in layer1 $N_1 = 25$, number of samples in layer2 $N_2 = 10$, the mini-batch size is set to 512.

## 7 Results

**Performance Comparison.** In this experiment, we compared our method with other baselines on a real-world dataset. Table 4 shows the performance of classification comparison with baselines.

As shown in Table 4, in our experiments, our proposed model achieved the best performance in terms of Precision, Recall, and F1-Score. Although CSDE had a higher Precision than our model using Mean aggregation, its Recall and F1-Score were lower than our model. Moreover, our performance was significantly higher than MDM, demonstrating the effectiveness of our approach on the real-world dataset.

**Table 4.** Results of classification comparison with baselines (Best in bold, second in underline)

| Methods | Precision | Recall | F1-Score |
|---|---|---|---|
| RF | 0.69714 | 0.81417 | 0.75112 |
| XGB | 0.75343 | 0.82573 | 0.78793 |
| MDM-LR | 0.69186 | 0.83641 | 0.75730 |
| MDM-XGB | 0.74254 | 0.82457 | 0.78141 |
| CSDE | <u>0.92915</u> | 0.86310 | 0.89491 |
| GSAR-MEAN | 0.92884 | **0.96102** | <u>0.94466</u> |
| GSAR-MAX | **0.93358** | <u>0.96085</u> | **0.94701** |

### 7.1 Performance across Different Features

In this experiment, we extracted user features, relationship features, and behavior features as three aspects of the features. Table 5 shows the performance of classification based on different features using Max Pooling Aggregation.

From the results in the first three rows, it can be observed that the choice of different individual features has a significant impact on the results. Among the user features, relationship features, and behavior features, the performance is optimal when utilizing behavior features, whereas the performance is worst when using user features. From the fourth to the sixth row, it can be seen that combining two different features together leads to better results compared to using a single feature alone, and there is no significant difference between different feature combinations. From the seventh row, it is evident that using the combination of all the proposed features yields the best performance for our model.

**Table 5.** Results of classification based on different features using Max Pooling Aggregation(Best in bold, second in underline)

| Experiment | Precision | Recall | F1-Score |
|---|---|---|---|
| $FU$ | 0.91985 | 0.95909 | 0.93908 |
| $FR$ | 0.92994 | 0.96044 | 0.94449 |
| $FB$ | 0.93119 | **0.96108** | 0.94590 |
| $FU + FR$ | <u>0.93203</u> | 0.95983 | 0.94573 |
| $FU + FB$ | 0.92983 | 0.96059 | 0.94496 |
| $FR + FB$ | 0.93184 | 0.96080 | <u>0.94610</u> |
| $FU + FR + FB$ | **0.93358** | <u>0.96085</u> | **0.94701** |

## 8 Conclusions

In this paper, we propose a method for detecting spammers based on Graph-SAGE graph neural network. The method leverages social attribute relationships of users to distinguish spammers from normal users. Even if spammers constantly change the content of their spam messages to avoid detection, they can still be identified by the different social attributes of spammers and normal users. Our approach designs and extracts user features, relationship features, and behavior features to represent the social attribute relationships of users. Experiments on the real-world dataset show the effectiveness of our model.

## References


1. Alvarez-Hamelin, J., Dall'Asta, L., Barrat, A., Vespignani, A.: Large scale networks fingerprinting and visualization using the k-core decomposition. In: Advances in neural information processing systems, vol. 18 (2005)
2. Benevenuto, F., Magno, G., Rodrigues, T., Almeida, V.: Detecting spammers on twitter. In: Collaboration, Electronic Messaging, Anti-abuse and Spam Conference (CEAS), vol. 6, p. 12 (2010)
3. Benevenuto, F., Rodrigues, T., Almeida, V., Almeida, J., Zhang, C., Ross, K.: Identifying video spammers in online social networks. In: Proceedings of the 4th international workshop on Adversarial information retrieval on the web, pp. 45–52 (2008)
4. Bollobás, B., Borgs, C., Chayes, J.T., Riordan, O.: Directed scale-free graphs. SODA **3**, 132–139 (2003)
5. Bozkir, A.S., Sahin, E., Aydos, M., Sezer, E.A., Orhan, F.: Spam e-mail classification by utilizing n-gram features of hyperlink texts. In: 2017 IEEE 11th International Conference on Application of Information and Communication Technologies (AICT), pp. 1–5. IEEE (2017)
6. Breiman, L.: Random forests. Mach. Learn. **45**, 5–32 (2001)
7. Cao, C., Caverlee, J.: Behavioral detection of spam url sharing: posting patterns versus click patterns. In: 2014 IEEE/ACM International Conference on Advances in Social Networks Analysis and Mining (ASONAM 2014), pp. 138–141. IEEE (2014)
8. Carreras, X., Marquez, L.: Boosting trees for anti-spam email filtering. arXiv preprint cs/0109015 (2001)
9. Chen, T., Guestrin, C.: Xgboost: A scalable tree boosting system. In: Proceedings of the 22nd ACM SIGKDD International Conference on Knowledge Discovery and Data Mining, pp. 785–794 (2016)
10. DeBarr, D., Wechsler, H.: Spam detection using clustering, random forests, and active learning. In: Sixth conference on email and anti-spam. Mountain View, California, pp. 1–6. Citeseer (2009)
11. El-Mawass, N., Honeine, P., Vercouter, L.: Similcatch: enhanced social Spammers detection on twitter using Markov random fields. Inform. Process. Manage. **57**(6), 102317 (2020)
12. Fakhraei, S., Foulds, J., Shashanka, M., Getoor, L.: Collective spammer detection in evolving multi-relational social networks. In: Proceedings of the 21th ACM SIGKDD international conference on knowledge discovery and data mining, pp. 1769–1778 (2015)
13. Geng, G.G., Li, Q., Zhang, X.: Link based small sample learning for web spam detection. In: Proceedings of the 18th international conference on World wide web, pp. 1185–1186 (2009)
14. Grier, C., Thomas, K., Paxson, V., Zhang, M.: @ spam: the underground on 140 characters or less. In: Proceedings of the 17th ACM conference on Computer and communications security, pp. 27–37 (2010)

15. Hamilton, W., Ying, Z., Leskovec, J.: Inductive representation learning on large graphs. In: Advances in neural information processing systems, vol. 30 (2017)
16. Hu, X., Tang, J., Gao, H., Liu, H.: Social spammer detection with sentiment information. In: 2014 IEEE International Conference on Data Mining, pp. 180–189. IEEE (2014)
17. Kiliroor, C.C., Valliyammai, C.: Social context based naive bayes filtering of spam messages from online social networks. In: Nayak, J., Abraham, A., Krishna, B.M., Chandra Sekhar, G. T., Das, A.K. (eds.) Soft Computing in Data Analytics. AISC, vol. 758, pp. 699–706. Springer, Singapore (2019). https://doi.org/10.1007/978-981-13-0514-6_66
18. Krestel, R., Chen, L.: Using co-occurrence of tags and resources to identify spammers. In: Proceedings of 2008 ECML/PKDD Discovery Challenge Workshop, pp. 38–46 (2008)
19. Lee, K., Caverlee, J., Webb, S.: Uncovering social spammers: social honeypots+ machine learning. In: Proceedings of the 33rd international ACM SIGIR Conference on Research and Development in Information Retrieval, pp. 435–442 (2010)
20. Li, C., Wang, S., He, L., Philip, S.Y., Liang, Y., Li, Z.: Ssdmv: Semi-supervised deep social spammer detection by multi-view data fusion. In: 2018 IEEE International Conference on Data Mining (ICDM), pp. 247–256. IEEE (2018)
21. Mandal, D., Medya, S., Uzzi, B., Aggarwal, C.: Metalearning with graph neural networks: methods and applications. ACM SIGKDD Explor. Newsl **23**(2), 13–22 (2022)
22. Markines, B., Cattuto, C., Menczer, F.: Social spam detection. In: Proceedings of the 5th International Workshop on Adversarial Information Retrieval on the Web, pp. 41–48 (2009)
23. Page,L., Brin, S., Motwani, R., Winograd, T.: The PageRank Citation Ranking: Bringing Order to the Web. Tech. rep., Stanford Digital Library Technologies Project (1998). http://citeseerx.ist.psu.edu/viewdoc/summary?doi=10.1.1.31.1768
24. Schank, T.: Algorithmic aspects of triangle-based network analysis (2007)
25. Skiena, S.: Implementing discrete mathematics: combinatorics and graph theory with Mathematica. Addison-Wesley Longman Publishing Co., Inc. (1991)
26. Yin, J., Li, Q., Liu, S., Wu, Z., Xu, G.: Leveraging multi-level dependency of relational sequences for social spammer detection. Neurocomputing **428**, 130–141 (2021)
27. Yu, D., Chen, N., Jiang, F., Fu, B., Qin, A.: Constrained NMF-based semi-supervised learning for social media spammer detection. Knowl.-Based Syst. **125**, 64–73 (2017)

# Lay Summarization of Biomedical Documents with Discourse Structure-Based Prompt Tuning

Yu-Hsuan Wu(✉), Chi-Min Chiu, and Hung-Yu Kao

Intelligent Knowledge Management Lab, Department of Computer Science and Information Engineering, National Cheng Kung University, Tainan, Taiwan
{p76104655,p76101720}@gs.ncku.edu.tw, hykao@mail.ncku.edu.tw

**Abstract.** Transforming complex biomedical texts into accessible lay summaries is a critical endeavor in Natural Language Generation (NLG). This study addresses the challenges associated with this task by employing a multi-aspect approach. Firstly, we undertake a comprehensive analysis of discourse structures within a diverse range of biomedical datasets and clarify underlying patterns and structures. Secondly, we designed the power of prompting strategies to integrate training on these varied datasets, thereby reducing the noise introduced by their diversity. This twofold strategy fine-tunes the model's training and enriches it with the ability to generate coherent and simplified lay summaries of biomedical content. Our experimental results clearly demonstrate the effectiveness of our study, underscoring its potential to make complex medical information more accessible to general readers.

**Keywords:** Natural language generation · Lay summarization · Discourse structure analysis · Prompt tuning

## 1 Introduction

In the realm of natural language generation, the domains of summary generation and text simplification have traditionally occupied distinct research trajectories, often discussed in isolation by scholars. However, the advent of global health crises, exemplified by the emergence of the COVID-19 pandemic, has underscored an imperative need: to render biomedical articles and research comprehensible to the broader public. These scholarly documents, typically authored by domain experts, are replete with specialized terminology and intricate concepts, thereby constituting formidable barriers for lay readers. In response to this challenge, the concept of biomedical lay summary generation has emerged as an auspicious avenue. Biomedical lay summaries endeavor to distill concise and simplified renditions of complex biomedical articles, rendering them more accessible and intelligible to a diverse audience. This task resides at the nexus of summary generation, and text simplification.


C.-Y. Lee et al. (Eds.): TAAI 2023, CCIS 2074, pp. 314–328, 2024.
https://doi.org/10.1007/978-981-97-1711-8_24

**Article:**
**The virus SARS-CoV-2** can exploit biological vulnerabilities (e.g. host proteins) in susceptible hosts that predispose to the development of severe COVID-19. To identify host proteins that may contribute to the risk of severe COVID-19, we undertook proteome-wide genetic colocalisation tests, ...

**Lay Summary:**
Individuals who become infected with **the virus that causes COVID-19** can experience a wide variety of symptoms. These can range from no symptoms or minor symptoms to severe illness and death. Key demographic factors, such as age, gender and race, ...

**Fig. 1.** The initial sentences of the article and lay summary of an eLife demonstrate distinctions in language usage and emphasis on background information.

In 2023, the BioNLP workshop@ACL organized the BioLaySumm competition [5], presenting a significant challenge in the field of biomedical lay summarization. Our research, conducted following the competition, focuses on analyzing its core tasks and primary dataset. This dataset comprises two distinct sub-datasets extracted from open-access biomedical journals, PLOS and eLife [6]. These journals cover a wide array of biomedical subjects, with PLOS encompassing biology, genetics, pathogens, and tropical diseases, while eLife predominantly focuses on life sciences. Each sub-dataset includes biomedical texts paired with manually-authored lay summaries. Notably, the creation process of these lay summaries varies between the two sub-datasets, with contributors independently composing summaries for PLOS and experts from eLife collaboratively generating summaries. We show the example of article and lay summary in Fig. 1.

Our examination of these sub-datasets revealed variations in biomedical themes, manual writing processes, and lay summary generation methods. We anticipated that these differences would also manifest in the stylistic and methodological aspects of the corresponding lay summaries. Consequently, our research adopts a discourse structure-based approach to thoroughly analyze and experiment with lay summary generation styles. Subsequent findings substantiate our initial observations, significantly enhancing lay summarization model performance in both learning and generation. Our approach, which integrates training for both sub-datasets, addresses resource inefficiencies and capitalizes on the limited availability of biomedical lay summary datasets. However, integrated training can introduce interference and bias due to differences in generation styles and methods. To mitigate these challenges, we employ specific prompt strategies during training to guide the model's understanding and adapt its learning for each dataset's unique lay summarization style and method.

In this research, following our comprehensive analysis and investigation of the dataset, we have introduced a comprehensive architectural framework for lay summarization. In comparison to leading methods showcased in the BioLaySumm competition, we have established that our method surpasses both the quality and stability of lay summarization. Our contributions, outlined in this paper, include:

1. A detailed examination and experimentation centered on the discourse structure of the BioLaySumm dataset.
2. Utilizing diverse prompt strategies to provide the model with supplementary information enhances its adaptability in lay summarization, while simultaneously mitigating interference and bias issues stemming from varying lay summary styles between sub-datasets during integrated training and knowledge sharing.
3. By employing the BioLaySumm competition's standard scoring, our method has consistently delivered superior results and enhanced stability when compared to outstanding teams in the competition. These findings affirm the exceptional performance of our approach in the realm of lay summarization.

## 2 Related Work

### 2.1 Text Simplification

Text simplification in the context of lay summarization involves the process of transforming complex, technical, or domain-specific content into more understandable and accessible language. This is a critical component of lay summarization as it ensures that the lay summaries effectively convey the core information from biomedical texts to a broader audience, including those without specialized knowledge in the field. The goal of text simplification is to bridge the gap between expert-level content and lay readers, facilitating better comprehension while maintaining the accuracy and integrity of the information.

The rapid advancements in neural network models over recent years have generated significant interest in the field of text simplification [9]. Several text simplification techniques and approaches have been explored in the related literature. These approaches often involve lexical [12], syntactic, and structural transformations to reduce the complexity of the text. Some methods employ controlled vocabularies or word substitutions to replace complex terms with simpler synonyms or explanations. Others focus on sentence and paragraph restructuring to enhance readability.

### 2.2 BioLaySumm 2023

BioLaySumm 2023 [5], organized within the BioNLP workshop@ACL, serves as a crucial initiative in the realm of biomedical lay summarization. It addresses the challenge posed by highly technical biomedical publications, aiming to make their content accessible to a wider audience. By harnessing natural language processing and machine learning, this competition focuses on generating reader-friendly "lay summaries" from complex texts, catering to non-experts and fostering advancements in biomedical abstract summarization. Using datasets derived from eLife and PLOS, BioLaySumm 2023 fills a gap in dedicated resources for this task, and as the competition concludes, it provides a basis for benchmarking and advancing future methods in biomedical lay summarization. We now shift our focus to an examination of the top-performing teams [4], serving as reference points for future comparisons with our proposed method.

1. **The Model of GPT Series** [14]: In their work, the Medicines Discovery Catapult (MDC) effectively employed this dataset to fine-tune various GPT series models, including the highly-regarded GPT-3.5-turbo (commonly known as ChatGPT) [10]. Within their implementation, the GPT-3 model, specifically text-davinci-003 (GPT-3), achieved top rankings in the competition. However, this method has limitations, notably underutilizing available data, particularly for LLM zero-shot techniques. Additionally, the inherent variability in GPT-series model-generated sentences introduces instability in reproducing lay summaries, leading to significant changes in the final output across iterations.
2. **Background Knowledge Grounding Augmentation** [13]: The approach presented in this paper involves collecting diverse biomedical knowledge and information available on the Internet, including sources such as Wikipedia, Simple Wikipedia, and the Unified Medical Language System (UMLS). This information is then combined with the dataset articles and fine-tuned on the Longformer-Encoder-Decoder(LED) [1] model. The objective is to leverage additional content information and enhance the effectiveness of lay summary generation. By incorporating a broader range of biomedical knowledge, the method aims to improve the quality and comprehensiveness of the generated lay summaries.
3. **Explicit Key Information Selection** [11]: VinBigData (VBD) JSC adopts a strategic approach by explicitly extracting vital information, or key sentences, from the source text before inputting it into abstract summarization models. In their most successful configuration, they fine-tuned the PLOS dataset with the Longformer model [1] and the eLife dataset with BioBART [17], aiming to optimize performance by adapting the fine-tuning process to each dataset's specific characteristics.
   - **ExSum(Lead)**: Extract the first three sentences (lead-3) and the last sentence of each article's section.
   - **ExSum(Key)**: Select the abstract, conclusion, and the lead-3 sentences of the remaining sections.

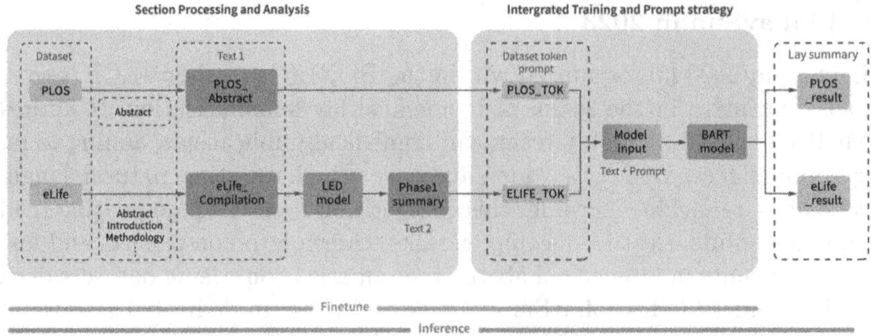


**Fig. 2.** The proposed architecture for our research

# 3 Methodology

This section introduces the proposed system architecture, which is shown in Fig. 2. In the initial phase of our proposed system architecture, we undertake research, analysis, and text discourse structure processing. Recognizing the constraints posed by model embedding, we prioritize the identification and extraction of crucial discourse structure elements essential for effective lay summary generation. Subsequently, we pursue an integrated training approach that combines the two biomedical datasets, PLOS and eLife, facilitating knowledge sharing. Through prompt tuning, we cultivate a lay summarization model characterized by exceptional adaptability to both datasets.

## 3.1 Discourse Analysis and Extraction

Biomedical research journals often contain excessively lengthy text content, often surpassing the token limits of conventional attention-based [15] Seq2Seq models such as BERT [3] and BART [7]. This frequently leads to issues of model truncation. Our dataset statistic Table 1 revealed that the number of retained words, post-conversion from the original text to lay summaries, is notably sparse. To address the issue of model truncation, we adopt a selective approach, prioritizing essential text content for lay summary generation while avoiding the inclusion of extraneous and potentially disruptive information. To achieve this, we conducted a comprehensive discourse analysis, segmenting the text into distinct sections, including Abstracts, Introductions, and more, which align with the field information provided in the official BioLaySumm dataset through "\n" separation. This section-based discourse analysis not only preserves text integrity and coherence but also enables more efficient adaptation to the token limitations of Seq2Seq models.

**Table 1.** The statistics of the eLife and PLOS training datasets, including the number of datasets, the average word count for articles and summaries, and the word compression ratio (%) from article to summary.

| Dataset | #Docs | Article #words | Sum. #words | Comp. % |
|---|---|---|---|---|
| eLife | 4,346 | 8,441.7 | 348 | 4.1 |
| PLOS | 24,773 | 5,864 | 176.6 | 3.0 |

### 3.2 Integrated Training and Knowledge Sharing

For our research, we recognize the substantial potential for knowledge sharing between the two distinct biomedical lay summarization datasets employed. Instead of separately training models on each dataset, we implement an integrated training strategy to harness the synergies between them. This approach not only optimizes resource utilization but also enables the model to gain insights from both datasets, promoting adaptability and robustness. By combining the valuable data from each dataset, we enhance our model's ability to discern the nuances in lay summary generation styles and methods. This integrated training methodology serves as a pivotal factor in our quest to achieve higher-quality lay summarization results.

### 3.3 Prompting Strategies

When integrating the two sub-datasets for training, addressing nuanced differences in biomedical topics and lay summary generation methods is crucial to avoid potential interference and bias during model training. To mitigate these challenges, we employ prompt-based fine-tuning methods, providing specific supplementary information to guide the model's generation process. We provide further details on these prompt strategies below, along with examples in Table 2.

**Dataset Discrete Prompt.** Incorporating the "Dataset Discrete Prompt" strategy involves prepending dataset-specific tokens to input artifacts before they are input into the model. For instance, the token **PLOS_TOK** is placed ahead of data originating from the PLOS dataset, while **ELIFE_TOK** is added in front of data from the eLife dataset. These tokens function as explicit markers, enabling the model to readily identify and distinguish between the datasets during both the training and generation phases. When a particular dataset is marked with such a prompt, it provides the model with crucial context, allowing it to discern the dataset in use, understand its thematic content, and grasp the nuances of lay summary generation style associated with that dataset. Subsequently, during the generation stage, the dataset discrete prompt guides the model in producing a lay summary that aligns with the specific style and theme of the dataset it corresponds to.

**Keywords List Prompt.** According to the research for latent prompt [18], text keywords as prompts are extremely effective for summary. Our prompt strategy harnesses the official dataset's keywords field, extracting and employing these keywords as prompts placed ahead of input articles. By utilizing dataset-specific keywords, this method encourages the model to focus on generating lay summaries that align with the essential concepts highlighted by these keywords. This approach serves as a guidance mechanism, directing the model's attention toward crucial information during lay summary generation. Additionally, these keywords assist the model in comprehending the text's overarching themes and differences between the two sub-datasets, akin to the dataset discrete prompt, enhancing the model's adaptability and the contextual relevance of the generated lay summaries.

**Table 2.** Show example based on two different prompting strategies.

| Prompt Strategies | Prompting Strategies Example (Article Inputs) |
|---|---|
| Dataset Discrete Prompt | **[ELIFE_TOK]** The virus SARS-CoV-2 can exploit |
| Keywords List Prompt | **(virus, biology, medical)** The virus SARS-CoV-2 can exploit |

### 3.4 Prompt Tuning

For prompt tuning, building upon the examples and methods from our prompt strategies Subsect. 3.3, we have determined that it is most effective to position the provided prompt at the beginning of the text. This approach is chosen to circumvent potential truncation issues that may arise if the prompt is placed at the end and subsequently fed into the Seq2Seq model, potentially leading to the truncation of essential prompt information. By positioning the prompt at the outset, we ensure its integrity and relevance are maintained throughout the generation process. This meticulous placement enhances the model's ability to interpret and respond to the prompt effectively:

$$y_i = \text{argmax} P(y_i|p, x_i) \tag{1}$$

where $y_i$ is the generated output for the $i$th input, $x_i$ is $i$th input example, $p$ represents the selected prompt we designed, $P(y_i|p, x_i)$ is the probability distribution over possible outputs $y_i$ given the input $x_i$ and prompt $p$.

## 4 Experiments

### 4.1 Evaluation Metric

In lay summarization, we assess beyond ROUGE [8] by incorporating readability metrics (FKGL**readability** and DCRS [2]). These metrics evaluate text simplification, ensuring lay summaries effectively convey complex information to a general audience.

1. Flesch-Kincaid Grade Level (FKGL): The FKGL metric 2 is a common tool for estimating the reading comprehension level necessary for a text. It accounts for factors like sentence length and syllables per word. A lower FKGL score signifies higher readability and a lower reading grade level.

$$\mathrm{FKGL} = 0.39 * (\frac{\mathrm{total\_words}}{\mathrm{total\_sentences}}) + 11.8 * (\frac{\mathrm{total\_syllables}}{\mathrm{total\_words}}) - 15.59 \quad (2)$$

2. Dale-Chall Readability Score (DCRS): The DCRS metric 3 as an additional readability measure. This metric assesses text simplicity by analyzing the presence of commonly used words. Specifically, it uses a list of 3000 common words; any word not found in this list is considered difficult. A lower DCRS score indicates greater text simplicity and improved language accessibility.

$$\mathrm{DCRS} = 0.1579 * (\frac{\mathrm{difficult\_words}}{\mathrm{total\_words}}) + 0.0496 * (\frac{\mathrm{total\_words}}{\mathrm{total\_sentences}}) + 3.6365 \quad (3)$$

### 4.2 Relevant Discourse-Structure Extraction

In this section, we delve into a comprehensive discourse-structure analysis of the eLife and PLOS datasets. Our primary objective is to examine the significance and relevance of the section structures within these two sub-datasets concerning lay summary generation. We strategically identify pivotal sections (**Abstract, Introduction**...) while excluding excessive text information, thus optimizing the subsequent integrated training process and mitigating truncation issues. As the text aggregated by the section structure often surpasses the token limit (2048 to 4096 tokens) of conventional Seq2Seq models, we employ the Longformer-Encoder-Decoder [1] Seq2Seq model, specifically designed for handling longer texts (>8192 tokens), to facilitate our research.

As we adopt the section as our standard unit for the discourse structure, our initial step involves filtering out less relevant and extraneous sections, such as "limitation" and "acknowledgment", which do not significantly contribute to lay summaries. This selective process is aimed at reducing subsequent experimental costs. We consolidate the retained, important sections and input this combined text into the Longformer model for fine-tuning. Following this, we generate lay summaries and assess their quality against ground truth data. This evaluation allows us to observe the impact of section-based discourse structure from both datasets on the quality of lay summarization.

Tables 3 and 4 results highlight the contrasting effects of section structures on lay summary generation within the two datasets. The datasets exhibit distinct section structures that lay summaries prioritize. In the case of PLOS, superior results are achieved by concentrating on the abstract section, while introducing excessive section text information leads to the dilution of critical training data. In contrast, eLife generates lay summaries by extracting information from various sections, avoiding a singular section focus. This confirms that the manual lay summary annotation methods differ between the two sub-datasets, leading to

**Table 3.** Evaluating section-based discourse structures in **PLOS** dataset's relevance to ground truth. ROUGE metric used. 'Abs.' stands for 'Abstract', and 'Intro.' for 'Introduction'.

| Section Combined text | Relevance ↑ | | |
|---|---|---|---|
| | R-1 | R-2 | R-L |
| All Sections | 48.98 | 17.00 | 44.62 |
| Abs. + Intro. + Result & Discussion | 48.64 | 17.11 | 44.61 |
| Abs. + Intro. + Methodology | 49.00 | 17.29 | 45.07 |
| Abs. + Intro | 44.19 | 13.28 | 40.89 |
| Abstract only | **49.15** | **17.38** | **49.83** |

**Table 4.** Evaluating section-based discourse structures in **eLife** dataset's relevance to ground truth. ROUGE metric used. 'Abs.' stands for 'Abstract', and 'Intro.' for 'Introduction'.

| Section Combined text | Relevance ↑ | | |
|---|---|---|---|
| | R-1 | R-2 | R-L |
| All Sections | **48.17** | **14.05** | **45.42** |
| Abs. + Intro. + Result & Discussion | 47.66 | 13.77 | 44.84 |
| Abs. + Intro. + Methodology | 47.41 | 13.27 | 45.30 |
| Abs. + Intro. | 47.49 | 13.00 | 45.36 |
| Abstract only | 46.47 | 12.96 | 43.87 |

different section structures emphasized by lay summaries, ultimately affecting the lay summary generation style.

Based on our discourse analysis, in subsequent experiments, we prioritized capturing the **abstract** section in the PLOS dataset, whereas eLife opted to process **multiple key sections' text** content as its initial step for both datasets. However, since eLife's selected sections are much longer than PLOS abstracts, we utilized the longformer trained on eLife's key sections to generate a 512-token lay summary. This approach aligns the text length with PLOS abstracts, facilitating integrated training in subsequent stages.

### 4.3 Integrated Training of Knowledge Sharing

As both datasets pertain to biomedical lay summarization tasks, our objective is to foster knowledge sharing through integrated training. However, as discussed in Subsect. 4.2, differences in discourse structure yield distinct lay summary generation styles, potentially leading to mutual interference during training. Thus, we carefully observe the impact of integrated training on both datasets at this stage. Notably, in both PLOS and eLife, the total text content after section extraction falls below 512 tokens. Consequently, we transition to utilizing the

**BART** [7] model as our primary model choice. BART currently stands as a robust Seq2Seq model, offering superior performance in short text tasks compared to Longformer.

**Table 5.** The impact of independent training of two sub-datasets and integrated training of two datasets.

| Approach | PLOS | | | | | eLife | | | | |
|---|---|---|---|---|---|---|---|---|---|---|
| | Relevance ↑ | | | Readability ↓ | | Relevance ↑ | | | Readability ↓ | |
| | R-1 | R-2 | R-L | FKGL | DCRS | R-1 | R-2 | R-L | FKGL | DCRS |
| $\text{BART}_{PLOS}$ | 49.03 | **17.49** | 44.85 | 15.00 | 11.66 | - | - | - | - | - |
| $\text{BART}_{eLife}$ | - | - | - | - | - | **48.24** | **13.60** | **45.38** | **10.11** | **8.41** |
| $\text{BART}_{Integrated}$ | **49.22** | 17.41 | **45.21** | **14.76** | **11.46** | 48.20 | 13.53 | 45.36 | 11.20 | 9.15 |

**Table 6.** The result of fixing the total number of **PLOS** dataset and adjusting the number of eLife data for integrated training. And inference in PLOS dataset.

| The number of eLife | R-1 | R-2 | R-L |
|---|---|---|---|
| 1500 | 48.82 | 17.14 | 44.85 |
| 2500 | 49.00 | 17.23 | 44.95 |
| 4346 | **49.22** | **17.41** | **45.21** |

**Table 7.** The result of fixing the total number of **eLife** dataset and adjusting the number of PLOS data for integrated training. And Infernece in eLife dataset.

| The number of PLOS | R-1 | R-2 | R-L |
|---|---|---|---|
| 1500 | 47.80 | 13.51 | 44.85 |
| 2500 | 48.03 | **13.58** | 44.95 |
| 4500 | **48.20** | 13.53 | **45.36** |

In our evaluation of dataset fine-tuning's effects on the BART model for lay summarization, we compared independent training on each sub-dataset with integrated training, as summarized in Table 5. Our findings show a noteworthy distinction: integrated training significantly benefits PLOS lay summarization by leveraging knowledge from the eLife dataset, leading to improved scores. However, for the eLife dataset, scores experienced a slight decline. This discrepancy suggests that when lay summaries exhibit distinct characteristics and generation methods across datasets, direct combination without proper preprocessing can introduce bias and noise, resulting in performance degradation.

To ensure a balanced ratio of data from both sub-datasets, we used 4300 data points from each. To explore knowledge sharing, we gradually introduced a small amount of data from one dataset into the other and observed the impact on evaluation scores. For example, we included 1500 eLife data points in a training set of 4500 PLOS data points. Similar experiments were conducted for the eLife dataset, with the results presented in Tables 6 and 7. These experiments demonstrate that introducing a moderate amount of data from different datasets can marginally enhance lay summary quality, showcasing the potential of knowledge sharing in improving lay summarization outcomes.

### 4.4 Prompt Tuning

To address potential issues of integrated training causing style interference, we've adopted integrated training alongside strategic prompts. Our prompt strategy explores various approaches to enhance the model's ability to generate precise summaries for both datasets. This includes prompts using dataset discrete tokens for recognition and additional prompts based on dataset-specific keywords within the data, enriching the model's understanding of the task.

**Table 8.** The impact of prompting strategies using integrated training on the BART model.

| Prompt Strategies | Relevance ↑ | | | Readability ↓ | |
|---|---|---|---|---|---|
| | R-1 | R-2 | R-L | FKGL | DCRS |
| No Prompt Adding | 48.71 | 15.47 | 45.29 | 12.98 | 10.31 |
| Keywords List Prompt | 49.58 | 16.10 | 46.10 | 12.97 | 10.25 |
| Dataset Discrete Prompt | **49.97** | **16.42** | **46.52** | **12.92** | **10.12** |
| Both Prompt | 49.66 | 16.15 | 46.20 | 13.03 | 10.20 |

Upon analyzing the indicator Table 8, when we incorporate prompt strategies during fine-tuning on the BART model, we observe significant enhancements in both relevance and readability compared to cases without prompts. Particularly, the utilization of dataset discrete prompts yields the most remarkable improvements during the fine-tuning process. These findings underscore the critical importance of enabling the model to accurately discern and comprehend the distinctive generative styles associated with both datasets.

### 4.5 Performance

To evaluate the effectiveness of our research methods in the context of lay summarization, we conducted a comparative analysis. Our evaluation method involves separately calculating the evaluation metrics for both datasets and then averaging the results to obtain the final score. We compared these metric scores from our research experiments with those obtained using basic architecture models and top-performing methods from the BioLaySumm competition. Our goal was to assess the impact of our current approach on biomedical lay summary generation within this dataset. To balance relevance and readability, we devised a comprehensive assessment metric (see 4). This metric involves subtracting the readability score from the average relevance score. A higher resulting value indicates a more harmonious balance between relevance and readability, highlighting a favorable synergy between these two aspects.

$$\text{Overall} = \left(\frac{R_1 + R_2 + R_L}{3}\right) - \left(\frac{\text{FKGL} + \text{DCRS}}{2}\right) \tag{4}$$

**Table 9.** The results of each method evaluation metrics

| Model | Relevance ↑ | | | Readability ↓ | | Overall ↑ |
|---|---|---|---|---|---|---|
| | R-1 | R-2 | R-L | FKGL | DCRS | Score |
| LED-8k | 45.01 | 13.06 | 42.97 | 12.56 | 10.61 | 22.09 |
| LED-16k | 45.35 | 13.14 | 43.13 | **12.24** | 10.51 | 22.49 |
| LED-Background Knowledge | 47.69 | 15.76 | 43.30 | 12.73 | 10.50 | 23.96 |
| Explicit Key Information | 48.29 | 14.69 | 45.02 | 13.01 | 10.17 | 24.41 |
| text-davinci-003 few-shot | 48.20 | 15.5 | 44.91 | 12.94 | 10.21 | 24.62 |
| Ours | **49.97** | **16.42** | **46.52** | 12.92 | **10.12** | **26.12** |

In Table 9, we showcase our method alongside other methods mentioned in the baseline section, along with the corresponding evaluation metrics. An examination of the table reveals that our method exhibits significant prominence across all evaluation metrics, indicating a notable performance improvement. Unlike large language models from the GPT series, which produce different responses each time, our method offers greater stability in lay summary generation, ensuring consistent results.

## 5 Ablation Study

In this section, we explore how dataset discrete prompts help the model recognize and adapt to the distinct themes and lay summary styles in our two datasets during integrated training. We evaluate the prompts' effectiveness in enhancing dataset recognition and improving the model's capacity to generate contextually relevant summaries for each dataset's unique requirements.

### 5.1 Reverse Dataset Discrete Prompt

To evaluate the model's ability to generate dataset-specific lay summaries as prompted, we conducted a reverse token experiment during inference, using prompts like PLOS data and ELIFE_TOK. The results, presented in Table 10, demonstrated lower scores and overall performance compared to the method without hints, affirming the effectiveness of our prompts in dataset identification and contextually appropriate summary generation. Additionally, the decreased scores when employing prompts from different datasets highlighted distinct generation styles between them, emphasizing the necessity of dataset-specific strategies in biomedical lay summarization.

**Table 10.** The impact of reverse the dataset discrete prompt.

| Prompt Strategies | Relevance ↑ | | | Readability ↓ | |
|---|---|---|---|---|---|
| | R-1 | R-2 | R-L | FKGL | DCRS |
| No Prompt Adding | 48.90 | 15.68 | 45.50 | 13.02 | 10.37 |
| Dataset Discrete Prompt | **49.97** | **16.42** | **46.52** | 12.93 | **10.12** |
| Dataset Discrete Prompt$_{reverse}$ | 47.83 | 15.67 | 44.81 | **12.79** | 10.52 |

## 5.2 Keywords List Prompt Analysis

In our examination of the keywords list prompt, we initially expected it to implicitly aid dataset differentiation due to the thematic differences between the two datasets. Additionally, we believed that keywords could provide supplementary information on text topics, potentially enhancing the model's focus on key content. Surprisingly, our results contradicted this hypothesis. As discussed in detail throughout this paper [16], the keywords column presented challenges, including missing values and coarse granularity, which hindered the model's learning process.

**Table 11.** Keywords field statistics. The first row indicates the number of examples with an empty list in the keywords field, the second shows the average number of keywords per example, and the last row is the counts of overall non-repeated keywords in each dataset.

| | PLOS | eLife |
|---|---|---|
| Num. of empty keywords field | 3471 | 2 |
| Avg. keywords per example | 16.71 | 2.28 |
| Num. of non-repeat keywords | 7235 | 31 |

- Coarse Keywords in the Datasets: Our analysis of the datasets revealed that the granularity of the keyword field is relatively coarse. Typically, the words found in this field represent broad themes or topics of entire articles, such as "biochemistry" and "cell biology". Regrettably, these keywords often fail to capture the nuanced details of an article, potentially leading to lower ROUGE scores.
- Missing Keywords in PLOS: Notably, the PLOS dataset exhibits a significantly higher number of empty keyword fields compared to the eLife dataset, as illustrated in Table 11. This discrepancy may result in inconsistent keyword prompts for instances from the two datasets.
- Low Keyword Diversity in eLife: We observed a substantial difference in the number of unique keywords and the average number of keywords per example between the PLOS and eLife datasets, as indicated in Table 11. Furthermore,

eLife provides keywords with an even coarser granularity for each data point than PLOS, potentially impeding our model's ability to capture article details within the eLife dataset.

## 6 Conclusion

This study presents a comprehensive analysis of two biomedical datasets, aiming to enhance the quality of lay summaries. Through in-depth exploration of the PLOS and eLife datasets, we achieved significant improvements in lay summary generation. Integrating information from both datasets and fine-tuning our model with strategic prompt tuning strengthened its ability to generate tailored lay summaries. These practices led to outstanding performance, surpassing other methods applied to the same datasets. Beyond score improvements, our study provides verification of each experimental step, enhancing research credibility and offering guidance for future endeavors in the field. By leveraging advanced models, our work highlights the potential of producing high-quality lay summaries and underscores the importance of dataset analysis and innovative approaches.

## References

1. Beltagy, I., Peters, M.E., Cohan, A.: Longformer: The long-document transformer. arXiv preprint arXiv:2004.05150 (2020). https://doi.org/10.48550/arXiv.2004.05150
2. Chall, J.S., Dale, E.: Readability revisited: The new Dale-Chall readability formula. Brookline Books (1995). https://books.google.co.uk/books?id=2nbuAAAAMAAJ
3. Devlin, J., Chang, M.W., Lee, K., Toutanova, K.: Bert: pre-training of deep bidirectional transformers for language understanding. arXiv preprint arXiv:1810.04805 (2018)
4. Goldsack, T., et al.: BioLaySumm 2023 shared task: lay summarisation of biomedical research articles. In: The 22nd Workshop on Biomedical Natural Language Processing and BioNLP Shared Tasks, pp. 468–477. Association for Computational Linguistics, Toronto, Canada, July 2023. https://doi.org/10.18653/v1/2023.bionlp-1.44, https://aclanthology.org/2023.bionlp-1.44
5. Goldsack, T., et al.: Overview of the biolaysumm 2023 shared task on lay summarization of biomedical research articles. In: Proceedings of the 22st Workshop on Biomedical Language Processing. Association for Computational Linguistics, Toronto, Canada (2023)
6. Goldsack, T., Zhang, Z., Lin, C., Scarton, C.: Making science simple: corpora for the lay summarisation of scientific literature. In: Proceedings of the 2022 Conference on Empirical Methods in Natural Language Processing, pp. 10589–10604. Association for Computational Linguistics, Abu Dhabi, United Arab Emirates, December 2022. https://aclanthology.org/2022.emnlp-main.724
7. Lewis, M., et .: BART: Denoising sequence-to-sequence pre-training for natural language generation, translation, and comprehension. In: Proceedings of the 58th Annual Meeting of the Association for Computational Linguistics, pp. 7871–7880. Association for Computational Linguistics, Online, July 2020. https://doi.org/10.18653/v1/2020.acl-main.703, https://aclanthology.org/2020.acl-main.703

8. Lin, C.Y.: ROUGE: a package for automatic evaluation of summaries. In: Text Summarization Branches Out, pp. 74–81. Association for Computational Linguistics, Barcelona, Spain, July 2004. https://aclanthology.org/W04-1013
9. Nisioi, S., Štajner, S., Ponzetto, S.P., Dinu, L.P.: Exploring neural text simplification models. In: Proceedings of the 55th Annual Meeting of the Association for Computational Linguistics (volume 2: Short Papers), pp. 85–91 (2017)
10. OpenAI: ChatGPT: a large-scale language model for conversational AI (2021). https://github.com/openai/chatgpt
11. Phan, P., Tran, T., Trieu, H.L.: VBD-NLP at BioLaySumm task 1: explicit and implicit key information selection for lay summarization on biomedical long documents. In: The 22nd Workshop on Biomedical Natural Language Processing and BioNLP Shared Tasks, pp. 574–578. Association for Computational Linguistics, Toronto, Canada, July 2023. https://doi.org/10.18653/v1/2023.bionlp-1.60, https://aclanthology.org/2023.bionlp-1.60
12. Qiang, J., Li, Y., Zhu, Y., Yuan, Y., Shi, Y., Wu, X.: LSBert: lexical simplification based on Bert. IEEE/ACM Trans. Audio Speech Lang. Process. **29**, 3064–3076 (2021)
13. Rosati, D.: GRASUM at BioLaySumm task 1: background knowledge grounding for readable, relevant, and factual biomedical lay summaries. In: The 22nd Workshop on Biomedical Natural Language Processing and BioNLP Shared Tasks, pp. 483–490. Association for Computational Linguistics, Toronto, Canada, July 2023. https://doi.org/10.18653/v1/2023.bionlp-1.46, https://aclanthology.org/2023.bionlp-1.46
14. Turbitt, O., Bevan, R., Aboshokor, M.: MDC at BioLaySumm task 1: evaluating GPT models for biomedical lay summarization. In: The 22nd Workshop on Biomedical Natural Language Processing and BioNLP Shared Tasks, pp. 611–619. Association for Computational Linguistics, Toronto, Canada, July 2023. https://doi.org/10.18653/v1/2023.bionlp-1.65, https://aclanthology.org/2023.bionlp-1.65
15. Vaswani, A., et al.: Attention is all you need. In: Advances in Neural Information Processing Systems, vol. 30 (2017)
16. Wu, Y.H., Lin, Y.J., Kao, H.Y.: IKM_Lab at BioLaySumm task 1: longformer-based prompt tuning for biomedical lay summary generation. In: The 22nd Workshop on Biomedical Natural Language Processing and BioNLP Shared Tasks, pp. 602–610. Association for Computational Linguistics, Toronto, Canada, July 2023. https://doi.org/10.18653/v1/2023.bionlp-1.64, https://aclanthology.org/2023.bionlp-1.64
17. Yuan, H., Yuan, Z., Gan, R., Zhang, J., Xie, Y., Yu, S.: BioBART: pretraining and evaluation of a biomedical generative language model. In: Proceedings of the 21st Workshop on Biomedical Language Processing, pp. 97–109. Association for Computational Linguistics, Dublin, Ireland, May 2022. https://doi.org/10.18653/v1/2022.bionlp-1.9, https://aclanthology.org/2022.bionlp-1.9
18. Zhang, Y., Zhang, X., Wang, X., Chen, S., Wei, F.: Latent prompt tuning for text summarization. arXiv preprint arXiv:2211.01837 (2022)

# An Empirical Analysis of Gumbel MuZero on Stochastic and Deterministic Einstein Würfelt Nicht!

Chien-Liang Kuo[1], Po-Ting Chen[1], Hung Guei[2], De-Rong Sung[1], Chu-Hsuan Hsueh[3], Ti-Rong Wu[2(✉)], and I.-Chen Wu[1,2]

[1] National Yang Ming Chiao Tung University, Hsinchu, Taiwan
[2] Academia Sinica, Taipei, Taiwan
tirongwu@iis.sinica.edu.tw
[3] Japan Advanced Institute of Science and Technology, Ishikawa, Japan

**Abstract.** MuZero and its successors, Gumbel MuZero and Stochastic MuZero, have achieved superhuman performance in many domains. MuZero combines Monte Carlo tree search and model-based reinforcement learning, which allows it to be utilized in complex environments without prior knowledge of actual dynamics. Gumbel MuZero enhances the training quality of MuZero by guaranteeing policy improvement, which allows it to learn with a limited number of simulations for tree search. Stochastic MuZero broadens the applicable domains using a redesigned model, which allows it to cope with stochastic environments. Recently, an approach combining Gumbel MuZero and Stochastic MuZero was applied to a stochastic game called 2048, discovering a counterintuitive phenomenon: agents trained with only 3 simulations performed better than agents trained with 16 or 50 simulations. However, this phenomenon has only been observed in 2048 and awaits further investigations. This paper aims to examine two questions, namely Question 1: whether this phenomenon also happens in another well-known stochastic game, EinStein würfelt nicht! (EWN), and Question 2: whether the stochasticity of the environment is the main reason for the phenomenon. To investigate these questions, this paper analyzes the training results using stochastic EWN and four deterministic EWN variants. The experiments confirm that the phenomenon also happens in the stochastic EWN, while not in the deterministic variants, suggesting that stochasticity leads to better performance of agents trained with lower simulations.

**Keywords:** EinStein würfelt nicht! · Gumbel MuZero · Stochastic MuZero · Monte Carlo tree search · Reinforcement Learning

## 1 Introduction

MuZero [1] was proposed by DeepMind in 2019, which combined Monte Carlo tree search and model-based reinforcement learning. Being different from its predecessor, AlphaZero [2], MuZero can be utilized in more complex environments by learning a

C.-L. Kuo and P.-T. Chen—Equal contribution.


C.-Y. Lee et al. (Eds.): TAAI 2023, CCIS 2074, pp. 329–342, 2024.
https://doi.org/10.1007/978-981-97-1711-8_25

model to predict rewards, policies, and value functions without requiring prior knowledge of game dynamics. Consequently, MuZero successfully achieved superhuman performance in many games, such as Go, Chess, and Atari games. Following the advent of MuZero, researchers have worked on improving and extending some of its limitations, particularly in improving its learning quality and applying it to stochastic environments. First, Gumbel MuZero [3] was proposed to address MuZero's deficiency of policy improvement. It uses a novel tree search algorithm combining the Gumbel-top-$k$ trick [4] and sequential halving [5] to sample actions without replacement. With these modifications, it successfully achieved marvelous results on Go, chess, and Atari with a small number of simulations for tree search. Second, Stochastic MuZero [6] was designed to extend MuZero to stochastic environments, by using a stochastic predictive model to learn and plan. It not only achieved state-of-the-art performance in two stochastic games, 2048 and backgammon, but also performed remarkably in a deterministic game, Go.

Recently, Kao et al. [7] proposed a new approach combining Gumbel MuZero and Stochastic MuZero to exploit the advantages of both methods. They evaluated the combined algorithm by applying it to 2048, a stochastic puzzle game. The experiment results showed that agents trained with only 3 simulations achieved an average score of 394,645, even outperforming agents trained with 16 or 50 simulations. This *phenomenon* is intriguing because it is intuitively considered that agents trained with fewer simulations should perform worse than the agents trained with more simulations. Kao et al. [7] attributed the cause for this phenomenon to the stochasticity of the game. However, no further investigation was conducted to verify their assumption.

In this paper, we aim to examine two questions, namely, *Question 1: whether the above-mentioned phenomenon also happens in other stochastic games*, and *Question 2: whether the stochasticity of the environments is the main reason for the phenomenon.* To answer these questions, we investigate another stochastic game, EinStein würfelt nicht! (EWN), and design a series of thorough experiments.

For Question 1, our empirical experiments demonstrate that, in the stochastic game, agents trained with fewer simulations perform the same or even better than agents trained with more simulations. This result is consistent with the counterintuitive phenomenon discovered in [7]. For Question 2, we propose four deterministic versions of EWN by removing the stochasticity in the game, e.g., removing dice. In all deterministic EWN versions, we observe that agents trained with fewer simulations perform worse than agents trained with more simulations. This result is opposite to the phenomenon happening in the original stochastic EWN. In conclusion, our observations strongly suggest that the phenomenon happens in multiple stochastic environments and that stochasticity is the main factor leading to better performance of agents with fewer simulations.

## 2 Background

In Sect. 2.1, we will introduce the game of EinStein würfelt nicht! (EWN). Then, in Sects. 2.2, 2.3 and 2.4, we will review MuZero, Stochastic MuZero, and Gumbel MuZero, respectively. Finally, in Sect. 2.5, we will review the approach that utilizes Gumbel MuZero in a stochastic environment.

## 2.1 EinStein würfelt nicht!

*EinStein würfelt nicht!* (EWN), designed by Ingo Althöfer in 2004, is a two-player stochastic game played on a square-shaped board with 5 × 5 squares. At the start of a game, the blue player places six *cubes* numbered from 1 to 6 on the blue side (lower-right triangular area), and the red player places another six cubes on the red side (upper-left triangular area), as shown in Fig. 1 (a). In the original rules, players can decide the placement of their own six cubes. However, in international competitions, such as the Computer Olympiad, the initial placement of cubes is usually randomly and symmetrically generated to ensure fairness. In this paper, we follow the rule of international competitions.

After setting an initial board, two players take turns rolling a six-sided dice and moving the cube corresponding to the rolled number. The player must move exactly one cube in each turn; skipping a turn is not allowed. All cubes must stay in the 5 × 5 squares. Players can only move cubes toward their opponent's corner in vertical, horizontal, or diagonal directions. Take Fig. 1 (b) as an example. When the rolled number is 5, the blue player can move cube 5 to the upper, left, or upper-left square. If another cube already occupies the destination square, the occupying cube, regardless of its color, is removed from the board. If the cube relevant to the rolled number is already removed, the player has to move the cube whose number is either the next-higher or the next-lower to the rolled dice number, as shown in Fig. 1 (c).

There are two winning conditions in EWN: (1) when one cube reaches the farthest corner of the opponent, the player who achieves this goal wins; (2) when one player has no cubes to move, the player who removes the last cube of the opponent wins.

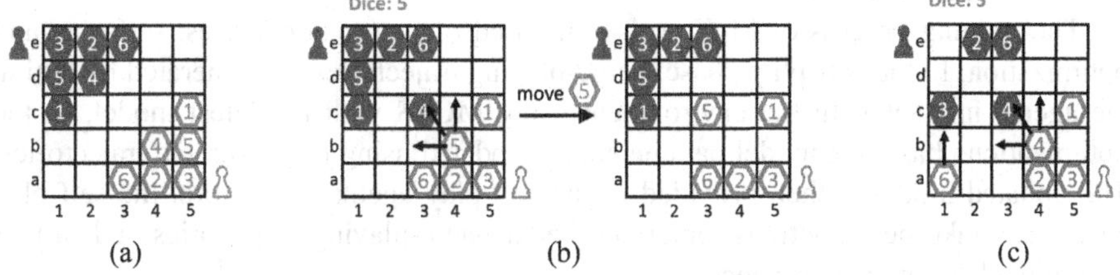


**Fig. 1.** Examples of the game rules in EWN. (a) An initial board placement. (b) The blue player has three possible actions when the rolled number is 5; then, the blue player moves the cube to the upper-left square, removing an opponent's cube. (c) The legal actions for the blue player when the matching cube (cube 5) is not on the board.

EWN is a popular game among computer game researchers. It has been adopted as an official game for competition by many international and domestic computer game tournaments, such as the Computer Olympiad held by the International Computer Game Association (ICGA), the tournament held by the Taiwanese Association for Artificial Intelligence (TAAI), and the tournament held by Taiwan Computer Game Association (TCGA). Developing an intelligent computer agent to play EWN is challenging because of the stochastic property of the game. The random six-sided dice play a key role in the difficulty of predicting future boards. An agent must take into account its opponent's strategy and future dice outcomes in order to play cleverly. In recent years, competitive programs are mainly implemented using Monte Carlo tree search (MCTS) or alpha-beta search [8].

### 2.2 MuZero

MuZero [1] combines Monte Carlo tree search (MCTS) with model-based reinforcement learning to learn the dynamics model through interacting with environments. The learned dynamics model allows the search algorithm to plan without a perfect simulator. Without any prior knowledge about the environments, MuZero achieves high performance in many domains, such as Atari games, Go, chess, and shogi.

The MuZero model architecture comprises three functions: the *representation*, *dynamics*, and *prediction functions*. These functions cooperate with the MCTS algorithm to perform multiple simulations to decide an action. Each simulation contains three steps [1]: *selection*, *expansion*, and *backpropagation*. First, the MCTS algorithm uses the representation function to transform an observation into an initial hidden state. Then, starting from the initial hidden state, the algorithm repeats the simulation process multiple times. In the selection step, the algorithm uses the pUCT formula to recursively select nodes until reaching a leaf node. In the expansion step, the algorithm uses the dynamics function to produce a new hidden state and its relevant reward and then uses the prediction function to obtain the policy and the value of the newly expanded hidden state. In the backpropagation step, the algorithm updates the statistics on all selected nodes using the value of the newly expanded hidden state. Finally, the algorithm chooses the most-visited child node of the root node as the best action. Since more simulations indicate that more subsequent states are considered, it is intuitive that MCTS with more simulations performs better.

The training process of MuZero is composed of two major phases: self-play and optimization. In the self-play phase, game-playing trajectories are generated by letting the agents interact with the environment using MCTS with the latest model. In the optimization phase, the model parameters are updated using the generated trajectories. The updated model is then provided to the self-play agents. Therefore, the self-play agents can take better actions, obtaining better game-playing trajectories and further improving learning performance.

### 2.3 Gumbel MuZero

The original MuZero algorithm does not guarantee policy improvement, and the training may fail when there are only a few simulations. Gumbel MuZero [3] is proposed to address this issue. By integrating the *Gumbel-top-k trick* [4] and *sequential halving* [5] with MCTS, Gumbel MuZero guarantees policy improvement, which significantly improves the learning quality even with limited simulations. Remarkably, it achieved state-of-the-art performance in Go, chess, and Atari games.

Here, we denote the available number of simulations as $n$. When $n$ is smaller than the number of legal actions, the Gumbel-top-$k$ trick [4] is used to sample $n$ different actions. To be more specific, for each action $a$, the algorithm calculates the sum of its relevant sampled Gumbel variable and policy logits, namely $g(a)+logits(a)$. Then, the algorithm selects the top $n$ actions with the highest $g(a) + logits(a)$ and performs a simulation on each of them. After the simulation, the algorithm calculates the transformed Q-value $\sigma(q(a))$ for each selected action, using a monotonically increasing transformation $\sigma$. Eventually, the algorithm chooses the best action according to the highest $g(a) + logits(a) + \sigma(q(a))$.

On the other hand, when $n$ is larger than the number of legal actions, sequential halving [5] with Gumbel is used to conduct simulations. For this case, the algorithm selects only $m$ actions at the root node. To elaborate, for each action $a$, the algorithm also calculates its $g(a) + logits(a)$. Then, the algorithm selects the top $m$ actions and allocates $n$ available simulations to them using sequential halving as follows. First, the selected $m$ actions are allocated with the same number of simulations. Then, half of the $m$ actions with lower $g(a) + logits(a) + \sigma(q(a))$ are removed. The remaining actions will continue to receive simulations repeatedly until only one action remains, namely the best action with the highest $g(a) + logits(a) + \sigma(q(a))$.

The model architecture and the training process of Gumbel MuZero are basically the same as those of MuZero, except for the training of the policy network. Unlike MuZero, which updates the policy network toward the MCTS search policy, Gumbel MuZero updates the policy network toward the target policy calculated from the Q-value of the actions.

## 2.4 Stochastic MuZero

The original MuZero model was designed only for deterministic dynamics. Stochastic MuZero [6] is proposed to expand its applicable domains by introducing the concept of *afterstates* [9] and utilizing a stochastic model instead of a deterministic one. Stochastic MuZero not only achieved superhuman performance in stochastic games, such as 2048 and backgammon, but also matched the state-of-the-art result that MuZero has achieved in a deterministic game, Go.

Stochastic MuZero constructs the search tree using *decision nodes* and *chance nodes* [10]. More specifically, decision nodes correspond to the hidden states, where actions are ordinarily selected using the pUCT formula. On the other hand, chance nodes correspond to the hidden afterstate, where chance outcomes are sampled from the chance probability prior.

Compared to the MuZero model, the Stochastic MuZero model introduces two additional functions: the *afterstate dynamics* and the *afterstate prediction functions*. The former receives a hidden state and an action as inputs and produces the next hidden afterstate. The latter receives a hidden afterstate as an input so as to predict the chance outcome probabilities and the afterstate value. To learn the stochasticity of environments, Stochastic MuZero's dynamics model takes a hidden afterstate and a chance outcome as inputs. Chance outcomes are modeled with a variant of Vector Quantized Variational AutoEncoder (VQ-VAE) [11] method.

Similar to MuZero, the training process of Stochastic MuZero is composed of two major parts, self-play and optimization. In the optimization phase, the VQ-VAE and the stochastic models are trained jointly.

### 2.5 Gumbel MuZero for the Game of 2048

Gumbel MuZero [3] ensures policy improvement with a few simulations; however, it was originally designed for deterministic environments. On the other hand, Stochastic MuZero [6] utilizes the stochastic model and chance encoder to learn the stochastic dynamics; however, it still requires more simulations to determine the best action. Therefore, Kao et al. [7] proposed a new approach combining Gumbel MuZero and Stochastic MuZero. To be more specific, this approach selects actions at the root node using a similar way to Gumbel MuZero; however, the search tree consists of decision nodes and chance nodes. Combining both algorithms allows this approach to learn in stochastic environments and achieve spectacular performance with a few simulations.

Kao et al. [7] applied their approach to the game of 2048, a single-player stochastic game, and achieved an average score of 394,645. In addition, they observed that the agents trained with only 3 simulations outperformed the agents trained with 16 and 50 simulations. Such a *phenomenon* that agents trained with fewer simulations perform better is counterintuitive, as it contradicts the previous training results [1–3]. Kao et al. [7] attributed this phenomenon to the stochasticity of 2048. However, they did not conduct further analyses to verify this assumption.

## 3 Our Designs

In this paper, we examine two questions related to the phenomenon that agents trained with fewer simulations perform better, namely *Question 1: whether the phenomenon also occurs in stochastic games other than 2048*, and *Question 2: whether the stochasticity of the environments is the contributing factor to the phenomenon.* To answer these questions, we choose EinStein würfelt nicht! (EWN) for investigation. For Question 1, we apply Kao et al.'s stochastic version of Gumbel MuZero [7] to EWN. For Question 2, we propose four deterministic versions of EWN. In this section, we will introduce two stochastic factors in EWN and how we modify the rules to obtain deterministic versions.

There are two stochastic factors in EWN: *initial boards* and *dice rolls.* On the one hand, randomly generated boards only affect the initial patterns of game boards. The stochasticity from random initialization can be simply removed by using a fixed initial board. On the other hand, the randomness of dice rolls directly contributes to the probabilistic transitions of the game. Therefore, if the stochasticity of dice rolls is removed from EWN, the modified version becomes a deterministic game, no matter whether the initial board is random or fixed. In Sect. 3.1, we will propose two methods for removing the stochasticity of dice rolls. In Sect. 3.2, we will summarize four deterministic versions of EWN based on the proposed two methods.

### 3.1 Removing the Stochasticity of Dice

In this section, we introduce two methods for removing the stochasticity of dice rolls in EWN. The first is to use a predefined sequence of rolled numbers. The second is to completely remove dice rolls and allow players to select the cubes to move unrestrictedly. The detailed rules of the two proposed methods are as follows.

**Fixed Order Dice.** In this method, the sequence of numbers rolled by the dice in the game is predetermined. To be more specific, the rolled number for each move is deterministically determined using a predefined sequence $\{1, 2, 3, 4, 5, 6\}$. For example, in Fig. 2, the first player rolls a dice and obtains a number of 1 at the start of a game. Then, the second player obtains a dice number of 1. In subsequent moves, both players obtain a number of 2, and so on. Note that in the seventh move of both players, the dice number is reset to 1.

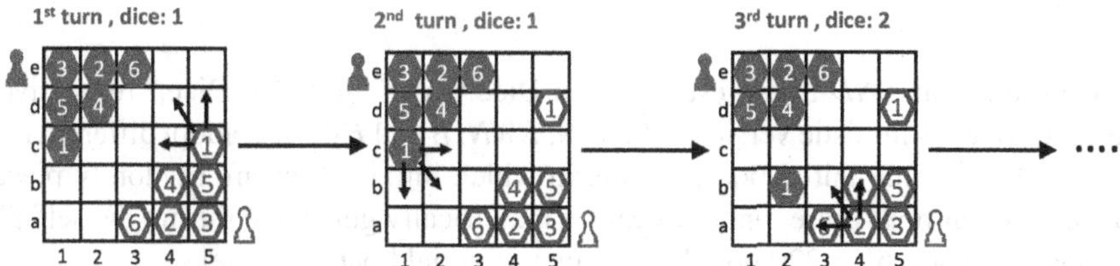


**Fig. 2.** Example of the gameplay in the Fixed Order Dice method.

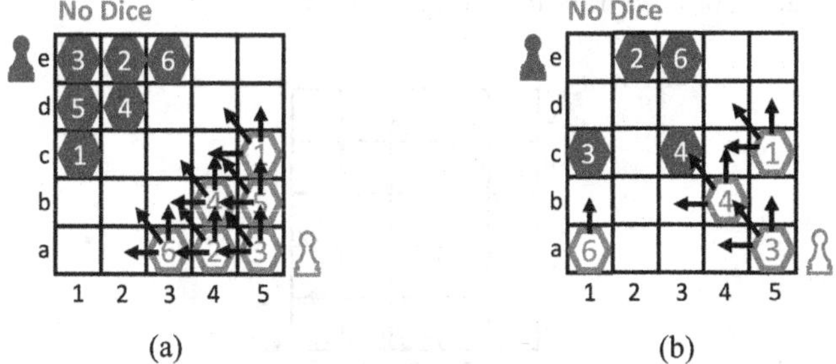


(a) (b)

**Fig. 3.** Examples of the legal actions in the No Dice method. (a) All 18 legal actions of the first player at the start of a game. (b) The legal actions for the blue player when there are only four blue cubes on the board.

**No Dice (All Movable).** In this method, the dice are removed from the rules, i.e., a player can move an owned cube that is still on the board regardless of its number. Figure 3 (a) illustrates an example of an initial placement in which all six cubes have three different movable directions, with 18 legal actions in total. Thus, the first player is able to choose one of the 18 legal actions to take. In the next turn, the second player can also choose one of the 18 legal actions. Figure 3 (b) illustrates another example that the blue player has only four cubes on the board, with 10 legal actions in total.

### 3.2 Deterministic Versions of EWN

In this section, we summarize four proposed deterministic versions of EWN, each combining one of the dice modifications with one of the initial board settings, including $EWN_{FD}$, $EWN_{ND}$, $EWN_{FD+Fs_0}$, and $EWN_{ND+Fs_0}$, as listed in Table 1.

**Table 1.** Comparison of four proposed deterministic versions of EWN.

| Version | Dice Rule | Initial Board Setting |
|---|---|---|
| $EWN_{FD}$ | Fixed Order | Random |
| $EWN_{ND}$ | No Dice | Random |
| $EWN_{FD+Fs_0}$ | Fixed Order | Fixed |
| $EWN_{ND+Fs_0}$ | No Dice | Fixed |

We use *FD* and *ND* to represent "Fixed Dice Order" and "No Dice," respectively. Our first two deterministic versions of EWN, $EWN_{FD}$ and $EWN_{ND}$, adopt different rules of dice but the same initial board setting in which initial cubes are randomly placed. Note that initial boards are randomly and symmetrically generated during the self-play training. There are $6! = 720$ possible symmetric initial boards in total.

Furthermore, in order to evaluate the performance of agents trained in completely fixed environments, we propose another two deterministic versions of EWN, $EWN_{FD+Fs_0}$ and $EWN_{ND+Fs_0}$, in which the game always starts with a fixed symmetric board $s_0$, as illustrated in Fig. 4, for both training and evaluation.

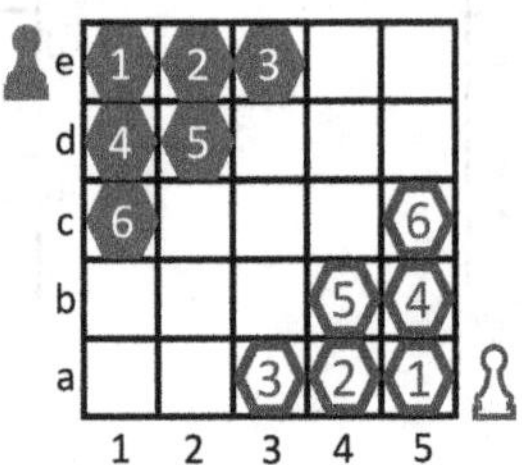


**Fig. 4.** The selected symmetric board $s_0$, used as the fixed initial board in $EWN_{FD+Fs_0}$ and $EWN_{ND+Fs_0}$.

All the modified versions of EWN eliminate the stochasticity of dice rolls, so there are no probabilistic transitions after a game starts. Thus, the modified versions become deterministic games. Nevertheless, they are similar to the original EWN since the rest of the game rules remain unchanged, which allows us to use the method in [7] to train agents with different simulations for them and compare their evaluation results with that of the original stochastic game to examine Question 2: whether the stochasticity of EWN is the key that leads to the intriguing phenomenon.

## 4 Experiments

In this section, we compare the performances between the agents trained with different hyperparameters under the stochastic EWN rules and the modified deterministic EWN rules. In Sect. 4.1, we will introduce the experiment setup, including the training and evaluation methods and the machine configuration. In Sect. 4.2, in order to answer

Question 1, we will describe the impact of simulation on the original stochastic EWN. In Sect. 4.3, in order to answer Question 2, we will analyze the impact of simulations on four types of deterministic EWN rules.

### 4.1 Experiment Setup

The experiment is conducted using a training framework based on Kao et al.'s work [7]. For the model architecture, all the model functions and the encoder are implemented using 3-block ResNet v2 [12], layer normalization, and $3 \times 3$ filter size. The encoder is designed with a codebook of size 32. The network input is comprised of 13 binary channels with $5 \times 5$ size, as shown in Fig. 5. For training, the Adam optimizer is applied [13], where loss functions are calculated by mean squared error. Each model is trained with two GPUs (GTX 1080 Ti), one CPU (Xeon E5-1650 v3), and 18 GB of memory for 45 h to reach around 1300 iterations.

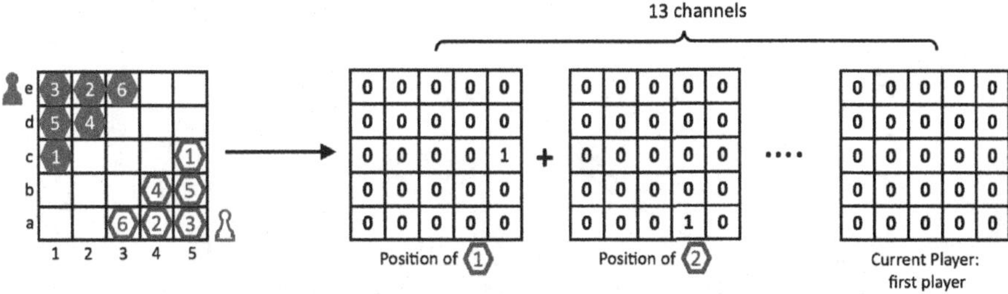


**Fig. 5.** Channel design of network model input. There are 13 binary channels with $5 \times 5$ size. The first to the twelfth channels indicate the positions of cubes 1 to 6 of the blue player and those of the red player, respectively. The last channel represents the current player, in which the first (blue) player and the second (red) player are indicated using channels filled with 0 and 1, respectively.

For evaluation on the random initial boards, an agent plays two games on each of 720 different initial boards, alternating as the first and the second players for a fair comparison, i.e., its winning rate is the average of 1,440 game results. For evaluation on the fixed initial board, an agent plays 100 games, with the agent and the opponent taking turns playing first. However, since the stochasticity has been eliminated, the game result becomes fixed if agents always play optimally. Hence, to increase the diversity of results, we implement softmax in the Gumbel search. To be more specific, the agent uses a softmax distribution to sample action from the top three actions with the highest transformed Q-values. Finally, for presenting the evaluation results, we calculate the Elo rating for each experiment by taking a high-simulation agent as the baseline. Note that we add an offset value to the original rating values to prevent them from being negative.

### 4.2 Gumbel MuZero for Stochastic EWN

To answer Question 1, in this section, we adopt the stochastic EWN rules to train two agents: *m6n6* and *m6n50*. To elaborate, *m6n6* indicates a setting of $m = 6$ sampled actions and $n = 6$ simulations during training. Note that 6 is chosen since there are at most six legal actions. For evaluation, we use $n = 50$ for both cases for a fair comparison, and we choose the 500th iteration of the *m6n50* agent as the baseline for the Elo rating. Similar to the findings in [7], both agents perform comparably in playing strength, as shown in Fig. 6. Moreover, as shown in Table 2, the *m6n6* agent reaches a 55% winning rate against the *m6n50* agent on the last iteration, i.e., the 1300th iteration. Our results demonstrate that under the stochastic EWN environment, training with low simulations, i.e., $n = 6$, can lead to the same and even a little better performance.

In addition, our best-performing *m6n6* agent achieves an exceptional level of performance, surpassing all other EWN agents at the 2023 Computer Olympiad. Specifically, it outperforms the 2022 champion [14] by a 65% winning rate.

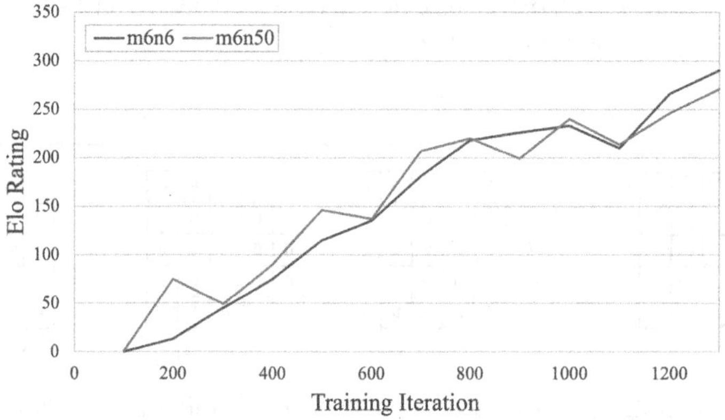


**Fig. 6.** Elo rating of the *m6n6* and the *m6n50* agents in the stochastic EWN environment.

### 4.3 Gumbel MuZero for Deterministic EWN

To investigate Question 2, we train and evaluate agents under four different deterministic EWN rules: $EWN_{FD}$, $EWN_{ND}$, $EWN_{FD+Fs_0}$, and $EWN_{ND+Fs_0}$.

$\boldsymbol{EWN_{FD}}$. In this case, we adopt the random initial board with the fixed dice order. Agents are trained using two settings, *m6n6* and *m6n50*. Note that 6 is chosen since there are at most six legal actions in this modified deterministic game. For evaluation, we choose the 600th iteration of the *m6n50* agent as a baseline. Figure 7 illustrates that there is a noticeable performance gap between the two agents. The agent trained with low simulations (*m6n6*) fails to reach comparable strength to that trained with high simulations (*m6n50*). This observation is inconsistent with the phenomenon observed in Sect. 4.2; however, it is consistent with what is usually seen in training other MuZero applications.

$\boldsymbol{EWN_{ND}}$. In this case, we adopt the random initial board with no dice. We train two agents: *m18n18* and *m18n50*. As Fig. 3 shows, the maximum number of legal actions becomes 18 since actions are no longer based on dice. We use the 500th iteration of *m18n50* agents as our baseline for evaluation. The result is illustrated in Fig. 8.

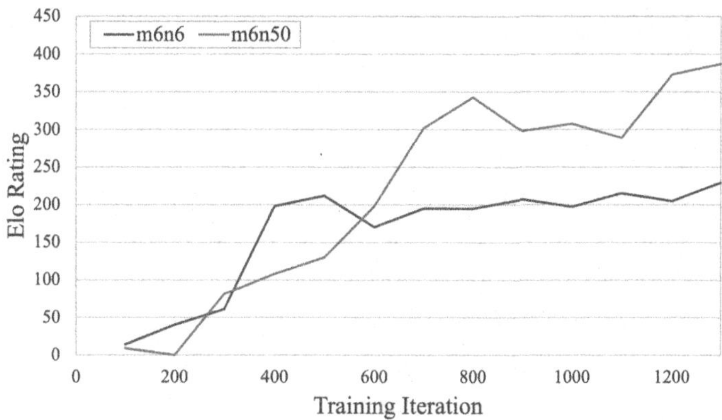


**Fig. 7.** Elo rating of the *m6n6* and *m6n50* agents in the deterministic $EWN_{FD}$ environment.

Apparently, the strength of the low-simulation agent is still far behind that of the high-simulation agent, which is consistent with the aforementioned $EWN_{FD}$ results.

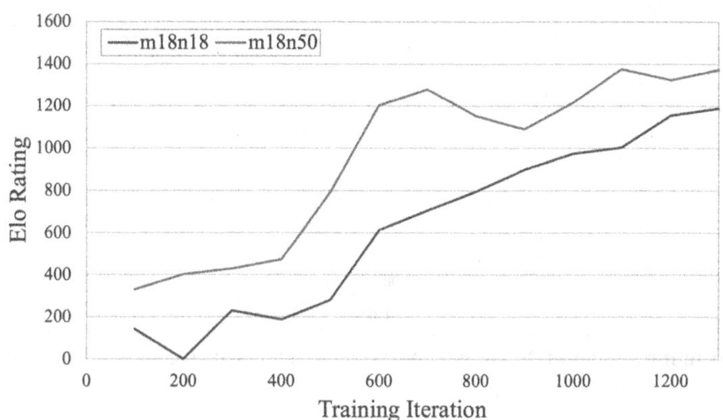


**Fig. 8.** Elo rating of the $m18n18$ and $m18n50$ agents in the deterministic $EWN_{ND}$ environment.

$\boldsymbol{EWN_{FD+Fs_0}}$. In this case, we adopt the fixed initial board with the fixed dice order. The maximum number of legal actions in this case is six, which is identical with $EWN_{FD}$. We evaluate two agents: *m6n6* and *m6n50*. Moreover, since we observe that the agents already converged at the 100th iteration, we conduct the evaluation within the first 100 iterations and select the 50th iteration of the *m6n50* agent as the baseline. Figure 9 shows that the performance of the *m6n50* agent has converged around the 70th iteration, while the *m6n6* agent still requires more time to learn.

$\boldsymbol{EWN_{ND+Fs_0}}$. In the last case, we use a fixed initial board with no dice for training. We evaluate the training of two agents: $m18n18$ and $m18n50$. Since the high-simulation agent converges at the 500th iteration, the evaluation is conducted within the first 500 iterations, and the baseline is the 200th iteration of the $m18n50$ agent. As shown in Fig. 10, the $m18n18$ agent performs significantly worse compared to the $m18n50$ agent.

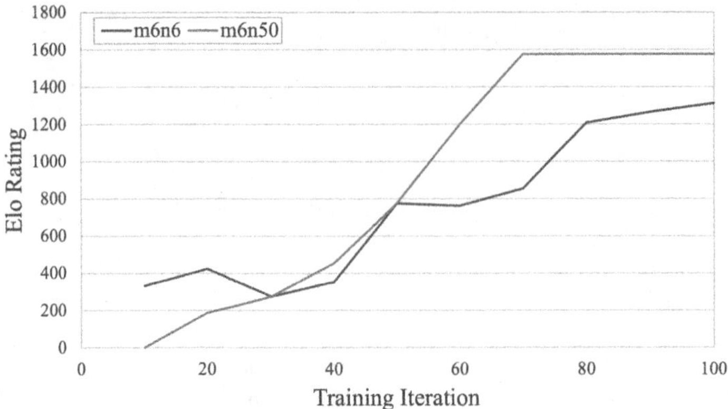


**Fig. 9.** Elo rating of the *m6n6* and the *m6n50* agents in the deterministic $EWN_{FD+Fs_0}$ environment.

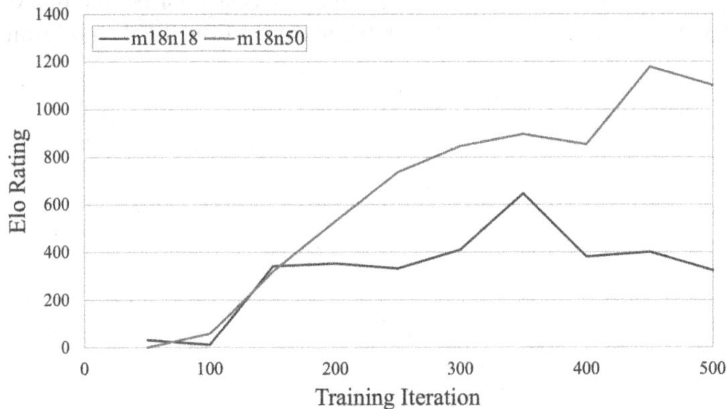


**Fig. 10.** Elo rating of the *m18n18* and the *m18n50* agents in the deterministic $EWN_{ND+Fs_0}$ environment.

### 4.4 Experiment Summary

To summarize, we answer Question 1 by demonstrating that training with lower simulations strengthens the learning performance in a stochastic EWN environment. Moreover, we answer Question 2 by redesigning deterministic EWN environments to demonstrate that the stochasticity of the environment is the key factor in the counterintuitive phenomenon.

We further evaluate the performance of agents trained in each environment by letting them play against each other. Table 2 shows the comparison between the performances of low- and high-simulation agents in their last trained iterations. We make them fight against each other directly. Apparently, the performance of the low-simulation agent is much more competitive under a stochastic environment. It can reach over 50% winning rates against a high-simulation agent. On the contrary, the low-simulation agents were completely defeated by the high-simulation agents under all deterministic environments. Finally, the experiments answer our questions.

**Table 2.** Comparison between the performance of low- and high-simulation agents in their last trained iteration. The winning rate is calculated by fighting against each other directly.

| Environment | $n_{low}$'s setting | $n_{low}$'s winning rate | $n_{high}$'s setting |
|---|---|---|---|
| $EWN$ | $\boldsymbol{m6n6}$ | 55% | $m6n50$ |
| $EWN_{FD}$ | $m6n6$ | 38% | $\boldsymbol{m6n50}$ |
| $EWN_{ND}$ | $m18n18$ | 45% | $\boldsymbol{m18n50}$ |
| $EWN_{FD+Fs0}$ | $m6n6$ | 40% | $\boldsymbol{m6n50}$ |
| $EWN_{ND+Fs0}$ | $m18n18$ | 0% | $\boldsymbol{m18n50}$ |

## 5 Conclusions

In this paper, we first propose four deterministic versions of EWN, in which the stochasticity of dice is removed. Utilizing the training paradigm proposed by Kao et al. [7], we then train and evaluate agents with different simulations in the stochastic and proposed deterministic EWN environments. The experiments show that in the stochastic environment, agents trained with fewer simulations perform better; conversely, in the deterministic environments, agents trained with more simulations perform better. This empirical result indicates that the stochasticity of the environments is a main reason leading to the counterintuitive phenomenon discovered in [7]: the agents trained with fewer simulations outperform the agents trained with more simulations. Furthermore, by using fewer simulations for training, our best-performing agent achieved an exceptional level of performance, winning the first place in the 2023 Computer Olympiad. Our work demonstrates that training with fewer simulations performs well in practice and is promising in stochastic environments.

In future research, we will conduct more experiments on other stochastic environments, such as the game of 2048, in order to further strengthen our conclusion. Besides, the exact explanation for why and how the stochasticity affects the performance of agents with different simulations will also be left for future work.

**Acknowledgments.** This research is partially supported by the National Science and Technology Council (NSTC) of the Republic of China (Taiwan) under Grant Numbers 110-2221-E-A49-067-MY3, 111-2221-E-A49-101-MY2, 111-2634-F-A49-013-, 111-2222-E-001-001-MY2; and Japan Society for the Promotion of Science (JSPS) KAKENHI under Grant Number JP22K12339.

## References

1. Schrittwieser, J., et al.: Mastering Atari, Go, chess and shogi by planning with a learned model. Nature **588**(7839), 604–609 (2020)
2. Silver, D., et al.: A general reinforcement learning algorithm that masters chess, shogi, and Go through self-play. Science **362**(6419), 1140–1144 (2018)
3. Danihelka, I., Guez, A., Schrittwieser, J., Silver, D.: October. Policy improvement by planning with Gumbel. In: International Conference on Learning Representations (2021)
4. Kool, W., Van Hoof, H., Welling, M.: Stochastic beams and where to find them: The Gumbel-top-k trick for sampling sequences without replacement. In: International Conference on Machine Learning, pp. 3499–3508. PMLR (2019)
5. Karnin, Z., Koren, T., Somekh, O.: Almost optimal exploration in multi-armed bandits. In: International Conference on Machine Learning, pp. 1238–1246. PMLR (2013)
6. Antonoglou, I., Schrittwieser, J., Ozair, S., Hubert, T.K., Silver, D.: Planning in stochastic environments with a learned model. In: International Conference on Learning Representations (2021)
7. Kao, C.Y., Guei, H., Wu, T.R., Wu, I.C.: Gumbel MuZero for the game of 2048. In: 2022 International Conference on Technologies and Applications of Artificial Intelligence (TAAI), pp. 42–47. IEEE (2022)
8. Chen, C.H., Chiu, S.Y., Lin, S.S.: Design and implementation of EinStein Würfelt Nicht program Monte_Alpha. Electronics **12**(13), 2936 (2023)
9. Sutton, R.S., Barto, A.G.: Reinforcement Learning: An introduction. MIT Press (2018)
10. Couetoux, A.: Monte Carlo tree search for continuous and stochastic sequential decision making problems (Doctoral dissertation, Université Paris Sud-Paris XI) (2013)
11. Van Den Oord, A., Vinyals, O.: Neural discrete representation learning. In: Advances in Neural Information Processing Systems, vol. 30 (2017)
12. He, K., Zhang, X., Ren, S., Sun, Ji.: Identity mappings in deep residual networks. In: Leibe, B., Matas, J., Sebe, N., Welling, M. (eds.) ECCV 2016. LNCS, vol. 9908, pp. 630–645. Springer, Cham (2016). https://doi.org/10.1007/978-3-319-46493-0_38
13. Kingma, D.P., Ba, J.: Adam: A method for stochastic optimization. arXiv preprint arXiv: 1412.6980 (2014)
14. Chen, C.H., Chiu, S.Y., Lin, S.S., Chen, J.C.: Monte_Alpha wins the EinStein Würfelt Nicht tournament. ICGA J. **44**(3), 111–113 (2022)

# Factor Analyses on Positive and Negative Evaluations of Games against Go Programs

Kyota Kuboki, Chu-Hsuan Hsueh, and Kokolo Ikeda(✉)

Japan Advanced Institute of Science and Technology, Nomi, Japan
{s2250002,hsuehch,kokolo}@jaist.ac.jp

**Abstract.** Analyzing users' preferences is important for many platforms to further improve users' satisfaction or make recommendations. This is the same for online game platforms. In this paper, we target a classical board game, the game of Go, and investigate the factors that make human players feel enjoyable when playing against Go programs on a website. In addition, we also investigate whether different players feel enjoyable in different ways. We use game records collected from the website, where players can evaluate games as enjoyable or not. We conduct statistical analyses using basic information, such as game lengths or players' win rates, as well as advanced analyses using information extracted by a strong Go program, such as the qualities of moves. The results show that some factors are generally common among players, while some factors show completely opposite preferences. For example, players generally prefer opponents with proper playing skills; meanwhile, some prefer close games and some prefer to win by large margins.

**Keywords:** Evaluation factor analysis · Player preference · The game of Go

## 1 Introduction

In recent years, the development of computer technology and the emergence of new methods have led to the rapid growth of AI. Researchers have employed AI in many fields. In the field of games, researchers have been devoted to making AI programs stronger than top human professionals. For the game of Go, AlphaGo [8] won against a top professional Go player in 2016, and a successor named AlphaGo Zero [9] beat AlphaGo the following year. These strong Go programs are valuable for players who aim to become stronger. In fact, many professional Go players utilize strong Go programs in their studies.

Meanwhile, some players, especially amateurs, play for fun. Many such players want to enjoy the gameplay rather than knowing the best moves or playing against stronger opponents. It is desired to have Go programs for such players, leading them to games that they find enjoyable. Some researchers created such Go programs based on

This work was supported by JSPS KAKENHI Grant Numbers JP23K11381 and JP23K17021. We would also like to thank Qinoa Inc. For providing the Go game records on Qinoa Igo.


C.-Y. Lee et al. (Eds.): TAAI 2023, CCIS 2074, pp. 343–357, 2024.
https://doi.org/10.1007/978-981-97-1711-8_26

common assumptions such as that players feel enjoyable when the skill levels do not differ too much [6, 7]. However, it is unclear whether those assumptions really hold. To our knowledge, there are no data-driven studies of what factors human players find enjoyable when playing games.

Moreover, different players may find different factors of games enjoyable. For example, some players may prefer close games, while others may prefer games that they win by large margins. Depending on the preferences of each player, it varies whether a game is enjoyable. Therefore, we consider it necessary to conduct player-by-player analyses to investigate the factors that make games enjoyable.

In this paper, we aim to analyze the factors that make a game enjoyable for each player and to clarify whether these factors differ from player to player. In cases where the factors differ, we investigate the tendencies of players. To achieve this, first, we collect game records that have been evaluated as enjoyable or unenjoyable by human players. Next, we perform statistical analyses on the collected games. We then analyze these games using the latest Go program and extract features for each game. Based on these features, we analyze the factors that contribute to enjoyable games. While some of the factors were generally common among the players, others were completely opposite among the players. A typical example has been discussed earlier, i.e., preferring close games or preferring wins with large margins.

## 2 The Game of Go

This section briefly explains the game of Go [1] in terms of the basic rules and terminologies. The board size is usually 19 × 19, and two players take turns placing black and white stones on the intersections on the board. The players aim to surround larger areas (called *territories* ) than the opponents.

A game ends when both players judge that there are no places worth playing and *pass* their turns consecutively. After that, the sizes of both players' territories are counted, i.e., the number of empty intersections within each player's territory. The player with a larger territory wins. A game also ends when one of the players *resigns*, usually when the player judges that there are no chances to win.

## 3 Related Work

### 3.1 Preference Analysis of Human Players in Games

One of the earliest studies to analyze player preferences and behavior within a particular game was that of Bartle's [3]. Bartle studied what players enjoyed doing on Multi-User Dungeons (MUDs). Bartle categorized players based on their preferences for objects (other players or the game world) and their corresponding behaviors (interactive or one-direction).

Tondello et al. [10] analyzed human players' preferences more thoroughly and introduced five player traits: aesthetic orientation, narrative orientation, goal orientation, social orientation, and challenge orientation. Their study demonstrated the effectiveness of the model in video games. However, since video games differ from board games in many aspects, their model is unsuitable for our study.

### 3.2 Analysis of Go Players

With the development of Go AI, researchers have employed the Go AI in various applications. One such application is to analyze game records to understand players' tendencies. For example, Gao et al. [4] presented a professional Go annotation dataset that includes rich in-game statistics calculated by a Go program, KataGo [11]. They showed sample tasks that could be done with the dataset, e.g., predicting mistakes during a game and predicting the outcome of a game.

Hayashita et al. [5] aimed to analyze the factors that make a game enjoyable for human Go players. First, they collected game records that have been evaluated as enjoyable or unenjoyable by human players. Next, they analyzed these games using KataGo and extracted many features for each game. Based on these features, they proposed several hypotheses about the factors that contribute to enjoyable games. However, their study did not differentiate the game records by player, possibly resulting in the strong influence of players with a large number of games. It is also possible that conflicting trends of players canceled each other out so that no trend was observed when viewed as a whole.

## 4 Approach

This section describes how we collect game records and analyze the games.

### 4.1 Collected Game Records

This study is collaboration research with Qinoa Inc., and we use game records and evaluations from Qinoa Igo [2], a website operated by Qinoa Inc. Qinoa Igo provides players with Go programs of various types and skill levels to play against. Players can evaluate games as *good* or *bad* once per game at any time point. According to Qinoa Igo's question statement, "did you find the game enjoyable, practice, etc.?", players evaluate good if they think so and evaluate bad otherwise. When a player evaluates a game as good or bad, both the game record at that time point and the evaluation are saved.

To analyze factors of enjoyment player by player, we only use game records that satisfy the following conditions, resulting in 6,911 games from 98 players.

- Games on 19 × 19 boards starting with empty boards
- Games with more than 50 moves
- Games played by players who played and evaluated 10 games or more[1]

### 4.2 Analysis Steps

We conduct the factor analyses of enjoyable games in two major steps. First, we conduct statistical analyses based on basic data such as each player's win rate and good rate (Sect. 5). Next, we conduct more advanced analyses using a strong Go program. In more detail, we let the Go program analyze (or, say, review) each game so that we can extract advanced features of each game for factor analyses (Sect. 6).

[1] Qinoa Igo saved players' IP addresses, and we used the IP addresses to distinguish players. Therefore, we could not identify the same player accessed from different IP addresses and could not distinguish different players accessed from the same IP address.

**The Used Go Program** We analyze the game records using KataGo [11], a powerful Go program based on AlphaGo Zero. For each state in a game, we can obtain from KataGo information such as the win rate, the territory lead by the player to move (e.g., a territory lead of 5 means that the territory size of the player to move is 5 intersections bigger than the opponent's), and the most and the second most promising moves. This study uses the following information.

- Information about a state
  - The (estimated) win rate
  - The (estimated) territory lead, etc.
- Information about a move
  - The rank in KataGo (more promising moves rank higher)
  - The (estimated) win rate after playing the move
  - The (estimated) territory lead after playing the move
  - The difference in the (estimated) territory lead from the pass move, which we call *gain*, etc.

**The Extracted Features of a Game.** We extract features for each game, either from simple statistics or based on KataGo. Note that a game on Qinoa Igo is played by a human player and a Go program. The following presents 4 features whose effects are easier to understand while we have extracted and analyzed more features.

- The game length (i.e., the total number of moves)
- KataGo's estimated territory lead at the end of the game for the human player, abbreviated as *human's lead*
- The promising-move rate of Qinoa Igo's Go program (i.e., the ratio of the moves by Qinoa Igo's Go program that match KataGo's most and second most promising moves), abbreviated as *program's performance*
- The number of unnecessary moves of Qinoa Igo's Go program (i.e., the number of moves by Qinoa Igo's Go program where the gains estimated by KataGo are lower than 0.5), abbreviated as *program's vainness*

## 5 Statistical Analyses

This section presents statistical analyses based on the basic data of the collected 6,911 games from 98 players. The games were evaluated as either good or bad by the players. The overall good rate of the games was 0.664. The result showed that the players were generally enjoyed, though there was still room for improvement. In addition, the human players' win rate was 0.865, which is very high. This indicates that the human players were generally stronger than Qinoa Igo's Go programs. The following subsections will

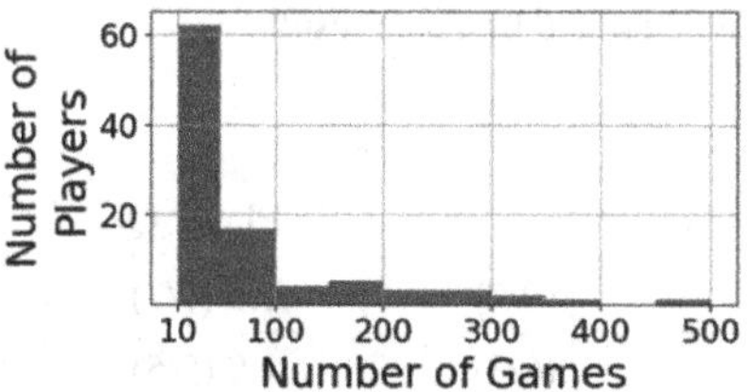


Fig. 1. The histogram of the number of games per player.

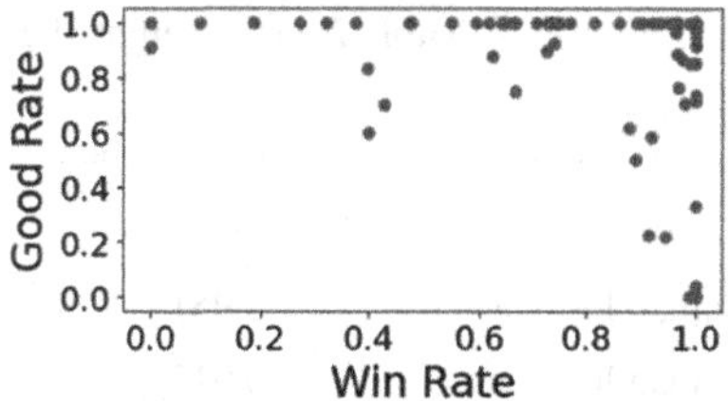


Fig. 2. The scatter plot of each player's win rate and good rate.

present more detailed analyses. Sub Section 5.1 shows the number of games per player. Sub sections 5.2, 5.3 and 5.4 show the relations between good rates and win rates, game results, and game lengths, respectively.

### 5.1 The Number of Games Per Player

First, we investigated the number of games played by each player, and Fig. 1 shows the results. Among players who played more than 10 games, 64 players played between 10 and 50 games, and 10 players played more than 200 games. The number of games played by each player differed greatly. When averaging the games from different players, we need to consider such differences in game numbers. Take the following as an example: Player X played 300 games and player Y 10 games. If we simply calculate the average over the 310 games without considering the number of games per player, the weights of the two players become 30:1. Namely, player X's results dominate the analysis. On the other hand, if we calculate the average of each player and then calculate the average of these averages, i.e., players X and Y weighing 1:1, too big influence comes from player Y, whose data are less reliable due to a small number of games.

To reduce the influence of players with a large number of games while still giving them more influence than players with a small number of games, we weighted different players' games as follows. Specifically, for a player with $n$ games, we set each game's weight to $\sqrt{10/n}$. For example, a player with 10 games has a weight of 1 per game, and a player with 40 games has a weight of 1/2 per game. In the following analyses, this weighting is applied.

Table 1. The weighted win rate and good rate of the target games.

| Win Rate | | Good Rate | |
|---|---|---|---|
| Average | Std | Average | Std |
| 0.725 | 0.406 | 0.840 | 0.234 |

**Table 2.** The weighted good rates separated by game results.

| Game Result | Good Rate | | | |
|---|---|---|---|---|
| | Overall | Player P's | | Player Q's |
| Human lost (resign) | 0.951 | - | (0/0) | 1.0 (7/7) |
| Human lost (pass) | 0.913 | 0.0 | (0/3) | 1.0 (5/5) |
| Human won (pass) | 0.876 | 0.667 | (24/36) | 0.571 (12/21) |
| Human won (resign) | 0.647 | 0.742 | (75/101) | 0.068 (7/103) |

### 5.2 Relation Between Good Rates and Win Rates

Table 1 lists the weighted win rate and good rate. Compared to the unweighted statistics on the whole target games, the win rate decreased from 0.865 to 0.725, and the good rate increased from 0.664 to 0.840. Note that compared to the unweighted statistics, the influence of players who played many games was reduced. We suspected that some players who played many games won almost all games and evaluated almost all games as bad. Except for such players, the general win rates were proper, and the games were generally favorable.

We further looked into each player's win rate and good rate, as plotted in Fig. 2. Note that some points overlap others in the plot. We found that many players evaluated only one of good and bad: 52 evaluated all their games as good, while 12 evaluated all their games as bad. All players with good rates of 0 had win rates higher than 95%, i.e., the players were much stronger than the Go programs. The result suggested that making Go programs stronger might help improve the good rate. In addition, among players with high win rates, some evaluated all their games as good. We considered two possible reasons: these players were satisfied with the current Go programs, or they evaluated the games irrelevantly to the gameplay.

### 5.3 Relation Between Good Rates and Game Results

Table 2 lists the weighted good rate for four categories of game results: (i) Human lost because of resignation, (ii) human lost because of owning a smaller territory counted after two consecutive passes, (iii) human won because of owning a bigger territory, and (iv) human won because the Go program resigned. Usually, a resignation is made when the player judges there is no chance of winning. Thus, the four categories from top to bottom roughly represent human players' losses by large margins in territories, losses by small margins, wins by small margins, and wins by large margins. The general tendency was that the good rate decreased from the top to the bottom. We interpreted that players tended to evaluate a game as good (or instructive) when they lost and as bad (or boring) when they won by a large margin.

However, we also observed that different players, even with similar skill levels, evaluated differently. Table 2 shows concrete examples from players P and Q, whose skill levels were estimated to be close. Player Q had a similar tendency to the overall one, though with a significantly lower good rate of 0.068 for the games that the Go programs

**Table 3.** Statistics of games where Go programs resigned.

| Game Length | #Games | Good Rate |
|---|---|---|
| 50–100 | 1479 | 0.591 |
| 100–150 | 305 | 0.584 |
| 150–200 | 834 | 0.626 |
| 200–250 | 881 | 0.671 |
| 250–300 | 421 | 0.665 |
| 300– | 76 | 0.665 |

**Table 4.** Statistics of games that ended by pass where human players won.

| Game Length | #Games | Good Rate |
|---|---|---|
| 50–100 | 0 | - |
| 100–150 | 0 | - |
| 150–200 | 0 | - |
| 200–250 | 98 | 0.968 |
| 250–300 | 933 | 0.922 |
| 300– | 556 | 0.818 |

resigned. On the other hand, player P had the opposite tendency, with the highest good rate of 0.742 when the Go programs resigned. The results showed an example that players had very different preferences.

### 5.4 Relation Between Good Rates and Game Lengths

From the investigation of game results and good rates, we found that the good rate of games in which the Go programs resigned was low. We considered two possible reasons: human players being much stronger than the Go programs and bad timings of resignation. In Go, the number of moves required to end a game (i.e., game length) differs depending on the game results. In particular, a game that ends by resignation may end early if the difference in playing skill is too large.

To find the cause of the low good rate in games that Go programs resigned, we further grouped games according to the lengths. Table 3 shows the results. For comparison, we did similarly for games that ended by pass where the human players won. Table 4 shows the results. For games that Go programs resigned, the good rates got lower as the games were shorter. Short games in this case mean that human players were much stronger than the Go programs. Big differences in territories had occurred at the early stages of the games. Namely, human players won easily and could not enjoy playing, making them dissatisfied. On the contrary, for games that ended by pass where human players won, the good rates got lower as the games were longer. We considered the reason to be that the

Go programs did not resign nor pass but continued to play even when the game results were clear, which was annoying and made human players unenjoyable.

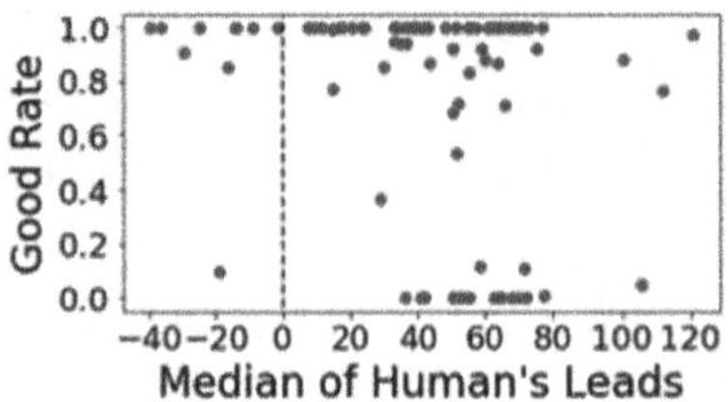


**Fig. 3.** The scatter plot of each player's good rate and human's lead median.

# 6 Advanced Analyses Using a Strong Go Program

This section conducts various analyses based on advanced features of games obtained from KataGo.

## 6.1 Relation Between Differences in Playing Skills and Good Rates

From the results in Table 2 and Fig. 2, we observed that the good rates were low when the human players were much stronger than the Go programs or when the Go programs had to resign because human players already led a lot in the territory size. In this subsection, we look at the win-loss results in more detail and use KataGo to analyze how much human players led in territories (i.e., the feature of human's lead) at the ends of the games. Since win-loss results were required, we excluded the games where players evaluated good/bad when the games had not ended, resulting 5,373 games from 82 players.

Even when the same player plays against the same Go program, the results (i.e., the territory lead) usually differ each time. We consider the median of the territory leads for a given player to be able to indicate approximately how much the player and the Go program differ in playing skills. Meanwhile, it is interesting to investigate the relation between the good rate and human's lead of each game, where the details will be presented in Sect. 6.3.

Figure 3 shows the scatter plots of each player's human's lead median (differences in playing skills) and good rate. We observed that some players evaluated all games only as good (46 players) or bad (10 players), similar to Fig. 2. For those who evaluated all bad, the medians of human's leads concentrated at 40–80. Such territory leads usually indicate big gaps in playing skills (roughly 4–7 handicap stones). On the other hand, when we looked at the players with good rates close to 1, we found a wide range of players, and many of them evaluated games to be good, even when the territory leads were between 40 and 80.

In order to clarify how each player evaluates good and bad differently, we conducted the following analyses that excluded players with extremely high or low good rates. Specifically, we targeted players with good rates between 0.1 and 0.9 and obtained 997 games from 21 players.

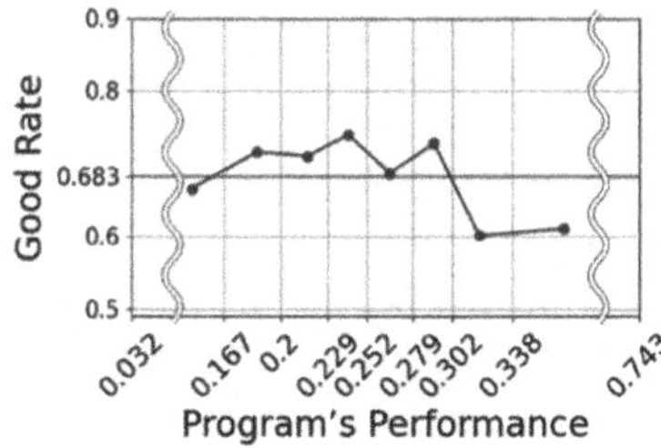

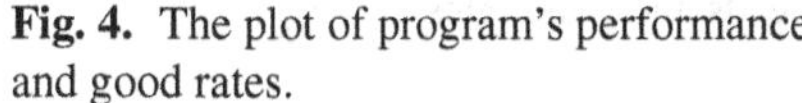


Fig. 4. The plot of program's performance and good rates.

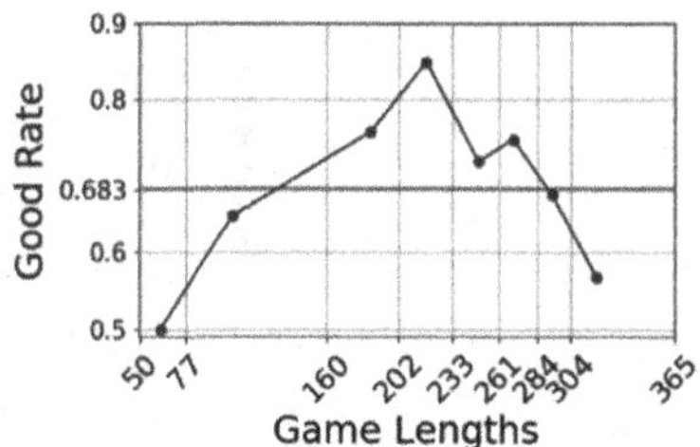


Fig. 5. The plot of game lengths and good rates.

### 6.2 Relation Between Single Features and Good Rates

According to the analyses so far, we confirmed that game results and playing skills of Go programs had big impacts on the evaluations of good and bad. Therefore, we further investigated three features, introduced in Sect. 4.2, that related to game results and playing skills: Program's performance, the game length, and human's lead.

We analyzed the overall tendency of players using single features. We plotted the features and the good rates following the steps below to show the tendencies.

1. For the target feature to investigate, we sorted the games according to the feature in ascending order.
2. We separated the games into several groups so that the *weighted* number of games in each group was the same. The weight of a game has been discussed in Sect. 5.1 (i.e., $\sqrt{10/n}$). The number of groups to separate was decided by the Sturges' rule based on the total weights of the games.
3. We calculated the weighted good rate and the weighted average of the target feature. We plotted the former as the $y$-axis and the latter as the $x$-axis.

**The Relation between the Program's Performance and Good Rates** Fig. 4 plots program's performance and good rates. The red line shows the overall weighted good rate. The values of program's performance were widely distributed, indicating two possibilities: (i) the provided Go programs had various skill levels, or (ii) even the same Go program might do well or poorly in each game. The good rate became low when the Go programs did too well (right end) or too poorly (left end). We considered it natural for human players to be dissatisfied when the opponent in that game was too strong or too weak.

**The Relation between the Game Lengths and Good Rates** Fig. 5 plots the game lengths and good rates. The curve had a clear mountain shape, where the good rates were low when the games were too short or too long. We suspected it to be a combination of two tendencies shown in Section 5.4: too quick resignation and too many unnecessary moves. More specifically, for cases the Go programs resigned too quickly (left end), players might not enjoy because the opponent was too weak. On the other hand, for cases the games were long (right end), players might be dissatisfied because the opponent did not resign despite a big difference in territory or because the opponent played many unnecessary moves in endgames instead of playing pass to finish the games.

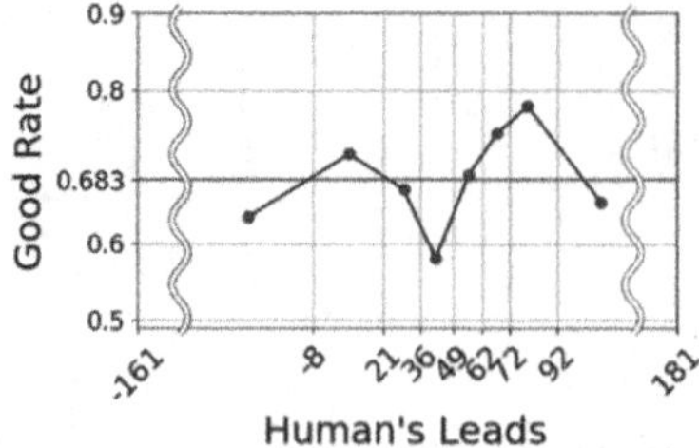


**Fig. 6.** The plot of human's leads and good rates.

**The Relation between Human's Leads and Good Rates** Figure 6 plots the human's leads and good rates. The good rates were low at the two ends and in the center (around $x = 40$). For the two ends, we suspected that human players did not enjoy when winning or losing by large margins in territories. Regarding the center where the good rate dropped drastically, we considered it unnatural and suspected that the result was a combination of different tendencies from different players.

### 6.3 Analyses of Individual Players Based on Two Features

Section 6.2 has shown the relations between single features and good rates, where the effects were summed up from several players. We found that the shape of the curve in Fig. 6 (human's lead and good rate) was hard to explain. We considered two possible causes of the unnatural shape: (1) different players had different preferences, which should not be summed up, and (2) the feature human's lead might influence human players' enjoyment in conjunction with other features, which should not be ignored. Therefore, in this subsection, we analyze player by player based on two features to see each player's tendencies or preferences.

**Human's Lead and Program's Performance** We first analyzed human's lead and program's performance together. We supposed the two features to have a relation because it is natural that human players' territory leads are smaller if more moves of the Go programs are promising moves.

Figure 7 shows players A and B's scatter plots of human's lead ($x$-axis) and program's performance ($y$-axis) in the games evaluated as good (blue circles) and bad (red crosses). Player A evaluated the games he/she lost ($x < 0$) as good more often than the games he/she won ($x > 0$), which might indicate that losing made him/her learn something and was favorable. Among the games that Player A won, good was more often evaluated when the Go programs played fewer promising moves (lower $y$). For different games with the same value of human's lead (i.e., the same $x$), lower $y$ values were likely to indicate that Player A also played fewer promising moves, or say, Player A played more bad moves. Similarly, we interpreted that Player A learned something from actually playing the bad moves and was satisfied with this. In contrast, Player B had more games evaluated as bad on the left side (losses or close games). We interpreted this to indicate that player B enjoyed winning games by large margins. In the games that he/she won, he/she evaluated many games as bad where the program's performance was high. Although the tendency to have more bad games in the upper parts of the figures was the same as Player A, we interpreted Player B to feel more comfortable winning when the opponent was weaker.

Scatter plots are suitable for seeing the tendency of each player in detail, but when there are many players, it is hard to analyze the tendencies at once. Therefore, we represented each player with two points (and the dotted line connecting the two points), where the circle point was the centroid of the player's good games and the cross point was the centroid of the player's bad games.

Figure 8 shows the 21 players whose good rate was between 0.1 and 0.9. We observed that circle points (good games) concentrated more on the center of the figure, while the cross points (bad games) were widely distributed. We interpreted that players generally preferred games with moderate territory differences and opponents with moderate playing skills. Despite the general tendency, we found differences in the relation between the circles and the crosses. Thus, we further grouped the players as follows. The red group contained players who preferred close games (circle points closer to $x = 0$ than cross points). The orange group contained players who were sensitive to the programs' performance (the dotted line being close to vertical). The blue group contained players who preferred to win by large margins rather than close games. To sum up, we concluded that players had general tendencies (preferring moderate territory differences with proper-level opponents), while players did differ from others.

**Human's Lead and Game Length** We also analyzed human's lead and game length together. The reason was that we supposed even with the same territory lead (say 50), it was not strange for players to feel differently when the games ended at different timings (say the 100th, 200th, or 300th moves).

Figure 9 shows 4 relatively characteristic players' scatter plots of human's lead ($x$-axis) and game length ($y$-axis).[2] Player B, who was discussed earlier (Fig. 7) to prefer to win by large margins, was likely to evaluate close games ($x \approx 0$) or long games (higher $y$) as bad. Player C, in contrast, seemed not to prefer to win by large margins or by Go programs' resignation early in the games. Instead, we suspected Player C to prefer close games or losses, though close games that were too long were likely to be evaluated as bad (this tendency was especially clear for Player E who will be discussed later). Player D was similar to Player C in that they tended to evaluate games as good when they lost while as bad when they won. But they were different in that Player D only evaluated the games he/she won by large margins in the middle games as bad. Player E seemed not to prefer to win by Go programs' resignation early in the games as Player C, but Player E more often evaluated games as good when the game lengths were between 100 to 300, regardless of the values of human's lead. Games with more than 300 moves were almost evaluated as bad. We suspected the reason to be that the Go programs played many unnecessary moves and did not resign even when the winners were clear or did not pass even when the territories were fixed.

Regarding Players C and E, their scatter plots helped to explain the seemingly unnatural M-shape in Fig. 6. Strong players like Player C often forced the Go programs to

[2] We suspected the reason why the data points for Players B, C, and E look like arcs to be that (1) The Go programs resigned early in the games when the human players already led a lot in territory. (2) After around 150 moves, if the human players led a lot, the Go programs resigned. (3) If the differences in territory were not large, the games proceeded to the ends.

resign quickly and evaluated such short games as bad. In such cases, the human's leads were around 30–50. Also, some players like Player E evaluated very long games as bad, where the Go programs hesitated to resign/pass and the human's leads were around 40–60[3]. We suspected these tendencies to be a possible reason for lower good rates around human's leads of 40–50 in Fig. 6.

Figure 10 shows the analyzed 21 players' centroids of good and bad games depicted in a similar way to Fig. 8, but the $y$-axis here is game length instead of program's performance. Similar to Fig. 8, circle points (good games) could be more often found around the center of the figure than the cross points (bad games). The results suggested that players generally preferred games with moderate territory differences and lengths. Nevertheless, according to the relation between the circles and crosses, we found several groups of players. The blue group contained players who preferred to win by large margins. The red group contained players who preferred close games. The orange group contained players who were sensitive to game lengths, dissatisfied either with Go programs' resignation in early games or with too-long games that might contain unnecessary moves. Again, we found both general tendencies among players (preferring games with moderate territory differences and lengths) and differences in players' preferences.

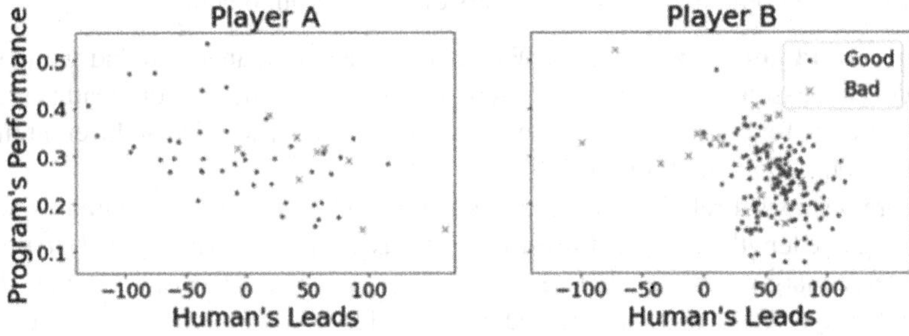


**Fig. 7.** Scatter plots of human's lead and program's performance for Players A and B.

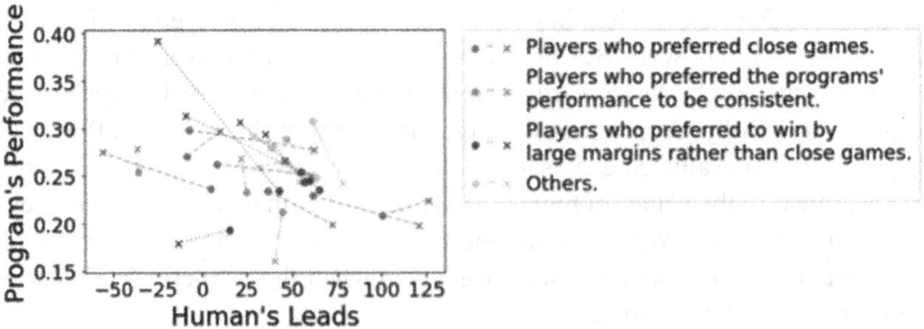


**Fig. 8.** Players' centroids of good and bad games plotted based on human's lead and program's performance.

[3] When the human's lead became larger than this range, probably the Go programs resigned earlier.

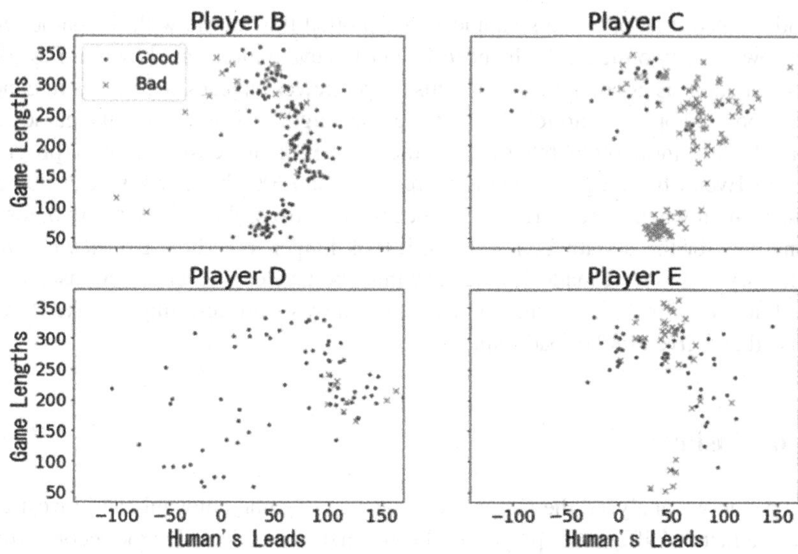


**Fig. 9.** Scatter plots of human's lead and game length for Players B, C, D, and E.

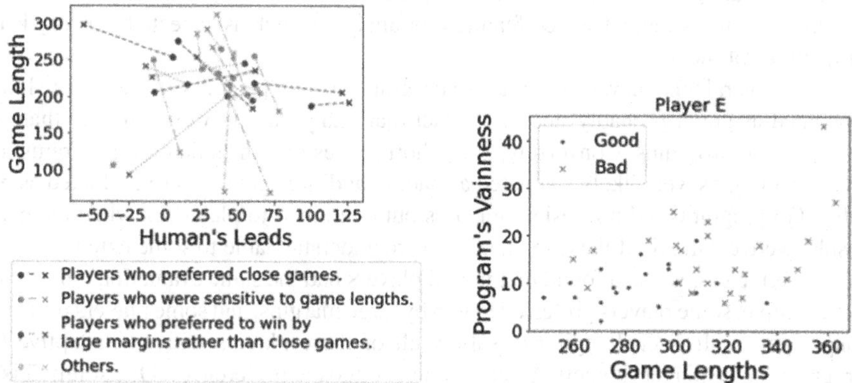


**Fig. 10.** 21 players' centroids of good and bad games plotted based on human's lead and game length.

**Fig. 11.** Scatter plot of game length and program's vainness for games ended by pass where Player E won.

**Game Length and Program's Vainness** For Player E's results in Fig. 9, we considered a possible reason for the bad games to be that the Go programs made many unnecessary moves and hesitated to resign or pass in endgames. To confirm this, we conducted a further analysis of games that ended by pass where Player E won.

To quantize how often the Go programs played unnecessary moves, we used the gains of moves, i.e., the differences in territory leads compared to the pass move, as explained in Sect. 4.2. A small gain means that the move has no different effects on the game compared to passes. We counted the number of moves with gains lower than

0.5 and defined it as program's vainness. We plotted this metric with the game length to see how these two metrics influenced Player E's evaluations, as shown in Fig. 11. In games evaluated as good, the Go programs played fewer unnecessary moves in general, which supported our assumption. When the game lengths exceeded 300, the games were evaluated as bad more often, regardless of the number of unnecessary moves (program's vainness). Even when the game lengths were lower than 300, the games were evaluated as bad more often when there were more unnecessary moves. We considered two possible explanations for the dissatisfaction. First, it took longer to end the games when many unnecessary moves were made despite the winner being clear, which was a waste of time. Second, longer games, even when unnecessary moves were few, might make Player E exhausted and give him/her bad impressions.

## 7 Conclusions

In this paper, we analyzed the factors that make a Go game enjoyable and investigated how these factors differ from player to player. First, we collected game records from a website providing human players with intermediate-level Go programs, where human players can evaluate games as good or bad. After performing statistical analyses using basic information, such as game results and game lengths, we employed KataGo, a strong Go program, to extract advanced features for analyses, such as expected territory leads or qualities of moves.

As a general tendency, games that Go programs won or played well were more likely evaluated as good, probably due to the fact that many players were stronger than the prepared Go programs. Conversely, very short games or games that Go programs lost by large margins were likely evaluated as bad. In addition, games were evaluated as bad when Go programs did not resign nor pass but continued to play even when the game results were clear. All of these tendencies were understandable to some extent.

Nevertheless, we also found that not all players had the same evaluation tendencies. For example, some players preferred to win by large margins, and some players preferred longer games. It is challenging to satisfy all of these players with non-adaptive Go programs since players sometimes have almost opposite preferences. One solution is to offer a variety of program options to suit different preferences. Another solution is to develop adaptive Go programs that refer to individual players' evaluation histories and game records.

In the future, we plan to conduct analyses using more advanced features. For example, in the game of Go, it is well known that there are players who are aggressive and like a lot of battles, while others may prefer to surround territories in peaceful ways. We believe that by inferring such advanced preferences of each player, the Go programs will be able to adapt to these preferences and improve the player's satisfaction.

## References

1. https://en.wikipedia.org/wiki/Go (game)
2. https://igo.qinoa.com/ja/

3. Bartle, R.: Hearts, clubs, diamonds, spades: Players who suit muds. J. MUD Res. **1**(1), 19 (1996)
4. Gao, Y., Zhang, D., Li, H.: The professional go annotation dataset. IEEE Trans. Games **15**(4), 517–526 (2023). https://doi.org/10.1109/TG.2023.3275183
5. Hayashita, M., Ikeda, K., Hsueh, C.H.: Factor analysis for Go AI to produce good games. Tech. rep., JAIST (2023), the 49th Meeting of the Game Informatics Research Group
6. Hsueh, C.H., Ikeda, K.: Playing good-quality games with weak players by combining programs with different roles. In: IEEE CoG 2022, pp. 612–615 (2022)
7. Liu, A.J., Wu, T.R., Wu, I.C., Guei, H., Wei, T.H.: Strength adjustment and assessment for mcts-based programs [research frontier]. IEEE Comput. Intell. Mag. **15**(3), 60–73 (2020). https://doi.org/10.1109/MCI.2020.2998315
8. Silver, D., Huang, A., et al.: Mastering the game of go with deep neural networks and tree search. Nature **529**(7587), 484–489 (2016)
9. Silver, D., Schrittwieser, J., et al.: Mastering the game of go without human knowledge. Nature **550**(7676), 354–359 (2017)
10. Tondello, G.F., Arrambide, K., Ribeiro, G., Jian-lan Cen, A., Nacke, L.E.: "i don't fit into a single type": a trait model and scale of game playing preferences. In: Lamas, D., Loizides, F., Nacke, L., Petrie, H., Winckler, M., Zaphiris, P. (eds.) Human-Computer Interaction – INTERACT 2019: 17th IFIP TC 13 International Conference, Paphos, Cyprus, September 2–6, 2019, Proceedings, Part II, pp. 375–395. Springer International Publishing, Cham (2019). https://doi.org/10.1007/978-3-030-29384-0_23
11. Wu, D.J.: Accelerating self-play learning in Go. arXiv, abs/1902.10565 (2020)

# Host's Assistant: Leveraging Graph Neural Networks for Daily Room Rate Prediction on Online Accommodation Sites

Hsiang-Yi Liang(✉) and Wen-Chih Peng

The Institute of Computer Science and Engineering, National Yang Ming Chiao Tung University, Hsinchu, Taiwan
{vivian0507.cs09,wcpengcs}@nycu.edu.tw

**Abstract.** Pricing has always been an important topic. It takes a lot of effort and time from the most traditional economic point of view. Therefore, many researchers are devoted to the research of automatic pricing models. In our case, we are focused on the prediction of accommodation prices. Unlike real estate price prediction, we primarily study the pricing issues faced by Airbnb hosts on a daily basis. Currently, existing methods predict prices based on room factors. However, we believe that the relationship between neighboring rooms has a significant impact on prices, which has not been adequately considered. Additionally, there is a lack of flexible mechanisms that adjust prices based on demand forecasting and variations during peak and off-peak seasons. To address these challenges, we have developed an advanced Room Price Interactive Forecasting System (RPics). In addition to incorporating data on individual room characteristics, our primary focus is on the impact of neighboring rooms. We utilize the framework of the model to simulate the effects of mutual influence and forecast demand patterns for different days, including simulations for weekends or peak and off-peak travel seasons. The overall framework enables us to adjust prices accordingly and achieve superior results.

**Keywords:** Graph Neural Network · Price prediction · Demand forecasting · Deep Learning · Attention Mechanism

## 1 Introduction

Determining the price of a product is crucial. To address this issue, we aim to build a seller pricing model. When a seller inputs basic product information, the model can calculate the most profitable price for that product and provide it as a reference for the seller.

Due to the complexity of pricing, we consider price prediction related to housing to be particularly challenging. Especially for online accommodation platforms, one needs to consider factors such as room type, location, and even neighboring rooms because travelers often compare rooms with nearby hostels. Furthermore, the daily room rates can vary based on the check-in date. For example, during the peak travel season, there is high


C.-Y. Lee et al. (Eds.): TAAI 2023, CCIS 2074, pp. 358–370, 2024.
https://doi.org/10.1007/978-981-97-1711-8_27

demand for hotel bookings. According to the law of supply and demand in economics, when demand is high, prices increase, and room rates go up.

The pricing system we proposed consists of four main components. The first part is feature engineering, where we use normalization and one-hot encoding to preprocess the room data, enabling better subsequent computations. The second part involves demand analysis, as demand is a significant factor influencing product pricing, and an analysis of room demand will impact the final results. The third part focuses on the graph structure. We recognize that room pricing is highly correlated with its neighbors, so we constructed graph neural networks to simulate the mutual influence effect. The detailed design of the graph structure will be presented in the later section. The final part is price prediction, which utilizes the results from our previous feature engineering and graph neural network to forecast the room prices.

In this paper, the experimental results demonstrate the effectiveness of our proposed strategy and model. The main contributions of this paper are as follows:

- We presented RPics, a new room price forecasting model based on graph neural networks, while the current price prediction systems often neglect the interrelationships among products.
- We constructed a suitable graph structure based on the room locations, emphasizing the influence of neighboring rooms on room prices and the relationships between neighborhoods.
- Our brand-new room pricing model based on graph neural networks integrates with a time series model. We aim not only to predict fixed room prices but also to consider the time-related factors that influence room prices based on previous pricing trends.

## 2 Related Work

We have surveyed many papers about graph neural network, because the gnn model may improve the accuracy of predicting the probability, and our system would be built on graph, how to build the graph is the first problem we will encounter. In the study [1], the features of each piece of data be set as a node feature, and those nodes who are closed will be connected by edges, so that an adjacency matrix of the graph structure can be established. After that, a computational graph of each node can be constructed, so that adjacent neighbors can send messages to each other, influence each other, and finally get node embedding by the neural network. Among studies [2–4], there are some convolutional neural network methods for processing message passing. The experimental results show that the node embedding obtained by these different methods has a certain degree of performance in the downstream task, which means node embedding is representative of the graph structure. In the study [5], the GraphSAGE model dealing with the graph problem in large scale. in the study [6], leveraging masked self-attentional layers to address the shortcomings of prior methods based on graph convolutions or their approximations. Beside the single graph, the heterogeneous graph with various node types and edge relations is more suitable to applied on the real-world task. Studies [7–9] have leading to good results, and making great achievements in this graph field. And there are some people working hard in the field of graph structure learning [10–12, 13], these models strengthen the influence of graph structure on embedding results, making them to be the significant turning point in this field.

# 3 Preliminary

Fig. 1.

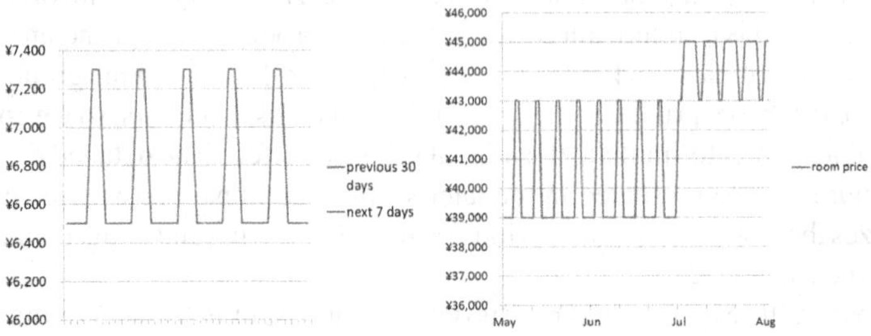


(a) Daily room price with in a months.

From this room price chart, we can find that prices are date-related and cyclical.

(b) Daily room price with in four month.

From this room price chart, we can find that prices are affected by peak season.

**Fig. 1.** Daily room price charts.

## 3.1 Problem Definition

The Host's Assistant aims to leverage the power of GNNs to capture relationships and dependencies among different listings and their surrounding neighborhood in a graph structure. Our room dataset $R = \{r_1, r_2, \ldots, r_n\}$, where $r_x$ represents the room data of room $x$, and $n$ is the number of rooms in the dataset. For each $r_x$, we got $r_x = (o_x, C_x)$, where $o_x$ is the basic feature of room $x$, and $C_x$ is the calendar data of room $x$. Then we can also represent the room dataset as $R = \{(o_1, C_1), (o_2, C_2), \ldots, (o_{|R|}, C_{|R|})\}$. To explain in more detail, the basic features of room include host_id, latitude, longitude, room_type, and so on. And about the calendar, $C_x = \{c_1^x, c_2^x, c_{|C|}^x\}$, where $c^x{}_t$ represents the calendar data of room $x$ at Day $t$. For each calendar data $c_t^x$, we got $c_t^x = \left(p_t^x, b_t^x\right)$, where $p_t^x$ is the room price of room $x$ at Day $t$, and $b_t^x$ is the available status of room $x$ at Day $t$. About the available status, indicating whether the room being booked for that day, is marked as true,$T$, or false, $F$. Then we can also represent the calendar data of room $x$ *as* $C_x = \{(p_1^x, b_1^x), (p_2^x, b_2^x), \ldots, (p_{|C_x|}^x, b_{|C_x|}^x)\}$. In addition, the final output we would like to get is the daily room price for the next week, $Y_x = \{y_1^x, y_2^x, \ldots, y_7^x\}$, where $y_t^x$ is the predicted room price of room $x$ at Day $t$. Overall, we have to use the above data to forecast the prices of these rooms for the next week.

# 4 Methodology

## 4.1 Architecture of Our Model

In the previous section, we said that the architecture of our dynamic pricing system can be divided into four main parts. (1) **Feature Engineering**, (2) **Demand Analysis**, and (3) **Relational Graph Neural Network**, (4) **Price Prediction**. We can see the overall architecture in Fig. 2.

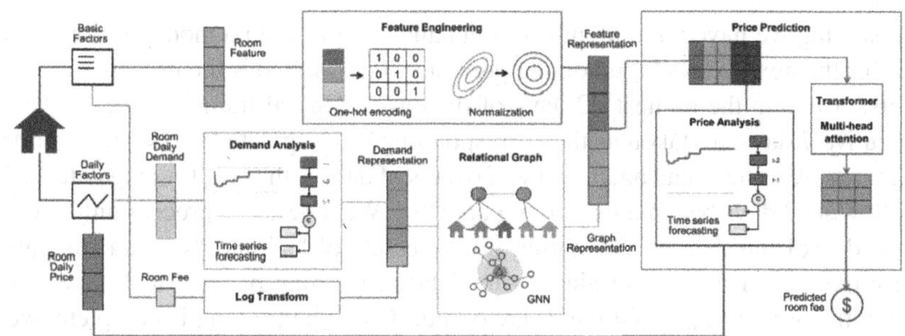


**Fig. 2.** Overview architecture of the RPics. The overall structure of RPics, with four main components, Feature Engineering, Demand Analysis, Relational Graph Neural Network, and Price Prediction respectively. To complete the house price forecasting problem.

## 4.2 Feature Engineering

Room features and the process of feature engineering are crucial in creating an effective and accurate prediction model.What we're doing here is extracting the effective part of the listing data, deleting the incomplete data, and then preprocessing the data. Features like room type, amenities, location, size, and other characteristics play a significant role in determining the room's perceived value and market competitiveness.

For these numerical features, min-max normalization is a commonly used technique. By scaling all numerical features to a similar range (typically between 0 and 1), the model can converge faster during training and avoid certain features dominating the others due to their scale.

For these categorical features, convert them to binary format using One-hot encoding. After performing feature engineering on both numerical and categorical features, the next step is to concatenate all the processed features into a single feature vector. This combined feature vector serves as the input to the model for predictions.

Finally, feature representations are learned from concatenated feature vectors using a Multi-Layer Perceptron (MLP) neural network. The MLP consists of multiple hidden layers and activation functions, allowing it to capture complex relationships between features and create a higher-level feature representation that is relevant for the prediction task.

### 4.3 Demand Analysis

In this part, we used the available status of calendar data as the daily room booking status to do the analysis. We employ a Long Short-Term Memory (LSTM) [14] neural network to predict the probability of the next week based on daily room booking data collected over a month. After training, the LSTM can generate predictions of the probability of booking a room for an event for each day of the week ahead. By leveraging the ability of LSTMs to model long-term dependencies, we aim to provide reliable predictions for the probabilities of events, leading to better decision-making and planning for a given scenario.

Assuming we have three months of data and want to train a model to predict room prices for the next 7 days based on the previous 30 days, here's the process:

First, we take the earliest 30 days of data as the initial training data "x," and the consecutive 7 days are taken as the corresponding training data "y." Next, we slide the window one day ahead and again extract 30 days of data as the new training data "x," and the following 7 days become its training data "y." We repeat this process until we reach the last day of the dataset, generating multiple sets of "x" and "y" data for training. We use the LSTM model to train on this dataset, learning patterns and dependencies between the 30-day input and the 7-day output. Once the training is complete, we can use the trained model to predict room prices for any future 7-day period by inputting the preceding 30 days of data. This approach allows us to leverage historical data and the sequence nature of room prices to make accurate predictions for the next 7 days. LSTM's ability to capture long-term dependencies makes it suitable for this time series forecasting task.

### 4.4 Relational Graph Neural Network

Constructing the graph in multi-relation is an important aspect of the Host's Assistant model for room fee prediction. The relational graph construction involves organizing the room listings and their relationships in a relational structure, which captures the spatial dependencies and neighborhood influences more effectively (Fig. 3).

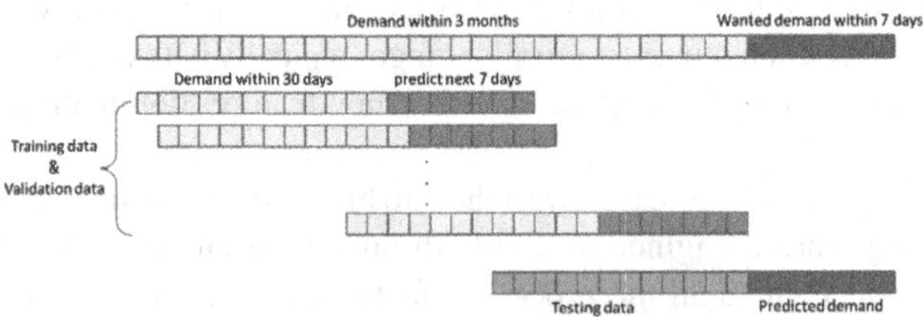


**Fig. 3.** Data cutting and training methods.

In the relational graph construction for the Host's Assistant model, the nodes represent individual rooms or the center of a neighborhood, and the edges capture various types of relationships among the rooms. There are three types of edges considered in the graph:

- Neighborhood-Neighborhood (NN) Edge: This type of edge connects centers of two neighborhoods in the relational graph. It signifies the relationship between different neighborhoods in the vicinity, allowing the model to capture broader neighborhood influences on room fees.
- Neighborhood-Room (NR) Edge: This edge connects a neighborhood center to individual rooms within that neighborhood. It represents the association between a neighborhood's characteristics and the specific room listings within it. By considering this edge, the model can factor in the influence of neighborhood features on room fees.
- Room-Room (RR) Edge (Meeting Requirements): This type of edge connects rooms within the same neighborhood that meet specific requirements. The requirements could be based on room type, property size, or other relevant factors. By considering this edge, the model can identify and leverage similarities between rooms that have met the given requirements.

The node features in the graph represent each room's characteristics and are created by concatenating the demand representation with the room's fixed price. This feature representation captures both the room's demand-related information and its base price, providing valuable information for the price prediction task.

Overall, the relational graph construction with these three types of edges enables the Host's Assistant to effectively capture and model complex spatial dependencies and neighborhood influences in the room fee prediction task. The graph's representation allows the model to consider local and global relationships, leading to more accurate and comprehensive predictions for room fees on online accommodation platforms.

We applied the relational Graph Neural Network [15] on our relational graph to leverage its capabilities in handling diverse relationship types. With this model, we can make use of different weights and trainable parameters to dynamically adapt the aggregation process to each edge type, allowing us to capture neighborhood influences, neighborhood-room associations, and similarities between rooms that meet specific requirements. This comprehensive approach will enable us to better understand the underlying patterns affecting room demands and prices, and make more accurate predictions. So, applying relational GNN on our relational graph will provide us with a powerful framework to analyze room demands and prices, effectively capturing the complex relationships and dependencies among rooms and neighborhoods (Fig. 4).

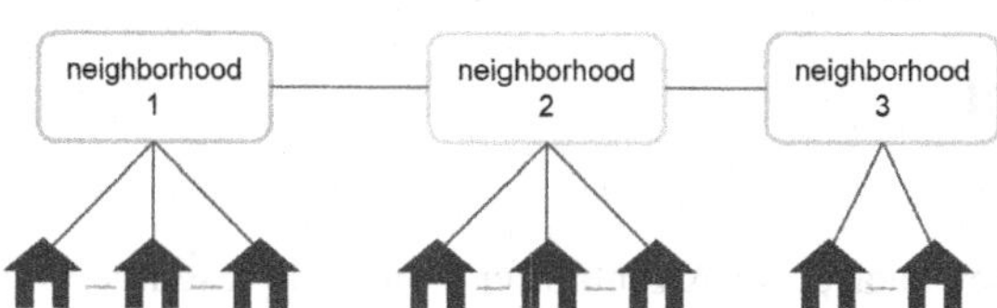


**Fig. 4.** Relational Graph structure. There are three types of edges. NN edges are in red color. NR edges are in blue color. RR edges are in yellow color.

### 4.5 Price Prediction

The first step in the final price prediction model is to study the historical room prices. We gather data for the past several months and extract the daily room prices. Understanding the price trends and patterns is crucial for accurate forecasting.

After we got the predicted daily room price, we concatenate these three representations (room feature embeddings, graph representation, and price forecasting) to form a comprehensive vector representation for each room.

This combined representation is then passed as input to a Transformer model, which is capable of handling sequential and relational data effectively. The Transformer model [15] learns the patterns and dependencies in the data and predicts the final room prices for the next 7 days. Query, Key, and Value Projections:

$$Q = XW_q, \quad K = XW_k, \quad V = XW_v \tag{1}$$

where $X$ is the input sequence, and $W_q$,$W_k$, and $W_v$ are learnable weight matrices for the Query, Key, and Value projections, respectively. Scaled Dot-Product Attention:

$$Attention\ Score\ \alpha_i = softmax\left(\frac{Q_i K_i^T}{\sqrt{d_k}}\right) \tag{2}$$

where $Q_i$ and $K_i$ are the Query and Key vectors for the $i$-th position in the sequence, and $d_k$ is the dimension of the Key vectors.

Weighted Sum of Values:

$$Output\ C_i = \sum_{i=1}^{n} (\alpha_i V_i) \tag{3}$$

where the sum is taken over all positions in the sequence, and $V_i$ is the Value vector for the $i$-th position. Multiple Heads:

$$Q^h = XW_q^h, \quad K^h = XW_k^h, \quad V^h = XW_v^h, \quad for \quad h = 1, \ldots, H \tag{4}$$

where H is the number of attention heads.

By integrating information from room features, graph relationships, and historical prices, the Host's Assistant's Transformer model can provide accurate and reliable predictions, helping hosts and accommodation platforms optimize their pricing strategies and improve overall performance in the competitive online accommodation market.

## 5 Experiment

### 5.1 Dataset

Inside Airbnb, open datasets of Airbnb offer a valuable resource for organizations and researchers seeking training data to develop and improve their machine learning models and algorithms. These datasets provide comprehensive information about Airbnb listings, including attributes such as property characteristics, geographical location, host details, pricing, availability, and guest reviews. By utilizing such open datasets as training data, organizations can leverage the wealth of real-world information to train their models for various tasks, such as price prediction, occupancy forecasting, customer sentiment analysis, and recommendation systems.

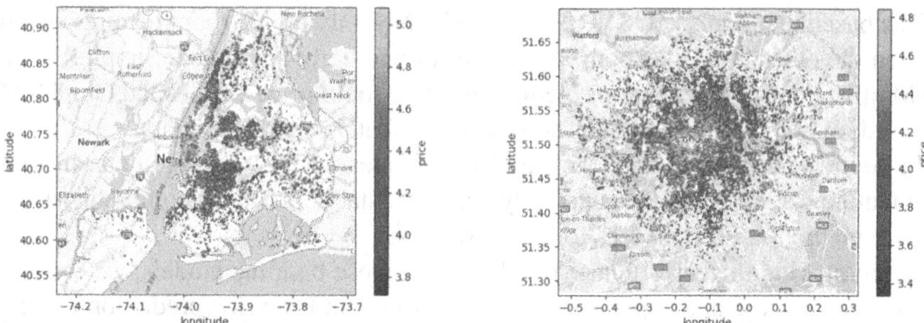


(a) Room price and location distribution in New York.
(b) Room price and location distribution in London.

**Fig. 5.** Room price and location distribution

The use of open Airbnb datasets as training data enables researchers and developers to harness the power of real-world data to build accurate and robust models, enhancing their understanding of the vacation rental market and enabling data-driven decision-making. Additionally, these datasets encourage collaboration and innovation by providing a standardized and accessible platform for experimentation and analysis within the research and data science communities.

In the data from Airbnb, it is common to find that neighboring room listings tend to have similar room fees. we can refer to Fig. 5a, and Fig. 5b. This similarity in pricing can be attributed to factors such as market competition, neighborhood characteristics, and pricing strategies used by hosts in the area. When many rooms offer comparable accommodations and amenities, hosts may adjust their prices to remain competitive and attract guests.

## 5.2 Baseline Model

A baseline model is essentially a simple model that acts as a reference in a machine learning project. Its main function is to contextualize the results of trained models. In our study, we compare the performance of our RPics with several baseline models for room fee prediction. The baseline models we consider are: Linear Regression (LR), Support-vector Regression (SVR), K-means Clustering (KMC), K Nearest Neighbor (KNN), Neural Networks (NNs), Recurrent Neural Network (SimpleRNN), Long Short-Term Memory (LSTM), Graph Convolutional Network (GCN), Graph Sample and aggregate (GraphSAGE).

Each baseline model utilizes different input data, as indicated in the Table1. The input data for each model is categorized into four parts:

- Room Features: Includes basic room characteristics such as accomodation, latitude, longitude, room_type, etc.
- Price: The reference price that the host can set.
- Daily Price Data: The historical daily room prices for the each room.
- Daily Demand Data: The historical daily room availability (booked or not booked) for the each room.

The baseline models LR, SVR, KMC, and KNN only utilize room features as input. NNs, on the other hand, use both room features and daily price data. SimpleRNN and LSTM utilize daily price data for predicting future room prices. GCN and GraphSAGE are based on graph representations and use room features and price data.

In contrast, our proposed RPics model integrates all the available data, including room features, daily price data, and daily demand data, to provide a comprehensive and accurate prediction of room fees for the next week.

By comparing the performance of RPics with these baseline models, we can evaluate the effectiveness and superiority of our approach in room fee prediction on online accommodation platforms (Table 2).

**Table 1.** Baseline input data comparing.

| | Room Feature | Price | Daily price data | Daily demand data |
|---|---|---|---|---|
| LR | O | O | O | O |
| SVR | O | O | O | O |
| KMC | O | O | O | O |
| KNN | O | O | O | O |
| NNs | O | O | O | O |
| SimpleRNN | X | X | O | X |
| LSTM | X | X | O | X |
| GCN | O | O | X | X |
| GraphSAGE | O | O | X | X |
| RPics (Ours) | O | O | O | O |

**Table 2.** Experiment result.

| MAE | New York | Boston | Tokyo | Taipei | London | Bangkok | Average |
|---|---|---|---|---|---|---|---|
| LR | 14.02 | 15.45 | 15.07 | 14.36 | 15.13 | 13.82 | 14.48 |
| SVR | 13.94 | 15.40 | 14.59 | 14.05 | 15.08 | 13.71 | 14.27 |
| KMC (k = 20) | 13.42 | 15.28 | 14.89 | 13.52 | 14.96 | 13.53 | 14.06 |
| KNN (k = 10) | 14.28 | 15.69 | 15.21 | 14.52 | 15.37 | 14.57 | 14.79 |
| NNs (3layer) | 13.19 | 14.93 | 14.35 | 13.28 | 14.61 | 13.14 | 13.71 |
| SimpleRNN | 12.73 | 15.06 | 14.51 | 13.41 | 14.74 | 13.08 | 13.69 |
| LSTM | **12.61** | 14.50 | 14.07 | **12.54** | 14.18 | 12.71 | 13.22 |
| GCN | 12.78 | 14.59 | 14.13 | 12.81 | 14.27 | 12.68 | 13.33 |
| GraphSAGE | 12.94 | 14.72 | 14.35 | 12.93 | 14.40 | 12.91 | 13.61 |
| RPics (Ours) | 12.69 | **14.33** | **13.98** | 12.71 | **14.01** | **12.63** | **13.20** |

### 5.3 Overall Performance

The table above presents the overall performance of different models for room fee prediction in various cities. The Mean Absolute Error (MAE) values are used as the evaluation metric, and lower values indicate better predictive accuracy.

Among the baseline machine learning models, Simple Linear Regression (LR), Support Vector Regression (SVR), K-Means Clustering (KMC), K Nearest Neighbor (KNN), and Neural Networks (NNs), the LSTM model stands out with the lowest MAE in New York and Taipei.

Moreover, the graph-based models, SimpleRNN, GCN, and GraphSAGE, demonstrate competitive performance, achieving lower MAE values compared to the traditional machine learning models.

However, our proposed model, RPics, outperforms all the other models across all cities, obtaining the lowest MAE values in New York, Taipei, and Bankok. RPics leverages relational graph neural networks and demand analysis, allowing it to capture complex relationships and demand patterns, resulting in highly accurate room fee predictions.

In conclusion, RPics provides a powerful and effective solution for daily room fee prediction on online accommodation platforms, delivering superior performance compared to traditional machine learning and graph-based models (Fig. 6).

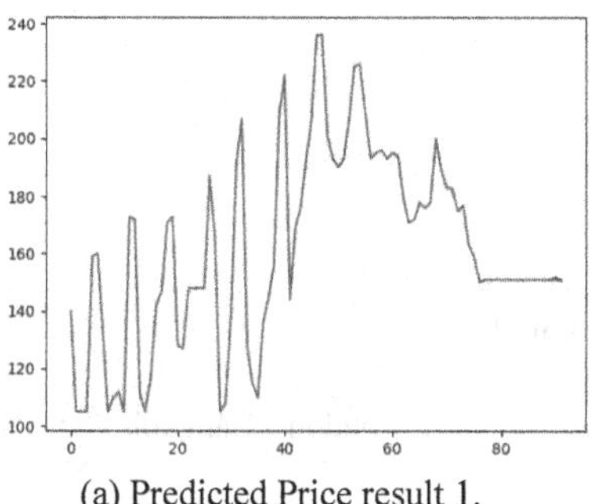

(a) Predicted Price result 1.

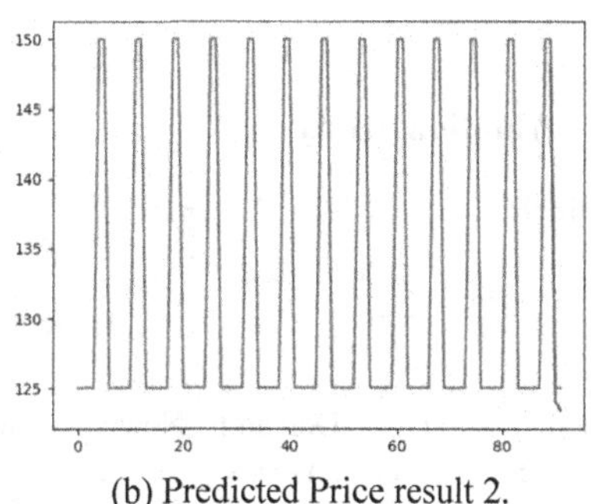

(b) Predicted Price result 2.

**Fig. 6.** Predicted Price result.

### 5.4 Comparison Test

- Weekday vs. Weekend Comparison: Weekdays show more consistent predictions with lower errors compared to weekends. This suggests weekends introduce some unpredictability, possibly due to small price fluctuations.
- Tourism Peak vs. Off-Peak Comparison: Predictions during peak and offpeak times are relatively stable. There's a slight increase in error during peak periods, indicating the model handles these variations well.
- Jump vs. Without Jump Comparison: Accounting for transitional periods (jumps) leads to higher errors. Excluding these points results in more accurate predictions, emphasizing their impact on forecasting.

- Effect of Training Data Duration: Longer training periods significantly improve prediction accuracy. Using 90 days of data yields the best results, highlighting the importance of extensive training data for precise predictions (Table 3).

**Table 3.** Comparison test.

| MAE | New York | Boston | Average |
|---|---|---|---|
| Weekday | 12.01 | 13.52 | **12.77** |
| Weekend | 12.89 | 14.37 | 13.63 |
| Peak | 12.67 | 13.86 | **13.27** |
| Off-Peak | 12.71 | 14.03 | 13.37 |
| Jump | 13.06 | 14.38 | 13.72 |
| Without jump | 12.57 | 13.76 | **13.17** |
| 90 days training data | 11.91 | 13.68 | **12.80** |
| 60 days training data | 12.04 | 13.90 | 12.97 |
| 30 days training data | 12.47 | 14.11 | 13.29 |

### 5.5 Ablation Study

Table 4.

**Table 4.** Ablation Study

| Room Feature | Graph relation | Demand analysis | New York | Boston | Tokyo | Taipei | London | Bangkok | Average MAE |
|---|---|---|---|---|---|---|---|---|---|
| O | O | X | <u>13.02</u> | <u>13.89</u> | <u>14.37</u> | <u>14.20</u> | **14.54** | <u>13.27</u> | <u>13.88</u> |
| O | X | O | 14.04 | 14.70 | 15.19 | 14.93 | 15.07 | 14.43 | 14.73 |
| X | O | O | 15.78 | 16.28 | 16.83 | 18.47 | 17.89 | 16.02 | 17.00 |
| O | O | O | **12.96** | **13.68** | **14.12** | **14.09** | <u>14.67</u> | **13.03** | **13.77** |

The ablation study results reveal the impact of individual components on the Room Price Interactive Forecasting System (RPics) for room fee prediction in different cities. The components evaluated are "Room feature," "Graph relation," and "Demand analysis."

Our model, which includes all three components, achieves the lowest Mean Absolute Error (MAE) values, indicating its superior predictive performance.

Removing any component leads to higher MAE values, showing the importance of each element in enhancing prediction accuracy.

Specifically, utilizing only "Room feature" or "Graph relation" results in higher MAE values, emphasizing that both components are valuable for accurate predictions. And we can see that "Room feature" is the most important component in this model. Similarly, considering only "Demand analysis" also leads to increased MAE values, highlighting the significance of incorporating room features and graph relations.

In conclusion, the complete model with all three components outperforms the ablated versions. Integrating room features, graph relations, and demand analysis is crucial for effective room fee prediction in different cities. RPics provides a comprehensive and robust framework for forecasting daily room prices, enabling hosts and accommodation platforms to optimize pricing strategies and respond to demand fluctuations.

## 6 Conclusion

This paper proposes an advanced model RPics, the House Price Interactive Prediction System, to address the pricing challenges that Airbnb hosts face on a daily basis. It not only considers the basic information of the basic room, but also simulates the analysis of the result of the interaction between room neighbors and the demand of customers. In order to simulate the mutual influence of housing prices among neighbors, we constructed a relational housing price network with rooms as nodes, and constructed them at the price level and demand level respectively. We also construct neighbor nodes so that houses in the same neighbor area can have stronger connections. Finally, the daily house price adjustment is made according to the house price trend, so that the house price has a cyclical change affected by weekends or peek seasons. Experiments on realworld datasets demonstrate the state-of-the-art effectiveness of our model. In the future, we hope that we can make the system be applied on Airbnb platform and other e-commerce sites. Not limited to just one platform, it can one day contribute to the world.

## Appendix A – Room Statistic

The Table 5 shows the number of listings for each room type in each city. The "Entire home/apt" category represents entire homes or apartments available for rent, "Private room" indicates private rooms in shared homes or apartments, "Shared room" includes shared rooms with other guests, and "Hotel room" represents hotel-style accommodations.

**Table 5.** Room statistic of each city.

| room type | New York | Boston | Tokyo | Taipei | London | Bangkok |
|---|---|---|---|---|---|---|
| Entire home/apt | 24278 | 2528 | 5433 | 1424 | 1278 | 10082 |
| Private room | 17874 | 1299 | 1845 | 829 | 1097 | 6176 |
| Shared room | 576 | 16 | 276 | 226 | 8 | 629 |
| Hotel room | 183 | 20 | 203 | 195 | 2 | 508 |

## References


1. Scarselli, F., Gori, M., Tsoi, A.C., Hagenbuchner, M., Monfardini, G.: The graph neural network model. IEEE Trans. Neural Networks **20**, 61–80 (2008)
2. Bruna, J., Zaremba, W., Szlam, A., LeCun, Y.: Spectral networks and locallyconnected networks on graphs. arXiv preprint arXiv:1312.6203 (2013)
3. Defferrard, M., Bresson, X., Vandergheynst, P.: Convolutional neural networkson graphs with fast localized spectral filtering. In: Advances in Neural Information Processing Systems, vol. 29 (2016)
4. Hamilton, W., Ying, Z., Leskovec, J.: Inductive representation learning on large graphs. In: Advances in Neural Information Processing Systems, vol. 30 (2017)
5. Schlichtkrull, M., Kipf, T.N., Bloem, P., van den Berg, R., Titov, I., Welling, M.: Modeling relational data with graph convolutional networks. In: Gangemi, A., et al. (eds.) The Semantic Web: 15th International Conference, ESWC 2018, Heraklion, Crete, Greece, June 3–7, 2018, Proceedings, pp. 593–607. Springer International Publishing, Cham (2018). https://doi.org/10.1007/978-3-319-93417-4_38
6. Velickovic, P., Cucurull, G., Casanova, A., Romero, A., Lio, P., Bengio, Y.: Graphattention networks. arXiv preprint arXiv:1710.10903 (2017)
7. Zhang, C., Song, D., Huang, C., Swami, A., Chawla, N.V.: Heterogeneous graphneural network. In: Proceedings of the 25th ACM SIGKDD International Conference on Knowledge Discovery & Data Mining, pp. 793–803 (2019)
8. Zhao, Y., Qi, J., Liu, Q., Zhang, R.: WGCN: graph convolutional networks with weighted structural features. In: Proceedings of the 44th International ACM SIGIR Conference on Research and Development in Information Retrieval, pp. 624–633 (2021)
9. Zhu, S., Zhou, C., Pan, S., Zhu, X., Wang, B.: Relation structure-aware heterogeneous graph neural network. In: IEEE international conference on data mining (ICDM), pp. 1534–1539 (2019)
10. Zhao, J., Wang, X., Shi, C., Hu, B., Song, G., Ye, Y.: Heterogeneous graph structure learning for graph neural networks. Proc. AAAI Conf. Artif. Intell. **35**(5), 4697–4705 (2021)
11. Jin, W., Ma, Y., Liu, X., Tang, X., Wang, S., Tang, J.: Graph structure learningfor robust graph neural networks. In: Proceedings of the 26th ACM SIGKDD international Conference on Knowledge Discovery & Data Mining, pp. 66–74 (2020)
12. Zhu, Y., Xu, W., Zhang, J., Liu, Q., Wu, S., Wang, L. Deep graph structure learning for robust representations: A survey. arXiv preprint arXiv:2103.03036 (2021)
13. Li, C.C., Wang, W.Y., Du, W.W., Peng, W.C.: Look Around! A Neighbor Relation Graph Learning Framework for Real Estate Appraisal. arXiv preprint arXiv:2212.12190 (2022)
14. Hochreiter, S., Schmidhuber, J.: Long short-term memory. Neural Comput. 1735–1780 (1997)
15. Vaswani, A., et al.: Attention is all you need. In: Advances in Neural Information Processing Systems (2017)

# Impression Effect of Using Politeness Theory by Educational-Support-Robot that Suggest the Number of Problems by Real-Time Dialogue System

Hiroki Kaede[1], Felix Jimenez[1](✉), and Tomoki Miyamoto[2]

[1] School of Information Science and Technology, Aichi Prefectural University, 1522-3 Ibaragabasama, Nagakute-Shi, Aichi 480-1198, Japan
is201028@cis.aichi-pu.ac.jp, jimenez@ist.aichi-pu.ac.jp

[2] Graduate School of Informatics and Engineering, The University of Electro-Communications, 5-1 Tyohugaoka, Tyohu-Shi, Tokyo 182-8585, Japan
miyamoto@uec.ac.jp

https://www.ist.aichi-pu.ac.jp/en/

**Abstract.** In recent years, educational-support-robots have attracted much attention. In conventional educational-support-robots, the number of problems to be solved by the learner is fixed. However, to promote spontaneous learning and enhance learning effectiveness, it is important of trying to solve a larger number of problems. The authors believed that it would be effective for the robot to suggest more problems to the learner by using politeness theory. Therefore, in this study, we construct a method for suggesting the number of problems. The robot is equipped this method with three types of politeness theory, and we investigate the impression effect that the robot suggested by each strategy has on the learner by comparing it with a robot with a fixed number of questions and a robot in which the number of questions is freely decided by the learner. The experimental results suggest that the robot that proposes the number of problems using the politeness strategy, PPS or NPS, is the most favorable and can keep the amount of learning as same as that of the conventional robot.

**Keywords:** Human-Robot interaction · Educational-Support-Robot · Collaborative Learning · Speech Recognition

## 1 Introduction

In recent years, educational-support-robots that assist human learning have attracted much attention [1]. Research on educational-support-robots can be divided into two categories: teacher-type robots, which assume the role of a teacher, and partner-type robots, which learn together with the learner. Previous studies have shown that collaborative learning with a robot is superior to on-screen agents in terms of advice [2], that it has a greater influence on the user when performing psychologically challenging tasks


C.-Y. Lee et al. (Eds.): TAAI 2023, CCIS 2074, pp. 371–380, 2024.
https://doi.org/10.1007/978-981-97-1711-8_28

[3], and that the child concentrates more [4]. In a research case study on educational-support-robots, Jimenez et al. [5] reported that learning with a robot has a higher learning effect than with an on-screen agent. With this in mind, many educational support robots have been developed.

In this study, we focus on a partner robot that solves problems together with the learner. In many conventional studies, the number of problems to be solved by the learner (hereafter referred to as the number of solved questions) has been fixed [6], and there are very few cases where the robot changes the number of solved problems by each learner. However, it is important to encourage learners to learn spontaneously in order to motivate them and give them higher learning effects [7]. Spontaneous learning is not forced by others, but the tasks are set according to one's own will [8]. To promote spontaneous learning with educational-support-robots, it is important to pay attention to the learner's own desire to solve a larger number of problems. The authors believe that it is effective to create a spontaneous learning environment for the learner by allowing the robot to decide the number of questions to be solved while talking to the learner before learning.

Therefore, in this study, we have constructed a method for suggesting the number of problems by a speaking robot based on politeness theory, which suggests the number of problems while conversing with the learner. Politeness theory is a systematization of linguistic considerations as strategies for establishing a good relationship with a partner [9, 10]. In this paper, we investigate the impression effect of the robot equipped with this method on the learner by comparing it with conventional robots that solve a fixed number of questions without conversation and robots that allow the learner to arbitrarily choose the number of questions to solve.

## 2 Politeness Theory

The politeness theory consists of several conversational strategies for maintaining good relationships with others [11]. In general, people have desires, called faces when they engage in conversation. Positive desire, such as the desire to be understood, seen, and liked by others, are called positive faces, while negative desires, such as the desire not to be disturbed or intruded upon by others, called negative faces. Behavior that satisfies the positive face is called positive politeness (PPS) and behavior that satisfies the negative face is called negative politeness (NPS). On the other hand, there are also behaviors that do not take these faces into account [11]. In this study, these are referred to as direct (DRC). Although there are several other strategies in the politeness theory. In this study, we use three types of strategies, DRC, PPS and NPS, which are applicable to educational-support-robots.

## 3 The Problem-Number Proposal Method

The Problem-Number Proposal Method is a conversation method between the robot and the learner, proposed by the authors, for the robot to encourage the learner to learn spontaneously.

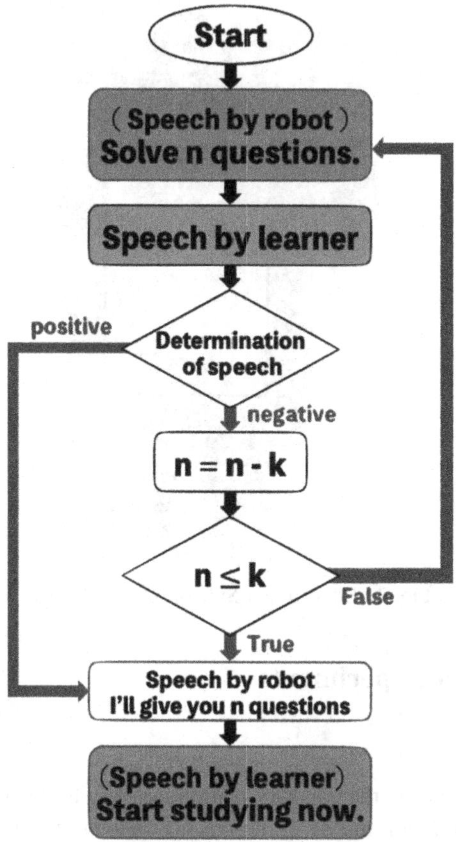


**Fig. 1.** The flowchart of The Problem-Number Proposal Method

The flowchart of the method is shown in Fig. 1. In this flowchart, the part shown by the red frame is the robot's utterance and the part shown by the blue frame is the learner's utterance. In our method, the robot proposes the number of problems $n_i$ to the learner before learning. The learner responds to the robot's proposal with an acceptance such as "Yes" or "OK" or a rejection such as "No" or "No thank you". If the learner accepts the robot's proposal, learning starts with the number of questions $n_i$. On the other hand, if the learner rejects the robot's proposal, that robot decreases the number of questions by $k$ and proposes again with the number of questions $n_{i+1}(= n_i - k)$. If the learner continues to reject the proposal, it continues to decrease the number of problems by $n_{i+2}(= n_{i+1} - k)$ and the number of problems by $k$. However, if $n - k \leq 0$ (the number of problems presented by the robot is less than or equal to 0), the number of problems immediately after the learner rejects the robot's proposal is forced to be presented as $n$ and the learner starts learning. This method allows the learner to spontaneously determine the amount of learning within his or her own learning capacity and is thought to increase motivation to learn.

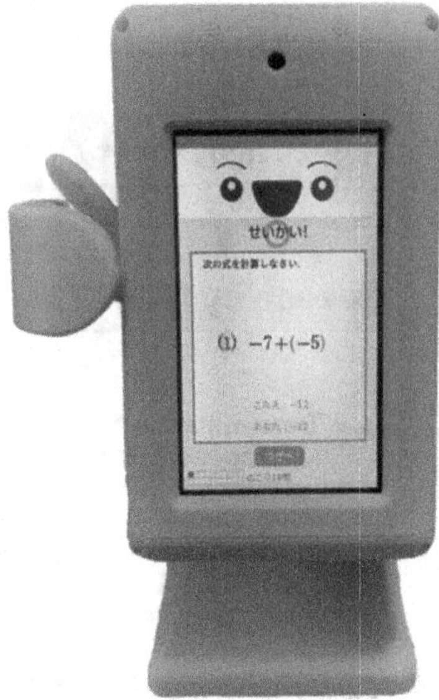


**Fig. 2.** Educational-Support-Robot: Rasby

# 4 Within-Subject Experiments

## 4.1 Robots Overview

For the experiment, we used the educational-support-robots Rasby, which consists of a hand equipped with a motor and an LCD panel, as shown in Fig. 2. The upper part of LCD panel is regarded as the head of Rasby, and by displaying the agent's face on that part, Rasby can perform various facial expression changes. The lower part of the LCD panel is considered to be the body of Rasby, and the belly can display problems, answers and explanations.

**Table 1.** Speech Method Based on Each Politeness Strategy

| | DRC | PPS | NPS |
|---|---|---|---|
| Solve $n_i$ problem | Solve 20 problems today | I have 20 problems for you today. Why don't we try our best together? | I have 20 problems for you today. If you don't mind, could you try this one? |
| Start studying now | Press the "Start" button to begin your study | Let's press the "Start" button and try our best study! | Press the "Start" button, and start studying, won't you? |

### 4.2 Learning System

The learners use the learning system, which is displayed on the lower part of Rasby's LCD panel. In the present study, the system is equipped with calculation problems of mathematics at the junior high school level, and the subjects are asked to solve them. Two types of mathematical problems have been prepared: simple ones for arithmetic operations with letters and ones for equation solving [12]. The reason for using middle-school level problems for the college students was that we were conducting a within-subjects experiment in which several types of robots were used continuously for a long period of time. If the task of having college students solve a reasonable number of college-level problems was repeated many times, the repetition effect would become stronger toward the end of the experiment, and the questionnaire scores and the amount of learning would be expected to decrease significantly. Therefore, in this experiment, middle school level problems were used to reduce the burden on the subjects, and the effect of the subjects' fatigue level was minimized.

### 4.3 Method

A within-subject experiment was conducted with 120 university students, in which the students and Rasby learn together. The duration of the experiment is from 2 May to 28 July 2023. In the experiment, the subjects experience a total of five different types of robots.

One of these is called conventional group in which the user does not talk to the robot but solves a fixed number of 20 questions as it is.

In three of the remaining for types, the robot asks the number of problems to be solved in line with each politeness strategy. The DRC (direct), PPS (Positive Politeness) and NPS (Negative Politeness) groups use The Problem-Number Proposal Method and talk with the subject. The remaining one is Any Number of Problems group, in which the robot talks with the subject, but does not use the method of suggesting the number of problems but asks the learner arbitrarily how many problems he/she wants to be solved and implements The Problem-Number Proposal Method.

Table 1. Shows how the robot speaks according to each politeness strategy in The Problem-Number Proposal Method. For example, in the PPS group, when suggesting the number of problems, the robot says: "I have 20 problems for you today. Why don't we try our best together?" The robot can achieve speech in line with the PPS. In this way, each group's robot speaking, and tone of voice are realized in accordance with each strategy. In our experiments, we set $n = 20$ and $k = 5$ in the Fig. 1.

### 4.4 Valuation Index

In this experiment, the Godspeed Questionnaire [13, 14], a questionnaire method for subjective evaluation in human-robot interaction, is used. In this experiment, we used the items assessing "likeability" and "animacy" in this questionnaire method. Positive impressions of the robot, such as likeability, are important for the continuation of bidirectional interaction. It has also been reported from conventional studies, that users tend to be more emotionally involved and more easily persuaded by things that they perceive as animacy [15]. Therefore, it is considered that users are more likely to listen to the advice from the educational-support-robot if the robot's animacy is high. Since each adjective pair in the questionnaire is on a five-point scale, the positive adjective side is quantified from 1 to 5 so that it becomes higher, and the average score of the five items of likeability is defined as "likeability" and the average score of the six items of animacy is defined as "animacy", and each group is compared with other.

An analysis of variance test was carried out. Significant differences were accepted when the significance level was 5%, and tests considering multiple comparisons were carried out twice in total on the mean values for likeability and animacy. Therefore, based on Bonferroni's method, The nominal level of significance for the whole experiment was adjusted to $p < 0.025$.

The average number of problems answered by the learners in each group is used as the indicator of the number of questions answered by the learners. However, since the number of questions is fixed for the conventional group, the average number of problems answered is always 20 (the maximum value of the average number of questions in this experiment).

To reduce the influence of order effects, a total of 120 different experiments were conducted in which each subject was tested in a different order form the others.

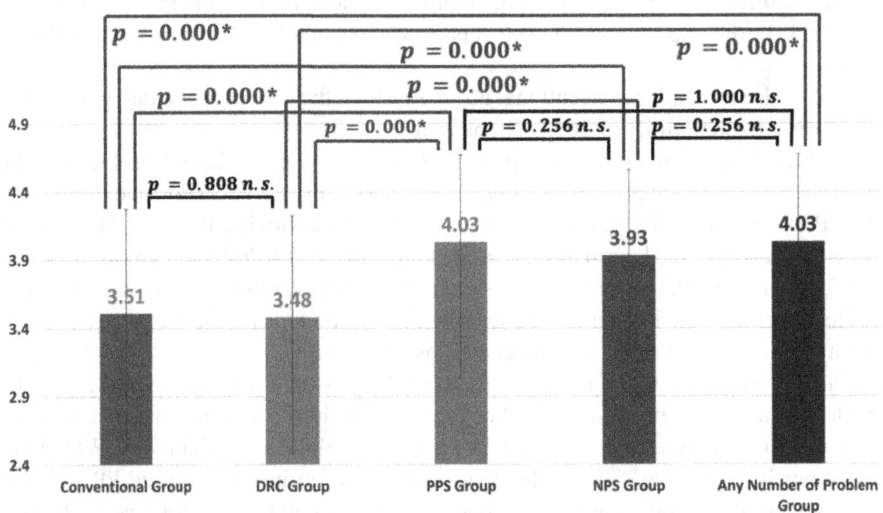


**Fig. 3.** Means and standard deviations of likeability for each group and results of the subtests.

### 4.5 Result

Figures 3 and 4 show the mean scores for likeability and animacy for each group and the results of the subtests in the analysis of variance. The graphs show that the group with Any Number of Problems group and the PPS groups had the highest scores on the likeability scale, followed by the NPS, conventional and DRC group. Any Number

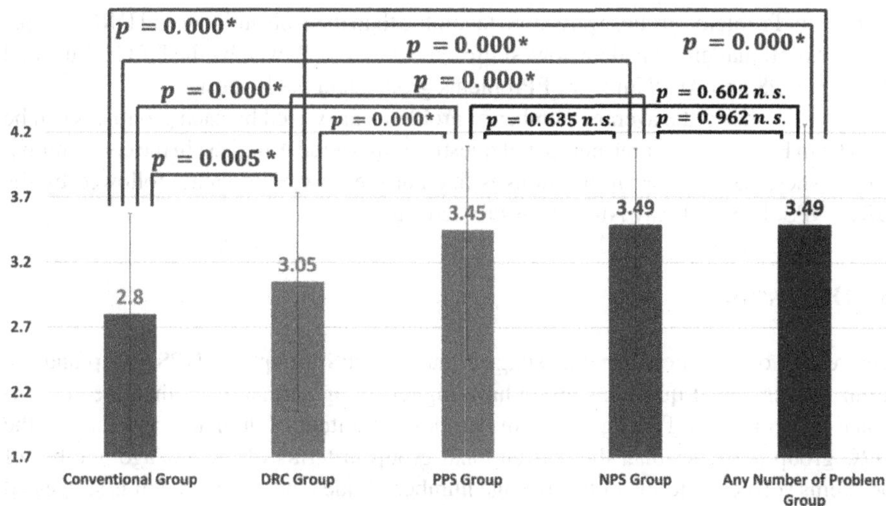


**Fig. 4.** Means and standard deviations of animacy for each group and results of the subtests.

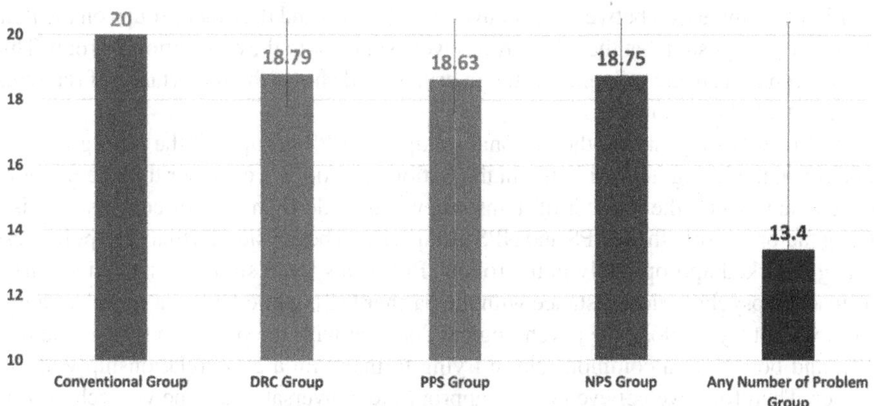


**Fig. 5.** Means and standard deviations of the average number of problems answered.

of Problems and the NPS group had the highest scores on the animacy scale, followed by the PPS, DRC, and conventional group. As shown in Figs. 3. and 4. The results of the upper test of analysis of variance for each item showed that the likeability (F-value = 27.2, Degree of freedom = (5, 119), p-value = 0.000), animacy (F-value = 23.4, Degree of freedom = (5, 119), p-value = 0.000), significant differences were found in both groups. Therefore, when the back-test of analysis of variance was conducted for each item, significant differences were found between the two groups of "conventional and DRC groups" and. "PPS group, NPS group and Any Number of Problems groups" in the item of likeability (Fig. 3). In the item of animacy, significant differences were found between "conventional group", "DRC group" and "PPS group, NPS group and Any Number of Problems groups" (Fig. 4). This suggests that the PPS, NPS and Any

Number of Problems groups were more favorable than the conventional and DRC groups. The conventional group had the lowest life expectancy, followed by the DRC group, and the PPS, NPS and Any Number of Problems groups had the highest.

Figure 5 shows the average number of problems answered by each group. As can be seen from Fig. 5, the average number of questions answered is highest in the conventional group where the number of questions is fixed at the maximum value, followed by the DRC, NPS, PPS and Any Number of Problems groups.

## 5 Discussion

The results of the questionnaires suggest that the PPS group, the NPS group and the arbitrary number of questions group have higher liking and animacy than the conventional group and the DRC group. Among these, the item of animacy suggest that the DRC group is higher than the conventional group in terms of the average number of problems solved. In terms of the average number of questions answered, it is suggested that the group using The Problem-Number Proposal Method maintains the same amount of learning as the conventional group, and the amount of learning is higher than that of the Any Number of Problems groups.

First, a comparison between the conventional group and the other groups on the item of animacy suggested that the other groups were superior to the conventional group. This can be seen as a strong influence of the interview and shows the importance of realizing bidirectional interactions.

The results suggest that the optional group, the PPS group and the NPS group are superior in the liking items. Firstly, in the optional group, we consider that the factor of being able to study the number of items one wants to do by means of conversation is a strong factor at work. In the PPS and NPS groups, it can be considered that each politeness strategy worked appropriately in the robots. PPS is a speech strategy that actively tries to close the psychological distance with the partner [12], while NPS is a speech strategy that does not try to close the psychological distance with the partner but to maintain it [12], and both have a common role in trying to maintain a good relationship with the partner. Therefore, we believe that the appropriate conversational tone was achieved in the educational support robot, and the participants had a good impression of the robot.

Looking at the average number of questions answered, when learning with robots using this method, many of the subjects who rejected the robot's suggestion (15% of the total) said that they were "just curious about what would happen if they rejected the suggestion". In other words, the fact that the average number of questions answered in Fig. 5 is about one question lower than that of the conventional group is due to the fact that this method was used multiple times in a short period of time in a within-subject experiment. In fact, among the five learning experiences of the subjects, 85% of the learning experiences in which the subjects refused the proposal of the robot using this method were the second and third times when this method was used, and the number of subjects who continued to refuse the proposal more than twice was 13% (excluding false recognition) of the total that. Of the 33 subjects (excluding false recognition) who requested to answer less than 10 questions in the arbitrary number of questions group, only 2 subjects answered less than 10 questions in the group using this method. From this data, it is considered that this method may promote spontaneous learning even in learners with low motivation to learn. Therefore, it is considered that this method can encourage learners to learn more spontaneously and can maintain the same amount of learning as the conventional fixed number of questions. However, in this experiment, problems designed for junior high school students were presented to college students. In other words, the fact that the robot presented easy problems may have prevented the number of problems from decreasing. Therefore, when initialy presenting the number of problems, it may be necessary to adjust the robot to present an appropriate number of problems according to the student's ability level.

## 6 Conclusion

In this paper, we constructed a method for suggesting the number of questions by the robot while conversing with the learner based on the politeness theory and reported on the impression effect of each politeness strategy and the average number of questions answered. According to the questionnaire results, the PPS and NPS and Any Number of Problems groups were suggested to have higher likeability and animacy than the conventional and DRC groups. In the item of animacy, it is suggested that the DRC group is higher than the conventional group. In terms of the average number of questions answered, it is suggested that the group using the proposed number of questions method maintains the same amount of learning as the conventional group, and that the amount of learning is higher than that of the group using the arbitrary number of questions method. If the PPS and NPS speech methods are used, we believe that the impression of the robot can be improved while maintaining the same amount of learning as that of the conventional robot with a fixed number of questions.

In the future, we will examine whether similar results can be obtained by changing the age groups and generations of the test subjects and the difficulty level of the problems. We also plan to test the effectiveness of this method by conducting long-term experiments to create an environment that more closely resembles real-life usage conditions.

## 7 Thanks

This research was supported by the Aichi Prefectural University President's Special Research Fund (2023).

## References

1. Jimenez, F., Kanoh, M.: Research trends on educational-support robots. J. Japan Soc. Fuzzy Intell. Inform. **26**(1), 2–8 (2014). (in Japanese)
2. Shinozawa, K., Naya, F., Yamato, J., Kogure, K.: Differences in effect of robot and screen agent recommendations on human decision-making. Int. J. Hum.-Comput. Stud. **62**(2), 267–279 (2005)
3. Bainbridge, W.A., Hart, J., Kim, E.S., Scassellati, B.: The effect of presence on human-robot interaction. In: Proceedings of the 17th IEEE International Symposium on Robot and Human Interactive Communication, 1–3 Aug 2008, pp. 701–706. Munich (2008)

4. Fridin, M., Belokopytov, M.: Embodied robot versus virtual agent: Involvement of preschool children in motor task performance. Int. J. Human Comput. Interact. **30**(6), 459–469 (2014)
5. Jimenez, F., Kanoh, M., Yoshikawa, T., Furuhashi, T.: Feasibility of collaborative learning with robots which prompts constructive interaction. J. Japanese Soc. Artif. Intell. **30**(3), A-F93-1-10 (2016). (in Japanese)
6. Miyauchi, K., Jimenez, F., Yoshikawa, T., Furuhashi, T., Kanoh, M.: Collaborative learning between junior high school students and robots teaching based on cognitive apprenticeship. J. Japan Soc. Fuzzy Intell. Inform. **31**(5), 834–841 (2019). (in Japanese)
7. Saichi, K.: Jihatsuteki Gakusyu no Sasekata. Child study **25**(8), 38–45, (1971–08). (in Japanese)
8. Kanade, S., Hamada, S.: Puratonteki Sugakukan ha Kodomo no Syutaiteki Gakusyu wo Hosyo suruka. J. Japan Soc. Math. Educ. **76**(3), 2 (1994). (in Japanese)
9. Goffman, E.: Interaction Ritual: Essays on Face Behavior. Pantheon Books (1967)
10. Miyamoto, T., Katagami, D., Shigemitsu, Y., Usami, M., Tanaka, T., Kanamori, H.: The effect of differences in linguistic behavior by conversational agents based on politeness strategies for development relationship with humans – psychological effects of joke at the first meeting. J. Japan Soc. Fuzzy Intell. Inform. **30**(5), 753–765 (2018). (in Japanese)
11. Brown, P., Levinson, S.C.: Politeness: Some Universals in Language Usage. Cambridge University Press (1987). https://doi.org/10.1017/CBO9780511813085
12. Chugakusei, T.D.: https://happylilac.net/sk1708021112.html. Last accessed 25 Apr 2023
13. Bartneck, C., Kulic, D., Croft, E., Zoughbi, S.: Measurement instruments for the anthropomorphism, animacy, likeability, perceived, intelligence, and perceived safety of robots. Int. J. Soc. Robot. **1**, 71–81 (2009)
14. Nomura, R.: Humans' subjective evaluation in human-agent interaction (HAI). J. Japanese Soci. Artif. Intell. **31**(2), 224–229 (2016)
15. Fogg, B.J.: Persuasive Technology: Using Computers to Change what We Think and Do. Morgan Kaufmann, San Mateo (2003)

# Effect of a Learning Support Model that Provides Autonomous Learning Support in a Teacher-Type Robot Based on the Learner's Perplexion State

Kohei Okawa[1], Felix Jimenez[2](✉), Shuichi Akizuki[3], and Tomohiro Yoshikawa[4]

[1] Graduate School of Information Science and Technology, Aichi Prefectural University, 1522-3 Ibaragabasama, Nagakute-shi, Aichi 480-1198, Japan

[2] School of Information Science and Technology, Aichi Prefectural University, 1522-3 Ibaragabasama, Nagakute-shi, Aichi 480-1198, Japan

jimenez@ist.aichi-pu.ac.jp

[3] School of Engineering, Chukyo University, 101-2 Yagoto Honmachi, Showa-ku, Nagoya, Aichi 466-8666, Japan

[4] Faculty of Medical Engineering, Suzuka University of Medical Science, 1001-1, Kishioka, Suzuka, Mie 510-0293, Japan

**Abstract.** In recent years, the introduction of ICT education has become active, and research on educational support robots has been attracting attention, especially in this field. However, it has been reported that the conventional educational support robots, which provide learning support through button operations by learners, cause excessive support demands from learners. To solve this problem, in this study, a perplexion estimation method was proposed that estimates the perplexed state of learners from their facial expressions through deep learning. Furthermore, an apprenticeship promotion model was constructed by combining the behavior model for providing learning support based on the cognitive apprenticeship theory and the perplexion estimation method to solve this problem. This paper investigates the effects of an educational support robot equipped with the apprenticeship promotion model for university students. The results of the subject experiment confirmed that the robot using this model provides the same learning effect as the conventional robot that provides learning support by button press. In other words, this model suggests that it is possible to accurately estimate the perplexed state of learners and achieve optimal learning support timing.

**Keywords:** Educational support robot · Deep learning · Collaborative learning · Human-robot Interaction

## 1 Introduction

Recently, research and development of educational support robots to support human learning have attracted significant attention in the educational field [1]. In educational robots, there is a "teacher-type robot" that instructs the learner on the content of learning like a teacher.


C.-Y. Lee et al. (Eds.): TAAI 2023, CCIS 2074, pp. 381–391, 2024.
https://doi.org/10.1007/978-981-97-1711-8_29

As a teacher-type robot in conventional research (hereinafter referred to as a "conventional robot"), we can cite the learning experiment of a teacher-type robot that acts based on the cognitive apprenticeship theory by Yoshizawa et al. [2]. Cognitive apprenticeship theory is a system that describes the process of craftsmen becoming proficient in intellectual acts from the point of view teaching their apprentices [3]. Experimental results show that robots that teach based on the cognitive apprenticeship theory can promote the improvement of learners' application skills. However, conventional robots provide learning support through the learner's button operation. The learner presses a button each time he/she needs assistance.

On the other hand, optimizing the provision of support provision in learning systems is an important issue in educational psychology research. In an environment where learners can request unlimited support, excessive use of hints [4] and search for hint patterns [5] occur regardless of the need for support. In fact, it has been reported that in an English vocabulary learning system that provides learning support in response to a learner's button presses, the learner becomes dependent on the support and does not learn English words at all [6]. In order to prevent these problems, it is necessary to utilize artificial intelligence technology so that the learning system can provide learning support autonomously according to the learner's situation [7].

In this study, we developed a perplexion estimation method (hereinafter referred to as "proposed method") that estimates the state of perplexion from the learner's facial expressions using deep learning. Based on this method, we develop a robot that provides learning support autonomously. In this paper, we construct an apprenticeship promotion model that combines the perplexion estimation method and a learning support model based on cognitive apprenticeship theory. Then, we investigate whether a teacher-type robot equipped with an apprenticeship promotion model can provide autonomous learning support to university students.

## 2 Perplexion Estimation Method

### 2.1 About This Method

In this study, we defined the perplexion state as a state in which the learner is in trouble because he/she does not know how to solve the problem. We constructed a perplexion estimation method to estimate whether the learner is in a perplexed state or not by transfer learning based on the seven emotion estimation methods developed by O. Arriaga et al. [8].

The facial expression data of the perplexion state was collected by filming the learner while he/she was learning using the learning system. Specifically, the expression data up to one second before the i-th button press in learning using the learning system were defined as the perplexion state, and the other expression data were defined as the non-perplexion state (Fig. 1). For example, in the case where expression data was acquired by shooting at 30 fps, the perplexion state is defined as the $n_i - 29$ frames from the $n_i$ frame when the button was pressed. Based on the timing of the learner's own button presses, we associate facial expressions with labels for the perplexed state. In other words, the facial expression data obtained is likely to be the facial expression of the learner when

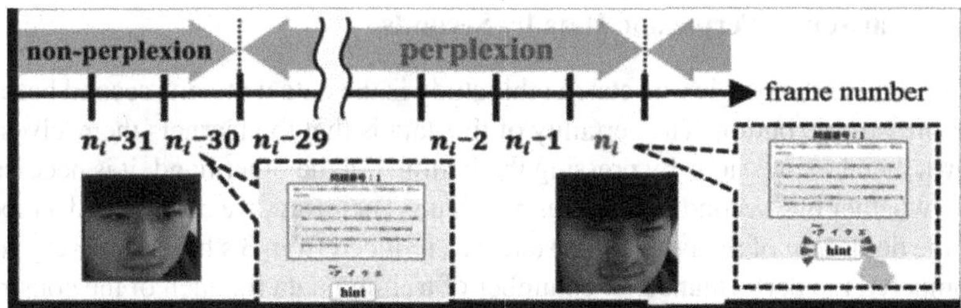


**Fig. 1.** Definition of state of perplexion

the learner requests learning support from himself/herself. We believe that the facial expression data is highly reliable.

The proposed method trains two classes: perplexion and other emotions (Fig. 2). The facial expression dataset for the perplexed state was trained from the collected facial expression data. For the other emotions, the FER2013 dataset and the collected non-perplexed state were trained as neutral. The accuracy of the perplexion estimation methods is shown in Table 1.

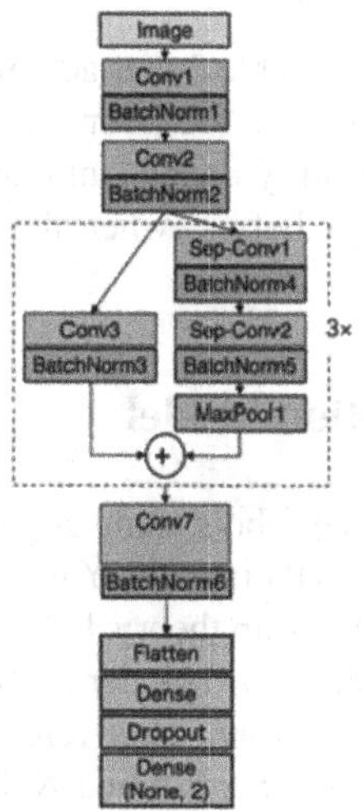


**Fig. 2.** CNN Model configuration

**Table 1.** Accuracy of Perplexion Estimation Method

| | Accuracy | Precision | Recall | F1-score |
|---|---|---|---|---|
| Score | 59.8% | 56.6% | 86.3% | 68.4% |

## 2.2 Comparison of Perplexion Data by Seconds

The definition of the perplexion state in this study is the data up to one second before the learner presses the button. The certainty of the data is that the learners themselves label their own facial expressions by pressing the button. On the other hand, it is necessary to confirm whether one second before is appropriate. Therefore, we constructed a model in which the definition of the perplexion state was reduced from 3 s before to every second and compared the performance. The number of training data for each of the constructed models is approximately 20,000–25,000 for perplexion data and 30,000–37,000 for non-perplexion data. The performance of each model is shown in Table 2.

**Table 2.** Comparison of performance

| Range | Accuracy | Precision | Recall | F-score |
|---|---|---|---|---|
| 0 to 3s | 62.5% | 58.2% | 99.7% | 73.5% |
| 0 to 2s | 58.7% | 55.7% | 81.9% | 66.3% |
| 0 to 1s | 59.8% | 56.7% | 86.7% | 68.4% |

The best performance shown in Table 2 was achieved by the model that defined the perplexion state as 3 s before. However, the error is only 1–3%, except for the F-score, which is increasing in a reproducibility-dependent manner. Therefore, in this study, we defined the perplexion state as 1 s before, when the blurring of facial expressions is considered to be the smallest.

# 3 Apprenticeship Promotion Model

As a previous study on teacher-type robots using cognitive apprenticeship theory, there is a study by Yoshizawa et al. [2]. In their study, Yoshizawa et al., proposed a behavioral model based on cognitive apprenticeship theory, believing that a robot that provides the same learning support for all problems will hinder the improvement of application skills. Yoshizawa et al.'s behavioral model (here-after referred to as "conventional model"), (1) Modeling, (2) Coaching, and (3) Scaffolding & Fading, which are said to be the core of cognitive apprenticeship theory, are switched for each problem based on the previous learning results. Participants experiments showed that the robot equipped with the conventional model was effective in promoting the learner's independence and was effective in helping the learner acquire applied skills. However, it is difficult to use the conventional model for a buttonless learning system, because it is a behavioral model that assumes the provision of learning support by the learner's button presses. Therefore, we have modified the model to utilize the baffling estimation method, which is the Apprenticeship Promotion Model.

The Apprenticeship Promotion Model provides a learning environment with less burden on the learner by switching the support phase based on the cognitive apprenticeship theory by judging whether the previous learning was correct or incorrect. In addition, the robot equipped with the model switches when to provide learning support according to the following phases (1) and (2). In the previous model, modeling and coaching were set up as separate phases. However, since this model assumes button operation, we decided to integrate them in the Apprenticeship Promotion Model.

(1). Modeling & Coaching

The robot shows how to solve the problem three seconds after the problem is presented. In addition, the learning system displays a hint button and provides a hint by pressing the button.

(2). Scaffolding & Fading

The robot provides hints to solve the problem when estimating the learner's state of perplexion using the perplexion estimation method.

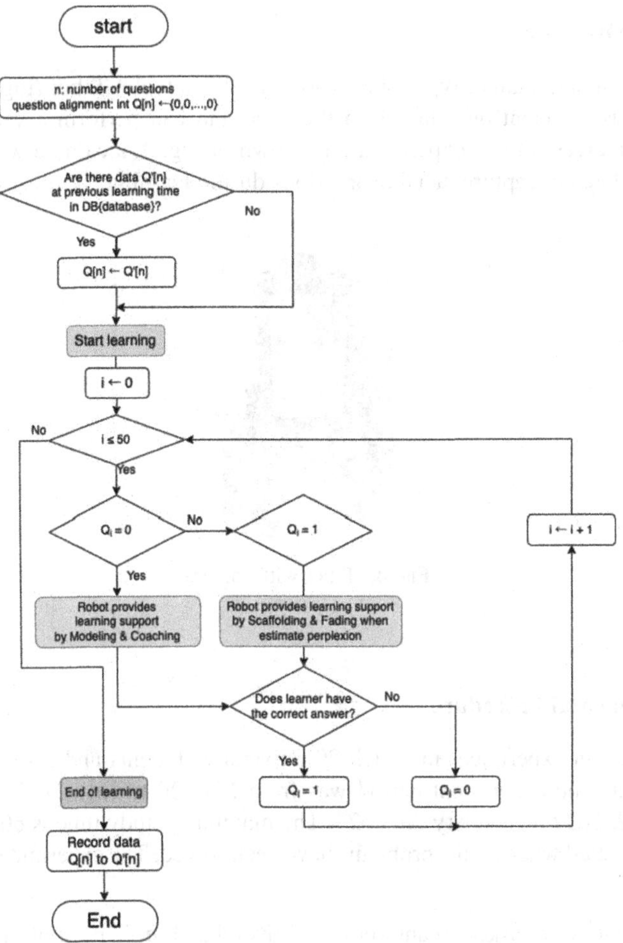


**Fig. 3.** Flow of the Apprenticeship Promotion Model

In (1), the reason for installing the hint button is to collect data for the perplexion estimation method. In order to improve the accuracy of the perplexion estimation method and to construct a user-specific model in the future, it is essential to collect data on the state of perplexion. Therefore, we made it possible to collect teacher data by setting up a stage in which the user presses a button. On the other hand, in (2), the button was removed to realize a fully autonomous learning support environment completely by a supervised robot. The core of the apprenticeship promotion model is (2) Scaffolding & Fading, which provides autonomous support during this phase.

A specific flowchart is shown in Fig. 3. Thus, in Fig. 3, Switch between the support phases by setting $Q_i = (0,1)$.

## 4 Participants Experiment

### 4.1 Robot Overview

For the experiment, a tablet-type robot whose head is a tablet Tabot (Fig. 4) was used. Tabot displays an agent on a tablet on the head and can perform a variety of facial expression changes. In this experiment, as shown in Fig. 4, a camera was installed on the subject's head to capture facial expressions during learning.

**Fig. 4.** Tabot with camera

### 4.2 Experimental Procedure

We conducted an experiment in which 20 university students and a supervised robot learn together. The experiment period was from May 20 to July 21, 2019, and from December 12, 2022, to January 25, 2023. The maximum study time is 60 min, and the study is completed when all the problems have been solved. The experimental procedure is as follows.

(1). Participants were asked to answer questions related to IT passport as a pre-study. One person works on 50 questions.
(2). Five times in about two weeks, the Participants work with a group of supervised robots assigned to them on the same problems as in the pre-training session.

(3). Three or four days after the fifth session with the robot, the Participants work alone on the same problems as in the pre-training session as a post-test.
(4). Five days after the fifth session with the robot, an application test was conducted. The participant will work alone on 20 questions related to the Basic Information Technology Engineer Examination.

In this experiment, we will verify whether the teacher-type robots equipped with the apprenticeship promotion model (hereinafter referred to as the "proposed group") can improve the dependence on support, which has been a problem for teacher-type robots equipped with the conventional model (hereinafter referred to as the "conventional group"). 10 participants were assigned to each group, equally divided into 4 males and 6 females.

### 4.3 Valuation Index

In this experiment, to verify whether the support-dependent environment can be improved compared to the conventional group, we recorded and compared the number of times the robot provided support and the transition in the number of points while studying with the robot.

### 4.4 Result

Figure 5 shows a graph that includes the number of times we provided forced assistance. Figure 6 shows the score transition for all five times when the robot and the student studied together. In each graph, the x-axis represents the number of learning sessions with the robot, the y-axis in Fig. 5 represents the number of assistance sessions, and the y-axis in Fig. 6 represents the number of points.

Figure 5 shows that even in the second learning session, the conventional group received more support than the proposed group because Coaching is a compulsory support program. In contrast, more than 80% of the problems in the Scaffolding & Fading

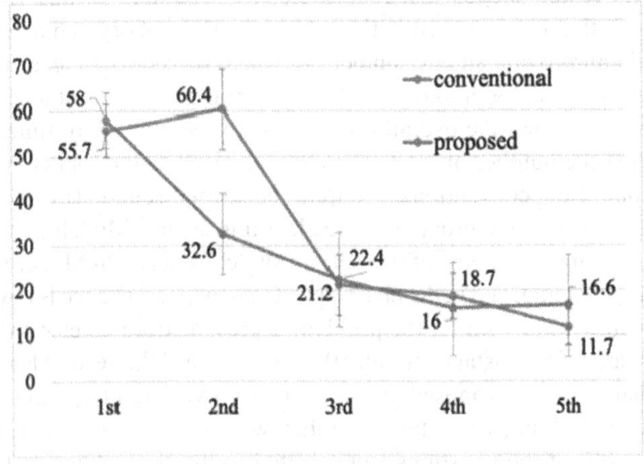


**Fig. 5.** Number of all support sessions

phase, as shown in Fig. 6, which means that the support is not forced support, but rather autonomous support at the time of estimating the state of perplexion. Therefore, the number of times of support was significantly different.

Figure 6 shows that although the scores were higher in the proposed group, a similar trend of change was observed. In other words, it was suggested that the same learning effect could be obtained when studying with a teacher type robot that removes buttons and provides assistant autonomously.

These results suggest that the proposed group can provide the same learning effect as the conventional group, which requires button operation, even though the number of times of support sessions is reduced at an early stage.

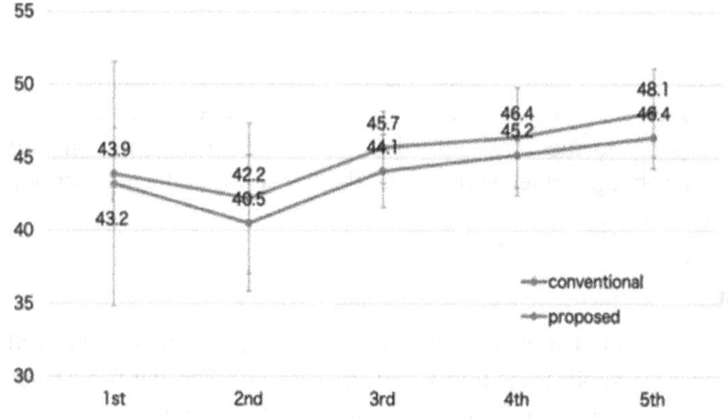


**Fig. 6.** Changes scores in collaborative learning

## 5 Discussion

The experimental results suggest that a supervised robot equipped with an apprenticeship promotion model that integrates cognitive apprenticeship theory and a perplexion estimation method can provide an environment in which learners can learn independently at an early stage while autonomously providing learning support without discomfort.

Figure 5, which shows the overall progression of the number of times support was given, shows that the number of times support was given to the robots in the proposed group is half that of the conventional group in the second round. This is mainly due to the fact that the conventional group has three learning stages: Modeling, Coaching, and Scaffolding & Fading. The conventional group switches between Modeling, Coaching, and Scaffolding & Fading, and in the phase up to Coaching, assistance is always provided for every problem within 4 s after the problem is presented. In other words, the learner is always provided with assistance for all 50 questions until the second learning session. On the other hand, in the proposed group, there are two learning stages: Modeling & Coaching and Scaffolding & Fading. In other words, in the second learning phase, approximately 80% of the questions were shifted to the Scaffolding & Fading phase, as indicated by the average score in Fig. 5. Since this stage provides assistance only for estimating the state of perplexion, there are some problems that are not assisted. So, it is highly possible that the second learning session provided an environment in which the learner could learn independently from the educator, which is the goal of the cognitive apprenticeship theory.On the other hand, if the learner continues to answer incorrectly without support as a result of being independent from the second study, there is a risk that the learner's motivation to learn will decrease. In order to assess the learner's motivation to learn independently, we believe it is important to check whether the learner is able to answer questions correctly without assistance. In the proposed group, the average number of questions answered correctly with support and the average number of questions answered correctly without support in the Scaffolding & Fading phase, excluding the first learning session, were tabulated (Fig. 7). It was confirmed that the number of questions answered correctly without assistance was higher on all occasions among the four study sessions, except the first time. In other words, it was confirmed that even in a learning environment that encourages independence at an early stage, as in the proposed group, the rate of correct answers did not decrease in the absence of support and continued to do so. In addition to this, Fig. 5 shows that the number of correct answers was similar to that of the conventional group, suggesting that the robots in the proposed group were able to encourage the learners to learn independently earlier.

We believe that the timing of support is important in realizing autonomous learning support. For example, early learning support does not give the learner time to think about the problem. Similarly, if the timing is too late, the learning time may be unnecessarily extended, and the learner's motivation may decrease due to frustration at not being able to solve the problem. If, as in the conventional group, support is provided by pressing a button when the learner wants it, there should be no concern about the timing of the support. On the other hand, in the proposed group, where learning support is provided based on the estimated state of confusion, the appropriateness of the support timing varies depending on the estimated timing. In other words, if the support is provided to the learner at a timing that is uncomfortable, it cannot be said that a teacher-type robot that provides learning support autonomously has been realized. Therefore, we examined the ratio of learning stages in all five learning sessions (Fig. 8). If many learners moved to Scaffolding & Fading after a certain number of opportunities for estimating perplexion, it was considered that the learning support was provided at a good timing. The Fig. 8 shows that, of course, all the problems in the first learning session start from Scaffolding & Fading increased, and in the last study, 92.8% of the problems were in the Scaffolding & Fading stage. This means that approximately 46 out of the 50 questions were provided with learning support when the state of perplexion was estimated. The fact that the learning results shown in the Fig. 8 were achieved while there was an opportunity for autonomous learning support to be provided is an achievement of autonomous learning support.

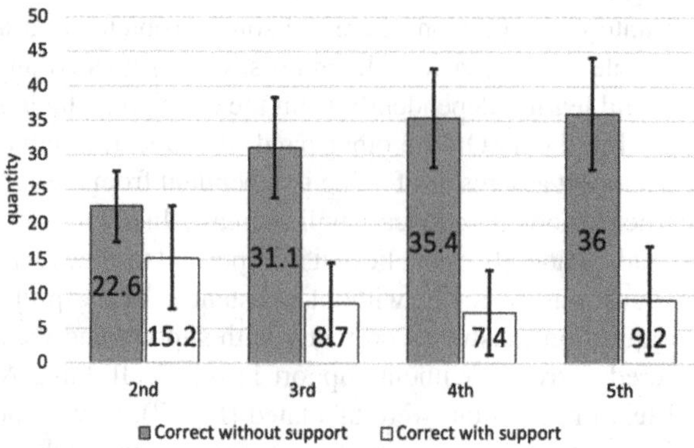


**Fig. 7.** Difference in number of correct answers with and without assistance

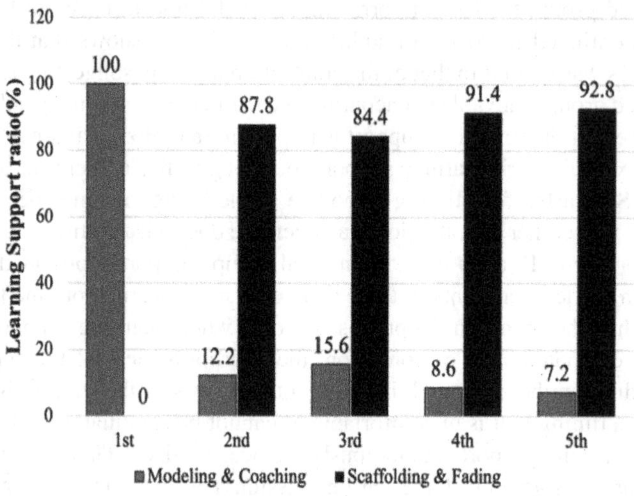


**Fig. 8.** Percentage of learning stages

## 6 Conclusion

In this paper, we conducted a comparison experiment between a robot equipped with an apprenticeship promotion model that combines a perplexion estimation method to estimate the learner's perplexion state and cognitive apprenticeship theory, and a robot equipped with a conventional model based only on cognitive apprenticeship theory.

To realize autonomous support for teacher-type robot, it is necessary to provide the same level of learning effect as robots that provide learning support by operating buttons, such as the conventional group. From the experimental results, we confirmed that the learning scores of the proposed group and the conventional group were similar (Fig. 6). Furthermore, the cognitive apprenticeship theory aims to allow learners to become independent. Figure 5 show that the number of support sessions can be reduced

earlier in the proposed group. We believe that we have achieved a teacher-type robot that autonomously provides learning support.

## References


1. T. Belpaeme, et al, " Social robots for education: A review, "Science Robotics, Vol.3, eaat5954, (2018)
2. R. Yoshizawa, et al," Proposal of a Behavioral Model for Robots Supporting Learning According to Learners 'Learning Performance", Journal of Robotics and Mechatronics, vol.32, no.4, pp.769–779, (2020)
3. A. Collins, et al, "Cognitive Apprenticeship: Teaching the Craft of Reading, Writing, and Mathematics", Essays in Honor of Robert Glaser, Ebaum, HiLLsdale NJ, (1989)
4. V. Aleven and K. R. Koedinger, "Limitations of student control: Do students know when they need help?", Proceedings of the 5$^{th}$ International Conference on Intelligent Tutoring Systems, (2000)
5. J. A. Walonoski and N. T. Heffernan, "Detection and Analysis of Off-Task Gaming Behavior in Intelligent Tutoring Systems", Proceedings of the 8$^{th}$ International Conference on Intelligent Tutoring Systems, (2006)
6. Jimenez, F., Kanoh, M.: Change in Learning Ability Using Scaffolding in EFL Vocabulary Learning System. Journal of Japan Society for Fuzzy Theory and Intelligent Informatics **25**(5), 880–888 (2013)
7. Roll, I., et al.: Improving students' help seeking skills using metacognitive feedback in an intelligent tutoring system. Learn. Instr. **21**(2), 26–280 (2011)
8. O. Arriaga, et al, "Realtime Convolutional Neural Networks for Emotion and Gender Classification", https://arxiv.org/abs/1710.07557, (2017)

# Author Index




C.-Y. Lee et al. (Eds.): TAAI 2023, CCIS 2074, pp. 393–395, 2024.
https://doi.org/10.1007/978-981-97-1711-8

**W**



**X**



**Y**

Printed in the United States
by Baker & Taylor Publisher Services

Printed in the United States
by Baker & Taylor Publisher Services